PLAIN FOLK IN THE NEW SOUTH

PLAIN FOLK

IN THE NEW SOUTH

SOCIAL CHANGE AND
CULTURAL PERSISTENCE
1880–1915

I. A. Newby

LOUISIANA STATE UNIVERSITY PRESS
BATON ROUGE AND LONDON

98 97 96 95 94 93 92 91 90 89   5 4 3 2 1

Designer: Diane B. Didier
Typeface: Plantin
Typesetter: The Composing Room of Michigan, Inc.
Printer: Thomson-Shore, Inc.
Binder: John H. Dekker & Sons, Inc.

The author gratefully acknowledges permission to publish passages from the Federal
Writers' Project Papers, no. 3709; the Southern Oral History Project Papers, no. 4007; and
the Chapel Hill Historical Society Papers, no. 4205, all in the Southern Historical
Collection, Library of the University of North Carolina at Chapel Hill.

LIBRARY OF CONGRESS CATALOGING-IN-PUBLICATION DATA

Newby, I. A. (Idus A.), 1931—
   Plain folk in the new South.

   Bibliography: p.
   Includes index.
   1. Rural development—Southern States—History.
2. Rural poor—Southern States—History. 3. Southern
States—Rural conditions. I. Title.
HN79.A13N48 1989   307.7'2'0975   88-17439
ISBN 0-8071-1456-1 (alk. paper)

The paper in this book meets the guidelines for permanence and durability of the
Committee on Production Guidelines for Book Longevity of the Council on Library
Resources. ∞

CONTENTS

ACKNOWLEDGMENTS

In preparing this study, I have accumulated obligations to many people. For their assistance, I wish to thank the staffs of the Southern Historical Collection at the University of North Carolina; the University of North Carolina Library, especially the North Carolina Collection; the Manuscript Department, Duke University Library; the South Caroliniana Library; the South Carolina State Archives; the University of Hawaii Library; Georgia State University Library; the University of South Carolina at Aiken Library; the Georgia State Archives; and the University of Georgia Library. I used, more briefly, material in the libraries at the University of California at Los Angeles, Emory University, and the University of South Carolina. I used the microfilm edition of the manuscript census at the Mormon Temple in Los Angeles and at the Federal Records Center in East Point, Georgia.

I am especially obligated to David L. Carlton for pointing me to the letters from cotton mill workers in the Coleman L. Blease papers. Several of my colleagues read portions of the manuscript in various versions and offered encouragement and helpful suggestions—Robert McGlone, Herbert Margulies, Doris Ladd, and Brij Lal. My thanks also to Tom Hamlen and to the others at the Kealani—especially Peter, Mark, and Kermit—for listening to me talk for several years about this study and the folk who are its subject.

I would like to dedicate this book to a group of my favorite people, my nieces and nephews—Nancy Jo, Miriam, Jeannine, and Jessica; Robert and Suzanne; Lesley and Stefanie; and Ben, Melanie, and Martha. They will not, I suspect, be much acquainted with the things I have written about here, though their parents probably will be.

NOTE ON CITATION OF
INTERVIEWS

Much of the documentation for this study derives from three sets of interviews in the Southern Historical Collection, Louis R. Wilson Library, University of North Carolina at Chapel Hill. The first of these sets consists of several hundred interviews made in the late 1930s by employees of the Works Projects Administration's Federal Writers' Project. They are not verbatim transcripts of the interviews but reports written later by the interviewers. On the merits of these interviews as historical sources, see Jerrold Hirsch and Tom E. Terrill, "Conceptualization and Implementation: Some Thoughts on Reading the Federal Writers' Project Southern Life Histories," *Southern Studies*, XVIII (1979), 351–62; Leonard Rapport, "How Valid Are the Federal Writers' Project Life Stories: An Iconoclast Among the True Believers," *Oral History Review* (1979), 6–17; and Terrill and Hirsch, "Replies to Leonard Rapport's 'How Valid Are the Federal Writers' Project Life Stories: An Iconoclast Among the True Believers,'" *Oral History Review* (1980), 81–92. In "Conceptualization and Implementation," Hirsch and Terrill wrote of the interviews: "There is evidence that some stories are inauthentic in significant detail. The life histories are most valuable as a source of qualitative evidence about hopes, fears, aspirations, [and] as the historical account of people not normally heard from."

For examples of these interviews, see W. T. Couch (ed)., *These Are Our Lives* (Chapel Hill, 1939); Tom E. Terrill and Jerrold Hirsch (eds.), *Such As Us: Southern Voices of the Thirties* (Chapel Hill, 1978); and Ann Banks (ed.), *First Person America* (New York, 1980). Most of the interviews include the names of the people whose experiences were recorded. A few of the names, however, are fictitious. I have used the interviews to reveal patterns of folk life, but the chronology of individual lives is not always explicit—age rather than birth date, for example, is usually given. I have used the three-reel microfilm edition of these interviews. For information on the Federal Writers' Project, see Monty N. Penkower, *The Federal Writers' Project: A Study in Government Patronage of the Arts* (Urbana, 1977); and Jerre Mangione, *The Dream and the Deal: The Federal Writers' Project, 1935–1943* (New York, 1972).

The other two sets are verbatim transcripts of interviews conducted in the 1970s for the Southern Oral History Project and the Chapel Hill Historical Society.

Because the quotations from interviews are so numerous, rather than footnote each individually, I have listed alphabetically below the names of those interviewed with the file number and location of the interview within the file in the Southern Historical Collection. Interviews in the Federal Writers' Project collection, file no. 3709, are cited as "FWP" by microfilm reel number. Those in the Southern Oral History Project collection, file no. 4007, are a part of the Piedmont Social History Project and are cited as "SOHP" and by box number. Those in the Chapel Hill Historical Society records, file no. 4205, are part of the Carrboro Oral History Project and are cited as "CHHS" and by box number.

Abbott, Mary, no. 3709, FWP reel 3
Albright, Frances Medlin, no. 4205, CHHS Box 5
Alexander, Fred, no. 3709, FWP reel 3
Andrews, Mrs. Bertram, no. 4205, CHHS Box 5
Austin, Ralph C., no. 4007, SOHP Box 3
Ball, Enoch, no. 3709, FWP reel 3
Belk, John, no. 3709, FWP reel 3
Belk, Martha, no. 3709, FWP reel 3
Bennett, Lula, no. 3709, FWP reel 3
Bland, Lessie Bowden, no. 4205, CHHS Box 5
Brady, Almeda, no. 3709, FWP reel 2
Brakefield, Sam, no. 3709, FWP reel 1
Bramblett, Henry T., no. 3709, FWP reel 1
Bramblett, Lelia, no. 3709, FWP reel 1
Brewer, F. B., no. 3709, FWP reel 2
Buchanan, Bessie, no. 4007, SOHP Box 4
Burchell, Everette, no. 4007, SOHP Box 1
Carden, Stella Foust, no. 4007, SOHP Box 1
Carnes, "Pa," no. 3709, FWP reel 3

Carter, Jessie Lee, no. 4007, SOHP Box 4

Cates, B. F. (pseudonym), no. 3709, FWP reel 2

Caudle, Alice, no. 3709, FWP reel 3

Cheek, Ella, no. 3709, FWP reel 3

Cline, Wilma, no. 3709, FWP reel 2

Conner, Will, no. 3709, FWP reel 2

Crowe, Herbert, no. 3709, FWP reel 2

Demry, Lulu, no. 3709, FWP reel 3

Dodson, Ila Hartsell, no. 4007, SOHP Box 4

Draper, Bob, no. 3709, FWP reel 2

Durham, Flossie Moore, no. 4007, SOHP Box 2

Dyer, George W., no. 4007, SOHP Box 3

Edwards, Mrs. Warren, no. 3709, FWP reel 2

Emerick, Annie Grady, no. 3709, FWP reel 1

Enlow, Curtis, no. 4007, SOHP Box 4

Everett, J. R., no. 3709, FWP reel 3

Evitt, Alice P., no. 4007, SOHP Box 3

Evitts, Ludie, no. 3709, FWP reel 3

Faison, Sarah Strickland, no. 3709, FWP reel 3

Farrington, Ollie, no. 3709, FWP reel 2

Faucette, Ethel M., no. 4007, SOHP Box 1

Fesperman, Clarence E., no. 3709, FWP reel 2

Fisher, Brother, no. 3709, FWP reel 3

Foster, Ernest, no. 3709, FWP reel 2

Freeze, Jones I., no. 3709, FWP reel 3

Gaines, Addie, no. 3709, FWP reel 2

Gattis, Mary, no. 4007, SOHP Box 2

Gibbs, Anthony, no. 3709, FWP reel 2

Godwin, Frank, no. 3709, FWP reel 3

Godwin, Molly, no. 3709, FWP reel 3

Graham, Molly, no. 3709, FWP reel 3

Griffith, Pauline Phillips, no. 4007, SOHP Box 4

Haithcock, Versa Vernon, no. 4007, SOHP Box 1

Hale, Mrs. John S., no. 3709, FWP reel 2

Herring, James, no. 3709, FWP reel 1

Holbrook, Lillian, no. 3709, FWP reel 2

Humphrey, Charles, no. 3709, FWP reel 2
Humphreys, Rose Bowden, no. 4205, CHHS
   Box 5
Jeffrey, Mrs. Jim, no. 3709, FWP reel 2
Johnson, Sallie Smith, no. 4007, SOHP Box 1
Jones, Louise Rigsbee, no. 4007, SOHP Box 2
Jordan, May, no. 3709, FWP reel 2
Kanipe, Rosa, no. 3709, FWP reel 2
Kay, Mollie Bowden, no. 4007, SOHP Box 2
King, Andrew, no. 3709, FWP reel 3
Lawrence, Mrs. J. C., no. 3709, FWP reel 3
Layton, Clara, no. 3709, FWP reel 2
Lee, Josie, no. 3709, FWP reel 2
Lee, Steve, no. 3709, FWP reel 2
Lester, Rachael, no. 3709, FWP reel 2
Lowe, Martin, no. 4007, SOHP Box 4
Lunsford, Georgia, no. 3709, FWP reel 3
McBride, Dewey, no. 4007, SOHP Box 1
McBride, Gladys, no. 4007, SOHP Box 1
McCoy, Betty, no. 3709, FWP reel 2
McDaniel, Swannie, no. 4007, SOHP Box 1
McNair, Margaret, no. 3709, FWP reel 2
Maddrey, Fanny Bowers, no. 3709, FWP reel 2
Maddrey, Roland, no. 3709, FWP reel 2
Martin, Frank, no. 3709, FWP reel 3
Martin, Sally, no. 3709, FWP reel 3
Mason, Lettie, no. 3709, FWP reel 3
Matheson, Mrs. M. A., no. 3709, FWP reel 2
Maynard, Ida, no. 3709, FWP reel 2
Michaels, Joseph A., no. 3709, FWP reel 1
Miles, Fannie, no. 3709, FWP reel 3
Moser, Dolly Hollar, no. 4007, SOHP Box 3
Murray, Charles, no. 4007, SOHP Box 1
Nolan, Nancy, no. 3709, FWP reel 1
Oakley, Maxie, no. 4007, SOHP Box 4
Oates, Nora I., no. 3709, FWP reel 2

Osteen, Letha Ann Sloan, no. 4007, SOHP Box 4
Owens, Nancy, no. 3709, FWP reel 2
Owens, William J., no. 3709, FWP reel 2
Pace, Lucy, no. 3709, FWP reel 2
Page, Ann, no. 3709, FWP reel 2
Parks, Paul, no. 3709, FWP reel 2
Parson, Mrs. Sim, no. 3709, FWP reel 2
Partin, Vinnie, no. 4205, CHHS Box 5
Peake, Lee, no. 3709, FWP reel 3
Pendergrass, Nellie Allen, no. 4205, CHHS Box 5
Pepper, Lil, no. 3709, FWP reel 3
Pharis, James W., no. 4007, SOHP Box 1
Pharis, Nannie, no. 4007, SOHP Box 1
Pierce, John, no. 3709, FWP reel 3
Pike, Homer L., no. 3709, FWP reel 1
Pope, Clarise, no. 3709, FWP reel 2
Prosser, John W., no. 3709, FWP reel 3
Reeves, Beatrice, no. 3709, FWP reel 3
Reynolds, J. H., no. 3709, FWP reel 2
Rhodes, Merton, no. 3709, FWP reel 2
Rice, M. D., no. 3709, FWP reel 1
Robinette, Jefferson M., no. 4007, SOHP Box 1
Rowe, Jennie, no. 3709, FWP reel 2
Sadler, Mrs. William J., no. 3709, FWP reel 3
Simmons, Ralph B., no. 4007, SOHP Box 3
Simmons, Susie, no. 3709, FWP reel 3
Sizemore, Thomas, no. 3709, FWP reel 3
Smith, Alice Thrift, no. 4205, CHHS Box 6
Stanley, Myrtle Ray, no. 4205, CHHS Box 6
Starnes, Abel, no. 3709, FWP reel 3
Stephenson, Sallie Jane, no. 3709, FWP reel 3
Tate, Clara, no. 3709, FWP reel 3
Thornton, Mrs., no. 3709, FWP reel 3
Thrift, J. Floyd, no. 4205, CHHS Box 6
Trammel, Naomi Sizemore, no. 4007, SOHP
  Box 4

xiv NOTE ON CITATION OF INTERVIEWS

Truelove, Eva, no. 3709, FWP reel 2
Vaughn, Walter, no. 4007, SOHP Box 4
Waldrup, Ann, no. 3709, FWP reel 1
Walter, Belle, no. 3709, FWP reel 3
Walter, Lottie, no. 3709, FWP reel 3
Warwick, Bessie, no. 3709, FWP reel 2
West, Julie, no. 3709, FWP reel 3
Westbrook, Will, no. 3709, FWP reel 2
Whitlock, J. T., no. 3709, FWP reel 2
Williams, Emma Clark, no. 4205, CHHS Box 6
Williams, Lonnie, no. 3709, FWP reel 3
Williamson, Ruth Jordan, no. 3709, FWP reel 2
Williamson, Theotis Johnson, no. 4007, SOHP
    Box 4
Willis, Emma, no. 3709, FWP reel 3
Workman, Lee A., no. 4007, SOHP Box 3
Wright, Lora League, no. 4007, SOHP Box 4

PLAIN FOLK IN THE NEW SOUTH

INTRODUCTION
PLAIN FOLK, "POOR WHITES," AND "WHITE TRASH"

"We started off farmin' and stuck to it up to the fall of 1913 and '14," Frank Martin remembered of sharecropping in North Carolina. "That year we planted cotton on a fourteen cent basis and got six cent for some and four and a half for the rest. Europe had got started in the war and the countries that had put in orders for cotton countermanded 'em and flooded our home market. Me and Sally made fourteen bales of cotton, thirty-one barrels of corn and three hundred bushels of potatoes besides a sight of peas. It was one of the best crop years I ever knowed . . . and we come out about the poorest we ever done. We worked let me tell you, we worked to make that crop."

"Law, I reckon we did," Sally Martin agreed. "I hoed seventeen acres of cotton myself without one lick of help . . . done my housework, and looked after three children. Many a night after supper I'd scour my floors or do my washin' and have it ready so's I could put it on the line before I went to the field at sun-up the next mornin'." She continued: "In gatherin' time I'd take my little baby to the field and put him in a wooden box at the end of a cotton row of a early mornin' when the frost lay thick as snow on the ground. Me and Frank picked every boll that went into eight bales of that cotton and I never got so much as two yards of ten-cent apron gingham." Martin explained, "Mr. Johnson, my landlord, got half of [the crop] because the land was his'n, and he took the other half to pay for what rashins he'd furnished."

The Martins had had a common sharecroppers' experience: they had failed to "pay out." Because of the vagaries of European politics, the bottom fell out of the cotton market, and the Martins' crop sold for less than the landlord advanced them for making it. Perhaps it was the uncharacteristically high expectations that caused their disappointment, which still rankled a quarter century later. In any case, after the landlord tried to take everything they owned, including their last pig, they quit farming. Martin looked for "public work," as poor folk called employment off the farm, and moved his family to a cotton mill at Henderson. "Mills was beginnin' to pay good," he remembered. "It wa'n't long till I was makin' $20 a week."

The Martins remembered the disappointments of farming in the New South. Addie Gaines recalled the hard living. Daughter of a Tennessee sharecropper who moved his family to South Carolina and then North Carolina in the early 1870s while she was still a child, Mrs. Gaines had a difficult life. "I've lived on a farm all my life," she remembered in 1939, when she was seventy-eight years old. "I've never knowed nothin' else. It's a mighty hard life, too. Them as farms knows. . . . Ma used to let us pick cotton for the neighbors. We got forty cents a day (daylight to dark). I've stooped over the rows until I'd feel like I'd growed crooked and could never stand straight no more. . . . I've et cornbread with molasses till I can't abide the thought of it now. We never had enough to eat at any one meal as I can remember."

"There was nine of us in family," Mrs. Gaines continued. "Pa couldn't earn enough farmin' to keep us in bread so he went to work in a cotton mill and put us to work there too. Law, you talk about farm life bein' hard! Child, you be thankful you never had to work for your livin' in a cotton mill."

M. D. Rice, who grew up in rural north Georgia in the 1880s and 1890s, remembered his life as a series of moves from one place to another. "I 'n Daddy 'n 'bout all our kin I knowed about was allus renters, sharecroppers, 'r worked on somebody else's place for wages," Rice recalled. "Reckon we never found 'ary place we wanted. Seems like come next year we'd find the right place to suit us, but we never did." Rice's family had migrated from "North Ca'lina" to "Georgy" shortly before he was born. As the oldest of seven children, Rice had gone to work in the fields while still a child. "I 'member I was allus strong for a kid and laid off corn ground for Daddy when I wasn't but twelve years old," he continued. "Wasn't long atter that I was doin' a man's work 'long with Daddy."

As far back as Rice could remember, his family had moved from tenancy to tenancy, seeking that "right place to suit us"; and he himself continued that pattern after marrying the daughter of a tenant farmer. In 1938 he recounted twenty-three moves in the forty-two years since he had married, during which time he had been, in sequence, a miner, agricultural laborer, sawmill worker, sharecropper, tenant farmer, sharecropper, small-town laborer, sharecropper, sawmill worker, farm foreman, and sawmill worker. For twenty-three of the twenty-four years from 1908 through 1931, he was a sharecropper, for twelve different landlords. "Seems like we've allus got some kind-a livin' off th' land," he said, looking back over his life, "'n I reckon hit'll allus feed us 'gin we tries hard'nuff."

Other folk moved often, too, but followed a different path. B. F. Cates, the only child of a North Carolina tenant farmer, began working in the fields as a lad about 1880. His father died, however, and after his mother remarried, Cates went to live with an uncle and work in his sawmill. "Wuz there two years," he recalled. "Can't say I liked it very much except that it got me offen the farm." Dislike of farm work encouraged young Cates about 1890 to go to the cotton mills, where he worked for twenty years, first at Haw River, then at Carrboro and Burlington and back at Carrboro again. He then quit the mills for a while and worked for a chair maker. "But it looks like I wuz destined to work in a cotton-mill," he said later, "and I worked at it again for four years." Still, Cates "often sighed for the independence of farm life." He "love[d] to see growing things: pigs, chickens, dogs, crops, flowers, and trees" and "to see the sun set, big and red behind the clouds." Of course, "there's a lot of hard work on the farm," he acknowledged, "but poor men all have to work hard"; and life in the mill was not fulfilling.

After more than a quarter century, Cates went back to farming, but five years of sharecropping for three different landowners made the mills more attractive. By the late 1930s, when he told his life story to an interviewer, Cates had worked at least thirty years in cotton mills, five years as a tenant farmer, and two years each at sawmilling and chair making; and during that time he had had more than a dozen employers. "They say a rollin' stone gathers no moss," he said of his experience. "But I ain't moved no oftener than most preachers and teachers. And . . . I had the habit of coming back where I'd been before."

The experiences of Frank and Sally Martin, Addie Gaines, M. D. Rice, and B. F. Cates were widely shared in the New South. But they were the experiences of people—roughly the poorer half of the white population—who had never evoked much sympathy and whose history has been more often overlooked or caricatured than studied systematically and evenhandedly. Alternately disparaged, patronized, and ignored, these people have never received what every group is entitled to—a sympathetic look into their history that seeks to understand them on their own terms. Historians, like other people, have stigmatized all or many of them as "poor whites," "white trash," "crackers," "rednecks," or "lintheads," and smeared them with the demeaning qualities those terms convey—benumbing poverty, social wretchedness, assorted bigotries, moral and physical degeneracy.

Few labels of wide currency have embodied, and still embody, more elitism and sanctimony than those, and only the kinds of racial and ethnic slurs no longer admissible in public discourse have served so widely as substitutes for informed and open-minded inquiry. Generally reserved for the kinds of people once disparaged as the "undeserving" poor—the most deprived of people whose life-styles openly flout middle-class notions of work, accumulation, and social discipline—those labels have become encrusted with the prejudices poor southern white people have always endured. "I had a little dog / His name was Dash. / I'd rather be a nigger / Than po'h white trash," some blacks used to chant. "I'd rather be a nigger an' plow ol' Beck, / Dan a white hill-billy wid a long red neck."[1]

Terms that embody such prejudices are not useful for historians and should be discarded. They are epithets at best, moral judgments at worst. Even the most neutral of them—"poor whites"—focuses attention exclusively on the economic aspect of identity and, in turn, on victimization and degradation.

There must be better designations. One that suggests itself is "working-class whites," which is literally accurate for the groups of concern here but is also problematical. E. P. Thompson has defined *class* not as a social category but an event that "happens when some men, as a result of common experiences (inherited or shared) feel and articulate the identity of their interests as between themselves, and as against other men, whose interests are different from (and usually opposed to) theirs." Thompson suggests that "the class experience is largely determined by the productive relations into which men are born—or enter voluntarily," and that "class consciousness is the way in which [class] experiences are handled in cultural terms."[2]

By these criteria the people constituting the poorer half of the white

1. Robert R. Moton, *What the Negro Thinks* (Garden City, N.Y., 1929), 21. For a discussion of the ambiguities of slave attitudes to "poor whites," see Eugene D. Genovese, " 'Rather Be a Nigger than a Poor White Man': Slave Perceptions of Southern Yeomen and Poor Whites," in Hans L. Trefousse (ed.), *Toward a New View of America: Essays in Honor of Arthur C. Cole* (New York, 1977), 79–96.

2. E. P. Thompson, *The Making of the English Working Class* (New York, 1966), 9–10.

population in the New South were not a class. They were instead a largely agricultural people with no sense of unity or common condition, and their social and political purposes were conservative rather than radical. In addition, *poor* is a relative term, and the working classes in the New South included groups differing widely in income, well-being, and productive relations. Skilled urban craftsmen and transport workers, for example, who formed the backbone of the region's labor movement, were not among the poorer elements of the population and had no sense of identity with folk they too thought of as "poor whites" or "trash."

A better designation is "plain folk," and it will be used in this study despite the risk of semantic confusion. This phrase is more accurate for present purposes than "working-class whites" and more neutral than "poor whites," "rednecks," and the like. Unfortunately, its most conspicuous usage in southern historiography, in Frank L. Owsley's *Plain Folk of the Old South*, is to designate an entirely different group of people from those studied here. Owsley's plain folk are the broad classes of nonslaveholding whites in the antebellum South, specifically the mass of substantial and small landowners and herdsmen, whom he pointedly distinguishes from "the destitute and frequently degraded poor white class."[3]

In contrast, the present study is concerned in uneven degrees with several categories of the poorest white people in the New South—those who made their living sharecropping, working in the cotton mills that began spreading across the South about 1880, or doing other kinds of low-paying, unskilled work on or off the farm. Collectively, those groups will here be labeled "plain folk," and subgroups of that general category will be termed "farm folk," "mill folk," and the like. The vast majority of plain folk were rural people—agricultural laborers, sharecroppers, tenant farmers, perhaps also even small and insecure landowners. Much smaller numbers were hunters, fishermen, or herdsmen, most of whom supplemented their livelihood by irregular cultivation of corn or garden patches. From time to time, many rural folk worked in logging, lumbering, sawmilling, rail-splitting, mining, turpentining, gristmilling, cotton ginning, or railroad construction—forms of employment that were largely seasonal or otherwise irregular, and in many areas dominated by blacks. The number of urban folk, including cotton mill operatives, was quite small compared to the total of rural folk. The number was growing, however, for plain folk in the New South were undergoing a major social transition. One group experiencing that transi-

3. Frank L. Owsley, *Plain Folk of the Old South* (Baton Rouge, 1949), viii.

tion, those who moved from sharecropping to cotton milling, is the focus of this study. (For the composition of the groups here designated "plain folk" and for statistical information on their general economic condition, see Tables I–IX in the Appendix.)

These people had no group consciousness and no name for themselves, but they are aptly described as "plain white folk." *Plain* suggests their standard of living and life-style without reference to such mischievous categories as "white trash" and "lintheads." *White* differentiates them from black southerners as it reminds us that they lived in a biracial society much concerned with race. And *folk* separates these people from middle- and upper-class southerners, and points toward the nature of their cultural distinctiveness.

Still, the categorization is not altogether satisfying. Plain folk have proven to be unexpectedly diverse people and difficult to set apart from others. Economically, culturally, and otherwise, people in the occupational categories noted above overlapped into other groups, and the lines between them and other southerners are therefore somewhat arbitrary. The folk exhibited an astonishing amount of mobility, moving from farm to farm and mill to mill and back and forth between the two, and into and out of other kinds of work as well. Moreover, there was often little distinction between work on and off the farm, and many folk combined the two, such as farming and cotton milling, with no regard for the neat categories of census takers or historians. In addition, there was more movement up and down the economic scale, into and out of the categories mentioned above, than most accounts allow for. Plain folk were people in motion, forever rearranging themselves, and their lives did *not* embody "most of the aspects of a separate caste," as one historian has recently said of "poor whites" in the New South.[4]

The social history of so large and diverse a people cannot be compressed into a single volume. The concern here is to understand how one group of plain folk, those who moved from sharecropping to the cotton mills, experienced the social and economic changes involved in that move. The period of this study is from about 1880, when cotton mills began to spread rapidly across certain sections of the South, until about 1915, when another series of transformations reduced the centrality of the farm-to-factory theme in the lives of mill folk. The intent is to focus on folk themselves—on the changes and continuities in their lives and on how they welcomed, resisted, and

4. J. Wayne Flynt, *Dixie's Forgotten People: The Southern Poor Whites* (Bloomington, 1979), 38.

otherwise reacted to forces trying to reorder their lives. Because cotton mills in the New South were concentrated in Georgia and the Carolinas, the study focuses on plain folk in those three states.

Many forces shaped the history of these folk, the most important of which were not economic or occupational but cultural. Plain folk were not "economic men," in the sense that they were not a people primarily concerned with work, accumulation, and otherwise maximizing their material condition. They were instead a cultural group, heirs to a folk, or folkish, culture, chiefly British in origin, that defined their values and aspirations, gave them a religious and social ethic, molded their family patterns and social relationships, and provided them with standards of conduct and measures for assessing themselves and other people. Their culture provided the means by which they understood and influenced the circumstances of their lives, and it largely determined the ways they reacted to social change.

Culture was the plain folk's major resource, and in the confrontation with social dislocation it served them better than history, ecology, or economic circumstance. Plain folk in the New South were products of a history that contoured their social and economic options. They were southerners in the aftermath of a military defeat that distorted political, social, and intellectual life in their section and left it with a spreading, corrosive impoverishment. Almost four of every ten white farm families in Georgia and the Carolinas in 1890 were sharecroppers or tenants, and more than four of ten in 1910.[5] An acute shortage of credit gave rise to a system of supply merchants, crop liens, and usurious interest rates that spread its tentacles far beyond the tenant and sharecropping populations. In an agricultural economy of one or two crops, many folk found themselves facing a creeping immiserization. The dimensions of their poverty are reflected in estimates that per capita income and wealth in Georgia and the Carolinas were about one-third of national averages and per capita income was nearly static for most of the New South era.[6]

Plain folk lived in an era of racial readjustment. The dislocations that

5. *Eleventh Census, 1890: Report on Farms and Homes: Proprietorship and Indebtedness,* 567, 569; *Fourteenth Census, 1920: Agriculture,* 201. These and other census figures should be taken as approximations only. In his study of the manuscript census of one Georgia county in 1880, Thomas A. Scott found that 22 percent of the heads of white families listed as farmers in the population schedules were not included in the agricultural schedules ("Cobb County, Georgia, 1880–1900: A Socioeconomic Study of an Upper Piedmont County" [Ph.D. dissertation, University of Tennessee, 1978], 32).
6. Richard A. Easterlin, "State Income Estimates," in Simon Kuznets and Dorothy S. Thomas (eds.), *Population Estimates and Economic Growth, United States, 1870–1950* (Philadelphia, 1957), 753; *Statistical Abstract of the United States, 1923,* 738.

accompanied emancipation and Reconstruction were still unresolved in 1880, and throughout the New South era, plain folk found themselves in growing economic competition with blacks and anxious lest that reduce them to the levels of the freedmen. Before the Civil War, whites supplied one-sixth of the labor that went into producing the South's cotton crop; by 1910 they produced two-thirds of the cotton grown in the section.[7]

The burdens of history were paralleled by those of physical environment. Planters in the black belt had preempted the section's best farmland and pushed plain folk into hill country, piney woods, or wiregrass areas, where soil was thin, eroding, and unproductive. The environment shaped the alternatives to farming, largely limited to extracting and processing the products of earth, forest, and farm. These jobs were unskilled, low paying, generally backbreaking, and often in out-of-the-way places that necessitated work camps or company towns and the socioeconomic relationships peculiar to such places. The warm, humid climate of the South, so attractive to sectional boosters, was less congenial to labor than to molds, fungi, bacteria, parasites, and insects, all of which infested and sometimes ravaged crops, livestock, and people alike. Folk therefore suffered a host of debilitating maladies, most of them chronic rather than acute, that affected their economic and social well-being no less than their health.

During the New South era, accelerating forces of industrialization and modernization began intruding upon these factors of environment and history, and plain folk bore a large share of the resulting dislocations. Spreading commercialization made the well-being of farmers increasingly dependent on commodity prices, credit costs, and other market forces they could not control or even influence. Monetary and banking policy, tariff rates, economic cycles, and decisions of distant capitalists had a growing, largely negative impact. Subsistence farming was increasingly precarious, even obsolescent, and more and more farm folk clustered at the bottom of the agricultural ladder.

On and off the farm, the fate of plain folk was coming to depend on how they adapted to forces of change, and on the surface at least, their prospects were unhopeful. The folk were poor, disorganized, unschooled, rural, and traditional people caught up in forces rendering all of those circumstances obsolete and limiting. Modernization was changing the objective conditions of their lives. Bred into traditional ways of subsistence farming and adapted to its rhythms and values, plain folk now found those conditions im-

7. U.S. Commissioner of Agriculture, *Report, 1876,* 136; Rupert B. Vance, *Human Factors in Cotton Culture: A Study in the Social Geography of the American South* (Chapel Hill, 1929), 60.

poverishing; and unless they became commercial farmers, they would become employees, on or off the farm. For those who remained in farming, this meant sharecropping, a form of tenancy first used on a large scale in the postbellum South to accommodate the needs of freedmen and planters. To become sharecroppers, rapidly growing numbers of farm folk adapted to unaccustomed forms of supervision and control. Becoming an operative at one of the new cotton mills, as increasing numbers of them also did, necessitated even larger adjustments. Yet plain folk had resources of their own in facing these transformations. What those resources were and how they used them are central concerns of this study.

The history of poor, powerless, and largely unliterate people is difficult to reconstruct, and for groups subject to continuing social prejudice the difficulty is compounded. For those groups, ordinary problems of source materials are aggravated by additional difficulties of cultural bias. Historians are social creatures, influenced like everyone else by the values and perspectives of their society. Their recasting of the history of slaves, ethnic minorities, and other groups, including women, is a recent example of the way they respond to current events. That example suggests that sea changes in historical treatment of social groups occur only when basic improvements take place in the status of the groups themselves. The abatement of popular prejudice serves, as it were, to legitimize the group and facilitate a new, more sympathetic look at its history. The result is sometimes clouded by tendencies to inflate and romanticize the group's past, but if that is resisted, the reexamination can be enormously fruitful.

Plain whites in the South are only beginning to benefit from this process. Unorganized and without group consciousness, they have no "movement" to assert their "cause" and no political or economic leverage with which to embellish their public image. Only a few years ago, F. N. Boney complained, not inaccurately, that while liberals, academics, and the media had largely dropped negative, stereotypical treatment of recognizable social groups, they had made no similar change in their treatment of the southern white working classes. In predictable roles of "nasty law enforcement officials, forlorn tenant farmers, select 'linthead' factory hands, and a mixed bag of unemployed rural thugs," Boney observed, southern "rednecks" commonly appear in the media and elsewhere as "the last dregs of our sick society, the ultimate bottom of the barrel."[8] Even today, they are one of the few recognizable social groups that the media can and do present in nega-

8. F. N. Boney, "The Redneck," *Georgia Review*, XXV (1971), 333.

tive, stereotypical fashion, and that academics and liberals can and do disparage by name.

This treatment rests on long tradition. Early in colonial America, descriptions began to appear of bizarre, depraved white people who were said to inhabit the backwoods of the South and live enmeshed in their own shiftlessness, immorality, and backwardness. "The inhabitants of our frontiers," Governor Alexander Spotswood of Virginia wrote in 1717, "are composed generally of such as have been transported hither as [indentured] Servants, and being out of their time . . . settle themselves where Land is to be taken up . . . that will produce the necessarys of Life with little Labour. It is pretty well known what Morals such people bring with them hither, which are not like to be much mended by their Scituation, remote from all places of worship."[9]

Here were the elements of an emerging stereotype. Then as now, "poor whites" were not simply whites who were poor, but a category of people set apart from everyone else by a plethora of undesirable qualities that added up to depravity and degeneracy. As Governor Spotswood indicated, "poor whites" were believed to descend from indentured servants, a group one historian described as including "rogues, whores, vagabonds, cheats and rabble of all descriptions raked from the gutters [of England] and kicked out of the country." When their indentures expired, the idea ran, this riffraff filtered into backwoods areas, squatting on land no one else wanted and living beyond the reach of social control and the cultural example of their superiors. Since they also lived, however barely, with no great effort, they lost all incentive for exertion, and thus for discipline and self-improvement, and "degenerated . . . into a besotted, ignorant, and vicious class, living apart in the dense recesses of the pine woods" and "multiplying with the usual fecundity of the poverty stricken."[10]

In 1897 historian John Fiske incorporated a mature version of these views in *Old Virginia and Her Neighbours*, and since then the stereotype has not changed.[11] Like most writers before and since, Fiske distinguished between "mean" whites, to whom the above description applied, and "yeo-

9. Quoted in John Fiske, *Old Virginia and Her Neighbors* (2 vols.; New York, 1897), II, 317.
10. Abbot E. Smith, *Colonists in Bondage* (1947; rpr. New York, 1971), 3; S. A. Hamilton, "The New Race Question in the South," *Arena*, XXVII (1902), 352.
11. The only element of this stereotype that can be tested empirically, the social composition of indentured servants, has been disproved. See James Horn, "Servant Emigration to the Chesapeake in the Seventeenth Century," in Thad W. Tate and David L. Ammerman (eds.), *The Chesapeake in the Seventeenth Century: Essays on Anglo-American Society* (Chapel Hill, 1979), 94. The most recent treatment of the larger subject is in Bernard Bailyn, *Voyagers to the West* (New York, 1986). On the origin and evolution of attitudes toward "poor whites," see

man" farmers and artisans, who, though poor, were sturdy, responsible, and deserving. This distinction too was part of the stereotype, and helped make it acceptable to modern scholars. Thus one historian divided "poor whites" in the antebellum South into "white trash" and yeomen, while another scholar distinguished between "yeomen farmers, artisans, and mechanics" and "the true 'poor-whites': indigent, shiftless, and generally inferior."[12]

One basis for the differentiation was economic. Thus one scholar described "poor whites" in the Old South as "a landless and relatively propertyless group" of people who were "shiftless, undernourished, ignorant, and had an inferiority complex." In most accounts, however, the key distinction was life-style. Yeomen were self-sufficient farmers who generally worked their own land; and more importantly, they were people who had internalized the economic and social values of the middle-class ethic. "The backbone of southern society," yeomen were thrifty, responsible, and law abiding, and committed to work, self-discipline, and conventional morality. "Poor whites," on the other hand, had "a tradition of improvidence, moral degeneracy, lack of ambition, and indifference to profitable labor." Theirs was a "state of aimlessness, of purposelessness, and of footlessness," in the words of one sociologist, "[that] expresse[d] itself not merely in laziness and general inefficiency but also in demoralizing habits, crime, insanity, and disease."[13]

The best way to understand these distinctions is to see them in context. The derogatory qualities attributed to "poor whites" are those that land-

Mildred R. Mell, "A Definitive Study of the Poor Whites in the South" (Ph.D. dissertation, University of North Carolina, 1938). The literary image of "poor whites" is traced in Shields McIlwaine, *The Southern Poor-White: From Lubberland to Tobacco Road* (Norman, Okla., 1939); and Silvia J. Cooke, *From Tobacco Road to Route 66: The Southern Poor White in Fiction* (Chapel Hill, 1976).

12. Avery O. Craven, "Poor Whites and Negroes in the Ante-Bellum South," *Journal of Negro History*, XV (1930), 14–25; A. N. J. Den Hollander, "The Tradition of 'Poor Whites,'" in W. T. Couch (ed.), *Culture in the South* (Chapel Hill, 1934), 404.

13. Clement Eaton, "Class Differences in the Old South," *Virginia Quarterly Review*, XXXIII (1957), 366; William B. Hesseltine and David L. Smiley, *The South in American History* (Englewood Cliffs, N.J., 1960), 195; and Edgar T. Thompson, "Purpose and Tradition in Southern Rural Society: A Point of View for Research," *Social Forces*, XXV (1940), 278. The traditional contrast between depictions of "poor white trash" and "yeomen" is graphically illustrated in D. H. Hundley, *Social Relations in Our Southern States* (1860; rpr. New York, 1973), 250–83 and 191–222. The favorable literary treatment of yeomen is reflected in Merrill M. Skaggs, *The Folk of Southern Fiction* (Athens, Ga., 1972). For favorable (and extensive) treatment of yeomen by historians, see Frank L. Owsley, *Plain Folk of the Old South;* Herbert Weaver, *Mississippi Farmers* (Nashville, 1945); and Blanche H. Clark, *The Tennessee Yeomen, 1840–1860* (Nashville, 1942).

lords, employers, and middle-class moralists have always ascribed to groups at the bottom of the socioeconomic scale—slaves, serfs, sharecroppers, unskilled or casual laborers, and any others whom they once thought of as the "undeserving" poor.

Such traits are of course in the eye of the beholder. Turned around and seen in positive terms, the shiftlessness, degeneracy, and other qualities attributed to "poor whites" become manifestations of the social and cultural phenomena that set plain folk apart from the middle classes. What bothered critics was the refusal of "poor whites" to live according to middle-class prescription. They lacked self-discipline and proper concern with appearances, and did not always honor the dictates of conventional morality. They also lacked acquisitive values, and thus the desire to save and possess and get ahead. Above all, they were unwilling to keep forever busy or make work the centerpiece of their lives. "Poor whites" were guilty of such transgressions; "yeomen" were not. For purposes of historical analysis, therefore, "poor white" is an unuseful social category. Like "welfare chiseler" or "hippie" today, it is a designation reserved for those whose life-style is deemed immoral or otherwise unacceptable. The point is not that such people did and do not exist—granting certain assumptions and definitions—but that the categorization impedes social analysis.

A brief look at one description of "poor whites" in the New South will illustrate this. In 1882 and 1883, an anonymous New Englander published in *Atlantic Monthly* an extended account of a trip he had recently made through the South. The account was notable for its effort to describe the section and its people objectively, and its publication was an effort to promote sectional reconciliation in the aftermath of the Civil War and Reconstruction. The account was also a striking illustration of the difficulties outsiders had understanding plain folk. "The traveler observes, nearly everywhere in the South," the New Englander wrote, "discouraging marks of ignorance and slovenliness on the part of those who cultivate the soil; of such wastefulness and want of foresight as would be fatal to any industry or enterprise." Thus, "plows and other utensils are left in the fields, exposed to the weather all winter. No adequate shelter is provided for horses or other domestic animals, and they are often insufficiently fed." Yet "when a poor man sees his only horse or cow die of exposure or neglect, he accepts the result of his own indolence as a mysterious dispensation of Providence, an occurrence for which he is in no degree responsible."[14]

14. "Studies in the South," *Atlantic Monthly*, XLIX–LI (January, 1882–January, 1883). The quotations are from XLIX (May, 1882), 677.

It was perplexing. "I have often tried to analyze this stolidity," the New Englander continued, "to discover its elements and sources, but have usually found it impossible to determine whether these people do not know that they cause their own misfortunes, or whether they know but do not care. . . . The poor white people do not appear to be a complaining class, but take ill-fortune with a stoical silence. Work for improvement, such as the construction of good bridges and roads, seems to be avoided as if it would be an impiety." Consequently, "the conditions of life and society in the South are in some respects peculiar, and to deal with them successfully will require a new development and advance in public spirit in the dominant classes, North and South."[15]

What the New Englander described was a way of life and work that embodied many of the cultural values of plain folk in the New South. Those values were not exclusive to folk, of course, but they were also not those of "the dominant classes, North and South," as the New Englander shrewdly observed. The folk reflected a number of qualities that offended the go-getting New Englander—an acceptance of things as they are and have been, an unconcern with accumulating and possessing, a greater concern with being than becoming, a personalism so infectious that even a standoffish New Englander was impressed by it. Above all, the folk evidenced an unwillingness to make work and material concerns the primary aim of life.

It was not, then, that folk were lazy or degenerate. Rather, their values and imperatives were not those of their critics. The truth was, as quintessential critic Walter Hines Page lamented in 1902, that "these men and women do not feel poor. They have a civilization of their own, of which they are very proud. They have for a hundred years been told to be proud of it." Page was writing of traditional, unprogressive southerners generally rather than plain folk specifically, but his comments aptly describe the latter. "Are they not independent?" Page continued. "What more could men ask? One in five is illiterate. But what matter? Some of the illiterate men are more successful than some others that can read. What does it profit a man, then, to read?" One of their schoolteachers told an astonished Page, "The ability to read was not a good test even of a man's intelligence, to say nothing of his character." Page complained, "What they are they regard as the normal state of society."[16]

But what group, one might ask, does not do that? Recognizing that all

15. *Ibid.* (1882), 677–78.
16. Walter Hines Page, *The Rebuilding of Old Commonwealths* (New York, 1902), 116–18.

social groups perceive themselves as normal is one of the essential steps in understanding plain folk and their history in the New South.

In recent years scholars and the media alike have begun to look beyond traditional stereotypes and into the lives of plain folk. The list of works already published on the history and present state of southern working classes is lengthy, growing, and impressive.[17] The success of several motion pictures, beginning with *Norma Rae* and *Harlan County: USA*, that sympathetically portray the struggles of southern workers for unionization, is evidence of another sort that perceptions are changing. Bigoted "rednecks" have not disappeared from the media as representative types of working-class southerners, but yokels and "good ol' boys" now seem more popular, and even they are beginning to share the spotlight with characterizations that embody some of the realities of life among southern workers and some of the positive dimensions of their culture as well. Indeed, certain elements of southern folk culture, especially "country" music in its many guises, have become nationally popular art forms.

All of this is related to the now-fashionable search for roots. White southerners, like other Americans, are suddenly interested in their personal and family histories, and more often than not those histories go back to folkish origins. Most southerners are only one, two, or three generations removed from the country and farming, and from poor or modest economic circumstances; and most of them certainly have plain folk in their direct or collateral ancestry.

The best fruits of this new interest have come from the burgeoning interest in folk life in Appalachia.[18] By comparison, the folk and folk culture of the Piedmont and lowland South, which are important concerns in this study, have received little attention. Perhaps lowlanders seem less quaint or remote and more difficult to romanticize, or perhaps their culture seems less exotic because it is less well preserved and therefore less distinctive. Yet folklorists have distinguished three primary foci of folk culture in the South—the cultures of mountain whites, lowland whites, and blacks—and have shown that each of those groups preserved its culture

17. See, for example, *Southern Exposure* (1973—   ); Flynt, *Dixie's Forgotten People;* Mimi Conway, *Rise Gonna Rise: A Portrait of Southern Textile Workers* (Garden City, N.Y., 1979); and John W. Hevener, *Which Side Are You On?: The Harlan County Coal Miner, 1931–1939* (Urbana, 1978).

18. For examples, see such publications as *Foxfire* (1967—   ); *Mountain Life and Work* (1929—   ); *Appalachian Heritage* (1973—   ); and *Appalachian Journal* (1972—   ).

through years of relative isolation.[19] In the mountains the barriers were geographical; in the lowlands they were social and economic; among blacks they were racial. Yet folk culture is no respecter of barriers, and the three groups interacted with one another and with the rest of society as well. The paramount fact about the two white folk cultures is thus their similarities, not their differences. The similarities pervade the form as well as the content of their cultures; the differences consist chiefly of the greater purity in which Appalachian culture survived and the greater degree of black influence in the lowlands. The recent success of Appalachians and Afro-Southerners in reclaiming their folkish pasts has encouraged lowland whites to do the same thing, and across the South today there are oral, family, and local history projects caringly collecting memories and otherwise preserving or recovering the history of ordinary people. The results are invaluable additions to the rich body of materials folklorists, antiquarians, and others have been collecting for more than a century; and they shed much new light on the history of plain folk.[20]

Although only a few historians have given plain folk the kind of attention their colleagues have bestowed on slaves, women, and other groups, many have produced impressive studies that bear on the lives of the folk.[21] In addition, a large body of recent work by young scholars, some of it still unpublished, suggests that interest in things affecting the history of plain folk and other members of the southern working classes is still rising.[22]

19. See, for example, B. A. Botkin, "Folk and Folklore," in Couch (ed.), *Culture in the South*, 570–93.

20. For examples, see B. A. Botkin, *A Treasury of Southern Folklore: Stories, Balluds, Traditions and Folkways of the People of the South* (New York, 1949); Henry Glassie, *Pattern in the Material Folk Culture of the Eastern United States* (Philadelphia, 1968); Newman I. White (ed.), *The Frank C. Brown Collection of North Carolina Folklore* (7 vols.; Durham, 1952–64); and *Southern Folklore Quarterly* (1937—   ).

21. See, for example, Edward Magdol and Jon L. Wukelyn (eds.), *The Southern Common People: Studies in Nineteenth Century Social History* (Westport, Conn., 1980), Gary M. Fink and Merl E. Reed (eds.), *Essays in Southern Labor History: Selected Papers, Southern Labor History Conference 1976* (Westport, Conn., 1977); Robert C. McMath, *Populist Vanguard: A History of the Southern Farmers Alliance* (New York, 1977); Melton A. McLaurin, *Paternalism and Protest: Southern Cotton Mill Workers and Organized Labor, 1875–1905* (Westport, Conn., 1971); Buel E. Cobb, *The Sacred Harp: A Tradition and Its Music* (Athens, Ga., 1978); and Bill C. Malone, *Southern Music / American Music* (Lexington, Ky., 1979). Jacquelyn Dowd Hall *et al.*, *Like a Family: The Making of a Southern Cotton Mill World* (Chapel Hill, 1987) appeared too late to be used in this study.

22. For examples, see David L. Carlton, *Mill and Town in South Carolina, 1880–1920* (Baton Rouge, 1982); Allen H. Stokes, "Black and White Labor and the Development of the Southern Textile Industry, 1800–1920" (Ph.D. dissertation, University of South Carolina, 1977); Steven H. Hahn, *The Roots of Southern Populism: Yeoman Farmers and the Transformation*

This interest is abetted by the shifting popular image of the white working classes and by the belated recognition of a large body of older scholarship, almost all by nonhistorians, on aspects of cultural and social life traditionally neglected by historians. As long ago as 1917, for example, Cecil J. Sharp published the collection *English Folk Songs from Southern Appalachia*, which opened a window onto the mind as well as the culture of mountain folk; and his example was soon followed by others. Presently there appeared an extended list of impressive works on folk culture and related topics in Appalachia and elsewhere, all of it distinguished by the serious and positive treatment accorded the subjects. Collectively, the works documented, for Appalachia at least, the richest and best preserved folk culture in the nation.

Social scientists, many of them gathered at the University of North Carolina under the aegis of Howard W. Odum in the interwar years, added important economic and sociological dimensions to these cultural studies. In such works as Rupert B. Vance's *Human Factors in Cotton Culture*, Margaret J. Hagood's *Mothers of the South: Portraiture of the White Tenant Farm Women*, and Arthur F. Raper and Ira De A. Reid's *Sharecroppers All*, published in 1929, 1939, and 1941 respectively, these scholars explored the lives of poor folk in their own day. At the same time, a host of works inspired by the New Deal and the New Dealers' discovery of southern poverty, exemplified by James Agee's *Let Us Now Praise Famous Men*, published in 1941, dramatized and humanized the plight of the poor. Today these works seem marred by their emphasis on victimization, but they nevertheless brought together a wealth of information on poor southerners and helped make the middle classes aware of the poor and their impoverishment.

A third stimulus to current interest in plain folk is the "new" history that originated in the work of French social historians and matured (for the working classes at least) in E. P. Thompson's *The Making of the English Working Class*. This "new" history has been especially fruitful because of its concern with working people as distinct from labor leaders, trade unions, and labor activism. It does not focus on the worker's relationship with his job, employer, or trade union, and it rejects the notion that economic factors define the worker's life and explain his behavior. Instead, it views workers as human beings in specific cultural contexts and studies their culture and

---

of the Georgia Upcountry, 1850–1890 (New York, 1983); and Charles Piehl, "White Society in the Black Belt, 1879–1920: A Study of Four North Carolina Counties" (Ph.D. dissertation, Washington University, 1979).

way of life rather than their employment alone. This approach neutralizes the tendency, so pronounced in some of the "old" history, to romanticize workers or distort their experience by dwelling exclusively on labor activism and class consciousness or, alternatively, on victimization by employers or impersonal market forces.[23]

The insights of this "new" history rest in part on imaginative use of social science. The things one needs to know to understand the history of working people, including those of the New South, are things social scientists have been studying for a long time—family composition and dynamics, social relations, group activity, work patterns, adaptation to social change, culture and its social functions, the meaning of poverty and powerlessness, techniques of social control, and other things too numerous to list. The relevant scholarship on these subjects is enormous and has been quite useful for this study, especially in such areas as culture and its social functions, the adaptation of rural folk to industrial employment, and the values and temperament of working people.[24]

In the course of this study, anthropologist Robert Redfield's common-sense definition of *culture*—a people's "total equipment of ideas and institutions and conventionalized activities"—has been used. It has been refined, however, with the distinction Sidney W. Mintz has drawn between culture and society. Culture, Mintz writes, is "a kind of resource" to be "*used*," whereas society is "a kind of arena" in which it is used. To understand the

23. The best introduction to the literature of this "new" history is David Brody, "Labor History in the 1970s: Toward a History of the American Worker," in Michael Kammen (ed.), *The Past Before Us* (Ithaca, 1980), 245–66. The best example of the literature of this school is Thompson, *The Making of the English Working Class;* and for American workers is Herbert G. Gutman, *Work, Culture, and Society in Industrializing America: Essays in Working Class and Social History* (New York, 1976). A good discussion of the relevance of this "new" history for southern workers is Michael J. Cassity, "Southern Workers and Social Change: Concepts and Prospects," *Georgia Historical Quarterly,* XLII (1978), 200–12.

24. On culture, see, for example, Clifford Geertz, *The Interpretation of Cultures* (New York, 1973). On the adaptation of folk to industrial employment, see, for example, Karl Polanyi, *The Great Transformation* (Boston, 1957); Sidney Pollard, *The Genesis of Modern Management: A Study of the Industrial Revolution in Great Britain* (Cambridge, Mass., 1965), especially 160–208; and Neil J. Smelser, *Social Change in the Industrial Revolution: An Application of Theory to the British Cotton Industry* (London, 1959). For a sampling of the voluminous literature on the values of the plain folk, see Robert E. Lane, *Political Ideology: Why the American Common Man Believes What He Does* (New York, 1962); Lee Rainwater, Richard P. Coleman, and Gerald Handel, *Workingman's Wife: Her Personality, World and Life Style* (New York, 1959); Edward C. Banner, *The Moral Basis of a Backward Society* (Chicago, 1958); Howard Newby, *The Deferential Worker: A Study of Farm Workers in East Anglia* (Madison, Wis., 1979); and William A. Rushing, *Class, Culture, and Alienation: A Study of Farmers and Farm Workers* (Lexington, Mass., 1972).

precise operation of that "resource," it is helpful to follow one of Clifford Geertz's admonitions. "Culture is not a power . . . to which social events, behavior, institutions, or processes can be causally attributed," Geertz has written, but "a context . . . within which [those things] can be intelligibly . . . described."[25]

To understand plain folk in the New South, it is necessary to come to terms with the unappealing or ostensibly dysfunctional aspects of their culture—their racism and traditionalism, for example, or their support for a political "demagogue" like Governor Coleman L. Blease of South Carolina. One's inclination to dismiss these things as bigotry or irrationality is unhelpful and a major obstacle to understanding. "When group behavior does not—and indeed, cannot—attain its ostensible purpose," Robert K. Merton has written, "there is an inclination to attribute its occurrence to lack of intelligence, sheer ignorance, [outdated cultural] survivals, or so-called inertia." Yet to do so "in no sense accounts for the group behavior" but is "simply a case of name-calling" and is no substitute "for an analysis of the actual role of this behavior in the life of the group." Merton continues, "*Apparently* irrational behavior may *at times* be found to be positively functional for the group." If "an activity of a group does not achieve its nominal purpose," that does not mean that "its persistence can be described only as an instance of 'inertia,' 'survival,' or 'manipulation by powerful subgroups in the society.'" The continuation of that behavior may instead, indeed often does, fulfill some positive function that is not immediately manifest.

There is much to recommend Merton's position to those who would understand plain folk in the New South. It grounds inquiry in social context, thereby increasing its complexity. It also points up the irrelevance of easy moral judgments and of the tendency merely to deplore social forms that violate one's sensibilities. "Any attempt to eliminate an existing social structure without providing adequate alternative structures for fulfilling the functions previously fulfilled by the abolished organization is doomed to

25. Robert Redfield, *The Primitive World and Its Transformation* (Ithaca, 1962), 85; Sidney W. Mintz, Foreword to Norman Whitten and John F. Szwed (eds.), *Afro-American Anthropology: Contemporary Perspectives* (New York, 1970), 1–16; Geertz, *The Interpretation of Cultures*, 14. I have found quite helpful Herbert G. Gutman's application of Mintz's idea in *Work, Culture, and Society in Industrializing America*. Oscar Lewis' "culture of poverty," which focuses too largely on passivity and victimization of the poor, is less useful. See Lewis, *Anthropological Essays* (New York, 1970), 67–80; and the critique of Lewis' model in Charles A. Valentine, "The 'Culture of Poverty': Its Scientific Significance and Its Implications for Action," in Eleanor B. Leacock (ed.), *The Culture of Poverty: A Critique* (New York, 1971), 193–225.

failure," Merton states. "To seek social change without due recognition of the manifest and latent functions performed by the social organization undergoing change, is to indulge in social ritual rather than social engineering."[26]

Critics and observers of "poor whites" have too often indulged in social ritual, and this remains a major obstacle to historical understanding. If plain folk are to be understood, they must first be accepted on their own terms, and many of those terms violate the assumptions with which historians, social analysts, and reformers approach the study—and needs—of poor, oppressed, working-class groups. To neutralize the difficulties this situation presents, plain folk have in the following pages been allowed to speak for themselves, and their words have been taken seriously. The results have been unexpected, often strikingly so.

26. Robert K. Merton, *Social Theory and Social Structure* (enlarged ed.; New York, 1968), 117, 119, 135. See also Merton's general critique of functionalist theory, *ibid.*, 73–138, and Clifford Geertz's insightful discussion "Ideology as a Cultural System," in *The Interpretation of Cultures*, 193–233.

PART I

BACKGROUND OF THE PLAIN FOLK

1

SHARECROPPING

"We'd never owned our own place and Pa hired out aroun' on the farms and sometimes he'd work at the sawmill or gettin' out wood for haulin'," Mary Abbott recalled of her childhood in rural Guilford County, North Carolina, in the 1890s. "We had a mighty hard pull. So when word come through that they was a big mill goin' to be put up at Concord and they was a-hirin' a lot o' folks to work, Pa said he was a-goin' down and see about it. Ma said if he was goin' we might's well all go along, so we got ready our stuff in the wagon, hitched up the ol' mule and started off." Mrs. Abbott remembered: "I mind well us a-goin'. I set between Mariah and Rose on the feather ticks on top o' the load, and when the wagon'd hit one of 'em mud ruts in the road or go over a bump we'd have to hold on tight to keep from fallin' off."

"Ev'ybody aroun' was crazy about goin' to the mill to make money," Mrs. Abbott continued; yet her own account reveals the uncertainty with which her father, and probably most other folk, approached the mills for the first time. Arriving before the mill and its village were completed, her father was forced to sell his mule to cover living expenses until the mill was running. "Pa said 's long 's he kep' Jeff [the mule] we'd have us a way to get back to farmin'," Mrs. Abbott recalled, "but now it looked like we'd have to stay on at the mill." An important link to the past was severed.

In endless variations across the New South the experience of Mary Abbott's family was repeated. "One day when I was about eighteen year old a man come ridin' up to our gate in a rubber-tire buggy. . . . His name, he give it, was Mr. Ab Newcomb, Super of the Cotton Mills," Rosa Kanipe remembered, relating her own introduction to mill work in Newton, North Carolina, about 1905. "He was out hirin' hands for the mill. To hear him talk you'd think all you'd have to do after movin' to the mill was to collect your money. I'd never seen a cotton mill in my life and had never dreamed of workin' in one. Maw invited him in. I could see she was kindly took with his nice ways." Mrs. Kanipe's mother asked Newcomb to stay for supper and talk with her husband, then at work in the field. "It was settled before he left," Mrs. Kanipe recalled, "that Lillian and me should go to the mill and board till spring," when the rest of the family would join them.

In the same year young Rosa and her sister went to Newton, four-year-old Jessie Lee, later Jessie Lee Carter, made a similar though longer trek from the Tennessee mountains to Greenville, South Carolina. "Some man from Brandon Mill," Mrs. Carter said, recollecting the event much later, "it must have been some big bossman come, and he was going around the country getting people . . . to come to work, because they just had made the mill. My daddy [Millard Lee] and my grandfather and my uncles begin to work in the mill as quick as they brought down here. They moved them here in two horse wagons." Mrs. Carter remarked: "It took them about a week to come down there and move us out here. I heard my daddy tell about that. They brought us to the house right over there at Brandon now, number fourteen. We moved in that house and [my daddy] lived there forty years and worked in the mill."

"He loved it," Mrs. Carter recalled. "He was never out a day without he was sick."

Not everyone was so eager. "Mr. Steele, the superintendent at the old Roberdel Mill, had heard about our bad luck and he come to see Frank about movin' to the mill," Molly Godwin recalled of the time she and her husband first thought about mill work. The Godwins, both children of North Carolina tenant farmers, had saved and bought a farm of their own only to lose it in a legal dispute that left them penniless. "Frank was ready to go but I wouldn't hear to it," Mrs. Godwin remembered. "I couldn't bear the thought of movin' to no cotton mill."

Still, they had to do something, and mill work was the most promising job available. A week after his visit, Superintendent Steele walked the couple through his mill to ease Mrs. Godwin's misgivings. "He took me all through that mill and I'd never heard so much racket in all my life," she recollected. "When we got back outside again he said, 'You've seen for yourself it's not bad, haven't you, Mrs. Godwin?' I said, 'Mr. Steele, it may not be what you call bad but it shore is scareful.'"

The cause of Mrs. Godwin's apprehensions may be imagined. Cotton mills were the largest things plain folk had ever seen. Full of strange, roaring machines crowded into vast rooms, they made more noise than the folk had ever heard, and more commotion too. The first impression they created could be awesome, even overwhelming. Added to this, the social prejudice against mill folk was strong and intimidating. "I caint do it, I caint do it," Mrs. Godwin was still insisting, even after Steele had shown her the six-room house he wanted the Godwins to move into and Mrs. Godwin to run as a boardinghouse while her husband worked in the mill. "I held out against movin' to the mill for a solid month," she remembered. "Funny, sometimes how long it can take you to make up your mind to do somethin' you knowed all along you had to do."

Not everyone gave in, however. Many folk went to the mills, looked around, even worked a while, and went back to the farm. "My folks moved one time to the mill," Merton Rhodes, a North Carolina tenant farmer, related in the 1930s. "I went up there on a visit. Pa wanted me to go to the mill one night to see how I liked it. I tell you the truth, there was such a buzzing and roaring in my head I couldn't make head or tail of it. No sir, no cotton mill for me. The farm is the place to raise a family." Will Conner, who began sharecropping in 1900 in North Carolina and was still at it in 1939, agreed with Rhodes. "No siree! No cotton mill for me," Conner said. "Farmin's what I was cut out for. I was some kind o' glad to get back on the farm," he added, recalling an eight-month stint he once worked in a cotton mill in Roanoke Rapids. "It's hard work [on the farm] . . . but I'll take it all to bein' stove up in a factory."

Will Conner and Merton Rhodes, like Molly Godwin, Millard Lee, and countless other folk in the New South, reached a crossroads in their lives and made deliberate choices to go one way rather than another. The choices they made were not the same, nor were they made with the same degree of freedom. For many folk, the new cotton mills offered hope or opportunity; for others they provided a desperate way out of a desperate situation; for others still, the very thought of mill work was intolerable. Those who went to the mills went for reasons of their own, and each brought his own hopes, disappointments, and anxieties. Their journey was a genuine folk movement, to all appearances disorganized and undirected; yet its regularities were real and important.

The vast majority of mill folk came directly from the farm, though many, like Mary Abbott's father, had also done other types of work. All were poor, though the levels of their poverty and the economic necessities that pushed them to the mills were not the same. Most went more in hope than in despair, though most, especially the men, would have remained on the farm had the choice been entirely free. Of those who stayed long enough to adjust to mill work and life, most, especially the women and children, came to see the mills as more attractive than the alternatives available to them, and the act of remaining was a conscious one. Going to the mills was a momentous move, its very momentousness serving to encourage expectation; and the move was easier and less disruptive than most accounts suggest.

"WE HAVE TO PAY WHATEVER THE MERCHANT OR LANDLORD CHARGES."

To understand the move, it is necessary to understand the folk who made it. Almost all of them were landless farmers—sharecroppers, tenants, or agricultural laborers, or the wives or children of men who were—though a few owned small farms or had done nonagricultural work all their lives. The vast majority came from the piedmont section of the states that stretch from Virginia to Alabama, where most of the mills were also located, or from the valleys and hills of southeastern Appalachia. Why did they leave the farm, these traditional, unventuresome folk? What pushed them toward the mills? What in their lives on the farm determined the ways they adapted to life and work in the mills? And why did others like them remain on sharecroppings that seemed to promise so little?

Answers to these questions lie in the history of landless farm folk in the New South and are therefore difficult to find because the history of those folk has been little studied—is in fact hardly known at all.[1] The recent scholarship on sharecropping, much of it revisionist and quite impressive, is largely concerned with the origin and spread of the system in the aftermath of the Civil War, or with institutional, economic, and racial aspects of the relationship between black croppers and white planters in the generation after 1865.[2] For the early postwar years, these emphases are probably

1. For convenience and readability, such folk will be referred to as sharecroppers and their farm experience as sharecropping, though a small minority of mill folk had never been landless farmers.

2. This literature is large. Among major works, which treat sharecropping in the New South in widely differing ways and with widely differing emphases, are Roger L. Ransom and Richard Sutch, *One Kind of Freedom: The Economic Consequences of Emancipation* (Cambridge, U.K., 1977); the critical literature Ransom and Sutch's work stimulated, especially the symposium in *Explorations in Economic History*, XVI (1979); Robert Higgs, *Competition and Coer-*

justified, for sharecropping became a major form of farm tenure in the South because freedmen and planters found in it ways to reconcile conflicting desires and complementary needs. By dividing large plantations into individual tenancies, sharecropping enabled freedmen to work individual crops and avoid the kinds of gang labor and overseeing they associated with slavery. It also gave them use of their landlords' tools and workstock, for most of them had no property at all. The freedmen's pay was not in cash but partly in kind (firewood, garden patch, pasturage, and the like), partly in supplies (periodic allotments of such staples as meat, meal, and molasses, or credit allowances for those and other necessities at a supply store), and partly a share of the crop. This arrangement satisfied the freedmen and eased the planters' chief problem, a shortage of liquid wealth. It also placed some of the risk for crop failure on the sharecropper.

The size of the freedman's share of his crop varied from one to three fourths, though after the system matured, the poorest croppers—those with nothing to offer but the labor of themselves and their families—generally received a third or a half of the crop. From this share was deducted the value of the supplies and allowances the cropper received during the year. A man with a mule, wagon, and other implements of his own could rise from the ranks of sharecropping and become a tenant farmer, though there were several intermediate grades between the "pure" forms of those tenure types. The differences between the types were substantial. A sharecropper was an employee, not a renter; therefore, he had no say in crop decisions and no property rights in the crop he made. A tenant farmer, on the other hand, was a renter and as such owned his crop, made his own decisions, arranged his own credit, and paid a set rent rather than a share of his crop.[3] Those distinctions, especially among white farmers, were less clear-cut than this dichotomy suggests.

This blurring was due to several factors, among them the economic circumstance of individual croppers, the size of a man's "field force" (the number of "hands" he could put in the field), and the custom of the neigh-

cion: *Blacks in the American Economy, 1865–1914* (Cambridge, U.K., 1977); and Joseph D. Reid, "Sharecropping as an Understandable Market Response: The Postbellum South," *Journal of Economic History*, XXXIII (1973), 106–30. See also the critiques of these and other works in Harold D. Woodman, "Sequel to Slavery: The New History Views the Postbellum South," *Journal of Southern History*, XLIII (1977), 523–54; and William N. Parker, "The South in the National Economy, 1865–1970," *Southern Economic Journal*, XLVI (1980), 1019–48.

3. On the legal aspects of sharecropping, see Harold D. Woodman, "Post-Civil War Southern Agriculture and the Law," *Agricultural History*, LIII (1977), 319–37; and Charles S. Mangum, *The Legal Status of the Tenant Farmer in the Southeast* (Chapel Hill, 1952).

borhood and of individual landlords and credit merchants as well. These things affected a man's ability to gain credit and thus the kind of deal a cropper could make with his landlord and credit merchant (who were often the same person in the black belt, but not in predominantly white areas).

To accommodate the cropper's need for credit and their own lack of liquid wealth, landlords and merchants worked out a lien system that became the controlling economic feature of sharecropping and other forms of farm tenure in the New South. At the beginning of the year, the cropper gave his landlord or credit merchant a lien, or mortgage, on his unplanted cotton (or tobacco) crop in exchange for credit to be advanced over the course of the crop year. The credit was in the form of supplies, fertilizer, and other necessities, and was repayable whenever the crop was harvested. As the cropper gathered his cotton, he turned it over to the lienholder, and at "settling up" time, the amount of his indebtedness was deducted from the value of his share. If the value was larger than the debt, the cropper had "paid out," and received the excess in cash.

This system evolved to meet the exigencies of a difficult situation. It functioned, however, to perpetuate the impoverishment and dependence that gave rise to it. The economic risks of sharecropping were high, and competition between credit merchants was largely inoperative. Credit charges were therefore depressingly high—the equivalent of 59.4 percent in annual interest in the 1880s according to the most systematic modern study. Contemporary estimates were lower than that, but the estimates then and now are imprecise. Credit charges were levied not in the form of interest surcharges but as markups over cash prices, and the markup on a given item was the same whether the charge was repaid a month later, six months later, or after an even longer time. Computed in terms of annual interest rates, the charges were usuriously high, but croppers thought not in those terms but of the amount of the markup. "I don't know what per cent we pay over cash price," a tenant farmer told the North Carolina labor commissioner in 1887. "We have to pay whatever the merchant or landlord charges, and it is generally very heavy—25 to 50 per cent."[4]

The amount of the credit, and thus the cropper's indebtedness, was

---

4. The annual interest estimate is that of Ransom and Sutch, *One Kind of Freedom*, 130. For lower contemporary estimates, see U.S. Commissioner of Agriculture, *Report, 1886*, 423–24; *House Documents*, 57th Cong., 1st Sess., No. 184, Vol. 10, pp. 160–61; and Charles Lee Raper, "The Use of Credit by the North Carolina Farmers," *South Atlantic Quarterly*, XIII (1914), 121. The tenant farmer is quoted in North Carolina Bureau of Labor Statistics, *Annual Report, 1887*, 133, hereinafter cited as NC *Labor Report* by year.

limited, however, and that reduced the burden of high interest charges. In eleven counties in the South Carolina upcountry in 1879, for example, the average value of all crop liens was $77, and in the entire state in 1885 the average was $99. In 1905, a student of the subject estimated that credit advances in Georgia ranged from $60 to $125 for a one-horse crop and $125 to $225 for a two-horse crop. These figures were low because croppers as well as merchants wanted to keep them down. Merchants wanted their creditors to pay out, and croppers wanted cash left over after settling up. Also, most farmers, white croppers probably to a much larger extent than blacks, grew most of their food and supplies and did not live off the "furnish" they received on credit. According to one modern estimate, Georgia farmers purchased 30 percent of their food and supplies in the 1880s, 60 percent of which they paid on credit. If that estimate is correct, 18 percent of their total food and supplies was subject to those high interest rates.[5] Croppers were less self-sufficient and more dependent on credit than other farmers, however, and spent a higher portion of their income on credit charges. Interest charges thus consumed a meaningful part of their income.

Sharecropping and the lien system also encouraged, or permitted, practices that kept farmers poor and dependent. Cultivation was unscientific, not intensive, and laxly done; the land was eroded, the soil depleted, and productivity impoverishingly low. In Georgia and the Carolinas, cotton farmers averaged three- or four-tenths of a bale per acre through the New South years, and sharecroppers even less.[6] Moreover, the system encouraged cotton to the neglect of other crops, thus adversely affecting food and feed supplies. The emphasis on cotton resulted from an effort to keep cash income up: but the increased production of cash crops depressed prices, and farm income remained low and uncertain throughout the cotton belt. Annual average cotton prices, which conceal significant seasonal variations, hovered around nine or ten cents in the early 1880s, and about a cent less from 1885 until the depression of the 1890s pushed them below five cents in

5. South Carolina State Board of Agriculture, *South Carolina Resources and Population, Institutions and Industries* (Charleston, 1883), 154; William J. Cooper, *The Conservative Regime: South Carolina, 1877–1890* (Baltimore, 1968), 137; Enoch M. Banks, *The Economics of Land Tenure in Georgia* (New York, 1905), 53; Claudia Goldin, " 'N' Kinds of Freedom: An Introduction to the Issues," *Explorations in Economic History*, XVI (1979), 21.

6. U.S. Department of Agriculture, *Bulletin No. 164: Cotton and Cottonseed Acreage, Yield, Production . . . by States, 1866–1952* (1955), 8–10, 23–25. Corn yields were equally low. See U.S. Department of Agriculture, *Bulletin No. 515: Corn Yields per Acre and Prices, by States, 50 years, 1866–1915* (1917), 2–3. On the lower yields of sharecroppers, see U.S. Department of Agriculture, *Bulletin No. 648: A Farm-Management Survey of Brooks County, Georgia* (1918), 17.

1894; and they remained below eight cents until 1900. During the next decade, cyclical fluctuations floated prices between seven and ten cents; in 1910 they jumped to fourteen cents only to fall back to a low of eight cents in 1914.[7] Cotton accounted for more than four-fifths of the cash income of cotton belt farmers, and at these prices sharecroppers had little hope of improving themselves economically. The scale of their operation kept their income at subsistence levels, for on fifteen or twenty acres of cotton, a one-mule cropper made no more than five to ten bales, a fourth or a half of which belonged to his landlord.

"THE POORER WHITES HAVE ABANDONED THEIR POOR FARMS AND WORK FOR SHARES ON THE LARGER AND BETTER FARMS."

How the sharecropping system spread among white folk in the fifteen or twenty years after the Civil War is not clear. "Before the war," an observer wrote in 1879, describing results of the spread in Polk County, Georgia, "the poorer whites owned and occupied small, poor places and produced nearly all they used of both food and clothing; but they produced very little cotton. . . . Now the poorer whites have abandoned their poor farms and work for shares on the larger and better farms, under the direction of landowners. As cotton is the profitable crop, these poor people produce cotton almost exclusively, and with it buy everything they need, except bread, and some buy even that. Families who in ante-bellum days only produced from 2 to 3 bales of cotton now produce from 5 to 20." To this observer, a field correspondent for the 1880 census of agriculture, this development was recent enough to be remarkable. "As producers of cotton," he wrote, as if reporting a novelty, "whites can be just as efficient as negroes in this part of the country. They need only to work under the direction of the most intelligent farmers, who, as a rule own most of the good land."[8]

This statement summarizes a major transition in the lives of plain folk. After the Civil War, black labor force participation dropped significantly, and work patterns among blacks began to approximate those among whites.

7. *Historical Statistics of the United States,* 517–18. Corn prices followed a similar pattern though with greater fluctuations. See Department of Agriculture, *Corn Yields per Acre and Prices,* 2–3.

8. Quoted in Eugene W. Hilgard, *Report on Cotton Production in the United States* (Washington, D.C., 1884), Pt. 2, p. 173.

Black sharecroppers showed that small farmers could produce cotton efficiently, and demand kept the price of the fleecy staple high. In the difficult
times that followed the war, cotton growing was therefore attractive to
landless whites; and sharecropping must have appeared to them as economic opportunity rather than as social decline. In a period of marked
transition, then, poor farmers of both races reacted to common circumstances in similar ways. Just as blacks preferred sharecropping to gang
labor, so many whites chose it over the alternatives available to them.
"Apparently the views of the landowners meant little to the white or the
negro landless class," a historian of Georgia agriculture has written, "for
both white and black labor preferred independency to efficiency and they
proceeded to force the owners to accept them as croppers and renters or not
at all."[9]

Sharecropping spread rapidly among whites in forms not unlike those
among blacks. On January 1, 1868, for example, John D. Williams, a
planter in the Laurens District of South Carolina, drew up a contract with
his black sharecroppers. In return for Williams' agreement to furnish them
land, workstock, and other necessities, including regular supplies of bacon
and corn at current prices, the croppers agreed to cultivate his land, perform other specified tasks, and obey certain rules of personal conduct. They
pledged "to be steady & attentive to there [sic] work at all times" under
threat of fines to be deducted from their share of the crop, to keep no
firearms or "ardent spirits," to "obey all lawful orders" from Williams or his
agent, and to be "honest—truthful—sober—civel—[and] diligent." When
the crop was harvested, Williams would get two-thirds and the croppers
one-third.

Such terms were unremarkable. What was remarkable was an addendum
to the contract covering Williams' white sharecroppers. "We the white
labores," it read, "now employed by John D. Williams on his white plains
plantation have lisened and heard read the forgoing Contract on this Sheet
of paper assign equal for the black laborers employed by him on said place
and we are perfectly Satisfied with it and heare by bind our selves to abide &
be controwed by it."[10]

Whether Williams treated his white and black croppers evenhandedly is
unknown. In written contracts that survive, strict rules of personal conduct

9. Willard Range, *A Century of Georgia Agriculture, 1850–1950* (Athens, Ga., 1954), 87.
10. The contract is printed in Rosser H. Taylor, "Post-Bellum Southern Rental Contracts,"
Agricultural History, XVII (1943), 122–23.

apply far more often to blacks than to whites, though the race of the crop-pers is not always clear. What is notable in the Williams contract is that its economic terms were the same for the two races. The specifics of sharecrop-ping arrangements varied widely, but the variations apparently depended less on the cropper's race than on his economic condition, family size, and reputation. "Can hardly tell you what are the regular rules of renting," William Evans, a tenant farmer in Maury County, Tennessee, wrote a cousin in North Carolina at the end of the 1869 crop year. "Every [landlord] seems to rent to suit himself & for as much as he can. Though so much per acre is prevailing more and more every year. From $4 to $10 per acre is common. We paid one third of grain, & 1/4 of cotton this year; but this farm is rented for $800 cash or about $4 per acre for next year."

For that reason Evans had been forced to move to another tenancy, and had just found a place in Williamson County when he wrote his cousin, who was also looking for a tenancy. "Glass furnishes horse feed during crop time," Evans wrote of his new landlord, "& part of the tools, & we give half cotton & third grain, but cultivate more cotton than anything else." He told his cousin: "If you were to get Glasse's [sic] place you would have to culti-vate cotton right smart. Renters have to do as they can & not as they would."[11]

By the late 1870s, sharecropping and other forms of landless tenure were well established among both races, and the patterns that characterized agricultural tenure in the New South were in place. On the basis of field reports from north Georgia, where white farmers were relatively more numerous than elsewhere, the state commissioner of agriculture estimated that 27 percent of the farm labor there in 1877 was wage labor, 42 percent was sharecroppers, and 31 percent was renters.[12] Thomas Sizemore re-membered the pattern among the poorest croppers in Greenville County, South Carolina, at that time. "After the war," Sizemore recalled, "Pa was a tenant farmer. We lived on the worst wore-out farm I ever hoped to see! Pa tried to raise cotton, he never bothered 'bout planting no garden nor to raise no meat, just got what we needed to live on at the store where he got credit on his cotton crop. He paid up if the crops was good; if not, he just stayed in debt till another year."

11. William Evans to William J. Covington, November 28, 1869, in Mary Ann (Covington) Wilson Papers, Southern Historical Collection, Louis R. Wilson Library, University of North Carolina at Chapel Hill.

12. Georgia Commissioner of Agriculture, *Fourth Annual Report, 1877*, lxxiv.

"COTTON'S A BORROWIN' CROP."

Over the years, a tightening economic squeeze enveloped agriculture in the New South, intensifying the impact of sharecropping on farm folk and encouraging many of them to look for other forms of employment. Farm population and the number of farms grew rapidly, but acreage did not, and the average size of farms shrank dramatically even as average values rose. In Georgia and the Carolinas, for example, farm population grew 54 percent between 1890 and 1910 and the number of farms 55 percent, but total acreage rose only 3 percent. As a result, average farm size fell 30 percent in North Carolina (to 88 acres), 33 percent in South Carolina (to 77 acres), and 37 percent in Georgia (to 93 acres). At the same time, average value increased markedly despite the long depression and only modest changes in general price levels, rising 75 percent in North Carolina, 119 percent in South Carolina, and 85 percent in Georgia. On a per-acre basis, the value of land and buildings on average farms rose 62 percent in Georgia between 1880 and 1900, 41 percent in North Carolina, and 76 percent in South Carolina, and then by another 156 percent, 138 percent, and 172 percent, respectively, in the first decade of the twentieth century.[13]

The significance of these figures may be seen in a specific case. In 1879 in Gwinett County, Georgia, the price of farmland averaged $5.52 an acre and the price of cotton 10.3 cents a pound. Twenty years later, the price of land had risen to $8.00 but that of cotton had fallen to 7 cents. By 1910 farm land in the county was selling on average for $17.27 an acre and cotton was bringing 14 cents a pound.[14] In three decades the cost of land had more than tripled while the price of cotton had risen 37 percent; and most of the latter increase came at the end of the period. It was more and more difficult to buy a farm.

The same pattern occurred in the price of mules. Acquiring one or more mules was the essential first step in climbing the agricultural ladder, for owning a mule was one of the things that set tenant farmers and "share tenants" apart from sharecroppers and agricultural laborers. The price of a

13. *Historical Statistics of the United States*, 458–63. These trends were present also in the 1880s and from 1910 to 1920, but I have used the 1890–1910 period for illustrative purposes because before 1890 the census counted rural rather than agricultural population (*Thirteenth Census, 1910: Agriculture*, 221, 495).

14. U.S. Department of Agriculture, *Circular No. 78: Conditions of Farmers in a White Farmer Area of the Cotton Piedmont, 1924–1926* (1929), 9.

mule fluctuated notably in the New South era, but along the general lines of other prices. It rose from a little over $60 to about $85 between the early and middle 1880s, fell to about $40 at the depth of the depression in the 1890s, but thereafter moved rapidly upward to more than $120 in 1910. It was thus always difficult for small farmers to acquire a mule, and became increasingly so over the years. As cotton and other prices rose moderately after 1898, the price of mules skyrocketed, doubling between 1899 and 1905, while the price of cotton rose about 55 percent.[15]

Small farmers had other problems, too. Apart from the high and rising prices of mules and land, more and more capital was required to farm successfully, and rise economically, in the New South. Economies of scale were increasingly achievable, but not, by definition, by small farmers. Even small amounts of operating capital could have had a marked impact on the income of sharecroppers. The price of cotton fluctuated meaningfully during the course of each year, being always lowest in the fall when the new crop flooded the market. Farmers able to hold their cotton until spring or summer benefited appreciably. Yet no cropper could hold his cotton, for the lien on his crop was due and payable when his crop was harvested—and when the price of cotton was at its lowest point in the annual cycle. Ten-cent cotton brought $50 a bale and eight-cent cotton $40. For croppers with several bales of their own, that difference might be the margin between paying out and ending the year in debt.

Seasonal price fluctuations had other adverse effects on those who farmed on credit. Farmers who ran out of corn before the new crop was harvested had to buy what they needed on credit at inflated, out-of-season prices and repay their debt in depressed, harvest-time prices. "We have to pay $1.25 per bushel for corn on time and in the fall sell ours at 75 cents to pay the debt," a North Carolina tenant complained in 1887. "How can we be in any other than a desperately poor condition; if we could borrow money or get supplies at 8 per cent we could prosper." Another complained: "We are sometimes forced to pay one and a half to two bushels of corn in fall for one borrowed in summer. Much of that kind of business [is] done."[16]

Despite these problems, farmers in the cotton belt could not diversify. The growing importance of capital and the effects of the money economy on even the smallest farmer made that impossible. To plant less cotton and

15. See the discussion in Gavin Wright, "Freedom and the Southern Economy," *Explorations in Economic History*, XVI (1979), 104–105.
16. NC *Labor Report* (1887), 132, 129.

more grain was to reduce cash income; and to improve their economic position in an age of commercialization, farmers needed more, not less, cash. Still, the more cotton farmers produced—in Georgia and the Carolinas, acreage increased more than 50 percent between 1880 and 1910— the more their efforts depressed prices. Yet cotton (in some areas, tobacco) was the only reliable cash crop farmers had and thus their only collateral for credit. "If you want to run a farm, and came to town here and gave a mortgage on your cotton crop there is no difficulty," a North Carolina landowner told the United States Industrial Commission in 1899, "but I have seldom known of any taken on the grains. You can always sell cotton. You leave home with a wagon load of cotton and you will go home that night with the money in your pocket; you load up your wagon with wheat or corn and come here with 100 bushels, and I doubt some days whether you could sell it."[17] Farm folk recognized this. "Frank always had wanted to do cotton farmin'," Molly Graham said of her husband, a small North Carolina farmer at the turn of the century. "Cotton's always cash, he'd say."

But not much cash. "Cotton went to six cents a pound and everything else went accordin'," Addie Gaines recalled of the hard times she experienced as a child. "We just worked and borrowed from then on and about perished. Pa kept on plantin' cotton and no good come of it. I don't know why in the world (unless it's because cotton's a borrowin' crop) folks keep on plantin' it instead of somethin' else. Seems like folks would learn to plant for their needs and raise somethin' else too, if they are so set on plantin' cotton."

"Folks" acted as they did not because landlords or credit merchants forced cotton upon them, but for more fundamental reasons.[18] They knew cotton, how to grow and market it, as they knew nothing else that brought cash, and to change to another crop would have required some new equipment and training, and new rhythms of living as well. Moreover, as contemporaries knew and economic historians have affirmed, "Cotton was the most profitable crop under the institutional arrangements that prevailed" in the New South, "and it was under those institutional arrangements that the economic actors, planters, laborers, and business men, lived."[19]

---

17. *House Documents*, 57th Cong., 1st Sess., No. 184, Vol. 10, p. 80.
18. Jacqueline Bull's search of the records of credit merchants "failed to reveal any lien notes which stated that cotton alone must be planted." See Bull, "The General Merchant in the Economic History of the New South," *Journal of Southern History*, XVIII (1952), 41.
19. Parker, "The South in the National Economy, 1865–1970," 1040.

"SHARECROPPIN'S A GOOD THING, A BLESSIN' TO THE PORE MAN THAT
DON'T OWN NO LAND."

The relationship between landlord and cropper was a fundamental aspect of
sharecropping, and one that did much to influence farm folk after they
moved to the mills. The relationship was an unequal economic partnership
in which each partner often regarded the other as an impediment to his
purposes, and it therefore contained intrinsic elements of tension. Yet the
defining features of the relationship came not from economic factors alone
but also from the paternalism—and sometimes even kinship—that leav-
ened it and muted its potential for harshness and exploitation.[20] The association was textured by cultural values, community customs, and personal
considerations.

The relationship between landlords and white croppers was close and
much more personal than that between planters and black croppers in the
black belt. Most white croppers worked for resident landlords who "ran"
no more than three or four croppers or tenants and supervised their own
farming operations. Many were farmers themselves, and spent all or part of
the time working crops of their own. White landlords, croppers, and agricultural laborers thus knew each other in the ways of people who work
closely together, and their knowledge was informed by the fact that they had
likely known or known of each other for much of their lives. Croppers did
not remain for a lifetime with the same landlord; on the contrary, they
moved frequently. Their moves, however, were typically short ones, generally within the same community; and landlords were a relatively rooted
group.

The relationship was also reciprocal. Croppers and landlords needed each
other even if the ties that bound them together were or could be competitive
or even antagonistic. Indeed, mutuality of need was the linchpin that held
the system together, and it accounts for the spirit of cooperation and deference that characterized many of these relationships. "I have learned one
thing in my experience in dealing with hired labor," a North Carolina
landlord wrote in 1887. "It pays to be kind and considerate to the hireling;
they will work better and stay better."[21]

20. There are apparently no systematic data on the extent of landlord-tenant kinship during
the New South era, but in Gwinett County, Georgia, in 1925, 23 percent of all white tenant
farmers were related to their landlord as were 8 percent of all white sharecroppers (Department
of Agriculture, *Conditions of Farmers in a White Farmer Area of the Cotton Piedmont*, 11).
21. NC *Labor Report* (1887), 94.

Well-treated tenants reciprocated that sentiment. "Mr. Spencer lets me farm jus' like twas my own land," Bob Draper, a North Carolina sharecropper said of his landlord of twenty years in the 1930s. "He hardly ever comes down here, for he says I'm a good farmer and know much how to tend a crop as he does and so run it like I please." Draper's judgment was not merely economic. "His folks is nice and familiar too," he said. "They know us on the streets [in town] same as here on the farm. Wherever we see 'em, town or country, they're social."

This reciprocation grew from the paternalism that encouraged many landlords to help deserving croppers. Some landlords gave tenants favorable credit terms. Others provided patches for their use and the tools and livestock to cultivate them. Still others helped with the purchase of a mule, a cow, or work implements and otherwise encouraged their croppers to rise up the tenancy ladder. Many allowed them vegetables, melons, or fruit from their fields and gardens, and in this and other ways helped improve the quality of their lives.

Instances of the landlords' consideration are rich in variety. "I rented most of my land in 1911 for one-fourth of all crops, cotton, corn, wheat, oats, pease," reported a Georgia planter who had five white and eight black tenants. "I am adopting the one-fourth system for the purpose of inducing my tenants to diversify and rotate their crops. . . . I also rent every tenant a few acres of bottom land thoroughly set in Bermuda, so that every tenant will have hay for his stock."[22] Sharecroppers reported other instances of this cooperativeness. "Some landlords would raise a row if their tenants went in the corn field to get a mess o' roas'n years," Draper said of his landlord, "but he lets us tote out all we want for the table. I've told him to help hisself to the corn down here and to go in my watermelon patch any time. . . . He lets me keep his team here and use 'em just like they was mine. If I want to plow my garden or little watermelon or 'tater patches or haul farm stuff to town, I'm welcome to use the mules."

Such instances of cooperation were more prevalent than most accounts suggest, and they are reminders that variety, not uniformity, was the characteristic feature of the sharecropping system. To understand sharecropping and why some folk, but not others, left it for the mills, it is necessary to look beyond the victimization the system permitted and to the actualities of individual experience. Croppers must be seen as individuals with some

22. Quoted in Robert P. Brooks, *The Agrarian Revolution in Georgia* (Madison, Wis., 1914), 97.

control over their own circumstance, and the system as one that permitted them and their landlords considerable flexibility.

The system's essence was discrimination, which grew from the judgment, predilection, or mere cavil of individual landlords and merchants, but also from the ways croppers reacted to the choices and circumstances they faced. Luck, temperament, general economic conditions, and even the weather might be major factors in individual cases, but the cropper had considerable room for maneuver. He could, for example, conform to the landlord and merchant's expectation of what a good tenant should be and reap certain benefits; or by confirming their prejudices about "no good white trash," he might get away with a great deal of "sorriness" at the price of poverty and social ostracism. "There is such a wide difference in the industry and thrift of tenants, also among the land-owners as to the per cent they charge their tenants on supplies furnished them," a North Carolina landlord observed in 1887. "I have tenants that I furnish the cash to buy what they need and charge them eight per cent on the money, and they buy entirely for cash. I have others that it would not do to furnish with money; they would spend it for things not necessary, and leave their supply of provisions short." It is not necessary to credit this landlord with disinterested wisdom to see that his system offered meaningful choices to his tenants. "Some tenants go much above the amount I have put down as the value of a one-horse crop," this landlord added. "[But] I have one tenant who runs a one-horse crop and makes fifteen to twenty bales of cotton, and his corn and meat besides."[23]

Merchants also dealt individually with croppers. "[We] size him up, and if he is pretty good, we sell him pretty cheap," P. H. Lovejoy, a Georgia merchant said in 1899 of his dealings with croppers and laborers. "We sell good men at 10 per cent [above wholesale]," but "we generally put a pretty good margin on cheap men because we have to take chances on them." This "pretty good margin" was about 25 percent above wholesale and much more than that in annual interest rates. Yet even Lovejoy, who had considerable faith in his own judgment, admitted that tenants did not always act predictably. "You can not [always] tell who is a good man," he said ruefully; "one may be good this year and bad next year." If "he is a hard case," that is, does not pay out at the end of the crop year and seems unpromising for the future, "we just take what he makes and quit." In other words, his debt was written off and he was refused further credit and employment.[24]

23. NC *Labor Report* (1887), 94.
24. *House Documents*, 57th Cong., 1st Sess., No. 184, Vol. 10, pp. 75–77.

These statements reflect the degree to which personalism infused share-cropping. In paternalistic, traditional societies, economic relationships involve trust, judgment, and ascription as well as economic calculation; and trusted croppers of known character often fared better than the letter of the law suggested. J. R. Everett, who was born "in a little tenant farmhouse in Edgecombe County, North Carolina," in 1892, remembered that when his father "gained a reputation for honesty," he "became able to get credit without giving crop liens or mortgages, as most other farm tenants of his class were forced to do."

These factors governed sharecropping contracts as well as store accounts, and help explain why croppers no less than landlords preferred oral agreements based on community custom, which everyone understood, over written contracts, which croppers might not be able to read. "The bargain is the law," William A. Graham said, detailing the system of oral contracts in effect in North Carolina at the turn of the twentieth century. He meant that whatever a landlord and tenant agreed to was legally binding on both. Graham, a landowner with tenants of his own, thought oral contracts better than written ones, for tenants as well as landlords. "The objection to the written law," he explained, "is that so far as your tenant is concerned it might as well be in Hebrew as in English. What does he know of what he is signing? He is the sufferer. The first thing was to get a verbal law so that if he did not know a letter he could understand what the contract was. The verbal law is the very thing for the poor uneducated. If you have a written contract, the written contract is the law, but if you have a verbal contract the laborer has his oath as to what it was."[25]

To see the potential advantage in this type of agreement for croppers is not to take Graham's statement as an assessment of how the system worked. It is instead to recognize that sharecropping functioned in a cultural context quite different from that of the present-day South. Of course oral contracts could be abused by cunning landlords and conniving merchants, especially where "the law" was cooperative or indifferent. But so could written contracts. In either case, the cropper's well-being depended on the honesty and goodwill of his landlord, as has always been the case in paternal relationships. "These verbal contracts are based on the general system," that is, community custom, explained Graham, "and if you know what wages are paid in the neighborhood, that will help [the tenant] or [the landlord] in his testimony" should a dispute be carried to litigation.[26] Knowing the prevail-

25. *Ibid.*, 437–38.
26. *Ibid.*, 438.

ing rate might also help a jury, already aware of community custom, evaluate the substance of a dispute.

Accustomed to the ways of sharecropping and to the values on which it rested, croppers tended to accept it at face value. "Sharecroppin's a good thing, a blessin' to the pore man that don't own no land," said Will Conner after thirty-five years of cropping in North Carolina and Virginia. "It gives him a home and rations, a chance to raise his own meat and vegetables and to grow a crop that's part his. Yeh, sharecroppin's all right." From his lifetime experience, Steve Lee added: "I see their side. Their farmin' is a investmint; if they got to farm at a loss, they just as well quit. The land's theirs, and they got to make some profit on it or at least break even. I see that and don't blame 'em."

As this comment suggests, croppers respected private property and the profit motive, and did not regard economic inequality as itself something to complain about. "The landlord figures if there is a lot made he's going to get his part of it," F. B. Brewer, a longtime North Carolina sharecropper said in the 1930s. "You can't blame him for that. If I owned a piece of land I would have the same attitude as that."

Yet experience was varied, and other assessments were less positive. "If you know anything about tenant farming you know they do without everything all the year hoping to have something in the fall," said Nancy Owens, who, with her husband William spent her life sharecropping in North Carolina. "Well, it's very little they ever have, but it's a hope to live and work for all the year just the same."

"The biggest problem I see," interjected William Owens, "is the landlord that has a bunch of tenant farmers on his place. They work like niggers all the year and he gits rich. They can't even make enough to eat on through the winter."

Attitudes toward landlords were equally varied. "All the men I ever worked for has been good to me," said Bob Draper. "I hear 'em talkin' 'bout landlords that's mean and hard to get along with, but I've never had no experience durin' my fifty-two years with sech as that." Steve Lee's more equivocal judgment was that "the landlords is fair, most of 'em. They's good ones and bad ones."

Other croppers were more critical. "You've been robbed! They've robbed you of thousands of dollars, and you know it!" Josie Lee interjected as her husband was making his more equitable judgment of landlords. William Owens, who had "had some pretty good landlords and some pretty bad ones," was equally emphatic. "I hate the thieving rogues anyhow," he said, "good or bad." Fanny Bowers Maddrey expressed a similar judgment after years of sharecropping in North Carolina. "I tell you the truth," she said, "landlords may be good men in a way, but when it comes to money every one's for self; he's after turnin' every dollar his way. Like the old sayin' says: 'Ought's . . . a ought, and five's a figger; all for the white man, and none for the nigger.' None's for the sharecropper, white or black."

At its worst, then, the system generated intense grievance. "I represent a large, and fearfully oppressed community, the territory on those extensive cotton farms near by," Mrs. J. W. Barnett, wife of a Spartanburg County, South Carolina, farm tenant, wrote Terence V. Powderly, head of the Knights of Labor, in 1886. "All the small farms have passed into the hands of a few individuals and they, and [illegible word] us all with the tyrants rod[.] [W]e are all fed three months, to do twelve months work." Mrs. Barnett described her own situation to illustrate the problem. "We pay for two thirds of the commercial fertilizer used, one third of the crop, from 35. to 1.00 per cent [that is, credit prices that were 35 to 100 percent higher than cash prices], for six months, on all we consume. Supplies are cut off as soon as the crops are laid by, and gather them at our own expense. When all is ready for the Market, then our employer takes all, everything, as you can readily see, and we are left to grapple with pitiless fate."[27]

These disparate assessments help explain why only some sharecroppers decided to leave farming and look for other kinds of work. The various opinions rest no doubt on differences of experience, and it would be interesting to know the proportions of sharecroppers who shared Mrs. Barnett's sense of victimization and Bob Draper's feeling of having always been treated fairly. One reason for the different reactions might have been differing expectations. Many farm folk had low expectations in life, which must have colored their reactions to experience. "All I ask of any landlord," said Will Conner, "is to be treated fair accordin' to the bargain me and him makes and to be spoke to like I was human. There ain't nothing to cussin' at a man like he was a dog." Respect, not income, was Conner's deeper concern. "Durin' the eighteen years with Mr. Long," Paul Parks, another North Carolina tenant farmer, recalled, speaking positively of the man who was his landlord from 1901 to 1919, "I never give him a short word, and he never spoke short to me."

Croppers had definite standards for measuring landlords. Good landlords

27. Mrs. J. W. Barnett to Terence V. Powderly, August 10, 1886, in Terence V. Powderly Papers, microfilm edition, Georgia State University Library.

were honest, "tolerable"—personable, familiar, considerate—and not given to intrusive supervision. Such men, paternalists in the best sense, were respected, deferred to, and looked to for advice and example. Insofar as individual croppers had internalized the values of the traditional, paternal system of which sharecropping was often a part, they wanted to attach themselves to such landlords and submit to the security of their direction.

The first measure of every landlord was honesty. Any man known or suspected of dishonesty or unfairness in dealing with tenants not only lost his tenants but, as word of his reputation spread, ran the risk of being unable to get good tenants to replace the old ones. Appearance as well as reality was important in this regard, for most croppers kept no or incomplete records of their credit accounts and did not know the credit costs they paid or even the amount of their indebtedness. The basic reason for their disadvantage was illiteracy or inability to figure easily, but many croppers made no effort to keep records, and landlords and merchants sometimes made it difficult to do so.

There was therefore frequent occasion for misunderstanding, error, and fraud at settling up time, and croppers often felt cheated, shortchanged, or otherwise unfairly treated. "Landlords never would itemize my account," recalled Steve Lee, "so I can't say where they've charged me too much or not. I'd ask sometimes when they was bookin' it how much the account was, and they'd tell me then. But when settlement time would come it was read out to me in a lump sum so I didn't know what was for what. Sometimes it seemed to run up mighty high, but I was helpless."

To avoid misunderstanding, at least some landlords helped their tenants keep and understand their accounts. "Soon as I started workin' for Mr. Spencer, he give me a book to keep my account with him in," said Bob Draper of a landlord for whom he sharecropped twenty years. "Course I couldn't write nothin' down myself, but Robert [an adopted son] set down what I told him, and there ain't never been no trouble at settlement time. Most times our books comes out together, but when there's five dollars' difference Mr. Spencer splits it between us, which satisfies us both."

Most landlords were less considerate, not necessarily because they were dishonest but because they were paternalists and as such considered it their prerogative and responsibility to keep the records of their own business. Many of them, as historian Jacqueline Bull once noted, thought it a reflection on their integrity for tenants to keep records of their own—an unsurprising reaction in a paternalistic society.[28] Many croppers acquiesced in

28. Bull, "The General Merchant in the Economic History of the New South," 53.

this stance, but those who did not could be outspoken in their complaints. "The main trouble with him was he wouldn't never give us no receipt for nothin' we paid him," Fanny Bowers Maddrey recalled of one of her landlords. "I kept an account book all the time, but he wouldn't look at it the end of the year when we went to settle. He figgered a little on a old envelop or a shoe box lid and told us what our share of the crop came to. So we just didn't know how we stood."

Croppers also resented landlords whom they considered unduly intrusive in their lives or work. As every mill owner eventually learned, plain folk found the reciprocities of the paternalistic relationship more congenial than those between employers and employees. They resented being treated as mere employees and told directly what to do. "The worst man I ever worked for was Lem Harris," recalled Will Conner. "He's a shot gun! You can't suit him. Sunday night just 'fore bed-time he drives round to tell you how and what to do first thing Monday mornin'. You start at it; he's there cussin' at you 'fore breakfast Monday mornin' for not doin' it another way. He's always cussin' you about somethin."

Wives as well as husbands resented the landlords' intrusion. "He was all time tryin' to meddle in our business," Fanny Bowers Maddrey said of a landlord who kept insisting that she and her husband go to the fields earlier and stay later than they wanted to. "All the woman's work here I got to do myself, and I'll get up and cook breakfast when I see fit," Mrs. Maddrey told the landlord. "I help Herman pick cotton till time to quit and cook supper," she also told him. "Then he quits and helps me do the jobs around the house. It ain't none o' your business when we start or when we quit. We ain't day laborers workin' for wages by the hour. Just so we tend to our crop and house it when time comes, there ain't nobody got no right to tell us when to set down or when to walk."

"THE ALMOST INSUFFERABLE INEFFICIENCY OF FARM LABOR, WHITE AND BLACK."

Landlords' complaints about farm folk are extraordinarily revealing of the work habits and attitudes folk took with them to the mills. According to the landlords, croppers and agricultural laborers were typically lazy, unmotivated, slovenly workers with no sense of their own or their employer's best interest, and were therefore responsible for their own poverty and social backwardness. But a careful reading of the landlords' complaints suggests a conclusion far more profound. The things landlords complained of were manifestations of premodern values deeply rooted in farm folk. Those values fitted folk poorly for the changing conditions brought on by commercialization and industrialization; yet folk clung tenaciously to them, for doing so gave a sense of security and stability in a world of rapid change. Those facts explain much of the history of plain folk in the New South.

"I have abundant opportunity to acquaint myself with tenants and hirelings," a landlord told the North Carolina labor commissioner in 1887, expressing some views widely held. "Am sorry to say that I am more and more impressed with the almost insufferable inefficiency of farm labor, white and black. The causes are: 1st. Want of intelligence or common sense to do anything whatever. The only way to get good work is to see it done there and then every time. Three-fourths of the laborers neither know nor care to know how to harness a horse or fix a plow to run properly. 2d. The next defect is want of moral character in almost all laborers. This may seem too sweeping—but so I find it." The landlord continued: "There does not seem to be one in twenty who cares whether his employer gets value for his wages or not. I could write a volume on my crosses and losses from careless and almost unprofitable laborers."[29]

Such encompassing complaints were numerous. "As to our labor system, it is mostly carried on in a slipshod kind of way," reported a landowner in whose community "the principal part of the farming lands are cultivated by white and colored tenants, about equally divided." He complained, "Everything [is] done in a careless and slovenly way." An employer of "a large number [of wage laborers] both white and black" added, "The great trouble with farm labor is the uncertainty of it." So troublesome was the problem that this landlord thought it should be "a criminal offence for a man to employ a wage-earner that has quit his employer before his time is out."[30]

Not only was farm labor bad; it was always getting worse. "Farm labor is fast becoming entirely unreliable, both white and colored," one landowner wrote in 1902. "The class, both white and colored, who have come out since the war don't care to work, and won't do it only when forced by want of rations. They won't stay on the farm if they can get work elsewhere," this landlord continued, illustrating the growing impact of employment off the farm, "won't comply with their contracts but a few days at the time; have no personal honor, and don't care to get a good name, but just catch little or short jobs in order to get a few days' rations." Other landlords agreed. "For the last two years labor has become considerably less reliable, both white

29. NC *Labor Report* (1887), 92.
30. *Ibid.* (1901), 35, (1902), 73.

and colored," one of them wrote. "It is unsafe for a farmer to start a crop with the expectation of properly cultivating it and save it in due time. Hands don't want to work regularly, not even for a week at the time, and all want railroad prices."[31]

Other landlords complained not of their croppers' work habits but of their personal qualities. The "moral status of farm labor [is] bad, caused by [a] bad system," one of them wrote the North Carolina labor commissioner in 1887. "The poor negro (and white too) will steal his own cotton and sell it in seed to buy necessaries of life under the belief that it is no harm to steal their own mortgaged crop." During the 1890s depression, another landlord wrote: "Both races are too much given to idling away their time, complaining of hard times, playing games, drinking whisky and smoking cigars, and expecting the government to feed them. They should go to work and make an honest living, which is within the reach of all."[32]

As this comment suggests, landowners, like other southerners, viewed social matters in moral terms, and many of them regarded poverty as evidence of personal weakness. Lack of self-discipline, ambition, and the drive necessary to get ahead was the croppers' problem, according to landlords. "A great many" white tenants "are honest, industrious and law-abiding," one landlord observed, "but they don't seem to aspire to anything better."[33]

Clearly, landlords saw the absence of certain values as setting croppers apart from themselves; and they were no doubt correct. Their complaints confirm a primary fact. Farm folk had not internalized the values or adopted the work habits a modernizing economy demands of workers. Landowners, who had such values and habits, wanted croppers who behaved as exemplary modern employees—disciplined, reliable, loyal, frugal, temperate, stable, ambitious, attuned to the clock. Those in their employ were traditional agricultural workers who were willing to work seasonally but not continually, in alternating rhythms of busyness and leisure, and with scant regard to punctuality and steadiness; who resisted close supervision and the kind of thoroughness demanded by modern employers; who had little commitment to progress and the spirit of accumulation on which it rested; who looked upon work as necessary because one had to live but not because it was morally or otherwise elevating. Moreover, when farm folk grew dissatisfied with their circumstance, they acted not in "rational," modern ways—

31. *Ibid.* (1902), 73, (1901), 76.
32. *Ibid.* (1887), 87, (1893), 69.
33. *Ibid.* (1901), 80.

by economic organization, political activism, collective protest, or self-improvement—but in traditional ways of the powerless. They worked indifferently, moved frequently, clung to accustomed ways, flouted economic and social values their employers honored.

To landlords, the croppers were thus "sorry" folk, and victims of their own lack of enterprise. "Even the small farmer and tenant who manage for themselves will not vie with the progress and improvement of the times," a North Carolina landlord wrote in 1887, "but go fishing, hunting, &c, and neglect a living. . . . It is hard to reach and awaken to energetic work this class of small farmer." Another complained: "Laboring people do not value time as they should. None of them put in more than half time, except in busy crop time." And another landlord concurred. "They work just enough to keep from starving and have no aspiration to lay by anything, even for the winter."[34]

No wonder they were poor. "Men who take hold of the farm in a business manner and stick to it six days in the week are doing well," a landowner observed in 1905. "But the man who works some, hunts some, loafs around town a great deal and drinks whiskey occasionally finds hard sailing."[35]

One telling measure of the landowners' exasperation was the frequent, even routine, practice of criticizing white and black croppers in the same language. In reading their complaints, it is usually impossible to tell whether they are directed at whites or blacks unless the landowners say specifically. In their remarks to the North Carolina labor commissioner, for example, landowners routinely lumped whites and blacks together and more often than not assigned them the same undesirable qualities.

That is a remarkable fact, and one that illuminates the racial anxieties of plain folk in the New South. Among landowners there was ongoing debate over the relative merit of white and black croppers and laborers, and the sentiments they expressed were not always flattering to farm folk. "A good white man is better than a good negro," a North Carolina landowner replied when asked which of the two made better tenants, "but a good negro is much better than a mean white man. If you can get an intelligent white man who you can depend on, he is the best class of labor, but if you get an unreliable fellow, the negro is better."[36] If that sentiment gave a nod to white superiority, it was not a nod farm folk found assuring.

Opinion varied widely, reflecting class as well as racial prejudice. "White

34. *Ibid.* (1887), 109, (1891), 86, and (1901), 76.
35. *Ibid.* (1905), 37.
36. *House Documents,* 57th Cong., 1st Sess., No. 184, Vol. 10, p. 434.

tenants and laborers are, as a rule, faithful to their work and good citizens; the negroes are shiftless," was the view of one landlord. "For tenants I prefer white men; for wage hands colored," was another's position. Another landlord had rented his land the previous year to two white and two black tenants. "The white and colored renters did almost equally well," he reported. "The whites worked with better judgment—the negroes did most work."[37]

The margin of superiority these views allowed farm folk was thin. Indeed, what stands out in the remarks is the willingness of many landlords to relegate "sorry" whites to categories usually reserved for blacks. "The white fellow that works for daily or monthly wages is no good," a Georgia landowner and credit merchant told the Industrial Commission in 1899. "There is no more move in him than in the darkey." The judgment was not merely economic. Whites at the bottom of the economic ladder had placed themselves in a "black" situation. "Laboring people always associate the idea of field labor with negro labor, because most of the laborers are negroes," another Georgian told the Industrial Commission, "and if a white man went into the field [as a laborer], he would have to work with the negroes."[38]

Perhaps it was to conceal these realities that white agricultural laborers so often made themselves intractable. "White hired hands are good laborers, with a few exceptions," a North Carolina landlord said in 1887, "but there is some work about the farm that I could never get white hands to do without complaining." A Georgia landowner said a few years later, "A white [agricultural laborer] does not obey me any more, and generally puts me to more trouble, and he is harder to please as long as he stays with me." Another North Carolina landlord remarked: "From my experience with colored laborers I prefer them to whites for farm hands. They are best under all circumstances and equally as reliable as the whites who hire themselves in that way, they work more cheerfully and are less disposed to complain."[39]

"I WORKED LIKE A NIGGER."

Farm folk who lived through the New South era saw things quite differently. They remembered their lives as full of hard work; and the differences between their views and those of landlords are further evidence of the

37. NC *Labor Report* (1887), 93, (1889), 88, 53.
38. *House Documents*, 57th Cong., 1st Sess., No. 184, Vol. 10, pp. 79, 449.
39. NC *Labor Report* (1887), 106; *House Documents*, 57th Cong., 1st Sess., No. 184, Vol. 10, p. 121; NC *Labor Report* (1887), 108.

cultural chasm that separated the two groups. Yet the differences are easily explained. Croppers remembered the hard work of such difficult tasks as land clearing and of peak periods of planting, hoeing, and harvesting, when work was demanding and the hours were from "can see" to "can't" for days or weeks at a time. Landowners, on the other hand, complained that croppers did little work other than cropping—ditching, terracing, fence mending, brush clearing, and otherwise keeping up the land and buildings—or that their work was done poorly, casually, or with no attention to the landlord's interests. It was the pace and irregularity of work, and the inattention to detail, that landlords lamented.

The difference, then, was one of perception—of what a cropper must or ought to do. Croppers expected to work, and did work, as long and hard as the crop demanded, but they expected to take things easier when the crop was in hand, and they did. Clarence E. Fesperman recalled the alternating pattern of work and rest on the "one-hoss, broken down, flea-bit" North Carolina farm where he grew up in the 1870s and 1880s. "We worked from Spring plowin' to past gatherin'—in from can't-see to can't-see, eighteen hours a day most of the time," Fesperman remembered. "We rested for the rest of the year. All we had to do after layin'-by was chop and split and get in the winter wood and kill hogs and ready the meat and do all our daily chores and tend to the animals and little things like that." F. B. Brewer, a tenant farmer near Wilson, North Carolina, said of farming: "There is plenty of hard work to it. I've had to work all of my life, but I don't reckon it ever hurt me in any way. . . . My father was poor and had to earn all he could get by the sweat of his brow. There were five of us kids and we all had to work. It won't long after I was born before I became familiar with the hoe."

The amount of labor needed to make a cotton crop was enormous but concentrated at certain times of the year. According to a Department of Agriculture estimate, between 127 and 154 man-hours and 59 to 66 mule hours per acre went into producing the 1918 cotton crop—far more than went into other crops that year. A man by himself could not make a cotton crop, no matter how hard he worked. "It takes to run a mule on a cotton plantation two and a half hands to the plow," an official of the Georgia Agricultural Society said at the turn of the twentieth century, "in other words, five hands to two plows." It would thus "take two good hands and a half-grown child to make a crop for one mule."[40]

40. U.S. Department of Agriculture, *Bulletin No. 896: The Cost of Producing Cotton* (1920), 40–41; *House Documents*, 57th Cong., 1st Sess., No. 184, Vol. 10, p. 49.

A cropper could therefore utilize a mule and a tenancy only if his family provided him the equivalent of one and a half hands besides himself. The critical factor was not how much cotton a man and mule could plow; it was how much his family could hoe and pick. The entire crop had to be hoed two or three times, and at the same time, corn and other crops needed plowing. Hoeing was thus largely done by women and children, as was most picking. No man could pick as much cotton as he could plow and do the other things he had to do during harvest-time. Without a wife and several nearly grown children, preferably sons, a farmer would have to hire labor to do some or most of the hoeing and picking, and since cotton prices were so low, that was a relatively expensive practice despite even lower levels of agricultural wages.

Picking was the bottleneck. Farmers planted only as much cotton as they could expect to get picked. "Cotton picking requires more hand labor than any other process in contemporary agriculture," Rupert B. Vance said in 1929; and his remark underscores the importance of the size of the cropper's work force. "We make it a point to secure tenants who have families of boys, thereby having labor under their control," Clarence H. Poe was told in 1904 by the owner of a large Richmond County, North Carolina, cotton plantation, two-thirds of whose tenants were whites.[41] Good pickers could pick up to 200 pounds of seed cotton a day and even more under optimum conditions, but the average for pickers, most of whom were women or children, was less than that. An average picker spent a week and a half to two weeks picking the 1,500 pounds of seed cotton necessary to make a 500-pound bale. So much labor was required that hired hands picked perhaps half of the South's annual crop. At 35 or 40 cents per 100 pounds, common rates in the 1880s, a picker made $5.25 or $6.00 for picking a 1,500-pound bale, and constant stooping made the activity the hardest sustained work in all of farming. "I dreaded picking cotton worse than anything else," F. B. Brewer remembered. Most farm folk would no doubt have agreed with him.

Sharecropping was a family enterprise. Croppers, like mill workers, were hired in families, and everyone except the too old and the too young worked as needed. The need, however, was a factor of the family cycle as well as the crop cycle, and was in turn a factor of the size and composition of the family. The number, age, gender, and sturdiness of the "hands" available for field

41. Rupert B. Vance, *Human Factors in Cotton Culture: A Study in the Social Geography of the American South* (Chapel Hill, 1929), 166; Clarence H. Poe, "The Rich Kingdom of Cotton," *World's Work*, IX (1904), 5490.

work were important. Newly married sharecroppers, those with no children or none large enough for field work, and those with few sons, had distinct disadvantages; and families with no man or grown sons to do the plowing could hardly farm at all. The wives of newly married and childless croppers were therefore compelled to do field work, and even a man and woman together were an inadequate work force for a one-mule crop. The wife's first pregnancy interfered with the couple's ability to make a crop, and that problem continued until the oldest children were large enough to work in the field. However welcome in other regards, pregnancy and childbirth in these years took women from the field when their work there was badly needed.

Individual examples illustrate the pattern. Ernest Foster was a tenant farmer in North Carolina when he married about 1909. He and his wife were determined to work hard and buy land of their own. Years later, Foster still marveled that his wife had "managed to stay in the fields until she felt the labor pains" that preceded the birth of their first child during the second year of their marriage, and that she was back at work a month later. "She worked with me in the field five days a week, and on Saturday she washed and scoured," Foster remembered. "She ironed at night and she kept our house clean." At the end of their fourth crop year, the Fosters owned seventy-five acres of land. Nancy Owens, who married her husband William, a tenant farmer near Wilson, North Carolina, about 1907, recalled a similar experience with hard work. "The first years after William and me got married were hard a-plenty," she recalled. "I worked like a nigger." Mrs. Owens' first child was born in August, in the middle of the crop year. "I won't worth much to William the whole year," she said, recalling her inability to work in the field. "He was good to me, too, and tried to keep me out of the field them first months when I was so heavy."

Each family adapted to conditions in its own way. "Women in those days did a lot of work in fields alongside their men, if there weren't a lot of small children," remembered Lola Canon, who was born in southern Appalachia in 1894. "If there were small children, they'd take a quilt, a bottle of milk and maybe a piece of bread to the field and find a shade to put the pallet down in, and then sit the baby on it while they worked. Women did more outdoor work then. That is what people call 'hard work.' People worked in those days from early to late."[42]

Within a few years, the children began to work. The oldest son always

42. "Aunt Lola Cannon," *Foxfire*, IX (1975), 275.

went to the field, but the oldest daughter might assume household and child-rearing responsibilities, and in that way free her mother for field work. Rosa Kanipe, who was born in western North Carolina in 1887, recalled the arrangement on her father's twenty-acre farm. "My job at home was to cook dinner after I was old enough," she remembered. "The rest of the family was in the field by six o'clock in the mornin'. I stayed at the house and took care of the little ones not big enough to work. I had to cook enough for dinner and supper. After dinner was over, I hitched a horse to the wagon, piled the younguns in, and drove to the fields. I'd take an old quilt along, take my hoe, dig out a round hole under a shade tree, spread the quilt over the hole and set the baby in it. That was to keep the baby from crawlin' off. It couldn't get out of the hole." Mrs. Kanipe continued: "I always hoed till seven, then I'd hitch up the horse, put the small children back in the wagon and start for home. The rest worked long as they could see. Supper would be ready to eat when they come in, and the milking done."

As children grew up, their mothers did less and less field work, and eventually none at all. Work in the field was increasingly difficult as women grew older, and farm folk, like other southerners, believed a woman's place was in the home. Some women, however, preferred field work to house-work. "My husband didn't want me to work in the field," remembered Lula Demry, who married a tenant farmer in South Carolina in the early 1880s, "but I was restless to help him and then I was lonesome out in the country." Out of choice rather than necessity, Mrs. Demry found someone to look after her small children and began to go to the field. "I went in the field to keep the hoe hands busy to start with," she recalled. "Then I got to picking cotton and hoeing right along with the Niggers." Her choice was more popular than one might expect. No less than seven-eighths of the white tenant farmer women Margaret J. Hagood interviewed in the 1930s ex-pressed a preference for field work over housework, and they took "a great deal of pride in the ability to work like a man."[43]

Still, it was practically impossible for a woman to operate a farm without a husband or grown son to do the plowing. The loss of a husband and father could thus be doubly catastrophic, and families who went to the mills were female-headed in disproportionate numbers. "My father died before I can remember," said Roland Maddrey, son of a one-horse farmer in eastern North Carolina, "and I had to take hold when I wa'n't big enough to see

43. Margaret J. Hagood, *Mothers of the South: Portraiture of the White Tenant Farm Women* (1939: rpr. Greenwood, 1969), 89.

over the plow handles. . . . After Ma was left with we four children she tried to fill Pa's place in the field till we was big enough to take hold. My oldest sister Cora . . . first learned me to bed up cotton rows, though she wa'n't much older'n me. . . . Cora had to help Ma with the plowin' at first, but soon as me and Early could reach the plow handles we went to work."

The pattern of child labor was less complex than that of women's work. As a rule, all children of "dirt farmers" did field work as the crop demanded from the time they were old enough until they left home. Whether or not individual children worked regularly in the field and the age at which they began to do so depended on family size and composition and the rank of the child among his siblings. Anthony Gibbs, who was born into the family of a small farmer in North Carolina about 1875, had what was probably a typical experience for boys. "Ma bossed me most of the time when I was a little fellow," he recalled years later. "I helped her wash dishes, churn and bring in wood. But as I began to grow bigger Dad gradually put me to work with him. I did the chores, then chopped and at twelve I began to plow." Mrs. J. W. Sadler, whose father had been "a poor man," had an experience shared by many girls. In the early 1880s, when she "was around eleven years old," she had to quit school and help her mother care for her younger siblings. "I worked mighty hard," Mrs. Sadler recalled, "washing, ironing, cooking, and all the other things that have to be done when there's a family as large as ours was." Child labor was not a social issue among farm folk but an integral part of making a living.

"AFTER GIVIN' THE FOURTH TO OLD MAN MUSSER FOR RENT THAR WAN'T ENOUGH LEFT TO FINISH PAYIN' ON THE MULE."

For all the hard work they did, farm folk were insecure, and their prospects were uncertain, which encouraged many of them to think about other ways of making a living. Their concern was security, not opportunity; and social mobility was a concept they would hardly have understood. This longing for security explained their desire to own land, yet the insecurity that produced the desire kept many of them from fulfilling it. "Since I been to myself," said Steve Lee, a longtime sharecropper, "I never tried to own no land. I've wanted to. I'd like to be independent, my own man, but looked like every time I'd lay up enough to start makin' a little pay-mint sickness or somethin' would overtake me." Lee's wife, Josie, added: "Oh, I wish I could have a home! It's somethin' I've wanted all my life!" Lee continued:

"We never will own, unless somethin' happens more'n I see. I've been handicapped because my field force has always been so small."

Acquiring land was a burdensome challenge for poor folk, and one from which many of them shrank. "I have thought that someday I would be able to own a farm," said B. F. Brewer, a lifelong sharecropper, "but it looks now like I never will. I will just have to go on and be contented with my lot in life, keeping up the other fellow's property. Some of us are destined to never have anything anyway. I guess I must be one of those."

Such unresisting acquiescence was widespread among farm folk. It rested on many things, among them the fear of risk and of the disappointments that striving, hoping, and then failing would bring. "I always aimed . . . to own a home some day," said Paul Parks, a North Carolina tenant farmer who several times had started saving for a farm. But Parks would not buy a place on credit, and something always came up to interfere with his plans. "I didn't want to make no down payments on land," he explained. "It was cash for a home or keep rentin'. I've kept rentin'. . . . My father owned land that way—with a down payment and so much a year to pay off the mortgage— and it was sold out from under him before I could remember."

Yet some farm folk did become landowners. "Our Pas had never owned no land but we was determined it wouldn't be that way with us," Molly Godwin said, remembering her marriage to Frank Godwin in North Carolina in the late 1890s. She and Frank therefore postponed marriage while he "worked at the carpentry trade" and saved "enough money to make a down payment on twenty acres of land." Even then, they married only after Frank built "a little house, two rooms," for them to move into.

Ernest Foster and his wife reversed this process. They married in 1909 and worked as sharecroppers while saving for a place of their own. "We said to each other that what little we had was ours, and we preferred it that way rather than using something that still belonged to someone else," Foster recalled of the first two years of his married life. "We worked, Lizzie and I, in the fields, side by side. We made most of our food and we saved. At the end of the second year we had only $300, but it represented many sacrifices." That winter Foster worked as a carpenter, saved most of his wages, and increased his nest egg to $500, which he put down on a 75-acre farm, agreeing to pay $500 more a year later. "For the first time we were in debt," Foster recalled, "and our nerves were under a heavy strain that year. We worked hard and we made a good crop." When the crop was sold, however, they had only $400 of the $500 needed to pay off the mortgage. Unable to get another carpentry job, Foster sold some of his potatoes, corn, and hay, and did whatever odd jobs he could find to raise additional money, almost dollar by dollar. His wife "sold a little milk and butter, eggs, fruit, and finally a hen," making her own contribution to the effort. They not only met the payment but had $15 left over.

Foster and his wife succeeded where others failed for reasons that tended to divide farm folk into two groups. Not only did the Fosters work hard, have good luck, and take advantage of Foster's skill as a carpenter, but they set about acquiring land with a determination and a set of social and economic imperatives most farm folk did not have. Foster and his wife began not with hope vaguely felt but with a firm expectation to succeed in their effort, and one can speculate that had their first effort failed, they would have tried again. Landownership was more important to them than to most other folk in the sense that they understood what it entailed and were prepared to make the sacrifices necessary to achieve it. Foster was thus an untypical sharecropper. The son of a small landowner—his father owned a hundred acres—Foster had a high school education as well as a skill, carpentry; and his ability to sell potatoes, hay, milk, eggs, and fruit in his first years of sharecropping indicates that he began farming with his own workstock, one or more cows, and other things that made property accumulation easier.

For every Ernest Foster who tried and succeeded, there were probably several Lee Peakes who tried and failed. Peake was still a young man in 1908 when the sawmill where he worked near Columbia, South Carolina, shut down, and he began sharecropping on cutover land belonging to his former employer. Peake and his wife were "the children, the grandchildren, and even the great-grand-children, of tenant farmers," but they resolved to do better. "I'll pay taxes on my lan' 'fore I die, I will," he told his wife. "This here fifty acres of cut-over lan' will be our'n in a year or two. Old man Musser has promise hit as soon as we can pay five hundred down." To accumulate that sum required sacrifice and hard work. "Yu'll hafter quit lookin' through that big Roebuck Catalogue, a-pickin' out rugs, shades, curtains, and other purty do-dads," he also told his wife, perhaps in jest. "And yuh'll hafter stop listenin' to the talk of these here stove agents and sewin' machin' agents comin' to our door." Peake pledged to "work all the harder" to achieve his goal, and his wife promised "to help with the hoein' and the pickin' of the cotton."

But despite every effort, the Peakes never realized their hope. In their second year of sharecropping, their mule, Old Sawmill, died, and they had to go into debt to buy another one. Still, the crop that year was passably good. Peake and his wife "picked eight bales of cotton off fifteen acres," and as Peake phrased it, "the cawn patch made a few nubbins. [But] after givin' the fourth to old man Musser for rent thar wan't enough left to finish payin' on the mule." The Peakes did not pay out at the end of the year, and over the next few years their problems multiplied. As their family increased, so did their living expenses, which, together with the kind of luck that caused their mule to die, prevented them from ever freeing themselves of debt. During World War I, Peake gave up his effort, and went to work as a laborer in town.

Croppers who acquired land did so in various ways. Some bought uncleared woods because that property was cheaper than cleared land. Others delayed marriage until they could buy land, or at least make a down payment. Leonard and Bessie Warwick used their earnings from the sale of illicit whiskey to buy a place in western North Carolina, thus putting to advantage what was surely the largest source of illegal income for farm folk in the New South. Still others used the labor of their children to purchase a few acres and added to them as conditions permitted.

Some folk acquired land through inheritance, though the holdings of small farmers were too small to be of much benefit to several heirs. Indeed, one cause of the spread of farm tenancy in the New South was the inability of many children of small landowners to acquire land of their own. It was also one reason many families went to the mills. "My father owned his home and a little farm near Creeksville," said Bob Draper, "but when he died it was divided up 'mongst the eight of us and done nobody much good." May Jordan's share of her father's North Carolina farm was eight acres, and Clarence E. Fesperman, another North Carolinian, received eighty dollars when his father's farm was sold and the proceeds were divided among his children. Each generation had to acquire its own land, which the economic squeeze on agriculture in the New South made more and more difficult.

The acquisition of property by farm folk is difficult to study quantitatively. The relevant sources—manuscript censuses, tax lists, and similar records of property holdings—are useful for studying individuals who remained in the same county or other jurisdiction. Like other Americans, however, farm folk moved so frequently that studies based on those sources are no more than suggestive. Only a quarter (26 percent) of the white tenant farmers and even fewer of the white farm laborers (15 percent) who lived in Cobb County, Georgia, in 1880 were still there in 1900, for example. Almost half of those who remained, however, improved their economic position, as measured by the acquisition of real property or the raising of their occupational status.[44] Yet such figures obscure more than they reveal, and the number of those who left the county for the cotton mills in nearby Atlanta or elsewhere in the country will never be known.

That many landless folk quit farming is suggested by information collected in the 1910 census to test the workings of the "agricultural ladder hypothesis."[45] That information showed a direct correlation between age, landownership, and farm size among white farmers in Georgia as well as elsewhere in the United States. The older the farmer, the more likely he was to own land and the larger his farm was likely to be. In Georgia and the Carolinas, only a quarter (28.7 percent) of young farmers (those less than twenty-five years old) owned their farms, compared with two-thirds (69.7 percent) of those of middle age (forty-five to fifty-four years old) and four-fifths (80.6 percent) of those in their retirement years (sixty-five and older).[46]

Whites who remained in farming thus tended to have some success. Yet the surplus agricultural population that plagued the New South functioned to keep farm income low, which in turn increased economic insecurity among farm folk as they were drawn into the money economy. Their economic plight encouraged many folk to look elsewhere for the economic and also social and psychological security they craved. Many found that stability in the cotton mills, and by the end of the New South era, the mills had had a meaningful impact on agricultural labor in some areas of the New South. "The principal agency in disturbing the stability of the laboring population was said to be the growth of cotton mills," Robert P. Brooks found in a survey of farm landlords in one group of North Georgia counties in 1911. "Many white tenant families have forsaken the country in order to place their children in the mills. Other heads of tenant families while remaining on the farm, send their children to the mills in the towns. . . . One planter based his preference for negroes [as tenants] on the fact that he was more likely to retain the young people of the black race."[47] Cotton mills had entered the lives of plain folk.

44. Thomas A. Scott, "Cobb County, Georgia, 1880–1900: A Socioeconomic Study of an Upper Piedmont County" (Ph.D. dissertation, University of Tennessee, 1978), 32.

45. On the hypothesis, see LaWanda F. Cox, "Tenancy in the United States, 1865–1900: A Consideration of the Validity of the Agricultural Ladder Hypothesis" Agricultural History, XVIII (1944), 97–105. For works supporting the hypothesis, see U.S. Department of Agriculture, Yearbook, 1916, 321–46, and Yearbook, 1923, 507–600.

46. Fourteenth Census, 1920: Agriculture, 367.

47. Robert P. Brooks, "Summaries," vol. II of "Questionnaires to Georgia Planters and Materials," in Robert P. Brooks Papers, University of Georgia Library.

2
TRANSITIONS

Folk went to the mills and adjusted to what they found there in ways that were culturally determined. The important thing they brought with them was not the meager group of possessions they piled onto the wagons that hauled them away from the farm but the cultural and social conditioning that had molded their lives. This conditioning formed the standards and expectations they brought to the mills; and because the mills and mill villages incorporated so much of the traditional, paternal, and rural South, this cultural and social baggage facilitated rather than impeded the transition mill folk were commencing. In the New South, the basic elements of mill life and work were not unique. On the contrary, most of them were commonplace; and recognizing that fact is another step toward seeing the mill experience as mill folk saw it.[1]

1. The experience of plain folk contradicted the model first put forth in Ferdinand Tonnies, *Community and Society*, trans. Charles P. Loomis (New York, 1957), originally published in 1887. Tonnies viewed traditional and modern societies as ideal contrasting types, and his followers viewed the transition from one to the other largely in terms of social disruption and discontinuity. Early studies of the impact of the Industrial Revolution on workers continued this tradition. See, for example, Karl Polanyi, *The Great Transformation* (Boston, 1957); and Sidney Pollard, *The Genesis of Modern Management: A Study of the Industrial Revolution in Great Britain* (Cambridge, Mass., 1965). More recently,

Few people, whatever their circumstances, order their lives as they please. The choices all people make are partly forced upon them; and the choices themselves are rooted in cultural factors that emanate from time, place, and experience. Those factors are the fundamental things that socialize people, mold their values, hopes, and expectations, and create the standards by which they and their contemporaries judge the circumstances of their lives and gauge their prospects for the future. "They were not a people bereft of standards and values," sociologist Glenn Gilman wrote some years ago of farm folk as they went to the mills in the New South. "They were, on the contrary, a people who had very little left of their heritage except its system of values. They clung to that system fiercely, hoping by means of it to build a bridge from the past to the future."[2] To appreciate the insight in this statement is to recognize that folk had minds of their own as they approached the mills, and they acted according to their own imperatives. In this and other ways, they were no different from other people.

The move to the mills was an encounter with economic and social change, and it required considerable adjustment. Farm life in the New South, however, including sharecropping, had also been changing, and folk who came to the mills had been making economic and social adjustments all of their lives. Subsistence farming had been growing obsolescent, and farmers found themselves nudged into the money economy whether they wanted to be or not. Chronic hard times and acute economic panics had had increasing effects on poor farmers. The old barter economy, in which work, produce, and even skills and livestock had been exchanged, had been declining, and such things were acquiring a market value. Even relationships between landlords and tenants were becoming more economic and therefore less personal in nature. Traditional self-sufficiency and the skills that sustained it were giving way to cheap consumer goods, and cash income was increasingly necessary even for subsistence. The folk were being pulled into

---

sociologists as well as historians have stressed the adaptive abilities of traditional folk confronted with modernization and industrialization. See, for example, Joseph R. Gusfield, "Tradition and Modernity: Misplaced Polarities in the Study of Social Change," *American Journal of Sociology*, LXXII (1967), 351–62; and Herbert G. Gutman, "Work, Culture, and Society in Industrializing America, 1815–1919," *American Historical Review*, LXXVIII (1973), 531–89.

2. Glenn Gilman, *Human Relations in the Industrial Southeast: A Study of the Textile Industry* (Chapel Hill, 1956), 128. Gilman's work is still the most insightful account of many aspects of the experience of mill folk.

the consumer society, and many offered little resistance. Their values were evolving.

New laws and ordinances, many of them reflecting shifting power relationships, were altering the rules of rural life. Fencing laws, requiring the enclosure of livestock rather than crops, were ending the open grazing by which many folk traditionally fed their livestock.[3] Other laws, also enhancing the rights of property or seeking to conserve diminishing stocks of fish and wildlife, restricted traditional hunting and fishing rights. Still other laws, symbolized by local-option prohibition ordinances, were regulating personal conduct and intruding the state into the lives of people as never before. The effect was to make social readjustment a continuing fact of life.

Technological change was having an impact, too, dramatically altering the substance as well as the pace of life in the view of those experiencing it. The railroad and telegraph, and then telephones and electricity, appeared suddenly in places previously isolated from the outside world and untouched by the gospel of "progress" spread by New South boosters. The effects rippled through the entire southern society. The appearance of railroads, for example, necessitated coordinated scheduling, uniform time, and thus standard time zones. The traditional practice of setting the time of day locally had to be abandoned. To accommodate the change, on November 18, 1883, people in Atlanta adjusted their timepieces twenty-two minutes.[4]

Cultural as well as geographical distances seemed to shrink, and folk found some of the ways of outsiders enticing. Some of them began to develop a sense of deprivation that made the circumstances of their lives appear limiting. Plain folk had thought little of themselves as poor in the sense of being deprived, and had never been much bothered by their lack of schooling or want of the economic and social skills valued by other people. Even poor health was something they had accepted as part of the natural order. Now, some folk became aware of these limitations, and that awareness perhaps encouraged them to go to the cotton mills. To whatever

3. See the informative treatment of these and related subjects in Steven Hahn, "Hunting, Fishing, and Foraging: Common Rights and Class Relations in the Postbellum South," *Radical History Review*, XXVI (1982), 37–64; and Hahn, "Common Right and Commonwealth: The Stock-Law Struggle and the Roots of Southern Populism," in J. Morgan Kousser and James M. McPherson (eds.), *Region, Race, and Reconstruction: Essays in Honor of C. Vann Woodward* (New York, 1982), 51–88. See also J. Crawford King, "The Closing of the Southern Range: An Exploratory Essay," *Journal of Southern History*, XLVIII (1982), 53–70.

4. Atlanta *Constitution*, November 18, 1883. On the changing meaning of time for new industrial workers, see E. P. Thompson, "Time, Work-Discipline, and Industrial Capitalism," *Past and Present*, No. 38 (1967), 56–97.

extent folk thought over the matter systematically, some must have concluded that the mills were better places to face the future than someone else's sharecropped land.

It is not clear that the folk thought in these terms, though many who went to the mills explained their going in ways compatible with that line of reasoning, stressing the greater income, better schools, or enhanced social life the mills seemed to promise. This suggests an awareness of larger social forces and an understanding that adaptations had to be made, in which case a move to the mills could be a rational act indeed. The explanations of those who went to the mills also suggest the possibility that they were more aware than those who stayed on the farm of the social and economic change around them and were more prepared to accept the challenges that change presented. Those who remained on the farm might have been less conscious of the change or less affected by it, or perhaps they thought the best way to deal with it was to seek security in the kind of life they already knew. This difference, if it existed, must not be overstated, for folk who went to the mills carried a full set of cultural baggage with them and maintained close contact with their rural roots. They also held onto much more of their past than they lost.[5]

"IT'S A HARD, UNCERTAIN SORT OF LIFE."

That the move to the cotton mills was not unique is important in understanding the move. As cotton mills were proliferating across the South, other economic currents were also stirring. A propertyless man contemplating his economic prospects in the rural South between the 1880s and the second decade of the 1900s would have been aware of those stirrings and (much more so than a woman) have felt he had a certain degree of choice in deciding his future. He could remain on the farm and hope to achieve security there. That option was risky, though less so if he had several sturdy sons. It also had the attraction of the familiar, and was the option most men

5. For a work that distorts the experience of mill folk by stressing victimization, see Frank Tannenbaum, *Darker Phases of the South* (1924; rpr. New York, 1969). More balanced but still with too much emphasis on victimization, if only by omission, are Melton A. McLaurin, *Paternalism and Protest: Southern Cotton Mill Workers and Organized Labor, 1875–1905* (Westport, Conn., 1971); and Dale Newman, "Textile Workers in a Tobacco County: A Comparison Between Yarn and Weave Mill Villagers," in Edward Magdol and Jon L. Wakelyn (eds.), *The Southern Common People: Studies in Nineteenth Century Social History* (Westport, Conn., 1980), 345–68. More successful is David L. Carlton, *Mill and Town in South Carolina, 1880–1920* (Baton Rouge, 1982).

chose. Most rural folk seem never to have given serious thought to any other occupation as a permanent form of work. Many of them, especially while they were young and unmarried, did, however, leave the farm for a while for work in mine or mill, or any other position that offered itself. However, most of the folk intended to return to farming and did so, often at the time, or soon after, they married and settled down. The result was that many farm folk—and perhaps most of the men among them—had worked at something other than farming, if only for one or two seasons when they were young and farm work was slack.

That point illustrates another fact relevant to understanding the mill experience: the division between on and off the farm in the New South was not a clear one, and many folk floated back and forth across that division. In the late fall of 1886, for example, a newspaper reporter found farmers around Anniston, Alabama, doing "a great deal" of digging and hauling of iron ore. "The best time for raising ore is in the dry part of the fall, after the farm work is finished," the reporter noted, "and the money made in this way, at a time when otherwise stocks would be idle, is a great help to the small farmers who avail themselves of it. Another benefit is to the common field hands who have to work in a crop during the spring and summer. They always find employment at good wages in the fall and winter raising ore or working in the various coalings of the [Woodstock Iron and Steel] company."[6]

Nothing better illustrates the growing desire for cash income than the efforts of farm folk to seek nonagricultural work wherever they could find it. All of the areas from which mill folk came, especially the Piedmont and southeastern Appalachia, were places of considerable economic activity in the New South era.[7] Between the 1870s and the second decade of the 1900s, the various forestry products industries—naval stores operations, logging, sawmilling, lumbering, and pulp wooding—came through the Carolinas and Georgia and, when the woods were cut over, pushed on to Florida, Alabama, and the Southwest. These industries offered unskilled jobs to thousands of black and white men, including many who later brought their families to the mills. The jobs were seasonal, sporadic, or otherwise temporary, however, and the pay for unskilled workers was low. Many men found

6. Atlanta *Constitution*, December 3, 1886.

7. For general information on social and economic conditions in the New South, see Rupert B. Vance, *Human Geography of the South* (Chapel Hill, 1932); C. Vann Woodward, *Origins of the New South, 1877–1913* (Baton Rouge, 1951); and Emory Q. Hawk, *Economic History of the South* (New York, 1934).

it necessary to combine or alternate them with farming in order to make a living. Still, these industries introduced many young men to work off the farm and to the attractions of cash income regularly received.[8]

Other forms of unskilled labor also appeared, among them mining, railroad construction and maintenance, and handling, transporting, and processing agricultural products. Sometimes different forms of employment existed in local combinations that facilitated movement to the cotton mills, which at first employed far more women and children than men. At High Point, North Carolina, for example, there were both furniture and cotton manufactories, and many men who worked in the former sent their wives or children into the latter.[9] In Columbus, Georgia, for a while the largest textile center in the South, there were not only fourteen cotton and woolen mills in the late nineteenth century but a variety of establishments providing an assortment of other jobs for unskilled workers: clothing factories, hosiery mills, cotton compresses, cottonseed oil mills, syrup refineries, and iron foundries, as well as plants for making ice, plows, fertilizer, candy, bricks, buggies, and wagons. Numerous other minor industries existed, too. In addition, five steamers plied the Chattahoochee River between Columbus and the Gulf Coast, and seven railroads connected the town with overland points. Men of various occupations there sent their children to work in the cotton mills. Durham, North Carolina, with tobacco and cigarette factories as well as textile and hosiery mills, is an example of a town where women and children as well as men could move back and forth between various industries.

Such variety was not the rule, however, for most of the early cotton mills were built in isolated areas at natural sources of water power, and many of the later ones were in unincorporated places, often just outside small towns or villages. Such mills were often near farming areas, and that fact explains why some farm folk went to work in them. Yet folk sometimes traveled great

8. These remarks are intended merely to suggest certain parallels and differences between working conditions in cotton manufacturing and in other industries. Information on those industries is voluminous but has been little studied and never comparatively. For examples, see *Senate Documents*, 61st Cong., 2nd Sess., No. 645, which contains 19 volumes of information on the condition of woman and child labor in various industries; *Senate Documents*, 64th Cong., 1st Sess., No. 415, eleven volumes of information collected by the Commission on Industrial Relations from 1910 to 1920; *House Documents*, 57th Cong., 1st Sess., No. 184, an additional 15 volumes of material collected by an earlier industrial commission at the turn of the century; and *Senate Documents*, 48th Cong., 1st Sess., No. 91, a major source of information on the relations between labor and capital in the early 1880s.

9. See Dan M. Lacy, "The Beginnings of Industrialization in North Carolina" (M.A. thesis, University of North Carolina, 1935), 124.

distances to find employment. The week's journey Jessie Lee Carter's family made from Tennessee to South Carolina in 1905 was not unique, which suggests that some of the folk who went to the cotton mills might have sought work at distant places had they found the work attractive—coal mining in Appalachia, for example, or iron mining and manufacturing in northern Alabama and southern Tennessee, or steel manufacturing in Birmingham. Large numbers of blacks from the Carolinas and Virginia did move to the coal mines in Virginia, West Virginia, and elsewhere, but relatively fewer whites did so; and miners throughout Appalachia, like the laborers in iron and steel manufacturing, were disproportionately blacks or immigrants.[10]

These facts suggest that plain folk had some choice in matters of employment and exercised that choice in ways of their own. "The native white who comes from the small farm is at best only a temporary employee who is enticed by cash wages during certain seasons of the year, and who as a general rule is a shiftless person," a national commission said of Alabama coal miners in the early twentieth century. "The native whites from the mountain country near by," the same commission said of West Virginia miners, "are irregular, being willing to work in the mines only at certain periods of the year when the farm and cattle grazing do not demand their presence at home. A large portion are also unsatisfactory as miners because of their lack of efficiency." As for the "very small" number of "native whites" who worked in the iron and steel industries near Birmingham, "they are for the most part, not adapted to conditions," the commission reported. "They come from the agricultural districts, and the majority are willing to work only during the winter months."[11]

In cotton mills and other industries across the New South, employers repeated such complaints, and to read them is to be reminded of the degree to which the move off the farm was a single regional movement and of the degree as well to which plain folk patterned their own employment. Most folk wanted to remain on the farm and did so even when they might have made more money elsewhere. For those who left, or wanted to leave, the attractiveness of specific jobs depended on a number of factors. The indi-

10. Thus blacks and immigrants constituted 42.4 percent of coal miners in West Virginia, Virginia, Kentucky, Tennessee, and Alabama in 1899 and 60.6 percent of the work force in the southern iron and steel district in 1910 (*Senate Documents*, 61st Cong., 2nd Sess., No. 633, Pt. 1, Vol. 2, p. 136, and 62nd Cong., 1st Sess., No. 110, Vol. 3, p. 89).

11. *Senate Documents*, 61st Cong., 2nd Sess., No. 633, Pt. 1, Vol. 2, pp. 216–17, 220, and Pt. 2, p. 151.

vidual's gender, age, physical condition, and family status were important, and race was too, for patterns of racial employment varied notably from one industry to another.[12] Most jobs in large industries were sweated, laborious, and even backbreaking, and only young men in good physical condition could fill them. In all of the jobs, hours were long and wages low, and much of the work was not only dangerous but in isolated places, so that the folk had to live in work camps and often away from their families. In sawmilling, mining, railroad maintenance, and the like, the wages of unskilled laborers were too low for a man to support a large family. That helped explain why the work force in those industries was disproportionately young, unmarried, and impermanent, and why many men, or families, combined farming and off-season work in those or other industries in whatever arrangement they could make.

"SHE 'DID NOT THINK OF WORK BY TIME.'"

Demographic factors alone do not explain why plain folk were willing to move to the mills and able to adapt to conditions there. Another part of the explanation is that what folk found in the mills and mill villages was familiar to them, or readily comprehensible, because conditions in the cotton textile industry had much in common with those on the farm and in other contemporary industries as well.

Working hours, for example, which were invariably long in New South industries, were no more so than those in busy seasons on the farm. The common workday for outdoor labor was sunrise to sunset, and for unskilled labor it was about the same—ten to twelve hours depending on the season, or longer or shorter according to the needs of the employer. In North Carolina tobacco factories in 1887, a normal day's work was ten to twelve hours, but as with other seasonal employment, it varied depending on the work at hand. The same was true in seafood canneries along the Atlantic and Gulf coasts, which, like tobacco factories, provided seasonal work for a labor force composed largely of women and children, including many

---

12. For example, in tobacco and cigar manufacturing in the South in 1890, 51.8 percent of the work force was black and 31.8 percent native white. In 1900 the corresponding figures were 44.9 percent and 38.7 percent (*Senate Documents*, 61st Cong., 2nd Sess., No. 633, Pt. 14, Vol. 2, pp. 145–46). The proportion of blacks to whites in the lumbering industries was approximately three to two, and about half the white workers were unskilled (Vernon H. Jensen, *Lumber and Labor* [New York, 1945], 76).

blacks and immigrants. In the lumber industry in 1915, the work week averaged sixty hours in the nation as a whole, but in some places in the South it was as long as seventy hours. In this and other industries, the workday was longer in summer than in winter because there were more daylight hours.[13] That was also the case in the cotton mills, some of which originally had no interior lighting.

These fluctuations in work time were reminiscent of farming, in which the length of the workday was always determined by what had to be done at a given time. On the farm, work was not a matter of hours or even of time, but of tasks, and the conditioning that this perception created carried over to nonagricultural work. A study of workers in seafood canneries on the Gulf Coast at the end of the New South era found pointed evidence of that fact. "Some families had no clocks," investigators from the Children's Bureau of the Department of Labor reported of the workers in 1919, "and did not know at what hour they began or ceased their work. One mother said she 'did not think of work by time.' They depended on the factory whistle or on the watchman to waken them, and usually worked as long as there was work to be done."[14] This condition resulted in short days (and short pay) as often as long ones, and was familiar to all workers in the New South.

The hours actually worked were throughout the country less than scheduled maximums. In tobacco factories in the late nineteenth century, for example, "the average laborer could . . . expect employment for less than 75 percent of the time during a normal year." West Virginia coal miners averaged 230 days of work in 1907 and 185 days in 1908, though a full schedule of 6-day weeks was about 310 days. A study of 42 lumber industry establishments (sawmills, planing mills, and logging operations) in Georgia and the Carolinas in 1915 found that they shut down an average of 33 workdays each, the equivalent of 5.5 weeks, and a significant minority of the work force worked less than 75 percent of the time. In 1888 the standard

13. Thus railroad section hands worked from "sunrise to sunset" at the turn of the century, and other railroad employees 10 to 12 hours (*House Documents*, 57th Cong., 1st Sess., No. 184, Vol. 1, p. 735). For detailed information on conditions of employment on railroads in North Carolina, see North Carolina Bureau of Labor Statistics, *Annual Report, 1887*, 163–71, hereinafter cited as NC *Labor Report* by year. On conditions in other industries, see NC *Labor Report, 1887*, 153–61; U.S. Department of Labor, Children's Bureau *Publication 98: Child Labor and the Work of Mothers in Oyster and Shrimp Canning on the Gulf Coast* (1922); and U.S. Bureau of Labor Statistics, *Bulletin 225: Wages and Hours of Labor in the Lumber, Millwork, and Furniture Industries, 1915* (1918).

14. Department of Labor, *Child Labor and the Work of Mothers in Oyster and Shrimp Canning*, 24.

workday in cottonseed mills in Atlanta was 12 hours, but the mills were closed several months during the year.[15]

Workers themselves also influenced the amount of time they worked. Astonishingly high rates of absenteeism and labor turnover were characteristic of all New South and other American industries. Unskilled workers were especially irregular even when work was available, and they moved from job to job with remarkable frequency. Of course the conditions just noted contributed to this situation, but worker dissatisfaction and insecurity, as well as an unwillingness to work so much, did too. All industries, including cotton manufacturing, had problems with "floating labor" and absenteeism. "Labor in the woods . . . is extremely shifting," the Bureau of Labor Statistics reported of the lumber industry in 1915, "an entire change of crews from two to five times a year [is] not uncommon." The case of a large, unidentified steel plant reported in a congressional study illustrates the national scope of this phenomenon. The plant had 16,997 employees on January 1, 1910, and hired 13,043 new workers over the next twelve months. Yet its payroll on December 31 was only 15,510. During the year, 20,509 workers had quit this plant, but 6,135 of them had returned before December 31 and been rehired.[16]

Lost time and labor turnover were also related to another feature of New South industry, the introduction of labor-saving machinery. Surveying this subject in 1886, the commissioner of labor noted recent innovations in the manufacture of bricks, brooms, carriages, and wagons and in a variety of other jobs at which plain folk worked. "In the manufacture of furniture from one-half to three-fourths only of the old number of persons is now required," the commissioner reported, summarizing the impact of recent innovations. "In the lumber business, 12 co-laborers with a Bucker machine will dress 12,000 staves. The same number of men, by hand process, would dress but 2,500." He also reported, "In a phosphate mine in South Carolina, 10 men accomplish with machinery what 100 men handle without in the same time."[17]

The impact of labor-saving devices was felt by craftsmen and artisans as

15. Nannie May Tilley, *The Bright-Tobacco Industry, 1860–1929* (Chapel Hill, 1948), 518; *Senate Documents*, 61st Cong., 2nd Sess., No. 633, Pt. 1, Vol. 2, p. 207; Bureau of Labor Statistics, *Wages and Hours of Labor*, 18–21; Atlanta *Constitution*, April 14, 1888.

16. The average turnover rate for all soft coal miners in the nation was 99.8 percent (*Senate Documents*, 68th Cong., 2nd Sess., No. 195, Pt. 3, p. 1263). For a study documenting high rates of turnover in contemporary industries outside the South, see Paul F. Brissenden and Emil Frankel, *Labor Turnover in Industry: A Statistical Analysis* (New York, 1922).

17. U.S. Commissioner of Labor, *First Annual Report, 1886*, 84–85.

well as by unskilled workers. "The greatest trouble I see with working people's interests in general is labor-saving machinery," a craftsman observed in 1900. "Constantly in all trades, machines are supplanting labor and nothing presents itself, comparatively, to afford employment." Labor-saving machinery brought, of course, mass production and the dislocation of craftsmen who could not compete with machine-made goods. "I worked in a wagon factory for fourteen years in succession," a North Carolinian told his state's labor commissioner in 1896, "put in full time and made some extra time up to the last four years, when labor-saving machinery and small wages drove me from the business. The business is running now with improved machinery and half the hands it used to employ, and a great deal less wages to those employed."[18]

"THE HABITUAL CIGARETTE SMOKER IS UNTRUSTWORTHY."

All of these conditions—long hours, irregular work, high rates of absenteeism, frequent moves, technological displacement—were widespread in the cotton mills, and this brief glance at the situation in other industries suggests that the universality of those conditions was part of the context in which folk reacted to life and work in the mills. Another feature of mill life, paternalism, also had a universal dimension. A large share of the New South's nonagricultural workers, especially those in large industries, lived in company-owned houses in company towns or work camps, kept pigs, cows, and gardens on company-owned land, received all or part of their pay in scrip or store orders rather than cash, shopped at company stores and had their accounts settled by payroll deductions, and were objects of company-sponsored "welfare" programs and company efforts to regulate their personal conduct.[19]

"My factory is out in the country about fourteen miles from town," a North Carolina tobacco manufacturer wrote in 1895. "I have prepared suitable tenant houses and placed them about 200 feet apart, giving to every house that much for garden space. Good, pure, cold well water, convenient for all—plenty of wood handy, and furnish pasture for one cow, and furnish

18. NC *Labor Report* (1900), 150, (1896), 193.
19. The history of company towns in the New South is little studied. David A. Corbin, *Life, Work, and Rebellion in the Coal Fields: The Southern West Virginia Miners, 1880–1922* (Urbana, 1981) is an interesting recent account that includes information on company towns in one of the areas mentioned here. An informative study of company stores made in 1934 is U.S. National Recovery Administration, Division of Review, *Work Materials No. 4: Report of the Committee on the Economic and Social Implications of the Company Store and Scrip System* (March, 1936).

hand and horse to do all the plowing for my hands [in their gardens]. All the above is free without any charge whatever." He also wrote, "I have a good school eight months in the year free to all, a good church and we have five more churches within two miles."[20]

Cotton mill folk would certainly have found those conditions familiar. "We never fail to grant them any reasonable favor," a North Carolina furniture manufacturer wrote of his employees, also in 1895, "frequently give them orders for clothes, and become responsible for the payment of such bills, and take the amount out so much per week, as they can stand, and when frequently they need it for rent or other urgent purposes, we advance the money and carry to debt until it suits them to pay it." Significantly, all this was done without a company town or company store. "We have a good set of men," this manufacturer continued. "We do not swear nor drink ourselves, and we forbid it of our employees."[21]

Moral policies of this sort were also characteristic of New South industry, at official levels at least. "Are you temperate in your habits?" "Are you addicted to the use of intoxicating liquors, morphine or opium?" "Do you ever play games of chance or gamble in any way?" These were questions prospective railroad employees might be asked about 1900, and presumably they referred to behavior employers intended to discourage. "All employees that smoke cigarettes must cease to do so or lose their positions," the South Carolina division of the Southern Railway announced, also at the turn of the century, "and . . . in the future no one will be engaged by the road who is a cigarette smoker." The Atlanta division of that company was already enforcing the latter rule, which, it explained, "is based on the ground that the habitual cigarette smoker is untrustworthy."[22]

To mention these policies is not to suggest that mill folk accepted at face value the paternalism they encountered in the mills and villages. In a paternalistic society, most people judge paternalists and their policies on what resembles an *ad hoc* basis. Certainly mill folk reacted to paternalism in ways that historians have found difficult to appreciate.

20. NC *Labor Report* (1895), 319.
21. *Ibid.*, 232–33.
22. *House Documents*, 57th Cong., 1st Sess., No. 184, Vol. 17, pp. 735, 804. There are numerous statements of policies regulating the moral conduct of employees in annual reports of the North Carolina labor commissioner from 1887 onward. See, for example, NC *Labor Report* (1887), 68.

"LET THE MAN THAT PLOWS PLOW."

Within the context of these forces, farm folk pondered their future. Many must have felt themselves caught up in multiple dilemmas. "Laborers of this community are in a suffering condition," one of the folk told the North Carolina labor commissioner in 1889. "The crops fell short this year, and the merchants have ceased to furnish the tenants with supplies because their farms will not produce enough to allow the tenants to settle their accounts. This leaves them to seek work otherwise, but none can be found."[23]

Tenants were not the only ones affected by these conditions. "I am sure that I would not exaggerate if I were to say that ninety per cent of the farmers in this county (and the land is fertile) would be only too glad to sell their land and find something else to do," a farm owner from eastern North Carolina wrote in 1899, complaining of low farm income. But no one stepped forward to buy the land, and few farmers had viable employment alternatives. One of the growing problems of landowners, especially those with small holdings who needed part-time or temporary help, was the pressure employment off the farm put on farm wages. "The great trouble," a landowner wrote in 1902, "is the factories, railroads, saw-mills and public works, paying more for hands than farmers can, and will give them short jobs, allow them to be in and out at their pleasure—no system—any hand can quit his job and get another the same day in any neighborhood."[24]

So farm owners sought economic alternatives, too. "I have a nice farm but see that I can't Meet my 'ends,'" one of them wrote Governor Coleman L. Blease of South Carolina in 1914, stating the problem in personal terms. "[H]ave been falling back for the last three or four years owning to the Drouth and scarcity of labor[.] If you have a good paying job that you could give me I would appreciate it Very Much."[25]

Every man's problem reflected his circumstances. Employers complained that wages were too high to make a profit, employees that they were too low to live on. Jobs were plentiful, insisted the former; no one can live on the wages they pay, complained the latter. These were predictable reactions to difficult times, and each reaction had its own validity. Poor farmers pushed out of farming found themselves in an imbalanced and underdeveloped

23. NC *Labor Report* (1889), 280.
24. *Ibid.* (1899), 59, (1902), 74.
25. W. H. Axson to Coleman L. Blease, October 9, 1914, in Coleman L. Blease Papers, South Carolina State Archives. These uncataloged papers are filed by counties.

economy, their very presence driving wages down just as their increasing production of cotton had helped undercut prices on the farm.

Bearing heavily on the movement to the mills was the pressure put on artisans by the efforts of displaced farmers to enter the skilled and semi-skilled trades. "There are so many cobblers [that is, inferior and untrained workmen] of all trades, that good mechanics can hardly get any work," a North Carolina sawyer complained in 1888. "Men who know a little something of use of tools, being driven from the farms by poverty, come to the towns and work at any and every price, and while barely making subsistence for themselves and families they are keeping the mechanics, who have learned their trade and have nothing else to depend upon, out of their legitimate work, and oftentimes causing their families to suffer. It is not right; there is something wrong somewhere. These farmers ought to be farming, and doubtless would be if they had a choice."[26]

The complaint was interested but legitimate, for impoverished farmers and farm laborers were crowding into an overcrowded labor force. "I frequently meet friends who inform me that they have been endeavoring to find other employment by which to earn money save that of farming," a North Carolina farmer wrote while the just-quoted sawyer was making his complaint. "They can get work that pays much better than farming [which pays nothing much at all], but most of those who have been raised on the farm like [farming] best."[27]

Not surprisingly, artisans resented this threat to their economic and social well-being. "Let each man of a trade work at his trade and no other," one urged in 1900. "If he is a farmer let him do nothing else. This will stop so much cutting wages." Another North Carolinian repeated this plea a year later. "Here a man can work his crop, and then pick up a saw and hammer and call himself a carpenter, and get a job," he complained. "Why? Because he will work for fifty and seventy-five cents a day, and the cheapest man is the one that is wanted. . . . So I think it best to let the man that plows plow, and the carpenter and bricklayer do the carpenter work and the brick work."[28]

Year after year from across the state, these and similar complaints reached the North Carolina labor commissioner in response to his requests that workingmen comment on economic conditions in their area. "My section has a surplus of young men seeking work," a carpenter wrote the commis-

26. NC *Labor Report* (1888), 117.
27. *Ibid.*, 408.
28. *Ibid.* (1900), 146, 104.

sioner in 1888. "There seems to be an over-supply [of laborers] in all lines," a blacksmith agreed. "The laboring people of this section need many things," a tinsmith added, "but most of all they need work. Not a third of them are employed with any regularity." Stating the problem in personal terms, a brickmaker reported, "I have been unemployed seven months the past year"; and a sawyer wrote: "I work by the day, put in just about half-time. Provisions are cheap enough here and house rent is low, and we get [a] very fair price per day if we could work every day."[29]

"OUR LABORERS ARE ALL COLORED."

Most folk who left the farm found themselves in competition not with skilled artisans but with unskilled blacks. Caught up in similar uprooting processes, poor blacks and whites were searching for alternatives to share-cropping or agricultural labor, and for the securities of steady income paid in cash. Unskilled whites and blacks found themselves in an economic competition in which their common impoverishment and mutual antag-onisms functioned to perpetuate their separate disadvantages.

Economic competition with blacks was not new for white plain folk, but it assumed large and immediate proportions for those who left or sought to leave the farm. As an important part of the context in which folk moved to the cotton mills, this competition helps explain why they were determined to keep the mills all-white. Racial and ethnic patterns among unskilled workers varied widely in major industries, often to the disadvantage of plain folk. Wherever unskilled and semiskilled workers were employed in large numbers in the New South outside the cotton mills, racial patterns were intricate, even crazy-quilt, and frequently at odds with common tenets of segregation and white supremacy. Employers very often reserved unskilled jobs for blacks, and in some cases that practice was reinforced by the refusal of even the poorest whites to do what they regarded as "nigger work." In other cases, such jobs were open to blacks and whites but only at "nigger wages," as whites contemptuously referred to pay levels unskilled blacks were forced to accept.

Because of the volatility of all things racial in the New South, generaliza-tions are difficult and risky. Employment patterns were always fluid and not generally subject to segregation laws until well into the twentieth century.[30]

29. *Ibid.* (1888), 60, 63, 126.
30. The only law formally segregating employment in the cotton mills seems to have been that enacted by South Carolina in 1915. See *South Carolina Code of Laws* (1962), Sec. 40-452.

Even when such laws appeared, however, they were not necessarily bene-ficial to unskilled whites. Excluding blacks from skilled and well-paying jobs, for example, might benefit whites who had the skills to fill such jobs but had the effect of crowding blacks into the only kinds of work many plain folk could do. Reserving the cotton mills for unskilled whites was thus doubly significant.

Racial factors were always important in employment, but they did not necessarily work to advantage for the poorest whites. "Our laborers are all colored except one man," a Columbus, Georgia, brick manufacturer re-ported in 1883. "I prefer them. I can manage them better, and they are better laborers than any other." In contrast, a North Carolina lumber mill operator "use[d] all white labor," while another "work[ed] both colors, and they seem[ed] to work together harmoniously." At the same time, "most" employees of a North Carolina building contractor, "especially brick layers and hod carriers," were blacks, while those at a sawmill in the same state were "mostly colored" and at a brick company "all colored." The manager of an ironworks, however, had "never had any experience with working negro labor."[31]

Across the New South this lack of pattern prevailed, and the operative factor in specific cases seems to have been the experience or predilection of individual employers. Thus, in thirty years at a Virginia charcoal furnace, one manager had "worked mixed labor, white and black, at all times" because he "found no difference in the color of the laborers" and "[could] not say that one [was] better than the other." In fact, he declared, "neither is reliable." A foundry and machine shop in Valdosta, Georgia, also employed both whites and blacks, but for other reasons and in different ways. "We have trouble in getting all of the common laborers that we need," the proprietor wrote in 1905. "Our remedy is that we have about half and half of white and black. We use home boys, working them in the most responsible positions and keeping the negro for the drudgery." A Tennessee pipe and foundry company executive had still another experience to relate. "We have been working about 150 negroes in our boiler shop and about 300 in our pipe shop for the past 16 years," he reported. "We have found them more reliable and efficient than the white labor in the South."[32]

It is uncertain whether this preference for black labor, which appears frequently in the sources from all parts of the South throughout the period

31. *Senate Documents*, 48th Cong., 1st Sess., No. 91, p. 489; NC *Labor Report* (1888), 171, 177, 183, 190, (1902), 125.
32. *Manufacturers' Record*, July 20, 1905, pp. 6, 8.

of this study, was influenced by the ability to hire unskilled blacks at low wages and keep them "tractable" by force of necessity and racial discrimination. But whether the explanation was racial or economic, the effect of this preference on unskilled whites was adverse. Moreover, the class prejudice involved was obviously important. On the basis of a survey of employer opinion, the *Manufacturers' Record*, certainly the most influential representative of employer views in the New South, concluded that "the class of whites likely to be available for the kind of labor largely monopolized by the negroes render no more satisfactory service and are less reliable and less efficient, though demanding even higher wages than the negro."[33] The prejudices plain folk encountered on the farm followed them into other forms of employment.

Behind such attitudes lay practices that excluded whites from some unskilled jobs and thrust them into competition with blacks for others. Such practices formed a pattern in the construction industry, which employed large numbers of men and grown youths at all levels of skill, and some who were unskilled, to, among other things, build new cotton mills and mill villages. "Particular in the building of new enterprises—mills and warehouses and stores," James L. Orr, president of Piedmont Mills in the South Carolina upcountry, observed in 1901, "you will see negro carpenters, negro bricklayers, and negro plasterers working along with white people." Another mill president (and former politician), Rufus B. Bullock of Atlanta, said in the same year, "All over the State, the two races work side by side on a brick wall or in the trench; the colored man on one side of the bench and a white man on the other, under the same contractor—very often a negro contractor."[34]

Were such statements mere propaganda from southern apologists trying to mislead inquiring Yankees on the Industrial Commission, to whom they were directed? Not according to H. F. Garrett, president of the Georgia Federation of Labor. "In some trades they are," Garrett responded when asked whether whites and blacks were employed together at equal wages. "Among the stone masons and the brick masons they are equal; the carpenters in some places are and in some places not."[35]

This does not mean that racial divisions in employment were disappearing. Rather, they might not be apparent at first glance. "We do not mix the races in our machine shop," reported the chief engineer of Eagle and Phenix

33. *Ibid.*, 5.
34. *House Documents*, 57th Cong., 1st Sess., No. 184, Vol. 7, pp. 485, 524.
35. *Ibid.*, 547.

Mills, one of whose jobs was to oversee construction of several large expansions of these mills and their villages at Columbus, Georgia, and Phenix City, Alabama. "[That] is done only where there seems to be a certain suitableness in it." That "suitableness" seems to have derived from an employer's intuition of what a given circumstance permitted or dictated. "If I want a man to do a certain thing I want a colored man every time," the just-quoted engineer, John Hill, continued, "while, on the other hand, if I want a man to do a certain other thing, I want a white man. I don't know that it hinges on the question of the whiteness or blackness of the man's skin; it hinges rather on the adaptability of the man to do the particular work that is required."[36]

The distinction was subtle indeed, and given the racial and class attitudes of most employers, it might logically lead to white skilled and black unskilled workers, to the disadvantage of unskilled whites and skilled blacks. "[For] such labor as can earn 60 to 70 cents a day," Hill explained, "there is perfect equality between white and black labor here in the South. But that does not mean at all social equality. . . . It means just 75 cents a day for a day's work, whether the laborer is white or black."[37]

If this treatment did not indicate social equality, as Hill insisted, it surely pointed to economic competition across racial lines; and if the equality Hill spoke of was preserved for unskilled labor, it was at wage levels blacks had to accept rather than levels they, like whites, thought adequate for decent living. "The colored man competes with the white man, and on all common buildings he is largely employed, tending to keep wages down," a North Carolina building contractor noted in 1888. White workers saw this, too. "Negroes should be excluded from all trades, especially bricklaying," one of them told the North Carolina labor commissioner, "as they tend to . . . lower a white man's wages until he can not live by his trade."[38]

There was truth in this conclusion even if it rested on the questionable premise that blacks could live more cheaply than whites and therefore did not deserve the same level of wages. The striking feature of the complaint, however, is not that it was wrongly premised but that it expressed an anomalous grievance—that white labor was victimized by a system of racial policies called white supremacy. "A negro apprentice seems to be preferred to a white one," a plasterer told the North Carolina labor commissioner, in a complaint frequently voiced. "My trade is badly abused by the colored labor," a painter reported, "consequently it keeps good men out of work.

36. *Senate Documents*, 48th Cong., 1st Sess., No. 91, p. 595.
37. *Ibid.*
38. NC *Labor Report* (1888), 187, (1900), 118.

The majority of capitalists will give employment to incompetent workmen [for which read *blacks*] because they work cheap."[39]

Such complaints were frequent because the conditions they protested were real. The superintendent of the cotton mill at Graniteville, South Carolina, illustrated that reality when he told the Industrial Commission of his own experience. "The white journeyman bricklayer in our section gets $2.50 a day," he said, "and we are able to employ a colored bricklayer for $1.75."[40] The difference in wages was 30 percent.

Racial competition was not restricted to outdoor work. "In some of our factories and workshops," a North Carolinian complained at the end of the nineteenth century, "the white men are obliged to work along with the negro or quit. This is unpleasant." Tobacco factories, especially, employed unskilled blacks and whites, and racial patterns there were important, for those places employed women and children and thus the kinds of families who went to the cotton mills. "In many of our tobacco factories," a man reported in 1900, "white girls are obliged to work by the side of stalwart, foul-mouth, male negro brutes, thus forcing self-respecting white girls to forego work in the tobacco factories or hear language that would shock a brute; thus many a pure white girl who is in sore need of work is, through self-respect, compelled to remain at home and idle away time that is precious to her, and perhaps afflicted parents and helpless little brothers and sisters."[41]

The racism behind this complaint should not obscure the way plain folk read it. To dismiss their reading, and the economic as well as the racial anxieties on which the report was based, is to ignore the largest dimension of the problem. The economic difficulties of plain folk were not a function of their racial views, however objectionable those views might be. Moreover, those difficulties would have been enlarged had mill folk welcomed blacks into the mills, for the employment of blacks would certainly have lowered the folk's wages. Economic realities thus influenced folk in matters of race, and those realities seemed to them all the more pressing because of the competition with blacks for unskilled jobs off the farm.[42]

39. *Ibid* (1900), 143.
40. *House Documents*, 57th Cong., 1st Sess., No. 184, Vol. 7, p. 488.
41. NC *Labor Report* (1899), 154, (1900), 119.
42. For an instance in which several hundred white women were replaced at lower wages by several hundred black women, see U.S. Department of Labor, Women's Bureau, *Bulletin No. 22: Women in Georgia Industries* (1922), 32. For a theoretical construction that explains much of the pattern of racial competition in New South employment, see Edna Bonacich, "A Theory of Ethnic Antagonism: The Split Labor Market," *American Sociological Review*, XXXI (1972), 547–58.

"DEAR GOV WE NEED HIS WORK FOR SUPPORT."

Most folk who moved to the mills were women or girls, who had special concerns of their own. Mill women and girls had to support themselves, often because there was no man in the family. Disproportionate numbers of them were widows or the dependent children of widows. For women in these circumstances, the New South could be a difficult place. They could not farm, and in the rural South there was no other way of making a living. On the farms and in small towns the jobs available to them—in agricultural labor, domestic service, food canneries, tobacco factories, and the like— were seasonal, menial, and low paying (many paid no cash at all), or given over to blacks. In none of these jobs could black or white women earn a decent livelihood. In larger towns and cities, other jobs were available— sewing for the garment industry, packaging cigarettes, or working in such places as box factories, confectionaries, and laundries. But those too had the characteristics of jobs reserved for women: they involved unskilled work for long hours at pay lower even than that of unskilled men. ·

A woman, in short, could hardly earn a living on her own. Custom decreed that a woman's destiny was marriage, motherhood, and unpaid work in and about the home. Outside work for wages was "unnatural," and married women did it only from necessity. Economic practice reinforced this custom. Wage rates embodied the notion of family income: a man worked to provide for his wife and children, a woman or child to supplement family income. For this reason as well as because they could do more of the kinds of physical labor most jobs required, men received significantly higher wages than women or youths. Except for the few kinds of agricultural labor paid for on a piecework basis—picking cotton, for example— these differences were universal. Years later, Stella Foust Carden still remembered that on the farm in Virginia where she grew up in the second decade of the twentieth century, "A man would get a dollar a day and a woman would get 50¢ and she'd do the same amount of work." One of the things Mrs. Carden liked about the cotton mills was that they paid by the position or piece, rather than according to the gender of the worker.

Men also recognized this discrimination as a problem. "No matter if a woman does as much and as good work as a man, she does not get much over half the man's wages," a carpenter told the North Carolina labor commissioner in 1888, probably with farm labor in mind. "This is not right, there should be no discrimination except in amount or quality of work whether it be woman or man." Such sentiment was not necessarily disinterested. It might reflect a man's awareness that discrimination against women had a harmful effect on the income of families, including his own. As another carpenter complained to the labor commissioner, "There is no employment in this town for girls, and I have five."[43]

It is difficult to know which was the greater problem, the scarcity of jobs or the level of wages. "There is hardly any work for women to do that they can earn a half a living at," a man from western North Carolina observed in 1888. "I know plenty of women who work for seventy-five cents per week, and that is the best they can do." Men "can hardly get wages enough to keep their families comfortable," another man wrote from the same area. "As for women, there is scarcely anything for them to do, and they get very little for it when they can get work. They have to work for about half price and take pay in trade or anything they can get. There are many poor women here who can hardly live."[44]

This situation existed in cities, too. In surveys in Atlanta in 1885 and 1886, newspaper reporters found few jobs of any kind available for women and those few at abysmally low wages. Their accounts of women sewing garments at home amid abject poverty for "starvation wages" are reminiscent of those of Charles Dickens in England in the mid-nineteenth century. "Why don't you demand more for your work?" a reporter asked a woman who supported herself and three small children sewing "drawers" at home for thirty cents per dozen pairs. "What's the use?" she answered. "I heard women beg for more but they are told that there are plenty of women who stand ready to work for the price that is now paid." Women forced into such work—the woman just quoted earned thirty-five to forty cents a day while staying at home and keeping her children—were quite poor; and their children were too small to work in Atlanta's cotton mills. "Generally . . . widows who have children to support," the reporter learned when he asked who the sewing women were. "A drunken husband, a deserted wife, or a widow left unprovided for is the usual story, where you find a woman making drawers at such a slavish price."[45]

The vulnerabilities of such women help explain the move to the cotton mills. Farm wives suddenly widowed and left with small children and no property might find themselves going there whether they wanted to or not. These women had lost not only their breadwinner but the manager of the family business, and probably most women had little experience managing

43. NC *Labor Report* (1888), 108, 109.
44. *Ibid.*, 74, 107.
45. Atlanta *Constitution*, November 22, 1885, and January 25, 1886.

business affairs. "I am the Widow of R. L. Smith," a Clinton, South Carolina, farm woman wrote Governor Blease a year and a half after her husband's death and just after she harvested the first crop she made on her own. "Mr. Smith died May the 4, 1913, and left me with five little Fatherless Children an a heavy bach [of] debts to be payed. . . . I tried to stay on Where Mr. Smith left me. [O]n Mr. R Lee Hunter place[.] I rent a three horse farm. And now here is how I stand[.] I pay three thousand lbs. of a lint Cotton for rent. [U]sed about two hundred and seventy five dollars Worth of guino [guano]. [A]nd the Haile struck My Crop and just allmost ruined it[.] [W]ont Make the rent and guino[."] The woman pleaded: "Dear Governor I want to stay on the farm[.] I could go to the Cotton Mill but dont see how we Could live[.] My health is bad[.] [M]y Children is small only have two could work. I have all ways lived on the farm and do trust I can remain until death. . . . [But] without help I Cant [continue to] farm."[46]

Some women, deprived of their husbands, had even less success than Mrs. Smith. Mrs. Vernon—she is not otherwise identified in her letter—lost the support of her husband because he was imprisoned. Her petition to Governor Blease for her husband's release illustrates the vulnerabilities of women with dependent children and absent husbands. "Give us back our husband and father," she pleaded. "My children can't make a living for us[.] I am not able to work my self and only two boys to make Eight a living[.] We have moved to a cotton mill and you know they dont pay children much wages. I think my husband has bin punish Enough almost three month[.] Dear Gov we need his work for support. My husband would [not] have done as he did if he had n't bin drinking."[47]

Such letters reveal the special meaning of cotton mills for poor women, some of whom were so misfortunate that just arriving at the mills was a struggle. In February, 1899, for example, the Atlanta Charitable Association was approached by an unnamed woman who "recently came down from Rome to work in one of the mills." She had secured a job by letter, but had spent all the money she had to bring herself and her children to Atlanta. When she arrived, "she had nothing with which to buy food or pay for a night's lodging," and her first payday was two weeks away. The charitable association gave her help.[48]

Six months after this incident, police found a "homeless, hungry, and barefooted" woman wandering about Atlanta. She too had come for a job in

46. Mrs. R. L. Smith to Blease, October 14, 1914, in Blease Papers.
47. Mrs. Vernon to Blease, February 10, 1914, in Blease Papers.
48. Atlanta *Constitution*, February 19, 1899.

the mills. "I came to Atlanta and worked for a while in a factory," she said, explaining her plight, "and I went to Gainesville [a few miles away] and worked for a while in a factory in that town. I returned to Atlanta last week to get work and have been wandering around ever since. I have no shoes and I have eaten only one meal, which a kind woman gave to me, in three days." Unable to get a job, the woman had become desperate and pitiful. "All I want to do now," she said, "is to go back home [to Banks County]. I will stay there and will be satisfied with a piece of dry bread once a day. A woman can't go out into the world and make a living honestly unless she has friends to help her. I will go back to the old farm and plow and hoe cotton or do anything to get a place to sleep and a morsel to eat."[49]

The story of Emma Foster of Palmetto, Georgia, illustrates another of the difficulties some women had in going to the mills. One day in 1900 Mrs. Foster walked into the Atlanta police station and told officers she wanted to give away her two-year-old child. "I have come to this city to work for a living," she explained. "My husband has deserted me and the child. I love the child and it is my love for it which makes me give it away. If I keep it I will have to leave it with other people and, as I cannot hire a nurse, you can imagine what sort of care will be taken of it while I am toiling in a cotton mill." Mrs. Foster continued: "My husband got tired of me and the baby saying we were a drag on him, and he left us. I tried to work and support myself and child but I could not do it and have the little girl minded."[50]

Finally, women might fall victim to other dangers in their effort to reach the mills. Thus, Ida Reeves, nineteen, went to Greenville, South Carolina, in 1903 "in search of work as a cotton mill operative." On her arrival, she met Charley Patterson, who offered to direct her to Poe Mills. Instead of doing as he offered, however, Patterson "led her into a body of woods and assaulted her," and then "threatened to kill her if she told what had happened."[51]

Despite such difficulties—and the representativeness of these episodes is unknown—poor and dependent women went to the mills much more readily than men. Mill work was an option for men even if their other options were unattractive, but for women (and dependent children) it was sometimes the only work available. The life of Ella May (later Ella May Wiggins) illustrates a common pattern. Born at the turn of the twentieth century, Mrs. Wiggins was the daughter of a small farmer who quit farming when

49. *Ibid.*, August 19, 1899.
50. *Ibid.*, September 18, 1903.
51. *Ibid.*, October 2, 1903.

she was ten years old and went to work in the logging camps of western North Carolina. Ella and her mother helped out by doing the washing of bachelor loggers. At sixteen, Ella married John Wiggins, and within a year her first child was born. Soon thereafter, before her second child came, a log fell on Wiggins, crippling him for life and thrusting on his wife the responsibility for making a living. Like many other women in similar circumstances, Mrs. Wiggins turned to the cotton mills. For ten years she worked as a spinner, during which time she bore several more children. Then her husband deserted her. On September 4, 1929, during the great mill strike in Gastonia, she was killed when someone from an antiunion group fired into some of the strikers. She was not yet thirty years old.[52]

Despite such tragedies, women who talked of their move to the mills were more likely than men to sound a positive note. "My old man died in the army, and we had to go to the field to put bread in our mouths," a woman whose three daughters worked at Exposition Mills in Atlanta once told Rebecca L. Felton. "I worked harder than any nigger for the man we rented land from, and we got precious little for what we made. Me and my children didn't have a decent shelter or decent clothes and we had no money to buy anything scarcely. It was a dog's life and I didn't see any chance until we heard about the cotton mill and we got along nicely."[53]

A woman who went from the farm to a mill in Augusta, Georgia, expressed other reasons for her move. "What we girls want is a husband and a home of our own, not a chance to scrape pots and pans in some farmer's kitchen, and be abused by his wife, who in all probability would expect a girl to do the work of a mule," she wrote the Augusta Chronicle in 1882. "It is not surprising that girls refuse to become scrubs in the country, when it is a well known fact that even farmers' wives are worked to a shoestring and die young. No sir, for one, I'll take my chance in the city, where I am regarded as an equal of all with whom I work and associate."[54]

The mills thus promised what many women sought—security and perhaps even a kind of emancipation. Certainly they were better than the alternatives for poor women who had to support themselves and their children. The work was steadier, the paydays were more regular, and the wages

52. Ella May Wiggins' life is summarized in John Greenway, American Folksongs of Protest (Philadelphia, 1953), 244–46.
53. Atlanta Constitution, June 30, 1903.
54. Quoted in LeeAnn Whites, "Southern Ladies and Millhands: The Domestic Economy and Class Politics in Augusta, Georgia, 1870–1890" (Ph.D. dissertation, University of California at Irvine, 1982), 194.

were higher and generally paid in cash. As one scholar recently pointed out, "Compared to all wage earners, mill workers were poorly paid, but compared to the wages of all women and children, they were in fact highly paid."[55]

Men also saw the advantages the mills offered poor women. "If a factory were started here, so that women and children could find employment, it would be a great help to the poor, and would benefit all business by putting more money in circulation," a carpenter wrote the North Carolina labor commissioner in 1888. "We need more avenues for the employment of women and children, especially the women, who are now without any employment," a woodworker agreed. "There is plenty of work here for colored labor—male and female, but none for white women and boys. We need good cotton mills."[56]

The plea for good cotton mills came not from a New South publicist or mill apologist but from a workingman who saw the plight of white women and children even as he was blind to that of blacks. The sentiment behind his plea was as popular among plain folk as it was among other southerners. "Sometime this fall two cotton factories will be in operation in Salisbury," another worker wrote the labor commissioner in 1888, "which, I hope, will prove a blessing to the poor white women."[57]

55. *Ibid.*, 195.
56. NC *Labor Report* (1888), 118, 126.
57. *Ibid.*, 127.

3

MOVING

The road from farm to mill was a two-way street. "Those who have usually followed working for wages have gone to farming themselves," one man wrote the North Carolina labor commissioner in 1901, describing the pattern among artisans in his community. "Those who have not farms of their own have rented lands and are farming. They usually pay one-third grain and blade fodder for rent, retaining two-thirds for themselves." Another man had written in 1888: "I am a carpenter by trade. Work was scarce in this section, and I concluded I would farm." This man had no land and tools of his own, however, and his only option was sharecropping. "Horse, land and implements were furnished," he wrote of his situation, "[and] I get half [of the crop]. Am compelled to trade with the landlord. He is [in] merchandising, and charges extravagant prices for everything I buy. At the close of the year he takes everything I make, and I come off in debt."[1]

Such men became farmers as reluctantly as others left the farm, and one result of this situation was that many folk floated into and out of farming as circumstances permitted or demanded. Thus Joseph A. Michaels, who was born in Burke County, North

1. North Carolina Bureau of Labor Statistics, *Annual Report, 1901*, 69, *Annual Report, 1888*, 72, hereinafter cited as NC *Labor Report* by year.

Carolina, in 1868, worked at various jobs as a youth, including gold mining and construction. In 1887 he and his father went to Glendale and then to Clifton, South Carolina, to help construct new cotton mills. When the Clifton mill was completed, young Michaels stayed on to help install the machinery, and then, with nothing else available, went to work in the mill as a weaver. "Wages were so cheap I could never earn more than forty five cents a day," he recollected of the experience. Because the pay was low and "the work was so hard," he quit and went to farming. In 1895 he married and returned to mill work, however, at Converse, South Carolina, where he remained for three years. Then, for two years Michaels alternated farm and mill work, farming during the spring, summer, and fall and returning to the mill in the winter. In 1900 he went back to Burke County, where for five years he was a monzonite miner, after which he farmed another year, again in Spartanburg County, and then went back to the cotton mill for two more years.

Michaels' experience illustrates the intimate and continued interchange of mill folk and farm folk. Moving to the mills was something individuals or families might do several times. The division between mill and non-mill folk was thus never absolute. August Kohn, who made an extensive investigation of cotton mills in South Carolina early in the twentieth century, was told by mill officials that no more than 10 percent of the farmers who went to the mills returned to farming, but that was only an impression. Moreover, the estimate ignored families that included mill and farm workers simultaneously as well as families in which the men did other kinds of work while their children were employed in the mills. Kohn himself noted that "mill help is shortest in the summer time, and this is because of the desire of a great many operatives, particularly those living in the mountainous sections, to spend the heated months in their former mountain homes."[2] Since Kohn reflected the views of mill owners, his statement suggests that the latter saw the mill-farm exchange as a problem.

That exchange relates to one of the important questions concerning the mill experience—the degree to which mill folk were isolated from other people. Were mill folk walled off from the rest of the world by barriers of physical and psychological segregation? There were such barriers, of course, yet much evidence suggests that the answer to that question is no. The interaction of farmers, mill folk, and other employment groups was extensive as well as intensive, and many mill folk remained farm folk at heart, suspended as it were between two ways of living. Mill folk were thus

2. August Kohn, *The Cotton Mills of South Carolina* (Charleston, 1907), 26.

never a separate caste despite their congregation in mill villages and the prejudices directed at them. On the contrary, they were constantly interacting with other people, forever moving into and out of mill work, perpetually rearranging themselves in relation to the rest of the local population.

These statements bear illustration. In Alamance County, North Carolina, cotton mills were numerous, small, and scattered, many of them in largely farming districts. There in 1900 every ninth mill worker lived in a family headed by a farmer.[3] Stated another way, in this county about one of every seven families that included a mill worker was headed by a farmer, and over half of those farmers owned their own land.[4] A sample of eighty-seven families headed by farm renters included thirty-eight cotton mill workers plus three workers in a pants factory.[5]

This degree of farm and mill integration might have been exceptional, but since so many mills were located in or adjacent to rural farm areas, it cannot have been unique.[6] Yet instances of considerable isolation of mill folk are also numerous. Arkwright mill village in Spartanburg County, South Carolina, for example, had a total population of 709 in 1900, almost all of whom were bound to the mill. More than half the population (359 people) worked in the mill, and almost all the others were housewives or dependent children in mill families. Only 29 white workers in this village (there were 3 blacks,

3. Actual figures were 354 of 3,174 mill workers (11.15 percent), including workers in families headed by women listed as farm owners or operators. Because of defects in the manuscript census (incomplete, inconsistent, or unclear listings, illegible pages, and the like), these and subsequent figures from the manuscript census are offered as approximations only. I have tried to neutralize these defects by counting large numbers of mill workers in several locations and offering the results as approximations. The figures from Alamance County are the result of an effort to count the total mill population there in 1900. In these and other figures derived from the manuscript census, the term *family* is synonymous with *household* (Manuscript Census, 1900, Schedule 1, Alamance County, N.C.).

4. A mill family is any family that included a mill worker. Actual figures were 151 of 1,096 mill families (13.8 percent) headed by farmers, and 80 of those 151 farmers owned their land. These figures are close to those compiled by Cathy L. McHugh. In her sample of 343 mill families in Alamance County in 1900, 53 (15.4 percent) were headed by farmers, 55.4 percent by mill workers, 5.2 percent by day laborers, and 9.3 percent by other nonagricultural workers; the remainder had no occupation listed (McHugh, "The Family Labor System in the Southern Cotton Textile Industry, 1880–1915" [Ph.D. dissertation, Stanford University, 1981], 20).

5. This sample was based on every fifth farm renter family in the county (Manuscript Census, 1900, Schedule 1, Alamance County, N.C.).

6. In a 1946 study of 128 farms in Gaston and Davidson counties in North Carolina, Francis E. McVey found that slightly more than half the farm households reported work off the farms by one or more members, and more than half of those employed off the farms worked in cotton mills ("The Impact of Industrialization upon Agriculture in Two North Carolina Piedmont Counties" [Ph.D. dissertation, University of North Carolina, 1946], 41).

all servants) were not mill workers, and most of those (the drayman, machinist, schoolteacher, "day man," and 5 store clerks, for example, and at least some of the 8 carpenters) certainly worked for the mill company. Of 119 families in this village, only 2 were headed by farmers.[7]

That degree of isolation was also untypical; for just as mill families in rural areas overlapped with farm families, so those in cities were integrated with laboring families of other sorts. Especially in the earlier decades of the New South era, there were relatively few mill jobs for men. It was partly for this reason that women headed a disproportionate share of mill families; and the consequence for male-headed families was that many of the heads did other kinds of work while one or more of the other family members worked in the mills. In 1880 the proportion of such households was more than two in five of all those with mill workers in the Columbus, Georgia, area, one in two in Augusta, Georgia, and one in three in Aiken County, South Carolina.[8]

What kinds of jobs did these fathers of mill workers have? Most were unskilled or semiskilled (teamster, drayman, laborer, peddler, wood hauler, huckster, policeman, fisherman, watchman, and the like), but many were skilled (blacksmith, carpenter, printer, machinist, plasterer, painter, miller, cooper, and sawyer, for example), and a few were white-collar or professional (bookkeeper, grocer, minister, teacher, mill superintendent). At Graniteville, South Carolina, 75 of 218 households in 1880 were headed by women, 25 of whom worked in the mill. Of the male heads of the remaining 143 households, 95 (66 percent) worked in the mills, but 18 (12 percent) were farmers, 7 were professional or white-collar workers (2 ministers, a trial justice, a clerk, a manufacturer, and 2 teachers), and the others (excluding 3 with no occupation) had a variety of skilled and unskilled jobs.[9]

The fact that a mill superintendent (the man who oversaw the actual operation of the mill) and an overseer (the supervisor of a basic mill operation such as spinning or weaving) sometimes put their children to work as operatives suggests another fact about mill workers in the New South: lines between labor and management were not always sharply drawn. In Moun-

7. Manuscript Census, 1900, Schedule 1, Spartanburg County, S.C.
8. Actual figures were 110 of 249 households (44 percent) in Muscogee County, Ga., and neighboring Russell County, Ala., where some Columbus operatives lived; 93 of 183 households (51 percent) in Augusta; and 109 of 316 (34 percent) in Aiken County, S.C. These are male-headed families only (Manuscript Census, 1880, Schedule 1, Inhabitants, Muscogee County, Ga., Russell County, Ala., Richmond County, Ga., and Aiken County, S.C.).
9. Manuscript Census, 1880, Schedule 1, Graniteville, S.C.

tain Island mill village in Gaston County, North Carolina, in 1880, for example, there were 30 male-headed families with mill workers. Of the heads of these families, 12 (including the night watchman) worked in the mill, but no less than 6 were mill officers or supervisors.[10]

"I WILL GO TO YOUR FACTORY . . . BUT I WOULD LIKE YOU WOULD TAKE US ABOUT THE FIRST OF OCT OR NOV SO I CAN GETHER MY CROP."

The aspect of this subject that attracted attention from contemporaries was the movement of workers between farm and mill. This movement was important to mill managers because it threatened their labor supply. It is important to historians because it indicates that mill workers were not isolated from the rest of the population and suggests that many farm folk went to the mills reluctantly. Equally important, the reaction of mill managers to the movement shows clearly that the mills did not have the abundance of labor they and New South publicists bragged about and that the labor they did have was not stolidly tied to the mills. There is every reason to believe that the judgment Marjorie A. Potwin, a mill social worker, made in the 1920s applied to the entire New South era. "There is a very constant inter-migration between mill village and farm," she wrote. This was one reason securing and retaining an adequate supply of labor was such a persistent problem. "A superintendent seldom has time for training, keeping up the machinery and improving the quality of his product," John F. Schenck wrote after years of superintending Cleveland Cotton Mills at Lawndale, North Carolina, "most of his time and energies being absorbed in the effort to procure and keep help."[11]

The farm-mill interchange was basically a manifestation of discontent, and its rhythms were tied to farm prices and the cycle of farm work. "Every fall, especially when there have been poor crops, we have a number of country people who have been broken up on their farms and who come into Graniteville with their families to put them into the mill," Hamilton H. Hickman, president of the Graniteville mill, told a congressional committee in 1883, describing a pattern that recurred throughout the New South era. Perhaps the realities behind that pattern prompted T. M. Foy to decide to

10. The six men counted as officers or supervisors were two mill superintendents, two "manufacturers," a "boss spinner" (overseer of the spinning room), and a mill bookkeeper (Manuscript Census, 1880, Schedule 1, Gaston County, N.C.).
11. Majorie A. Potwin, *Cotton Mill People of the Piedmont: A Study in Social Change* (New York, 1927), 18; NC *Labor Report* (1908), 220.

quit farming in the summer of 1889, well before his crop was harvested, and seek mill work for himself and his family. "I will go to your factory if all is still rite with you but I would like you would take us About the first of Oct or Nov So I Can gether my Crop," Foy wrote a North Carolina mill owner in August. "[I]f you Agree to do so I will not deceive you," he continued, obviously concerned to get the job. "[Y]ou may depend on my Coming[.] I Will do as I say[.] So if it is all rite let me no."[12]

The other side of this coin was the return of mill workers to farming when crop prices improved. "Let cotton bring in any year ten cents a pound, and cotton-mill managements are likely to face a shortage of operatives," the *Manufacturers' Record* observed in 1901, prompted by just such a circumstance. Between 1898 and 1903, while the number of cotton mills grew rapidly, the price of cotton rose, and it remained up for several years. The result was a labor shortage in the mills, and the repeated alarms of mill managers revealed a great deal about this shortage as well as about the continuing interchange of mill and farm folk. "Our people come largely from the country, often driven to town by the low price of cotton," C. L. Pierce of Eagle and Phenix Mills said in 1905, "and when the year following cotton sells from 10 to 12 cents, the same families go back to the farm. Our people are constantly changing. Out of a force in our mills of 1800, not more than 50 percent are permanent help. To make up the other half of a full quota we are forced to hire about 4000 new people annually."[13]

In 1906 the *Manufacturers' Record* queried mill officials on the labor situation and published the responses of several dozen. Almost all of the officials complained of a lack of workers and blamed the situation on high farm prices. "Farmers are, fortunately, so prosperous that they have stopped moving to the mills," J. H. Webb of Eno Cotton Mill in Hillsboro, North Carolina, wrote, perhaps ironically; "in fact, families are leaving the mills and returning to the farms." W. C. Farber of Middleburg Mills in Batesburg, South Carolina, remarked, "This section is short of help, and from what I learn the entire State is in the same fix, the same being caused by a great many operatives returning to their farms, and with 10-cent cotton they will remain there."[14]

Not even higher wages stemmed the tide; and mill officials thought the

12. *Senate Documents*, 48th Cong., 1st Sess., No. 91, p. 737; T. M. Foy to Morgan and Malloy, August 30, 1889, in Mark Morgan Papers, Manuscript Department, Duke University Library, Durham, North Carolina.
13. *Manufacturers' Record*, September 14, 1905, p. 214.
14. *Ibid.*, May 24, 1906, pp. 520, 521.

combination of higher wages and labor scarcity "demoralized" their workers by making them restive and demanding. Moreover, the officials' complaints show that even workers who remained in the mills benefited from the rise in farm prices and the labor scarcity that produced—a pointed illustration of the reciprocal relationship between mill and farm folk. "Every Southern factory hand has got two or three jobs in his or her pocket, rendering them careless, unsteady and inefficient," a Mississippi mill official complained in 1906. "To quote the words of one of North Carolina's oldest and largest manufacturers, 'you can't look cross-eyed at them or they are gone.' "[15]

A North Carolina mill official agreed. "The demand for mill help" has been "so abnormal," John T. Schenck wrote in 1908, "that said commodity became not only very expensive, but unduly insolent and frightfully unreliable. . . . A deserved correction or reprimand too often resulted in the loss of a hand and the stopping of a machine. Lying out and loafing without excuse, leaving without notice, borrowing from a mill money to move to it and procuring from it advancement to live on just long enough to make a similar deal with another mill, just for the sake of roving over the country —utter disregard of contracts to stay at a mill or come to it—all these events and conditions became so common that they ceased to excite any surprise."[16]

Effects of the labor shortage were widely felt, even to the extent of idling machinery. Petitioning the state government for help in 1906, the South Carolina Cotton Manufacturers' Association estimated that "fully 20 per cent of the spindles in the State are idle for lack of labor." Summarizing the results of its aforementioned survey, the *Manufacturers' Record* estimated that "at least 10 percent of the spindles of the South are idle" because of the worker shortage. The Charleston *News and Courier*, another booster of the textile industry, expressed the belief that the mills of South Carolina could employ "about two or three thousand [additional] families" in the summer of 1906 "without throwing anybody out of employment."[17]

Behind this shortage, and the farm-mill interchange itself, lay the lure of the farm after a stint in the mills. The lure was strong year round—in the spring when new crops were starting, and in the late summer and fall when

15. *Ibid.*, 520.
16. NC *Labor Report* (1908), 220.
17. South Carolina Commissioner of Agriculture, Commerce, and Immigration, *Third Annual Report, 1906*, 44; *Manufacturers' Record*, May 24, 1906, p. 519; Charleston *News and Courier*, rpr. in Atlanta *Constitution*, June 4, 1906.

harvest labor paid about as much as mill wages. "One reason why we are short of help just now is that many cotton mill operatives have gone into the country and are hired out at farm work," an Atlanta mill president told a reporter in the summer of 1903. "They enjoy the fresh air and like the country life, while prices for such work are unusually good at present and farm laborers can make as much money as they could in the mills in town. So they go out to the country seeking recreation as well as work during the summer months and when fall sets in they will return and resume their places at the spinning frames and looms."[18]

Evidence of this preference for farming, especially among men, is substantial and persuasive. Lee A. Workman, whose family moved to a cotton mill in Newton, North Carolina, during World War I, remembered that his father had never adapted to mill life. "When it come springtime, he'd go back over there to that old homeplace, and he'd stay over there a couple of months and make cradles," Workman recalled. "He'd tell Mr. Stamey, the superintendent, 'You can just get somebody else to run these frames, because I'm going back to make cradles for my friends.'" But he would "come back in the wintertime and work in the mill," and he continued that pattern despite the protest of his employers. "He told them, 'If you dont want [me] to do that, I'll move back to the country and take the family.'" But since the family included four other workers, the mill tolerated his behavior. Still, after two years, he brought his family back to the farm. "He loved the country," Workman explained. "He wasn't a city boy. He wanted to get back over there in the country where he could have his horses and mules and the cows and plenty of milk and all that good stuff to eat, tomatoes and cucumbers and onions." His freedom to move was due in part to the fact that he owned his own farm even while he and four of his children worked in the mill.

Edgar R. Rankin, who interviewed one hundred mill families in the course of a study of Gastonia, North Carolina, in 1914, found considerable ambivalence in their discussion of the merits of farm and mill. "In the main . . . they preferred life at the mills," Rankin wrote of the workers he interviewed. "The general reason for this preference seemed to be that an easier living could be made at the mills, and employment could be had for the entire family the year round." Yet, Rankin continued, "in many of these people . . . I found a deep-seated love for the simple, outdoor life in the country rather than for the at best somewhat shut-up life at the mills. Many

18. Atlanta *Constitution*, August 9, 1903.

would prefer to live in the country if conditions were favorable to their so doing and they could be comfortably situated." As a housewife told Rankin, "[I] would prefer to live in the country if conditions were favorable, and I owned my own home, with no rent to pay, but under the present conditions and circumstances, owning no land and with rent to pay, I would rather live at the mills, where all of our family can get work."[19]

A dozen years later, Alexander R. Batchelor studied a mill village in Whitmire, South Carolina, where he was a minister, and found similar attitudes. In his survey of village families, Batchelor did not raise the subject, but members of several families volunteered the information that they would return to farming if they could make a living at it. "In six of the twelve cases the statement was simply made that, 'they would rather be on the farm,'" Batchelor wrote. "In one case the mother in the home, especially, wished to return to the farm; and in another case the father wished to go but the mother refused to leave the mill. She said it was 'too lonesome' on the farm. . . . One man who was getting old was heart hungry to get back to the farm. He had no grown children to take his place, and being on his feet all day in the mill was too hard on him."[20]

These were not the only connections Batchelor found between farming and mill folk. One family in his sample had recently purchased a farm from earnings in the mill and was then saving to get started in farming. Another man "farmed on the side," his son doing most of the work on a small farm near the mill. A third family, however, had just moved to the mill because the "boys in the home did not like the farm, [and] wanted to go to the mills."[21]

Both mill folk and farm folk, then, debated the merits of both locations, and the debate never ceased because the conditions that prompted it persisted. The assessments were remarkably candid. "More money can be made at the mills; more enjoyment can be had in the mountains," a woman whose family had moved to Loray Mills in Gastonia from Madison County told Rankin.[22] "As to which I like better, the cotton mill or sharecroppin', one's bout as good as the other far as I know," said Bob Draper. "They's more money at the mill, but a better livin' on the farm. Unless a man's

19. Edgar R. Rankin, "A Social Study of One Hundred Families at Cotton Mills in Gastonia, North Carolina" (M.A. thesis, University of North Carolina, 1914), 20–21.
20. Alexander R. Batchelor, "A Textile Community" (M.A. thesis, University of South Carolina, 1926), 18–19.
21. *Ibid.*, 19–20.
22. Rankin, "A Social Study of One Hundred Families at Cotton Mills," 8.

mighty sorry he can raise good somethin' t'eat on the land, while he has more spendin' money in the mill—and he spends it too. All he does at either one is jus' about break even." Charles Murray had also had both mill and farm experience. His father, a farmer as well as a weaver, had moved his family back and forth between farm and mill near Graham, North Carolina, while Charles, who was born in 1897, was a child. "I liked farming the best, so far as work business," the younger Murray said of his early experience. "But I had a little more money when I went to the mill work. I'll just tell you the truth, when I first come on I didn't know what money was, 'til I got up in my teens. Farming, you just don't know what money is."

The farm-mill interchange was facilitated by the fact that most folk went to mills near the countryside in which they had always lived. The move, therefore, did not take them far from the relatives, friends, and communities they had known all their lives. It was easy to go back, whether to visit or to raise a crop, and easy to maintain ties to the land. When Lawrence B. Graves made a study of the early cotton mills in Newberry County, South Carolina, he located and interviewed 35 people who had worked in mills there before 1900. All of the 35 went into the mills from Newberry or adjacent counties—1 from Newberry town, 2 from other cotton mills, 2 from farms they owned, and 30 from farms they rented or sharecropped. That degree of proximity was untypical, however. Of 72 families at Saxon Mills near Spartanburg, South Carolina, in its initial year at the turn of the century, 26 came from other mills, 26 from nearby farms, and 20 from the mountains farther removed.[23]

The roots of mill folk in nearby farm communities, including an attachment to the land, were not severed by moving a few miles away. Among the 100 families in Rankin's sample were 34 whose heads were sons of farm owners. Since the average holding of the fathers of these men had been 76 acres, which was too small to divide among several children, the sons who went to the mills were perhaps those who lost out or sold out to a sibling who inherited the family farm. The ties between the mill families and landowning farmers must have been substantial, for 9 of the families in Rankin's sample owned farms of their own.[24] That too must have operated to undercut the isolation of mill folk.

Mill families that also owned small farms were sprinkled about the New South. August Kohn interviewed operatives who owned farms and rented

23. Lawrence B. Graves, "The Beginning of the Cotton Textile Industry in Newberry County" (M.A. thesis, University of South Carolina, 1947), 48.
24. Rankin, "A Social Study of One Hundred Families at Cotton Mills," 10.

them out while they worked in the mills, and operatives too who began as farmers but went to the mills and accumulated some money, went back to farming and lost out again, and returned once more to the mills. William A. Graham, president of the North Carolina Farmers' Alliance, told the Industrial Commission of farmers who had worked in the mills to buy their land. "A man will buy a piece of land, contract for it," Graham explained, "and rent that land to some other man, and he will go to the cotton factory and make the money to pay for it. I know of instances right among my own people. It is not that they prefer factory labor, but it is the long credit on farms, sir."[25]

The mills themselves facilitated this interchange. As New South publicists so often insisted, many cotton factories were built in the cotton fields. At least a few mill owners, Charles H. Phinizy of Augusta Mills, for example, were also planters, and a few mills operated cotton plantations and produced some of the cotton their operatives spun. A larger number of mills operated cotton gins to which nearby farmers brought their cotton.[26] Cleveland Cotton Mills was one such, ginning and purchasing the cotton of local farmers, even storing cotton for them for later sale. These mills also had agents in contact with other gins and cotton dealers in a constant effort to buy cotton at the cheapest possible price. Because of these activities and the fact that some of the operatives were farm owners and others the children of nearby farmers, it seems certain that some of the cotton spun in Cleveland Cotton Mills was produced by the families of the spinners themselves. It seems equally certain that this situation was far from unique and perhaps even commonplace.

Still other mills operated farms to supply their own company stores. Sallie Jane Stephenson, whose family moved to an Anderson, South Carolina, cotton mill in 1890 when she was an infant, remembered that "the first job Pa ever had after we moved to the mill was managing a farm." She recalled: "The company owned all that land through there. They raised a lot of truck and sold it at the company store. Raised some cotton too. And hogs."

Personal experiences illustrate other aspects of the continuing interchange. Mary Gattis was born in 1909 in the mill village of Bynum,

25. Kohn, *The Cotton Mills of South Carolina*, 26–31; *House Documents*, 57th Cong., 1st Sess., No. 184, Vol. 10, p. 435.
26. *Senate Documents*, 48th Cong., 1st Sess., No. 91, p. 702. For other examples of cotton mills operating cotton plantations and ginning their own cotton, see Broadus Mitchell, *The Rise of Cotton Mills in the South* (Baltimore, 1922), 139.

North Carolina, to a couple that worked in the mill. In 1913 her father moved his family to the country and farmed for the next five years. But every winter he and his two oldest sons worked in the mill, the three of them walking back and forth each day from the farm.[27]

Another woman interviewed in the Piedmont Social History Project, on condition she remain anonymous, recalled that her family, which included her four sisters and brother, moved to a Durham, North Carolina, hosiery mill in 1911 after her father, a farmer, had been disabled by a falling tree. When her father recovered, he rented a farm near Durham which he traveled to and from each day while he and his family continued to live in the mill village and his children continued to work in the mill. Other mill workers lived in the country but boarded in the mill village during the week. "Three of us work in the cotton mills and our [widowed] mother works at home," an unnamed woman wrote the North Carolina labor commissioner in 1891. "We walk from home to the mills, six miles, each Sunday evening so as to be ready for work Monday morning, and then home when Saturday evening comes."[28]

The farm-mill interchange was reinforced by continuous recruitment of mill labor from the farm. "There are constantly on our pay-rolls whole families of 'green help,' fresh from the farms, obtaining their first experience in tending to the frame or loom," John A. Law of Saxon Mills said in 1905.[29] Even well-established and well-managed mills were always looking for laborers, and many found the countryside the best place to look. Many mill owners believed workers recruited directly from the farm were less likely to be "floaters" than those recruited from other mills.

One such official was W. M. Nixon, president of an Atlanta textile firm. "For cotton mill work, a green hand out of the country is really to be preferred over an experienced person who has learned his trade but likes to move," Nixon said in 1903. "If you can take a family from the country and give the older members employment and make it to their liking sufficiently to keep them, say, a month, teach them their work and pay them for it, the chances are they will remain with you for a long time to come." But it was a continuing activity. "At various times I have sent men out in the surround-

27. In an insightful study of the Bynum mill community, based largely on interviews, Douglas DeNatale found a "continuum between mill and rural life" there ("Traditional Culture and Community in a Piedmont Textile Mill Village" [M.A. thesis, University of North Carolina, 1980], 39).

28. NC *Labor Report* (1891), 195.

29. *Manufacturers' Record*, September 14, 1905, p. 213.

ing country in an attempt to bring people here to learn the mill work," Nixon added. "Once or twice I have made these trips myself. We get some operatives in this way, and they usually stay with us."[30]

Other believers in this policy of recruiting only farm folk were H. F. and John F. Schenck, father and son, who ran Cleveland Cotton Mills through the New South era and whose surviving correspondence provides many insights into the problems of recruiting mill labor. The Schencks's two mills were relatively isolated, and their labor force came largely from nearby farms. They were frequently short of workers despite constant attention to that problem. "Our lack of hands has embarrassed us and bothered us a good deal in trying to get off orders promptly," John Schenck wrote in the early fall of 1898. "It is a difficult matter to get hands this time of the year, because almost all laboring people are busy on their farms."[31]

In the depression of the 1890s, when their New York business partner was urging that the mills be closed for a while, the Schencks argued against a shutdown because their workers would leave and be difficult to replace. "Some of them are good farmers who own small farms," the elder Schenck wrote, "and I fear nearly half of them will at once go to their farms and to other mills."[32] Significantly, this letter was written in January, when farmers were beginning to prepare for a new crop.

A week later Schenck was still wrestling with the problem but had decided to close the mills for a week despite his fears. "We do not know how our families will take this," he wrote. "There will be no trouble to get rid of the farming help we have at our mills, but we would not find it easy . . . to replace them." By "farming help," Schenck seems to have meant not only the farm owners and their families but other men who farmed while their children worked in the mills. These farm-related workers, Schenck thought, would not be so badly hurt by a temporary shutdown because they could fall back on their farms. Moreover, if the shutdown ended before they planted new crops, they were more likely to return because their farms kept them from readily moving elsewhere. Workers with farm ties were thus more stable than those without them. "My opinion has always been that when I get hands from other mills who have been floating around from Mill to Mill," Schenck wrote, "that I get hands that are unreliable and will not

30. Atlanta *Constitution*, August 9, 1903.
31. John F. Schenck to J. E. Reynolds, October 1, 1898, in H. F. Schenck Papers, Manuscript Department, Duke University Library, Durham, North Carolina.
32. H. F. Schenck to Reynolds, January 30, 1894, in Schenck Papers.

compare with these we have selected from the respectable farmers around us."[33]

This farm-connected labor force had other advantages for the mills. When the Schencks had considered shutting down their mills in August, 1893, the younger Schenck had believed the workers would be little affected if the shutdown coincided with the harvest season. "Should we decide to shut down all, or a portion of our mill two or three weeks from now," he wrote in early August, "our hands can find employment in picking cotton for several weeks."[34] A family could earn about as much picking cotton as working in the mill, and the diversion might even have a salutary effect on morale.

These views governed the Schencks's recruitment of workers. In 1892 Christopher Buff wanted to farm while others in his family worked in the Schencks's mills. "If you still wish to move here we give you an opportunity, provided you can come *right away*," John F. Schenck wrote, answering Buff's inquiry. "Your brother says you would like to get a farm. We do not know but think it quite sure that you can get land to work near this place." Schenck expressed an eagerness for such a family. "Let us hear from you by return mail, or if you think best come up yourself to see us."[35]

The Schencks showed the same solicitude to other prospective workers from the farm. "I am glad you have determined to learn a trade for, from your inclination, I think you would like it, would succeed at it, and would be much more useful than you could possibly be to continue on the farm," H. F. Schenck wrote a man who had evidently inquired about a job. "I am sorry I have no opening for you now, that it would justify me to pay you a fair price. . . . But at a place like this there generally is constant changes and if you were here, as opening occurred you would stand your chance to advance." Schenck continued: "I feel confident that [with] your ability to grasp the intricacy of running machinery, if you were here, you could in a short time render yourself competent to fill almost any place in our mill. . . . I am so confident of us suiting each other that I do not want you to make any other arrangement til I see you. Cant you come down some day soon and see me."[36]

33. H. F. Schenck to Reynolds, February 6, 1894, in Schenck Papers.
34. John F. Schenck to Reynolds, August 7, 1893, in Schenck Papers.
35. John F. Schenck to Christopher Buff, July 2, 1892, in Schenck Papers.
36. H. F. Schenck to Ambrose Cline, April 5, 1889, in Schenck Papers. The other side of this story of recruiting farm families is the resentment it generated among farm landlords. For

"THE GREAT SCARCITY OF LABOR"

As the Schencks's letters suggest, recruiting and retaining labor were nev-erending problems, though they varied from mill to mill, year to year, and even season to season. Only in the early 1880s and the depressed years of the mid-1890s was there a general abundance of workers, though the decade after 1898 was the only period when mill spokesmen throughout the South complained of an acute shortage. But even in day-to-day operations, all mill managers worried about how many workers would show up each morning.

The problem of labor supply had many causes, most of them only indi-rectly related to the willingness of farm folk to go the mills. The movement in and out of mill work and the related problem of "floating" labor (workers moving frequently from mill to mill) kept a meaningful portion of mill folk in a kind of perpetual transit. An outbreak of illness, a change in manage-ment, the opening of a new mill nearby, rumors of a shutdown (which caused anxious workers to look for other jobs), announcement of a pay cut or a change in operating policy, even Monday morning blues—these and countless other things caused disruptions in the labor supply.

To help neutralize the effects of such disruptions, mill owners began systematic recruitment of new workers, chiefly from the surrounding coun-tryside but also from Appalachia and elsewhere. This effort developed slowly, perhaps because of the early abundance of labor and perhaps also because mill officials believed the supply of folk eager for mill work was inexhaustible. The abundance of labor in the early years seems clear enough. In 1881, N. J. Bussey of Eagle and Phenix Mills, then the largest such organization in the South with a work force of 1,800, described labor as "very abundant." Speaking chiefly of women and girls, who constituted three quarters of his work force, Bussey said, "If our mills employed 5,000 instead of 1,800 hands there would be no difficulty to secure them. No effort is necessary to induce them to work. They flock to our mills whenever they are wanted." Similarly, Charles H. Phinizy, president of Augusta Mills, told a congressional committee in 1883 that his and other mills in Augusta had

discussion of an effort by supporters of Governor Benjamin R. Tillman of South Carolina to pass a law restricting the hours of labor in cotton mills in order to lower earnings of mill workers, see Graves, "The Beginning of the Cotton Textile Industry," 86ff; and Gustavus G. Williamson, "South Carolina Cotton Mills and the Tillman Movement," *Proceedings of the South Carolina Historical Association, 1949*, 36–49. August Kohn interviewed landlords who refused to employ farm tenants who had worked in cotton mills (*The Cotton Mills of South Carolina*, 28).

"never had any scarcity of help." He added, however, that "up to this time we have never had the competition for labor that we are going to have."[37]

The concern was well placed, for when mill construction resumed on a large scale not long after Phinizy spoke, some of the new mills had problems attracting workers. When John H. Montgomery opened a new mill at Spartanburg in 1890, he had unexpected difficulties securing the five hundred workers he needed. "All the machinery is in position ready and waiting for operatives," Montgomery wrote while his mill sat idle. "The only remedy I have to suggest is time and patience. The necessary help is in the surrounding country and will sooner or later find its way to this or some other cotton mill." Montgomery used the occasion to remark on the larger problem as a whole. "There is no denying the fact that there are at present more cotton mills in this Piedmont section than experienced help to operate them," he said. "Very few mills within my knowledge have had during the past summer and present fall sufficient numbers of operatives, and this being the case makes it all the more difficult for us to get our supply, all of us looking to the farm, the source from which the deficiency in the aggregate must come." In "less than a year" Montgomery had secured the workers he needed.[38]

This difficulty disappeared during the mid-1890s, when cotton sometimes fell below five cents a pound. When Massachusetts Mills opened its Lindale plant near Rome, Georgia, at that time, many more workers sought jobs than the mill could employ. "We had no trouble in getting operatives," an official said at the time.[39]

Once cotton prices recovered and mill construction resumed late in the 1890s, however, the problem returned on so large a scale that it became a major concern of industry leaders. By 1899 newspapers were running stories on the scarcity of labor throughout the Piedmont, and mill officials were sounding alarms. "The only problem that now confronts the southern manufacturers is the great scarcity of labor," D. G. Sunderland, president of the Southern Association of Hosiery Manufacturers, said in 1900.[40]

By this time the larger mills had begun systematic recruitment of workers. Word of mouth and periodic rides by superintendents into the coun-

37. Atlanta *Constitution*, February 17, 1881; *Senate Documents*, 48th Cong., 1st Sess., No. 91, p. 700.
38. William W. Thompson, "A Managerial History of a Cotton Textile Firm, Spartan Mills, 1888–1958" (Ph.D. dissertation, University of Alabama, 1960), 58.
39. *Manufacturers' Record*, May 15, 1896, vi.
40. Atlanta *Constitution*, September 27, 1899, January 12, 1900.

tryside were no longer sufficient to people the mills. Not only were there more mills, but the new mills were larger and more concentrated than the old ones, and supplies of laborers willing to go to them had been exhausted in many localities. The number of textile mills in Georgia and the Carolinas had leaped from 231 in 1890 to 411 in 1900 and rose again to 549 in 1905, while the average number of wage earners in those years rocketed from 27,954 to 83,120 to 106,005.[41] By the turn of the century, the largest mills had more than 100,000 spindles, and individual mills employing 500 to 1,000 workers were not uncommon.

It was these largest mills—Pelzer, Pacolet, and Piedmont in the South Carolina upcountry, for example—that undertook the organized recruitment of workers. Their agents and publicists appeared at circuses, town celebrations, and wherever else people gathered, distributing circulars, making speeches, importuning individuals, and otherwise spreading the word about the mills. They told of things they thought would impress poor folk: good wages and working conditions and the securities of mill life. In 1907, for example, a circular from Pacolet Mills near Spartanburg advertised 500 openings for "steady employment for over 300 days in the year." Experienced youths from twelve to sixteen years old could earn 50 cents to $1.25 a day, according to the circular, men and women 75 cents to $1.50, and "old men" 75 cents to $1.00. The mill provided "good, comfortable houses at 50c a room per month," the circular continued, and "wood, coal and provisions laid at your door at market prices." Pacolet was a healthy place free from malaria, as the circular described it, and the mill itself was heated in winter and run in summer with windows open "to give nice cool air through the mill." Pacolet's village was a place of "good water, a splendid system of free schools, churches of different denominations; in fact everything that appeals to one who wishes to improve the condition of his family."

The last idea—that mill work promised better things for poor folk— underlay the appeal. "If you are a poor man there is no better location for you to select than Pacolet," the circular read. "It behooves every man to either educate his children or place them in position to learn good trades." "We will advance you your transportation and if you remain with us six months the same will be given you. . . . We want families with at least three workers for the mill in each family."[42]

Such appeals were often effective. "A man come through there one time

41. *Census Bulletin 74: Census of Manufacturers: 1905 Textiles* (1907), 24.
42. The circular is printed in Kohn, *The Cotton Mills of South Carolina*, 23.

and he had a letter with him from the super' at Spartan Mills," recalled Susie Simmons, who heard of the mills while her husband was mining coal in Virginia. "He showed us the letter and said that we could get a job in Spartanburg if we wanted to. The old man [her husband] and Charlie [their son] come first and worked at Spartan Mills about two months before they sont fer us."

Yet so many folk held back that the labor problem increased as the number of mill jobs multiplied. "Raw labor is still abundant in the aggregate," a group of New England mill men reported after a tour of southern cotton mills in 1900, "but in many districts the scarcity of skilled help has been quite apparent during the past year, and even a full complement of raw help has not been easily secured. . . . New mills cannot start without a fair proportion of skilled help and their late and current increase has created considerable competition for it."[43]

As cotton prices rose and farming became more attractive, the number of mills increased rapidly, and every new mill required a core of experienced workers to begin production. The mills reacted variously to the problem of securing an initial labor force. There were experienced workers who for many reasons applied for work at new mills, and nearby mills thus suffered losses, at least for a while. Thus, when the number of mill jobs multiplied dramatically at West Point, Georgia, at the turn of the century, the mills had a major problem securing workers. One desperate superintendent even wrote the police chief of Atlanta asking for help. "Do you know of some respectable families in your city who would make cotton mill operatives?" he inquired. "I would prefer widows and families of girls." The immediate cause of the problem was the opening of a major addition to Lanett Mills in 1900. Not only did Lanett's local agents search "eagerly" for "every man, woman and child that has ever had any experience in a cotton mill"; but other agents were dispatched to Alamance County, North Carolina, where an extended mill strike was underway, and successfully recruited some of the strikers. "Two [rail] cars were side-tracked here yesterday, another this morning and still another is expected tomorrow morning," read a press report, "containing families from the cotton mill regions of North Carolina, principally from Graham, North Carolina. These people will immediately be housed in the new cottages recently erected by the company, and put to work in the new mill."[44]

43. Atlanta *Constitution*, November 30, 1900.
44. *Ibid.*, April 29, 1901, December 10, 1900.

Another device frequently used in staffing new mills was hiring managers and overseers from other mills who brought skilled workers with them. Thus when Olympia Mills, the first southern mill powered exclusively by electricity, opened in 1894, the owners hired the superintendent of a Baltimore mill who brought with him "a number of experienced operatives" who "serve[d] as leaders to the other help." Inexperienced help in the new mills came from whatever sources were available, a surprising number from among workers who constructed the mill and installed the machinery.[45]

As these examples suggest, securing labor was a highly competitive business. Because experienced workers were scarce and in such great demand, many—perhaps most—mills found it necessary to look for workers in the villages of other mills. Those who disliked this practice called it "enticing" labor and condemned it; but in spite of the condemnation this practice was a fixture of mill life certainly in and after the late 1890s and probably beginning at a much earlier date. "Too many superintendents keep a man on the road hunting help and holding out inducements, thereby getting [workers] dissatisfied, and, in many instances, get families to moving around from mill to mill, doing no good," a Gaston County mill official complained to the North Carolina labor commissioner in 1898. A Surry County manufacturer agreed. "The mills should stop sending out runners and drummers and robbing other mills of their hands," the latter said. "Such practice is bad for the mills and worse for the hands."[46]

These complaints continued throughout the New South era. "Manufacturers should stop this thing of enticing help from other mills, which is demoralizing what help we have, and should all pull together to get new labor in," another North Carolina mill official told the *Manufacturers' Record* in 1906. "Instead of enticing help from each other's mills," still another mill man said, "there should be some kind of an agreement not to employ operatives from another mill without they can show an honorable discharge by the mill from which they come. As it is, there are men regularly employed by many of the larger mills to visit other mills to get help and many times to entice them away, leaving their employer in debt."[47]

Industry leaders and trade associations took up this cause. In 1902 officials from several mills in Alabama, Mississippi, and Columbus, Georgia, met and "arranged for a general agreement [to end enticing] under certain

45. *Manufacturers' Record*, June 8, 1894, p. 310. See Graves, "The Beginning of the Cotton Textile Industry," 47, for examples of construction workers becoming mill operatives.
46. NC *Labor Report* (1898), 401.
47. *Manufacturers' Record*, May 24, 1906, p. 520.

well defined restrictions just to both [workers and mills]." Enticement "injure[s] all concerned by its demoralizing effects on labor," these men declared, denouncing mills that "even go so far as to pay the transportation of labor from other concerns." The men who signed the agreement hoped all other mill men in the three states would do likewise.[48]

Apparently none did. Three years later, representatives from several mills in south Georgia made a similar agreement and asked other mill men to sign. A year later, in 1906, an association of mill officials from throughout the South "unhesitatingly denounce[d] the practice existing among cotton manufacturers whereby competing mills seek to acquire each others help," and further condemned "the system which provides for the furnishing of transportation to mill hands of competing firms." The following month the Southern Soft Yarn Spinners Association adopted a similar resolution, again "condemning the practice now prevalent among the various cotton mills throughout the country of enticing away the help from other mills, paying transportation, etc., believing that it is no less harmful to the laborers than to the mills themselves."[49]

The practice, however, seems to have increased, because its cause—the rising need for experienced workers in an industry that was expanding rapidly and upgrading its product—continued. Enticement, of course, was hardly unusual. Recruitment of labor is an integral part of capitalist enterprise. Southern mill officials seem to have reacted so strongly to the practice for two reasons. First, it violated their paternalistic notions of labor-management relationships, according to which it amounted to tampering with their "people." Second, it gave workers a degree of independence and raised the possibility that the mills would have to increase wages, shorten hours, or provide other incentives for their labor to stay. The first of these things threatened the image mill officials cultivated for themselves; the second challenged their prerogative in areas where it had always been absolute. Mill officials sought to neutralize the first of these threats by various displays of paternalism and to resist the second through a united front against any of their number inclined "to depart from established custom."

That was the phrase Fred B. Gordon, president of the Georgia Industrial Association, an organization of textile officials, used in the course of denouncing an "experiment" in which T. C. Duncan, who owned several mills in South Carolina, reduced the workday in his mills from eleven to ten hours

48. Atlanta *Constitution*, February 22, 1902.
49. *Ibid.*, February 2, 1905, May 18, June 17, 1906.

in an effort to make mill work more attractive. This is a "matter of great importance," Gordon told his fellow mill owners, this "reported inclination of certain cotton mills in our association and in other southern states, to depart from established custom as to hours of labor and other important matters of mill management, doing so without consulting neighboring mills, and apparently from selfish motives to especially attract help, or gain some other supposed advantage." Such actions, "independent of some agreement or understanding on the part of all the mill interests of the state, will prove a costly experiment," Gordon warned. "Once it becomes evident that we cannot stand together for the principles for which we have contended for years, our concert of action will be gone."[50]

Since mill owners resisted market mechanisms in dealing with labor shortages, they had to use other devices. Whenever mills closed for any reason, including strikes, major accidents, or natural disasters, recruiting agents from other mills were on the scene immediately, trying to hire away workers. Thus in the spring of 1896, when operatives at Eagle and Phenix Mills went on strike, F. C. Foy, an agent for the newly constructed mill at Alabama City, near Gadsden, appeared with the announced intention of recruiting 450 skilled workers from among the strikers. He had at least some success according to press reports, for in early April "a hundred former operatives of the Eagle and Phenix mills left yesterday for Alabama City," their transportation paid by Foy. "An immense crowd of several hundred friends gathered to see them off at the Columbus and Phenix City depots," the report read, and "another party will leave in a day or two."[51]

In Augusta, in the winter of 1898, recruiting agents used the same strategy during a prolonged strike. "For some days there have been in the city representatives from [South] Carolina mills needing skilled and efficient operatives," the Augusta *Chronicle* reported in the middle of the strike, by which time the recruiters had had some success. "Twenty-nine operatives and their families have gone to Columbia to work in a factory there," the newspaper stated. "Another mill on the Charleston and Western Carolina [railroad] is trying to get 100 expert spinners, and promises to take care of, by finding employment for, the families of such as go." Meanwhile, the Columbia *State* reported on November 27 that "about 150 hands have come

50. *Ibid.*, May 16, 1905. By the time Gordon spoke, Duncan had ended his "experiment" and reverted to the eleven-hour workday. The shorter schedule had proved to be "a losing move" (*ibid.*, May 3, 1905).
51. *Ibid.*, April 4, 6, 10, 1896.

to this city so far [from Augusta] and most of them have found work in the Richland and Granby cotton mills."[52]

Two months later, as this strike continued, one of its leaders "received a letter from Mr. Oscar Elsas, vice president of the Fulton Bag and Cotton company asking for 380 hands to work in their mill in Atlanta." The request was for 50 carders, 180 spinners, and 150 weavers. This unusual offer was due to Elsas' desire to begin a night shift at his mill, for it was always difficult to get mill folk to work at night.[53]

At least a few of the Augusta strikers went to Elsas' mill, which presently began to operate around the clock. But within a few months the night shift had to be discontinued in part because other mills, aware of the general dislike for night work, had themselves lured Elsas' workers away. "There are a number of runners from other mills in the state, and some of them near Atlanta, who are constantly among the employees of the Fulton Bag and Cotton Mills and are soliciting the employees to go to those mills and secure work," a reporter wrote. "Their argument, it is said, is that the operatives can by working at other places secure day work," and because the argument "prevailed in many instances . . . a large number of experienced men have been taken from the Fulton mills."[54]

This kind of wholesale raiding was exceptional. More common was the recruiting of individuals or families by agents taking advantage of whatever opportunity presented itself. "They'd come to the house," Alice P. Evitt, who worked in mills in and near Charlotte, North Carolina, recalled of her own experiences with recruiting agents in the early years of the twentieth century. "They'd come in and talk and try to get us to come by," she said of agents from mills where she and her family had formerly worked. "They'd just say they'd liked our work and all. They'd love for us to come back. They'd pay our movin' bill and everything. But we always left it up to mother about movin'. . . . Sometimes they'd make one of us mad in the mill, and we'd move on account of that."

The fact that this kind of enticement was frequently successful was one reason mill officials tried to keep strangers out of their mills and villages. When Bessie Van Vorst was on her muckracking tour of southern mills, for example, she was denied permission to go inside an Anniston, Alabama,

52. Atlanta *Journal*, November 26, 1898; Augusta *Chronicle*, November 26, 28, December 3, 1898.
53. Atlanta *Journal*, January 21, 1899; Augusta *Chronicle*, January 21, 1899.
54. Atlanta *Constitution*, July 12, 1899.

mill. "You see," the superintendent told her, "we have some difficulty keeping our help, and we're always afraid folk might be prowlin' around to get some of our hands away from us."[55]

The antagonism between officials of one mill and agents of another could be intense, and was occasionally the cause of serious dispute. At least one agent, representing Bibb Manufacturing Company of Macon, Georgia, was charged with violating that state's contract labor law, which had been enacted in Reconstruction to prevent the loss of black farm labor. The charge was later dropped, but not until officials of the company agreed "not to hire an employee of another mill unless they [sic] come to them with a clean bill of health."[56]

The experience of another agent, Wiley J. Smith, was more spectacular. In the fall of 1904, Smith, of Whittier Mills near Atlanta, went to Porterdale Mills at Covington, Georgia, "to see some friends, but not for the purpose of inducing them to leave Porterdale," as Smith said later in telling his story to police. Late on the second night of his visit, a "crowd of Porterdale toughs" went to Smith's hotel room and, according to his account, forcibly took him outside and down to the river, where they tried to push him into the water. When he resisted, they tarred him. One of them "stepped up and poured the black sticky stuff over my head," Smith said later, "it running down my face and into my eyes, blinding me so that I could scarcely see anything." Then the group escorted him to the edge of town and released him, saying, in Smith's words, "that they had marked me so as to recognize me next time I put my foot in their town. They told me to run. I refused. They then began firing pistols at me in rapid succession."[57]

A. M. Kale, superintendent of Mims Manufacturing Company near Charlotte, was less fortunate even than Smith. One day in 1905 Kale went to the house of an operative at a nearby mill, Hardin Manufacturing Company, "it is said," read a press report, "for the purpose of inducing [the operative] and his family to move to his mill." Earl Carpenter, son of the owner of the Hardin mill, "learned of the object of Kale's visit and confronted him with the charge. A fight ensued in which both drew pistols. Kale shot Carpenter in the breast, inflicting a dangerous, if not fatal, wound, and Carpenter, in turn, fired at Kale, the bullet striking him squarely in the forehead, passing directly through the brain, causing instant death."[58]

Alice P. Evitt, who was interviewed in the 1970s, still remembered this

55. Bessie Van Vorst, *The Cry of the Children: A Study of Child Labor* (New York, 1908), 40.
56. Atlanta *Constitution*, June 10, 1907.
57. *Ibid.*, October 9, 1904.
58. *Ibid.*, March 16, 1905.

incident though she gave a different account of it. "Mr. Carpenter owned that whole place, the mill, and everything there," she recalled. "He had a son, Earl Carpenter. There was a feller up there at High Shoals. He'd slip up there and hire they hands, and they'd slip there and hire his. This Earl caught him one evening down there in a buggy beside the road and shot him—killed him. He accused him of comin' to hire hands."

"I HAVE MADE UP MY MIND TO GO TO A COTTON MILL."

The move to the mills was, finally, the result of a family of farm folk making a conscious choice about its future. All of the forces just described were refracted through that act, and if those forces were controlling in fundamental ways, the individual act still determined the immediate pattern. The typical event involved a poor farmer moving his family a few miles down the road, certainly no farther than the next county, to a mill employing five, ten, or twenty score, where he and two, three, or more of his children went at once to work. His family was likely to be large, including perhaps three to six children, and he made the move as soon as the oldest children were large enough to work in the mills. "I write you for to know if you co[u]ld give me a Job," George Wallace addressed a North Carolina manufacturer in 1889. "I have made up my mind to go to a cotton Mill & Wold like to have a Job With you as you have been Recommended to Me as a good Place[.] I am a bout 29 years old have a boy a bout 10 years ould" and "a girle that Will Soon be large a nuff to go in a Mill."[59]

A few years later, Will Westbrook took a similar step. "I kept on farmin' till 1900," Westbrook recollected, "and seein' I wa'n't gettin' nowhere atall I decided to come to the mill. Farmin' was too uncertain for a man with a wife and five children to take care of." Westbrook had been married thirteen years, so his oldest children were at or near the age of mill work, and as they became old enough, all of them followed their father into Proximity Mill at Greensboro, North Carolina.

Always this emphasis on numbers appears. Mill officials, like rural landlords, were first concerned with the size of a man's "force." "When Mr. J. W. got ready to open up his mill back in '86, he didn't have but thirteen houses for his hands," recalled Jones I. Freeze, whose family was among the original work force in J. W. Cannon's first mill in Concord, North Carolina. "Mr. J. W. figured if he hired big families, he could get enough hands in them thirteen houses to work his mill. . . . I reckon that's howcome he

59. George Wallace to Morgan and Malloy, November 27, 1889, in Morgan Papers.

wanted us. Anyway he wrote my father a letter asking him to move his force to the mill—hit was ready to start work. . . . Soon as the mill opened my father and all the younguns that was old enough commenced to work. There was nine of us younguns, five girls and four boys and everyone of us 'ceptin' one got their start in that same mill. . . . I was too little to go to work right away, but whenever I was nine or ten I began."

Failed farming looms no less large than family size in memories of going to the mills. "The crops were kind of failing at that time," Pauline Phillips Griffith said, explaining her parents' move to Judson Mill at Greenville, South Carolina, in 1915. "It was a necessity to move and get a job, rather than depend on the farm," even though, as Mrs. Griffith recalled vividly of her parents, "they would have preferred to stay on the farm." Stella Foust Carden's family moved to a Virginia mill the same year for much the same reason. "He thought he could make a better living at public work than he was," Mrs. Carden remembered of her father. "He was a farmer but yet he was more of a hired hand on the farm. He worked for wages." Of his life on a western North Carolina farm before he and his family moved to a Charlotte mill in 1907, Jefferson M. Robinette recalled, "We were just renters and [it was] hard getting along."

There were countless variations on this pattern. The most common involved the family that moved to a mill because it lost its breadwinner. Flossie Moore Durham, born in 1883, was still a child when her father, a Chatham County, North Carolina, tenant farmer, died and left his wife and eight young children. "We didn't stay [on the farm] but a few months after he died," Mrs. Durham remembered, "just gathered that crop and then we moved to Bynum," where the older children went to work in the mill. Flossie joined them when she was ten years old.

Mollie Bowden Kay's experience was somewhat different. When a grown son left home about 1910 and was no longer available to help on the farm, Mollie's aging father moved his family to Carrboro, where Mollie, sixteen, went to work in a hosiery mill. Similarly, the move of Bessie Buchanan's family to Erwin Mills in Durham was due to the disability of her father, who was a Wake County sharecropper. "My father had the TB, and he couldn't work on the farm," Mrs. Buchanan recollected. "He thought he'd get to a textile place where we children could go to work."

"I'D HEARD RIGHT SMART LITTLE ABOUT THE MILL WORK."

Behind individual experience lay intricate patterns. How did folk learn about the mills and come to entertain the possibility of going to them? How did they decide to go? Did those who decided to go resist their own decision? How and why did they select one mill over another?

The answers to all of these questions begin at the same point: folk generally went to the mills in families. They thought about mill work as a family unit, were recruited and employed by the family, and experienced mill life as a family group. There were deviations from this pattern in urban mills, a few of which had no villages at all, and among single workers and those who lived outside the villages, but even there the family pattern was controlling. That arrangement was essential to the mills' functioning as they did, and mill folk no less than their employers found the family-centered pattern not only practical but desirable. Family hiring enabled everyone in the group to contribute to family income, and going to the mills in family groups eased the social and psychological transition. Folk had been hired as families on the farm, and family employment was a social form they recognized and accepted. Moreover, given the nature of the mills and the jobs they provided, there was no other realistic option. Most of the early mills were spinning mills that made coarse goods only, which required little skill. Most of the work could be readily learned and performed by women and children.

The evidence that folk regarded mill work in family terms is extensive, and comes from workers as well as employers. "[I]'ve herd say that you wanted hands," W. M. Miller wrote a North Carolina mill owner in 1889. "[M]e and my wife would like to have room in your factory if can ag[r]ee." J. R. Nelson wrote the same mill owner: "I presume you are starting up a new mill and being in want of a situation I hast to write you for a position. I have two experienced Weavers also and Spinner and i hope you will endever find Employment for me and famly[.] [C]ould com at once." Sallie A. Goodman also wrote in the same year: "I write you this Morning to See if you will give me work for my children[.] I have three good hands[.] [T]hey can do any kind of work in the mill[.] [T]hey are good Experince hands[.] [T]hey have been at work in the factory eight years[.] I want you to give them work if you possible can for I am a widow and have to look for my self[.] [T]he Dam has wash a way hear and we are out of work."[60]

The correspondence of mill owners shows the same emphasis on family. "Mr. Oates received your letter of March 3rd and handed it to me recommending you and your family should we need another family," John Schenck wrote a prospective employee in 1892. "At that time we did not need another family—but now we do." Schenck also wrote the proprietor of

60. W. M. Miller to Mark Morgan, September 19, 1889, J. R. Nelson to Morgan, March 11, 1889, and Sallie A. Goodman to Morgan, August 27, 1889, in Morgan Papers.

a mill that had recently closed because of a major accident: "We would like to get a good family. We are in need of a family say of four girls—or boys—to work on twisters, reels, spoolers, &c."[61]

Under such a system, large families might be even more valued than they had been on the farm. "I understand from Mrs. Ellick Broyes, that you had written to her and informed her, that a family from Tuckaseege wishes to move here which can furnish 8 or 9 hands," John Schenck wrote Mrs. Pink Early in another of his recruiting efforts. "I would be glad if you would write me at once, giving me the name of the family who wishes to come; also state how many boys, and how many girls they are, and what are their ages, and what each hand can do in the mill. Also please state if this is a first-class family and good people."[62]

This family emphasis helps explain how farm folk decided to go to the mills and why they went to particular mills. Proximity was probably the most important factor in most cases. Many folk simply heard of a new mill being built near town or in the next county and decided to write or go there to see it. "Long before the mill was ready we had hundreds of letters from . . . operatives in small mills and people tired of farm work," an official of Massachusetts Mills said after that company opened its mill at Lindale, Georgia, during the depressed years of the 1890s. "When we were ready to start the machinery we notified the operatives we wanted to come to work."[63]

Folk also heard about the mills and came to consider mill work through recruitment by mill agents and through family or neighborhood connections. The interviews show repeatedly that folk chose particular mills because of a relative. Nellie Allen Pendergrass' family chose the mill at Carrboro when her father died because Nellie's uncle was already working there. He brought them to nearby Carrboro. When his sister was left a widow, in other words, this man arranged employment for her and her children. The presence of such a relative at the mill and in the village must have made moving there easier than it would otherwise have been.

Pauline Phillips Griffith's move with her family to Judson Mill also involved a relative. "I had an aunt that lived here, and she worked in the plant. She's the one that got the jobs for them at the time," Mrs. Griffith explained. Indeed, when the family first went to the mill, they lived in the

61. John F. Schenck to J. L. Burke, March 26, 1892, John F. Schenck to R. R. Haynes, March 15, 1893, in Schenck Papers.
62. John F. Schenck to Mrs. Pink Early, November 5, 1897, in Schenck Papers.
63. *Manufacturers' Record*, May 15, 1896, vi.

same house with Pauline's aunt. "She lived on one side and us on the other," Mrs. Griffith remembered. "There was just a hall in between."

Sometimes extended families went to the mills together. "It just got to where those old hills wore out up there. You couldn't make a living on it, hardly," recollected Martin Lowe, who decided to move to Poe Mills in 1912. "I told my father, 'I believe I can find a place where I can make a better living,' and I come to the mill." How did Lowe make his decision? "Well, I'd heard right smart little about the mill work. I'd seen some people that were working at a mill and went back, and then they was always wishing that they'd stayed at the mill when they went back to the mountains. . . . I've never begrudged it a day that I come to the mill at all." Lowe talked over his decision with his own as well as his wife's relatives, and while none of the former went with him, all of the latter did. "My wife's family all come when I did. Yes, I brought them all," Lowe said, referring to his wife's mother, three brothers, and three sisters.

A neighbor rather than a relative led other families to a particular mill and was the immediate impetus for their going. Such a neighbor helped increase the recruiting agents' effectiveness. When an agent persuaded one family from a neighborhood, or one member of a kinship network, to go to his mill, he might use them to send back word on the advantages of mill employment. In the sample of 135 mill families Alexander R. Batchelor studied at Whitmire, South Carolina, in 1926 were 15 who came from the same community in Virginia. "Evidently one family came and wrote back recommending the work and the town," Batchelor wrote. "A number of these families have come within a few months. There were six families together in one section of the village."[64] When Jefferson Robinette's family decided to quit their tenant farm, they moved to a certain mill in Charlotte because several families from their community in western North Carolina were already working there. "The man there that run the mills, he wanted some help, and they come back up there and hired [my father] to go to Charlotte," Robinette recalled. "The man that owned the plant that we went to work in hired [an agent] to go out and hire help for him. And so he just went up there in the mountains and picked up help, families that didn't know nothing about working, and took them and trained them. . . . There was two sisters, myself, and I had a brother and a sister then younger than me. We all went in in the same plant at the same time, all green just the same way, and learned to work in that plant."

64. Batchelor, "A Textile Community," 16.

Deviating from the usual pattern, many individuals went to the mills on their own. John Pierce went at the turn of the century because of his childhood experience in a sharecropper's family. "We moved from one man's farm to another, never satisfied nowhere and hardly havin' enough to barely live on," Pierce remembered. "I got tired of that and when I got to be my own man I come to the mill." Lillian Holbrook first went to the mills in 1918 when she ran away from home to avoid a marriage her father was trying to force her into.

Some workers in the New South era went to work in the mills because they were born into a mill family. There had been cotton mills in the South since long before the Civil War, and even as early as the 1880s and 1890s, there were second- and even third-generation mill workers.[65] Thus James Herring, who was born in Athens, Georgia, about 1870 and worked in the cotton mills there off and on for about thirty-five years, was a third-generation mill worker. Long before the Civil War, Herring's maternal grandfather had begun working for the Athens Manufacturing Company; and he continued there after the war. "My grandmother kept house while my grandfather, my mother, two uncles, and three aunts worked in the mills," Herring recalled. Herring's paternal grandfather was a plantation overseer in antebellum days, but after the Civil War, he took his family to the Athens Manufacturing Company's mill. Thus both of Herring's grandfathers and both of his parents had worked in the mill. "Mother was a spinner and father was a beamer," he remarked; and when Herring himself was still a child he also entered the mill. "To make a good textile worker," he said years later, "you had to start young, say around the age of eight."

"I MADE UP MY MIND THAT I WAS GOING TO ESCAPE THIS DRUDGERY."

Explanations remain elusive. For every individual who went to the mills, many others in the same circumstance remained on the farm. Thus decisions hinged not on economic factors—poverty was a necessary but not sufficient element—but on less concrete matters of temperament, outlook,

65. On mills in the Old South, see Richard W. Griffin, "North Carolina: The Origin and Rise of the Cotton Textile Industry, 1830–1880" (Ph.D. dissertation, Ohio State University, 1954); Ernest M. Lander, *The Textile Industry in Antebellum South Carolina* (Baton Rouge, 1969); Griffin, "Poor White Laborers in Southern Cotton Factories, 1789–1865," *South Carolina Historical Magazine*, XLI (1960), 26–40; Martha T. Briggs, "Mill Owners and Mill Workers in an Antebellum North Carolina County [Randolph]" (M.A. thesis, University of North Carolina, 1975); and James C. Bonner, "Profile of a Late Ante-Bellum Community," *American Historical Review*, XLIX (1944), 663–80.

and individual psychology. The operative factor seems to have been the way an individual read his circumstance and the experience from which that circumstance derived. Was the individual resigned to his condition in life? If so, a move to the mill was less likely than if he had some sense of mastery over life or some hope that things could be better. A certain mixture of hopeful seeking, grim determination, and calculated willingness to take a risk seems to have been common to those who went to the mills.

Whatever the individual's immediate situation, going to the mills was an act of will by people not given to calculation. Poor, traditional folk generally seem inclined to hold onto the familiar wherever possible, and plain folk in the New South had many reasons to want to maintain the life they knew. Their society had long ago rationalized rural life and farm work, and now reinforced that rationalization with prejudicial stereotypes about mill work and "lintheads." This outlook had to be transcended, or at least neutralized, by those who went to the mills.

For a surprisingly large number of folk, gaining a fresh outlook was easier than it sounds. Many folk rejected popular myths about the superiority of farm life, and those people seem especially to have found the mills attractive. Many mill folk retained deep attachments to the farm, but many, perhaps even most, never looked back to the farms or did so only to affirm the decision to leave. "I was glad to move," Lessie Bowden Bland recalled of her family's going to Carrboro about 1910 while she was still a teenager. "[Our farm] was way out in the country, you know, and no way to get anywhere." Mrs. Bland's recollection of farm work was also negative. "Oh, I used to work, let me tell you," she said, "pick cotton and things like that."

This sentiment and others much stronger appear frequently in the interviews. "Farming be damned!" exclaimed J. T. Whitlock, who grew up on a farm near Union, South Carolina, in the 1880s and 1890s. "You could work your head off and still not get results. That is, none except a hell of a lot of blisters." When his father died, fourteen-year-old Whitlock went to work in a nearby hosiery mill. The wages were low and the hours long, he remembered, but "it was a damn sight better'n work in the fields; and I was getting paid for it!"

Hard work, loneliness, and economic insecurity were things many mill folk associated with farm life, and for such folk the mills represented lighter work, sociability, and a degree of security. "I alwayes [sic] detested the loneliness and the hard work of farm life," Lettie Mason said, recalling her youth in rural Wake County, North Carolina. "Picking cotton, hoeing corn, planting tobacco, pulling fodder, gathering peas, milking cows, feeding the stock, and the thousands of other chores to be done about a farm. . . . I made up my mind that I was going to escape this drudgery as soon as I got old enough to go it alone in the city and that is exactly what I did." The city was Durham, and her first job there was in a hosiery mill.

Severing rural roots was thus easy for some folk and facilitated their move to the mills. The prejudices against mill folk, however, were more difficult to overcome. News that a family was going to the mills often occasioned displays of ostracism, which must have had an effect. All of the workers Lawrence B. Graves interviewed in his study of the early mills in Newberry County remembered having problems as soon as their decision to go to the mills became known. One of them, "a lady who asked that her name not be mentioned," Graves wrote, "relates that as she and her family were leaving their farm in the southern part of Newberry County moving to the mill village, all the family connections gathered and tried to persuade them to remain on the farm. She said it was 'worse than a funeral.' "[66] Similarly, Sallie Jane Stephenson recalled that her family's decision to move to an Anderson County mill about 1890 "pretty near killed some of our relatives. Some of 'em stopped ownin' us right then," she recalled, "and we finally stopped ownin' them."

Whatever one's economic needs, to open oneself to such ostracism was hard indeed. The courage it took can only be imagined, for plain folk were sensitive people, and conformity to accepted norms was important to them. Of course necessity could overcome matters of image, but plain folk had mechanisms that probably reduced the significance of social prejudice. The farm-mill interchange and the overlapping of mill and farm families must have helped lessen prejudice, as did the nature of social and economic stratifications in the rural South. Extended families always included people of various economic grades; everyone had "poor relations" and well-off kinfolk, too, which undercut class divisions in the South. It would therefore be interesting to know what proportion of all white people in an area as large as the Piedmont had relatives in the mills. If the degree of kinship is extended no farther than cousins, that proportion was probably high enough to undercut some of the prejudice mill folk would otherwise have felt.

That prejudice is best seen as a special manifestation of the general prejudice against "poor whites," which all folk recognized and had ways of reacting to. "The country-mill distinction is practically nonexistent at the

66. Graves, "The Beginnings of the Cotton Textile Industry," 49.

tenant-millhand level," John K. Morland wrote of mill folk in York, South Carolina, in the 1940s, "for the tenants and millhands share a similar status."[67] Furthermore, in certain important ways, social stereotypes, like their racial counterparts, are of more concern to those who formulate and dispense them than to those who are their objects.

A decision to move to the mills was a serious one and was not easily made. "I could have money at the mill," Tom Rampey told his landlord in the South Carolina upcountry as he thought aloud on the pros and cons of the mills. "I ought to be able to save enough in no time to buy a few acres of my own." But economics was not the only thing at stake. "How do I know how long the mill job will last? . . . I don't know the folks who own the mill. They don't know me. I don't like to work for folks I don't know. I don't like to live in a house either that belongs to a stranger."[68]

Despite his misgivings, Rampey went to the mills, and his soliloquy is a reminder that the move involved an ending as well as a beginning. He stayed in the mills, however, suggesting that, above all, the move was a continuation.

67. John K. Morland, *Millways of Kent* (Chapel Hill, 1958), 177.
68. Quoted in Gustavus G. Williamson, "Cotton Manufacturing in South Carolina, 1865–1892" (Ph.D. dissertation, Johns Hopkins University, 1954), 169.

PART II

MILL WORK

4

ADAPTATIONS

"We had a strange sort of time gettin' used to the mill. Specially Will and them two boys that worked," Ella Cheek recalled long after she and her husband and their children had moved to a cotton factory in Seneca, South Carolina. The Cheeks were sharecroppers whose move was occasioned by a tornado that destroyed their house and crop, and the sudden dislocation might have made their adaptation more difficult than usual. "Will would come home of a night and say, 'I don't know as I'll be able to stand the racket much longer. Work I'm used to and don't mind but such a racket is liable to put a body crazy.'" Cheek adapted, however, if only from necessity. "I expect if he was to quit the mill now," his wife said in the 1930s, "he'd feel lonesome without the noise."

Will Cheek's experience was not unique. Recollecting their first days at work, mill folk invariably bared the consuming bewilderment that gripped them all. For many, like Will Cheek, the roaring noise of uncovered machinery commanded their memories; for others, it was the total picture of commotion and sound—machines and people bound together in incomprehensible activity, the workers oblivious of the furious cacophony about them. Still others were astonished by the size of the mill—two, three, or four stories tall—and the size of the work force too, fifty, a hundred, even several hundred people. They were un- sociable folk to all appearances though at ease among themselves, at work at baffling tasks. It was the largest group of people many newcomers had ever seen at one time under the same roof, and it was difficult for newcomers to fathom the purpose of what they saw.

One easily became disoriented. Children, many of whom went to work without any idea of what a cotton mill was, were simply astonished, and sometimes sorely afraid. "Law, I didn't know what, I just looked and looked and looked 'till my eyes got tired seeing so many different things," Letha Ann Sloan Osteen recalled of her first day at Poe Mills, where she went to work as a child just before the turn of the century. "[I was] just out of the country, [and] didn't know nothing but a one room schoolhouse."

This feeling too was widely shared. "I was scared to death," Bessie Buchanan recalled of her first day at Erwin Mills just after the turn of the century. "I heard that machinery roaring. Ooh, it scared me near about to death." Nothing better illustrates the fortitude of mill folk than their refusal to succumb to such feelings. "I had to stay there," Mrs. Buchanan recalled. She remembered "getting up so early in the morning" and the reason for her successful adjustment. "My father carried me. He worked in the mill, and my older sisters worked in there." With these family members as sources of assurance, nine-year-old Bessie overcame her initial amazement and readily took to mill work. "I really enjoyed it, I'll tell you the truth," she said years later. "It was something to do."

Adults frequently showed the same resourcefulness. "I looked it over. I thought I never would learn it, I'll tell you that," said Martin Lowe of his first impression of work at Poe Mills, to which as a young man he brought his family in 1912. "It looked like there was too doggone much machinery. . . . But I was always a fellow to take hold of anything though, and try it, and I made it and made a success of it."

Mountain folk, the "greenest" of the newcomers, had special problems. "I never had seen no town nor nothing before I went to work in that textile plant," recalled Jefferson M. Robinette, who as a teenager in 1907 moved with his family to a Charlotte mill. "Just from up there in the mountains and go where there's a lot of folks. I didn't know whether I was a-walking or a- running." Seasoned workers did not make the adjustment easy; "green hands" were open targets for jests. "We got used to it pretty quick," Robinette recollected of his family's experience. "Of course they pulled a lot of stunts on us, the folks in the mill there did."

Occasionally the stunts had tragic results. "[Amos] and me was doffers and the other doffers played tricks on us," Jennie Rowe recalled of her own and her brother's initiation into mill work at Lawndale, North Carolina. "You know how they always is about new hands. We was awful green without no learnin' nor nothin'. One day [Amos] got mad at the way they picked on him and had it out with another boy at dinnertime. That little boy—he won't but twelve year old—stuck a knife in [Amos'] heart and he was dead before the doctor got there."

MACHINE TENDING AND KNOT TYING

Mill work was simpler and easier to learn than it appeared to be. Indeed, learning to live with noise and commotion, and developing habits of attentiveness and regularity proved far more difficult than the work itself. Between the 1870s and 1890s, technological advances in spinning, weaving, and other processes eliminated what skill remained in cotton manufacturing and reduced mill work to a series of tasks involving little more than tending machines. This was one reason cotton manufacturing spread rapidly across the New South. As the mill boom accelerated, manufacturers took eagerly to the newest machinery. After 1890, the new southern mills were "thoroughly up to date in all respects," a study of the industry noted in 1900, often incorporating improvements in machinery and construction "not yet introduced in the manufacturing regions of the North."[1]

The effect was to simplify mill work. After the Draper loom, with its automatic filling-changing and warp-stopping mechanisms, appeared in the 1890s, even weaving, the most skilled task in the manufacturing process, was itself no more than "machine tending and knot tying." Thenceforth, most jobs in southern cotton mills, which produced coarser goods than those in New England and thus required less skill, were ideally suited to plain folk looking to leave the farm. The work was light compared to farm labor, and most jobs could be learned in a few days or weeks, even by folk with no experience in factory work. Thus Eliza Jackson Barden, who went to work in the cloth room at Eagle and Phenix Mills as a teenager in 1878, learned to weave in "about a week and a half" when she transferred to the weave room; and Addie Priscilla Jones, who was fifteen when she trans-

1. *Twelfth Census, 1900: Manufactures: Textiles*, 28; Marvin Fishbaum, cited in Irwin Feller, "The Diffusion and Location of Technological Change in the American Cotton-Textile Industry, 1890–1970," *Technology and Change*, XV (1974), 573n.

ferred from spinning to weaving at the same mill, learned to weave in four weeks.[2]

The process of cotton manufacturing began in the picker, or breaker, room, often physically apart from the rest of the mill, where bales of cotton arrived from the warehouse.[3] There, pickers, always strong men before machines were perfected to perform their tasks, removed the metal ties from the bales, which weighed about five hundred pounds each, and began the transformation of cotton into cloth. From several bales at once, the pickers took chunks of raw cotton and fed them into hoppers, which mixed them to produce a blending of texture, color, and other things affecting the uniformity of the finished product. The mixed cotton then went to an opener, which loosened the fibers and, by means of air pressure, began the process of removing dirt, trash, and other foreign matter. Like picking, opening was a sweated, disagreeable task requiring considerable strength; and openers, like pickers, were sometimes blacks.

From the opener the cotton went to a lapper, a machine that further untangled and cleaned the fibers and rendered them into laps, thin sheets of batting, several of which were meshed together to enhance the uniformity of texture. The laps then went to carding machines, which combed the fibers to make them parallel while continuing the removal of foreign matter. The cotton emerged from this process in the form of sliver—loose, untwisted rope, coiled into cans—and was then placed onto drawing frames. There, pairs of rollers moving at uneven speed further straightened the fibers and drew them into finer slivers, several of which were then combined, and the process was repeated one or more times. The sliver then passed to a slubber, where it was further compressed, given a slight twist, and wound onto bobbins. Now called slubbing, the loose roping passed through a series of roving frames, where it was further compressed and twisted by machines called speeders, and rendered into roving.

Bobbins of roving were then placed onto creels and run between rollers turning at uneven speed, which fed them onto the spinning frames. Spin-

2. The phrase "machine tending and knot tying" is from Ben F. Lemert, *The Cotton Textile Industry of the Southern Appalachian Piedmont* (Chapel Hill, 1933), 33. On textile machinery, see U.S. Department of Commerce, Bureau of Foreign and Domestic Commerce, *Miscellaneous Series No. 37: The Cotton-Spinning Machinery Industry* (1916), especially 36–47; and Melvin T. Copeland, *The Cotton Manufacturing Industry in the United States* (1917; rpr. New York, 1966). On the experience of the two mill workers, see *Senate Documents*, 48th Cong., 1st Sess., No. 91, pp. 598–99.

3. This summary follows that in Holland Thompson, *From the Cotton Field to the Cotton Mill: A Study of the Industrial Transition in North Carolina* (New York, 1906), 118–36.

ning itself (using ring spindles) consisted of a single continuous operation in which the roving was drawn out, twisted, and wound into thread and onto bobbins turning at 5,000 to 10,000 revolutions a minute. The speed of the bobbins and the tension it created caused the thread to break occasionally and the bobbin on which the thread was winding to stop and remain "down" until a spinner came along and twisted the ends together and restarted the bobbin. That task constituted the work of spinners. The bobbins were located on frames, commonly 104 on each side at this time, and spinners were paid according to the number of sides they attended. A child might begin tending a single side, but experienced spinners tended 6 or 8 sides—624 or 832 bobbins, or spindles, respectively, arranged on each side of an alley, which they walked up and down "keeping their work up," as they called the process of checking for broken threads and "down" bobbins.

When a bobbin was full, it was doffed—removed and replaced—and the new one started up. Doffing was the mill job most often held by young boys; indeed, the vast majority of small children who worked in the mills—those under thirteen or fourteen—were either doffers or spinners.

Bobbins of yarn went from the spinning frames to spoolers, operated by girls or young women, which rewound the thread evenly onto spools, and if the mill produced ply yarn, twisters then rendered two or more threads into one, according to the ply desired. If the yarn was shipped elsewhere for weaving, the spools went to a warper, where perhaps one or two thousand of the ends—individual threads—were drawn into a single skein, tied together to prevent tangling, and baled for shipment.

If woven on the premises, the yarn went through several additional processes before arriving at the weaver's loom. Threads intended for the warp went to a beam warper, where they were wound onto cylindrical beams and passed on to a slasher to be sized. That is, the several hundred threads on each beam were sent through a solution to stiffen, strengthen, and smoothen them, and then wound onto loom beams. These were then adjusted onto the looms, the separate threads being drawn into the harness of the looms in what was perhaps the most tedious operation in the mill. The filling, as threads in the woof were called, came directly from the weaving frames on bobbins placed by the weavers in the shuttles. Once all this was accomplished, the weaving commenced. After the introduction of automatic looms, which became standard in southern mills about 1895 to 1905, the weaver's task was to mend broken threads and replace empty bobbins in the shuttle, which required strength and judgment but little skill. An experienced weaver could operate eighteen or twenty automatic looms compared to four or six of the old ones, and pay was by the "cut," commonly forty to sixty yards of cloth.

The woven cloth was wound upon a beam, sewn into strips, and passed through a machine that sheared off loose threads and ground off rough places. It was then sent through a steam jet, ironed, and folded into bolts, and the bolts were stamped and baled for marketing.

THE TYPICAL OPERATIVE WAS A TEENAGER.

The composition of the work force was determined by the skill and strength necessary to accomplish this work. In mills that wove as well as spun, which were typical though not universal, the largest groups of workers were weavers and spinners, who together constituted half or more of the work force.[4] The division of jobs according to gender and age, a conspicuous feature of mill work, was one consequence of hiring workers according to the minimum level of skill and strength necessary to accomplish given tasks. If children could fill a job, they were employed to fill it, for theirs were the lowest wages in the mills. If they could not, women were hired. Only tasks requiring strength or mechanical skill, or entailing supervisory responsibilities, were necessarily filled by men. The result was a work force made up largely of women, children, and youths.

Counting mill workers was never an exact science, but according to census figures, almost three quarters (71.4 percent) of all workers in the mills of Georgia and the Carolinas in 1880 were women or children, the latter defined as boys under sixteen and girls under fifteen. Over the next three decades, these proportions changed notably, though the distribution remained distinctive. Weaving, a task performed chiefly by men and always by adults (persons sixteen and over), became relatively a larger part of the industry, while spinning, a task of children and women, became relatively smaller. At the same time, machinery became more complex or ran more rapidly, and the average grade of the product of southern mills—the fineness of the yarn spun—rose meaningfully.[5] Each of these factors necessitated greater experience, attentiveness, and skill in workers. Only men or strong women could efficiently operate the Draper looms, for example, and

4. For a list of mills in Georgia and the Carolinas at the turn of the century and the number of looms and/or spindles in each, see *Manufacturers' Record*, February 22, 1900, pp. 72–73.

5. The average grade of yarn produced in southern mills rose from less than 15 in 1890 to more than 17 in 1900, compared with an average of 25 for New England mills in the latter year. The figure is equal to the number of hanks—lengths of yarn 840 yards—to a pound (*Twelfth Census, 1900: Manufactures: Textiles*, 41–42).

as mill machinery improved, the cost effectiveness of employing small children decreased—a development that accelerated the effects of child labor reform. Finally, as more and more men were employed in the mills, relatively fewer wives and mothers found it necessary to work outside the home.

Thus, while the work force in Georgia and Carolina mills grew rapidly, from 11,491 in 1880 to 78,757 in 1900 and 123,767 in 1909, the proportion of men (males sixteen and over) increased from 28.6 to 42.5 to 53.5 percent, respectively. At the same time the proportion of women (females fifteen and over in 1880, and sixteen and over thereafter) declined from 47.6 to 32.4 to 28.6 percent, while that of children went from 23.8 to 25 to 17.9 percent, respectively.[6] These trends continued in the second decade of the twentieth century, especially the declining proportion of children, as child labor legislation began to have significant effect.

Behind these patterns lay the actualities of the workplace. A few jobs were filled exclusively by children and many more by women or men only, while others might be held by women or children and still others by women or men. Only an occasional job, such as sweeper, was filled by children or men, and then only men too old for other work. "Women [and girls] were in the spinning and the spooling, and the boys done the doffing," Flossie Moore Durham remembered of the spinning mill where she worked in the 1890s. "Men worked in the card room mostly."

The youngest workers were often, even generally, not on the payroll. They were "helpers," children as young as six or eight, who went to the mills irregularly to "help out" an older relative working on a piecework basis. Most of them "helped" at spinning, enabling an older sibling to tend more sides and thus increase family income. A 1907–1908 study of women and child labor cited the example of a twelve-year-old spinner who tended five sides on his own and was assisted in tending five others by two sisters aged nine and eleven. The boy was paid for tending ten sides, and neither of his sisters appeared on the payroll.[7]

"Helping" was the way many children began mill work. "I am advised that we have quite a number of children in the mill under 12 years of age, who are not on our pay-roll, and could not in any way, as I consider it, be considered in our employ," J. H. M. Beaty, general manager of Olympia

6. Figures compiled from *Tenth Census, 1880: Manufactures*, 104–106, 159–61, 173–74; *Twelfth Census, 1900: Manufactures: Textiles*, 61; and *Thirteenth Census, 1910: Manufactures*, 41. These figures should be taken as approximations. The work force fluctuated from season to season, large numbers of workers were part-time workers, and not all workers appeared on the payroll.

7. *Senate Documents*, 61st Cong., 2nd Sess., No. 645, Vol. 1, p. 190.

Mills in Columbia, South Carolina, wrote the mills' attorney in 1907, describing the situation in his factory. "They are brought in by some older member of the family, whom it seems would rather have them in the Mill than to have them in the village with no one to look out after them. These little fellows help around the machines considerably, and while I can see no harm in this I would like to have your advice in this matter. Right now I do not see how it would be possible to keep them out of the mill, without keeping some of the older members of the family out also. The people themselves would object to this most seriously."[8]

When they went on the payroll, occasionally as young as seven or eight but typically about twelve, boys were likely to be doffers and girls spinners, especially those who were very young. If they were a bit older, boys might start as sweepers or waste gatherers, or at some other light, irregular work, and girls as spoolers, winders, or "drawing-in girls." Throughout the New South era, these tasks—especially doffing, spinning, "helping," and sweeping—constituted the work of child laborers. All involved light work but long hours each day.

By their middle teens, youths of both sexes moved into places alongside adults. Because they required great strength, picking, twisting, beaming, and filling were jobs almost always held by men, as were all positions requiring mechanical skill—engineer, machinist, loom fixer, card grinder, and electrician. All other occupations—as carders, speeders, slubbers, spoolers, warpers, weavers, drawing-frame operators, and the like—were open to men and women, though women tended to dominate most such jobs except carding and weaving. Weaving was the most prestigious and highest-paying job a woman operative could fill. Mill work was not subject to the kind of sex discrimination plain folk were most familiar with—pay differentials for women and men doing identical work. By the turn of the century, most mill workers were paid on a piecework basis—the number of machines tended or cuts of cloth produced—with no sex or age differentials, though jobs generally filled by men paid more than those held exclusively by women and children. For this reason, and because men held all the skilled and supervisory jobs and worked more regularly, the average man made substantially more money than the average woman. Still, there was less discrimination against women in cotton manufacturing than in any other form of employment open to plain folk in the New South, and many women

8. J. H. M. Beaty to William Elliott, Jr., June 14, 1907, in William Elliott, Jr., Papers, South Caroliniana Library.

operatives made more than some men working in the same mill. Also, most female workers were quite young because women generally quit work when they married or soon thereafter, and if they later returned, it was often as "spare hands," that is, part-time or occasional workers.[9] Yet the discrimination was real. "I was a spinner at first," Alice Caudle recalled, "then I learned to spool. When they put in them new winding machines, I asked them to learn me how to work 'em and they did. If I'd a-been a man no telling how far I'd-a gone. It was mighty convenient for 'em—having a hand that could do all three."

Neither men nor women usually worked in the mills in old age. As Flossie Moore Durham said of the mill where she went to work in 1893, "Didn't any old people work here then." Mill work was enervating and unhealthful, and the hours were long, all factors that bore heavily on people of advancing age; thus few folk over fifty or sixty continued at it. Those who did were given less demanding (and lower-paying) jobs as sweepers, elevator operators, watchmen, or handymen of some sort. Virtually all such individuals were men, for a woman who wanted to lighten her workload returned to spinning, tending only as many sides as she comfortably could.

There were few opportunities for operatives to advance to supervisory jobs. An overseer, occasionally called a foreman, supervised each basic mill operation, and where the number of operatives under him was large, he had an assistant, called a "section," or "second," hand. The number of such positions, the lowest supervisory jobs in the mill, was small. Every mill had a boss spinner and every weaving department a boss weaver, as overseers were familiarly known. Large mills might also have a boss carder, boss spooler, and overseer of the cloth room, as well as a boss dyer; and sometimes there were bosses of reeling, winding, warping, and a few other functions. But a typical mill had no more than four to six overseers, not all of whom had assistants. Thus a mill with several hundred operatives might have no more than ten or twelve supervisory positions to which operatives could aspire.[10] Occasionally a superintendent, who oversaw an entire mill, had worked as an operative, but that was exceptional and more often than not part of his management training. The chief executive officer of each mill, variously the president, treasurer, or chairman of the board, handled financial affairs and matters of policy rather than day-to-day operations. He

9. The work forces in a number of mills in Georgia and the Carolinas are listed by position, sex, and age in U.S. Commissioner of Labor, *Eleventh Annual Report, 1895–96*, 186–99, 231–39, 251–60.
10. For examples of the numbers of supervisors and operatives in individual mills, see *ibid.*

was typically an owner, investor, or owner's representative, and almost none of the men who held these positions ever worked as operatives.

Mill workers were young, astonishingly so. Of 2,470 female operatives counted in manuscript census reports of seven counties in 1880, 51.7 percent were under twenty-one, as were 55 percent of 1,539 males. Moreover, many in both groups were small children. Of the females, 1 in 10 (9.55 percent) was twelve or younger, and of the males 1 in 7 (14.1 percent).[11] This picture changed little until well into the twentieth century. In 1900, census takers counted 22,046 children fifteen or younger employed in mills in Georgia and the Carolinas (28 percent of the work force), of whom 5,141 (6.5 percent of the work force) were ten or eleven years old. No children under those ages were reported, though in the words of a census study, there were "many children under 10 employed."[12]

The typical operative, then, was a teenager, especially in the first half of the New South era, a fact obscured by statistics that count as adults all workers who had passed their sixteenth birthday. In 152 southern mills examined in depth in a 1907–1908 study, three-fifths (60.8 percent) of the work force was under twenty-one years of age, and that after the rise previously noted in the proportion of adult males. The reasons for this anomaly were, first, that everyone past his sixteenth birthday was counted as an adult, and second, that as the average age of male workers rose over the years, the average age of females declined. More than half the female mill workers counted in the manuscript census reports of 1900 were minors; and as the 1907–1908 study noted, the number of females in the mills declined each year after age eighteen as women married and became housewives and mothers.[13]

Another factor influencing the social history of mill work was the size of the mills. Compared to other factories, cotton mills in the New South were small, but by the standards of plain folk and the New South, they were quite large. In North Carolina, where there were no large mills to distort the figure, the average cotton factory in 1880 employed less than fifty oper-

11. The counties are Muscogee (Columbus) and Richmond (Augusta) in Georgia, Russell in Alabama, Aiken and Spartanburg (not yet a mill center) in South Carolina, and Gaston and Alamance in North Carolina (Manuscript Census, 1880, Schedule 1).

12. *Census Bulletin 69: Child Labor in the United States* (1907), 43, 48.

13. The proportion of female workers under twenty-one counted in the manuscript census reports of 1900 ranged from 76.3 percent in Spartanburg County to 46.4 percent in Richmond County, and tended to cluster about the 60.8 percent in Alamance County and 61 percent in Gregg Township in Aiken County. The relatively low figure in Richmond County is explained by the high portion of families there headed by females (Manuscript Census, 1900, Schedule 1; *Senate Documents*, 61st Cong., 2nd Sess., No. 645, Vol. 1, pp. 41–42).

atives, while those in Georgia and South Carolina employed a little more than 140. The latter figure is misleadingly large, however, for Eagle and Phenix Mills in Columbus, by far the largest mill in the South at the time, employed more than 1,600 operatives. This establishment was counted as one mill though its workers were actually located in four separate factories. In South Carolina, where there were only fourteen mills in 1880, the size of the average work force was enlarged by the three mills in Horse Creek Valley, which together employed more than half the operatives in the state. Although these averages seem small by today's standards, they should be measured by the standards of other manufactories at the time. In 1880 the average tobacco factory in North Carolina employed less than thirty workers, and the average sawmill in Georgia about five.[14]

During the New South era, the average size of the mills grew. By 1909, a typical mill in the three states employed about 225 workers, but almost a third (29 percent) of all workers were in mills employing between 250 and 500 workers each, and more than a third (35 percent) in mills employing over 500 each. Even though the average mill was still small, the average worker had become part of a rather large work force.[15]

"[THE YOUNGER FOLK] HAVE LEARNED HOW TO WORK IN THE
MILLS, . . . BUT THE OLD FOLKS ARE NO HELP WHATEVER."

The written history of mill workers has focused so exclusively on degradation, victimization, or, less frequently, heroic resistance, that it comes as something of a shock to learn that the workers themselves had other views of their experience. In their own estimation, they were no more the flotsam of southern industrialization, haplessly tossed about by impersonal forces of poverty, oppression, and economic transformation, than they were the progeny of rural degeneracy. Nor were they stupefied automatons sheepishly following the dictates of all-powerful employers. And least of all were they heroic activists caught up in class struggle with exploitive capitalists.

Mill workers were instead, in their own minds at least, ordinary people

14. Average numbers were 45.5 workers per mill in North Carolina, 144 in South Carolina, and 141 in Georgia (*Tenth Census, 1880: Manufactures*, 104–106, 173–74; 159–61, 209–10, 317–19, 354–55). On the size of work forces in tobacco factories and sawmills, see *ibid.*, 104–106, 159–61.

15. In Georgia and the Carolinas, 391 of 544 mills (71.9 percent) employed 250 or fewer workers in 1909. In Massachusetts, in contrast, 58 percent of all workers were in mills employing more than 1,000 workers, compared with 9.9 percent of workers in the three states (*Thirteenth Census, 1910: Manufactures*, 45).

making the best of things as they found them—living, working, enjoying, and suffering very much like everyone else. They looked upon mills and mill work through lenses of experience and culture and their own immediate needs, and what they saw was more hopeful and helpful than anything else available to them. More often than not, therefore, folk thought of their mill experience in positive terms. And those who remained in the mills long after the New South era looked back nostalgically to the relaxed, informal atmosphere of the earlier period and contrasted it favorably with the rushed, impersonal conditions brought on in later times by speedups, scientific management, and the assorted uncertainties of the 1920s and 1930s.

Indeed, what seems most characteristic of the New South period was its utterly unmodern and unrationalized ways—the casual, unsystematic, even chaotic conditions that prevailed in the workplace. Mediated by factors of personalism, family, and the small size of mills, the system, or rather lack of system, functioned on a manageable, human scale. The operative forces were things folk understood and used in adapting themselves to the mills.

Informality characterized getting a job. Mills had no personnel office and hardly anything we today would call a personnel policy. Generally, overseers were responsible for hiring and firing workers, but since "help" was so often in short supply, superintendents and even presidents also concerned themselves with recruiting and retaining workers. Overseers always had discretion in job assignments, work rules, and even wages, and workers thought of given jobs in terms of individual overseers. They knew or quickly came to know their overseer, called him by his first name if they were adults, and developed individual strategies for dealing with him.

The vast majority of workers got their jobs by going to a mill, locating an overseer or a superintendent, and asking for employment. "There was always work," Bessie Buchanan recalled of her years in the mills in the 1890s. "They'd hire anybody then." And they would fill positions on the spot. "It wasn't no job at all to get a job then," said Martin Lowe, who went with his family from the mountains to Poe Mills in 1912. "It was hard for them to get the help to run the mills." Lowe continued, "Hadn't none of us never been in a mill and we got a job. Put us right in there to learn." Everette Burchell, who began doffing as a twelve-year-old in 1914, also remembered the ease with which he found employment when as a teenager he began moving from mill to mill in North Carolina and Virginia. When he left one mill, Burchell simply presented himself at another and "nine times out of ten" was put immediately to work. This helped ease the introduction to mill work.

Yet not everyone adapted. Men, especially middle-aged men who had spent their lives farming, seem to have had the most difficulty adjusting to mill work, and a considerable minority of those who tried it failed. Mary Abbott believed her father's death was due to his inability to adapt to the mills. "Pa never'd took rightly to workin' in the mill," she recalled, "an' after Ma'd tell how when he was on nights an' tryin' to sleep in the day he fretted like and she allus blamed that for him takin' sick, like he did an' dyin'. After he was dead, I'd hear Ma a-sayin' how when he was sick an' spring'd come she'd pull his bed over to the window an' prop him up, an' even if they wasn't no way to see the country there, he'd talk to Ma about what they'd be doin' now if they was on the farm an' things like that."

Such instances were no doubt extreme. More representative was the family head who "had acquired habits which made it impossible for him to be active and quick enough to be a spinner or weaver." The man's "fingers had been so gnarled and roughened by agricultural work," wrote Lewis W. Parker, a South Carolina mill owner, "as to be unsuitable for the tying of small threads"; and at the mills he became dependent on the labor of his children. A North Carolina mill official wrote similarly of the parents of families newly arrived at his village who "either can't work or don't know how" to do mill work and could not be taught. "We have several families in our mills who come directly from the homes on the farms, who, on their arrival, had to be supported for awhile by the mill until the younger folks could earn enough," this official wrote the North Carolina labor commissioner in 1902. "Since [the younger folks] have learned how to work in the mills the whole families are doing well and are well pleased, but the old folks are no help whatever, as stated, but they claim they can't make anything on a farm."[16]

That some men failed as mill workers while their children succeeded no doubt intensified their personal as well as family difficulties. Yet there were positive options available to men who could not do mill work, such as farming near the mill or doing other outside work while their children remained in the mills. The mills themselves provided jobs for many such men. In April, 1893, Cleveland Cotton Mills employed 118 operatives inside the mill, 32 of them men (probably men and grown boys over sixteen or eighteen). They also employed 3 wagoners, 2 carpenters, a machinist, an engineer, a shipping clerk, and 8 mercantile clerks, as well as two superin-

16. Lewis W. Parker, "Conditions of Labor in Southern Cotton Mills," *Annals*, XXXIII (1909), 59; North Carolina Bureau of Labor Statistics, *Annual Report, 1902*, 168, hereinafter cited as NC *Labor Report* by year.

tendents, three bosses, and a bookkeeper.[17] All of these jobs were held by white men, and since some of the operatives lived in farm families, it seems quite likely that at or near these small, rural mills there were enough jobs for men who could not or would not do mill work themselves but whose children did. This conclusion is reinforced by the fact that there was also a number of irregular jobs for men in every cotton mill community—wood chopping, hauling, and day labor in agriculture and other occupations.

This pattern, too, eased movement into the mills. Having a combination of mill and nonmill workers in the family accommodated the needs of many folk in the transition. Yet not all men could make the accommodation, and the result was "mill daddies," as they were known, able-bodied men who worked irregularly or not at all and lived off the earnings of their children and sometimes their wives as well. These men were objects of derision and scorn; and the frequent, exaggerated depictions of them created an impression that their numbers were large. "Numbers of men throughout [Georgia] put their wives and children in cotton mills as operatives and make them earn money for them to spend in drink," an Augusta labor leader told the Industrial Commission in 1900. "There are numerous instances in [Atlanta] where families come into town and the father puts the children in the mills and he does nothing, just lives on what those children make," the president of the Georgia Federation of Labor told the same commission. "There are numerous instances of that kind. . . . They do not do anything but lay around and their children work in the mills and support them. They go down when the children get paid and get the money and buy the children something and the balance goes for whiskey."[18]

Mill workers, too, often described such men, and in similar language. "Many an old drunkard has signed a contract stating his child is over twelve years of age in order that the companies may work them, and so that he himself may lay around a barroom or the stillhouse drunk," a carder wrote the North Carolina labor commissioner in 1904, "and it is all right with the company, for child labor is much cheaper than grown people." A beamer wrote in a similar vein, "I know of several parents who have put their small children in the factory, while they idle away the hours at the public places in town."[19]

Despite such rhetoric, the actual number of "mill daddies" was appar-

17. H. F. Schenck to E. M. Ward, April 10, 1893, in H. F. Schenck Papers, Manuscript Department, Duke University Library, Durham, North Carolina.

18. Atlanta *Constitution*, March 22, 1900, July 5, 1903; *House Documents*, 57th Cong., 1st Sess., No. 184, Vol. 7, p. 545.

19. NC *Labor Report* (1904), 206–207, (1891), 177.

ently small and the phenomenon itself misunderstood and misrepresented. Of 660 southern mill families whose budgets the labor commissioner studied in 1890, 14 were headed by idle men. In 1,567 families studied in depth in the 1907–1908 investigation of woman and child labor, 37 male heads were present and idle, 68 were present and "incapacitated," and 59 had deserted their families. Investigators who made this study believed idle fathers were more common in mill families than in the general population, and they were probably correct, for cotton mills were among the few places in the New South where women and children could support themselves. Of 1,096 male-headed households with one or more mill workers counted in the manuscript census reports of Alamance County in 1900, the number of men with no occupation was 52; 4 of the men were less than fifty years of age. At Arkwright mill village in Spartanburg County, also in 1900, 14 of 104 male heads of households had no occupations listed, and 4 of these were under fifty years old. In Gregg Township in Aiken County, South Carolina, the same year, 226 of 706 male heads of households containing at least 1 mill worker did not work in the mills. Thirty-three of these men had no occupations listed, and 18 others were infirm or over fifty years old.[20]

Many men brought their families to the mills because they were unable to do sustained, heavy labor. Because they worked intermittently in or about the mills or villages, however, they do not appear in the records as idle. Other men went to the mills with their families because they could do no physical labor at all but were still able to be up and about. Both groups whiled away time in the social centers of the villages—the store, depot, or other places idle men gathered. Moreover, mill work itself was irregular, and all or part of the work force was idle from time to time. Mill workers were frequently absent; and mills sometimes had more hands than they could use at one time. In addition, farmers, carpenters, and other men who headed mill families also worked irregularly and would have spent at least some of their idle time in the villages.

Casual observers might mistake all of these groups for "mill daddies," especially those whose purposes were served by exaggerating what was actually a small but very human problem. What the critics generally saw was not heartless men living off their children but evidence of the irregular work patterns of plain folk. Concentrated in mill villages, idle men aroused

20. U.S. Labor Commissioner, *Seventh Annual Report 1891–92*, 866–96; *Senate Documents*, 61st Cong., 2nd Sess., No. 645, Vol. 1, pp. 439, 453; Manuscript Census, 1900, Schedule 1, Alamance County, N.C., Spartanburg County, S.C.; and Gregg Township, Aiken County, S.C. The sample of families studied by the labor commissioner was not scientific though an effort was made to make it representative.

the censuring spirit of critics in ways they did not in the countryside. But idleness was certainly no greater in the one place than in the other.

"Mill daddies" were the most obvious victims of the transformation of farm folk into a factory proletariat. These were men who could not make the transition successfully and who had no workable alternative to becoming charges on their families. Many were alcoholics and "sorry" or "lazy," as their critics charged. But those states were manifestations of deeper problems. Some men saw the move to the mills as evidence of their own failure, as men and fathers as well as farmers, and what they found in the mills confirmed their misgivings. Even men who worked in the mills with their children or at other jobs nearby lost their economic centrality in the family. Yet they, like society as a whole, counted as one of the measures of manhood the ability to provide for one's family. In and out of the mill, however, the wages for unskilled work were too small for that. At Cleveland Cotton Mills in 1893, for example, men commonly earned between 60¢ and $1.00 a day and women between 50¢ and $1.00; outside, wagoners received 85¢ and the two carpenters $1.00 and $1.25, respectively.[21]

Whatever the difficulties of individual men, putting one's children in the mills without going in oneself did not necessarily mean a loss of interest in the children and their well-being. "I am not in the mill, but I represent it with my children," H. W. Baughn of Mayodan wrote the North Carolina labor commissioner in 1900. "I don't favor the docking of hands for being too late getting in to work," Baughn wrote; nor did he approve the 69-hour week his children had to work. He suggested instead a 10-hour day and a division of child workers into two groups, one to work in the morning and attend school in the afternoon, and the other to follow the opposite schedule.[22] Such a suggestion made far more sense for folk who needed the earnings of their children than did those of reformers who wanted to exclude all children from the mills regardless of the effect the exclusion would have on family income.

"I WANTED TO WORK. WHEN THEY PUT ME OUT OF WORK, I CRIED. I DIDN'T WANT TO GO TO SCHOOL."

There is no analogue to "mill daddies" among women and children who went to the mills. No doubt many women avoided the condition by never

21. H. F. Schenck to E. M. Ward, April 10, 1893, in Schenck Papers.
22. NC *Labor Report* (1900), 114–15.

working in the mills in the first place. Not even widows who headed mill families typically worked in the mills; instead, they kept house while their children worked, though some of them also kept boarders or otherwise contributed to family income.

Because of the distinctive composition of the mill work force, most folk who went directly from farm to factory were young, a substantial majority of them under twenty-one and probably an overwhelming majority under thirty-five. When a typical family moved to the mills, the children who were old enough went to work immediately, the mother kept house, and the father also went to work, probably in the mill but often somewhere else. Female-headed families went to the mills only when their children were old enough to work. Unmarried youths of both sexes also went to the mills in large numbers.

Despite the widespread impression to the contrary, children and youths had the least difficulty adjusting to mill work, though of course not everyone fit the general pattern. "We were brought to work and stuck in the factory, and that's the only way to put it," an anonymous woman told interviewers of her introduction to mill work in 1911. As a child, this woman had gone with her family from a farm in North Carolina to a Durham hosiery mill, where she went to work with no knowledge of what mill work involved. She disliked it intensely, and after a few days and a spat with her boss quit for a job in a nearby tobacco factory.[23]

"It was a horrible place as I look back at it now," another unnamed woman told Mary O. Cowper, a North Carolina social reformer, of her introduction to mill work, also in a Durham hosiery mill, early in the twentieth century. "We worked eleven hours a day," she recalled. "The stools we sat on had high small tops with no backs, and every body that used snuff and tobacco (and nearly every body did) had to spit on the floor." Moreover, this woman remembered, the pace of her work was rapid and the volume so burdensome that she was unable sometimes to take a rest break for an entire morning or afternoon. "I hated to hear the whistle blow to go to work," she said, "and the only glad moment of the day was when it blew to go home."[24]

One approaches the recollections of mill workers expecting to be overwhelmed by views and experiences of this sort, but they are exceptional.

23. Her interview is in SOHP Box 4.
24. Mary Cowper, "Writings and Notes on the Textile Industry" (Typescript in Mary O. Cowper Papers, Manuscript Department, Duke University Library, Durham, North Carolina).

The woman just quoted left the mill she disliked for work in a bag factory, which she "really enjoyed."

To see the initiation of children and youths into mill work as the workers themselves recalled it is eye-opening. Even those who went to work with no prior acquaintance with cotton manufacturing seem to have had only temporary problems. "It wasn't so hard [to learn to spin]," Bessie Buchanan remembered, "but it was for me because I'd never seen it done and never knew nothing about it." James W. Pharis was also thrown on his own in an unfamiliar position. "Back in them days, you just had to learn more or less yourself," he said, discussing his first mill job, which began when he was no more than eight or nine years old. "You didn't have much system in textile plants. So you just had to put you in there and you just had to learn it."

Clara Tate, who began spinning in a North Carolina mill when she was thirteen, was likewise perplexed for a time. "I was scared of my job, of myself, and of my boss," she recalled of her first mill experience. "They put a woman on with me till dinnertime to show me and in the even' they sorta turned me loose by myself. When I'd get messed up she'd come around to help me but I felt so ashamed I didn't know what to do." Exhibiting the resourcefulness so much in evidence in the ease with which plain folk adapted to mill work, young Clara determined to overcome her dismay and learn the job. "If that was my job I wanted to keep it up without any help," she recalled. And she did.

Mary Abbott found the mill strange at first. "I'd go along with Pa at six o'clock in the evenin' and work till six o'clock in the mornin', and for them twelve hours I got ten cents every night I worked," she recollected. For a child of seven, such a schedule might have been disorienting, but little Mary got along. "When I first worked I wa'n't near big enough to reach up to the frame, and they had a box for me to stan' on to make it and I pushed the box along as I worked," she remembered. "I took on right quick to learn, and before long I could spin right up with some of the big ones. The boss told Pa I was peart, and when folks come visitin' at the mill he'd bring them to see the youngun that could spin good." The pride in her accomplishment is evident.

For children who grew up near the mills, the introduction to mill work involved none of these anxieties. On the contrary, these children eased so gradually into mill work that it is difficult to say when they began. A few had been taken to the mills while they were infants by parents unable to afford babysitters. "I was born and reared on the cotton mill hill here," Clarise Pope recalled of her childhood in Hickory, North Carolina, in the second decade of the twentieth century. "Mammy and Pappy worked in the mill. Us children were too little to leave, so we had to go along. We were dumped in the bobbin bin and had to stay there 'till they were through with their work." President Charles Estes of King Mill in Augusta described the custom there in 1886. "Some few mothers take their children to the mill with them to keep them under their eye, and likely as occasion may require allow them to assist them, but that is quite rare."[25]

In many places village children wandered into and out of the mills, visiting parents or siblings at work, bringing them snacks or lunch, or simply satisfying youthful curiosity. No doubt they were fascinated by what they saw, for they returned repeatedly, and on their own volition, many of them began to learn the simpler tasks.

In 1915, when she was a teenager, Ethel M. Faucette went to work in a North Carolina mill where her older siblings were already employed. For some time, young Ethel had carried lunch to her relatives, and while in the mill she had begun to learn their jobs. "I was already learned when I went to work, 'cause I'd work every day on [my sister's] job while she ate her lunch," Mrs. Faucette recalled of her role as a "dinner toter." In saying "I liked the work," she must have spoken the truth, for she worked in the same mill from 1915 until it closed in 1954. "I wish it was running now," she said at age eighty-two, "I'd be at work."

Such reactions to mill work were commonplace. Rose Bowden Humphreys began working in Carrboro in her early teens despite her family's desire that she remain in school. "I wanted to do it, I just wanted to," she explained. "I had some friends working and I wanted to be with them. And then I could have my money to buy what I wanted." Because her family insisted that she stay in school, young Rose at first worked only in the summer; but when school began, her family would, as she said, "make me go back to school, and I'd go back, and then first chance, I'd slip off again." Her family soon relented, and she quit school and worked until she married. "I just loved it," she said.

Ironically, when southern legislatures began passing child labor legislation, some children had to be "put out" of the mills over their own objections. "I learned how to spin at Saxapahaw," Alice Thrift Smith recollected of her introduction to mill work in 1909, when she was about ten years old. "My oldest sister was working there and she was a spinner and after I got out of school in the evening I would go in the mill and help my father. He was

25. Augusta *Chronicle*, June 8, 1886.

cutting quills. And I would go in there. Well I learned how to spin from there." The next year, however, Alice's family moved from Saxapahaw to Carrboro, and the bosses there, she remembered, "said I couldn't come in and help. I would have to be on the payroll so they put me on the payroll. And I worked there, I don't know how long—several months—and then when they come over, they said I couldn't work unless my father signed me up for being twelve years old [she was eleven]. Well, he wouldn't do it. He said he didn't want me to work no way then, you know." So "they put me out then and wouldn't let me work. And then when I got to be twelve, I went in and went to work." Mrs. Smith recalled: "I wanted to work. When they put me out of work, I cried. I didn't want to go to school. . . . I just wanted to work and make some money."

Such instances of young children wanting to go to work despite parental objections occur too frequently to be aberrations. Louise Rigsbee Jones, who was born in 1897 and grew up in the Bynum mill village in North Carolina, liked school, but when she was fourteen or fifteen she wanted to quit and go to work. "I wanted to go to work in the mill," she recalled. "I was old enough to work." But she was also the youngest child, and her parents insisted she stay in school. "I just begged my mama to let me quit school and go to work down here." Her mother refused, however, and not until Louise was eighteen or nineteen was she able to go to work in the mill.

Children who lived in the mill villages learned mill work for a variety of purposes, and some of them worked without ever being formally employed. Lee A. Workman was too young for mill employment during the two years his family worked in a North Carolina mill during World War I, but he learned mill work anyway and earned his spending money by filling in for friends. "I'd go in of a night and run the twisters, do twister work while my friends went to the moving picture show," he explained. "They'd say, 'Lee, what about running my frames tonight while we go to the show?' And he'd give me fifty cents. And I kept on working till I bought me an eleven-dollar bicycle."

One attraction of mill work was that it allowed children to quit school. "I'd go in there and mess around with them, they'd spinnin'," Alice P. Evitt said of the mill in Charlotte where her mother and older sisters worked early in the twentieth century. When she was no more than seven or eight years old, Alice had begun visiting the mill and learning her sisters' work. "I liked to put up the ends and spin a little bit, so when I got twelve years old, I wanted to quit school," Mrs. Evitt remembered. "My daddy didn't want me to quit, and he said, 'Well, if you quit school, you've got to go to work.' So I quit and went to work." Her workday lasted from 6:00 A.M. to 6:00 P.M. with forty-five minutes for lunch. "But I loved it," she said, "I enjoyed it."

Besides bringing release from school, mill work offered children and youths unlimited opportunity for social intercourse and carried with it a sense of accomplishment and responsibility. Moreover, village life revolved around mill work, and not to work was to be outside the center of things. For youths with few social alternatives, that was unattractive.

Also making mill work tolerable was its alternating periods of busyness and inactivity, which permitted rest and socializing. This pattern was especially pronounced in the early years and smaller mills, and in the jobs assigned to children. Doffing required perhaps twenty to forty minutes of each hour, and there were regular, extended periods in which doffers sat about or went outside and played. "We didn't do nothing," Everette Burchell said, describing his work as a doffer in the second decade of the twentieth century. "We used to catch up with the work and then we'd play till time to go back to doffing," Betty McCoy recalled of her work at Louise Mills in Charlotte, where she began doffing in 1914 at twelve. "I don't believe I realized I was working because all the rest of the children were working and I would a lot rather been in the mill than to stayed out because I'd been so lonesome."

Spinners, too, had time to rest. As long as their bobbins were "up" and no threads broken, they had nothing to do but check their sides periodically. "I don't think I ever got tired," Nannie Pharis said of her work as a spinner, which she began when she was nine years old just after the turn of the century. "If you caught up and didn't have nothing to do you could sit down a few minutes and watch your work." During these breaks, "We'd talk to one another. Maybe one in the next alley to me. They wasn't very strict. They looked after us, I think, very well. . . . I worked hard but I enjoyed every minute of it." Jessie Lee Carter, who began spinning in 1913 at twelve, had even less difficulty at work. "Oh, we didn't have to work hard then," she remembered. "I've set [down] half an hour at the time before I'd go up and down my alley, and then maybe wouldn't find just two or three threads down. It run so good then. I have left the mill—they had a Brandon Company Store. . . . I have left my sides and went up there to that store and played all the way up there and all the way back, for people that wanted coca colas." She commented: "They's just five cents a bottle then. And I'd bring back ten, five in each arm like this, in a paper sack. The help in the mill'd send me after it. I have went down my alley when I come back and I wouldn't have a thread down."

Other jobs were equally light and irregular. Lora League Wright, who went to work at twelve as a spooler at Poe Mills, recalled her work schedule this way: "When we would, what they would call catch up, we'd spool all the yarn that was there and then we would wait. And sometimes it'd be a half an hour and sometimes a hour 'till they doffed the yarn off of the spinning frame and brought it back to the spooler room you see. So we had time to rest, but we had to work eleven hours to start with."

What is surprising in these accounts is the positive attitudes toward the jobs themselves. When Lottie Walter was eleven years old, in 1903, she began spinning in a Concord, North Carolina, mill, and thirty-five years later was still there enjoying the work. "Why it's more like home than this," she said, comparing the mill and her residence. "Many a night I would rather have just stayed there all night than to come home." Miss Walter's younger sister Belle had followed her into the same mill when only nine years old. "I cried to go because Lottie was working and I wanted to do everything she done," Belle Walter said, explaining how and why she went to work so young. "Most of the time I stayed in the mill ten hours a day, but I didn't work steadily all the time. I used to play with the other children in the mill; then sometimes I would get mad about something and I'd get my little old bonnet and march home. The overseer would go to Papa [who also worked in the mill] laughing and say, 'Well, tell her to come back to work when she's over being mad.' And I would. Maybe somedays I would tell Mama I wanted to stay home to play, and she would let me."

Emma Clark Williams first went to work after school hours in a Carrboro hosiery mill about 1905. "I went in when I was six years old, going on, you know, and turning stockings and just pretending to work, I think," Mrs. Williams recalled. Stockings were sewn with their seams on the outside, and the work she referred to consisted of turning finished stockings inside out. For every hundred dozen they turned, Emma and the other children earned ten cents. "All of us used to do it together," Mrs. Williams recollected. "We had more fun." Speaking more generally, she added: "The people here were very good to their children. They never exploited them or anything like that. Didn't pay them much, but they didn't do much. It was real fun. . . . I loved to work in the mill. I loved the odor, and I liked the activities, I guess." She said that she was never pressed to work harder.

One explanation for these positive reactions was the family system of mill employment. Most workers, and probably a large majority of children and youths, went to the mills with other members of their family. No doubt that made the work easier to accommodate to, just as it preconditioned young folk to view mill work in a positive way. Mill children grew up expecting to contribute to family income in due course, and going to work carried with it assurances that they were fulfilling an obligation they respected. This explains the uncommon pride with which so many mill workers remembered their wages and their first payday. "I remember the first check I drawed was for forty cents," Ollie Farrington said of her first job at age nine, about 1905. "I was so proud of it I rushed home as fast as I could and gave it to Papa. At nine years old I gave him my check," Miss Farrington remarked in 1938, "and at forty-two I still bring my check to him."

It was even commonplace for two or more family members to work in the same room at the same task. Occasionally the number of relatives was so large that mill work was virtually a family activity. This was the situation at Brandon Mill in Greenville when Jessie Lee Carter went to work in 1913. Young Jessie's father and six of her siblings were already at work in the mill, as were a number of other relatives. Her uncle Bob Mace, the boss spinner, recruited her for the job. "When I got twelve years old," Mrs. Carter recalled, "my uncle come to my daddy, and [asked if] daddy'd let me quit school and go to work. And he did." Her work day was 6:00 A.M. to 6:00 P.M. with half an hour for lunch and half the day off on Saturday, but Jessie took readily to the job. "Oh, I enjoyed working," she recalled. "I'd rather work than eat when I was hungry. It took me, I guess several weeks to really spin good. My oldest sister was a spinner and she run eight sides. I went from one side to two and on up until I got to eight."

Certainly, one of the things that helped Jessie along was the presence of so many relatives. Not only did one of her sisters teach her to spin, but the entire spinning room was a gathering of kinfolk. "All running in the mill in the spinning room, in two sections, wasn't anything that worked on it but kin people," Mrs. Carter recalled. "All of us was aunts and uncles and cousins. So we all was kin-folk that worked up there. 'Til they married off." Also, "I had two brothers worked in the card room. My daddy worked in the card room. And I had one sister to work in the card room. And I had three sisters working in the spinning. Four with me when I went to work."

Mrs. Carter's memories of her early years in the mill were positive. "I'd rather work than go to school," she recalled. "I never did learn to read and write. But I loved to work. Yes, I did. I really enjoyed it. I had an aunt that was young like I was and me and her, we chummed together. And so we worked close together. Her sister had married my Uncle Bob, the section hand, and he never said anything to us. He let us play all we want to. I was all right. He didn't bother us. He was a mighty good section hand." His effectiveness was of course helped by his kinship with so many of his workers. "He'd get out and brag about it," Mrs. Carter recalled. "He'd run his work where all his people was kin-people. He could boss if he wanted to, but he didn't want to because he was a good man. He'd tell you—of course everybody then, they did their work. They didn't have to be told to do it. They enjoyed doing it."[26]

26. For a list of 64 members of one extended family who worked between 1879 and 1945 at one South Carolina mill, see File 333, Graniteville Manufacturing Company Papers, University of South Carolina at Aiken Library. The individuals were descendants of 6 folk who entered the mill in 1879. Dora Clark of Warrenville, S.C., who compiled the list, added this notation: "This is not near all."

5

HOURS AND DAYS

Time softens memories of distant experience, and the recollections herein are mostly memories of elderly folk recalling their childhood and youth. Yet the testimony is important as well as impressive. Its common themes, positive tone, and humanizing dimensions are fresh reminders that the history of mill folk is full of the singular and unexpected. Moreover, contemporary testimony was sometimes equally positive. In 1883, for example, Eliza Jackson Barden, a twenty-two-year-old weaver at Eagle and Phenix Mills, told congressional investigators she got along at her work "splendidly." Similarly, Addie Priscilla Jones, also a weaver at Eagle and Phenix, answered "I like it very much" when questioned about her job, and "I do" when asked if she felt "rather attached to the mill."[1]

Mill folk, then, could be as involved in their work as other people; and seen as one of multiple responses to their circumstance, that fact is essential to understanding their experience. Their day began early but no earlier than on the farm, about five or six o'clock, depending on the season, when the mill bell (or whistle) woke them up. During the next hour, housewives (or housekeepers), who were gen-

1. *Senate Documents,* 48th Cong., 1st Sess., No. 91, pp. 598–600.

erally not mill workers, prepared breakfast and saw that the workers in their households were up, dressed, and fed when a second bell beckoned them to the mill. It rang only a few minutes before work time, for all workers lived within a short walk of the mill. They were not clock watchers, or had not been when they arrived from the farm, and they depended on the bell to regulate time for them. Mill officials used that habit to manipulate their hours, but that is only one reason published schedules are imperfect guides to working time.

Officially, in the early years, work began about 6:00 A.M. or daylight, whichever came first, and continued until 6:00 P.M. or twilight, whichever came last. This long day was interrupted once, by "dinner time," as the lunch break was always called, generally half or three-quarters of an hour, but sometimes an hour or longer. On Saturdays the day was usually shorter by two or three hours or sometimes more, so work weeks averaged sixty-six to seventy-two hours. Over the years this total fell, and by 1910 the scheduled week was typically sixty to sixty-four hours.[2] The reduction generally resulted in earlier closings, especially on Saturdays.

Within these totals was some variation. "We work eleven hours, or a little over eleven hours, a day [on average]," A. S. Matheson of Eagle and Phenix Mills told a congressional committee in 1883. "We do not light up at nights but very little. We work longer in the summer than in the winter, but taking the summer and the winter together, we may average a little over eleven hours for the year." This schedule was due in part to cost. Working only during daylight saved the expense of "lighting up," and resulted in better work as well. "The lights are not strong enough to distinguish the threads in the colored work," Matheson said of his mill, "and when we work with that light, when day-light comes, it takes as much time to straighten out the warp as was saved by working at night." A few years later, in 1889, Eagle and Phenix Mills was operating ten hours a day in midwinter and eleven and a half hours the rest of the year. The shorter winter hours, an official explained, enabled "female operatives, who in many instances live a considerable distance from the mill, [to] go home at night before it is too dark."[3]

Yet many mills did "light up" in the winter, their workdays beginning before daylight and ending after dark. "Stoped work by lamp light March 5th 1878 friday night," Henderson Monroe Fowler recorded in his diary at

2. In 1908 the scheduled week in southern mills averaged between 60 hours in Virginia and 64 in Georgia (*Senate Documents*, 61st Cong., 2nd Sess., No. 645, Vol. 1, p. 261).

3. *Senate Documents*, 48th Cong., 1st Sess., No. 91, pp. 537–38; Atlanta *Constitution*, August 7, 1889.

Alamance Mill as the days grew longer. "Lit lamps Monday night Oct 14th 1878," he added as they shortened in the fall.[4]

A minority of mills ran night and day. For some this was a matter of policy, for others a periodic response to good times or special orders. Atlanta Cotton Mill was one of the former. There in 1881 the shifts changed at 6:30 A.M. and 6:30 P.M. with forty-five minute dinner breaks at noon and midnight. The machinery ran on as the shifts changed, incoming workers taking over directly from those departing.[5]

It was difficult to secure workers for the night shift, and mills employed various strategies to make that shift more attractive. Some divided the twenty-four hours unevenly, with the night shift working less than the day shift for the same pay, while others worked the night shift only five nights a week but paid workers for six. At Cleveland Cotton Mills in 1901, the day shift worked twelve hours and the night shift ten, and the machinery shut down in the interval. Other mills offered substantial pay differentials to night workers. At one such mill in South Carolina, visited by the English traveler T. M. Young in 1902, spinners received ten cents per side during the day and twelve and a half at night while warpers earned eighty-five cents per day and a dollar per night.[6]

Schedules were not inflexible. Atlanta Cotton Mill ran sixty-six hours a week at the turn of the century, but instead of eleven hours a day for six days, it operated eleven and a half hours on weekdays (6:00 A.M. to 6:00 P.M., with thirty minutes for dinner) and stopped at 3:00 P.M. on Saturdays. The workers preferred the long weekdays and short lunch breaks, an official told the Industrial Commission, because they wanted the early closing on Saturday. At least occasionally, workers influenced their work time in other ways. Sometime during the 1880s, Rufus B. Bullock reduced the workday in the Atlanta mill he managed from twelve hours to eleven in a successful effort to improve the quality of work. "We got better results and a more finished product in 11 hours than we used to get in 12," he said of the experience. "When an employee is very fatigued, it makes bad work, as to spinning and weaving especially." When Augusta Mill reduced its workday from twelve to eleven hours at about the same time, the change was made only after the workers agreed to produce as much in the shorter day as they

4. Henderson Monroe Fowler Diary and Account Books, Vol. IV, in Southern Historical Collection, Louis R. Wilson Library, University of North Carolina at Chapel Hill.
5. Atlanta *Constitution*, June 16, 1881.
6. North Carolina Bureau of Labor Statistics, *Annual Report, 1901*, 216, hereinafter cited as NC *Labor Report* by year; T. M. Young, *The American Cotton Industry* (London, 1902), 73.

had in the longer. "When the Augusta factory reduced the hours," explained Otis G. Lynch, who had been an overseer there at the time, "we beat the old [production] record with the same machinery" immediately. "It was a part of the agreement," he continued, "that if we kept the product up to the same standard as before, we should have the reduced hours, and we did keep it up to the standard and above from the first." Among the reasons for the success were "increased activity on the part of the operatives and more promptitude."[7]

How frequently such reductions occurred is unknown, but they all had favorable results. J. F. Hanson, president of Bibb Manufacturing Company in the 1880s, voluntarily reduced the work week in his mill from seventy-two to sixty-five hours with, by his own account, no loss of product. As a result Hanson became an advocate of the ten-hour day. In 1889, while the Georgia legislature debated a proposal to limit mill hours, an unnamed mill owner, probably Hanson, wrote a legislative committee of his own experience with reduced hours. "We are getting better production in 10 hours and 50 minutes," he said, "than when we ran 12 hours."[8]

A number of mills across the South made similar reductions with a variety of motives. In 1886, for example, Pilot Mills in Raleigh, North Carolina, and the several Holt mills in nearby Alamance County reduced the work week from seventy to sixty-six hours, perhaps as a way of attracting laborers. "We gave our help this reduction of hours," a spokesman said, "without their asking or demanding it," but no doubt with happy consequence. "L. S. Holt adopted the 11 hour System Monday Sept 6, 1886" is the laconic way one of Holt's overseers recorded the event in his diary.[9]

Even before the turn of the century, legislation limiting the hours of work began to have a modest impact. The first law on the subject in the three states under examination became effective in Georgia in 1890, but like all such laws in the New South, it set maximum hours high (eleven per day, sixty-six per week). Moreover, it permitted mills to extend even these hours to make up lost time, and contained no special provisions for enforcement. Three years later South Carolina implemented a similar law, and in 1903 North Carolina followed suit.

7. *House Documents,* 57th Cong., 1st Sess., No. 184, Vol. 7, pp. 530, 521; *Senate Documents,* 48th Cong., 1st Sess., No. 91, p. 751.

8. Mercer G. Evans, "The History of the Organized Labor Movement in Georgia" (Ph.D. dissertation, University of Chicago, 1929), 410; *Senate Documents,* 61st Cong., 2nd Sess., No. 645, Vol. 1, p. 170.

9. Raleigh *News and Observer,* December 16, 1900; Henderson Monroe Fowler Diary.

The South Carolina statute reduced the work week at Newberry Mills by three and a half hours, and there were no doubt many such examples across the state. More importantly, when the North Carolina law was enacted, mills in that state were running up to seventy-five hours a week and the average of all mills was perhaps sixty-nine hours. In such places, the reduction to sixty-six hours must have seemed like meaningful relief. In subsequent years, the legislatures of all three states moved toward the sixty-hour week, and the possibility of such legislation often prompted mills to reduce their hours in an effort to avoid restrictive legislation. Thus, in April, 1907, a group of mills in Charlotte announced plans to reduce work hours from sixty-six to sixty over the ensuing eight months. At the time of the group's announcement, Erwin mill folk in Durham were already working sixty-two or sixty-three hours, and some of the mills owned by the Holt and Cone interests in the state had adopted a sixty-hour schedule.[10]

Only South Carolina had a law making a sixty-hour week the legal norm before 1911. In 1909 the Census Bureau reported that all workers in South Carolina were in mills that, officially at least, ran sixty hours, compared to 42 percent in Georgia and 16 percent in North Carolina (including negligible numbers in each state in mills running less than sixty hours). Unfortunately, the remaining workers in the last two states were lumped into a single category of sixty to seventy-two hours, which is too extended to be helpful.[11]

"FOR SEVERAL YEARS WE HAVE LOST BETWEEN 25 AND 30 DAYS ON ACCOUNT OF ONE THING AND ANOTHER."

Actual working time had no necessary relationship to these totals, however. The chief reason for that anomaly was the irregularity of mill operations. Throughout the New South era, mills were "down" for a few minutes or hours or one or two days at a time; or "standing" for days, weeks, or even months at a time; or on "short" time, running two or three days a week or every other day or week; or on "slack" time, with only part of the machinery operating. Some of the lost time was made up by overtime, often on the day

10. Lawrence B. Graves, "The Beginning of the Cotton Textile Industry in Newberry County" (M.A. thesis, University of South Carolina, 1947), 59; Holland Thompson, *From the Cotton Field to the Cotton Mill: A Study of the Industrial Transition in North Carolina* (New York, 1906), 133; Atlanta *Constitution*, April 7, 1907.
11. The laws of the three states on hours and related matters are printed in U.S. Commissioner of Labor, *Twenty-Second Annual Report, 1907*, 286–99, 960–71, and 1224–36. The information on hours in 1909 is from *Thirteenth Census, 1910: Manufactures*, 218, 902, 1144.

it was lost; and slack periods might be followed by days or weeks of overtime or even, if things looked suddenly bright, addition of a night shift. Also, to a surprising degree, mill operations were tied to the rhythms of the cotton crop, so that work was unevenly distributed over the course of the year.

There were other factors at work as well. Mechanical breakdowns plagued the mills; natural phenomena disrupted power supplies; economic conditions produced cycles of boom and bust; even strikes and holidays sometimes occasioned meaningful stoppages. Collectively, these things produced major reductions in the time mill folk actually worked, so much so that "down" time was probably a larger concern to folk than overwork itself.

One major cause of shutdowns was acts of nature, a consequence of the fact that most mills, especially those built before 1900, were powered by water and for that reason located along waterfalls or wherever rivers could be dammed or their water flows otherwise exploited.[12] This explains the concentration of mills in places like Columbus, Augusta, and Columbia, all of which were on the fall line; and in the piedmont and upcountry of the Carolinas, where narrow, rapid rivers provided easily developed power sites.

This pattern enabled the mills to utilize a cheap and generally reliable power source, but it had important disadvantages. Many of the rivers were really creeks whose water flow varied enough from time to time to interfere with mill operations. In winter, the bodies of water sometimes froze; in spring, they often flooded; in late summer, drought reduced them to a trickle. Dams eased the problems somewhat, and most mills eventually installed steam generators, but neither solution was completely effective. Even electricity was no panacea, for that too was unreliable at times, especially at first. "These constant interruptions in power have been most annoying and irritating," Lewis W. Parker of Monaghan Mills in Greenville, South Carolina, complained in 1914 after his mill switched to electric power. "We did not have these interruptions when we drove the mill by steam."[13]

The problem could be considerable. In the four years between March 1, 1878, and February 28, 1882, Graniteville Mill was closed a total of forty-five days, almost two weeks a year, "by reason of protracted droughts and low water," to use the words of President Hamilton H. Hickman, "and

12. Of 64 cotton factories reported on in North Carolina in 1883, all but 12 were powered by water (*Manufacturers' Record*, November 10, 1883, p. 368).
13. Greenville *Daily News*, July 17, 1914.

during much of the time when it was run, the speed was too slow to develop its full capacity." In 1879, the worst of these years, the stoppage totaled seventeen days, all between May and August, not including the even larger number of days the mill ran below capacity because water flow was insufficient to generate full power. The Schencks had similar problems at Cleveland Cotton Mills a decade later. "For several years," John F. Schenck wrote in the summer of 1893, "we have lost between 25 and 30 days [each year] on account of one thing and another interfering with our running by water."[14]

These problems appeared even in Augusta, where a canal regulated the flow of water from the Savannah River and distributed energy among several mills, and at Columbus, where the falls of the Chattahoochee River created an almost ideal source of natural power. In the winter of 1886, the Chattahoochee partially froze and stopped the Columbus mills for a while. President W. H. Young of Eagle and Phenix Mills was astonished by "the extraordinary spectacle of large blocks of ice floating in the river . . . obstructing the flume of one mill and causing its stoppage for nearly a day." In the following spring, a "great freshet" on the same river submerged several buildings at Young's mills under several feet of water. Altogether in 1886, Eagle and Phenix Mills lost fourteen days from high water, and some of its departments lost much more time. The woolen mill, for example, was idle six and a half weeks.[15]

As this incident suggests, mills built in river bottoms were subject to periodic floodings. Indeed, Eagle and Phenix Mills routinely removed machinery from exposed floors whenever flooding threatened. "The belting will be placed back in the wheel pits tomorrow," an official of these mills announced as floodwaters receded in 1900, "and the machinery removed from the weaver room placed in position again." Meanwhile, other mills experienced the same floods. "All the mills were forced to close down because of the high water," read a dispatch from Augusta on the same day the waters were receding in Columbus, "and will suffer the loss resulting from idleness for several days."[16]

This problem persisted throughout the New South era, though efforts to

14. Annual Reports of President H. H. Hickman, 1882, 1879, in Graniteville Manufacturing Company Papers, University of South Carolina at Aiken Library; John F. Schenck to J. E. Reynolds, August 23, 1893, in H. F. Schenck Papers, Manuscript Department, Duke University Library, Durham, North Carolina.
15. The annual report of President Young is summarized in Columbus *Daily Enquirer-Sun*, February 3, 1887.
16. Atlanta *Constitution*, February 15, 1900.

combat it were partially effective. "For the first time in many years," a newspaper reported in 1904, "the mills at the lower falls of the Chattahoochee river at [Columbus] have not lost a single day from high water this spring. Usually the mills lose a few days each February or March, due to a booming river."[17]

More isolated mills had the same problem. "Rain began falling Sunday 2 ocl[ock] AM," Henderson Fowler wrote in his diary at Alamance Mill, "& by 2 PM the water was 6 inc[hes] in the weave room Jan 12 1879[.] Factory Standing until Tues at 12 oclock." The incident was not unique. "Biggest freshet ever here," Fowler wrote on another occasion, "[water] over the looms heavy damage to looms & to flower & corne[.] [T]ook the bridge and bell fences old dy[e] hous[e] from of[f] the dam . . . April 23, 1883." For several days the mill was idle. "Started Cards & Cap frames friday Apr 27th," Fowler continued. "Weave room Standing yet in bad order for running[.] May the first looms doing very well." Three years later, he recorded a similar incident. "Hardest raine ever fell the first day of July 1886[.] [W]ater in the factory 2 ft deep & lots of mud."[18]

Even efforts to control these problems sometimes caused difficulties of their own. The mills constructed dams to regulate the flow of water, and the dams sometimes gave way, perhaps because of poor construction. That happened in 1901, for example, to the dam on the Seneca River supplying power to the Orr and Anderson mills in South Carolina. Orr Mills had to close down while the dam was reconstructed, but Anderson Mills, which had emergency generators, continued running. The generators, however, produced only part of the power necessary to run the mill at capacity, so the superintendent divided the work force into day and night shifts and ran at half capacity twenty-four hours a day. The great Charleston earthquake of 1886, in another instance, destroyed the dam that powered the mill at Langley, closing the mill for five months.[19]

Mills occasionally experienced overwhelming disasters. The most spectacular occurred in 1903 and bore most heavily on a group of mills in Georgia and South Carolina originally owned by John H. Montgomery, who had been killed in a mill accident a few weeks earlier. Not long after work began on the morning of June 1, a tornado "burst with the fury of the fiends of hell" on Gainesville Cotton Mill, blowing away 2 stories of the mill and

17. *Ibid.*, April 10, 1904.
18. Henderson Monroe Fowler Diary.
19. Augusta *Chronicle*, December 31, 1901, September 3, 1886; Atlanta *Constitution*, February 1, 1887.

200 nearby buildings, most of them houses in the mill village; and then bounced over to the village of Pacolet Mill No. 4, where it destroyed 40 homes and damaged as many others. When the storm was over, some 70 people were dead or dying, 200 were injured, many of them seriously, and several hundred were left homeless, their household goods and personal possessions gone. Most of the victims were mill folk.[20]

Before the debris from this disaster was cleaned away, another group of Montgomery's mills, near Spartanburg, South Carolina, bore the brunt of an even greater calamity. On June 6, after several days of torrential rains, waters of the Pacolet and Tyger rivers burst forth, some forty feet above normal, in a sudden tide of destructive fury. "The operatives had gathered to their work before the waters rose," a reporter wrote of the scene. "They suspected nothing until the water reached the first floor, then hurried exits were made and the people crowded on a hill which fortunately was convenient. From that point they saw [Pacolet] Mill No. 1 crumble and then collapse with a mighty crash," and continued to watch as Mill No. 2 "became a total wreck" and the lower floors of No. 3 were inundated, though that mill remained standing.[21] Not far away, the Converse and Clifton mills, at Clifton, were also destroyed, and before the waters subsided, six to eight other mills sustained major damage. At Greer, water rose six feet inside Arlington Mill, and at Newry Mill near Calhoun it reached the second floor.

The operatives and their villages were also devastated. Together the mills that were destroyed or heavily damaged employed six thousand people, about sixty of whom died in the disaster; most of the rest were uprooted at least temporarily. Their misfortune was eased, however, by the fact that the affected mills were part of two of the largest holdings in the South. The companies supplied emergency food and other assistance, and immediately paid the workers the back wages they had coming. More importantly, they announced plans to rebuild the mills, and for that purpose wanted to hold onto the workers. They employed many of the men and grown boys to clean away debris and help construct new mills and villages, and arranged for other operatives to work in other mills. Many employees of the demolished Gainesville Mill went to work at Pacolet No. 4, which escaped damage,

20. Montgomery had died in an accident at Pacolet Mill No. 4 (Atlanta *Constitution*, November 1, 1902). Exact totals of deaths and injuries and the amount of property destruction from the tornado are not clear from newspaper accounts. See Atlanta *Constitution*, June 2–6, 1903, for a running account of the disaster.
21. Atlanta *Constitution*, June 7, 1903. For accounts of the disaster, see *ibid.*, June 7–10, 1903; and *Manufacturers' Record*, June 11, 1903, pp. 415, 421, and June 18, 1903, pp. 433, 438.

while many of those in the Carolina mills were sent to other factories owned by the Pacolet and Clifton companies. The undamaged mills began night shifts where possible, or divided workers into groups and spread the work among them.

For the remaining operatives, the companies made other arrangements. They sometimes farmed out orders to mills they did not own, arranged for those mills to employ displaced workers, and helped workers relocate if they agreed to return when the destroyed mills reopened. Finally, employees for whom no work could be found but who agreed to return to work when the mills reopened were furnished rent-free housing, credit at company stores, and half pay as long as they were idle.

Despite these enticements, some operatives left the affected mills. When the undamaged Pacolet Mill No. 4 reopened, three days after the tornado, some of its operatives refused to return to work. "Some few of the younger persons who have been working in the mill up to the time of the storm," read a newspaper report on the reopening, "walked out yesterday because their nervous condition filled them with fear. Some few idlers outside had filled their minds with the idea that the mill was unsafe." J. A. Young, superintendent of the mill, was understandably concerned. "In a few days normal conditions will assert themselves among the former employed who survived the storm and as many as can be induced to go to work immediately will be urged to do so," Young told a reporter. "Once employed again, their minds will be relieved of the fearful picture which has been constantly before them since the fateful disaster."[22] Whether things went as Young expected is unknown, but according to one report, sixty families left Gainesville after the tornado and went to work in Atlanta.[23]

"COTTON IS SOMEWHAT SCARCE AND SO HIGH."

Economic factors were another cause of lost time. The national economy was unstable during much of the New South era, and the textile industry was vulnerable to destabilizing forces of its own. The industry grew more rapidly than the market for its products, and prices of those products were

22. Atlanta *Constitution*, June 6, 1903.
23. *Ibid.*, August 9, 1903. One other form of disaster, fire, must be noted. In annual surveys of southern mills, *Manufacturers' Record* reported three mills burned in the year ending August 31, 1896, and four in the following year (*Manufacturers' Record*, September 11, 1896, pp. 108–109, September 10, 1897, p. 93). If these figures are representative, perhaps a few hundred workers were burned out of their jobs each year.

low and inflexible. More importantly, these prices did not respond to changes in cotton prices, which fluctuated meaningfully from year to year and sometimes markedly from season to season. This disparate relationship was significant because the cost of cotton was the largest item of operating expense for every mill, and a major influence on profits. In the year ending February 20, 1886, for example, Enterprise Mill in Augusta spent $292,171.36 on cotton and $86,922.08 on wages, a ratio of more than three to one; and in 1904 Eagle and Phenix Mills spent $957,748 on cotton and $511,501 on wages, which was 30 percent and 56 percent, respectively, of total operating costs. Overall, in the mills of the three states, wages accounted for just under 20 percent of the expenses of operation in 1909, while materials, largely cotton, accounted for more than 70 percent.[24]

The price of cotton was therefore of great concern to mill owners, and acquiring adequate supplies of cotton at favorable prices was one of their chief interests. A new crop came on the market each September, and since most farmers were obliged to sell immediately, from then until mid-December, when the harvest ended, the price dropped and remained low. This was of course the time for mills to buy, but just when and how much were questions not easily answered. The key to success was correctly predicting the market—waiting until the price hit bottom—for at six, eight, or ten cents a pound, a change of one or even half a cent represented a significant change in operating expense. To wait for price declines, however, was risky. Price levels were partly a matter of supply, which directly depended on the size of the crop, and partly also of local circumstance. Wherever mills were concentrated, they consumed more cotton than local farmers produced, which created local shortages and encouraged competitive bidding, both of which drove up the price. To buy from distant dealers was to face other costs, including those of transportation and of dealers' profits.

It was just as difficult to decide how much cotton to buy. The amount consumed in individual mills varied from year to year, sometimes greatly, according to economic conditions, special orders, the time machinery was "down," and even such unpredictable factors as short-term influences on overseas markets. The date at which next year's crop would be on the market was also important, for bad weather often delayed planting or maturation for two or three weeks, and during the delay cotton was always scarce and high priced. A mill that bought more cotton than it needed incurred

24. Augusta *Chronicle*, March 11, 1886; Atlanta *Constitution*, January 6, 1905; *Thirteenth Census, 1910: Manufactures*, 46.

extra capital and storage costs; one caught short with orders to fill had to enter the market in spring or summer, when prices were high and rising. Contracts signed in the fall when prices were low might have to be filled with cotton bought in the summer when they were high.

These calculations determined the frequency with which mills closed or went on extended periods of slack time, especially during summer, because they had little or no cotton and were unwilling to buy at current prices. So frequently did this occur that some mills seem to have had regular vacations. "Local cotton mills . . . will close down on the evening of July 31 and will remain closed until Monday August 10," a Greenville newspaper reported in 1914. "This is the usual summer vacation when the machinery is rested and gone over by machinists and when the operatives are given a vacation." Some people also spoke of a mill "season," beginning in the fall and continuing into the spring, during which the new crop brought lower prices and plenty of cotton, and mills ran full time until scarcities appeared again. "Until the new crop comes in we will run only five days in the week," the superintendent of Charleston Cotton Mill announced at the beginning of August, 1884. "The evident backwardness [that is, lateness] of the crop and the difficulty of buying the grades we need at reasonable prices forces us to spin out our supply of cotton." When the supply ran out, the mill would close.[25]

As the number of mills increased, so did the problem of cotton supply. In early August, 1889, the Southern Plaid Manufacturers Association urged its members to curtail "both spinning and weaving, [for] thirty days between now and the new crop time." This was necessary "in order to avoid buying cotton at the present high prices," the association announced. "No more cotton will be bought until the new crop is marketed."[26]

Apparently such pronouncements were intended in part to influence the price of cotton, but if so, they were ineffective. The following spring prices rose "so rapidly" and unexpectedly that many mills found themselves "without a sufficient supply of cotton . . . and the consequence is that they will have to close their factories." Surveying the situation in Georgia, the Atlanta *Constitution* spoke of the "woeful effect" shutdowns would have on "many operatives," who would find themselves "without employment for the greater portion of the year"; but the newspaper expressed the belief that the mills had little choice. "Several prominent mills in the state have already

25. Greenville *Daily News,* July 15, 1914; *Manufacturers' Record,* August 2, 1884, p. 717.
26. Atlanta *Constitution,* August 7, 1889.

been forced to shut down," the *Constitution* reported, "and others will follow suit very soon."[27]

During the long depression of the 1890s, the source of the problem shifted from high cotton prices to glutted markets for finished goods, but the result was much the same. Across the South, mills closed for varying periods. Lanneau Cotton Mill in Greenville closed for the month of August, 1893, "on account of the general condition of business," while Camperdown Mill, also in Greenville, began a three-day week. The knitting mill at Scotland Neck, North Carolina, stopped entirely for six weeks the following winter, while Bibb Manufacturing Company in Macon operated for "several months" on half-time. The spinning department at Eagle and Phenix Mills also ran half-time because of the lack of markets for finished goods.[28]

During the depression, trade associations worked to limit production and spread available work among the various mills. They seem to have had little success, but their effort revealed much about the irregular nature of mill operations. Thus, in the summer of 1896, delegates to a convention of the Southern Textile Manufacturers Association resolved that the entire industry should close down for sixty days. Such a shutdown, however, "would work a serious hardship on the workmen employed by the mills," so the delegates urged instead that all mills "curtail their production 50 percent during the next ninety days." In response to this plea, 215 mills, representing about four-fifths of the spindles in the South, reportedly agreed to an average curtailment of 38.1 percent during July, August, and September. "A number of mills in each state report that they will close down entirely for different periods," read a newspaper survey of the situation, "some until August 1st, others for 60 days, and a few will remain idle until October 1st. . . . A majority of the mills will adopt the plan of running a portion of every week, as this method is generally preferred by the operatives." Only a few mills would continue to run full time.[29]

When the depression ended, the problem reverted to fluctuating cotton prices. "I have been in this business a good many years," one mill official said in the late summer of 1900, after the price had risen from eight to nine cents and promised to go even higher, "but I do not recall where conditions were more perplexing for the cotton manufacturers." The 1900 crop was

27. *Ibid.*, May 24, 1890.
28. *Manufacturers' Record*, August 4, 1893, p. 8, August 18, 1893, p. 40, and February 16, 1894.
29. Atlanta *Constitution*, June 30, 1896, July 10, 1896.

late reaching the market, and when prices reached ten cents in early September, many mills consumed whatever cotton they had and closed down. The Sibley, King, and Augusta mills in Augusta closed for two or three weeks, for example, and the mill at Langley, South Carolina, operated at half-time for about a month. Together, these mills employed more than three thousand operatives.[30]

These recurring problems were complicated by events in faraway places. Many of the mills that closed down in the late summer of 1900 made cheap, coarse goods, the principal markets for which were overseas, especially in China, where the Boxer Rebellion and its aftermath disrupted trade and threatened to eliminate the market for Western goods altogether. "No class of people read the news from China with more anxiety than the cotton mill men," one mill owner said in July, as unsold goods piled up. "This glut is attributable to three causes," a newspaperman declared. "A great deal of the product of the American mills, especially those of the south, is sold in India, China, and South Africa. The famine in the first and the wars in the other two [the Boxer Rebellion and the Boer War] have practically put a stop to trade."[31]

The consequences were felt across the South. By mid-September many mills in South Carolina were on a part-time schedule, among them the largest manufactories in the state and all of those "which find their principal market in China and the orient." Included were "the three [mills] at Piedmont, the three at Pelzer, the three at Clifton, the two mills of the Anderson company, the Belton mill, the Abbeville, Newberry, Reedy River, Whitney, Pacolet, and Glendale mills and the Orr mills at Anderson."[32]

The price of the coarse goods these mills produced was too low to return a large profit when cotton was high. Yet according to press reports, mills buying cotton on September 19 paid eleven cents a pound, four cents (or 57 percent) more than they paid a year before. Despite sporadic shutdowns, the fundamental problem, which was the capacity of the industry to produce more than it could sell at a profit, persisted. Only a few months after the closedowns just noted, the Southern Cotton Spinners Association was again urging collective action against overproduction. In February, 1901, this organization asked all mills with night shifts to abolish them and those with day shifts to close one day a week for four months beginning March 1.[33]

30. *Ibid.*, September 1, 12, 1900; Augusta *Chronicle*, September 12, 30, October 7, 1900.
31. Raleigh *News and Observer*, July 13, 1900; Augusta *Chronicle*, September 16, 1900.
32. Atlanta *Constitution*, September 16, 20, 1900.
33. *Ibid.*, February 17, 1901.

Mills reacted to such pleas according to their interests, and the problem persisted. When cotton prices rose in the spring of 1903, mills in South Carolina began closing or running on slack time as early as April, five months before the new crop was marketed. "Only a few" mills had enough cotton to operate full time until the new crop came in, a reporter wrote. As for the others, "It is a question of but a few weeks before they will have to buy cotton at the prevailing high price, which is the highest known for two years, or will have to shut down or curtail. The cotton crop in this section is now exhausted and whatever cotton is raised by the mills will have to be brought from a distance." According to this newspaperman, "After August 1, at the furthest, every mill will be out of cotton entirely and the entire crop will be exhausted."[34]

The economics of this situation, which persisted for the remainder of the New South era, were complicated by several factors, all of which had the effect of reducing the work time of operatives.[35] Despite the public lamentations, most mills were highly profitable (though profits might vary widely from year to year), and mill officials decided to run or close down for a time with both eyes on profit ledgers. This was neither surprising nor sinister, and explains some of the creative ways mills handled cotton purchases and operating schedules.

Because of short-term fluctuations in cotton prices, mills sometimes deliberately overbought cotton for speculative purposes and, when the market worked to their advantage, found it more profitable to shut down and sell their cotton than to remain open and manufacture it. During the 1902 crop year, for example, President Tracy I. Hickman of Graniteville Manufacturing Company purchased a large amount of cotton at 10 cents a pound, and while he held it, the price rose from 11.5 cents in May, 1903, to 17.5 cents in January, 1904, with no equivalent change in the price of manufactured goods. The increase was such that Hickman decided to close his mill and sell his cotton—3,500 bales (about 1,750,000 pounds)—on which he realized a profit of several cents a pound. While the mill was idle, he gave the operatives half pay to keep them from moving away, and used the time to install new machinery and overhaul the old. The cotton sale ensured his company's profitability, which was 11 percent on invested capital that year,

34. *Ibid.*, April 26, 1903.
35. In October, 1909, for example, mills in Alamance County, N.C., agreed to go on a four-day week until February, 1910 (New York *Times*, October 31, 1909). Also in 1909, the South Carolina labor commissioner reported that "some few small plants" in his state had been idle all year, while "others" had closed down from two weeks to four months (South Carolina Commissioner of Agriculture, Commerce, and Industries, Labor Division, *Second Annual Report, 1910*, 22, hereinafter cited as SC Labor Division by year).

and payment of the regular 7 percent dividend as well. So in spite of the shutdown, which was longer than Hickman planned because the new crop was late, and payment of half wages to an idle work force, the company had a successful year, even adding to its capital reserves despite the expenditure on new machinery.[36]

A variation of this pattern figured in the closing of the Pacolet mills at Gainesville, Georgia, between January 30 and May 17, 1904. Ostensibly, the closing was due to "the high price of cotton and the low price of goods," but actually other considerations were involved. When it closed, the mill had on hand "thousands of bales of [finished] goods" made from seven-and-a-half- and eight-cent cotton, which it could sell for a profit of three or four cents a pound. But feeling this profit was too little, mill officials held onto the goods and sold their cotton instead. The sale of 3,000 bales (about 1,500,000 pounds) netted a profit of well over $80,000, which enabled the company to pay its regular dividend despite being closed for three and a half months and operating on half-time for a while after reopening. While idle, the workers received half pay and free rent on condition that the head of each family report to the mill once a week and agree to return his "force" to the mill when it reopened. This arrangement enabled the family to put its children in other mills while their half wages continued at Pacolet, and guaranteed Pacolet a work force when it started up again.[37]

"WE WERE SO URGED BY HELP TO GIVE THEM 3 DAYS HOLIDAY WE SHUT DOWN LAST NIGHT."

The mills, then, closed frequently for a variety of reasons. When Eagle and Phenix Mills went into receivership in 1896, work there was interrupted for months. When the main engine at Spartan Mills exploded in 1904, four months passed before a new one was installed. When Sibley Mill in Augusta sustained major fire damage in the summer of 1884, it closed for two months. Alamance Mill was idle "from the last of August 1884 to the 16th of Sept 1884" while workmen "covered the factory with tin." The Cannon mills in North Carolina shut down for a while because of a shortage of coal occasioned by the 1902 coal strike.[38]

36. Annual Report of President Tracy I. Hickman, 1904, in Graniteville Papers; Atlanta *Constitution*, May 22, 1903.
37. Atlanta *Constitution*, January 28, February 4, May 17, 1904.
38. *Ibid.*, June 14, 1896; William W. Thompson, "A Managerial History of a Cotton Textile Firm, Spartan Mills, 1888–1958" (Ph.D. dissertation, University of Alabama, 1960), 72; *Manufacturers' Record*, August 30, 1884, p. 75; Henderson Monroe Fowler Diary; Atlanta *Constitution*, November 22, 1902.

Mills also closed for holidays, religious observances, and funerals. "The Small twin child of W. E. Holt died on the 19th of Apr 1882 & was buried the 22nd . . . Factory Standing," Henderson Fowler wrote of a tragedy in the family of the owners of Alamance Mill. Apparently all mills observed the Christmas holiday, and in some at least the holiday was several days. In 1890 Alamance Mill closed from Thursday, December 25, to Monday, December 29. A year later, the closing was three days, December 24–26, and in 1892, when Christmas fell on Sunday, the mill was idle on December 26 and 27. At Durham Hosiery Mill in 1896, the holiday lasted from Friday, December 25, until Monday, December 28.[39]

At least some mills observed Thanksgiving, Easter Monday, Labor Day, and the Fourth of July, and many closed a day every summer for a picnic at company expense. "We give them all the holidays," President Charles H. Phinizy told a congressional committee of the practice at Augusta Mill in 1883, "and generally in May we stop the whole mill and give them a big picnic." At Eagle and Phenix Mills, however, Christmas Day and a spring picnic were the only holidays. Custom thus varied from mill to mill, but workers expected the convention at a particular mill to be honored. "Factory running on Ester Monday," Fowler wrote on one occasion at Alamance Mills. "Such was never the case before[.] [H]ands all mad & not much good done that day 1879." Apparently, management got the message. "Ester the 10th of April," Fowler recorded in a subsequent year. "Standing on Monday."[40]

Unfortunately, no overall figures for the amount of time lost by mill closings are available. In his annual reports the North Carolina labor commissioner sometimes reported summaries, usually by county, of the average number of days the mills reported operating in the preceding year. The summaries are unweighted and not very useful; but they suggest that the time lost was considerable, though it varied considerably from year to year. In 19 of 27 counties in 1894, the average length of operation was 275 days or less, and in 10 of the counties it was 250 days or less. In 1887 the mills seem to have lost less time, though the information as arranged in the commissioner's report is not very specific.[41]

As to overall losses, it is difficult to know if individual mills were typical.

39. Henderson Monroe Fowler Diary; Time Book, 1890–1901, Vol. XI of Alamance Cotton Mill Records, in Southern Historical Collection, Louis R. Wilson Library, University of North Carolina at Chapel Hill; Time Book, 1896–1898, Vol. I of Durham Hosiery Mill Company Papers, Manuscript Department, Duke University Library, Durham, North Carolina.

40. *Senate Documents*, 48th Cong., 1st Sess., No. 91, pp. 702, 512; Henderson Monroe Fowler Diary.

41. NC *Labor Report* (1894), 52, (1887), 144.

Because of gaps in the sources, it is also difficult to follow the situation at individual mills over long spans of time. From 1890 to 1900, the weaving room at Alamance Mill was idle a total of 495 days, an average of 45 days a year, and the spinning room was idle 458 days, or almost 42 each year. Within these totals, however, were marked variations, caused in this case by the depression of the mid-1890s. From 1895 to 1897, weavers at Alamance lost an average of 73 days each, and spinners 72, from shutdowns; while in the other 8 years of the period, their losses averaged 22 and 16 days, respectively. These figures count only full days the weaving or spinning room was idle, and therefore omit those days on which the rooms closed for part of the time or on which only part of the machinery was operated. Those days were numerous but are impossible to count because of the nature of the records.[42]

At the end of the New South era, the situation at Alamance Mill had not changed. In the 4 years between September 14, 1908, and September 13, 1912, the weaving room lost 42, 78, 50, and 33 workdays respectively—209 days altogether and a yearly average of 52. Again, spinners fared somewhat better, losing 19, 84, 50, and 21 days, a total of 168 days and an annual average of 42. Spinners lost the equivalent of 7 weeks each year and weavers almost 9 weeks.[43]

At Eldorado Cotton Mill in Ansonville, North Carolina, the situation was much the same. There, during the 39 months from June, 1898, through August, 1901, the mill was idle 219 days, or more than five and a half days per month. In 1899 and 1900, the 2 full calendar years covered by the payroll from which this information was derived, the mill was idle 73 and 80 days, respectively, including extended periods in both years.[44]

In a survey of southern mills in 1896, the *Manufacturers' Record* reported that 52 of 386 mills, representing 8.5 percent of the spindles in the section, closed down entirely during August. Twenty-eight additional mills were idle for the entire year, and a "large number" of others stopped for unspecified periods during the twelve months. A year later, 31 of 414 mills, representing about 4 percent of the spindles in the section, closed during August, and 40 other mills were idle the whole year. A dozen years later, 91 mills in the section closed for the whole of August, and "many thousands of [additional] spindles were idle during a considerable part of the season. Some of

42. Time Book, 1890–1901, Vol. XI of Alamance Cotton Mill Records.
43. Time Book, 1901–1912, Vol. XV of Alamance Cotton Mill Records.
44. Eldorado Cotton Mills Time Book, 1898–1903, in William Alexander Smith Papers, Manuscript Department, Duke University Library, Durham, North Carolina.

the mills have part of the time run mainly to retain their help," the *Manu-facturers' Record* reported, "while many shut down altogether for several months at a time."[45]

These overall figures are revealing, but they obscure the variety of actual experience. A glimpse into that variety at one mill is provided by the correspondence of the Schencks in the early 1890s. The twenty-five to thirty days the mills were closed each year during this period because of problems with water power was not the extent of the time the mills lost.[46] In the year ending May 28, 1892, for example, Mill No. 2, the larger of the Schencks's mills, lost a total of twenty-eight workdays because of mechanical problems, including lack of power. For twelve days the water was too high, and that was by far the largest single cause of lost time. In March, 1892, Mill No. 1 "stopped one day for repairs continued from last week's break down," while Mill No. 2 "stopped 1/4 day and ran 3/4 day with exceedingly low speed." The low speed was "caused by a coupling on one of the gate shafts giving away, so that gate couldn't be drawn on one wheel." In early April, "warp production fell off considerably" because "some of our twister hands were out." In May, Mill No. 2 "stopped 1/4 day to sew some large driving belts and others which had become slack because of dampness of weather." A week later the same mill stopped three days, "one because of high water and the other time for sluicing out saw—repairing flood gates and wheel gate, and cleaning up machinery &c." In August a fire stopped half the mill for half a day, and later in the month, another fire caused the loss of several hours. In January, 1893, the stream froze over, idling the mills two days and forcing them to run an unstated number of additional days on partial power. "In fact sometimes we can run only half the spinning," H. F. Schenck wrote of the latter period.

When power was low, more often owing to drought than to freezing or flooding, the Schencks did whatever they could to keep the mill going. They sometimes ran one part of the mill for a while and then another; at other times they ran part of the mill in the day and part at night. "Water is still getting lower and the weather still dryer," John F. Schenck wrote of one such occasion in late August, 1893. "On Monday we put 6 frames on sewing, two on rope—and these are all we are running. We are running just so much of Carding room to keep these going—and we are running openers and Lappers every other night. We are not running quite one half of Spin-

45. *Manufacturers' Record*, September 11, 1896, p. 108, September 10, 1897, p. 93, September 15, 1909.
46. The following account is taken from letterbooks in the Schenck Papers.

ning and Carding room at once. Yet the water hardly holds up. We have divided the help into two squads. One set works one day and the other next day. Several hands are left out entirely." During low-water season two years later, the mill ran only four days a week for several weeks so that the cotton gin, which the Schencks also operated, would have sufficient power to gin the cotton local farmers brought to the mills.

In spite of the loss of so much time for reasons they could not control, the Schencks often shut down their mills when they could have kept them running. "We were so urged by help to give them 3 days holiday we shut down last night," the elder Schenck wrote on Christmas Eve in 1891. A year later, the Christmas break was two days plus an additional half day "for work on Pump." The mills also stopped during these years on the Fourth of July and Thanksgiving, and on election day in 1892 and 1894.

These practices suggest the extent to which cultural factors influenced economic relationships in the mills. Every year, the Schencks closed their mills for religious revivals. In August, 1892, the closings were two days "for protracted meeting" and another half day "for baptizing." The following July, "No. 1 stopped all week to allow hands to attend preaching," and there were two subsequent stoppages, totaling two and a half days, for the same purpose. During August of the next summer, 1894, both mills "stopped all week to allow the hands to attend a protracted meeting," and a year later they again "stopped all week to allow the hands to attend a series of meetings."

Funerals were another cause of shutdowns. In November, 1892, the mills stopped "2 days for the Burying of an old Lady who had died on the hill," and the length of the stoppage suggests that a period of mourning was part of the observance. The following February, "Mill No 2 stopped 1/4 of a day to attend burial service of a girl that at one time was one of the mill hands"; and in May, "Mill No 1 stopped 1 day to attend the burial services of an old man who died on the hill."

Such incidents embody the personalism that mediated employee-employer relationships in the mills. The Schencks were unsentimental businessmen who in the 1890s ran their mills twelve and a half hours a day, including dinnertime, and paid women as little as forty cents for a day's work. They also ran their mills and villages with a firm, even arbitrary, hand. But they were obviously sensitive to the cultural context in which their mills operated and in which their employees lived and worked. By accommodating to that context, the Schencks enhanced not only their profit but the morale of their workers as well. Indeed, without such consideration mill work might have been intolerable. This was one way the Schencks and other paternalists let their employees know that they regarded the mill folk as something more than cogs in an economic wheel. "I have given the hands half holiday this week to attend a series of meetings at this place," the elder Schenck wrote on August 9, 1897. "I had promised them this a good long while ago." The "half holiday" lasted four full days.

"THESE LONG BURDENSOME TEDIOUS HOURS"

The attitudes of workers to the hours they worked were complex. The standard of comparison was farm and other unskilled work, and by that standard, mill hours were long despite gradual reductions. Farm work was notably irregular over the course of the year, and in most forms of work off the farm, the trend toward shorter hours ran ahead of that in the mills. "Everything in the city works 10 hours except cotton mills," H. F. Garrett of the Georgia Federation of Labor told the Industrial Commission in Atlanta in 1900. Garrett was himself a machinist and worked ten hours a day, six days a week—a schedule that seems only slightly better than that of nearby textile workers, who worked perhaps sixty-six hours a week.[47]

Yet the difference was important to mill folk, who perceived things in relative terms; and to many of them long hours were the most objectionable feature of mill work. "I think it is very hard for a woman to work 12 and 1/2 hours a day for 40¢," an operative wrote of her situation at Cleveland Cotton Mills in 1891. A weaver from Randolph County agreed. "I think we have to work too many hours per day," he said. "I think ten hours a plenty." A feeder-tender, also at Cleveland Cotton Mills, concurred. "The ten-hour-a-day system would be a great relief to those who are confined to cotton mills. The long confinement that we are compelled to work under the twelve-hour system keeps us nearly exhausted. . . [.] [W]e don't gain the rest our bodies require till work time is at hand again."[48]

Yet even these sentiments were not unanimous. Mill workers who testified before a congressional committee in 1883, for example, had no criticism of their work schedule. "Do you not object to the number of hours you have to work?" Addie Priscilla Jones was asked. "No, Sir. That is to our advantage," she answered, with piece-rate wages in mind. Della Barnes, like Addie Jones a weaver at Eagle and Phenix Mills, was equally forthright.

47. *House Documents*, 57th Cong., 1st Sess., No. 184, Vol. 7, p. 521.
48. NC *Labor Report* (1891), 168, (1891), 188, 170.

"No, Sir; I am very well satisfied on that point," she answered when asked if she objected to the hours she worked.[49]

Such attitudes might be explained by the flexibility some operatives had in the hours they actually worked. "Sometimes I could stop early—thirty minutes, twenty minutes, something like that," Bessie Buchanan recalled when asked how she had managed to make dinner for her husband and work in the mill too. "I'd catch up my work, and come out and get everything ready for twelve o'clock," when dinnertime began. "You had so much work to do then, and if you got your work caught up you could come home." This custom also affected quitting time. "Sometimes I could get two hours off," Mrs. Buchanan continued. "Lots of times I'd catch up about four o'clock, and I'd get to go home because [blank space in transcript] I had done all they required me to do."

Obviously workers wanted shorter hours, but efforts at reduction might have undesirable side effects. In the New South era, laws intended to regulate cotton mills and benefit operatives had many loopholes and were therefore unenforceable, and their passage provoked owners to protect themselves through practices that hurt their workers. Laws or even the threat of laws reducing hours, for example, prompted mills to pay workers on a piece-rate basis, which many workers, especially at first, disliked intensely. Under that system, reductions in hours resulted in comparable reductions in pay unless the mills made voluntary adjustments in rates. Whenever the choice was theirs, workers chose long hours over reduced pay, and often said so. "We the undersigned cotton mill operatives," about three thousand workers petitioned the South Carolina legislature in 1905, "having understood that there is now pending before your honorable body a Bill to reduce the hours of labor in cotton mills to ten hours per day, or sixty hours per week, respectfully request you not to pass such a Bill, as it will injure us by reducing our wages without giving us any benefit whatever. We are not overworked, and are satisfied, and only ask to be let alone."[50]

But wherever they could, mill workers opted for shorter hours. Three years before Coleman L. Blease became governor in 1910, the South Carolina legislature passed a law ostensibly limiting mills to a work week of sixty hours; and mill folk took the new law at face value. The law, however,

49. *Senate Documents*, 48th Cong., 1st Sess., No. 91, pp. 600–601.
50. *South Carolina House Journal*, 1905, p. 407. Of course many mill folk also signed petitions supporting legislation restricting hours. Large numbers of the approximately 3,000 people who petitioned the Georgia legislature on that subject in 1887, for example, were mill operatives. See Atlanta *Constitution*, September 15, 1887.

permitted the mills to ignore the daily and weekly limits in making up lost time. It also said nothing about how long mills could run their machinery or how long workers could work "voluntarily." The law was thus "worse than useless," in the words of the state's chief labor official.[51] It raised the expectations of workers without shortening their hours, and its chief consequence was friction on the job and resentment among operatives. The workers felt the law promised shorter hours and regular quitting times, and the mills appeared to be violating that promise.

In 1913 alone, "many hundreds" of workers complained to Blease about violations of the law. "We would like for you to have the law in regards too working mill operatives amended, so as to read that they the Mill Co should not run their Wheel over 60 hours per week," C. P. Lockey of Drayton Mills wrote Blease, pointing to a change that might have made the law effective. According to Lockey, the mills started up earlier and ran later than their schedules called for or the law permitted—in fact, ran as many as sixty-seven hours a week. "What we want along this line, he said, "is to force them to run their wheel 60 hours per week and no more, so that we will have these long burdensome tedious hours shortened."[52]

Blease received a stream of such complaints. "Did you Know that the majority of the Cotton Mills through this Section Are now gaining about 30 thirty Minutes each day on their laborers?" G. P. Stephens of Saxon Mills in Spartanburg asked the governor. "If not this is a fact—this thirty moments represents just two hours and ten moments per Week, *to we poor* people who need all the open air, and exercise And time to Study our books and attend to other matters helpful to us that we Can get." C. M. Cooper of Whitmire wrote: "I want to tell you What is the Matter[.] They Wants the Card Room hands to run till 10 oclock at night and Start up at 6 in the Morning[.] 6:30 is Starting[.] I am not able to Work all day and till 10 oclock at night[.] Now to get to the Point[.] [T]hey Wanted me to work last night and I did not feel like working and this Morning they Sent Me and My wife back home because we did not Start at 6." He continued: "The Boss told me that Was What he Sent me out for[.] Now it Dont look like they can Forse a Man to go to Work before Starting time but hear if you dont they Wont let you Work and they dont Want you to Stop at Noon."[53]

51. SC Labor Division, *Third Annual Report, 1911*, 16.
52. SC Labor Division, *Fifth Annual Report, 1913*, 3; C. P. Lockey to Coleman L. Blease, December 29, 1913, in Coleman L. Blease Papers, South Carolina State Archives.
53. G. P. Stephens to Blease, April 7, 1911, C. M. Cooper to Blease, December 1, 1914, in Blease Papers.

"I know of a Cotton Mill That is Running about 65 hours a Week," James Metcalf of Duncan Mills in Greenville told Blease. "They are Paying Their Loom fixers a day over time every 2 Week to Start up looms at 20 minutes until 6. oclock in the Morning and haft past 11 at noon and fired me out Because I was Talking to some of the hands about Reporting it to you. . . . They are Running from 65 to 70 hours per week."[54]

T. V. Blair of Pelzer explained to the governor how some mills circumvented the law. "You know it is against the law to run over 60 hours a week," Blair wrote, reflecting the widespread misunderstanding of the letter of the law. "They are starting up here fifteen minutes after 5 oclock and trying to force the help to run the extra time in the morning and at noon[.] [A]ll that dont run the extra time they take 1-1/2 hours away from them each day for not working it[.] [T]hat is the piece hands[.] [A]nd they are forcing the hands to go out at 11 o'clock too[.] [T]hey turned two off friday for refusing to go out at eleven oclock." The last complaint referred to the practice in some mills of giving regular workers an extended lunch hour while spare hands ran some of the machinery. In this way a mill could run perhaps twelve hours a day without requiring its workers to work longer than the legal limit of ten hours. Thus, in 1913 Simpsonville Cotton Mill employed extra hands to come in between 11:00 A.M. and 1:00 P.M., during which time regular workers had an extended break. Their workday stretched out over a twelve-hour period.[55]

Other mills ran all or some of their machinery during dinnertime without hiring extra workers, instead encouraging regular workers to remain on the job. "It [is] the practice of most of the mills to allow the wheels to run during the dinner," the state's chief labor official reported in 1912; and though that practice was not illegal, it was the source of much resentment. "This Department has had numerous complaints from operatives who claim that certain mills are working them over the legal limits each day," the official reported as early as 1909, "and that when the machinery was allowed to run during the dinner hour they were compelled to come back in before the whistle blew to start up their machinery, saying if they did not do this the overseers would take their regular looms from them and give them to those who would come back and start up of their own accord." The following year, factory inspectors visited many mills in which "the engine wheel was run during the noon hour" but could find no workers willing to say they were

54. James Metcalf to Blease, April 27, 1913, in Blease Papers.
55. T. V. Blair to Blease, November 30, 1914, in Blease Papers; SC Labor Division, *Fifth Annual Report, 1913*, 40.

forced to work more than ten hours a day. "The superintendents [and] overseers did not ask the weavers to stay in and run their looms," the inspectors were assured, "but allowed those who so desired to start up their looms at any time they wished."[56]

Many workers were required to remain at work during dinnertime but were afraid to complain for fear of losing their jobs. "In case there is Any thing said About this letter," J. B. Riddle, "a poor Cotton Mill operator" at Watts Mill in Laurens County, wrote Blease, complaining of too much overtime, "I hope you will Not Tell Any one Who Wrote this to You." Many workers, however, benefited from leaving the machinery on, and this was a traditional practice in weaving rooms. "We frequently run the mill at dinner time to oblige the weavers, who are on piece work, as it enables them to earn more," President Stewart Phinizy of Algernon Mill in Augusta wrote in 1886. "No day hand is required to work during that time."[57]

Typically, weavers left their looms running when they went to dinner. The Draper looms stopped automatically when threads broke or shuttles emptied; otherwise, the machines ran on their own for half an hour or longer. A weaver could therefore take a hurried lunch break without interrupting his work and, since he was paid by the piece, might welcome the opportunity to do so. That was no doubt one reason weavers refused to confirm the complaints of other workers about having to work during dinnertime.[58]

But other operatives did not accept the extra work, and in South Carolina, they bombarded state officials with an "ever-increasing intensity . . . of complaints." The "majority" of the complaints "were anonymous for obvious reasons," as officials acknowledged; but that made redress difficult. In the summer of 1913, for example, an operative at Woodruff Mills, identified only as Cooper, complained of being forced to work illegally long hours. "I looked up Mr. Cooper as soon as I got there and he told me that he had said nothing about the mill working overtime," an inspector reported. In the cloth room where Cooper worked, the inspector found the kind of irregular schedule that was no doubt the basis of Cooper's complaint (and one that illustrated the irregularity of mill work and the ineffectuality of the state's hours law). During August, the mill had lost a total of ten hours and fifty-

56. SC Labor Division, *Fourth Annual Report, 1912*, 21, *First Annual Report, 1909*, 34, *Second Annual Report, 1910*, 21.

57. J. B. Riddle to Blease, January 17, 1912, in Blease Papers; Augusta *Chronicle*, June 6, 1886.

58. Augusta *Chronicle*, June 6, 1886; SC Labor Division, *Second Annual Report, 1910*, 21.

one minutes on six different days, ranging from nine minutes on August 29 to six hours on August 9 and including three days when the loss exceeded an hour. To make up the loss, the mill ran overtime on fourteen days in August, recouping a total of nine hours and thirty-five minutes. The overtime ranged from two minutes on August 15 to forty-five minutes on five different days. Altogether, on seven days in August, the operatives had to stay at least thirty minutes beyond their scheduled quitting time, for which none of them received any overtime pay.[59] All of this was legal, but the basis for complaint is apparent.

"YESTERDAY IS THE FIRST DAY IN ABOUT 2 MONTHS WHEN WE HAVE HAD A MILL FULL OF HANDS."

Every day in the mills had its own distinctiveness. As they arrived in the morning, workers might not know whether they would work all or only part of the day, or whether they would have to stay overtime; and management never knew if too few or too many workers would show up. If too many appeared, the overseer "sent out" some of them—"excused" them for the day. If too few came, he or someone else went looking for absentees or spare hands about the village.

Sometimes more informal remedies sufficed. Work loads were often light enough for workers to tend one or two extra machines; or since most workers knew how to do more than one mill task, some might shift from one job to another to even out the work force for the day. "If any of the hands was sick or anything and had to be out, we'd double up work," Jessie Lee Carter recalled of her early years at Brandon Mill. Or, since employment was a family affair, another member might fill in for an absentee. "When a father or a mother, or an older sister or brother were sick," James Herring explained, "a younger one was sent to work in that person's place and the youngster continued to hold the place until the absent one returned." Schoolchildren often filled such a role, again showing how family employment gave mill and family alike a certain flexibility.

The work force constantly fluctuated. Employment was not the kind of committed circumstance it often is today, and even the number of persons necessary to staff a mill varied according to the work load carried by individual workers. A spinner who tended eight sides one day might be replaced the next by four children tending two sides each. Individual work orders

59. SC Labor Division, *Eighth Annual Report, 1916*, 22, *Fifth Annual Report, 1913*, 15–21.

might necessitate the addition or dismissal of workers, or the transfer of workers from one task to another. Securing workers and matching them with the work at hand was thus a recurrent problem. "We have usually been short of help from one cause or another here," H. F. Schenck wrote his business partner in 1891, "and I have added houses and taken in families that should 8 or 10 hands be out from sickness or any cause we might have enough." But Schenck's success in attracting additional hands merely changed the nature of his problem: too many workers showed up for work, and since he was reluctant to turn anyone away, he had to account to his business partner for the increased labor costs. "[This] week no one seemed to be out and help was rather flush," Schenck wrote, explaining the overrun. "I have often been compelled to stop machines for want of help—thus cutting production."[60]

Most of the surplus workers Schenck spoke of were spare hands who worked no more than one or two days a week, or a week or month from time to time. These part-time workers were of several types: housewives and other members of mill families who preferred irregular or occasional work because they had family or other responsibilities; farmers, farm laborers, or other men who went to the mills when work at their regular jobs was slack; children who alternated between school and mill work; mill folk whose health or stamina made it difficult or impossible for them to work regularly; and folk in or about the mills who refused to work all the time because they did not have to. President Estes of King Mill complained of an employee who worked four days a week and spent the rest of his time fishing and hunting. The man did this, he told Estes, because he could live on what he made in the four days, and he preferred to spend the rest of his time doing something else.[61]

Other spare hands were not part-time workers but a labor reserve such as the one Schenck tried to build up as insurance against absenteeism and labor turnover. Just as airlines today overbook their planes in order to fill them, so mills tried to keep more workers than they could use at any time. "We have had more help at times than we know how to keep busy," John F. Schenck wrote in the spring of 1892, "but we are reluctant to dismiss hands, especially at this season when sickness like last Summer's may return and cut down our help to our great disadvantage." The caution was prudent, for inevitably, things soon changed. "We have been extremely short of hands,"

60. H. F. Schenck to J. E. Reynolds, undated (ca. December 1, 1891), in Schenck Papers.
61. Augusta *Chronicle*, December 18, 1898.

H. F. Schenck wrote less than two months later. "We have been compelled, frequently to put our roper and line hands on other work. Two families left us yesterday, leaving the mill shorter of help than it has ever been." Again pointing to the irregularity of the work force, the younger Schenck wrote a month after the just-quoted complaint from his father, "Yesterday is the first day in about 2 months when we have had a mill full of hands."[62]

"THERE IS NOT MUCH . . . SENSE IN PUTTING IN A SHORT-TIME WORK WEEK ON THE STATUTE BOOKS WHEN THE PEOPLE CLAIM IT BY DIVINE RIGHT ANYWAY."

This irregularity was a major fact of mill life in part because it grew out of traditional habits of mill folk. "Absenteeism is easy to understand and hard to combat among employees who have been accustomed in the country only to seasonal occupations . . . [and] long periods of idleness," Marjorie A. Potwin, a social worker, wrote of mill folk in the 1920s. "This . . . actuates the mill operatives to take a day or so of leisure every now and then on general principles." For this reason, Potwin thought, "there is not much common sense in putting a short-time work week on the Statute Books when the people claim it by divine right anyway. Those who try to explain absenteeism only as a consequence of fatigue and a long working day miss the real point in the case. By every right of his inheritance and custom the worker, only now in the transition state from an agricultural to an industrial society, believes that he has to work just when and only when and for how long he pleases. He does not take easily to regulation."[63]

Workers, then, might or might not show up for work; and Monday mornings were perhaps the worst time of the week for overseers. "They'd come in there over a weekend and talk to them," recalled J. Floyd Thrift of recruiting agents coming into Carrboro mill village, where he was an overseer, "and maybe Monday morning you'd go in and there'd be two or three families a-moving out." This was only part of the picture, however. "Most men had the Monday drunks, I reckon," Myrtle Ray Stanley said of workers in the village, also in Carrboro, where she worked in the second decade of the twentieth century. The delinquents were not fired, however; there were

62. "Report of Cleveland Cotton Mills" for week ending May 14, 1892, H. F. Schenck to J. E. Reynolds, July 5, 1892, John F. Schenck to Reynolds, August 3, 1892, in Schenck Papers.

63. Marjorie A. Potwin, *Cotton Mill People of the Piedmont: A Study in Social Change* (New York, 1927), 149.

too many of them. To fire them, moreover, would result in the loss of the other workers in their families, for dismissed workers would surely move away and take their families with them. This was another advantage of family employment, and one mill folk used for their own purpose. "Oh, no," Mrs. Stanley recalled, "if they do [fire them] they'd hire them back the next day when they sober up."

This problem was largest on payday weekends. Officials at an unnamed mill complained to investigators for the 1907–1908 labor study of "a considerable falling off in the number [of workers] who report for work directly after pay days, and on one particular Monday following pay day, at the time of this investigation 150 looms were idle at one of the mills. Accustomed to just enough to live on and nothing more, many of these people would not work when they had money in hand."[64]

The extent of Monday morning absenteeism of this sort is impossible to quantify because records generally fail to differentiate between types of workers (adults and youths, for example) or to note the cause of absenteeism. In the two weeks ending September 8, 1900, illustrating this problem, Warren Manufacturing Company in Warrenville, South Carolina, operated ten and three-quarters days. During that period, the fifty-eight weavers on its payroll missed a total of thirty-one days, an absentee rate of less than 2 percent. Twenty-one of these absences occurred on Monday, September 3, which suggests an instance of "Monday drunks" but these absences may instead indicate slack time on that day in the weaving room. The mill had not run at all the preceding Monday.[65]

Absenteeism and the related problems of coaxing and disciplining workers were continuous concerns. At Fulton Bag and Cotton Mills, the day frequently missed was Saturday, not Monday. "We have a certain element that will not work on Saturday at all," Vice-President Oscar Elsas told the Industrial Commission in 1900. "That seems to be the greatest day to lay off." The diary of Henderson Fowler, apparently an overseer at Alamance Mill in the 1870s and 1880s, illustrates other aspects of the problem of absenteeism as management saw it. A man might suddenly take himself and his family out of the mill over unpredictable things and to the frustration of his overseer. Thus "John Allred took 7 hands out of the Mill Monday Morning Oct 11th 1886 on ac[coun]t of a little fuss between his son John & Webb out side of the mill about a dog." An employee might persist in

64. *Senate Documents*, 61st Cong., 2nd Sess., No. 645, Vol. 1, p. 513.
65. Warren Manufacturing Company Payroll, in Graniteville Papers.

objectionable behavior and have to be disciplined, again to the disruption of work: "Hubbert went to Co Shops Thursday 19th got drunk lost his hat fell in the creek got turned off the 20th took him on looms got drunk again left for good Sunday 22th 1878." Or workers might simply take time off for their own diversion. Thus, there was an "Exhibition at Oake dale the 30th of May" to which "Jim May John May John Isley Bob Clapp L Anderson Bob Sharp all went without leaf," and as a result, "Sharp Jim May J May and L Anderson was turned out of a job next morning 1884."[66]

However justifiable such discipline was from management's standpoint, the dismissal of several employees interrupted production schedules. "The only rows that we have had were before the holidays set in which we promptly nipped in the bud by discharging several of our hands who were drinking whiskey," H. F. Schenck wrote his business partner during the Christmas season of 1899. "This will make us a little scarce of help for some little time until we can replace the help that is discharged."[67]

Fairs, parades, and other festivities were occasions for missing work. When a fair came to Athens, Georgia, in November, 1886, for example, the doffers at Athens Manufacturing Company requested time off to attend. When the request was refused, "they determined to strike for their rights," a newspaper reporter stated, "so on Thursday when the bell rang [after dinner] not one of the boys appeared. The looms were at a stand still, and for a time it seemed that the factory must close down. After some delay, however, enough boys were collected to partially do the work." In the aftermath, "Two of the leaders in the strike were discharged," but the event seems more like truancy than a labor dispute. Perhaps it was to avoid a similar disruption that Cleveland Cotton Mills in the spring of 1894 "stopped 1 day for the hands to go to the Circus."[68]

Excitement of any kind disrupted work. When Mary Hedgecock, "an inspired fortune teller," appeared outside Fulton Bag and Cotton Mills in Atlanta in the summer of 1904, for example, mill officials faced an unexpected problem. "Yesterday morning a great crowd of mill operatives is said to have gathered about Mrs. Hedgecock's boarding house on the lower end of Decatur street to have their fortunes told," a newspaper said of the incident, "and when the mill whistle blew, announcing work time, large

66. *House Documents*, 57th Cong., 1st Sess., No. 184, Vol. 7, p. 571; Henderson Monroe Fowler Diary.
67. H. F. Schenck to J. E. Reynolds, December 26, 1899, in Schenck Papers.
68. Atlanta *Constitution*, November 17, 1886; "Report of Cleveland Cotton Mills" for week ending April 7, 1894, in Schenck Papers.

numbers of these people, men and women, remained about the place and failed to go to work." Mill officials had to call the police and have Mrs. Hedgecock arrested. The charge against her was "keeping large numbers of operatives from their work."[69]

In the fall of 1900, the Reverend George R. Stuart, an evangelist once associated with Sam Jones, went to Salisbury, North Carolina, to preach a revival. So great was the response that Stuart preached to three thousand people at one time in the canvas "tabernacle" erected for his meetings. Apparently some in the congregation were operatives from Salisbury Cotton Mill, for in the spinning room there one Saturday morning during the revival, "some one began talking salvation to a friend," and the word spread. "Others took up the work and soon the machinery of the entire room was standing still and it stood for some time while sinners were converted, Christians strengthened, and a general good time was had." In the words of a newspaper account, "Persons who witnessed the scene never saw anything like it before. . . . The desire to attend the tabernacle was so great among the employes that the mill closed down this morning at 9 o'clock for the day to enable all to attend the morning and evening services."[70] One wonders if that was the purpose all along.

Family responsibility was another cause of absenteeism. "I can remember my Daddy," Vinnie Partin said. "He would always get off from the mill on the day we were going to kill hogs." Illness had the same effect. "Last week we had about 18 hands out of mill—Some with typhoid, Rheumatism, general break-down from Exceedingly hot weather and other causes," one of the Schencks wrote in the summer of 1892, "and some out because sickness in the family demanded some help to wait on those who were helpless."[71]

A special dimension of this problem was the willingness of workers to quit on the spot in sudden disputes with their bosses. "Sometimes matters turn up that we cannot control," H. F. Schenck wrote on such an occasion, "such as the strike we had, three of our first-rate hands having left us. Our anxiety to make wick instead of cancelling those orders caused us to take a hand out of the dye house" and give him other work. The hand objected to the reassignment, and he and two other dyehouse workers walked off the job.[72]

Changes in work or pay policies, especially changes that were unexpected

69. Atlanta *Constitution*, August 13, 1904.
70. Raleigh *News and Observer*, November 8, 11, 1900.
71. H. F. Schenck to Reynolds, July 26, 1892, in Schenck Papers.
72. H. F. Schenck to Reynolds, October 11, 1898, in Schenck Papers.

and unsatisfactorily explained, produced many such disruptions. In the summer of 1889, for example, Sibley Mill announced a pay reduction for some of its operatives in the name of equalization. The day the reductions were effective "about forty" operatives absented themselves from work, idling "about two hundred" looms. As was usually the pattern in such incidents, "several" of the absentees returned later in the day and others went back subsequently, but management learned anew the cost of actions workers considered arbitrary. When Isaetta Mills, also in Augusta, announced a wage cut in 1896, so many workers quit that the entire mill closed down for a time. And when Revolution Mills in Greensboro, North Carolina, announced its intention to pay weavers by the piece rather than by the day, "practically all" the affected workers walked off the job.[73]

"I ALWAYS THOUGHT THE JOB OVER YONDER WAS BETTER THAN THE ONE I HAD."

Absenteeism coexisted with another phenomenon, what mill owners called "floating labor," the frequent movement of workers from one mill to another. "Everybody done that, I mean, back when I was a kid," Letha Ann Sloan Osteen recalled. "Why you'd look out the door any which a way and there's trucks backed up to the houses and people are moving and then in two or three hours or the next day, there's another family in there. It just went on constantly."

The reasons were numerous and complex. For some folk, moving was adventure, for others escape or protest, and for others still, a phase of life, as it were. Young folk were apparently the largest group of floaters. As a teenager, Everette Burchell "just wanted to see some of the country," and in the second decade of the twentieth century, he moved from mill to mill about North Carolina and Virginia. "It was something new," Burchell recalled. His movement was made easy by the ways of mill life—the shortage of workers, on-the-spot hiring, readily available housing, the interchangeability of mill jobs. And marriage did not necessarily end the practice. "All the new married people, there ain't never no dependence to be put in 'em when they got a job, how long [they would remain at it]," Letha Ann Sloan Osteen said. "My husband," Mrs. Osteen recalled, "he was one of these here scat-abouts."

He was not exceptional. Versa Vernon Haithcock, who was born in 1906

73. Atlanta *Constitution*, June 25, 1889, November 21, 1896; Raleigh *News and Observer*, February 27, 1901.

and spent his lifetime working in mills, once counted twenty-six places he had worked. "I can't answer that," Haithcock said when asked why he had moved. "I guess I always thought the job over yonder was better than the one I had." His reason for moving was not dissatisfaction, at least not in the usual sense, for on several occasions he returned to mills he had previously left; and he could remember no occasion on which he had moved because of objectionable bosses or working conditions.

No doubt much of this movement, however, expressed dissatisfaction. "If folks don't treat me right, I light out," an Atlanta worker told a reporter in 1899.[74] "I never did have to take anything," Swannie McDaniel said, recalling her years as a mill worker. "If they don't treat me right, I just walked out. I could always walk into another door."

Yet the relationship between dissatisfaction and frequent moving was often indirect and is not easily established. When mill workers moved, they did not usually look for other forms of employment. This was partly due to a lack of alternatives, but it had the effect of limiting the effect of their moving if the purpose was protest. Yet most moves were probably related to specific complaints. "They wouldn't do it," Alice P. Evitt remembered when she asked for time off after she had spent the day at a parade instead of resting for the night shift on which she worked. "I got so sleepy in the night, I couldn't hold my eyes open. They wouldn't let me off, and I just quit and went home, and we moved." She was twelve or thirteen at the time.

Many folk described their reason for moving as wanderlust, in which case the frequent moves may be seen as continuous with the ways of sharecroppers. Alexander R. Batchelor interviewed a man at Whitmire mill village in the mid-1920s who always kept "moving money" on hand so he could leave on the spur of the moment. Whenever he went to a new mill, the man told Batchelor, the money he received on his first payday he put aside to cover the expense of his next move. He therefore never felt confined.[75]

Most moves were to nearby mills. Martha Belk and her husband moved so often that, in Mrs. Belk's words, they "lived in a waggin' "—"a waggin' a-movin' from one mill to another." They moved within a limited area in the South Carolina upcountry. "We'd not no more'n get good settled in Pac'let before we'd up and move to Union," Mrs. Belk recalled. "Get settled good there and, whoosh!—off to Pac'let. And then back again." It had obviously been Mr. Belk's idea to move so often.

74. Atlanta *Constitution*, January 2, 1899.
75. Alexander R. Batchelor, "A Textile Community" (M.A. thesis, University of South Carolina, 1926), 10.

"THEY HAVE SHIFTED AND CHANGED AND STARTED AND STOPPED UNTIL
SCARCELY ANY OF THE ORIGINAL FORCE IS LEFT."

Absenteeism and labor turnover were extensive phenomena, and it is not always possible to distinguish between them in the records. Nor is it necessary to do so to see that mill folk missed work frequently. At the Morgan-Malloy Cotton Mill in Laurel Hill, North Carolina, there were 41 people on the payroll during the second half of October, 1881. Ten of the 41 (22 percent) worked full time, but 15 others (37 percent) were absent 2 or more days. During the next 2 weeks, there were 43 people on the payroll, 14 of whom (33 percent) missed no work at all while 19 (44 percent) missed 2 or more days. At the same mill a year later, between August 5 and September 4, 1882, only 4 of 48 workers worked the full 25 days the mill operated. Some of the absenteeism was due to turnover, for during the month, 8 workers left the mill and 9 new ones were hired.[76]

This payroll, though it did not record reasons for absences, also showed that some workers scattered their time off in small bits through the month, while others were absent for a single extended period. Anna Terry missed 7 consecutive days but no other time during the period, while Ella Penfield, who lost a total of 3 days, was off 1 whole day and 4 half days. Moreover, members of the same family (individuals with the same surname listed consecutively on the payroll) varied their schedules. Jeff Musselwhite, for example, worked the entire 25 days, while "Mrs. Musselwhite," listed next on the payroll, missed 4 days and Babe Musselwhite, whose name was the next entry, was absent 6.5 days. Eliza Hodge missed no work, but the four other Hodge women or girls (Matilda, Novella, Mary, and Stella) missed, respectively, 3, 1, 7, and 8.5 days. Together, these 5 individuals provided the equivalent of about 4 full-time workers—a pattern that illustrates another way in which mill folk, or at least those in large families, used family employment to advantage.[77]

Evidence from later years shows a similar pattern. In the 2 weeks ending September 8, 1900, the Warren Manufacturing Company ran 10.75 days. Of 163 operatives in the carding and spinning rooms of this mill for whom information on the payroll is clear, 55 (34 percent) missed no time at all, but absenteeism was high among all groups of workers in the mill. Thus, only 9 of 19 spoolers worked more than 7 days during the 2 weeks, while 13 of 53

76. Time Book, 1881–1884, in Morgan-Malloy Cotton Mill Papers, Manuscript Department, Duke University Library, Durham, North Carolina.
77. *Ibid.*

spinners (25 percent) missed at least 2 full days in addition to the 1.25 days the mill itself was closed.[78]

These figures are consistent with other kinds of evidence. In 1906 an officer of Springstein Mills in Chester, South Carolina, complained that of eighty-one employees in the spinning room of his mill, only twenty-one had worked full time during the most recent pay period. Also, three-fifths of the female industrial workers, most of them textile operatives, studied by the Women's Bureau in South Carolina in 1921 missed at least some time during the two-week survey period; and three-fourths of those women lost at least ten hours—one or more days. In a more systematic study of nine southern mills in 1922, researchers found that male workers missed more than a fifth (20.7 percent) of the possible work time during the year, and female workers more than a fourth (27.4 percent).[79]

Because of the high rates of absenteeism and turnover, mills had to employ more workers than they could use at one time. The treasurer of an unnamed mill told the *Manufacturers' Record*, for example, that in 1882 his mill carried an average of 423 names on its monthly payrolls, though only 335 hands were needed to run the mill. Similarly, President Estes reported that King Mill had 1,085 names on its payroll at the time a strike commenced there in the fall of 1898, though the mill employed no more than 787 workers at any one time. During the two weeks preceding the strike, Estes said, 253 of the 1,085 employees had worked full time while the other 732 had, on average, worked 7 of the 12 days the mill operated.[80]

Estes' mill apparently had sufficient labor despite the absenteeism of which he complained, but that was not always the case. When the Atlanta Cotton Mill opened in June, 1879, it had far more workers than it could employ. In the first five months of operation, the mill had on its payroll more than three times as many workers as it had positions to fill. It was soon plagued by absenteeism and turnover, however. By November the workers there had "shifted and changed and started and stopped until scarcely any of the original force [was] left." As the superintendent told a reporter, "some of the places have seen four or five changes," and the workers were very unreliable. "The consequence is that on some days," the reporter noted, the superintendent "is not able to bring the factory up to more than

78. Warren Manufacturing Company Payroll.

79. *Manufacturers' Record*, May 24, 1906, p. 521; U.S. Department of Labor, Women's Bureau, *Bulletin No. 32: Women in South Carolina Industries* (1923), 12, and *Bulletin No. 52: Lost Time and Labor Turnover in Cotton Mills: A Study in Cause and Extent* (1926), 15.

80. *Manufacturers' Record*, June 14, 1884, p. 504; Augusta *Chronicle*, December 18, 1898.

two-thirds of its capacity." In his first annual report to the stockholders of this mill, President H. I. Kimball reported that the mill had had "much expense and trouble in the procurement of help and the frequent changes and losses which must inevitably follow such changes."[81]

One result of such a situation was the constant employment and re-employment of workers. In 1904, in what was apparently an extreme example, Eagle and Phenix Mills had a total of 4,986 employments though its work force was no more than 1,800. The only contemporary effort to measure this phenomenon was made by Charles W. Stiles during the course of his investigation of hookworm disease in the mill villages. Examining the records of an unnamed mill, Stiles counted 712 names on the payroll for January 1, 1907, and an additional 797 added during the ensuing twelve months. On the basis of this information and that from other mills, he estimated that the 91 mills he investigated, which had a nominal work force of 28,893, employed a total of 50,786 people during the year. For every 100 positions in those mills, he estimated, 175 persons had been employed during the twelve months.[82]

Such figures should not obscure the fact that most workers did not move so frequently. The 1907–1908 labor study estimated the number of "itinerant" employees "in most mills [as] at least 25 to 30 per cent," but the value of the estimate is compromised by the absence of a precise definition of *itinerancy*. Although many mill workers moved frequently, that is, every one or two years, a larger number did not. At the Morgan-Malloy Cotton Mill, for example, 37 percent of the workers who were on the payroll in 1873 were still there in 1883 and 21 percent in 1889. At Alamance Mill 50 of the 67 names on the payroll on January 1, 1890, were still there after 1 year, 30 were still there after 5 years, and 17 after 10 years. At Royall Cotton Mills in Wake Forest, North Carolina, of 183 names on the payroll on March 7, 1903, 86 (47 percent) were there a year later and 64 (35 percent) two years later, though 7 of the 64 were missing from the intermediate payroll. On March 7, 1908, five years after the initial count, 35 (19 percent) members of the original work force were still at the mill. Of 244 names on the payroll of this mill in 1908, only 35 (14 percent) were there five years earlier.[83]

81. Atlanta *Constitution*, November 20, 1879, July 22, 1880.
82. *Ibid.*, January 5, 1905; Charles W. Stiles, *Hookworm Disease Among Cotton-Mill Operatives* (Washington, D.C., 1912), 23.
83. *Senate Documents*, 61st Cong., 2nd Sess., No. 645, Vol. 1, p. 127; Cathy L. McHugh, "The Family Labor System in the Southern Cotton Textile Industry, 1880–1915" (Ph.D. dissertation, Stanford University, 1981), 78; Time Book, 1890–1901, Vol. XI of Alamance Cotton Mill Records (figures exclusive of four duplicate names on the first payroll); Time Book,

"ACTUAL AVERAGE WORKING HOURS WERE FEWER THAN IN THE NORTH."

During their days and weeks of regular work, mill folk put in long and straining hours. But over the course of a year or a cycle of years, the hours they actually worked were not long, were even moderate, by standards of the time. The conclusion Jack Blicksilver reached some years ago concerning mill workers in the South during the second decade of the twentieth century seems amply justified for the whole of the New South era. "Actual average working hours," Blicksilver wrote, "were fewer than [those of mill workers] in the North." Work schedules in New England mills were of course significantly shorter than those in their southern counterparts; but absenteeism and turnover rates were also significantly lower, and workers there worked less irregularly.[84]

The predominating pattern prevailed even in mills that went for long periods without shutdowns or other interruptions. At Enterprise Mill, a full work year was 312 days (365 days less 52 Sundays and 1 holiday, probably Christmas), and in the fiscal year ending February 20, 1886, the mill actually ran 305.5 days. That seems to suggest a picture far different from the one sketched above. The time lost during the year amounted to only a week and a day; but according to President J. P. Verdery's annual report, the "average number of hands" in the mill during the year was 412 and the "number of days" they worked totaled 106,808.25. The meaning of "average number of hands" is not altogether clear, but if the phrase refers to the average number of people on the payroll at any one time during the year, Verdery's figures may be used to calculate that an "average" worker in his mill worked 259 days during the year. That amounts to 53 days—almost 9 weeks—less than the 312 days in the full work year.[85]

It is quite possible that the amount of time most workers lost from all causes during a given year was within the range suggested by that figure. If so, typical operatives missed perhaps six to twelve weeks of work over the course of a typical year. Many of these workers were dependent children, and some of the adults had other jobs during the time they lost. When an Atlanta mill closed for a time in 1885, for example, "the operatives were

1903–1907, and Time Book, 1907–1910, Vols. XX and XXI respectively of Royall Cotton Mill Company Papers, Manuscript Department, Duke University Library, Durham, North Carolina; Potwin, *Cotton Mill People*, 73.

84. Jack Blicksilver, *Cotton Manufacturing in the Southeast: An Historical Survey* (Atlanta, 1959), 69.

85. Verdery's report is summarized in Augusta *Chronicle*, March 11, 1886.

provided with work on the company's farm or in improvements about the city." And when "a very large number of the North Carolina cotton mills" shut down in the late summer of 1904, "a great many" of their employees found "work on the farm and so . . . fared pretty well."[86]

These examples suggest what for most workers was the other side of the coin of the work time they missed. Lost time meant not so much leisure or idleness as lost pay. And lost pay was one of the things that kept so many mill folk impoverished and that made absenteeism and frequent movement problematical responses to their situation.

86. Atlanta *Constitution,* September 27, 1885; Raleigh *News and Observer,* September 6, 1904.

6

ON THE JOB

Cotton mills were objects of great interest in the New South, and they attracted hosts of visitors. Among the visitors were apologists and critics of varying degrees of insight and persuasion, most of whom saw what they wanted to see. "Seated or standing by every loom was a bright girl or woman or boy" whose "appearance betokened content-[ment]," a visitor wrote of the mills at Griffin, Georgia, in 1900, "and contentment is happiness. One could not but notice the general buoyancy of the spirit of the operatives, their clear complexions and healthful appearance—a marked difference to those in New England mills." This pleasant scene harmonized, the visitor thought, with the physical amenities of the mills. "Light, ventilation, comfort are the predominating features," he wrote, "and this means preservation of the eyes, fresh air in summer and warmth in winter."[1]

A woman who toured Eagle and Phenix Mills was even more taken with what she saw. A "pretty girl of fifteen summers, with waves of golden brown hair snugly held back with jaunty side combs" looked to the visitor "coquettishly happy as she busily [worked] her shuttle" while across the room "her probable sweetheart [was] busy with his heavier

1. Atlanta *Constitution*, February 9, 1900.

goods." Elsewhere, "the many clean-faced children" about the mill were "far better cared for in learning industrious habits, side by side with their older sisters," than they would have been if "left to roam at large with idle street urchins."[2]

The mills, or perhaps what they represented, spurred imagination, but not everyone's imagination was of the same bent. "In the southern cotton mills where the door shut out the odor of the magnolia and shut in the reeking damps and clouds of lint," a mill critic wrote, "where the mocking bird outside keeps obligato to the whirring wheels within, we find a gaunt goblin army of children keeping their forced march on the factory floors."[3]

Only occasionally did visitors react to the mills in unexpected ways. Child-labor reformers, who were persistent critics of the mills, were sometimes surprisingly balanced in what they said about mill workers. "Operatives speak very highly of mill authorities, and appear reasonably well satisfied, though some complain about low wages," a North Carolina reformer wrote in 1916 of one of the mills he had recently visited. At another mill, this spokesman continued, "the employees, almost to a man, declared themselves well satisfied," though at a third mill, "the people are miserable" and "none stay there who can get away."[4]

That kind of variation is one key to the disparate accounts of mill visitors; for discerning visitors found varied conditions among mills and workers alike. "The types of operatives" Mary Applewhite Bacon encountered in a tour of southern mills early in the twentieth century, for example, included "quiet, self-respecting men going steadily about their work" and "women neatly dressed and contented-looking." But they also included men "whom ignorance and poverty have brutalized in mind and body" and women "whose personal appearance shows an inner life equally regarded and wretched." In "the long, long alleys of the spinning room" of one mill, "the little children" looked to Bacon "more pallid and listless" than those she had seen elsewhere, "more stunted in body, perhaps because of the climate; though some of them, indeed, [were] less than twelve years of age." But "in a little open space" in the same mill, Bacon was "cheered by a group of doffers using their off period for a game of marbles on the worn, uneven floor." At another mill, the atmosphere was more depressing. "A few of the children" there were "rosy and healthy-looking," but "most [were] pale and dull-eyed" and "their unkempt hair and little cheap calico gowns [were] covered with lint."

2. *Ibid.*, February 17, 1896.
3. *Journal of Labor* (Atlanta), January 18, 1907.
4. "Aged 12, Has Worked Two Years," *Child Labor Bulletin*, IV (1916), 173.

Bacon's portrait of mill workers reflected her willingness to look beyond outward appearances. "There is neither resentment nor suspicion in the faces," Bacon wrote of the operatives, who in all the mills she visited were open, talkative, and candid in their assessments of mill work. "No, ma'am the work ain't so hard," one woman told her. "Hit's jes' tejus an' confinin'. But a body can make mo' at it than they can" doing other work. "I like it very well," one woman added. "The managers is all mighty kind," another said, "an' our super is a good man. He was raised in a mill himself, an' knows how a po' person feels." When asked if she liked her work, a spooler answered: "Yes, ma'am, I do. I'd another sort rather be here than a-workin' in the field, or he'pin' ma around the house. Besides, you don't get no pay for that sort o' work."[5]

These judgments are all relative. "It is not doing well that makes people happy, but doing better," Charles B. Spahr suggested in trying to explain the "cheerfulness" he found among mill workers at Lindale, Georgia, at the turn of the century. "These workmen, though not doing so well in point of wages as workmen in the North, were doing better than they had done on their farms a few years before." And that, he believed, determined their frame of mind and their attitude toward their circumstance.[6]

"THE PEOPLE HERE MOVE AND ACT SLOWER."

One thing responsible for many of the visitors' positive assessments of mills and mill workers was the informality of the work scene—the moderate and uneven pace, the infectious socializing, the evident absence of tension. Mill work was not laborious by the standards of mill folk; no one who had ever picked cotton for any length of time thought machine tending was hard labor, however long the hours or disagreeable aspects of the workplace might be. That is why so many operatives insisted their work was easy and they "liked" it. Speedups and stretch-outs appeared in southern mills after the New South era, and to workers interviewed in the 1930s and 1970s, the appearance of those practices was a watershed in the history of mill work. "I don't think they worked us as hard then as they do now," Theotis Johnson Williamson said, contrasting her situation at Erwin Mills in the second decade of the twentieth century with that of mill folk she knew in the 1970s. Moreover, the work rules Mrs. Williamson remembered were more re-

5. Mary Applewhite Bacon, "The Problem of the Southern Cotton Mill," *Atlantic Monthly*, XCIX (1907), 224–31.

6. Charles B. Spahr, "America's Working People: The New Factory Towns of the South," *Outlook*, LXI (1899), 512–13.

laxed. "I think we done as we pleased then," she recalled, "'cause there weren't no fence around the mills, and if we wanted to go home and get a biscuit or anything we'd go home. And I worked for some wonderful people."

Bessie Buchanan agreed. "They're doing more in eight hours now in these textile plants than we did in twelve hours then," she said. "The way they're working now is much harder on the poor class of people than it was when I was growing up." J. H. Reynolds, who worked before and after the stretch-outs began and was still at work when he was interviewed in the 1930s, was even more emphatic in his contrast of past and present. "I thought I was a hard working man before then but I didn't know nothin' about work till this thing come about," he said. "Now, I am doin' almost twice the amount of work"; and stricter work rules made mill work "worse than bein' in jail."

This is not to suggest that mill work was ever undemanding, or that at given times and places in the New South era it was not exhausting and even debilitating. When the Knights of Labor petitioned mill owners in Augusta in 1886, they asked in part that "operatives be not over-worked, as is the case in certain departments at this time." Workers in those areas "cannot do justice to themselves or the work," the petitioners said. "This complaint is made by some of the very best and most honest men in the mills. They strive with all their might to keep up, but hot weather is at hand; they cannot stand it."[7]

There are no objective measurements of such things, but much evidence suggests that the pace and intensity of mill work in the New South were relatively and absolutely moderate. Moderation was the price mill folk exacted for the long hours they had to work. According to census reports, the number of spindles per operative in southern mills was barely half that in New England mills—33 compared to 69 in 1880, and 44 compared to 79 in 1900. In North Carolina and Massachusetts, both extreme examples, the respective figures in 1900 were 37.4 and 84.5. As census analysts stated, "The number of persons employed by a mill of a given size is much greater [in the South] than in the great factory towns of the North."[8]

These disparities reflected differences in machinery, finished products, and composition of the labor force. But they also reflected the slower pace of work in southern mills. T. M. Young, an Englishman who visited mills in

7. Augusta *Chronicle*, April 17, 1886.
8. *Twelfth Census, 1900: Manufactures: Textiles*, 49.

the South and New England early in the twentieth century, found the productivity of weavers in a North Carolina mill varying as much as one-third per loom, suggesting differences of pace as well as of skill. Young also found the machinery running slower in southern than northern mills, which also affected the pace of work. One Massachusetts mill he visited produced 1.35 pounds of yarn per spindle in a work week of 58 hours, while a branch of the same mill in the South produced 1.42 pounds per spindle in a work week of 67 hours and 15 minutes.[9]

Mill officials recognized such laxness and used it to justify long hours. "It will require ten per cent more time for equal results in processes involving labor alone in the south than in the north," John Hill of Eagle and Phenix Mills said in 1889. "The people here move and act slower, and moving slower do not become weary so quickly. All of the disadvantages of the south will give us no net advantage by eleven hours in the south over ten hours in Massachusetts." Summarizing the views of mill officials on this point, an agent of the North Carolina labor bureau wrote, "The trouble is, the Southern laborer is disposed to take things easy and it [will] take years to get him out of the old ruts."[10]

The cycle was thus complete. Workers worked slowly in part because their hours were long, and mill officials insisted on long hours because their workers worked slowly. As machinery improved and workers became more efficient, however, the pace of work in southern mills increased. "Year by year they've been adding new machinery and making one man gradually increase his work until he was doing that of two," an unnamed Augusta operative told a newspaper reporter in 1898. "When I started a man worked 16 cards at 75 cents per day, now he runs 32 for 80 and 90 cents." Significantly, this operative complained more of the cut in pay rates this change represented than the increase in work. Another Augusta operative made the same complaint about the pay of spoolers. "When I came here to work in the mills," Robert Glover said, also in 1898, "so much was paid per box; then the box was double, then a third more was added, yet the spoolers had to fill that box at the same cost [that is, pay]."[11]

What lay behind these complaints was the grievance that workers were not sharing the benefits of improved technology and productivity. As better machinery increased productivity, the mills adjusted pay scales downward,

9. T. M. Young, *The American Cotton Industry* (London, 1902), 62 and *passim*.
10. Atlanta *Constitution*, August 7, 1889; North Carolina Bureau of Labor Statistics, *Annual Report, 1894*, 65, hereinafter cited as NC *Labor Report* by year.
11. Augusta *Chronicle*, October 17, November 24, 1898.

which, more than increased work loads, was what workers resented. "New looms have been placed in Nos. 1 and 2 mills, and the speed on them increased, which increases the output," a labor columnist wrote of Eagle and Phenix Mills in 1899, "and I will add here that increased speed on machinery demands closer attention and more active work to keep the machine in operation." Yet "the mills are vastly more benefited by the introduction of this new machinery than is the operative," the columnist concluded.[12]

There is other evidence of increasing work loads. In August, 1885, Pelzer Mills employed 24 hands per 1,000 spindles, but in August, 1909, the number of workers had dropped to 12. Lest that drop be interpreted as simply the result of speedup, however, it should be noted that the composition of the labor force also changed over the same period, the proportion of women, for example, dropping from 52 to 28.9 percent.[13] The rising proportion of men in the mills was one reason the southern textile industry increased its productive capacity far more rapidly than its work force. Improved machinery, more efficient workers, and increasing work pace were other reasons.

"THEY WOULD SING AND PICK THE GUITAR AND THE BANJO."

The slow, uneven pace of work encouraged socializing on the job. The workers knew one another, and most of them were children or youths for whom work was itself a kind of social activity. "Oh, yes, they was all . . . . [sic] one big family," Flossie Moore Durham said when asked if she and her friends socialized in the mill. The result, in many mills at least, was a relaxed, informal atmosphere. "We could talk, and had a lot of fun," Rose Bowden Humphreys remembered. "Yeah, we could talk. Oh, we would talk and talk at our work. I loved it. . . . Emma [Williams] and me were close friends. All this time she and I worked side by side. Oh, it was just a group of people that had more fun. I don't believe young people [today] have the fun we had."

Vinnie Partin recalled the same kind of atmosphere. "We knew everybody. Carrboro was a very small place and we knew everybody. And we would get caught up with our work and then we'd go around in each other's alley, you know, in the room, and talk." Mrs. Partin also remembered that

12. Columbus *Daily Herald*, April 16, 1899.
13. South Carolina Commissioner of Agriculture, Commerce, and Immigration, Labor Division, *First Annual Report, 1909*, 17.

workers played practical jokes on one another, and even did some of their courting on the job. She herself had married a fellow worker in 1917. "He worked in the Winding Room too," she said. "I worked on one side of the machine and him on the other." Nellie Allen Pendergrass had similar memories. At times, she said, "all of us would sing [mostly church songs]. And we also went barefooted. All of us worked barefooted in the mill. . . . We'd catch up our work, you know, and then we could set down and talk."

These memories are no doubt colored by the frequent interruptions in work. When the mill stopped unexpectedly, usually because of mechanical problems, it was customary to keep workers in or near the mill if the interruption was expected to be brief. Folk used these breaks to rest, clean their machinery, and socialize. "There was a crowd of 'em that picked guitar and the banjo and different string instruments," Ethel M. Faucette recalled of the workers at Glenco Mill in Alamance County in the second decade of the twentieth century. "We run by water then, had water wheels—that was the power that run the mill—and when the water'd get low, maybe they'd stop off for a hour or two. Well these gang of boys would get their instruments and get out there in the front of the mill, and they would sing and pick the guitar and the banjo, and different kind of string music. And maybe they'd stand [that is, the mill would be idle] an hour or two and [then] the water'd [begin] goin' up, and they'd start back up."

These were reminiscences of childhood and youth; it is more difficult to document the socializing of adult workers. Yet adults were no less sociable than youths, and they considered socializing an important compensation for the tediousness of work and its long hours. "At work, the women have an excellent opportunity for expanding their social contacts," Sybil V. W. Hutton wrote after interviewing mill women in Greer, South Carolina, after World War II. "The 'visiting' done by women in the mill is a major part of their social lives." As one woman told Hutton, "I do enjoy the fellowship with the women in the cloth room. We have the best time talking, even if we aren't supposed to."[14]

"I HAD [LINT] IN MY EYES, MY HAIR'D BE WHITE. AND MY EYELASHES."

The spirit behind this socializing influenced the ways mill folk adjusted to noise, lint, humidity, and other disagreeable conditions in the workplace.

14. Sybil V. W. Hutton, "Social Participation of Married Women in a South Carolina Mill Village" (M.A. thesis, University of Kentucky, 1948), 55.

Like long hours, those conditions were intrinsic features of the mills and had to be tolerated because work was necessary. A remark by Harriet H. Robinson, who as a child worked thirteen and a half hours a day in a New England mill, illuminates the point. "I do not know why I did not think . . . of my work in the mill as drudgery," Mrs. Robinson wrote of her experience. "Perhaps it was because I *expected* to do my part towards help-ing my mother to get our living and had never heard her complain of the hardship of her life."[15]

To fret over what cannot be changed is to risk demoralization, and mill folk were not demoralized. The experience of William G. Raoul illustrates the importance of background and expectation in making necessary adjust-ments. Raoul came from a middle-class Georgia family, and in his early twenties, about 1895, he decided to learn mill work from the bottom up and become an overseer. He had never done "continuous manual labor" or work of any kind under mill conditions, and he was appalled by what he experienced at Exposition Mills. "They put me in the picker room, at the only heavy physical labor in a mill," he wrote later. "There are the bales of cotton received, the hoops cut, the bale broken apart and shaken to pieces, and fed into a hopper, from which it is drawn toward the powerful beater revolving at about eighteen hundred revolutions a minute."

The experience was horrifying. "The roar of the machines is deafening," Raoul wrote of the picker room. "It is impossible to hear a word, unless shouted within a few inches of the ear. No other room in the mill can compete with this for noise except the weave shop. The dust and lint is stifling, until you learn how to keep the mouth strictly shut, and to allow the lint to accumulate in the nostrils and eyebrow, and lips even." All this Raoul endured twelve hours a day and sometimes longer. "My muscles were not used to this heavy work," he recalled, "and on the second day every joint ached, and my ears rang as though I had taken an overdose of quinine. It was a very ancient mill, and frequently the antiquated machinery would give way somewhere, and everything would have to stop. I would pray for these intervals, and when the lessening roar of the big belts gave the signal to stop, I would throw myself down in the soft piles of cotton and hope it would never start again." Raoul soon moved to the card room, where work was less difficult, but after two months he left the mill.[16]

15. Quoted in Holland Thompson, *From the Cotton Field to the Cotton Mill: A Study of the Industrial Transition in North Carolina* (New York, 1906), 245.

16. William G. Raoul, "Proletarian Aristocrat" (Typescript autobiography in Southern Historical Collection, Louis R. Wilson Library, University of North Carolina at Chapel Hill), 43–44.

Raoul's reactions are understandable but were not shared by most mill workers. The majority of workers, whom Raoul considered a "mindless mass" and "the least capable of the working class," approached the disagreeable aspects of mill work as conditions to become used to and live with. Those conditions could be hateful in the extreme. "We do not have any more showing than negros in slavery time," S. E. Arthur of Langley Mills wrote Governor Blease in 1914. "The mill gates are locked when mill starts and are kept locked and if you have cause to go out you must go to your overseer and get a pass and give same to man at the gate who will unlock gate and let you out." Also, "The windows are nailed down in the mill. [T]hat is some parts[,] and we learn that A. H. McCarrel Superintendent are going to have them nailed down in all parts of the mill[.]" Arthur continued: "[N]ow as to the Toilets in 30 minutes after the mill starts the seats are wet from pipes over head and other causes which could easily be void if they had men here who cared for the help[.] [T]he floors are wet and you get your feet wet unless you get there be fore the mill starts[.] . . . I ask your Honor to treat this letter confidential as you know I will lose my position should they know I wrote it."[17]

The mills were dank, sweltering places because cotton manufacturing required still, humid air. The passage of cotton through the machinery generated static electricity, which caused fibers to curl, tangle, and break; and to control that problem, the mills closed all or some of the windows and installed humidifiers to pump moisture into the workrooms. The most commonly used humidifiers simply injected steam into the air—a process that accomplished the immediate purpose of keeping the air moist but did nothing to solve other problems. The primitive devices had no means of measuring air moisture or of removing lint, dust, and other impurities. Investigators for the 1907–1908 labor study found those devices "still largely in use" and saw "much dust and lint" in "a large majority of the mills" they visited. The humid, impure atmosphere created by these conditions, investigators believed, were conducive to "pulmonary, bronchial, and catarrhal infections."[18] "It was awful hot," Alice P. Evitt said simply. "You'd come out of there, your clothes was plumb wet."

Yet conditions were not the same everywhere. "The weaving-rooms at Cooleemee were an agreeable surprise," T. M. Young, the English traveler,

17. S. E. Arthur to Coleman L. Blease, January 19, 1914, in Coleman L. Blease Papers, South Carolina State Archives.
18. *Senate Documents*, 61st Cong., 2nd Sess., No. 645, Vol. 1, pp. 361, 365; Melvin T. Copeland, *The Cotton Manufacturing Industry in the United States* (1917; rpr. New York, 1966), 93.

wrote of a mill near Winston-Salem, North Carolina, in 1902. "It was, as I have said, intensely hot out of doors . . . but in the weaving rooms the air was pleasantly cool, far cooler and fresher than in some of the Fall River mills. The ceiling was high, the windows were wide open, and the air was moistened but refreshed by humidifiers which threw out a very fine spray of cold water."[19]

Lint clung to the moist air and then settled onto floors, machines, and operatives alike. "Oh it was full of it," Myrtle Ray Stanley recalled of the mill where she worked. "I've seen where the sun would shine through the window and I'd see great gobs [of lint] that big. You couldn't see it unless the sun was shining." At the end of the day, "I had it in my eyes, my hair'd be white. And my eyelashes," Mrs. Stanley continued. "When I'd wake up in the morning, my eye could just be like that and just pull out strings of it."

Lint was even in the drinking water. "There was always that bucket sitting up on the big post place, and a dipper in it," Flossie Moore Durham remembered. "I can almost see anybody go there now, take that dipper and knock the lint back off of it, and get them a drink of water." Because of the problem, most folk got a drink as soon as a fresh bucket was brought in, "before it got lint on it." How did workers adjust to the lint? "It didn't bother us," said Vinnie Partin, who wore a dust cap to keep it out of her hair. She meant that it was something else to endure in the mill.

The same was true of noise. "You learnt to spin and you learnt to hear," remarked Jessie Lee Carter. "Maybe you'd work in the mill about a week before you learned good. But then you could hear everything. I could holler from my sides maybe to over to my aunt's—she was my mother's sister, but she was as young as I was—and I'd holler to her and I'd say, 'I'll beat you down my alley.' And she'd say, 'No, you won't.' We'd holler to each other over the frames." Frank Thompson, who went to work at Carrboro in 1909 when he was about twenty years old and whose memories of mill work were less positive than those of some of the others quoted here, made the same point. "Anybody that wasn't used to the noise couldn't talk much," he recalled, "but after you stayed in there a good long while, you could talk just as good as you could anywhere."[20]

The adjustment of Beatrice Reeves, who went to work when she was "a little youngun seven year old," best expressed the ingenuity with which mill folk adapted to circumstances they could not control. "Lots of folks said the noise nearly drove 'em crazy," she said, "but I wove it into a song of my own,

19. Young, *The American Cotton Industry*, 61.
20. Quoted in Marc S. Miller (ed.), *Working Lives: The Southern Exposure History of Labor in the South* (New York, 1980), 9.

and you know I loved the noise till three year ago when I had my operation and my nerves went to pieces."

Unsanitary conditions were of less concern than noise and lint. Workers shared some of the responsibility for a healthful environment, but management, to whom clean toilets, floors, and the like were matters of expense rather than hygiene, had a larger responsibility. The worst mills were bad, indeed. "That was the nastiest mill that I ever went in and ever heard of," Myrtle Ray Stanley said of a Hillsborough, North Carolina, factory where she worked for a while in the second decade of the twentieth century. "It was worse, a whole lot, than Carrboro. It [Carrboro] was pretty clean. But, law, that was the filthiest place. Outside the toilets, filthy, and dirt and lint. I've seen lint that deep [perhaps two feet]."

One reason for unsanitary toilets was the practice of charging the cost of cleaning them to the operating expense of the rooms in which they were located. Where that was the custom, an overseer could increase the profits of his room by skimping on sanitation. Yet many mills had adequate, well-tended toilet facilities. "The accommodations for the help in the way of wardrobes and toilet-rooms" at Olympia Mills were "the most complete to be found in any mill, every care and consideration being taken for the comfort of the employes."[21] The "wardrobes" were dressing rooms in which workers might put on aprons, head covers, or other garments to keep lint off themselves and their clothes, or at day's end, freshen up, comb the lint out of their hair, or change clothes before leaving the mill.

Next to toilets, the chief source of insanitation was the "promiscuous spitting" of snuff and tobacco juices on the floor. "Every body that used snuff and tobacco (and nearly every body did)," a worker recalled in the 1920s, "had to spit on the floor for there was no where else to spit. Later, I remember, when the Health Department made them put spittoons in negro men took tools like shovels and scraped the snuff up from the floor. Only those who saw it can imagine what it looked like." This condition, however, evoked little complaint at the time, perhaps because almost everyone was responsible for it. "Ninety per cent of the operatives—kids and all—used to use snuff," an Augusta mill official told Broadus Mitchell in the second decade of the twentieth century. "We would get from the loom boxes, where they would leave them, a barrel of snuff boxes a week in cleaning."[22]

A final disagreeable aspect of the workplace, the monotony of most mill

21. *Manufacturers' Record*, June 8, 1894, p. 310.

22. Mary Cowper, "Writings and Notes on the Textile Industry" (Typescript in Mary O. Cowper Papers, Manuscript Department, Duke University Library, Durham, North Carolina); Broadus Mitchell, *The Rise of Cotton Mills in the South* (Baltimore, 1922), 171.

tasks, seems to have been more important to mill critics than to workers themselves. Mill work was simple and repetitive to the point of tediousness, yet workers seldom complained of monotony. They viewed mill work in terms of their total activity in the mills rather than as the rote tasks they were hired to do, which afforded them a quite different perspective from that of outside observers. Their day consisted of much more than the routines of spinning, weaving, or other tasks. The alternating rhythms of rush and rest, the intervals of play and socializing, and the opportunity periodically to move about all functioned to break the monotony of work itself and were no doubt engaged in for that purpose. The periodic interruptions of mill work had the same effect, as did high rates of absenteeism and closedowns of the entire mills. Because of the constant turnover of workers, there were new people to get to know or, alternatively, new workplaces and bosses to get accustomed to. This too broke routines and helped keep interest and anticipation alive.

Workers had other devices for preventing monotony, such as learning new jobs within the mill and transferring from one room—and boss—to another. "I done ever'thing there was to be done from sweepin' the floors and reelin' to spoolin' and spinnin'," Ann Waldrup recalled of her experience in mill work, which began in Athens, Georgia, in the 1870s. Jones I. Freeze recalled a different progression. "At first I doffed," he said, but "you keep a-goin' up, so I went to the spinning room and on to the weaving room. Then they put me to fixing looms." After a while he became an overseer.

"A PISTOL, A DIRK, AND A PAIR OF KNUCKS."

If the workplace was often sociable and relaxed, it was also often the site of tension and disputation, its rhythms occasionally disrupted by flashes of violence among workers. Mill folk were friendly by nature but temperamental and easily offended as well, and given at times to volatile, unreflective behavior.

The nature and extent of on-the-job violence are difficult to learn. Disputes and divisions occur in all large groups of people, but only exceptional incidents appear in historical records. Extraordinary events, however, generally reflect ordinary social forces, and that was true of outbursts of violence among mill workers. A few examples, the representativeness of which is unclear, will illustrate the point. One day in the early summer of 1904, Marion Carden, a twenty-year-old spinner at Atlanta Woolen Mills, walked by Paul Lipsey, a fellow employee, and slapped him on the head. The reason for this mischief is unknown, but Lipsey, "a sickly appearing little boy of 11 years," responded by throwing a spool at Carden and hitting him. Carden "then turned and caught [Lipsey] up in both hands, lifted him high in the air and slammed him down on the floor with much force," badly bruising the child's face and head. Someone had Carden arrested for this bit of brutality, and at his trial Carden "admitted throwing the boy to the floor, but [said] he did not lift him higher than 3 feet." He was ordered to pay a fine of $15.75 or serve thirty days in the city stockade.[23]

On Christmas Eve in 1901, Dunk Locklear and Langdon Bowie had a fight in the Anchor Duck Mill in Rome, Georgia, where both worked. During the fight, Locklear, who was thirty years old and six feet tall, grabbed "a piece of scantling 4 feet long" and advanced upon Bowie, "an 18 year-old boy belonging to one of Rome's most prominent families." "After warning" his onrushing attacker, in "self-defense" Bowie pulled a gun and shot Locklear, who died three days later.[24]

Boys in the mills were especially prone to violence. In the summer of 1904, Press McKinney and Clarence Edmondson "engaged in a fight" at Fulton Bag and Cotton Mills, where they were both employed. McKinney, who was only eleven years old, apparently lost the fight, perhaps because Edmondson was two or three years older and no doubt a stouter boy. McKinney "went to his brother immediately after the fight, borrowed a knife, and without warning, cut [Edmondson] with it." Two weeks later, when the story disappeared from the newspaper, Edmondson was "at the point of death" and McKinney in jail on a charge of assault with intent to commit murder.[25]

Death occasionally resulted from violent encounters. In the early morning hours of December 9, 1900, Cliff Harnesberger, a night watchman, and Charles Boyce, an operative, were playing cards in the engine room of Thomaston Cotton Mill in Georgia. During the game the two men "became involved in a difficulty over 50 cents." Boyce, who "was somewhat intoxicated, drew his knife and a desperate encounter ensued, during the progress of which Harnesberger was cut three or four times in the back." Harnesberger "drew his pistol and fired upon his antagonist three or four times, but Boyce continued to use his knife until Harnesberger tripped him up and ran off." A while later, Boyce was found in the engine room "lying on his

23. Atlanta *Constitution*, June 25, 1904.
24. *Ibid.*, December 28, 1901.
25. *Ibid.*, August 31, September 1, 15, 1904.

back dead, with two pistol shot wounds in his body just over the heart. His left coat sleeve was on fire and in his right hand he grasped an open knife."[26]

These incidents were certainly extreme, but they are relevant to understanding mill folk at work. The pathology that turned trivial disputes and boyhood fights into deadly encounters was something to guard against, for workers and bosses alike. No doubt such incidents encouraged both to develop strategies in personal relationships designed to avoid offensiveness. No doubt they also served to rationalize the belief that violence was a proper, or at least predictable, response to certain kinds of provocation. Certainly the incidents just described suggest that some folk believed murderous violence was sometimes necessary and appropriate. They also indicate that many of the men and boys among the mill folk were armed and willing to use their arms.

Among boys and men of all classes in the New South, carrying pocketknives—some the size of daggers—was almost universal, and not the least benefit in having a knife was its usefulness as a weapon. Men and boys in the mills carried knives as a matter of course, and that fact was surely known to everyone. Handguns were less numerous and probably not generally carried to work, but they too were widely owned and readily available. In December, 1905, illustrating how extreme this phenomenon of carrying weapons might be, John McAlister was arrested at Middle Georgia Cotton Mills at Eatonton because police mistook him for a fugitive murderer. When police searched him, they found he was carrying "a pistol, a dirk and a pair of knucks."[27]

The above incidents hint at the fact that workers on the job were sometimes intoxicated or partially so. How common this was is unknown, but in view of the widespread drinking in and about the villages, it seems likely that drinking on the job was not extraordinary. Some mills considered it enough of a problem to ban it in their written rules, and probably all of them officially forbade the practice. Individual overseers, however, may have tolerated drinking that did not interfere with work. Drinking is no doubt one explanation for the sudden outbursts of violence and the senseless brutality they sometimes involved. It is also no doubt something that made mill work more tolerable for men, especially those who had difficulty adjusting to the mills. But for folk who did not drink, that activity must have injected tension into the workplace.

26. *Ibid.*, December 10, 1900.
27. *Ibid.*, December 19, 20, 1905.

"IT . . . CUT MY LEFT ARM OFF, PULLING IT OFF AT THE ELBOW JOINT."

Drinking might also have added to accidents on the job. The mills were not safe places to work. There were no meaningful laws regarding dangerous machinery, fire protection, accident reporting, or other safety matters, just as there were none concerning ventilation, air quality, or sanitation.[28] Neither mill officials nor mill folk made up for the deficiency. Machinery and belting ran uncovered at high speed, and antiquated, poorly maintained machines remained in use long after they were reasonably safe to operate. Boiler explosions, belts breaking or falling off their shafting, and bobbins flying off their frames were among the resulting hazards.

Most accidents and injuries were probably due to carelessness and ignorance of bosses or workers, though quantitative information on accidents and their causes is unavailable. "It seems to me that we are having more accidents now than I have ever known before," J. H. M. Beaty of Olympia Mills wrote in 1907, "most of them coming from carelessness in the operative cleaning machinery while it is in operation." The occasion for Beaty's remark was "another woman having one or two of her fingers clipped off by disregarding the rules for cleaning up." The woman was "an experienced hand" who "knew better" than to clean her machines while they were running, Beaty complained. "I do not know of anything we can do to prevent these people taking such chances as this woman did."

There was, however, much Beaty and his mill could have done, for they were partly responsible for the woman's accident. Like other mill officials, Beaty required workers to clean their machines but did not pay them for doing so. Pay was based on the amount of cloth or yarn produced or the number of machines tended. The only safe way to clean machinery was to wait until it was stopped, but to wait meant working overtime without pay. One way to avoid that situation was to clean the machinery while it was running. "It is to the advantage of the operative running speeders to keep their machines in operation as they are paid by the piece," Beaty said of the accident just mentioned. "Several of the accidents we have had lately were of this class of machines and was caused by the operative trying to get their production and clean up at the same time."[29]

One solution to this problem would have been to permit operatives to

28. See *Senate Documents*, 61st Cong., 2nd Sess., No. 645, Vol. 19: *Labor Laws and Factory Conditions*.
29. J. H. M. Beaty to William Elliott, Jr., May 28, 1907, in William Elliott, Jr., Papers, South Caroliniana Library.

shut down and clean their machines individually during work time, but the mills, and probably most operatives too, wanted the machines to run continuously. "I was wiping out the head of the spinning frame by order of Mr. Broadwax [the boss spinner]," said John Edward Robertson, a doffer at Orange Mills in South Carolina, describing an accident that befell him in 1887. "He told me to clean off the frame, and while I had my hand in it, he hollowed 'Why in the Devil don't you start the frame.' As I was about to take my hand out to start the frame, it started itself, and cut my left arm off, pulling it off at the elbow joint, and which remained in the Spinning frame some thirty minutes afterward."[30]

Young Robertson had been working in the mill less than three days when he lost his arm, and his inexperience as well as the overseer's determination to keep up production contributed to the accident. The same combination was responsible for the injury eleven-year-old William Cody Hilton sustained at Fulton Bag and Cotton Mills in 1903. Young Hilton was employed in the carding room to do "a job that until a few months prior had been operated by men"; and his employment was a clear instance of a mill putting profit ahead of safety. "When the work was done by men," a reporter explained, "the job paid the sum of $1 per day," but "this wage was reduced to 60 cents per day and boys substituted for men." If "one boy was unable to do the work and two boys were necessary, the 60 cents was divided equally among them . . . and if three boys were required the wage was further divided," and each received twenty cents. On his third day at work, young Hilton was "caught in the machinery while pulling waste from a card." He had been "unable to reach the waste even by standing on tiptoe and . . . it was necessary for him to get over in the waste box" to do his work.[31]

Children and youths seem to have been disproportionately victims of accidents. Thus, in 1907 eleven-year-old Eva Rackley was injured while playing in Granby Mills in Columbia. Eva, a spooler, was "running from Elisa Mason and slipp down and hurt her left arm above [the] wrist." And Ross Hampton Owen, "a child only seven years and nine months of age," lost "one or two fingers" and had his "hand stiffened permanently" when he caught it "in the gearing" at Gainesville Cotton Mill in 1906.[32]

Some, probably most, mills had modest compensation plans, the purpose

30. "Statement of John Edward Robertson, Commonly Called Eddie, July 5, 1887" (Typescript in Finley-Henderson Family Papers, South Caroliniana Library).

31. Atlanta *Constitution*, November 22, 1903.

32. *Ibid.*, December 30, 1902; "Immediate Report of Accident, Granby Cotton Mills, July 3, 1907" (Typescript in Elliott Papers); *Journal of Labor* (Atlanta), January 19, 1906.

of which was to help the injured and avoid damage suits. The plans varied but typically paid doctors' bills and a small cash settlement, or perhaps wages during recuperation, at least for a while. When John Edward Robertson lost his arm, the mill paid his doctor's fees and gave his father "10 doll[ar]s to buy nourishment" for the young man.[33]

Such policies were meaningful only when injury was slight and recovery rapid. For workers with incapacitating injuries or lengthy convalescences, an accident was a financial as well as a physical disaster. "My wife got Badly hurt in the mill an the Company has Refused to help us," John Brown of Gray Mills in Spartanburg County wrote Governor Blease in 1913. "I cant leave her to work an i am in Bad sape[.] My Wife is in Beed [bed] an has Bin for 3 moths[.] The Gray Mill Company offered to pay her time an all expenses an tha have refused to comply with contract."[34]

Other mills were more generous. In 1894, Athens Manufacturing Company gave Mary Vincent "one lot of land & fifty Dollars in Cash in full payment for injury Sustained while in their employment by the dislocating of one of [her] eyes by a flying Shutter." The company also agreed "to place on said lot a Dwelling 32 feet long by 16 feet Wide Also to dig a Well and build a picket fence on the Strect side of said lot[,] Plaster the Dwelling and paint the Same & build a nice Porch over the front Door."[35]

Such generosity might have been explained by the paternalism of Robert L. Bloomfield, owner of the mill, or by the threat of legal action, or both. Certainly Mrs. Vincent, whose husband had deserted her and their small child, seemed to drive a hard bargain. Injured operatives sued the mills in numbers sufficiently large to cause some mills a problem. In the papers of William Elliott, Jr., an attorney for several South Carolina mills, are records of several such suits and of the reaction of mill officials to them. Sometimes the mills acknowledged the validity of a claim and settled out of court, as in the case of Wesley Adams, who received one thousand dollars from Olympia Mills early in the twentieth century.[36] In other instances, mill officials thought, perhaps correctly, that the suits were frivolous. This might have been the meaning of President Lewis W. Parker's remark concerning Addie Waltern's suit for one hundred dollars against Richland Cotton Mills in 1907. Mrs. Waltern "was walking down one of the aisles," according to her

33. "Statement of John Edward Robertson," in Finley-Henderson Family Papers.
34. John Brown to Blease, March 3, 1913, in Blease Papers.
35. A copy of the agreement is in Box 11, Chicopee Manufacturing Company Papers, University of Georgia Library.
36. A copy of the settlement is in Elliott Papers.

claim, "when she received a blow in the side because . . . the aisle was too narrow." An incensed Parker wrote the superintendent, "It was not a case of the aisle being too narrow, but . . . of the woman's being too large to try to go through the aisle."[37]

Parker was "exceedingly anxious to break up the disposition in Columbia to institute suits for damage." Not only did the suits cost money but they besmirched his reputation as a paternalist. To deal with the problem, Parker had his attorney prepare a "form of release" to be signed by injured workers. In return for signing the form, workers received some immediate compensation from the mill but gave up all rights to future claims. "I think it very important," Parker said, "that in the case of every accident before the employee returns to work he should be required to sign such release as a condition to the payment of his time during the period he was out of employment consequent upon the accident. I favor the general policy of paying this time in every case, provided the imposition is not too great and provided the accident is such as does not amount to criminal negligence."[38] Parker's concern is a reminder that relations between labor and management were a crucial factor in the workplace.

37. William Elliott, Jr., to J. S. Moore, May 16, 1907, Lewis W. Parker to Moore, May 16, 1907, in Elliott Papers.
38. Parker to Moore, June 18, 1907, in Elliott Papers.

7

INTERACTING WITH
BOSSES

Mill workers and bosses interacted in a complex, variegated workplace, and the nature of their interaction was kaleidoscopic and not easily summarized. The controlling factors were simple and easily stated; it is their applications and ramifications that are difficult to compress. The key elements were those that dominate workplaces everywhere.[1] Bosses wanted to extract from workers as much labor as was consistent with high profits and minimum levels of discord; and workers wanted to make a living with as little difficulty as was consistent with other aims they valued highly. Members of each group wanted to get along effortlessly but were willing to risk bother and tension, and even serious trouble at times, to accomplish a larger purpose. Both

1. In understanding this subject, I have benefited from Richard Edwards, *Contested Terrain: The Transformation of the Workplace in the Twentieth Century* (New York, 1979); Robert Blaumer, *Alienation and Freedom: The Factory Worker and His Industry* (Chicago, 1964); Michael Argyle, *The Social Psychology of Work* (New York, 1972); E. P. Thompson, "Time, Work-Discipline, and Industrial Capitalism," *Past and Present*, No. 38 (1967), 56–97; Daniel Nelson, *Managers and Workers: Origins of the New Factory System in the United States, 1880–1920* (Madison, Wis., 1975); Sidney Pollard, "Factory Discipline in the Industrial Revolution," *Economic History Review*, XVI (1963), 254–71; and Alex Inkeles, "Making Men Modern: On the Causes and Consequences of Industrial Change in Six Developing Countries," *American Journal of Sociology*, LXXV (1969), 208–25.

boss and worker could and did cause the other great difficulty, but both had compelling reasons for wanting to avoid difficulty and for conceding much to accomplish that, too.

Ultimately, the relationship hinged on power, but compromise and accommodation were important elements in its actual operation. This is not to suggest the relationship was equal, for it clearly was not. But inequality is a complex phenomenon, especially between interdependent groups, and does not preclude effective use of ingenuity and resourcefulness on the part of the weaker group. Certainly mill folk had their own arsenal of sticks and carrots for dealing with management, and if they were often ineffectual, even at times self-defeating, in their use of it, the same could be said of management's handling of its own much greater store of weapons.

The relationship always depended on specifics of place and time. No two mills were the same; indeed, because overseers had so much discretion, conditions varied widely from room to room in the same mill. Much depended on the chemistry between specific groups of workers and their overseers, and that hinged on factors of personality, sensitivity, and experience. Much more depended on larger matters: how often and why work was disrupted, whether efforts were underway to push workers beyond what they thought proper or customary, whether times were good or bad, whether there was a shortage or a surplus of workers locally.

Many mills were relaxed, their workplaces free of tension and festering grievance. "Everything is carelessly done," child-labor reformer Alexander J. McKelway, who was certainly no mill apologist, wrote of Athens Manufacturing Company in 1913. "The workers do pretty much as they please, and the lack of anything modern was very evident. The doffer boys play inside and outside the mill, in the summer they go in swimming and play baseball."[2]

To northerners familiar with New England mills, this informality was striking. Journalist L. A. Coolidge was "impressed particularly" during a tour of southern mills by "the easy way in which the operatives go about their work and their comfortable familiarity with the men in charge," and by the number of children at work as well. The two things were no doubt related. "The men in charge of mills know their hands by name and talk to them in a pleasantly informal and democratic way," Coolidge told his northern readers. "Work is taken easily. There is time to stroll about, to sit down occasionally, to run to a window once in a while for a bit of light and air. You

2. A. J. McKelway, *Child Labor in Georgia, No. II* (n.p., n.d.), 20, copy in Georgia State Archives.

will see girls tending the speeders perched nonchalantly on boxes at the end or the sides, clapping their heels as though they had nothing to do in the world." This atmosphere, Coolidge believed, was "one of the things which keeps the operatives contented with their meagre pay and long hours."[3]

Other mills, however, were as repressive and tension ridden as functioning workplaces can be. Fulton Bag and Cotton Mills and most of the Augusta mills were places of recurrent disputes and worker complaints, including several long, bitter strikes. Many large mills in the South Carolina upcountry, on the other hand, avoided open, sustained labor disruptions despite the grievances some of their workers reported to Governor Blease. This difference was no doubt due in part to the success or failure of individual paternalists. But more objective factors were also involved, among them the size and location of individual mills and how long their work force had been in mill work. Large mills, urban mills, mills located near one another, and especially large mills concentrated in cities where cotton manufacturing went back two or three generations were the most likely places of discontent among workers. This formulation suggests that mill workers were molded by their work, and that traditional ways gradually succumbed to modern industrial relationships.

"WHEN HE'D COME THROUGH THE MILL WE'D ALL JUST HANG AROUND JUST LIKE HE WAS OUR DADDY."

Mill folk encountered management on two levels. The more familiar level was that of immediate bosses, especially overseers and section hands, but in small mills the superintendents as well. At a much more distant level were presidents and owners—often the two were the same—and in large mills the superintendents, too. Encounters with working bosses were intimate and regular, often in antagonistic circumstances. These were the men who imposed rules and exacted work, gave orders and handed out fines, and it was they who usually personified things that aggrieved—and pleased—workers. Owners and presidents were distant overlords whom workers might never know personally. In the spring of 1902, President L. A. Thomas walked through King Mill just after most employees had walked out in a labor dispute. Seeing a nonstriking weaver still at his looms, Thomas approached him. "I congratulate you on your spunk," he said, referring to the weaver's rejection of pressure from other workers to join the strike. "Yes, by ———, I am going to [remain at work], but what in the hell

3. Quoted in *Manufacturers' Record*, February 11, 1898, p. 48.

have you got to do with it?" Thomas answered, "Nothing at all, except that I happen to be the president of the company." The man asked: "Are you L. A. Thomas? I am proud to meet you, sir."[4]

This distance between workers and high officials abetted the paternalistic stance of the latter. Freed from the day-to-day business of running their mills and thus from the disagreeable tasks of exacting labor from their employees, these men might come in contact with mill folk only in the role of generous overlords—rescinding decisions of lower bosses, excusing breaches of errant employees, dispensing largess at annual picnics, acting as philanthropists through the churches, schools, or clubs they sponsored in the villages. The most successful high-ranking officials understood the psychology of their employees and played to the paternalism that was expected of them; when they appeared among the folk, as they often did, it was as kindly, familiar patriarchs rather than as capitalists extracting surplus value. This stance was not pose alone, for in such men self-interest and natural bent coincided, indeed reinforced each other, and they exploited the advantage that combination gave them.

Mill folk responded positively to such men. "We all were a friend to him because he was our daddy," Bessie Buchanan remembered of "Mr. Bill" Erwin, owner of Erwin Mills, where she went to work as a child. "We loved him just like he was our daddy, because when he'd come through the mill we'd all just hang around just like he was our daddy." Among the reasons for this attitude was the familiarity with which Erwin and his family treated mill folk. Not only did Erwin himself talk pleasantly with workers but others in his family took evident interest in their lives. "I knew them all," Mrs. Buchanan said. "Bess, his daughter, taught me in Sunday school." Theotis Johnson Williamson, who went to work in Erwin's mill some years after Mrs. Buchanan, was equally positive in her recollections. "He was a wonderful person," Mrs. Williamson said of Erwin. "He'd come in the street and talk to you just like I'm talking to you. He'd stop. . . . Anybody wouldn't think that the man had the money, the job and everything that he had. And we've been to his house and picked grapes off his vines."

Such sentiments appear often in reminiscences of mill folk. "He was just a real nice fellow," Martin Lowe said of F. W. Poe, at whose mill he began working as a young man in 1912. "Real nice. He'd stop and talk with you. He'd stop and talk with a sweeper just the same as he would anybody else. He was just a nice man."

The relationship with overseers and other immediate supervisors was

4. Atlanta *Constitution*, April 9, 1902.

more varied. "They were real good, we liked them," Lessie Bowden Bland recalled of the bosses she worked for at Carrboro; "they were real thoughtful about us and all." In the same vein, Nellie Allen Pendergrass remarked, "They wasn't hard on us." Indeed, the boss spinner for whom Mrs. Pendergrass had gone to work as a child had been "good" to her. "He had a bunch of children working for him," she recalled; and he had not tried to inhibit their socializing as long as they kept up their work. Likewise, Alice Thrift Smith remembered that her bosses were "good" and that she had gotten along "just fine" in her work. "I sure was treated well," she recollected. "We would talk. And we would catch up with our work and then we would go sit down and talk. We had a good time."

These easy relationships with bosses were sometimes the result of kinship or simply friendship between bosses and workers. The boss spinner under whom Jessie Lee Carter worked was her uncle, and there are many examples of such relationships in the records.

Not all bosses were accommodating, however. "Back then, the boss man would get you for nothing," Alice P. Evitt recalled. "Maybe your work'd be runnin' bad and you couldn't keep it up good. You'd be workin' as hard as you could, and it would get all messed up. Some rollers choked up on it and you couldn't help yourself. It wasn't your fault, and they'd just raise cane with you about it. People doin' all they could do, that's all they could do." She continued: "They thought they could do more than they could do. They'd get on 'em and holler at them. You could hear them all over the plant—much fussin's that made—you could hear them holler at people. I never had one holler at me like that."

What, besides "messed up" work, caused such bother? "A lot of them go in there and they'd talk," Mrs. Evitt said of workers malingering in the restroom while "their work'd be going bad." The bosses would "go to the door and holler at 'em make 'em come out of there" and resume their work. Still, "if your work was caught up, you could go on and do what you want to do around. They didn't care. . . . You could go around and talk, or sit down. They had what they'd call cotton boxes at the end of the frame. You could sit down on them and rest a little bit. Just so you kept up your job."

"PEOPLE BACK THEN, THEY TRIED TO WORK WITH THE BOSS AND THE BOSS TRIED TO WORK WITH THEM."

Many bosses recognized that the workplace was an arena of conflicting interests and sought to accommodate to what mattered to workers. "People back then, they tried to work with the boss," Mrs. Evitt observed, "and the boss tried to work with them." For example, workers wanted to tend the same machines everyday and asserted a kind of proprietary right to do so. Assigning a worker's machines to someone else was thus one of the worst things a boss could do. "If they'd take their springs from 'em, they'd get mad at 'em—the sides or anything—they get mad and take 'em back," Mrs. Evitt recalled of the practice. "They's not supposed to take 'em. Whatever you run that's yours long as you stay there."

Bosses saw advantage in honoring such customs. "The boss man wouldn't let them," Mrs. Evitt said, describing an incident in which new workers tried to take over the machines of older workers. "He'd take them off. They could go work on the others or go home or whatever they wanted to do. He wouldn't let them take them." Workers appreciated such an act. "You worked with them," Mrs. Evitt said again, "and they worked with you."

This kind of reciprocity was explicit in the permission to socialize as long as work was running on schedule. It was implicit in the acquiescence in many smaller things that affected worker morale. Thus one worker might be permitted to "cover" for another while the latter left the workplace to buy a soft drink, smoke a cigarette, or run home for a minute. Workers who smoked had special problems. Cotton and cotton waste were highly flammable, and the risk of fire in the mills was high. All mills therefore prohibited smoking on the job and rigidly enforced the prohibition. Some even threatened to dismiss anyone bringing matches inside the mill. These stringent rules and the absence of scheduled work breaks forced smokers to fashion their own ways of having a cigarette. The most common was to go outside the mill to smoke, which required the acquiescence of overseers if not higher management itself. Everette Burchell remembered that he and a fellow worker took turns covering each other's work so that each could run out behind a nearby corn mill, "take two or three draws off a cigarette and then run back to the mill."

Workers viewed such privileges, once established, as rights, and efforts to withdraw them invariably caused difficulty. At one of the South Carolina mills she studied in the 1920s, Lois MacDonald found there had recently been confrontations over the "slack habits" of workers. The workers had been accustomed to "leaving the mill during work hours to cross the street and buy sandwiches and drinks," and when management issued "strict regulations" to end the practice, about eighty workers left the mill, though "a part of them" later returned "and promised to abide by the rules."[5]

5. Lois MacDonald, *Southern Mill Hills: A Study of Social and Economic Forces in Certain Textile Mill Villages* (New York, 1928), 44.

These examples suggest that one of the strategies management used to coax work from operatives was accommodating to some of their ways and values. The details of labor-management relations, in other words, were influenced by the cultural context in which they occurred. This influence was so great that it spawned the popular belief that only southerners could manage mill folk and entice them to work readily. "It was an accepted tradition that while northern men made good southern Superintendents, they could not be used as overseers," William G. Raoul wrote in his auto-biography.[6] The problem was, the idea ran, northerners did not understand mill folk and could not accommodate their peculiar ways.

Although Raoul was himself a southerner, his own experience was an object lesson in the meaning of the idea. After his two months at Exposition Mills, Raoul had gone to Lowell, Massachusetts, to learn mill management, and then returned to Georgia, where he got a job as an overseer at a mill in Roswell. "It was about the slackest twisted mill I was ever in," he wrote, imbued perhaps with Massachusetts efficiency. When Raoul fired an em-ployee for not doing his job, the employee appealed to the superintendent, who ordered him reinstated. "The damned mountain town was isolated," Raoul wrote of the incident. "Everybody was kin to somebody else, had lived there all their lives, and there wasn't anything else to do but work in the mill. Thus firing people was unknow[n]." When Raoul refused to re-instate the employee, he was himself dismissed.[7]

Such incidents suggest why mill officials from outside the South found it necessary to learn the ways of mill folk and the South. One who did so was Thomas Lang, superintendent of West Point Manufacturing Company, located across the Chattahoochee River from West Point, Georgia, in Lang-dale, Alabama. Born in England, Lang managed textile mills there before he went to West Point in 1878. By the turn of the century, he had absorbed the outlook of southern mill paternalists and become a notable example of that fraternity. The "slow and careless ways" southern workers once had, Lang told a reporter in 1900, disappeared under the discipline of mill work, and once their ways changed, they were model employees. "Their hesitancy to duty has been corrected" by experience, Lang explained, "and they are always willing to have their attention called to individual faults when po-litely pointed out to them, but will very quickly resent any manner that is not in keeping with their natural independence, which is a very marked

6. William G. Raoul, "Proletarian Aristocrat" (Typescript autobiography in Southern Historical Collection, Louis R. Wilson Library, University of North Carolina at Chapel Hill), 59.
7. *Ibid.*, 80.

feature in the southern people, no matter what their station in life may be."
Southern operatives were therefore "tractable," and "management is affec-
tionately drawn to them and a spirit of paternalism is created, and a feeling
engendered that becomes in every sense mutually beneficial."[8]

The element of reality behind this sentiment was far more difficult to
achieve than Lang's statement suggests. The atmosphere he describes was
in fact never fully achieved, as the plight of bosses who violated certain
cultural norms makes clear. In 1901, H. F. K. Booth, superintendent of a
knitting mill in Griffin, Georgia, directed one of his employees, Lavonia
Moore, "to do a certain bundle of work," which Mrs. Moore "refused to
do . . . without a ticket for it." An argument ensued in which, according to
Booth, Mrs. Moore "used strong language to him, whereupon he laid his
hand upon her shoulder and in turn was attacked by her with a needle,
which she drove into his hand." Mrs. Moore had a different version of what
happened. Booth had "grabbed the chair she was sitting in at her machine
and attempted to roughly upset her," according to her account. "She arose
protesting and he pushed her against the wall, grabbed her wrists, pulling
her to the office, where he again assaulted her and then roughly put her out
of doors." While this was happening, she "used the needle she had as best
she could, as it was her only weapon."

Such an incident was not an ordinary dispute between labor and management, as its aftermath showed. Folk in Griffin seem to have disliked
Booth—perhaps he was an overbearing supervisor. What he had done could
be considered abuse of a white woman under his charge—a far more serious
action than manhandling a mill worker. The result was an uproar, the
nature of which Booth probably understood since he acted to defuse it.
Specifically, he went to Mrs. Moore's home to apologize for his conduct, but
when he arrived there, "two outside parties" "roughly handled" him and
"ordered [him] to leave town." Booth retreated hastily but remained in
town, with the Griffin Rifles, the local militia unit, on alert to prevent
trouble. When the story disappeared from the newspaper, Booth was
"being guarded at his home on Taylor street by friends."[9]

The conduct of mill employees was thus something to be wary of. Volatility was sometimes turned against bosses. In 1896, for example, the boss
weaver at Mill No. 3 of Muscogee Manufacturing Company in Columbus
accused one of his hands, Bose Faulkner, "a boy of about sixteen years of

8. Atlanta *Constitution*, February 1, 1900.
9. *Ibid.*, February 28, 1901.

age," of "misplacing some cloth," and discharged him for suspected thievery. Young Faulkner "fancied" himself "greatly wronged" by the action and, in the words of a newspaper reporter, " 'tanked' up on mean whiskey and swore that he would have revenge." When the mill opened the next morning, he appeared in the weaving room and began wildly firing his "big Colt's revolver." The arriving weavers panicked, but perhaps because of the "mean whiskey," no one was hit. Poor Faulkner, however, inept to the end, was arrested and charged with shooting a firearm inside the city limits and, for good measure, with larceny of the missing cloth.[10]

A different and more characteristic problem faced Lem McDonald, a second hand at Exposition Mills, after he allegedly slapped fifteen-year-old Elizabeth Strickland for refusing to carry out one of his orders. Elizabeth appealed to her father, who charged McDonald with battery and had him arrested.[11] This kind of incident was probably a fixture of labor-management relations, for it grew out of the distinctive composition of the mill work force. More than half of all mill employees were dependent children or youths, and fathers who put their children in the mills did not in their own minds surrender control of the children. Nor, as they saw the situation, did they give up the right to protect them from abuse. The family, that is, continued to function in traditional ways, and if the mills often used that fact to advantage, they also sometimes experienced its disadvantage. The mills expected parents to discipline their children in as well as out of the workplace. But the other side to that coin was that children used parents as buffers against unwarranted discipline or abusive bosses.

Alice P. Evitt related an instructive example in her remarkable memoir. "Back then the boss man would get on you for nothing," she recalled. "Out to Highland Park, they was awful bad about that. My daddy was about to get in trouble—'bout to whoop one of them bosses about gettin' on my sister so much. He'd get on her [whenever] she'd go to the bathroom. He'd holler and go on at her that way, and [my daddy] didn't allow men to do like that." The family quit that mill and moved away. "[My daddy] was about to get in trouble," Mrs. Evitt repeated. "He was about to whoop [the boss man], or try to whoop him."

This was not a unique event. "They'd do all them spinners that way," Mrs. Evitt continued. "After I went to work in there, they knowed my daddy, they never did holler at me or nothing like that. . . . Back then, the

10. Columbus *Daily Enquirer-Sun*, May 8, 1896.
11. Atlanta *Constitution*, February 27, 1907.

bosses, they just thought they could boss you around and make you do as they say do. They would them that would listen to them, but we never did listen to them, cause my daddy told us not to. So, he knowed we wasn't goin' to do nothin' wrong, but he wanted us to do our work right. They was just mean to people back them days. I never had them be mean to me that way." One's willingness to accept Mrs. Evitt's account of such incidents is enhanced by her ability to make discriminating judgments about "mean" behavior. "When I wanted off and couldn't get off," she said, "that wasn't being mean, they just needed me."

Not all parents were as discerning as Mrs. Evitt's father. In 1903 John Burnett, boss carder at Bibb Manufacturing Company, credited one of the children in his employ with less time than the child thought he had worked. The child disputed with Burnett to no avail, and then appealed to his father, W. T. Padgett, who "took up the row, and began abusing Burnett," who "made every effort to avoid trouble." Burnett was unyielding, however, and the incident rankled Padgett. One night thereafter, while he was drinking, Padgett went to Burnett's home and, being refused entrance, stood outside and "abused Burnett loudly and emphatically." Burnett went out to remonstrate, but Padgett came at him threateningly, and Burnett "pulled his pistol and fired at his adversary three times." The first two bullets missed, but "the third . . . struck Padgett on the left nipple," and he later died.[12]

Family ties, treatment of women, and racial mores, like paternalism and slow, irregular work, were among the cultural forms that intruded into labor-management relationships. All were troublesome to mill officials, but accommodation to these forms was an integral part of the structure of control. Mill folk were generally respectful of the larger prerogatives claimed by management in the workplace, and one reason mill owners were able to exploit that fact was their accommodation to folk in lesser things. One of the keys to understanding mill work in the New South lies in recognizing and appreciating the compromise involved in that exchange. Workers and owners had differing priorities, and each group was willing to grant something to the other in return for considerations of its own. Management's priorities were money, power, and the prerogatives necessary to achieve and hold onto those things; those of workers were social and cultural traditions ill-suited to a contest with the rich and powerful.

12. *Ibid.*, November 13, 23, 1903.

"THEY LOAFED AND DID AS THEY PLEASED, AND THE RESULT WAS WE HAD
TO CLOSE DOWN."

Mill folk were troublesome employees, and they often resisted management, with varying degrees of success. In 1899, loom fixers at the Swift,
Hamburger, and Muscogee mills in Columbus joined together in an effort to
be relieved of routine cleaning duties they had to perform on "dead" time.
For a long while, they tried to negotiate the matter with their superintendents to no avail, and when nineteen of them simply refused to do the
cleaning, they were summarily dismissed. In 1891, in another kind of
incident, about fifty workers walked out of one of the mills in Concord,
North Carolina, fearing exposure to smallpox brought in by new workers.
Upon hearing their complaint, the superintendent ordered them to return
to work at once, threatening to dismiss those who did not and force them to
vacate the company's houses immediately. Apparently believing the threats,
all workers "came back in time," the superintendent stated, "& I let them
go to work except the one that started the bolt. I discharged him and made
him get out of the Company's House."[13]

Other incidents had more ambiguous results. The night shift that Fulton
Bag and Cotton Mills instituted in 1898 had to be discontinued after a few
months in part because workers would not work at night despite inducements from management. "The men and boys and some of the women
would stay awake all day and could not work at night," an official of the mill
told the Industrial Commission of the incident, "and the labor [cost] advanced so proportionately to our total poundage cost that we could not
afford to run the mill at night any longer. As an evidence of it, we kept a
record of the number of cuts from each loom, and although a weaver might
get off only a half cut per loom per night, they would still expect the full cut
prices when the week came around, claiming it was the greater amount. So
as to make the night run a success, we gave in to them for several weeks,
hoping to gather a large body of hands so that we could make it go." He
continued: "We found it an utter failure. They loafed or did as they pleased,
and the result was we had to close down the night run."[14]

13. Columbus *Enquirer-Sun*, October 15, 1899; Allen H. Stokes, "Black and White Labor
and the Development of the Southern Textile Industry, 1800–1920" (Ph.D. dissertation,
University of South Carolina, 1977), 168.
14. *House Documents*, 57th Cong., 1st Sess., No. 184, Vol. 7, p. 571.

On other occasions workers had more success in challenging management. In 1886, weavers at Algernon Mill accused overseer D. E. McGaw of "abusive and tyrannical" conduct and of cheating them in "that he does not put down to the weaver [all] the cloth that he is entitled to." When McGaw proved unresponsive to their complaints, they staged a walkout and remained out until McGaw resigned his position. The resignation was arranged by higher officials as a way of appearing not to give in to the workers, but the workers had made their point. Other workers staged slowdowns to the detriment of overseers they disliked. "The hands, in the last weeks, have been doing little or no work," a reporter wrote after interviewing the boss spinner at Riverside Mills in Augusta in 1886, "neglecting their duties to such an extent that the production has fallen off in his department at least one-third" and "the superintendent was blaming [the overseer] for the falling off in the production."[15]

"I HAVE BEN GOIN TO NIGHT SCHOOLS FOR A NUMBER OF YEARS OF WHICH I HOLD A TEXTILE DIPLOMA."

The effort to turn mill folk into a disciplined work force foundered on the absence of the work ethic among them. Mill officials recognized this fact about their workers, and some of them understood its nature and consequence. The problem, as August Kohn stated in 1907, was that mills could not "by any persuasion, pay or premiums, induce their operatives to appreciate the old-time maxim that 'keeping everlastingly at it brings success.' "[16]

The difficulties were multiple, as mill representatives saw them: mill folk lacked economic and social discipline because they did not honor loyalty, thrift, perseverance, and contractual obligation, and they did not honor those things because they had no appreciation of the values of material accumulation. They were not consumers, in short, and therefore had little of the drive that motivated people to work, save, and accumulate.

The North Carolina labor commissioner regularly asked employers to comment on the needs of working people, and his annual reports are filled with lamentations from mill owners and superintendents on these points. What were mill workers most in need of? "To be taught and in some way *compelled* to observe the sacredness and binding force of a contract,"

15. Augusta *Chronicle*, June 12, 20, 1886.
16. August Kohn, *The Cotton Mills of South Carolina* (Charleston, 1907), 22.

thought John F. Schenck of Cleveland Cotton Mills, and to "know that the greatest promotor of contentment and happiness is constant and honorable employment." To see "that honest labor is far better for them and the country than useless, loitering and slothful lives," a Craven County mill official suggested. "To be fed on some food which will give them the inclination, or desire, to work six days a week, save their money, and rest more than a few days in one place," another mill representative replied.[17]

The folk lacked acquisitiveness. Discussing his difficulty in recruiting and retaining labor, the superintendent of Atlanta Cotton Mill complained especially of women workers. "They actually seem to have no idea of work," he said, meaning the kind of disciplined work required in modern industry. He stated that "there is nothing like regularity" among them. "They come in two or three days on time, but they know nothing of the steady, plodding, faithful work" that characterizes model employees. The latter, unlike his own workers, the superintendent explained, "never lose an hours time in three months of work" and "are thrifty, careful, and ambitious." The only way to reform his own workers, the superintendent thought, was to imbue them with the consumer spirit. The women needed to be taught the advantages of steady income—that it "could be used to improve the house, to make the home happier, and better, and to add a hundred little comforts." They needed to know that "it would buy better clothes, a few books or pictures, a scrap of carpet, and would make [them and their] family happier and better." It "would [also] allow for a little saving each week," the superintendent continued, and "at length enough might be accumulated to buy a little home." Working women "have more money and can fix up more" than those who are idle, he said, clinching his argument, and are "much more apt to catch good husbands."[18]

One way to make work more attractive might have been to make it more remunerative, but the logic as well as the self-interest of mill owners prevented wage increases. "In a great many cases," William H. Williamson of Pilot Mills said in 1907 after a period of rising wages, "it seems the higher wages received, instead of being an incentive for doing more work, and becoming expert in their work, have just the reverse effect. Owing to the increase in wages, it seems a great many [workers] try to do as little as possible just to get along. We find, also, quite a number of operatives do not

17. North Carolina Bureau of Labor Statistics, *Annual Report, 1908*, 22, *Annual Report, 1896*, 121, *Annual Report, 1907*, 247, hereinafter cited as NC *Labor Report* by year.
18. Atlanta *Constitution*, November 20, 1879.

work regularly, finding that, with the increase of wages, they can live on four or five days' work, whereas, before, it required six days."[19]

These complaints are understandable and even contain an element of truth, but the mill owners would have been more convincing had they acted to encourage the qualities they wanted mill folk to have. If the rewards of work, thrift, and personal discipline were what mill representatives said they were, their employees would never know it from their mill experience. Large numbers of workers, for example, received no pay at all in the usual sense of the word. Children, youths, and even dependent adults, especially women, gave their pay to a parent, who might or might not return a small portion of it to them. Often, the parent received the pay directly from the mill. "About the best thing I can suggest for the improvement of operatives and by these I mean all minors, is some way to compel their lazy, loafing fathers to allow them (the minors) a certain proportion of wages earned," a North Carolina mill executive wrote the labor commissioner in 1896. "I have tried this experiment . . . under such a system the efficiency of my help, sixty per cent of whom are children from twelve to eighteen, has increased fully twenty-five per cent, if not more. I simply conferred with the heads of families and arranged for the children to receive a certain proportion of their wages, with the result that practically without an exception every one began to work more diligently in order to run their wages above the limit where their portion began."[20]

The success of this experiment points to another side of the subject. Mill folk did not think in terms of careers and advancement, for theirs was not a progressive view of life. The kind of security they sought generally came not from accumulation but from the absence of threats to self-respect. Not everyone fits this formulation, of course. Those distinguished by ambition and improvement almost always left the mills. "Successful" workers thus disappear from the record as mill folk, and mill work is studied through the experience of folk who remained at it rather than those who left it. Yet the latter were mill folk too, if only for a while. Of course there were middle-class people who worked one or two summers in the mills to earn spending money—Olin D. Johnston, who later became a United States senator from South Carolina, for example. But the concern here is with folk from the operative class who moved up from the mills because they learned and followed middle-class values. In view of the large turnover of mill workers,

19. Cathy L. McHugh, "The Family Labor System in the Southern Cotton Textile Industry, 1880–1915" (Ph.D. dissertation, Stanford University, 1981), 20.
20. NC *Labor Report* (1896), 131.

this group was probably large enough to take account of, but its size cannot even be guessed.

It is possible only to glimpse the experience of such folk. That glimpse comes not from evidence that a minority of operatives had savings accounts, owned real property, and the like but from bits of information about operatives trying to leave the mills for reasons that reflect ambition and the desire for self-improvement. Among the folk who wrote Governor Blease was Floyd W. Garrison, "a Mill Boy of 34 years of age," who worked at Orr Mills in Anderson. "Per haps I had Better Explain My Silf," Garrison wrote the governor in 1913. "I have Ben Goin to Night Schools For a Number of years of Which I hold a Textile Diploma having 21 years Experance as an operator[.] Furthermore I have about 16 Months Studys Under Certain Members of the Local Bar of Which I Wish to Complete During this year and Will Need Some Funds Besides or in Addition to My Wadges of Which I Earn in the Mill." Garrison continued: "This Seems Necessary In Order for Me to Get Certan Books that I Will Need to Enable Me to Make a Complete Success as to this I Am Determining to Do[,] And Were thankin Per hap you Would give Me an appointment of Some Kind that of Which Would Be of More Pay than My Present Salary of $35 Per Month[.] [I]f you haven Nothing of this Kind Per Haps you could Find a Side Line of Which I Could Run In Addition to My Present Work of Which it Would Be of Great Help to Me thrue My Work. . . . I am also a Graduate in Book keeping."[21]

The letter is remarkable for many reasons. It reflects not only aspiration and perseverance but ineffectuality in using those qualities to gain concrete rewards. It therefore reflects the difficulties mill folk had improving themselves. The lack of money for books and for attendance at regular schools, and the unlettered writing too, certainly inhibited advancement. The unwillingness to quit the mill—to seek opportunity and fortune elsewhere— suggests a fear of risk that had the same effect. Even the decision to write Blease itself might be evidence not of capacity for individual daring but of lingering reliance on an overlord. The letter thus pictures an individual struggling between two worlds.

A. H. Walker, who grew up at Pelzer and "was forced to work at an early age" because his father was "very feeble," was another such individual. In 1912, at age twenty-four after twelve years in the mills, Walker too wrote Blease for help. "Mill work does not agree with me," he told the governor,

21. Floyd W. Garrison to Coleman L. Blease, December 4, 1913, in Coleman L. Blease Papers, South Carolina State Archives.

asking for assistance in obtaining "a good out-of-door position" where he could "get plenty of fresh air." Listing his qualifications, Walker noted: "I have a very good common education. Of course I was compelled to do all my studying at night school. . . . What I want is something I can make a mark at. I believe I have the talent."[22]

W. H. Bishop, employed at Duncan Mills, also wanted to move up from mill work. "I am a graduate student in the C T Ludwig Detective Schooling," he wrote Blease, "and I Will Reply [apply] to you for a Job[.] . . . I would like for you to instruction Me[.] I am a Man age 37 years," and "a Sicterson of Greenville." An accompanying letter attesting to Bishop's graduation from Ludwig, a correspondence school in Kansas City, was dated August 23, 1912, five months earlier than the letter to Blease. Bishop was obviously having a hard time finding work as a detective.[23]

"THEY MUST BE RESPECTFUL BOTH IN LANGUAGE AND DEPORTMENT TO THEIR RESPECTIVE OVERSEERS."

Controlling workers was the basic problem of mill management. Paternalism, accommodation, and efforts to inculcate middle-class values were helpful in handling that problem but insufficient to solve it, and the mills developed more formal instruments of control. One was written contracts. Neither workers nor mills regarded their relationship as primarily legal, and for this reason written agreements between them were exceptional. "Employees are frequently averse to signing contracts," investigators for the 1907–1908 labor study reported. "The reason seemed to be a feeling that they were signing away some part of the independence which constitutes such a marked trait of character of southern mill operatives." In place of written agreements, most mills posted work rules and declared them binding on all employees, whom they agreed to pay at "regular" rates. "The above regulations are considered as a part of the contract with each person entering the employment of Graniteville Manufacturing Company," read rules posted in that mill in 1889, "and a strict compliance therewith will be required."[24]

Such an arrangement had little advantage for workers, for mills changed rules and pay rates at their own discretion. Yet written contracts were hardly

22. A. H. Walker to Blease, February 10, 1912, in Blease Papers.
23. W. H. Bishop to Blease, March 24, 1913, in Blease Papers.
24. *Senate Documents*, 61st Cong., 2nd Sess., No. 645, Vol. 1, p. 243; File 147, Graniteville Manufacturing Company Papers, University of South Carolina at Aiken Library.

better, perhaps even worse, for they put in writing inequities oral agreements merely implied. Thus, when Jennie Richardson contracted to work as a quiller at Pilot Mills in 1896, she agreed to obey "the rules and regulations governing [the] department" in which she worked and to accept "the regular [but unspecified] wages of the mill." She also pledged "to give a notice of not less than 10 days" before quitting and agreed that upon failure to do so, "on account of the difficulty of ascertaining the exact damages sustained" by the mill as a result of her failure, "the damage shall be whatever [back pay] is due" her at the time. She further agreed "to perform her work in a faithful and workmanlike manner, and to be promptly at work, except in case of sickness or necessity." The mill, however, reserved the right to discharge her "without giving her any notice, for any misconduct, violation of any rule, or for bad, and imperfect work."[25]

A year earlier F. R. Eastman signed a similar contract, also with Pilot Mills, to work as a beamer-warper. In his contract, Eastman agreed to "work in a faithful and workmanlike manner [and] to the satisfaction" of the mill, and if he were responsible for any interruption of work, he "agree[d] to allow" the mill to deduct from his daily wage "10 cents per loom for each loom standing a day, and pro rata amounts for looms standing a fraction of a day." He, too, pledged to give a ten-day notice and to forfeit all back wages if he quit without doing so. Finally, he acknowledged the mill's right to discharge him "on account of any misconduct or nonperformance of duties" as well as its right to "be the judge of such misconduct and nonperformance."[26]

Contracts were often with heads of families rather than with individual workers, and covered all members of the family, workers and nonworkers alike, who lived in company housing. Such agreements generally specified the number of workers the family was to furnish rather than the names of specified workers, perhaps requiring all children above twelve to work in the mill. The contracts also covered company housing, generally obligating the family to vacate its house whenever the mill asked.[27]

Parents who did not work in the mills might sign contracts for their children who did. Thus in 1896 Rufus King signed a contract for his son Walter to work as a quiller at Pilot Mills. The elder King agreed "to make

25. Legal Papers, 1893–1915, in Pilot Cotton Mill Papers, Manuscript Department, Duke University Library, Durham, North Carolina.
26. *Ibid.*
27. See the model contract printed in *Senate Documents*, 61st Cong., 2nd Sess., No. 645, Vol. 1, p. 242.

said Walter King perform his work in a faithful and satisfactory manner, and not to allow him to absent himself from the mill unless he is sick, or for some other reason satisfactory" to the mill. He also pledged "to make" his son "work a notice of two weeks" and to forfeit all back pay due him if he failed to do so, and agreed that if Walter "disobeys the rules of the mills, and does anything mean, or becomes insubordinate," Walter would owe the mill five dollars.[28]

These contracts reveal problems mills had in managing workers. Obviously the basic problem was undependableness—the tendency of workers to quit suddenly and frequently, do "imperfect" work, and commit acts of indiscipline in the workplace. These problems were of such magnitude that mill owners thought it necessary to develop a structure of grossly inequitable controls to try to neutralize them. The threat of dismissal was not enough to achieve the control desired, so it was reinforced by a number of strategies designed to ensure discipline in the workplace and inhibit free movement of workers from one mill to another.

The first step in disciplining workers was posting work rules. In some mills, the rules had a paternal gloss; in others, they were simple listings of dos and don'ts. At Graniteville in 1889, each overseer was "required to use his best endeavors to create and preserve a general good feeling among his help, by encouraging kindness one to the other, at the same time requiring strict obedience to all rules laid down." He was also admonished to avoid "violent, abusive, or profane language," and whenever "enforcement of discipline [was] necessary," to exercise "patience and moderation both of language and deportment." Rules in the spinning room at Spartan Mills in the 1890s, on the other hand, were a simple list of don'ts, some of which were aimed at supervisors. "Dont Let Sexian Hand curse Before their Help or Put their Hands on thim," the boss spinner was admonished, and "Dont Let Head Doffers put their Hands on Doffers or curse thim."[29]

Work rules were statements of management ideals as well as mirrors of management's problems. "All the operatives will be *required* to be *promptly* at their stations for work at the *last tap of the bell*," read one rule in effect at Graniteville in 1889. "They must be respectful both in language and deportment to their respective overseers, comply with their directions respecting their work, and observe every rule of the room in which they are employed.

28. Legal Papers, 1893–1915, in Pilot Cotton Mill Papers.
29. File 147, Graniteville Papers; William W. Thompson, "A Managerial History of a Cotton Textile Firm, Spartan Mills, 1888–1958" (Ph.D. dissertation, University of Alabama, 1960), 63.

They must [also] be *particularly* attentive to the *cleaning* and *oiling* of the machinery on which they are engaged, and neatness in their own person and habit is enjoined." Moreover, "they are not to absent themselves from their work without the consent of their overseer, or person in charge of the room, except in case of sickness, when they are required to send him word of the cause of their absence." And "during working hours they must not leave the room without the permission of their overseer—this is strictly enjoined."

Not just work itself but the deportment of workers was outlined in rules. At Graniteville, "want of capacity, or unfaithfulness in the performance of duty," was enjoined alongside "intemperance, profanity, or improper treatment of overseers, or associates." Each of these was "deemed sufficient cause for dismissal." Workers who damaged mill property through carelessness would have repair or replacement costs deducted from their wages, and those willfully doing such damage would be charged double the cost to the mill and dismissed as well.[30]

At Olympia Mills in 1907, employees were forbidden "to touch any machine or machinery which they have not been ordered to operate or work upon"; and the boss spinner at Spartan Mills in the 1890s was directed to make sure his workers worked carefully and thoroughly. "Dont Let Spinners Leve their work Down at Stopping time," his instructions read. "Dont Let Doffers do Bad doffen or Leve Down ends"; "Dont Let Sweepers Leve Flore Durty at Stoping time"; and "Dont Let Spoolers Hands tye Long knots or Make Bad Spools."[31]

Many rules were aimed specifically at children. At Olympia Mills, for example, rules in effect early in the twentieth century forbade "running, wrestling, scuffling, or indulging in any kind of play in any part of the [mill]," and banned employees from "any part of the [mill] where their own work or where necessity does not require them to be." At Saxon Mills a few years earlier, spinners, no doubt many of them children, were directed not to "get in Back ally and talk in bunches," not to "Lay out at the Winder When Running or Stop at Noon," not to "fuss in Side of the Mill or in Side of the Fence of the Mill," and not to "Stay in Warter house till work get down or go at doftime." And spoolers were not to "go to the Warter house in Crouds or Carry Eney Bobbins or Waste with thim."[32]

30. File 147, Graniteville Papers.
31. A copy of the rules at Olympia Mills is in William Elliott, Jr., Papers, South Caroliniana Library; and the rules at Saxon Mills are in Thompson, "A Managerial History of a Cotton Textile Firm," 63.
32. Copy of rules at Olympia Mills, Elliott Papers; Thompson, "A Managerial History of a Cotton Textile Firm," 63.

Adolescent workers were a problem, too, though they seem not to have been singled out by rule makers. "The worst thing in a factory is a sixteen-year old boy," President Hamilton H. Hickman of Graniteville said in 1883. "He will give more trouble than anybody else. . . . It is the sixteen-year-old boys that give us nearly all the trouble we have."[33]

Workers could be troublesome outside their work stations, too. Overseers at Graniteville were "especially enjoined to detect and report any person writing on or defacing the walls of any part of the factory, or using cotton or waste in the water closets." The fine for these infractions was five dollars for the first offense and dismissal for the second.

Whether such rules were written in response to specific events is unclear, but scattered pieces of information suggest that the mills' concern with security against their own employees was not entirely misplaced. Some mills were enclosed in fences; and if the fencing sometimes functioned to keep workers inside the mills during work hours, it also kept them outside at other times. Apparently all mills had night watchmen, one of those functions was to guard the mills against arson, vandalism, and other forms of destructiveness.

Evidence of sabotage of mill property by workers is scant, apparently because sabotage itself was rare. It did occur, however, suggesting that worker dissatisfaction occasionally overflowed into calculated acts of vengeance. In the same year Graniteville mill posted the aforementioned rule against willful destruction of property, someone entered the mill one night and "cut the warps in all but fifteen of the looms in the weaving room." The fifteen not cut "were near where the watchman had to pass to wind up his clock, and were left untouched to prevent attracting the watchman's attention." President Hickman did "not believe the vandal act was that of any employe," and perhaps it was not. But only a disgruntled employee or former employee would seem to have motive for such an act. The destruction forced the mill to close for several days.[34]

Another such incident occurred at the cotton mill in Savannah, Georgia, in the summer of 1904. Someone piled cotton around each of the machines on the ground floor, connected the piles with rows of additional cotton, and about 3:00 A.M. on July 25 started "an incendiary fire." The cotton was arranged so that "the flames [could] communicate more readily with the different machines filled with the inflammable cotton," and only swift ac-

33. *Senate Documents*, 48th Cong., 1st Sess., No. 91, p. 741.
34. Atlanta *Constitution*, March 21, 22, 1889.

tion by firemen prevented a major conflagration. But as the fire on the ground floor was extinguished, another broke out on the floor above, and while firemen were diverted to the second blaze, "the cotton rolls connecting the machinery [on the ground floor] were removed . . . and made away with, thus destroying that much of the evidence of incendiarism."[35]

"WHAT IS KNOWN AS DOCKING IN COTTON MILLS IS NOTHING BUT ROBERY."

The mills enforced their rules ultimately by dismissing workers, but that action was self-defeating if the worker was skilled and productive or if no replacement was available. Mill officials therefore created a series of intermediate punishments, the most important of which was a system of fines— "docking" their pay, the workers called it. The practice was widespread, though not universal, and it apparently diminished over the course of the New South era. Of 152 mills reported on in the 1907–1908 labor study, 100 imposed fines, mostly for poor work, insubordination, or absenteeism. In some mills, employees who worked in the morning but did not return after dinner were fined the amount they earned that morning. In others, those absent one day were fined a fourth of their earnings from the previous day and those out a week lost a quarter of what they had earned the preceding week. A Monday absence might mean the loss of the previous Saturday's earnings. Workers who came in late might be docked a half day's pay regardless of how little time they lost; or they might be laid off for a while for violating work rules. In 1907 and 1908, operatives were fined for such forms of misconduct as "disorder, fighting, mischief, impertinence to the overseer, throwing bobbins to hit employees, and insulting persons who pass by the mill." They were also docked for "loitering, remaining too long in toilet rooms, opening windows without permission, not cleaning machinery, and violation of other mill rules or disobedience to overseer's orders."[36]

Workers resented this system. "What is Known as Docking in Cotton Mills," one of them wrote Governor Blease, "is Nothing But Robery." Two others wrote: "I think it is Rediciouls for iny one to Work hard and Some one to Rob them out of it. We have ben employed By the Brogon Mill and We Stayed out on the 24th and Went in on the 25th and they talked Rough to us and We quit and they docked us $5.00 Each. And we have been to See the

35. *Ibid.*, July 26, 1904.
36. *Senate Documents*, 61st Cong., 2nd Sess., No. 645, Vol. 1, pp. 333–35; *Journal of Labor* (Atlanta), August 27, 1906; Charleston *News and Courier*, March 6, 1897.

Lawyers and I think they are employed by all of the Mills here And Would like for you to look into the Matter as We are poore Boys and Wouldnt like to loose that Much Money."[37]

No information is available on how much pay individual workers lost through fines over meaningful periods of time and what portion of mill payrolls were recouped as a result of the system. In 1914 the management of Fulton Bag and Cotton Mills reported that fines there totaled no more than $10 in a weekly payroll of $11,500, and that the cost of deducting them exceeded the amount collected. Mill folk gave a different impression. "The Westervelt Mills claim they are in debt a half Million dollars," one of that firm's employees wrote Governor Blease. "They are docking the weavers from 25c to 50c on a 2. two cut of cloth. [T]hey dock each and every Weaver 25c to as high as 2.00 two dollar a week and deduct it from his wages and we cant help our Selves. Mr Blease please help us[;] please look in to this[.] I offer for proof every weaver in the weave Room[.] Mr Blease it is a Shame." The employee continued: "The poor people is here and it Seeme like they cant get away from the mill[.] [T]hey are in debt at the Stores and Seems like they want to Stay to get out of debt. Mr Blease it looks So hard for us and it Seems like we cant help our Selves[.] [T]hey dock us for first class cloth[.] [I]t is just like I tell you."[38]

"WHEN WE MAKE FORTY CENTS PER DAY WE CAN *LIVE*, BUT THAT'S ABOUT ALL."

Docking was part of a larger system through which wages and pay schedules were used to try to control workers. Both income levels and control mechanisms were integral parts of the system. Concerning the former, the key factor was not individual wages per task, day, or pay period, nor the average wage of an "average" worker whatever the base of calculation. Those factors were important, of course, and in all those forms wages were low. Stories of children earning 10¢ or 20¢ a day are true as well as numerous, as are those of adults making no money at all as "learners" and 40¢ or 50¢ a day as experienced hands. After the turn of the century, $1.00 a day was still an exceptional wage. Investigators who totaled the earnings of workers in 151 mills for one week in 1907 found those earnings ranging from less than $2.00 to more than $12.00, but at intervals of $1.00 each, the greatest

37. S. M. Miller to Blease, April 26, 1914, Claud Abbott and Henry Kirby to Blease, May 26, 1911, in Blease Papers.
38. Atlanta *Constitution*, June 3, 1914; Albert Burnett to Blease, January 10, 1914, in Blease Papers.

frequency occurred between $4.00 and $4.99. About 12 percent of the workers surveyed earned less than $2.00 during the week, and more than half (53 percent of males and 58 percent of females) earned less than $5.00. Two-thirds (68 percent) of the females and half (48 percent) of the males over sixteen made less than $1.00 a day.[39]

These earnings were recorded after the hard times of the 1890s had abated and some improvement in wages had occurred. They are therefore a reminder of how low wages of individual workers were in absolute terms. Yet family income was a more meaningful indicator of economic well-being (and a more important instrument of social control), and it presents a more positive picture. In 1,567 mill families in 1907, net cash income averaged $822 a year, a not inconsequential sum for the time and place, though the average figure obscured wide variations among individual families. Not surprisingly, the variations had less to do with wage levels than with family composition. In families with working fathers, income averaged $900, while in those with working mothers the figure was $672, fully 25 percent less—striking evidence that mothers generally worked in poorer families only. The amount earned by working fathers and mothers, $306 and $187 respectively, attests not only to wage differentials between men and women but to the fact that working mothers worked fewer days than working fathers.[40]

These figures show that children earned large, vital shares of family income. Children under twelve who worked provided 13.5 percent of their families' income in 1907, twelve- and thirteen-year-olds provided 17.6 percent, and fourteen- and fifteen-year-olds 22.9 percent.[41] About 19 in 20 of the children fourteen and older were at work in the 1,567 families studied in 1907, as were 17 in 20 of all twelve- and thirteen-year-olds.[42]

The key indicator of economic well-being was not cash income but total compensation for families. Compensation included not only cash wages or the face value of trade checks, or "tickets," but the value as well of everything else the family received, including housing and other subsidies, gardens and livestock products, and income from boarders and nonmill work. From total compensation figures must be deducted the cost of fines at work

39. *Senate Documents*, 61st Cong., 2nd Sess., No. 645, Vol. 1, p. 305.
40. *Ibid.*, 316.
41. *Ibid.*, 432.
42. Actual figures in 1,567 families in the southern states were 96.9 percent of male children over sixteen; 93.9 percent of female children over sixteen; 96.2 percent of all children fourteen and fifteen; 87.6 percent of all children twelve and thirteen; and 15.6 percent of all children under twelve (*Ibid.*, 424–25).

and overcharges at company stores and of losses absorbed by trading company checks with outside merchants. For most of these amounts, debit and credit alike, quantitative data are lacking, though available information suggests that indirect income was significantly large. Among the families studied in 1907, for example, 3 in 8 (36.7 percent) had gardens, 1 in 4 (26.3 percent) kept boarders, 1 in 4 (26.2 percent) owned milk cows, 1 in 10 (10 percent) raised hogs, 1 in 6 (17.2 percent) had chickens, and 1 in 25 (3.9 percent) owned rental property (from which they received an average rent of $113.07). The cash value of the income from these sources is unknown, but for many families it must have been enough to neutralize the worst consequences of low wages.[43] Probably also alleviating the effects of low wages in some families were hunting, fishing, berry and fruit picking, bartering with neighbors, and gifts of farm produce from neighbors or rural relatives.

Housing subsidies were an important source of indirect compensation. The vast majority of mill folk received free housing or were charged nominal rent—25 to 50 cents per room per week was the common range—throughout the New South era. In 1890, 660 southern mill families, including 380 in Georgia and the Carolinas, spent an average 11 percent of their income on rent; and in 1899 and 1900, the amount deducted for rent at Eldorado Cotton Mill at Ansonville, North Carolina, was 9.2 percent and 9.4 percent of the payroll, respectively.[44]

Despite the suggestiveness of this information, meaningful estimates of family compensation are impossible to calculate. Most companies did not operate stores, but where they did so, there was often no competing store available, whether because the company excluded competition by paying in checks redeemable only at its own store, or, as was often the case, because there was not enough business to support two stores. Where competing stores did exist, some company stores charged more. The experience of sharecroppers suggests that independently owned stores did not solve the problem of folk needing credit; and it is easy to overestimate the exploitive role of company stores. In 1907 and 1908, investigators for the study of woman and child labor, who were certainly not apologists for the mills, found company-owned stores in 57 of 152 mill villages. They also found "very little difference in prices at company stores and nearby independent stores."[45]

43. *Ibid.*, 505.
44. U.S. Commissioner of Labor, *Seventh Annual Report, 1891*, 1619–21; Eldorado Cotton Mill Time Book, 1898–1903, in William Alexander Smith Papers, Manuscript Department, Duke University Library, Durham, North Carolina.
45. *Senate Documents*, 61st Cong., 2nd Sess., No. 645, Vol. 1, p. 602.

Mill folk viewed wages and other forms of compensation in the context of immediate circumstance and experience. Mill work paid more than share-cropping and provided jobs for women and children; and with it came cash income, regular paydays, and usually better housing and other fringe bene-fits. Moreover, except during the depressed years of the 1890s, the secular trend in take-home pay during the New South era was upward, and effects of the drop during the depression decade were partially offset by deflation. According to one calculation, which adapted levels to a scale on which those of 1914 equaled 100, average money wages in North Carolina mills rose from 45 in 1880 to 58.9 in 1890, only to fall to 46.2 in 1899. They then rose to 70 in 1904 and 87.4 in 1909 on the way to 100 in 1914.[46] Changes in real wages were less dramatic but followed the same course.

These trends no doubt affected the way mill folk looked at wages. The upward trend must have encouraged the belief that conditions were improv-ing, whatever the actualities at given times. Furthermore, wages of indi-viduals tended to rise over time, also encouraging positive attitudes. Experi-enced workers tended more machines or transferred into higher-paying jobs—from spinner to carder to weaver, for example—and mechanically minded men might become loom fixers or machinists, all with meaningful increases in wages. Age and wage levels thus correlated, at least for a number of years in each worker's life. In a group of North Carolina mills in 1907, for example, the average wage amounted to 5.2 cents an hour for boys eleven to fifteen years old compared with 13.7 cents for men twenty-five to twenty-nine, and corresponding figures for girls and women followed a similar pattern.[47]

Workers' comments on wages were often relative and based on family earnings. "I think we can do better here than on a farm," a Cleveland County operative wrote the North Carolina labor commissioner in 1891. "For my own part I know that I am doing a great deal better than farming." This positive assessment rested not on the man's wage alone, which was 75¢ a day after two years in the mill, nor on his overall earnings, which had been $200 the preceding year. It rested instead on his family's income. Three of his five children worked in the mill, and he and they together earned $1.85 a day. In addition, he paid no house rent and received other fringe benefits

46. Andrew W. Pierpont, "Development of the Textile Industry in Alamance County, North Carolina" (Ph.D. dissertation, University of North Carolina, 1953), 128. See also Harry M. Douty, "The North Carolina Industrial Worker, 1888–1930" (Ph.D. dissertation, Univer-sity of North Carolina, 1936). On comparative wage levels in southern and New England industries, including textiles, see Richard A. Lester, "Trends in Southern Wage Differentials Since 1890," *Southern Economic Journal*, XI (1945), 317–44.
47. *Senate Documents*, 61st Cong., 2nd Sess., No. 645, Vol. 1, p. 317.

free or at reduced charge. The difference between this man's own earnings and the total compensation his family received was the margin between livability and want.[48]

For men with no one to help them, however, the story was different. "I . . . ask you if you can give me a Job of eny kind that I can make a living at," J. D. Brown of Pelzer Mills wrote Governor Blease in 1912. "I cant live at the wages I am Making here[.] I get $120 [that is, $1.20] a day and have a Wife and one child to keep up[.] I am a Poor Cotton Mill boy and if you can give a Job of eny kind I sure will appresha it." George Dewey Cartin, an Aiken County operative, was equally desperate. "My father is Det and i want to Make a liven for My Mother," Cartin wrote Blease in 1914, asking for a job as a "ditetiff" (detective). "I cant Make but 75 cents a day in the Mill and 1 wat you to due all you can for Me[.] [I] am 17 teen years old."[49]

Other workers agreed. "I think if the employers would give the hands better wages it would be better for all," a Cleveland County operative wrote in 1891. "The help could then support themselves better and be able to school their children. When we make forty cents per day we can *live*, but that's about all."[50]

"THE MAYOR . . . WILL PUT FINE UNREASONABLE ON A PERSON & THE MILL PAY THE FINE & THEN THE PARTY HAS TO WORK IT OUT."

Whatever the actual level of wages, the compensation system was the centerpiece of the owners' effort to control workers. It was not that wages were low because mill owners wanted to keep workers dependent. Rather, low wages and the manner of payment functioned to reinforce the worst effects of social and economic dependency. The fact that workers accepted important features of that system and even used them for their own purposes did not lessen the extent to which the system functioned to keep them subordinated.

The whole purpose of this system was to tie the worker's finances to those of the mill, and its prominent feature was the payment of compensation in kind and to the family or household. A significant part of every worker's income was in the form of free or nominal house rent, free garden plots and pasturage for livestock, free schooling for children, free or reduced doctor's

48. NC *Labor Report* (1891), 171.
49. J. D. Brown to Blease, June 30, 1912, John Dewey Cartin to Blease, June 16, 1914, in Blease Papers.
50. NC *Labor Report* (1891), 172.

fees, free water, reduced rates for fuel and electricity, and subsidies to churches, clubs, and civic and recreational activities. Where these benefits were not available, cash wages never made up the difference, and workers were poorer for their absence. Even the principal source of outside income in the villages, keeping boarders, came indirectly from the mills.

None of these forms of compensation involved many cash transactions. In most mills, such things as rent and the cost of utilities were deducted from workers' pay; and fuel supplies and even pay for keeping boarders were often handled through the company store in what amounted to a modified system of barter. In addition, many mills paid little or none of their payroll in cash—a practice especially prevalent in small, isolated mills in the first half of the New South era. Many other mills paid only a portion, perhaps a third or a half, of their wages in cash, or only as much as workers specifically asked for. This practice was due in part to the shortage of cash in the New South and the dearth of banking facilities, but it fitted neatly the desire of mill owners to envelop the economic affairs of their workers in those of the mills and their mercantile subsidiaries in the villages.

Payday was an occasion not so much for dispensing money as for balancing accounts, letting mills and workers alike know how they stood with each other. That circumstance, too, meshed with the desire of mill owners to keep cash away from their employees, for it conformed to the belief that mill folk would not work if they had money in their pockets. Another device that served the same purpose was long pay periods, infrequent paydays. In the early years, many, perhaps most, mills had monthly pay periods, and semimonthly periods were still common at the end of the era, though weekly paydays were probably the rule by 1910.[51]

Mills that did not pay in cash used various forms of scrip, checks, or tickets, and the specifics of this system varied widely. "The way the hands are paid off here," a Cumberland County mill worker wrote the North Carolina labor commissioner in 1890, "is, at the first of every month you get a ticket, the ticket is full of numbers. At the end of the month you must bring up your ticket. All the numbers punched off from the ticket are deducted from that month's wages. The ticket can be given in exchange for goods nowhere but at the company store." Checks were more widely used than tickets but operated in much the same way. Where they were in use,

51. When the North Carolina labor commissioner first collected information on payment of wages in 1887, monthly pay periods were more common than any other pay periods in those mills reporting; a few mills paid "daily" or "irregularly." In subsequent years, weekly or semimonthly pay periods became the rule. See *ibid.* (1887), 145, 147, and (1894), 54.

the mill paid in checks generally redeemable only in merchandise at the company store, though some mills would cash the checks in whole or part if the operative requested, and in some places the checks were negotiable elsewhere in the community, though usually at a discount. "Wages are paid [weekly] in trade checks, which are worth par value in cash the 10th of each month," a Randolph County mill owner wrote of his own system. "We would settle with the cash all the time if we had a bank convenient to us, but to pay weekly in cash would require an extra hand on the road most of the time to keep a supply of money on hand." The mill at McAdenville, North Carolina, was using a variant of this system in 1900. The mill paid monthly in checks, but the checks were cashed "immediately whenever [operatives] want it." Moreover, the owner reported, operatives "are not compelled to trade it out at the store, because the store does not belong to the mill. If at any minute they want the money the treasurer will pay them. Hence it is that our checks pass in that country current as greenbacks or silver."[52]

Workers who described their experiences to the North Carolina labor commissioner were more negative in their reports. "The trade check system is used here," a Gaston County operative wrote in 1887. "If the hands trade their checks to any other firm, and they present them for cash, this firm demands a discount of 10 per cent. The best trade check used in this county is not worth over 75 per cent. Some of the checks used in this country are almost worthless [outside the company store]." A Lincoln County operative described a different system, one in which a worker could get a check for his earnings at the end of each day. "A girl works for fifty cents per day," this worker wrote, "has three in family to support, gets a check for each day for work, and buys her supplies from the company's store. When the four weeks are ended [and pay day comes], she has no checks and gets no cash."[53]

These practices were so widespread and their restrictive nature so apparent that mill officials who shunned them pointed to that fact as evidence that they treated their employees equitably. "We pay our operatives fairly well," William H. Young of Eagle and Phenix Mills told a congressional committee in 1883, "and we pay them punctually; we never fail to pay them at the very time when their wages are due, and we never pay them in anything but money." His company, he boasted, had no "pluck me" stores, as operatives called company stores where prices were high and they were forced to trade.

52. *Ibid.* (1890), 82, (1887), 151; *House Documents*, 57th Cong., 1st Sess., No. 184, Vol. 7, p. 503.
53. NC *Labor Report* (1887), 152, (1889), 282.

"We give no [store] orders to anybody," Young said. "We pay the operatives the money and they do with it what they please." In 1900 James L. Orr of Piedmont Mills near Greenville made the same statement for the same purpose. "We pay absolutely in cash to everyone," he told the Industrial Commission. "We pay the whole amount to them and they dispose of it as they please."[54]

Two linchpins held this system together. The first, withholding pay for one pay period, encouraged indebtedness to the company, for it required the worker to work two weeks, a month, or even two months before his first payday. The second required workers to give notice equal to the length of a pay period when they decided to quit, and imposed a fine on those who failed to do so equal to the amount of back pay held by the company.

At worst, the results of these practices were bad indeed. "I have known families to work in a mill for years and years without ever drawing a cent in cash," Joseph A. Michaels said after half a century in and out of the mills. "On payday the father would be given a blank ticket, showing the family earnings for the month, and the amount of the debt" and because of continued indebtedness would have to remain at the mill even if he wanted to leave. "Mill owners were none too anxious to have the debt paid off quickly," Michaels continued. "The mills were content to keep the debt hanging as a sword over the heads of their hands. . . . If a family tried to gain their freedom by leaving the village, they would be stopped; and even if they succeeded in getting away they could be brought back. The laws were so writ that a cotton mill worker, or tenant farmer, who owed a debt was a serf."

This reference to serfdom is no doubt overdrawn, but Michaels' statement that the mills used indebtedness to try to hold onto workers was certainly valid. In extreme form, the use of debt to compel labor amounts to peonage of the sort planters and other employers of black labor in the New South were sometimes guilty of.[55] No one has ever documented such a charge against mill owners, though they too used the force of law to threaten indebted workers. Occasionally at least, they also used indebtedness to secure and hold onto laborers. "The mayor of this town is connected with the mill—& we have no showing whatever," a Hartsville mill worker wrote Governor Blease in 1914, "as he will put fine unreasonable on a person & the

54. *Senate Documents*, 48th Cong., 1st Sess., No. 91, p. 511; *House Documents*, 57th Cong., 1st Sess., No. 184, Vol. 7, p. 483.
55. See Pete Daniels, *The Shadow of Slavery: Peonage in the South, 1901–1969* (Urbana, 1972).

mill pay the fine & then the party has to work it out. Please do not make this letter public if so please hold my name."[56]

Such an arrangement was singular if not unique. But this system of indebtedness did not always work as mill owners hoped, for it too could be undermined. "The hands will come to our mills and get in debt as soon as possible, and when their credit becomes in the least limited, they will get mad with the manager of the store and move away from the mill, and when they move away they almost always consider their debts paid," a North Carolina mill official complained in 1901. "I have known some families to move as many as six times in a year. You may ask why we let them get in debt at our stores." The official continued: "It is because they get sick, and a great many times are too lazy to work and play off sick, and think we are compelled to let them have rations while sick, as they are in our employ, and as soon as they get able to work, instead of working to pay their debt, which we allowed them to make through sympathy with them in their sickness, they will play off sick again, or else not properly do their work in order to get the Superintendent to turn them off, as they know it would take them some time to pay their bad debt; then they will move away to some other mill where they will follow the same scheme."[57]

"I CANT LIVE AT THE WAGES I AM MAKING HERE."

The attitudes of workers toward this system of compensation were generally negative. "Wages are about as good here as at any mill in the State and I think better than at many of them," a North Carolina operative wrote in 1887. "The only trouble about wages is that they are not paid in cash—trade checks are issued with which employees are expected to buy what they need at the company's store—which is not right."[58]

It was not only the injustice but the function of the pay policies that mill folk condemned. Desiring to lay before Governor Blease "a fiw facts that are of the Most vital importance too our Mill people," C. P. Lockey, of a Spartanburg County mill, listed what he thought "at least 80 percent of [his] coworker[s]" wanted in the way of reform. "1st We want a law forcing the Cotton Mills to pay off every Saturday," Lockey wrote, "there-by giving the poor people the chance to take advantage of the opportunities that's af-

56. G. T. McDaniel to Blease, January 5, 1914, in Blease Papers.
57. NC *Labor Report* (1901), 217–18.
58. *Ibid.* (1887), 150.

forded the Consumer through competition for cash purchases. . . . 2) We want a law Making it a Misdemeanor punishable by a heavy fine for any Cotton Mill Co, or agent there of too deduct any amount what so ever from the wages or pay of any Mill operative for any thing what so ever, if said operative does not give satisfaction let said company dispose of services and not force upon the heads of an already oppressed people this miserable *dockage system*[.] [I]n other words Dear Sir," Lockey told the governor, "they take the bread from the mouths of the men and women and little children of our state too fatten the dividen of these Yankee capitalist along with the other stock holder in our Cotton Mills."[59]

Other workers had other complaints. "The Brandon Mills has thair pay day every too Weeks on the first an 15 of Each Month," J. B. Crippen wrote Blease in 1913, "holding back too Weeks an if the people get in tough times and go to the office and draw out $10.00 15.00 or $20.00 the awditer charge Such pursons 5 cts on the dollar[.] Now is this a legal transaction for a man to have to pay the Co . . . 5 perct for the privilege of Spending thair own hard Earned dollar[?]"[60]

Workers not only protested the pay policies of the mills but also refused to succumb to their intended purpose. Refusal to concede control is one explanation of absenteeism and labor turnover. It is also part of the significance of the "sorriness" that caused mills to dismiss some workers despite large debts at the company store, and of the casual way in which workers went about their work. Those who decided to quit their jobs far enough in advance might miss so much work that the earnings they forfeited were minimal, or they might run up debts to the company large enough to make up for part of the forfeited pay. More commonly, they provoked their bosses into discharging them. Whenever a worker was fired for cause, the custom was to "give him his time," that is, pay him his back wages, and order him out of the mill and village. The opening this allowed workers to escape the forfeiture of pay was so widely utilized that the mills developed protections against it. Thus the contract Rufus King signed for the employment of his son Walter at Pilot Mills in 1896 provided that "if in the opinion of the [mill] . . . Walter King had acted in bad faith in order to be discharged, with a view to being discharged in order to get his money," the mill had the right to discharge Walter and still keep five dollars of the pay due him.[61]

59. C. P. Lockey to Blease, December 29, 1913, in Blease Papers.
60. J. B. Crippen to Blease, April 20, 1913, in Blease Papers.
61. Legal Papers, 1893–1915, in Pilot Cotton Mill Papers.

"IF A HAND WAS TO QUIT ONE, THEN THE OTHER MILLS IN TOWN
WOULDN'T HIRE HIM."

A second series of control policies was intended to prevent free movement of
workers between mills. Forfeiting back pay did not prevent workers from
quitting their jobs suddenly and frequently, so the mills tried to hold folk by
preventing them from finding work elsewhere. The result was an elaborate
system of agreements among mills not to hire workers from other local mills
or workers known to be floaters or troublemakers. This system was not
always effective and did not prevent mills from raiding one another's work
forces. But when it was effective, mill folk suffered. An extreme example
was the pass system in effect in Augusta in the 1880s. Under that system,
when an employee wanted to quit, he had to notify his boss two weeks in
advance and work out his notice. At the end of the time, the boss might give
him a pass—a paper attesting to the worker's satisfactory service and stating
that "in leaving [he] has complied with all the rules of the company."[62] The
mills defended the policy as rewarding good workers with letters of recom-
mendation that worked to their advantage. Bosses were under no obligation
to give workers passes, however, even for satisfactory service. Indeed, they
might have compelling reason not to do so if they could find no replacement.
But without a pass, the worker could get employment in no other mill in the
Augusta district and was therefore excluded from several thousand jobs.

The function of the pass system is obvious. "An overseer can make
himself so unpleasant to a man that he is compelled to quit without notice or
commit murder," a worker told a reporter, "and if he does quit the pass is
refused him and he cannot get employment. I have known a boy to be
discharged from one room, and when he obtained employment in another
the overseer followed him down and had him discharged because he was
working without a pass. . . . I knew a young lady . . . that worked out her
notice in one room in order that she might get work in another, and the pass
was refused her."[63]

Various versions of this system existed wherever mills were concentrated,
though the zealousness with which the Augusta mills policed their agreement was apparently exceptional. Until 1901, for example, when they ostensibly abolished the practice, mills in Gastonia, North Carolina, "re-

62. Augusta *Chronicle*, June 6, 1886.
63. *Ibid.*, May 1, 1886.

quired a written pass or permission before any one mill would employ anyone leaving any other mill."[64]

A concomitant of this system was blacklisting, the refusal of mills to hire workers known to cause trouble. For mill officials, troublemaking included everything from joining a union or going on strike to insubordination or disagreeableness. Charles J. Trippe, an overseer at Laurens Mills in up-country South Carolina, was fired and blacklisted because he displayed Governor Blease's picture in his workroom and refused to remove it when ordered to do so. Three months later, he was still unemployed despite his efforts to find work at a number of mills. "It seems that they have all got me boycotted," he wrote Blease, asking for help.[65]

Knowledge of individual workers was generally confined to given localities, however, and this plus the general need for workers neutralized some of the effect of blacklisting. It was necessary simply to move beyond the reach of a local agreement to escape its effect. "I got mad and quit," Alice Caudle recalled in Concord, North Carolina, early in the twentieth century. "In them days there was an agreement here in the mills that if a hand was to quit one, then the other mills in town wouldn't hire him, so I went over to Albemarle and I got me a job in the knitting mills."

64. *American Federationist*, VIII (1901), 182.
65. Charles J. Trippe to Blease, April 3, 1911, in Blease Papers.

PART III

VILLAGE LIFE

8

BONDS OF FAMILY LIFE AND WORK

For mill folk, family life and work were bound inextricably together, the one infusing the other in ways that make it impossible to separate their basic elements for discrete analysis as aspects of work or social life. Family employment and residence in villages owned by the mills, together with the paternalism of mill owners, bound mill folk to their employers in relationships far more organic than those normally binding industrial employees and employers. This too made control of workers easier than it would otherwise have been, though the extent to which such control was the calculated purpose of these organic relationships is unclear.

The family was the basic institution of folk life, and mill owners as well as workers acknowledged that fact and accorded the family a central place in the operation of mill and village alike. Mill folk honored the family as an idea as well as an institution, and one of the reasons they accepted so much of the owners' paternalism in and out of the mills was its consonance with family forms and expectations.

In the mills and villages, the family proved to be strong as well as flexible, and instead of collapsing under pressures of economic and social transition, it grew stronger and more important for individual and community alike. Not only did its traditional forms and functions persist but they became explicit instruments of social policy. Work as well as life revolved around the family, which more than anything else eased the effects of long hours, low pay, and virtual powerlessness. Management adjusted the patterns and demands of work to family imperatives; workers arranged their family concerns to meet the dictates of work.

Mill owners worked consciously to preserve traditional roles in families they employed, for those roles made mill governance easier; and mill folk accepted, even encouraged, the policies that purpose abetted. The contracts or understandings that governed the employment of most workers assigned heads of families explicit responsibilities that enhanced their authority. Each head agreed to furnish a specified number of workers and see that they showed up for work and honored mill discipline, and each was accountable for the conduct of members of his family in and out of the mill. Family heads were interested parties in work disputes involving their children or other dependents, and the mills acknowledged and acted in accordance with that interest. Perhaps family heads often sided with management in such disputes, just as parents of schoolchildren often supported teachers in disciplinary matters. Certainly children who misbehaved in the mills had to answer to parents as well as bosses. Frances Medlin Albright, who went to work in a North Carolina mill in 1930, heard older workers recall that in bygone years misbehaving children had been routinely reported to their parents, and workers as well as supervisors had done the reporting. There was a positive side to that practice, for it permitted family heads to intercede in disputes in behalf of their children, and sometimes to protect them from arbitrary supervisors. No doubt the anticipated reaction of family heads was one of the factors supervisors weighed in imposing discipline on dependent workers.

This consideration was of consequence. Scattered evidence indicates that mill children, like schoolchildren, were sometimes slapped or otherwise corporally punished for misdeeds or poor work, though such punishment seems never to have been official policy. "They didn't allow that," Jessie Lee Carter said when asked if children were whipped in the mills. Work rules at Spartan Mills in the 1890s directed supervisors not to "put their hands on" employees in the spinning room, most of whom were probably children or youths. Such a rule suggests that the prohibited practice sometimes occurred.

Despite their playfulness and mischievousness, most mill children were obedient in fundamental things on the job. "When the bossman told them to do anything, they went ahead and done it," Jessie Lee Carter said of children in the mill where she worked, "just like it'd been their parents telling them to do it. Children minded that worked in the mill." A writer in the *Labor Advocate* noted after a tour of cotton factories that "the children . . . do not complain of cruelty by overseers. They say they are not cuffed or flogged or in any way maltreated, though many taskmasters use abusive, even profane language in enforcing their orders."[1]

There were other instructive examples of management's use of family authority. In the summer of 1893, Cleveland Cotton Mills was operating at a loss, and the Schencks faced the necessity of having to close down for a while or reduce operating costs. The only large cost item they controlled was wages. Pressed by their business partner to act quickly but knowing that even a brief closure would cause some of their workers to move away, they decided to offer the workers a choice between shutting down and working at reduced pay. Accordingly, they called "a meeting of the hands and heads of families," explained the situation to them, and assured them that the temporary measures would be ended as soon as business conditions permitted. No doubt, too, they made it clear that they themselves preferred to reduce wages and continue operating. To decide the matter, only the heads of families, including some who did not work in the mills, were permitted to vote, and the vote of each counted equally regardless of the number of workers in his family.

No one seems to have considered this procedure extraordinary, and certainly it was not *pro forma*. That the voters followed their own and not the Schencks's convictions is evident from the fact that at Mill No. 2, fifteen of thirty-six family heads voted to close down rather than work at reduced wages. The younger Schenck, who considered such a vote foolishly contrary to the workers' own interests, attributed it to "cussedness" and unreasoning opposition to pay cuts of any kind. In this instance, the cut would have amounted to 25 percent. But he followed the letter if not the spirit of his exercise in worker consultation. "We will run a part of Mill No. 2—so as to keep up our regular sewing twine orders," he wrote after the vote, "and use such hands as we need of those at No. 2 who voted to run on at reduced wages—and let those who voted to shut down live at ease for a while and see how they enjoy it."[2]

A somewhat similar incident occurred in connection with the effort of William Erwin to defeat a move to unionize workers at his mill in West

1. *Labor Advocate* (Birmingham), August 30, 1902.
2. John F. Schenck to J. E. Reynolds, August 12, 17, 1893, in H. F. Schenck Papers, Manuscript Department, Duke University Library, Durham, North Carolina.

Durham, North Carolina, in the summer of 1900. As soon as he heard that an organizing effort was afoot, Erwin called a meeting of the heads of all families with workers in his employment and warned them of the harm that would come to anyone joining a union. Specifically, he promised to fire any worker who did so. His strategy was calculated, for at the meeting, "the doors were closed against the young men, who were the leaders in the labor organization"; only their fathers or mothers were allowed to attend. Erwin's tactic was not altogether successful, for the organizing effort continued; but with knowledge of the union's plans, Erwin precipitated a strike before the workers were prepared for it, and the union effort failed.[3]

The authority of family heads was solidified by pay policy. Many mills paid family heads the wages earned by their children and other dependents; and even where that was not the case, dependent workers generally turned their pay over to the heads. On the payroll at Royall Cotton Mills in the early twentieth century, workers were listed and their earnings totaled by family unit. For the pay periods that included March 7 of each year between 1903 and 1906, the proportion of employees listed in family groups of 2 or more workers was 55, 67, 59, and 74 percent, respectively, and their earnings were clearly treated as family entities. From each family's collective earnings, the paymaster deducted house rent and other bills, and paid the remainder in a lump sum, making no distinction between the earnings of individual family members.[4] Such a system surely concentrated power as well as authority in family heads and compensated in some degree for the inability of men to support their families on their own earnings. A man who earned only a fourth or a third of his family's income still controlled its purse strings.

"IT WASN'T A WOMAN'S PLACE TO WORK IN THE MILL THAT HAD FAMILY."

Mill managers also sought to preserve the family roles of women. Employers and employees alike believed the proper place of wives and mothers was at home. Thus women in those categories who worked in the mills were generally in the poorest families, most of them female headed, and they worked because they had to. So strong was custom in this regard that not even female heads of mill households typically worked in the mills. A large majority—perhaps as many as 7 in 10—did not do so, despite the fact that

3. Raleigh *News and Observer*, August 26, 1900.
4. Time Book, 1903–1907, Vol. XX of Royall Cotton Mill Company Papers, Manuscript Department, Duke University Library, Durham, North Carolina.

their families had less income than those with male heads.[5] Female-headed households did, however, provide a disproportionate share of mill workers, probably more than a third of the total; and a disproportionate share of families with mill workers was thus female headed—perhaps 1 in 5 in self-contained villages and 2 in 5 in urban mills.[6] Such figures show just how extensively female heads of households used mill employment to cope with economic problems caused by the absence of husbands and fathers. They also point to the fact that especially in the early years, mill households were disproportionately female. Thus, no less than 64 percent of the people in a sample of mill families in Augusta, Georgia, in 1880 were female. And in the small, rural village of Bynum, North Carolina, the proportion was even higher. There, in 1880, 9 of 14 households were headed by women and those households included 8 males and 49 females. Only 18 of the 93 people in this village were males.[7]

In male-headed families, patterns were more conventional. Wives and mothers in those families rarely worked in the mills.[8] Moreover, most

5. Twelve of 23 female heads of households counted in the manuscript census of 1880 at Vaucluse Mill in Aiken County were mill workers, but that proportion was rare. At nearby Graniteville, the figure was 25 of 75, and at Langley in the same county 10 of 42. Comparable figures for Richmond County in the same year were 26 of 112 and for the Columbus area 58 of 215, for an overall proportion of these five localities of 28 percent (Manuscript Census, 1880, Schedule 1, Aiken County, S.C., Richmond and Muscogee counties, Ga., and Russell County, Ala.). In her sample of mill families in Augusta, Ga., in 1880, LeeAnn Whites found that 38 percent of widowed heads of households worked outside the home ("Southern Ladies and Millhands: The Domestic Economy and Class Politics in Augusta, Georgia, 1870–1890" [Ph.D. dissertation, University of California at Irvine, 1982], 209). In 1900 the proportions of female heads of households working in the mills were 19 percent in Alamance County, N.C., 18 percent in Gregg Township in Aiken County, and 9 percent in a sample in Spartanburg County. In Richmond County, however, the proportion was 41 percent, reflecting an important difference between urban mill districts and self-contained mill villages (Manuscript Census, 1900, Schedule 1).

6. Forty-two percent of mill workers counted in the Columbus area and 30 percent of those in Richmond and Aiken counties in 1880 were in female-headed households (Manuscript Census, 1880, Schedule 1). The number of female-headed families with mill workers was 215 of 464 households in the Columbus area (42 percent), 112 of 295 in Richmond County (30 percent), 140 of 456 in Aiken County (31 percent), 51 of 131 in Gaston County (39 percent), and 71 of 178 in Alamance County (40 percent), according to Manuscript Census, 1880, Schedule 1. In LeeAnn Whites's sample of Augusta mill families in 1880, 40 percent were headed by women (Whites, "Southern Ladies and Millhands," 196).

7. Whites, "Southern Ladies and Millhands," 196; Douglas DeNatale, "Traditional Culture and Community in a Piedmont Textile Mill Village" (M.A. thesis, University of North Carolina, 1980), 17.

8. Of 2,455 women whose husbands did mill work in Alamance County, Gregg Township, and a Spartanburg County sample in 1900, only 231 (9 percent) were themselves mill workers. The Spartanburg County sample is every third household (Manuscript Census, 1900, Schedule

working wives were young and newly married or in households with another woman (grandmother, aunt, maid) who did the housework. No doubt most such women, especially those in the latter category, preferred mill work to housekeeping, but even they did not work if they had small children. Only 71 of the mothers in 1,294 mill households in Alamance County in 1900 with children under ten were at work in the mills, and only 5 of those in 224 households in a Muscogee County sample.[9]

These patterns are corroborated by the testimony of former mill workers, whose interviews reveal the cultural underpinnings of female employment patterns. "She worked in the mill a little, but Daddy wouldn't let her work," Stella Foust Carden, who grew up in North Carolina in the second decade of the twentieth century, recalled of her mother. "He made her stay home and take care of the family. He told her one time she got her a job and went to work, 'Now I want to tell you something. You're going to quit and stay home and look after the children, or I'll quit. There's one of us going to be here with them.' So she quit." Jessie Lee Carter's father had the same idea. "My daddy said it wasn't a woman's place to work in the mill that had family," Mrs. Carter remembered. "She's supposed to be home. And that's the way my husband felt." J. Floyd Thrift summarized the pattern at Carrboro thus: "The mothers didn't work often. The mothers would have to stay at home and do the cooking and take care of the children."

Nothing better illustrates the preference of mill folk for traditional social forms and their effort to maintain those forms in the face of changing and sometimes desperate circumstances than these patterns. Women could and did contribute to family income, but most did so in traditionally female ways. They kept boarders, tended gardens and milk cows, raised chickens and pigs, took in sewing and sometimes washing and ironing. Seventy-seven percent of the 1,567 families investigated in 1907 had income from one or more of these sources, and it is likely that that proportion was higher in earlier years.[10]

Women did what they had to do to help their families make a living. Swannie McDaniel's mother worked in the mills, even when her children

---

1). In urban centers the figures seem to have been higher. Fifty-six of the 203 wives in LeeAnn Whites's sample of Augusta families (28 percent) worked outside the home (Whites, "Southern Ladies and Millhands," 210).

9. Manuscript Census, 1900, Schedule 1, Alamance County, N.C., and Muscogee County, Ga. In Augusta in 1880, where a higher portion of mothers worked, 23 percent of the children in mill households had mothers who worked (Whites, "Southern Ladies and Millhands," 223).

10. *Senate Documents*, 61st Cong., 2nd Sess., No. 645, Vol. 1, p. 500.

were small. "We took care of ourselves," her daughter recalled. "We knew we had to behave ourselves. . . . We didn't get into no meanness because we knew better." Other women hired maids to do their housework and free themselves for the mills. "You could get a nigger to work for you for a month for five dollars," Flossie Moore Durham remembered. Nellie Allen Pendergrass' mother, newly widowed, moved her family to Carrboro about 1909 and not only went to work in the mill but took in washing and ironing to eke out a living for her family of small children. As the children grew up, each of them went into the mill, and their mother eventually quit, though she continued the laundry work at home.

Individual arrangements were thus infinitely varied. Myrtle Ray Stanley's mother took in "lady boarders," single women who worked in the mill during the week and returned to their families in the country on weekends. Ila Hartsell Dodson's mother worked as a weaver and left the housework to Ila's grandmother. "She worked till two months before I was born," Mrs. Dodson recalled. "And I told her that's the reason I always wanted to weave, because I wove before I got here."

Despite this variety, overall patterns are clear. Girls in mill families worked in the mills, but their mothers generally did not. Thus, in 1,567 families in 1907, 93.9 percent of girls over sixteen were at work compared to 16.6 percent of their mothers. Alma Sizemore's story illustrates the pattern. Orphaned while she was a teenager, Alma and her younger sister Naomi were sent by relatives to work at Victor Mills in Greer, South Carolina. Not long thereafter, in 1901, Alma married Jim Wilson, who also worked at Victor. She continued to work, but only for a while. As soon as she had enough to pay for a set of furniture, she and her husband moved back to the country and went into farming.[11]

As a result of this pattern, working women were generally single, or, less often, widowed, deserted, or divorced. Thus, in samples counted in the manuscript census of 1880, only 18 percent of female workers over twenty-one in the Columbus area, 27 percent in Richmond County, 47 percent in Aiken County, and 6 percent in Alamance County were listed as married.[12] In 1900 the proportions were 28 percent in Alamance County, 48 percent in

11. *Ibid.*, 424–25. Alma Sizemore's story is related by her sister, Naomi Sizemore Trammel, in SOHP Box 4.

12. Exact figures were 58 of 324 in the Columbus area, 56 of 211 in Richmond County, 186 of 396 in Aiken County, and 10 of 168 in Alamance County. In Vaucluse and Graniteville in Aiken County, the proportions were somewhat higher than one-half. These figures are approximations because census listings are inconsistent and because some of the women listed as married had no husband present (Manuscript Census, 1880, Schedule 1).

Richmond County, 18 percent in Gregg Township, and 32 percent in the Spartanburg County sample.[13] Those listed as widowed or divorced in 1900 were 10 percent of the total in Alamance County, 11 percent in the Spartanburg sample, and 29 percent in Richmond County.[14] The reasons for such significant variations probably relate in part to differences in the ways census takers recorded marital status and to the fact that divorce was unusual among plain folk and altogether illegal in South Carolina.

Most mill families were nuclear. Of 4,587 households counted in the 1900 census in 5 counties, 52 percent were nuclear in form, 20 percent female headed, 14 percent extended (male headed with one or more extra relatives), and 14 percent boarding (male headed with one or more apparently unrelated boarders).[15] What distinguished the nuclear families was the small proportion in which the father was the only breadwinner—21 percent in Alamance County in 1900, for example, and 18 percent in the Spartanburg sample.[16] Regardless of their form, however, mill families were generally large—5 to 7 people on average, including 2 to 4 workers and often also an extra relative or boarder.[17]

The mills, then, did not alter family structures or functions; rather, they provided ways for certain types of families to earn a living. This was especially true of families with female heads, those in which fathers and husbands could not or would not work, and those with disproportionate numbers of daughters. Because of the nature of the sources, it is often difficult to distinguish among widows, deserted women, and unmarried mothers, and to identify families of derelict husbands and fathers. The pervasive impression that such families were more numerous in mill communities than elsewhere in the South was no doubt correct, but those families were not products of mill conditions. On the contrary, they went to

13. Exact figures were 146 of 522 in Alamance County, 385 of 806 in Richmond County, 134 of 289 in Gregg Township, and 67 of 211 in the Spartanburg County sample (Manuscript Census, 1900, Schedule 1).

14. Manuscript Census, 1900, Schedule 1. Divorce on any grounds was not legal in S.C., and that too undermines the value of these figures.

15. The counties were Alamance, Muscogee, Spartanburg, Richmond, and Aiken. The Aiken figure is for Gregg Township only, and the Muscogee and Spartanburg figures were samples of every third household (Manuscript Census, 1900, Schedule 1).

16. Exact figures were 276 of 1,294 families in Alamance County and 136 of 770 in the Spartanburg sample (Manuscript Census, 1900, Schedule 1).

17. The 4,587 households in five counties included 23,688 people, an average of 5.2 per household, and 10,854 mill workers (2.4 per household). In 1,567 mill families studied in 1907 and 1908, the average size was 6.6 people and the average number of workers per family was 3.8. Of these families, 23.5 percent had no father present (*Senate Documents*, 61st Cong., 2nd Sess., No. 645, Vol. 1, pp. 420–21).

the mills because mill employment was the best available solution to their economic problems. "There was but one thing that impressed me unfavorably among this great throng of factory operatives," a reporter wrote after touring Fulton Bag and Cotton Mills in 1903. "The proportion of 'grass widows' struck me as being too great, but the excuse for this is that being deserted by heartless men . . . this is the only place they can congregate to make an honest living."[18]

Family and household arrangements were often determined by low wages. Individuals, who could hardly support themselves living alone, pooled their resources in joint living situations. They boarded, often with relatives but often, too, with unrelated families. Newly married couples often lived with one of their parents, sometimes until long after their children began to arrive. Both husband and wife frequently worked while the mother of one of them kept house and tended their children. Two or more widowed or deserted women, or women with disabled or derelict husbands, formed households, one of them keeping house and tending the small children while the others took the older children and worked in the mills. In boarding or otherwise extended households, a young woman might make enough money to eke out a living for herself and an elderly parent. A woman with no other means of support might run a boardinghouse; or a family with only one or two workers might take in boarders to supplement an otherwise meager income. Unmarried adult siblings also formed joint households. All of these combinations appear frequently in manuscript census listings—mute testimony to the adaptations mill folk and their families made to economic and social necessity.

"IN THOSE DAYS MOTHERS DIDN'T ASSERT THEMSELVES."

If the role of women was primarily traditional, it was also changing. Family, mill, and village alike were patriarchal institutions that assigned subordinate, deferential positions to women. In each, men held, or were supposed to hold, positions of authority and leadership, and women as well as men endorsed that ideal, even when conditions prevented its realization. "Most men and women say that women should stay in the home and not go 'around fooling with outside things,'" Lois MacDonald wrote, summarizing the views of folk she interviewed in a Carolina village in the 1920s.[19] Individual

18. Atlanta *Constitution*, December 20, 1903.
19. Lois MacDonald, *Southern Mill Hills: A Study of Social and Economic Forces in Certain Textile Mill Villages* (New York, 1928), 77.

workers agreed. "In those days mothers didn't assert themselves," Maxie Oakley said with her own mother in mind. "She went along with Daddy's decision." Stella Foust Carden remembered the same behavior. "She didn't complain. She went along," Mrs. Carden recalled of her mother's reaction to the frequent moves her family made at her father's behest. "He was the one making the living, and she went along with him. Then there were some places she didn't like too well, but she didn't say nothing about it."

These statements were of an ideal, the achievement of which depended on individual family dynamics that are not clearly revealed in the interviews. "I just don't know, because they didn't talk in front of us children," Bessie Buchanan answered when asked who made decisions in her family. "But I guess [my father] made most of the decisions because he did all the transacting business." Alice Thrift Smith, on the other hand, remembered her parents making family decisions together; when her father died in 1913, her oldest brother assumed the man's role in family councils, and as a teenager, Alice had to have her brother's approval to go out on social occasions.

Consciously, then, mill folk worked to preserve traditional sex roles and divisions of labor. Men almost never did housework. "Oh, no," Nannie Pharis said of her father on this point. "I never did know of it, if he did." Moreover, mill work did not always free women from traditional responsibilities. Women who worked during the childbearing years, for example, did not escape the responsibilities of child rearing. When they became pregnant, some women stopped work immediately, but others worked until a few weeks before delivery. Such differences were probably due to economic circumstances, for pregnancy was not a condition women wanted to display in public. Perhaps most women worked until their pregnancy became apparent. Nannie Pharis, who worked during her childbearing years, quit work about six months before the birth of her child and returned when her baby was about a year old. Ila Hartsell Dodson's mother worked until two months before her daughter was born.

For such women, the mills granted, in essence, unpaid maternity leave. "You could come back when you got able to go back to work," Letha Ann Sloan Osteen recalled. "Stay out and have your baby and then go back to work when you got able." It was "easy to go right back on your own job," Mrs. Osteen continued, "because they took care of their people." Some women, again perhaps for economic reasons, returned to work before their babies were weaned, and the mills accommodated their special needs, too. A few women brought their babies to work and cared for them in the mills. "We had a neighbor, her name was Miss Lamb," Jessie Lee Carter recalled, "and she had a nursing baby, and she worked. She'd take that baby in her roping boxes and she'd take a quilt and she'd lay him in that roping box and she'd work 'cause [the mills] didn't have any help. Now that's how bad they were for help." Other mothers left their babies at home and returned every few hours to nurse them. Investigators for the 1907–1908 labor study found instances of women leaving the mills two or three times a day for that purpose.[20]

Despite the persistence of traditional roles, mill work set in motion changes in the economic and social positions of women just as it did for men. Mill work was attractive to many women because it relieved them of housekeeping chores. "I'd a-heep ruther do it than house work," was the way Alice Caudle described her preference after years in the mills. The option implicit in her remark was a real one. Of 2,105 working women and girls about whom investigators gathered information in 1907 and 1908, only 41 did all the housework in their home, and 871 did some—spending on the average 45 minutes a day. The other 1,193 (57 percent) did no housework at all.[21]

There might have been some psychological cost in relief from traditional duties, for most folk accepted the notion that public work, especially when done at the expense of housekeeping and mothering, was undesirable, even unnatural, for women—particularly married women. At least some married women would have agreed with Carroll D. Wright, one of the nation's first experts in labor matters, when he wrote in 1880 that "the employment of married women is the very worse feature of factory employment." Wright meant that such employment endangered the home and therefore the moral fiber of the nation.[22]

No doubt many women who quit mill work when they married did so not because they preferred housework but because they shared this view or honored husbands who did so. That at least is implied by the fact that many women who recalled mill work with fondness quit when they married and never returned. And the fact that marriage would likely result in the end of mill work and of the element of independence it provided might help account for the disproportionate number of unmarried women in the mills.

20. *Senate Documents*, 61st Cong., 2nd Sess., No. 645, Vol. 1, p. 541.
21. *Ibid.*, 540.
22. *Tenth Census, 1880: Manufacturers*, Pt. 2, p. 552. For similar views expressed by the Georgia Federation of Labor at the end of the New South era, see Mercer G. Evans, "The History of the Organized Labor Movement in Georgia" (Ph.D. dissertation, University of Chicago, 1929), 253.

Surely some women made conscious decisions not to marry and were able to remain single because they supported themselves. Sixty percent of the adult female workers counted in four counties in the manuscript census of 1900 were listed as unmarried, presumably indicating that they had never been married.[23] Mill work offered women folk an economic, and therefore social, option not otherwise readily available. As a reporter stated ungrammatically in 1885, "The cotton factory, after a girl becomes an experienced hand, is one of the best places they find to earn a living."[24]

If the reporter's statement suggests the limited opportunities available to women, it also suggests that women might regard mill employment as opportunity and their success at it as achievement. "When I got married, my husband was [working] in Clinton, South Carolina," Alice P. Evitt recalled. "I went there, and I run twelve sides there—I made $1.44 a day there—I raised my wages some. So I spun there and liked to run frames too. So I run frames and wherever I'd make the most—in the card room or the spinnin' room—if I changed jobs, that's where I'd go."

The independence and sense of security success at mill work gave to women was by no means absolute. Wages and hours were such that individuals could not live independently, but the ability to pay one's way or help support one's family despite the absence, infirmity, or dereliction of a husband or father must have been personally satisfying.

"NEAT WHITE COTTAGES" AND "VILLAGE[S] ON STILTS"

These patterns and practices were encouraged by residence in company-owned villages that clustered about the mills. Approximately nine of every ten cotton mills in the New South owned residential villages for their operatives, and about the same proportion of mill folk lived in company-owned housing.[25] These villages were to some degree isolated from neighboring communities and functioned simultaneously as home and refuge for mill folk, and work camps as well. Company towns they were, and thus arenas in which mill folk confronted management's ceaseless effort to control them and make them model citizens and workers.

But to see the villages as merely instruments of control or repression is to

23. Totals were 1,096 of 1,828 women in Alamance, Spartanburg (sample of every third household), and Richmond counties, and Gregg Township in Aiken County (Manuscript Census, 1900, Schedule 1).

24. Atlanta *Constitution*, November 22, 1885.

25. According to the trade journal *Cotton*, 89 percent of all southern mills owned villages in 1920 (Jack Blicksilver, *Cotton Manufacturing in the Southeast: An Historical Survey* [Atlanta, 1959], 74).

miss the richness of the life they sustained. They were diverse places. Each had its singularities, even uniqueness, its own history and circumstance, its specific combination of people and institutions. As mill folk differed individually, so did their families and households differ, and so too the communities they constituted. A village might be old or new, large or small, city slum or model of benevolent paternalism, apart from other communities or integrated with them.

Because of this diversity, visitors found whatever they hoped to find, and descriptions of individual villages are mostly exposés of poverty and social wretchedness or portraits of material well-being, civic advancement, and social harmony. The social state implied by one or the other portrayal was typical of many villages, but it is impossible to quantify the quality and textures of life, and generalizations are hazardous. Most descriptions of villages were implicitly or explicitly comparative, but the standards on which the comparisons rested are rarely apparent. In addition, the villages underwent significant evolution between 1880 and 1915, and if typical ones existed in those years, those in 1915 were much different from those in 1880. At the end of the New South era, the villages were larger, more rounded communities, and probably more tolerable places to live. Moreover, more of their inhabitants had a generation's experience in village life, which brought adjustment to its ways; and the fruits of village welfare work, a curious blend of paternal uplift, physical improvement, and efforts at social control, were much more evident.

The villages could be unappealing, even repelling places. Just after the turn of the century, two reform-minded "gentlewomen" described them as "pest-ridden, epidemic-filled, filthy settlement[s]" where mill hands lived their "horrible honey comb of lives, shocking morals and decency." Less sensational writers found similar conditions, especially in urban mill districts, which were not truly mill villages, though the mills owned all or some of the housing in them. Thus a newspaper columnist, who was not hostile to mill interests, described some mill housing in Columbus, Georgia, in 1899 as "germ-breeding and poverty-engendering 'shacks'" whose bare floors and walls, broken windows, and battered doors bespoke the human misery they might otherwise have obscured. In these "rookeries," the reporter said, lived "families (often large ones) sleeping, eating, cooking in a single room, in health or sickness, with no sanitary guards whatever."[26]

Such slums were the worst mill communities, for even the most repelling

26. Mrs. John Van Vorst and Marie Van Vorst, *The Woman Who Toils, Being the Experiences of two Gentlewomen as Factory Girls* (New York, 1903), 217; Columbus *Weekly Herald*, February 5, 1899.

rural villages were less crowded and unhealthful. What these writers described were therefore extreme, not representative conditions. More common were those utterly drab places scattered about the Piedmont and up-country, the villages of small, rural, and generally older mills. These were often poorly constructed, with little regard for physical comfort or livability and none at all for aesthetics or the amenities of living. The village locations were determined by mill sites, with the result that they were often remote, frequently in clearings in the woods, perhaps precariously perched on sloping hillsides or riverbanks miles from other communities, even sometimes miles from rail connections.[27] "When the mill is built in the woods, the trees are left for shade," Holland Thompson wrote of such villages in North Carolina, "but oftener some bare, worn-out hillside is the site of the village. Little grading is done, and the supporting pillars on one side [of the houses] may be six feet higher than on the other." The unappealing sight this type of construction created was worsened by monotonies of architecture, color, and layout. Houses of the same size were generally identical, and in many villages every building was painted the same dull color. Moreover, the houses were generally arranged in rows—two, three, or four rows in a typical village—and their monotonous appearance might be unrelieved by trees, shrubbery, or anything else except the wells spaced at regular intervals between houses or the privies placed at uniform distances behind them on otherwise barren lots. "Often streets and sidewalks are neglected," Thompson said of these villages, "and the whole atmosphere may be depressing."[28]

The village at Cooleemee, North Carolina, which the English traveler T. M. Young visited just after the turn of the century, had many of these features. "In a woodland clearing beside the broad, rushing stream," Young came suddenly upon "two groups of buildings." In one group, at the end of a rail spur, was the mill itself, a structure of three stories that, with its "tall and slender iron chimney," dominated the clearing; and nearby stood a cotton warehouse and the village store. Apart from these were "many small buildings of wood—the dwelling-houses of the mill people, and a little hotel"—no doubt a boardinghouse—"in which the officers of the firm lived." The dwellings were detached frame houses, each "nicely painted,

27. See, for example, the description of the Troup factory in north Georgia in Atlanta *Constitution*, January 2, 1881. This factory, ten miles from the nearest town and rail connection, employed 80 workers, who lived in a village of 18 or 20 houses.

28. Holland Thompson, *From the Cotton Field to the Cotton Mill: A Study of the Industrial Transition in North Carolina* (New York, 1906), 140–41.

and provided with a little piazza or 'stoep.' " Young states that "none of them had a garden, or even an enclosed yard," and "a minute's walk" from any of them the woods began. The houses lodged on a steep, ungraded slope, their fronts so far off the ground a man could stand upright underneath one of them, creating the effect "of a village on stilts." The houses had four or six rooms each and rented for twenty-five cents a room per week. Young wrote, "I saw nothing of any school or recreation room," or any other buildings. He encountered a part-time preacher at the settlement, however, which led him to believe there was a church nearby.[29]

This village was two years old when Young visited, and the missing buildings were added in subsequent years. Soon the village had four churches, a public hall, improved roads, and "a steel bridge over the river for the benefit of the people living in this vicinity."[30] That was the general pattern of growth. When mills and villages were constructed, only essential facilities were built at first—the mill itself, one or two warehouses, a store, and a minimum number of houses for the workers. Once the mill was profitable, however, new buildings appeared—more houses, a church, a school, eventually a community building (the first structures used for these purposes might be converted residences). In time, other buildings and facilities were added, especially if the mill itself was enlarged, as happened quite often; and trees, shrubbery, flowers, fences, and additional buildings appeared about the village. In this way, the villages grew much like other hamlets, and most of them eventually assumed a more comfortable appearance and the substance of settled communities. By 1910 the largest mill villages had five to ten thousand residents.

The village of Granite Mills on the Haw River in Alamance County, North Carolina, perhaps went through such a phased growth. One of several enterprises owned by Governor Thomas M. Holt and his family, Granite Mills had almost 9,000 spindles and 500 looms in 1891 when it was visited by a newspaper correspondent. The correspondent found the mill surrounded by 100 "well-constructed and neatly painted brick and frame dwellings"—a flour mill, a store, "a beautiful and conveniently arranged office," "sundry store and ware houses," and "an attractive and comfortable chapel, in which Governor Holt and the operatives worship[ed], and whose pulpit [was] filled at the governor's expense." The settlement, the visitor thought, had "the appearance of a large, thrifty and beautiful village."

29. T. M. Young, *The American Cotton Industry* (London, 1902), 60–61.
30. *Manufacturers' Record*, October 13, 1904, p. 301.

Overlooking it from an eminence across the river was Governor Holt's "princely mansion," which sat on twelve acres of grounds so "highly improved and embellished" as to remind the correspondent of Central Park.[31]

Such beauty might have been in the eye of the beholder, for the correspondent was an enthusiast for economic development through cotton mills. This degree of attractiveness was not typical, but after the depression of the 1890s, the new mills that sprang up across the South were generally larger than the older ones and their villages more adequate places to live. By that time, mill owners were coming to believe that better villages and housing would help them attract more and better workers, and as a consequence the size and quality of mill housing, as well as the appearance and completeness of mill villages, improved. This improvement was doubly significant because these larger villages housed disproportionate numbers of mill folk.

One such village was that of Courtenay Manufacturing Company at Newry, South Carolina. When a correspondent for the New York *Tribune* visited this recently built village in 1895, he found not only an imposing mill of four stories with a tower of ninety feet but a well-constructed, pleasing hamlet of several hundred people. The workers' cottages were "all lathed and plastered," he noted, "neatly painted inside and outside and attractive in appearance." The largest, with eight rooms, were boardinghouses; and those with six rooms were divided into three-room apartments. Most, however, were single-family homes, probably with three or four rooms each. That kind of mix was characteristic of sizable villages: large families lived in single-family homes, small ones in duplexes, and single workers in boardinghouses. Each house at Courtenay had running water, still a rarity in 1895, and the village's "excellent drainage system" indicated an early instance of concern with health and sanitation. The houses were arranged in four rows and spaced apart to allow "plenty of ground around each" for a yard and garden. Down the middle of the village, which included a general store, a market and icehouse, an office building, and five cotton warehouses, ran a rail spur from the Southern Railway a mile and a half away.[32]

Some of the large villages were showcases of paternalism. Early in the twentieth century, the village housing employees of Granby, Olympia, and Richland mills had 10,000 inhabitants living in "neat white cottages, all wired and equipped with electric lights, the plumbing and drainage con-

31. Atlanta *Constitution*, April 9, 1891.
32. The description of the Courtenay village is reprinted in *Manufacturers' Record*, January 24, 1896, pp. 395–96.

nected with a fine sewer system." There were also "schoolhouses and churches, a fine fire department, a company store where operatives may or may not trade," streets "laid out with excellent sidewalks and lighted with electricity," and an assortment of civic, educational, recreational, and other social programs.[33]

Among the model villages were those at Pacolet and Pelzer in the South Carolina upcountry. In 1895 a visitor found Pacolet an hour and a half's ride from Spartanburg through pine woods and cotton fields. Situated on a bluff overlooking the Pacolet River, the village already had the physical and social features associated with model communities. It was apart from other communities, and only mill folk lived there. In 1901, Pelzer, on the Saluda River, boasted a thousand "tasteful and well constructed cottages," which averaged four rooms each and for which the residents paid fifty cents a room per month. Each cottage had garden space, running water, and sewerage connection, all included in the price of the rent, and each family had free access to a common pasture for livestock. There were several churches, a graded school, and numerous other buildings in the community, and a varied assortment of social, improvement, and recreational services. "The entire town, from end to end," one visitor thought, "[was] as tidy and tasteful as a good housewife's guest-chamber."[34]

"SOME HAVE VERY COMFORTABLE HOUSES, OTHERS HAVE NOT."

The quality of mill housing was as varied as the physical features of the villages. In the early years, houses were often poorly constructed and overcrowded, as the complaints of mill folk to the North Carolina labor commissioner illustrate. "The tenements are all double and roughly put up, neither ceiled nor plastered," a card grinder wrote of his village in Rutherford County in 1890. "The mill here has not been running very long and has not made much money as yet. The company says they will improve houses when they get straightened out."[35]

There were various problems. "The houses are roomy enough," a

33. *Ibid.*, December 11, 1902, p. 383. For a fond remembrance of this village by a former resident, see Alvin W. Byars, *Olympia-Pacific: The Way It Was, 1895–1970* (Columbia, S.C., 1981).

34. Edward Porritt, "The Cotton Mills in the South," *New England Magazine*, n.s., XII (1895), 579–80; Leonora B. Ellis, "A Model Factory Town," *Forum*, XXXII (September, 1901), 62–63.

35. North Carolina Bureau of Labor Statistics, *Annual Report, 1890*, 92, hereinafter cited as NC *Labor Report* by year.

Cleveland County operative reported in 1891, "but are not sufficient to keep us warm and dry." Another operative from the same county, a feeder-tender whose family of thirteen included six mill workers, reported a similar problem. "The tenant houses at this place are all good frame houses and ceiled," he wrote, "but only one fire-place to some of them; some of the families would be greatly benefited with another chimney."[36]

Others complained of crowding. "We need more house room," a Randolph County weaver told the commissioner. "A good many of the hands have to live in one room, and a good many families have to live in a house with another family. I live in a two-room house; I occupy one room and another family the other room, which is not pleasant." This man, who was married but had no children, also considered his rent too high. For the one room, he paid $1.25 a month from wages of $1.00 a day. In the preceding year he had earned $260—his wife did not work in the mill—and his annual rent was thus 6 percent of his income.[37]

This weaver's complaint suggested the extent to which attitudes toward housing might have been shaped by farm experience. In mountain districts, rural families often lived in one room, but the one room was a detached house generally well removed from other houses. That arrangement precluded the sense of crowding that came from eating, sleeping, and living in a single room in a house with another family in a village where the houses themselves might be bunched together. Sharecropper families in the flatlands almost never lived in one-room houses, and it might be that plain folk considered two rooms—one for cooking, eating, and living and the other for sleeping—the minimum acceptable measure of adequate housing. "Some families lack room to keep themselves and house decent," a boss weaver told the labor commissioner in 1891. "This is the case at all factories of my acquaintance. Some are worse than this [village in Richmond County]. I think every family should have at least two rooms, as it is not pleasant or healthy to cook and sleep in the same room."[38]

Rural standards also influenced attitudes toward rent. Mill rents were low or, in a sizable minority of cases, free. But sharecroppers paid no rent at all. Moreover, rural and even town rents were so low that it is easy to overstate the significance of low rents in the villages. Indeed, in 1907 and 1908, investigators estimated mill rents to be two-thirds of those for equivalent

36. NC *Labor Report* (1891), 168, 170.
37. *Ibid.*, 188.
38. *Ibid.*, 190.

housing outside the mills.[39] It was these standards that caused the weaver to complain that fifteen dollars a year was too much to pay for one room.

There were still other complaints. "I think the tenements that mill hands have to occupy are, as a general thing, built upon a plan that is deleterious to health," a Buncombe County beamer wrote in 1890, "being built to get as many in one house as possible, not studying comfort. While some have very comfortable houses, others have not." A loom fixer from the same county agreed. "Our houses are small and inconvenient in arrangement," he told the commissioner, and "rent is too high." Also, he added, "the water we drink is very unhealthy on account of filth."[40]

Variety makes generalization hazardous. Investigators in 1907 and 1908, who were inclined to accentuate the negative features of mill life, thought village housing "far from being ideal," but compared to that available to "other laboring people having about the same income, it [was] at least not inferior, and the rents [were] lower." Sanitary conditions, they reported, were "generally better than the average among other laboring people."[41]

These conclusions, which were far more positive than those of contemporary critics, rested on detailed study of the housing of 1,567 families, almost all (91.5 percent) of which lived in mill-owned quarters and nearly as many (87.6 percent) of which in single-family homes. The vast majority of homes (82.5 percent) had 3, 4, or 5 rooms, with 4 rooms being typical. The average family paid $3.57 a month, or 4.8 percent of its annual earnings. Almost all the homes were heated by open fireplaces and lighted by kerosene lamps, and 1 in 20 (5.2 percent) had indoor running water.[42]

These conditions are best understood comparatively. Because the houses of sharecroppers and mountain folk were generally small and poorly constructed, it is likely that most rural folk who moved to the mills thereby improved the size and physical quality of their housing and appreciated the improvement. The 1907–1908 investigators studied the housing of 844 families in mountain regions from which mill folk came. More than half the families (55 percent) lived in log houses, many with only one room and almost a third (32 percent) with no windows. To move, as many Ap-

39. *Senate Documents*, 61st Cong., 2nd Sess., No. 645, Vol. 1, p. 521.
40. NC *Labor Report* (1890), 75–76, 74.
41. *Senate Documents*, 61st Cong., 2nd Sess., No. 645, Vol. 1, pp. 536, 533.
42. *Ibid.*, 519–20, 527. Housing continued to improve during the New South era. See Blicksilver, *Cotton Manufacturing in the Southeast*, 74–75, and Harriet L. Herring, *Welfare Work in Mill Villages: The Story of Extra-Mill Activities in North Carolina* (Chapel Hill, 1929), 31 and *passim*.

palachian families did, from such houses to, for example, the new Saxon Mills village, which opened in upcountry South Carolina in 1901, where all single-family houses had four rooms each, must have seemed an improvement.[43]

Evidence on what the move to the mills meant in terms of housing for individual families is, however, scanty. None of the interviews with mill folk treat the subject. Edgar R. Rankin, who studied 100 mill families in Gastonia, North Carolina, in 1914, found that 45 of them had lived in houses of 3 or fewer rooms before going to the mills—3 in 1 room, 15 in 2 rooms, and 27 in 3 rooms. In the mill villages, in contrast, only 12 of the families lived in houses of 3 or fewer rooms—none in 1 room, 3 in 2 rooms, and 9 in 3 rooms.[44]

Despite such improvement, mill housing was crowded by modern standards, though not necessarily by those of mill folk. The early crowding eased over the years, but among the 1,567 families studied in 1907 and 1908, the average family, of 7.1 persons, lived in 4.2 rooms with 2.7 people in each bedroom. It is not apparent that such a family considered this overcrowding. Mill folk seem not to have shared modern, middle-class notions of privacy and individual space. Children slept together two or three to the bed with no regard for gender (or social or psychological consequences) until puberty, after which boys slept with brothers and girls with sisters, though not necessarily in different bedrooms. Houses were too small and families too large to divide the sexes in that way. Families that boarded with other families, typically couples with or without small children or women with one or more children, probably had bedrooms of their own as a rule. An individual boarder likely slept in a room with one or more members of the family he boarded with unless the family had other boarders, in which case the boarders occupied a room of their own. It was probably sleeping arrangements that motivated many families to have male or female boarders only.

Boarders were generally crowded, in boardinghouses as well as in family homes. When the Elsas, May Company built a sixty-room "hotel" for unmarried workers at Fulton Bag and Cotton Mills in 1889, it designed the

43. *Senate Documents*, 61st Cong., 2nd Sess., No. 645, Vol. 1, p. 123. On the Saxon Mills village, see Marjorie A. Potwin, *Cotton Mill People of the Piedmont: A Study in Social Change* (New York, 1927), 45. For a study that sensationalizes contrasts of mill and mountain housing and views the mill villages as a vast improvement for mountain folk, see Thomas R. Dawley, *The Child That Toileth Not* (2nd ed.; New York, 1913).

44. Edgar R. Rankin, "A Social Study of One Hundred Families at Cotton Mills in Gastonia, North Carolina" (M.A. thesis, University of North Carolina, 1914), 9.

building to sleep four people per room, males in one wing and females in another. According to one report, a family near this mill boarded thirty people in its twelve-room house.[45]

Such crowding was due to the mills' desire to house their workers in the least possible space and to the need of mill folk to keep rent costs low. At first, mill officials tried to insist that every family or household supply at least one worker for each room it occupied. The effort was generally unsuccessful, but the principle behind it influenced housing policy throughout the New South era. The mills assigned housing on the basis of family size, and families were moved within the village as their size changed. At Saxon Mills in the second decade of the twentieth century, newly married couples lived in two-room "bungalettes" until their families were large enough to justify additional space.[46]

Mills preferred families with several working-age children largely because such families made maximum use of living space. Occasionally at least, mills used rent policy to encourage such use. At Pacolet Mills in the 1880s, for example, the company charged one dollar a month for each room of housing, but waived the charge for one room for each worker a family furnished. A family of four workers thus received a four-room house free, while a family with three workers paid one dollar a month for the same house. Households supplying more than one worker per room received a bonus of one dollar a month for each extra worker. This practice not only encouraged families to put children to work but prompted them to take in boarders as well. Perhaps it also discouraged absenteeism, for families could in effect be charged for members who did not work. "This system," an observer wrote in 1895, "led to some overcrowding, as many families were willing to pinch themselves on house accommodation in order to secure a little extra money."[47]

"IT IS IMPOSSIBLE TO RENT HOMES OR TO OBTAIN ACCOMMODATIONS NEAR . . . THE MILL."

Mill folk did not own their homes. Critics of the mill system blamed this circumstance on calculated mill policy and used it to explain the vulnerability of mill workers to employer pressure and to account for the absence of labor activism. Troublemaking workers, that is, risked their

45. Atlanta *Constitution*, August 1, 1889, November 5, 1905.
46. Potwin, *Cotton Mill People*, 74.
47. Porritt, "The Cotton Mills in the South," 580.

homes as well as their jobs. The absence of home ownership also explained for some observers why mill folk were irresponsible, of roving disposition, and uninterested in keeping up themselves and their communities. The mills did encourage workers to live in mill houses and, whenever such houses were available, made that a condition of employment. The requirement, however, was less meaningful than it seems, and the absence of home ownership must be seen in its context.

Mill folk did not look upon home ownership as the middle class did, and to approach the subject from the perspective of that class is to miss the meaning of company-owned housing. It was not that such housing had no ill consequences. Workers could be and often were evicted from their homes for matters of labor activism or personal conduct as well as work performance, and with significant results in every instance. Surely, the possibility of losing one's home as well as one's job encouraged a sense of insecurity and therefore dependence and conformity. And there were other undesirable possibilities. Elderly folk might lose their homes when they were too old to work, for village housing was for mill workers. In addition, mill officials used housing policy to enforce the rule that children work in the mills and nowhere else—a practice that increased the isolation of mill folk and restricted economic and social opportunity among youths.

These things did not determine the way mill folk looked at company housing, however. That view was a product of experience, circumstance, and perception. Those mill folk who owned their homes—4.9 percent of the 1,567 families studied in 1907 and 1908—were mostly town or farm families who lived near a mill and sent one or more of their members to work there. Poor people in the New South rarely owned their homes, however they made their living or wherever they lived. In Charlotte, Durham, and Raleigh, for example, all sizable towns with cotton mills, home tenancy rates were 66, 71, and 70 percent respectively in 1910; and in Georgia and South Carolina in 1920, more than two-thirds of all homes were rented. These rates were inflated by the high incidence of tenancy among blacks, but they are reminders that the lack of home ownership did not set mill folk apart from other poor people.[48]

Mill folk had reasons to consider home ownership more burden than opportunity. To buy a house on mill wages required years of saving from an already low income in order to pay cash, as was the general rule of home

48. *Senate Documents*, 61st Cong., 2nd Sess., No. 645, Vol. 1, pp. 519–20. On home tenancy generally, see J. G. Gullick, "The Homeless Multitudes in Urban Areas," *University of North Carolina Extension Bulletin*, II, No. 9 (Chapel Hill, 1923), 24–33.

buying in the New South, or to make a down payment and assume the risks of a mortgage. Because most families had little or no savings and mill work was irregular, those risks were high. That part of the family's income set aside to help pay for a house was unavailable for day-to-day living expenses, so that the family had to voluntarily accept a reduced standard of living until the house was paid for. Low rents in the mill villages made that option even more unattractive than it might otherwise have been.

There was another consideration as well. Buying a home entailed giving up the freedom to move between mills—a freedom that meant much to mill folk inasmuch as it was the most available means of protest they had. This freedom was facilitated not only by the absence of home ownership but by the ready availability of village housing as well. Frequent movement pulled mill folk farther into the vortex of dependency. But folk thought in immediate and concrete, not long-range and abstract, terms; and standing up and resisting an exploitive employer was an unpromising venture.

For families that did not move frequently, mill housing also had advantages. When mills closed down or ran on reduced schedules, they canceled rents or reduced them proportionately to time worked. At Alamance Mill, for example, where a five-room house cost sixty cents a week, the company regularly canceled rent when the mill was idle or ran on short time. Thus during Christmas week in 1908, which ended on December 26, the mill ran two days and collected no rent. Similarly, the mill shut down entirely for the four weeks ending August 20, 1910, and collected no rent; during the following week, when operations resumed on a limited basis, only families for whom work was available paid rent. Altogether, in the five years from 1909 to 1913, the mill collected no rent during twenty-two weeks, the equivalent of one month a year.[49] Had the workers affected by these practices rented from private landlords or been paying off mortgages, their rents or payments would have continued during the stoppages, to their financial disadvantage.

Within the range of available options, then, mill folk found village housing policies attractive. Sliding rent scales eased the impact of irregular work, as did the practice of forgoing rent for families or individuals out of work and for those who were ill or victims of unexpected misfortune. Also, wage cuts were often cushioned by across-the-board rent reductions, as occurred at King Mill in the fall of 1898. Workers living in private hous-

49. Rent Book, 1908–1920, Vol. XXII of Alamance Cotton Mill Records, in Southern Historical Collection, Louis R. Wilson Library, University of North Carolina at Chapel Hill.

ing—about a third of the total in this urban mill—received no benefit from the rent reduction. It was for reasons of this sort that at least a few families who owned their homes when they went into mill work persuaded the mill to buy the homes and rent them back to them.[50]

Another way of understanding the value of village housing is to look at the situation of mills that owned too little housing to accommodate their employees. This was common in urban mills, a few of which owned no housing at all. Because wages were low and hours long, workers had to live within walking distance of the mills. Moreover, the workers preferred to go home for dinner or have it brought warm to them by "dinner toters." Such conveniences, like low rents, were facilitated by company-owned villages. Atlanta Cotton Mill, which opened in 1879, owned no housing at all, and its difficulty in recruiting and maintaining a labor force was related to that fact. "Those who seek employment in the mill," a reporter wrote of the difficulty, "are unable to accept the place that is open to them for the reason that they find it impossible to rent homes or to obtain accommodations near enough to the mill to render their employment at all possible." The mill, the reporter believed, would have to build housing suited to the special needs of mill workers if it wanted to remain in business. "The cheap homes provided for the operatives must be in close proximity to the factory itself," he wrote, "for the work is of such a nature and the hours so fixed that an operative, male or female, cannot afford a long tramp in the dark and perhaps in the rain."[51]

Wherever a mill was built, and especially in towns or cities, property values, and thus rents, rose in the neighborhood, and private landlords always charged more than the mills for comparable housing. In 1888 the president of Exposition Mills said that houses equivalent to those his company rented for $1.50 a month cost $6.00 in nearby neighborhoods. That great a disparity was exceptional, but the point is pertinent. Low rents helped mill folk survive on low wages, and mills without sufficient housing had difficulty recruiting and retaining workers. Thus when Fulton Bag and Cotton Mills decided to institute a night shift in 1899, it immediately constructed a hundred new houses. This mill owned housing for only about half its work force, and not only were its houses "overflowing with operatives" but its perennial shortage of workers was due in part to the unavailability of affordable housing in the neigttorhood. "At present some of the operatives

50. Augusta *Chronicle*, October 17, 1898; Herbert J. Lahne, *The Cotton Mill Worker* (New York, 1944), 39.
51. Atlanta *Constitution*, January 2, 1880.

have to walk a mile to their work," a spokesman said of the decision to build the new houses in 1899. "There is not a house to rent within three-quarters of a mile of the mills." Indeed, "On Decatur street opposite the mills, [rents] are higher than they are a mile nearer the center of Atlanta."[52]

Company-owned housing was thus always in demand, and that fact neutralized the coercive potential in the requirement that mill workers live in company houses. In isolated villages, there was nowhere else to live, and to live outside the village was to forgo the fringe benefit of what was, in effect, subsidized housing.[53] It was also to forgo housing that was generally better than mill families could otherwise afford. As investigators for the 1907–1908 labor study concluded, living conditions in mill villages offered more "comfort and convenience" and were "much better" than those among mill workers "in many of the larger towns." Living conditions in mill districts in towns and cities, especially in privately owned housing, were often deplorable. In the 1920s, Paul Blanshard contrasted the "beautiful and modern" village of Bibb Manufacturing Company in Columbus, Georgia, with the "dingy slum of unpainted shanties" across the river in Phenix City, Alabama, where many mill workers lived in privately owned houses. The contrast was not always that great, but the larger point remains: in material terms, there were many reasons for mill folk to prefer village housing to other quarters available to them.[54]

52. *Ibid.*, April 8, 1888, January 26, 1899.

53. Occasionally one finds charges that mill rents were higher than those for nearby comparable houses. C. C. Houston of the Atlanta Federation of Trades told the Industrial Commission in 1900 not only that the houses of Fulton Bag and Cotton Mills were "ramshackle structures" in "deplorable" states of repair but that company rents were "much higher . . . than the same houses cost in the community near the mill" (*ibid.*, March 21, 1900).

54. *Senate Documents*, 61st Cong., 2nd Sess., No. 645, Vol. 1, p. 538; Paul Blanshard, *Labor in Southern Cotton Mills* (New York, 1927), 46–47.

9

PATERNALISM

Mill villages were more important as social institutions than as physical settings. They were the locales of folk life, and to approach the texture and substance of that life it is necessary to know the villages as social entities. Bessie Buchanan recalled that folk in the village she grew up in at Durham early in the twentieth century were "much happier" than people in the 1970s when she was interviewed. "It's because there's so much meanness going on now," she explained. "I think the fear between us now and [the absence of it] then [is the difference]. We weren't afraid to play in the streets till nine o'clock at night. But at nine o'clock every family had his little brood in the house, and the mothers knew where the children was at."

This sense of security was reinforced by feelings of belonging to a community that cared. "Everybody knew each other," Mrs. Buchanan continued, "I knowed everybody." She knew too that the mill owner cared about the village and its people. "They taken care of people," she recalled. "If a family was in need of anything, [the owner, William Erwin] seen that they was taken care of . . . out of his own expense." Moreover, "if a person come in here and they didn't act like and do like he thought they ought to, you'd see them getting out. So it was a clean community. . . . That's why we liked it, because we wanted to be a big family."

Flossie Moore Durham had similar memories of the village at Bynum, where she began work as a spinner in 1893. "We had a real good life over there on the hill," she recalled. "Every house was filled, and the people was all friendly and they was all nice. And Mr. Luther Bynum [the owner] was looking after it, and he wouldn't have anybody over there that drank. Anybody got drinking, they left there right now. Didn't have no drinking and cutting up over there. Things was kept quiet and nice. And it was a good place over there to live." Frank Thompson spoke in the same vein of the village at Carrboro, to which he and his family moved in 1907. "We never locked our door there," Thompson remembered. "Everybody seemed to behave themselves all right. Better than they do now. Once in a while there'd be somebody'd get drunk and get locked up. They'd fire them if they got drunk. I never heard of any stealing."[1]

Such reminiscences sound a cautionary note even if they do not tell the whole story of village life. Students of mill life have dwelt so largely on oppression and social wretchedness that it is necessary to remind ourselves that mill villages were functioning communities of ordinary human beings living and dying, working and playing, loving and hating, succeeding and failing—and always "making do" with whatever they had. The villages shared the satisfactions and problems of all human communities, and had problems and possibilities peculiarly their own, for they attracted poor and uneducated people in disproportionate numbers, and people too with no experience in village living. They had more than their share of broken or malfunctioning families, and exceptional numbers of teenagers, females, and unmarried adults of both sexes. They were also small communities in the late Victorian age and in the New South at a time of economic and social transition.

For all their problems, the villages were vibrant, even exciting places to folk who had never lived in organized communities. There were people in the villages—friends, neighbors, relatives—and what seemed like endless rounds of activity to folk whose lives had always been isolated—talking, visiting, working, helping, and just sitting around, and also gossiping, intruding, backbiting, and feuding. As folk settled into the villages, group activity developed, social institutions emerged, the social senses grew.

Life went on, held together at first by little more than grim determination, cultural commonalities, and the hope that mill employment would bring a more secure life. Family helped, too. Some villages were home to

1. Quoted in Marc S. Miller (ed.), *Working Lives: The "Southern Exposure" History of Labor in the South* (New York, 1980), 7.

extended kinship groups. At the Saxon Mills village in the 1920s, for example, 80 of the 168 families were related to at least one other family. Similarly, in the villages at York, South Carolina, in the 1940s, John K. Morland found "only a few nuclear families" not related to other families there. Morland wrote, "There is a tendency in each of the mill sections for kindred groups to rent houses in close proximity." In admittedly exceptional cases, he found a sixty-five-year-old woman living within sight of the homes of all eight of her children, who were married and living on their own. He also found a twenty-nine-year-old man who had sixty-five relatives, not counting his wife and children, in the villages of York, about half of them in one village. "A few family names dominate each village," Morland reported, and this pattern gave "a strong feeling of security to mill people."[2]

The paternalism of mill owners and officials was another source of village cohesion as it mediated the worst features of village life and made easier the transition from farm to factory of the constant streams of newcomers. Thus, life not only continued but improved over the years, and mill villagers were probably more secure and more hopeful in their own ways than most other plain folk in the New South.

"THE COMPANY OWNS EVERYTHING AND CONTROLS EVERYTHING, AND TO A LARGE EXTENT CONTROLS EVERYBODY."

As a fundament of village life, paternalism was rivaled only by work itself and the material conditions of life.[3] It permeated everything and manifested itself as soon as one entered the village. Its most apparent expression was property. The company owned not just the mill, the operatives' houses, and perhaps a company store and other auxiliary buildings but all other structures as well, including churches, schools, and community buildings (though these might be deeded to village groups beholden by that act to the company). The company owned all the land, even streets, pastures, parks, and cemeteries. It commonly supplied villagers with water, and fuel too for a charge. It provided them with gardens, pasturage, and street lighting if these things were available, and even saw that their privies were cleaned. It

2. Marjorie A. Potwin, *Cotton Mill People of the Piedmont: A Study in Social Change* (New York, 1927), 67–68; John K. Morland, *Millways of Kent* (Chapel Hill, 1958).
3. I will use the term *paternalism* to encompass 1) the array of welfare, social, and labor policies mill owners, superintendents, and other supervisors used in dealing with mill folk, 2) the congeries of attitudes and beliefs that justified those policies, and 3) the personalism that accompanied the implementation of the policies. Together these things made the relationship between mill folk and their employers quite different from the strictly economic relationships that characterize modern capitalist enterprise.

decided if and under what conditions they could keep livestock in the village; and introduced or failed to introduce at its own behest physical and aesthetic improvements, community services, welfare and educational programs. It might also own and operate a company store and other retail services—gristmill, flour mill, barber shop, icehouse, savings bank, meat and vegetable markets—though these were generally contracted out to other parties. It hired and fired, or caused to be hired and fired, everyone who worked in the village outside as well as inside the mill—preachers, teachers, social workers, tradesmen, policemen, skilled and unskilled laborers—and denied admission to the village to anyone, and where possible any idea, it deemed objectionable. The villagers' entire economic and much of their social life could be conducted through the company or its officers, lessees, or agents. The ideal was self-containment—the insulation of villagers from the outside world.

In the most inclusive sense, the company governed the village. "It has no mayor, no alderman, no police, no prison, no judge, no court, [and] no magistrate," a visitor wrote of the village at Piedmont Mills in 1895. It therefore had, or so the visitor thought, "no whisky, no gambling, no theatre, no dancing, no rioting and no disorders of any kind." Another visitor was similarly impressed with the village at Pelzer. "No municipality imposes taxes," Leonora B. Ellis wrote of this village in 1901, "and no mayoralty elections, aldermanic squabbles, or ward politics keep the people in a ferment." Liquor was prohibited, and any "disorderly element" that appeared was "quickly detected by the watchful management, and . . . banished with small ceremony." As a result, this author concluded, "order and peace uniformly prevail[ed]."[4]

From such appearances it was easy to conclude, as did investigators in 1907 and 1908, that the mill owner's power was "dictatorial" and his authority "almost unlimited" or, like other observers, to view the village system as despotism, benevolent or otherwise. "His will is supreme in the village," the investigators wrote of the mill owner, "his decisions final, so long as they do not conflict with the laws of the State." As a consequence, "All the affairs of the village and the conditions of living of all the people are regulated entirely by the mill company. Practically speaking, the company owns everything and controls everything, and to a large extent controls everybody in the mill village."[5]

4. *Manufacturers' Record*, September 20, 1895, p. 121; Leonora B. Ellis, "A Model Factory Town," *Forum*, XXXII (September, 1901), 62–63.

5. *Senate Documents*, 61st Cong., 2nd Sess., No. 645, Vol. 7, pp. 537–38.

According to some critics, mill officials developed this system for malevolent purposes. "The mill village was a vehicle perfectly calculated from all angles to restrict the development of the workers into independent free-acting citizens," a scholar wrote in 1944. "As the industry in the South became assured of financial success, the early paternalism [which had evidenced "a genuine concern for the welfare of employees new to the ways of industrial life"] became transformed into a deliberate tactical pose of the employer in which the restrictive [features] of the mill village system were brought to the fore. It became a means of producing and assuring what the Southern employer liked to call 'contented' workers." And, this author believed, paternalism largely succeeded in its purposes.[6]

Such assessments rest largely on theory and appearance. Their very statement, however, is a useful reminder of the need to distinguish between appearance and reality—between theoretical power and the ability to translate that power into social goals. The difference was substantial in the case of mill owners, and company policies and regulations are imperfect guides to the actualities of village life. Moreover, the purposes of mill paternalists were more utilitarian than malevolent, and their endeavors far less objectionable to mill folk than to critics of the mill system. The villages were neither socially idyllic places (as apologists implied) nor concentration camps (as talk of dictatorial power and malevolent purpose suggested). They were instead distinctive communities of working folk in the New South.

"AN OUNCE OF LOYALTY TO THE COMPANY AND GOOD CHARACTER"

Paternalism was an integral feature of life in the New South, pervading relations between classes, races, and sexes, as well as employers and employees. Traditional notions of hierarchy and social place permeated the society, and it would have been remarkable had pronounced forms of paternalism not appeared in the mills and villages.

The essence of mill paternalism derived not from the exploitation it facilitated but the reciprocal relationship it defined. That relationship, between owners and folk, was unequal but mutually dependent. The two groups needed each other, recognized that need, and were prepared within limits to accommodate to each other. Mill owners and officials defined and rationalized these mutualities in a well-developed ideology that explained

6. Herbert J. Lahne, *The Cotton Mill Worker* (New York, 1944), 63–64.

and justified their position. Mill folk, less cerebral and articulate, intuited the mutualities from a "structure of feeling" that explained and rationalized their dependency and enabled them to acknowledge and act on it without losing their sense of individuality and self-worth.

The ideology of mill representatives is easily delineated, for it was developed and elaborated in public discourse. The counterpart among mill folk, however, must be inferred from acts and utterances largely concerned with other things. In the village as on the job, mill folk had the resources of the weak. They could ignore, evade, or otherwise compromise the exhortation and example of the most determined paternalist, and do much the same for every effort to reform and uplift them. Mill officials as well as mill folk recognized these resources, and the purpose of both elements of village paternalism—the "sticks" of regulation and restriction and the "carrots" of welfare and uplift—was to overcome the obstacles they presented to the development and maintenance of abundant supplies of willing labor.

The problem, as mill owners saw it, was that mill folk were enthralled by traditional ways and preindustrial values that inhibited individual and group improvement in the villages and productivity and profit in the mills. These results, moreover, were of a single piece; the one could not be rectified without rectifying the others. The need was to make the folk over, to wean them from traditional habits and values and inculcate them with others of modern, progressive, capitalist, middle-class society. This was a daunting, indeed impossible task, the very difficulty of which helps explain the multiple, confused, and sometimes contradictory elements of village paternalism, which sought at once to force, pressure, nudge, coax, and bribe folk to do and be as paternalists desired.

It was a worthy effort or not according to one's assessment of its ends and means. Certainly the ways of mill folk inhibited accumulation and economic advancement; and certainly, too, the devaluing of schooling and "reform" limited their prospects in other ways. Mill paternalists sought to remedy these things, which they saw as deficiencies. In this sense, they sought to "improve" the folk—make of them better citizens, consumers, and workers—while, not incidentally, enhancing their own profits and reputations as doers of good. These purposes were not in their view selfish. On the contrary, each was essential to larger ends of economic development and social progress. However self-serving this attitude appears and was, and however much it invites cynical reading, mill owners were not the first or last group to see their own interest in elevated terms. The flaw in their vision was not self-interestedness or cynicism but the contradiction on which the vision rested: had they succeeded in "uplifting" mill folk and making them over as they said they wanted to do, the folk would not have been content to remain in the mills.

Thomas F. Parker of Greenville was one of the most successful and most self-conscious practitioners of mill paternalism. He was certain the two facts were related; and his statement of paternalist ideology may be taken as representative. His villages were showcases of welfare work and social up-lift, and his faith in the efficacy of those things was unfailing.

"Its motive has been a genuine desire to help the operative, and methods have been found profitable alike to the employees and employers," Parker wrote of mill paternalism. "It has endeavored to inspire each employee with a desire to do his best and to furnish him with the means of doing it in a helpful environment." Whatever was good for workers was equally good for management. "After all," Parker also said, "what we need in our villages is not so much numbers as efficiency, general intelligence, and character; for unintelligent, unskilled labor is in the long run not only unprofitable but dangerous to capital." That was the goal, but not yet the reality. "We have yet much to learn," Parker wrote, "about dignifying labor."[7]

Parker did not, then, play down the "selfish" motive behind paternalistic endeavor. On the contrary, he insisted that welfare work was "largely a business necessity." He said in a revealing passage, "Most mill superinten-dents know from experience that any illiterate child who goes to the average village school for a year is thereby increased in mill efficiency besides being made a better citizen in general; and what the school does for the child, other agencies can do for young men and women in the village." If every mill had adequate welfare programs vigorously pursued, "the villagers would be revolutionized," that is, transformed into efficient workers and exemplary citizens. "And not only would they retain a true friendliness toward the management" when that transformation occurred, but they would also "escape the future control of demagogues and labor agitators."[8]

Still, the advantages to management were products of larger purposes and responsibilities. "The Monaghan Mills," Parker said at the dedication of a new YMCA building in one of his villages, "recognizes that in collecting a large number of people under new conditions for its own purposes it assumes to them and to the State a certain moral obligation for their wellbe-ing. It recognizes further that its main dependence for success is not in its

7. Thomas F. Parker, "The South Carolina Cotton Mill Village—A Manufacturer's View," *South Atlantic Quarterly,* VIII (1910), 328–37.
8. *Ibid.*

buildings and machinery, but in its leadership and in its workers . . . and that what elevates these latter promotes the company's interest. To Monaghan workers the management always extends the hand of friendship to help them help themselves; it never professes to offer them any charity, but it gives them always friendly interest and it only asks of them the same." Parker told an assemblage of workers, "An ounce of loyalty to the company and good character is worth a pound of cleverness."[9]

The goal, then, was loyal workers with good character. Of course, Parker's rhetoric was part of the standard fare of public ritual in the New South, and it may be misleading to read too much meaning into individual passages. Yet the ideals Parker spoke, of social reciprocity and uplift, were not unlike those of contemporary Progressive reformers, and it is with those people that mill paternalists belong. Men like Parker wanted to help the folk, genuinely, and make a profit doing so. The problem was that mill folk had imperatives of their own. They were traditionalists bent on preserving continuities in their lives as much as possible. Mill owners, on the other hand, as both employers and village paternalists, wanted folk to break with important elements of their past. The unwillingness of folk to do so was underscored by the fact that the move to the mills had already distanced them from vital parts of their past. They were therefore doubly concerned to hold onto whatever they could of the rest.

Folk had other concerns as well, the most immediate of which were earning a livelihood and meeting the demands of day-to-day living. In those concerns too, they had values and interests of their own. Folk viewed the social and economic position of mill owners, and the prerogatives that went with it, as legitimate. They also agreed with some of the goals paternalists wanted to accomplish in the villages. They did not therefore respond negatively to men like Parker. They were too dependent on their employers to reject outrightly their paternalist machinations, and they found things in paternalism they hoped to turn to their advantage.

"MR. BLEASE IT LOOKS SO HARD FOR US AND IT SEEMS LIKE WE CANT HELP OUR SELVES."

The attitudes of mill folk toward paternalism and paternalists may in part be deduced from their comments on mill owners in interviews. That those

---

9. *Manufacturers' Record*, January 15, 1905, p. 8. For another illustrative statement of paternalism, see John T. Woodside, typescript autobiography in Southern Historical Collection, Louis R. Wilson Library, University of North Carolina at Chapel Hill.

memories were so vivid after so many years suggests the depth of feeling on which they rested. That they were so positive should not be surprising, even if allowance is made for the tendency of older folk to recall the past in positive terms. In hierarchical societies, attachment to a powerful overlord and marrying one's identity with his are common devices by which weak, dependent people cope with insecurity. Those devices, in effect, are what many mill folk used with regard to paternalistic employers. Their action was distinctive only in the degree to which some of them merged their interests with those of their employers. Attachment to and identification with "big" men—landlords, employers, and charismatic politicians or preachers, for example—were not unusual in the New South.

The pattern was exemplified by the attachments plain folk generally and mill folk specifically developed for Governor Blease of South Carolina. Their letters to "Coley," as they spoke endearingly of the governor, open many windows onto the folk mind. One reveals the ways poor people identified with powerful figures and used that identification in dealing with dependency and insecurity. It likewise reveals the deep cultural sources of that identification, thus shedding light on not only the relationship mill folk developed with paternalistic overlords but the way they tried to hold onto cultural forms as well. More specifically, this window onto the folk mind shows the potential willingness of folk to accept the leadership, example, and being of paternalistic employers. That acceptance could not be induced by coercion or threat. On the contrary, it had to be rendered willingly; and to induce it, employers had to tap into fundamental elements of folk psychology. What those elements were and how that process worked are revealed in the correspondence to Blease.

Folk wrote Blease to ask favors, report problems, or simply voice their admiration for a man they considered great and praiseworthy. They never approached him familiarly, without due deference, despite his own earthiness and bluntness of public speech and his pose as just one of the "boys." The governor's appeal to them was cultural in the profoundest sense. Blease said what they wanted to hear in language they understood and in a manner they found endearing. His enemies were their enemies, his causes theirs. Indeed, "Bleaseism" was, more than anything else, the political expression of the cultural concerns of plain folk and of the effort of folk to hold onto traditional ways. Its concerns were not political in the conventional sense of centering on issues of economic self-interest, for the deepest concerns of folk were not economic. They were instead intensely personal and specifically cultural.

In writing the governor, folk were always careful to establish their dependent condition and appeal to him from positions of weakness. Such a pose established a claim on Blease's attention, appealing as it did for help as a matter of benevolence, not right, the granting of which would validate Blease's claims to magnanimity and to the allegiance of the supplicant he helped. Dependency, in other words, led to supplication rather than assertiveness—a consequence often found in paternal, hierarchical societies. "I Would like to Ask some information of You if You Will permit a poor Cotton Mill operator to step in and take up a few Moments of Your spare time," one man wrote the governor; and that pose appeared again and again. "I Am a poor man working in the Cotton Mill"; "I am a poor land renter got nothing a wife and three little childerns"; "I am a poor old Solger"; "I am only a Poor Renters Son havent got any thing and Never have had any thing"—these were typical bases for approaching the governor.[10]

Such statements represented an effort to turn dependency—poverty, weakness, poor health, widowhood, sudden misfortune, or simply inability to do for oneself—to advantage, which is another characteristic of dependent folk in hierarchical societies. The effort was not calculated. Rather, it grew from unquestioning faith in Blease's ability to accomplish whatever was asked of him and from the naïf's assumption that it was proper to ask anything. Such was the folk image of the power and role of a paternal overlord. Thus, when one man found himself in economic difficulty, he asked Blease to "help me or point me out Some Aid in Borrowing Some Eight hundred or a thousand Dollars." When fire destroyed a small farmer's home, his wife wrote the governor to "ask Mrs Blease if she has any clothes and bed clothes and bed covering she could spair." A mill worker from Horse Creek Valley wanted to be relocated in a new job. "We have been awrangl At this Mill for Some time and We do Not no how long be fore the Mills troubles Will be settled," he told Blease. "I am down here in a destute condition With Nothing to eat and I cannot Get No Work to do. [A]nd I wont you to interseed to some of the Cotton Mills in your town for me and my family and fix Some Way to help us get away from here. [F]or I See No help but to starve without help."[11]

10. J. B. Riddle to Coleman L. Blease, January 17, 1912, W. A. Mooney to Blease, May 6, 1913, A. S. Watson to Blease, April 12, 1913, R. A. Clem (?) to Blease, May 9, 1913, and M. T. McDonald to Blease, April 9, 1913, in Coleman L. Blease Papers, South Carolina State Archives.

11. S. J. Widener to Blease, October 6, 1914, Mrs. J. B. Nunnamaker to Blease, November 19, 1914, and M. W. Snipes to Blease, n.d., in 1914 Aiken County folder, in Blease Papers.

Such pleas were not unlike those children address to parents. "Mr. Blease please help us," a Greenville mill worker wrote in a time of need. "Mr. Blease it looks So hard for us and it Seems like we cant help our Selves." A "poor Widdow" wrote in a similarly instructive passage: "I appeal to you Just as a Child does to its Father." Another mill worker wrote: "We need shoose and clothes and Cant get them[.] My little children are haf to go with out iny shoose becaus we ant got the money to get them with[.] We are in det to the copany and they take out all he Make [note: the letter was probably written by the worker's wife] and we Cant hardly get sompathen to eat Much less Cloths and shoose[.] Mr Blease plese send Me some Money[.] . . . [S]end me 25 dollars iny how."[12]

Whether Blease helped these supplicants is unknown, but one can readily imagine the sense of gratitude and obligation assistance of any sort generated. The possibilities created by an unfortunate situation provided an opening for mill paternalists, who regularly helped mill folk in times of pressing need. A bag of groceries, extra credit at the store, and help with medical or burial expense, especially when accompanied by a kind word or even an admonition to do better in the future, were regular features of village life. So was assistance in dealing with drunken husbands or overbearing overseers, hiring needy relatives, or handling problems with "the law." Speaking of officials at Exposition Mills in 1899, a villager whose grandchild had recently died told a reporter: "There never was any kinder people in the world. Mr. Jeter, the mill superintendent, sent us a coffin over here last night and money to pay the funeral expenses with it. The burial won't cost my daughter a cent. And when [my] other [kin]folks were sick Dr. Turner and Dr Elkin to[o] come out from town and attend them. I reckon he [J. D. Turner, president of Exposition Mills] paid for it. We didn't. We never were asked to."[13]

This was one of those unequal exchanges mill folk made with their employers. In return for benevolence in time of need, many folk allowed their sense of gratitude to become a feeling of obligation so enthralling as to mire them deeper in the morass of dependency. That feeling tended to smother critical thought about their situation and to encourage unquestioning identification with their benefactors.

The folk's admiration for Blease rested not on what he did for them but on what he was and said and symbolized. "Coley is the riseing star of the

12. Albert Burnett to Blease, January 10, 1914, Mrs. S. J. Vaughn to Blease, January 5, 1914, and F. M. Meadow to Blease, November 23, 1912, in Blease Papers.
13. Atlanta *Constitution*, January 2, 1899.

morning, the onely Gov we had sence B R Tilman," a "wool hat one gallas boy" from Laurens County wrote. "According my judgement Colie ahead of Tillman[.] [W]e never had such a Gov as C. L. Blease is been so far," this man continued. "I voted for you 3 times before and I'll do so again if it is nessary[.] . . . I read some of your peaces [in a local newspaper.] [M]akes the hair rise on my head[.] I walk the floor[.] I cant hardly keep from coming to Columbia[.] . . . I have one of your pictures[.] [R]eads under it Mayer Cole L Blease & I got another one the other day reads under Gov Blease & in 3 years from now Ill get one reads senator Blease & they cant help them selves."[14]

Hanging Blease's picture in the home, a practice that was quite widespread, was a concrete act of fealty and identification. "I am writing you for your Picher," a Laurens County man wrote the governor. "I wount to Shoe [show] the men who my Man is[.] I am for you ever Day and I wount one of your Picher to Put in my home[.] Sent it to Me Soon." An operative at Gray Cotton Mill in Woodruff wrote similarly, "I Want one of your photygraph fore the honer of my house an the honer of my Wife an Chilldren an to show tha pore peeple thare friend."[15]

A similar expression of the devotion, also widespread, was naming children after the governor. "I have got a fine Boy named after you," Queen Daisy Gosnell wrote to "Mr Cold l Bleece." "He Was Born September the 12 day in the year 1912[.] [H]e Was Born close to the time you Was elected as govener and i Wanted to name him after you and i Wated tell he Was too Months old and Wee named him after you and Me and My husban are Borth are for you[.] My husban is a Bleace Man from hed to foot." A Laurens County operative also wrote: "I have got 5 Boys and 4 girls[.] [T]he Baby is 6 monts old an I Name Him Cole L[.] I like the Name But Like the Man the Best[.] I work for you in Every Campain you have Run[.] I Was Put of[f] a Job in Greenville for voting for you the Last time But I Will Lose a Job Eny time to vote for you[.] . . . I Hope the Boy that I Name after you Will Be as Gratier Man as you ar[.] He is fine Boy[.] I Will Have his Picter Taken an Send it to you an I Hope you Will Precate [appreciate] your Name Sake."[16]

The task of mill paternalists was to tap the reservoir of trust and commitment these letters reveal. The wonder is not that they sometimes succeeded in doing so but that they ultimately failed to do so completely. "Paternalism

14. R. L. Holland to Blease, March 25, 1912, in Blease Papers.
15. C. E. Alverson to Blease, September 14, 1913, William Rodgers to Blease, September 11, 1913, in Blease Papers.
16. Charlie Gosnell and Queen Daisy Gosnell to Blease, January 18, 1913, in Blease Papers.

can function to reduce anxiety in its emphasis on taking care of the worker," John K. Morland wrote in his study of mill folk in the 1940s. "The workers know that if they are loyal to the company, cooperate with the bossman, and do a reasonably good job in the mill, they can be sure of their jobs and their houses. Many of their problems are solved for them if they submit to the system."[17] Yet they did not submit, if submission be defined as assenting to the values and purposes of paternalists.

The paternalists encountered obstacles they never overcame, and the reasons for their failure seem apparent. Their relationship with mill folk was exploitive, and that plus the arbitrary exercises of power it permitted compromised their pose as selflessly benevolent men. Indeed, the letters mill folk wrote Blease often complained about and asked help against their employers, and are therefore impressive evidence of the limitations of paternalism as well as of the ability of mill folk to make discerning judgments about their situation.

Mill paternalism had a dual nature, and most folk were inclined to accept at face value many of the things it entailed. On the one hand, it imposed rules, responsibilities, and inequalities on folk; but on the other, it promised security, benevolence, and for those who wanted it, uplift. Both sides of that equation were important, and mill folk insisted as the price of their acquiescence in the burdens of paternalism that their employers deliver the benefits it promised. Those benefits were not just jobs, housing, and other material things but expressions of benevolence that brought psychological assurance. These included spoken, friendly greetings, expressions of concern for one's problems, inquiries about one's family, token gifts, and expressions of gratitude at appropriate times. Benevolent treatment also included tolerance for the ways of the folk—from slow work and absenteeism to taking snuff and tobacco. In short, an employer must act as a paternalist was supposed to act if he wanted to be accepted as one, and he must play by the rules of the game as folk understood those rules.

That was not always easy, even for well-intentioned men; and those who failed, as was apparently the case with the employers of many of Blease's correspondents, could expect not only sullen disdain from their employees but the transfer of their loyalties to another "big man." Blease was thus an alternative to failed paternalists, as it were, and his appeal to mill folk disillusioned with their employers was made stronger by his pillorying public attacks on mill owners generally. Publicly identifying with Blease was thus doubly satisfying for mill folk seeking psychological as well as

17. Morland, *Millways of Kent*, 50.

cultural security. It not only affirmed an identity deeply felt but provoked the ire of mill officials whose power mill folk perceived as exploitive and therefore illegitimate. The fact that North Carolina and Georgia had no counterparts to Blease—a politician who stirred mill folk to political awareness—is probably explained not by the fact that paternalists in those states were more successful than those in South Carolina but by the absence of a political figure who berated mill owners successfully, that is, in language and cultural imagery that stirred the passions of mill folk.

ON UPLIFT AND WELFARE

A major manifestation of paternalism was the effort to "uplift" folk in the villages. The purpose behind the effort was not to achieve a narrowly moral or religious goal or simply to improve individual behavior, though those concerns were present; it was instead to turn mill folk into a reservoir of willing laborers. That transformation, mill owners came to believe, could best be achieved through welfare programs designed to cultivate the social senses, elevate cultural tastes, and raise material desires among mill folk. Achieving those goals would make the villages more desirable places to live; and more important, it would encourage villagers to merge their sense of well-being with loyal service to the company. The effort to accomplish these things was audacious in purpose and sometimes in execution, and the resulting programs came to have a significant impact on village life.

Before folk went to the mills, most had little experience with organized social activity. Among sharecroppers and mountaineers alike, social bonds beyond the family were few and relatively weak. Both groups had commonalities of identity through kinship and perhaps religious affiliation, and to a lesser extent through racial awareness, community affinities, and similarities of day-to-day existence. But neither knew much about sustained, purposeful group activity involving anything more than the work they did and the diversions they occasionally enjoyed in small collectivities. Even their churches involved no group activity except worship itself, and there as elsewhere folk were followers, not leaders. When they arrived in the villages, few of them had ever joined any organization except a church, and fewer still had participated in organized efforts to achieve social goals.

The social instincts and experience of the folk therefore worked at cross-purposes with the goal of mill owners to form them into effective social and economic units. The move to the mills was a venture into the unknown, and once made, holding onto traditional ways was an important source of security. The move therefore encouraged not the values mill owners preached—individual initiative, ambition, and the disciplines of the work ethic—but something akin to their opposites. A kind of social atomism prevailed among newly arriving villagers, encouraging suspicion of strange people and new ideas, and resistance to social innovation of any sort. Concrete matters and personal relationships composed the social vision of those folk. The present, not the future, and security now, not opportunity in the long run, were their concerns; and things as vague as "progress" or as impossible to comprehend as wealth had no meaning for them. Welfare to them was not a collective concern but something individuals and families arranged on their own through landlords, employers, or others in position to provide the necessary services and assurances.

Where such values prevail, group consciousness is undeveloped, and leadership and therefore collective action on anything not viscerally felt (like racial prejudice) cannot emerge. Cooperation in the interest of abstractions like democracy, civil rights, civic improvement, and economic opportunity is impossible. The tendency in the villages was therefore toward social stasis. Work had to be done in order to live but not in order to accumulate or try to rise above one's "raising." Schooling and "culture" were alien, as was the concept of social mobility, and those who sought such things were looked upon as pretentious social climbers. Experience—tradition—was the proper guide to the present. The future would, it was hoped, be like the past, but whether it was or not, it would take care of itself.

These beliefs were tendencies, not absolutes, in folk thought; and village welfare work—what we today call social work—was an effort to reshape them to the purposes of mill owners. The owners reasoned, and hoped, that group activity would encourage mill folk to take up modern ways; that exposure to "elevated" culture would kindle among them a sense of social refinement; and that life in improved villages with modern conveniences would arouse in them a desire for higher standards of living. And once under way, those processes would, mill owners also hoped, encourage folk to see that "the good life" was achievable only through disciplined labor and loyal service to the employers who made it possible.

"TRYING TO BUILD UP CHARACTER AND CREATE AMBITION"

Welfare work began slowly.[18] It grew in part from Progressive impulses, and gathered strength as those impulses spread across the South. Before the

18. The standard work on the subject is Harriet L. Herring, *Welfare Work in Mill Villages: The Story of Extra-Mill Activities in North Carolina* (Chapel Hill, 1929).

mid-1890s, it consisted largely of building churches and schools and encouraging villagers to worship and see that their children learned to read and write. The focus of paternalism in those years was pragmatic—establishing the owners' authority and offering minimum security to folk in a society with little wealth. Owners saw that sick villagers had a doctor or patent medicines; they "carried" disabled workers for a while at the village store; and they helped bury the dead, dispensed occasional favors, and enforced rules of personal conduct. They did not, however, articulate a vision of social uplift or see their villages as agencies of civilization. On the contrary, they were preoccupied with the business of cotton manufacturing. "Uplift" and help in socializing new villagers they left to preachers and villagers themselves.

In these early years, work itself and the organization of life around the demands of the mills were the most important social activities in the villages, and those activities centered on the family. Folk had to adapt family routines to work schedules, deciding who would go to the mill and who would be responsible for work at home, and if necessary dividing family members between day and night shifts and adjusting living arrangements accordingly. They had to learn to live by the clock, or more accurately the mill whistle or bell, rather than by the sun and the seasons. Workers had to be up and at work on time, which necessitated learning to reckon in minutes and hours. Meals had to be prepared and served on time, almost to the minute, for dinnertime might be no more than half an hour. Housework revolved around the goings and comings of family workers.

Meanwhile, folk learned to live with one another, with neighbors even in the same house; and as they did, familiar kinds of social activity emerged. With so many people about, work and goods could be swapped and borrowed, help received and given, the value of neighbors made manifest. Specialists appeared. One woman sewed; another midwived, tended small children, or knew the secrets of folk medicine; others had vegetables or milk to barter or give away. Men whose children worked in the mills might be carpenters or wood haulers or have their own mule and plow the gardens of other villagers. Those who worked in the mill might also know about livestock raising, hog killing, or tool mending, or even how to make illicit whiskey. Youths might play the fiddle or guitar or have other social skills. All such things encouraged social intercourse, and community took root in the villages. Circumstances demanded that it do so, and nudged the process in specific directions.

The resulting adaptations are obscurely documented. Perhaps appearances became more important. Certainly it was necessary to acknowledge the presence of other people, and perhaps also their ways of doing and being. Newcomers grew sensitive about "country" clothes and shoes and ways. No doubt mill work itself caused them to bathe and change clothes more often than they had in the country. Perhaps village living also encouraged circumspectness in speech, less casual housekeeping, more attention to sanitation, and other changes too various to list. Suddenly life was more involved. Folk who had never handled money might now have regular income in cash or trade checks to be managed from one payday to the next. Males and females of all ages, married and unmarried, worked and lived in unaccustomed closeness, and that situation too had to be managed.

That the changes this new way of life involved were difficult is suggested by the number of folk who went back to the farm or moved back and forth between farm and mill. It was uncomfortable for many to live so close to other people. "Manufacturers could increase the welfare of their operatives very greatly by building better houses and giving more land to each family," a boss beamer-tender told the North Carolina labor commissioner in 1891. "The greatest mistake, in my opinion, is in crowding the houses too close."[19] For many folk, however, crowding was an attraction that opened opportunities for social intercourse. Women and youths especially found this proximity appealing, and they were the aptest pupils of village welfare workers.

The pace of these changes was casual and undirected, and they hardly filled the needs of employers yearning for better workers or those of paternalists enamored of human engineering and social uplift. By the 1890s, mill owners came to believe their interests as employers meshed with their purposes as paternalists, and they began not only to build better villages but to give increasing attention to the kind of life their villages sustained. Their interest in church and school expanded to concern with the physical well-being of villagers and moved on to a long list of activities concerned with social well-being.

The resulting programs varied enormously from village to village, but by the second decade of the twentieth century, when the movement that produced them matured, almost all villages and urban mill districts had at least some company-sponsored social programs beyond those of church and school. In their most complete form, in the largest villages, the programs encompassed a range of services and activities far more extensive than those available to most members of the working classes in the New South. At

19. North Carolina Bureau of Labor Statistics, *Annual Report, 1891,* 318.

Pelzer, a widely publicized model village, for example, there were 5 churches for a community of about 7,000 people in 1901 and a subsidized, graded school that the company required all children between the ages of five and twelve to attend for ten months a year. There was a lending library with more than 5,000 volumes "of approved standard literature" and current copies of about 25 newspapers and magazines. In the manner of the times, the library included a "ladies reading room" and a "gentleman's reading and smoking room." The company arranged regular programs of concerts and lectures for villagers and a lyceum course for those interested in more systematic learning. There was a league of baseball teams, each uniformed at company expense, and a bicycle race track, where the Smyth Wheel Club, made up solely of mill employees, gave frequent public exhibitions. There was even a militia company, the Smyth Rifles, composed of young men from the several Pelzer mills, reportedly the only military unit in the state made up entirely of mill workers. For parades and concerts, the company financed a brass band with 36 members. For vocational training, it provided industrial and manual arts classes. For housewives and girls, there were home demonstration clubs and classes in sewing, cooking, and other appropriate activities; for the frugal, there was a savings bank and the opportunity to purchase stock at twenty-five dollars a share in the largest store in the village, already largely owned by operatives. There were also troops of Boy Scouts and Girl Scouts, YMCAs and YWCAs, Sunday schools, and daycare centers for small children of working mothers.[20]

Pelzer was exceptional. Indeed, no more than a handful of villages had a range of services approaching the array of programs there. From the long list of possibilities suggested by the Pelzer example, more typical villages chose programs according to their size and resources and probably also according to the interests of their owners and their perception of the wants and needs of their villagers. Religious and educational programs were almost universal, but some owners stressed physical improvements—paved sidewalks and streets, screen doors, running water, and the like—while others gave attention to group activities of various sorts, encouraging athletic clubs, fraternal organizations, garden clubs, or classes in "practical" subjects. Some encouraged social activities such as dancing and picnicking, and some brought motion pictures to their villages. Still others focused on

20. Ibid.; Manufacturers' Record, February 21, 1901, pp. 78–80; U.S. Bureau of Labor, Bulletin No. 54: Housing of Working People in the United States by Employers (1904), 1224–26; Thomas R. Dawley, The Child That Toileth Not (2nd ed.; New York, 1913), 99–114.

social self-help, encouraging burial unions and medical insurance programs, or sponsoring contests for the best flower or vegetable gardens.

In urban mill districts, much of the welfare work centered on settlement houses or institutions rather like them. Such was the case at Fulton Bag and Cotton Mills, where, early in the twentieth century, one institution combined the various functions of daycare center, kindergarten, welfare agency, and recreational facility, all for the purpose of fostering "self-activity, independence and honesty" in mill folk. "It is trying to build up character and create ambition," a reporter wrote of the house after touring its facilities and interviewing the staff, "so that pauperism will be unknown and those people will be energetic, intelligent, and upright." In the daycare center, children of working mothers received, at a cost of five cents a day per child, "the best training in cleanliness, obedience, etc.," and had their "moral and spiritual development" nurtured as well. They learned, too, the value of respecting rules and obeying orders. "If he 'helps' the privileges may be enjoyed, but if he transgresses the nature, punishment follows," a teacher said of the child in the center. "If he is not willing to cooperate he may be deprived of the privilege 'to help,' for work is a reward, not a punishment." Discipline was "just," and intended to make the child "desire to be a good member of his little social world." "The jails, the prisons, [and] the reformatories," the teacher told the reporter, "are filled with men who are there because they were weak, more than because they were evil." Children remained at the center from 5:45 A.M. to 6:15 P.M. to accommodate the workday of their mothers.

In addition to the daycare center, which accepted children up to eight years of age, the settlement house offered night classes in "elementary" subjects. It also provided Saturday afternoon sewing classes; a gymnasium class; a health clinic, where volunteer staff members learned that mill folk had "many superstitious beliefs and practices, especially in reference to disease"; a Sunday school and weekly Bible drill; a reading room and library of 150 books; a Friday "entertainment," at which children learned "how harmlessly they may engage in the pleasures of life"; and a "penny provident" savings department to teach "the necessity of providing for the future." The "need for [the savings department] is eminent," a staff member told the reporter, "for the value of money is unknown. It is wasted on every hand, even the very young children being given pennies with which to play or spend for candy, gum or some useless trifle, thus the habit of wastefulness is begun and it continues through the succeeding years."[21]

21. Atlanta *Constitution*, November 5, 1905.

A different kind of institution was the Eagle and Phenix Club, operated for employees of the giant mill of that name. The creature of President Gunby Jordan, the club was less concerned with welfare (the mill sponsored other programs for that purpose) than with social, recreational, and educational activity. To house the club, the company acquired and renovated an old public library building. When it opened in the spring of 1899, the clubhouse included "reading rooms, bowling alleys, billiards tables, reception rooms, and other appliances for physical culture and enjoyment, with a spacious hall for lecture courses during the winter." The reception room was "elegantly fitted with leather furniture" and "adorned with pictures and draperies." The library contained "all standard works of fiction and general literature, as well as reference and technical and textile books" and "the complete works of many of the most popular authors." The gymnasium housed "a Medart standard vaulting horse, parallel bars, pulley weights, dumb bells, Indian clubs, etc.," as well as "ten pin alleys, pool and billiard tables, and Manhattan pool." The bathhouse was "fitted up with fine porcelain tubs, shower baths and all accessories which go to make up a modern and complete bath." The combination lecture hall and gallery was "roomy" enough to seat 600 people.

The club was incorporated under Georgia law, and membership was limited to male operatives over sixteen. However, Wednesday nights were set aside for female employees of the mill, and they and the ladies of members could attend dances and open house twice a week and other activities as well. The membership fee was 25 cents a month, the company making up the shortfall in operating expenses of about $200 a month in 1900. At the end of that year, there were reportedly 300 members, which suggests considerable interest in the club. (At the time, the company employed about 1,800 operatives, probably more than half of them females, and a sizable portion of the males were under sixteen.) The members elected a governing committee, which in turn engaged a full-time director. Mill officers were honorary members.

The club's activities were educational as well as recreational, and reflected the interests paternalists thought mill folk needed exposure to. During the first year and a half, the lyceum course included "a class on the mandolin under a professor of music" and a course in mathematics as well. Most lyceum lectures, however, held on Saturday nights, were on "industrial subjects and other topics of special interest to members of the club." During the winter season of 1899, offerings were varied. Bob Burdett appeared in the stage play *Rise and Fall of the Mustache*. "The Sapphos, Columbus' peerless female quartette" gave a concert, as did the Ottumwa

Male Quartette. Serviss gave his "wonderful illustrated lecture on 'Travels,'" and Dinsmore introduced mill folk to "the Wonders of Chemistry." One night in December, 1899, Hart, the strong man, entertained. On another occasion, 250 members and their ladies enjoyed a "splendid" sit-down "supper and soiree" at which "a full string band produced splendid music" and "the evening was given [over] to the dance[,] and cotillion, the lancers, and the merry waltz rapidly succeeded one another." An out-of-town visitor thought the club and its activities "the most perfectly equipped and thoroughly uplifting venture in social ethics and practical humanity" he had ever seen.[22]

One wonders if folk agreed with that assessment—either those who attended the club's activities or those who stayed away. Presumably tastes varied, and presumably some folk found the offerings edifying as well as diverting. Unfortunately, the reporters who wrote so much about the club in its early years never talked to mill folk about it, though one reporter did note that members "who have heretofore inclined to the sociability of saloons have found more congenial amusement at the club house."[23]

The purposes of the club are easier to state than its effects are to estimate. According to Gunby Jordan, who founded and guided the club while he was president of Eagle and Phenix Mills, its purposes were multiple. Overall, Jordan said, the varied activities were intended to "educate each member to broader views of life, higher aspirations in his own vocation, and thus incidentally obtain for the corporation . . . [an employee] sound in mind and body, imbued with that keen emulation to better his condition, and incidentally that of his employer." More specifically, Jordan continued, the club's recreational activities were designed to be "attractive without offering any forms of dissipation." The gymnasium "offer[ed] opportunities for healthful exercise . . . by those who are closely confined during the working hours"; and the bathhouse gave members "an opportunity for approaching Godliness through its nearest of kin, cleanliness." The library "encourage[d] the members not only to read but to direct their reading in such channels as will be of benefit to them and encourage them" in "the business to which they are devoting their lives." The lyceum encouraged "good fellowship" as well as "an interchange of ideas between those who have given more thought and had more experience in textile lines and others who desire to learn."[24]

22. Columbus *Enquirer-Sun*, September 17, November 5, December 17, 1899; Atlanta *Constitution*, December 30, 1900.
23. Atlanta *Constitution*, December 30, 1900.
24. *Manufacturers' Record*, June 23, 1899, pp. 336–37.

"MY IDEA IS TO GET THE PEOPLE READING AND GET THEM INTERESTED IN BOOKS."

An instructive feature of welfare work was the establishment of lending libraries in villages across the New South. Indeed, no welfare program was complete without a library, for the idea that folk could be reformed through schooling and the mysteries of the printed word was one of the founding principles of welfare work. The folk were, of course, largely unschooled and unbookish, and except for the Bible and an almanac never read books. Mill paternalists, however, were imbued with the Progressives' faith in the efficacy of right knowledge, and they were certain that reading "approved" literature would make their villagers better people and better employees. Not only should mill folk read; they should read the right things.

That attitude of course gave rise to censorship, which characterized the practices of public and private librarians and library committees across the New South. This was a censoring age, and mill owners, like other upright people, did not want their employees, or anyone else for that matter, to have access to unacceptable literature, whether the unacceptability was moral, racial, economic, or otherwise. Moreover, most folk approved of censorship, certainly in moral matters and probably in other matters, too. "The [motion] picture was censored before they were shown," Bessie Buchanan recalled approvingly of the practice in her village, "and if it wasn't a clean picture that picture didn't go on the screen."

Yet there was more than censorship involved in the selection of books for village libraries, for mill paternalists genuinely believed that reading good books would uplift mill folk, and their definition of *good* was broader than one might expect. That point is graphically revealed in the remarkable correspondence of the Schencks of Cleveland Cotton Mills.[25] By 1893, the Schencks had built and were subsidizing a church and a school in their village, and at that point decided to start a lending library. They arranged to purchase a small collection of books—less than one hundred volumes initially—and add to it gradually through mill funds and a modest fee for library users. The books, the younger Schenck pointed out to their New York business partner, should be carefully selected, for mill folk would have to be enticed into reading them and otherwise supporting a library program.

25. The following account is based on letters from John F. Schenck to J. E. Reynolds, November 29, 1893, January 2 and 24, and February 2, 1894, an undated book order, probably February, 1894, from John F. Schenck to Montgomery Ward, and an order dated May 20, 1895, from H. F. Schenck to Bloomingdale Bros., in H. F. Schenck Papers, Manuscript Department, Duke University Library, Durham, North Carolina.

"These people, like all country folk in this state," John Schenck wrote, "have very little taste for reading thoughtful and elevating literature, have done very little of it, and they have to be *coaxed* into taking an interest in a library." He proposed to organize a library club and, through the club and a deposit scheme, give villagers a sense of participation in a worthwhile enterprise. Specifically, he proposed that instead of paying regular membership fees each borrower be required to purchase and deposit in the library each year one book costing at least forty cents. The book would remain the property of the donor, who could withdraw it if he left the mill's employment, but while on deposit, it would be treated as part of the regular collection and be available for borrowing by other members.

The Schencks's business partner demurred at the deposit proposal, thinking it gave club members too much control over the collection. The younger Schenck, who was superintendent of the mills, dispelled the New Yorker's misgivings. "Of course the management and sole ownership of these books should not be given to the hands," he wrote. "We will give them merely the *use* of them—and that in a systematic way." Schenck "thought it wise to offer [club members] the *full use of books* under certain regulations and conditions" but was not proposing that they have any control over the library. "We merely require each member shall deposit a book worth at least a certain amount annually, for the purpose of increasing the library," he wrote, "and also as a security against the abuse or loss of books of the library."

If members had to buy books for the library, Schenck pointed out, they might want a voice in its governance. "If we require each member to make an *absolute gift* to the library our library would not be a free one as we wish it to be and we certainly would not get so many members," Schenck explained. "We have all agreed that the control and management of the library should be wholly in me. . . . But it certainly would not be fair for this to be the case if every member of the association had to contribute to the library. . . . We ought not to tax them without giving them representation."

Control was one concern, and it remained firmly in John Schenck's hands. Another was the selection of books, and that too was his prerogative. The books must be "suitable interesting and profitable to our little community," Schenck wrote. "*Most* of our readers will be children *in fact*—and *almost all* children in *Education*," and that circumstance must govern the choice of books. It was necessary, he thought, "to select such as will be interesting [and] instructive, and will cultivate a taste for good literature. What historical works we get . . . should be such as are written for youths, brief and comprehensive, telling a plain simple narrative of historical events, interspersing novel and thrilling incidents here and there. My ideal history for beginners, whether old or young, is one in the style of 'Tales of a Grandfather' [by Walter Scott]. . . . The works of fiction . . . should be those of standard authors, simple in style but somewhat educational. Of course we should have a few solid books for such as may be inclined toward such reading," and "a few books on practical subjects" as well. "My idea," Schenck wrote, "is to get the people to reading and get them interested in books—and then have them assist in adding to the library every year such good literature as it appears the readers will be able to appreciate."

Accompanying these remarks was a list of books Schenck wanted to purchase. It is predictable from the remarks just quoted; but if it is representative of the contents of village libraries generally, it indicates that those libraries were no more agencies of thought control than were libraries in other small towns across the New South. Schenck's list includes a history of the United States by Edward Eggleston, of England by Charles Dickens, and of Scotland by Walter Scott; Jacob Abbott's biographies of George Washington, Benjamin Franklin, Christopher Columbus, David Crockett, Daniel Boone, and John Paul Jones; and Lydia Farmer's books for boys and girls on "famous rulers." In fiction Schenck asked for *Aesop's Fables, Robinson Crusoe, Arabian Nights, Tom Sawyer, Huckleberry Finn, The Scarlet Letter, Uncle Tom's Cabin, Around the World in Eighty Days,* and *Our Country.* He also asked for other popular works by George Eliot, Walter Scott, Edgar Allan Poe, William Makepeace Thackeray, Emily Brontë, James Fenimore Cooper, Charles Dickens, Jules Verne, Charles and Mary Lamb, and Susan Coolidge. Among the "practical" books he listed were such titles as *Mechanic's Complete Library, Complete Practical Machinist, Chambers Cyclopedia, Allen's New American Farm Book,* and a "cheap unabridged Dictionary."

A few months later, Schenck submitted another list that included some of the same titles and a number of new ones as well. Among the latter were *The Wandering Jew, Black Beauty, The Last Days of Pompeii, Child's History of Rome,* George Bancroft's *Life of Washington, Ben Hur, Grimm's Household Stories, Smith Family Robinson, Jane Eyre,* and Bryce's *American Commonwealth.* More interesting than Schenck's lists, however, were the titles ordered by library users in payment of their membership fees. Among these were *The Count of Monte Cristo, Dr. Jekyll and Mr. Hyde, The Vicar of Wakefield, Roland Oliver, King Solomon's Mines,* Thomas Carlyle's *French Revolution,* the histories of Josephus, Shakespeare's works, Rollin's *Ancient History,* Ralph Waldo Emerson's *Essays,* Cooper's Leather Stocking tales, and more of Walter Scott's novels.

Perhaps this list justifies Schenck's boast in January, 1894, that his library was "exceedingly" popular. Certainly if folk in any numbers and with any regularity in this small, rather isolated village read or listened to readings from the books on these lists, their literacy and cultural levels were higher than mill folk have been given credit for. And certainly, too, the village libraries were active instruments of acculturation.

"THE SOUTHERN COTTON MILL VILLAGE HAS PROVED TO BE A CIVILIZING AND ELEVATING FORCE."

Another way of seeing the nature and purpose of welfare work is to look at the attitudes of village social workers. These workers had only a limited impact before 1915, for they were employed in only a few of the larger villages at that time. But those villages were pacesetters, and professional social workers articulated the purposes of the welfare movement better than the volunteers (often mill officers' wives and schoolteachers) who staffed most of the programs. Like mill paternalists, professional social workers shared the missionary's desire to make other people over; and they, too, wanted to help mill folk achieve what they (the social workers) considered a better life. But also like paternalists, they knew mill folk, lived and worked among them, and understood the limitations of their own ability to move them. The social workers therefore had little of the arrogance or fondness for coercion that characterized more distant reformers. If some of them succumbed to cultural and social condescension, the best developed insight into the ways and minds of villagers. One who did so was Marjorie A. Potwin, a New Englander with a doctorate in social work who became community director at Saxon and Chesnee mill villages at Spartanburg, South Carolina, in 1916. "The mill people have their own idea of what constitutes the good life," Potwin wrote in 1927. She observed that they could not be forced to do things against their will: "They simply do this or that very largely because it is their natural expression of an inherent spiritual or social or occupational tradition." They accepted or rejected things "according to ingrained principles," not as a result of the social worker's prodding. It was not that they were contentious or perverse, Potwin concluded; rather, "as they see it, right is right and wrong is wrong."[26]

Realizing that characteristic of folk was the beginning of wisdom for social workers. It signaled an awareness that folk were unimpressed with

26. Potwin, *Cotton Mill People*, 17, 15.

much of what social workers offered them; and that awareness in turn encouraged a wholesome humility or at least lowered expectations. "In a great many mill communities the operatives do not appreciate the efforts of the officials who are constantly trying to better living conditions," one advocate of welfare work wrote in 1915, and it would take "years," he thought, "to bring about the desired results." This writer suggested, "The great mass of the operatives will have to be taught to appreciate the efforts of the mill owners," and to accomplish that "there must be a spirit of thorough cooperation."[27]

That spirit had to come largely from social workers, and to achieve it they had to know mill folk and understand their ways. To be effective, one of them wrote after several years of village experience, the social worker "need not of necessity be highly trained." He might better be "a man from the local village with whom the people are acquainted and with good common sense," and "he must be able to avoid antagonizing the people."[28]

Welfare workers were mirror images of the paternalists who employed them. James L. Carbery, who began working for Thomas F. Parker at Monaghan Mills in 1910, described his goals in language almost identical to that Parker used in stating his own purposes. His work, Carbery wrote in 1915, "has as its object the mental and physical improvement and moral uplift of humanity; the development of strong character and individuality, which must of necessity lead to greater efficiency and better citizenship." Its success, he said, "will also doubtless affect favorably and lessen the restless desire of the average operative to move from place to place, and in time transform him and his family into more efficient help and better citizens."[29]

Others expanded on these goals. According to M. W. Heiss, who was president of the Southern Textile Social Service Association, the purpose of village social work was to improve the quality of home life as well as the efficiency of workers. This was to be done by teaching household skills to homemakers and imbuing their daughters with "dignity and refinement," as well as a sense of "the seriousness of married life, and the sacredness of the home." Boys and men must learn "to be self-reliant, honest and trustworthy," and all workers must come to know the value of "wholesome recreation and diversion." The success of these efforts, or so Heiss believed, could be impressive indeed. "The southern cotton mill village has proved to

27. *Manufacturers' Record*, February 4, 1915, p. 49.
28. *Ibid.*
29. *Ibid.*

be a civilizing and elevating force," he wrote in 1924. "It has within the scope of a very short time elevated an entire people."[30]

Such optimistic assessments were a staple of social work literature. "Several years ago the Arcade Mill village had a 'bad name,' " read one report of what happened at a mill in Rock Hill, South Carolina. "The operatives were restless and shiftless; they were constantly moving; often on Monday morning there was not sufficient help to start the mill; in many instances the officers were forced to bail them out of the city police station." Fortunately, President Alexander Long, who suffered the consequences of this situation, "believe[d] in investing money in character." He began a program of welfare work, and his village was transformed. "The citizenship gradually improved," and soon "good help was plentiful in the mill."[31]

Such results were singular if not unique. Jennings J. Rhyne, who studied five hundred mill families in his native Gaston County, North Carolina, in the 1920s, found that most folk in those families did not "respond with any feeling of gratitude" for the welfare and social programs "because they argue that all the money being spent on them is due them anyway as wages and some of them would rather have it in the [pay] envelopes. Most of them feel that they earn it as truly as their cash wages." Also, Rhyne found, "workers seem to move to a mill village lacking welfare work with the same readiness as to a mill that has its community houses, social workers, health supervisors, and other welfare activities."[32]

"CAUSING THEM TO BECOME BETTER OPERATIVES AND CITIZENS"

The truth about mill folk and their response to the welfare programs was more prosaic than critics or enthusiasts suggested. Welfare programs differed from one another, as did the men advocating them. These differences affected responses to welfare endeavor. Entertainment and recreation programs, for example, probably had built-in advantages over lyceum lectures and night-school classes. And individuals who responded enthusiastically to one program might be indifferent or even opposed to others. A housewife who saw no need for sewing classes might find a "tomato club" interesting and the idea of going to a dance or moving picture morally objectionable.

30. M. W. Heiss, "The Southern Cotton Mill Village: A Viewpoint," *Social Forces*, II (1924), 345–50.

31. *Manufacturers' Record*, February 4, 1915, p. 49.

32. R. W. Edmonds, *Cotton Mill Labor Conditions in the South and New England* (Baltimore, 1925), 17; Jennings J. Rhyne, *Some Southern Cotton Mill Workers and Their Villages* (Chapel Hill, 1930), 34–35.

Even where programs had meaningful effect, it might not have been the effect mill owners intended, for folk had great capacity to assimilate change to their own purpose. Levels of schooling and school attendance grew notably during the New South era, and mill folk came to read more and more; but social workers often complained that they read pulp romances and other "trash." Church participation might have grown, too, after the holiness and charismatic denominations appeared in the villages, but they hardly represented the kind of religion mill officials wanted to encourage. Probably health improved as well, in areas outside the respiratory diseases, but social workers still complained of adherence to folk remedies and patent medicines laced with alcohol. Housewives learned more of the practices social workers wanted them to learn, but they still served traditional foods prepared in traditional ways, clung to old practices of child rearing, and took too much snuff and advice from "granny women."

Part of the success in preserving folkways stemmed from the overriding demands of life and work. After ten or twelve hours in the mill, workers might understandably wish to forgo a visit to the village library or lyceum lecture; and after a week of sixty or sixty-five hours, they might easily resist Saturday afternoon sewing class or baseball practice. Just as understandably, housewives might spend their leisure time "just sitting" and resting or visiting with neighbors or relatives.

For many reasons, then, welfare programs had limited effect, which neutralizes their significance as instruments of social control. Where they succeeded, they encouraged "modern" values (education and the values of the work ethic, for example), or alternatively, they increased dependence on the paternalists. In which of these ways one reads the successes depends in part on one's own perspective.

In the papers of the Graniteville Manufacturing Company at the Aiken campus of the University of South Carolina, for example, there is an undated petition signed by 500 villagers urging the company to construct a new building to house the village library on one floor and an athletic hall on the other. The library, grown to 2,000 volumes, was overflowing its old quarters; and the village apparently had no athletic training facilities. In urging the company to act, the petitioners offered justification that the most ardent paternalist would have endorsed, and they did so in language the most committed devotee of the work ethic and self-improvement would have praised. "A building which could be properly equipped for a library, reading rooms, etc, where the daily and weekly papers and magazines could be kept on file would have a marked tendency toward uplifting the people," the petitioners said. "It would be educational in its nature, thus causing them to become better operatives and citizens, enabling them to do better and more intelligent work, thus redounding in a great measure to the benefit of your company." An athletic hall would benefit company employees by "promoting the health of their physical bodies, thereby having a tendency toward making them more regular in their labor, and better able to bear their sometimes onerous duties." It would also provide a place for "young men and boys" to gather, thus "tend[ing] in a great measure toward keeping them out of probable mischief, and off of the streets where many of them may now be found."[33]

Was this the language of folk who had absorbed the message and dependencies of paternalism? Was it the words of those who had internalized the values of self-improvement and the work ethic? Or was the petition merely a designing ploy of folk who wanted a library or a gymnasium and thought the best way to get what they wanted was to link it with the other enterprise and plead for both in the language they thought company officials would find convincing? If it was such a ploy, the petition might be likened to some of the things the slaves once did in "puttin' ol' massa on"—telling "the man" what he wanted to hear in order to get him to do what they wanted done. Certainly the petition validated the view mill officials had of themselves as disinterested paternalists, and it was no doubt more effective for that reason. Still, the meaning of the petition is ambiguous, and as such the paper is a proper monument to the uncertain legacies of mill paternalism and welfare work.

33. File 143, Graniteville Manufacturing Company Papers, University of South Carolina at Aiken Library.

10

SOCIAL LIFE

Despite the effort to bring mill folk into a larger social orbit, the family or household remained the focus of their lives. The best way to understand their social life is therefore to approach it through the rhythms of family living.

Families began with marriage, which was itself the culmination of courtship. Courting and romantic love, basic aspects of folk life, are especially difficult to study. Plain folk seldom talked of personal emotions, especially those relating to love, romance, and sexuality. They were embarrassed, even shamed, at the prospect of discussing anything relating to sexual intimacy in their lives. Apparently they were close-mouthed not only in interviews with strangers but among themselves too, at least in respectable company, and perhaps even with their mates. And they did not like to display sexual affection in public, even after marriage. Men thought that behavior was unmanly, and women considered it unladylike if not morally compromising.

This attitude suggests that folk had difficulty handling personal emotions, perhaps because of larger insecurities. Perhaps they were so conditioned to limited expectations that they could not trust or examine straightforwardly the ecstasies they experienced in falling and being in love. One defense against acts and feelings that might end in disappointment was the public reserve that manifested itself as nonchalance or joking indifference about love. Perhaps, too, plain folk had difficulty relating intimately to each other; certainly many of them suffered hurt or disappointment in love. It seems likely that few of them expected bliss in marriage, in keeping with their low expectations in other areas of life. "I'll have to say it for Eugene Lester," Rachel Lester, a North Carolina mill worker, said of her husband of many years. "He provided for me as well as he knowed how and never beat me as long as he lived. Plenty men do beat their women you know."

Were these the standards that made married life tolerable? Probably not, for Mrs. Lester's was admittedly a loveless marriage. Clara Layton, another North Carolina mill worker, looked back over her marriage somewhat differently. "I don't know as it was too young," she said, answering an inquiry about getting married at seventeen in 1911. "I could've waited a year or two and done a sight worse. Been married twenty-eight years and me and my man still get along." Was that a matter-of-fact evaluation or a way of understating a love deeply felt?

Such ambiguity is characteristic of the way most folk discussed their courtship and marriage. Their discussions were summary to a degree that suggests indifference to the events themselves; and folk rarely mentioned the emotions those events involved. Many, perhaps most, young couples "slipped off" and were married without the knowledge of their parents, because they knew or suspected the bride's parents would object. Grooms rarely had this problem, which suggests that parents thought it a son's prerogative to marry when and whom he pleased, but not a daughter's, especially if she was a young daughter still living at home. Such "girls," their parents believed, were too emotional, too susceptible to a man's persuasion, to know their interests or make wise choices in affairs of the heart. Thus the courting of daughters, but not of sons, was supervised carefully and often prohibited altogether. Most courting, like most marriages, thus involved a degree of furtiveness, which probably reinforced the tendency to associate sex and sexual feelings with sin and shame. When Ethel M. Faucette decided to be married at nineteen about 1916, she told no one in her family. "Because my people were against it—they didn't want me to marry," she explained. "And I slipped off and married him—I was old enough, they couldn't help it." When she returned and told her parents, however, they accepted her action. "They didn't do nothing," Mrs. Faucette recalled. "They said we was married and that's all there was to it."

The rituals and routines of courtship and marriage are difficult to pinpoint. Flossie Moore Durham was married in 1901 at home with family and friends attending. After the ceremony, she and her husband rented a horse and buggy and "just went out to ride, that's all. . . . Come back then and et down at his aunt's."

Addie Gaines met her future husband "at a big camp meetin' over at the church." When "the meetin' was over we got acquainted," she recalled. "I didn't think I was goin' to like him much, he was so tall and ganglin'. He shore wasn't much to look at but he kept on comin' to see me and I finally give in and married him." Ruth Jordan Williamson, whose father was a small farmer in North Carolina, was equally unrevealing in describing her marriage, which occurred in 1905. "When I was about twenty years of age, I met Ell Russell Williamson, a young farmer, and it was a case of love at first sight," she said. "We saw each other nearly every day and night for three years, or until we were married."

What they did when together Mrs. Williamson did not say. Nor did Clara Layton, who met her future husband at a Methodist singing school. "I went with him six months before my folks ever allowed him to come to the house," Mrs. Layton remembered. "When they seen they couldn't do nothing about it they quit objectin'." Paul Parks, the son of a North Carolina tenant farmer, was equally laconic about the courtship that preceded his marriage about 1898, when he was twenty-three. "I met a girl I wanted," he said. "I concluded I just well get married. After a couple of months, I broached it to her. She told me I'd have to wait three years. But I didn't. She had me the next year."

Compared to Park, Lillian Holbrook was positively loquacious in describing her courtship. The daughter of a North Carolina tenant farmer, Mrs. Holbrook ran away from home just after World War I to keep from having to marry an older man at her father's insistence. At a cotton factory in Winston, she lived in a boardinghouse with other mill workers, one of whom she presently married. "We got to talkin' to each other after meals and sometimes we'd go for a walk after workin' hours," she recalled of their courting. "I reckon we done like most anybody else'd done. We got married a month later and he moved in with me. I don't recollect when I was ever so happy. It seemed like somethin' in a dream . . . like most times never come true. It was so nice, coming home from the mill together, eating together, going to the show."

Nora I. Oates, who was born into a North Carolina mill family before the turn of the century, remembered the custom among teenagers of her day. On paydays the boys would buy chewing gum "and go see their best girl friends," Mrs. Oates recalled. "They would chew their gum and rattle the change in their pants pockets. You know there were no picture shows to go to then so we would go to a box party or in the summertime we would go to a lawn party." The boys apparently had difficulty making their feelings known to girls. "The young men would write the girls a letter and ask if they could call on them on Wednesday night," Mrs. Oates continued. They would send the letter by a small boy who waited for a response. Mrs. Oates received her first note when she was fifteen. "There was a young man working in the mill," she remembered. "All the girls were trying to catch him. I was young and at that time I was pretty, so he sent me a note one Sunday evening asking me if he could take me to church that night. . . . I wanted to go but I was ashamed to let my folks know that I even thought of a man. I asked my father if it would be all right and he said yes so we went to church." Three months later, she and the young man married.

James W. Pharis remembered the routine of courting at the mill village in Virginia where he married in 1911. "The way they dated back in them days—and everybody done practically the same thing because it was a habit with all of them," he recalled, "they'd date Wednesday night, Saturday night, and Sunday evening. Sometimes they'd stay until nine-thirty on Saturday night, being the end of the week. You seen a boy visit a girl on Wednesday night. And they stayed at home, too [that is, the girl was not allowed to go out]. Nine o'clock, nine thirty was late bedtime. I've heard remarks made of neighbors, 'You know that boy stayed up there last night to see that girl until nearly ten o'clock.' "

These examples suggest that courtship was brief and circumspect. Under prying eyes, courting couples were the talk of the village. Many youths no doubt found this embarrassing, for they had difficulty articulating and displaying personal emotions. In addition, there was little social activity in the villages; so courting consisted chiefly of meetings at church, the girl's home, or the homes of friends if the girl's parents objected to her dating. Courting, then, was not easy in the villages, which encouraged early marriage. Moreover, youths of both sexes had reasons of their own for wanting to leave their parents' home, and the availability of mill housing and employment removed what might otherwise have been practical obstacles to doing so. Finally, there were no other satisfactory outlets for sexuality, at least for respectable women.

The most important aspect of courtship seems to be its briefness. Most young men and women apparently were married not long after they acknowledged their attraction for each other. This suggests that parental interference had little effect and that mill youths often married because of adolescent infatuation rather than mature love. If so, that motivation is further evidence of their difficulty in coping with emotion and was no doubt one reason so many of their marriages ended in disappointment.

"COURSE HE'S GOT SENSE ENOUGH TO STAY OUT TILL YOU'VE GOT IN BED."

Marriage was a major transition in life, perhaps the most important transition of all for women, yet it was marked by little ceremony or evident sense of significance. Marriage, like courtship, involved a display of emotions that made folk uncomfortable; moreover, most folk disliked being the center of attention. They therefore wanted to downplay the ceremony. In addition, marriage was expected, almost inevitable, and practically necessary in the lives of plain folk, and not something to make a fuss over. It was difficult to live singly; and to most folk, "old maids" were pitiable and unfulfilled, and bachelors eccentric at best. Life itself revolved around family affairs. So plain folk married as soon as they wanted to, and a large minority of them married more than once.

Almeda Brady, the daughter of a North Carolina tenant farmer, married in the 1890s. Before doing so, she worked in a cotton mill to earn money to set up housekeeping. After eight months, when she had enough money, she quit the mill one Friday and married on Sunday morning. "We come on back home that day for dinner and spent the night there," she said of her wedding day. "The next day we went to his folks. Me and my man never knowed there was such a word as honeymoon, and after we'd spent a night with both families we went to the house on Mr. Caviniss' place where we was goin' to [sharecrop]." Fred Alexander made even less of his wedding day, which was a Saturday. "We went on off after supper [which they had with his new in-laws], but I was back at work Monday mornin'," he recalled. "That [Monday] night when I went up to Mr. Whitlock's I got Mattie and took her to a house I had done rented."

John W. Prosser and his wife recalled their wedding, which occurred in 1914, with more than the usual detail. Son of a South Carolina blacksmith and a mill worker for a while, Prosser had been twenty-one and his bride fifteen. "I got 'er young so I could raise 'er to my notion," he said of his bride's age. "And it wasn't so very hard to get 'er, neither. I just told 'er, 'I got a mule and a buggy, and I got a good place to carry you to. Won't be so much work for you to do neither.'" Recalling her response to his proposal, Mrs. Prosser said: "I told him I'd try it for a while. Me and 'im got married

292 PLAIN FOLK IN THE NEW SOUTH

at my house. Had a big supper, too. Wasn't nobody hardly invited, but the house was full, and the yard was full. Yes ma'am, all stayed for supper, and all the men got drunk." Prosser confirmed: "And I got drunk too. Her brother give me the whiskey." On the couple's wedding night, two of Mrs. Prosser's friends "fixed up a room all nice for us." They also told her, "Course he's got sense enough to stay out till you've got in bed." Prosser remembered: "And I stayed out, too. Next mornin' we stayed in bed till the sun was way up and comin' in at the window. [My wife] wasn't used to cookin' breakfast 'cept by lamplight, and she said it seemed so strange to her to be a-cookin' breakfast and the sun a-shinin' in at the window." Such was the way plain folk recalled their wedding night.

They married young. Information in the population census of 1900 indicates that the vast majority of married male mill workers in Aiken, Alamance, and Spartanburg counties had married between the ages of eighteen and twenty-five, with the highest frequencies at twenty, twenty-one, and twenty-two. Females married younger, a large majority between sixteen and twenty-two, with the greatest frequencies in the late teens. There were of course numerous exceptions, but they clustered just outside these ranges. About one in nine of the women married at fifteen or younger, and one in thirty of the men at sixteen or younger.[1]

Newly wed mill folk generally moved into a house or apartment of their own, though many lived with relatives for a short while and a few for a much longer time. Within about a year, their children began arriving, and most mill folk eventually had large families. In Spartanburg and Aiken counties in 1900, 436 women over forty-five who were heads or wives of heads of mill households had given birth to a total of 3,030 children, an average of just under 7 each. Of those children, however, 810 (26.7 percent) were dead. Only 44 of the women (10 percent) had 2 or fewer children, and only 12 were childless, while 56 (12.8 percent) had more than 10 children and 3 had 15.[2]

Information on how these children were spaced is imprecise. Two to three years between births was probably average, though births were sometimes much closer in time. At Langley in 1880, for example, the wagoner W. B. Conger, forty-three, and his wife, thirty-seven, had ten children, one of

1. Of 1,431 male workers who married at thirty or younger in the three counties, 1,117 (78 percent) married between eighteen and twenty-five. Of 1,491 female workers who married at thirty or younger, 1,046 (70 percent) married between sixteen and twenty-two. Of the females, 165 (11 percent) married at fifteen or younger—the youngest, according to census takers, at nine. Of the males, 49 (3.4) percent) married at sixteen or younger, the youngest at fourteen (Manuscript Census, 1900, Schedule 1, Aiken and Spartanburg counties, S.C., and Alamance County, N.C.).

2. Manuscript Census, 1900, Schedule 1, Aiken and Spartanburg counties, S.C.

them a three-month-old infant. Ages of the other children were fourteen, thirteen, twelve, eleven, eight, seven, six, five, and four—the nine of them born in about ten years. The oldest four of these children worked in the mill, and one can imagine that their income was needed. Similarly, James Baggett, thirty, and his wife Sarah, thirty-five, both of whom worked in a Columbus mill, had closely spaced children, aged seven, six, four, three, and one. One can imagine, too, that Mrs. Baggett worked because of economic necessity.[3]

Such spacing was exceptional. More typical was the family of carpenter John E. Griggs, fifty-three, like Baggett of Russell County, Alabama, and his forty-seven-year-old wife. Their ten children were twenty-two, twenty, nineteen, sixteen, thirteen, eleven, nine, seven, four, and two years of age. The twenty-two-year-old son and the sixteen- and thirteen-year-old daughters worked in a cotton mill in Columbus; the twenty-year-old daughter was "at home," no doubt helping her mother with housework; the nineteen-year-old son was a farm hand (perhaps he preferred farming to mill work, or perhaps he farmed a few acres to help feed the family); and the eleven-year-old son went to school.[4]

As the example of Mrs. Griggs suggests, bearing and raising children were the principal concerns of most mill women from the time of marriage until old age approached. Mrs. Griggs was somewhat unusual in that her first child was born when she was about twenty-five (though it is possible she had one or more older children no longer at home when her family was listed in the 1880 census). The twenty-year span between the birth of her first and last child was not unique, however. If her youngest child married and left home at twenty, Mrs. Griggs would have been sixty-five when all her children were gone. Long before that, however, if her family was typical, she would have had grandchildren in the neighborhood, and they would have been an intimate part of her daily life. One can easily believe, if Mrs. Griggs were a conscientious wife and mother, that her children, family, and household consumed all of her life after marriage.

"THE MORNING OF THE DAY [HER] BABY WAS BORN [SHE] PICKED 45 POUNDS OF COTTON."

Family expansion began with pregnancy, which in the New South era was far more dangerous and subject to complications than it is today. The first

---

3. Manuscript Census, 1880, Schedule 1, Aiken County, S.C., and Russell County, Ala.
4. Manuscript Census, 1880, Schedule 1, Russell County, Ala.

pregnancy was probably welcome. Women folk grew up expecting to marry and become mothers, and to whatever degree they looked forward to motherhood, pregnancy represented fulfillment.[5] Certainly reactions to first pregnancies were not complicated, as they might be to subsequent ones, by concern over "another mouth to feed" or previous difficulties with childbearing.

Women folk had to work, at home if not in the fields or the mills, and generally continued to do so during pregnancy. "One mother prepared the family meals, did a big washing, and churned on the day her baby was born," investigators for the Children's Bureau of the Department of Labor found in a study of white farm women in an unnamed north Georgia county in 1918. "Another carried 2 gallons of water 100 yards uphill an hour before labor began. A third washed and scrubbed on the day of her confinement." In a county in the North Carolina low country, investigators from this agency found the same pattern in 1916. "A mother of five children," they wrote, giving what was apparently an unusual example, "continued her housework, field work, and chores up to the date of confinement, and the morning of the day the baby was born picked 45 pounds of cotton and cooked a big dinner for her family of seven."[6]

Such experiences must have taken a psychological as well as a physical toll. "Receptive-dependent needs" are aroused by pregnancy, Therese Benedek has written, and as a result, "pregnant women thrive on the solicitude of their environment and suffer, sometimes unduly if such needs are frustrated."[7] Certainly women folk did not always experience such solicitude during pregnancy, which might have contributed to the burdens they bore.

Nor did the women receive prenatal medical care unless they became ill or experienced complications. They did, however, by the end of the New South era, generally have a doctor present at childbirth. Of 509 white women who gave birth in the north Georgia county just mentioned between 1916 and 1918, only one delivered her child in a hospital. Two-thirds, however, had a physician in attendance, though in 41 instances, the physician arrived after the baby was born. One of the women gave birth with no one else present.[8]

5. On the psychology of pregnancy, see Therese Benedek, "The Psychobiology of Pregnancy," in E. James Anthony and Therese Benedek (eds.), *Parenthood: Its Psychology and Psychopathology* (Boston, 1970), 137–51.

6. U.S. Department of Labor, Children's Bureau, *Publication No. 120: Maternity and Infant Care in a Mountain County in Georgia* (1923), 21; U.S. Department of Labor, Children's Bureau, *Publication No. 33: Rural Children in Selected Counties of North Carolina* (1918), 34.

7. Benedek, "The Psychobiology of Pregnancy," 142.

8. Department of Labor, *Maternity and Infant Care in a Mountain County in Georgia*, 9–10, 14.

More than a quarter of the women in this sample were attended by midwives, a practice that remained widespread among rural folk after it largely disappeared from mill villages. "Certain mothers expressed a preference for midwives rather than doctors," the Children's Bureau investigators reported of rural white women in the Georgia county, "giving as reasons the smaller charge for services, the longer stay (the midwife often gave nursing care and helped with housework), and a prejudice against having a man attend them in confinement."[9]

The complications attendant upon pregnancy and childbirth were numerous. In 1918, many mothers told the Children's Bureau investigators of illnesses incident to childbirth ranging from "childbed fever" and "milk leg" to "gathered breasts," hemorrhaging, and even, in three cases, difficulties "due to retention of parts of the placenta" after delivery. Many other women simply said they had had "a hard time" during confinement or "had not been well since"; and investigators concluded from the way women reacted to their experience that the average woman's "tendency is rather to accept as unavoidable many of the complications of childbirth." They reported similar conditions in a county in the North Carolina low country in 1916: "Many women endure a lifetime of ill health which they date from a particular confinement."[10]

A frequent complication was miscarriage or stillbirth. About half the 509 women studied in the Georgia county in 1918 had at some time experienced miscarriage, stillbirth, or death of an infant. No less than 6.3 percent of the pregnancies of these women had terminated in miscarriages, and 3.1 percent in stillbirths. And of the 1,774 babies born alive to these women more than a year before the date of the study, 135 (7.6 percent) had died during their first year.[11] Those figures represent 17 percent of all pregnancies.

"THE YOUNGUNS STARTED COMING AND IN NO TIME WE HAD FIVE OF THEM."

How did mill women react to the social role their maternal position dictated? What did they think of pregnancy, childbearing, and children, and of having their lives consumed in the duties of wife, mother, and housekeeper? Most mill women were ultimately ambivalent about their lives. They loved children, their own and other folks', too, and wanted desperately to be good mothers. But they disliked repeated pregnancies, feared childbirth, and

9. *Ibid.*, 17.
10. *Ibid.*, 18–19; Department of Labor, *Children in Selected Counties of North Carolina*, 27.
11. Department of Labor, *Maternity and Infant Care in a Mountain County in Georgia*, 31.

wearied of the ceaselessness of housework. Many had abusive or irresponsible husbands, loveless marriages, and uncaring or disappointing children. They were thus constantly reminded that the burdens of marriage and home life were unequally distributed. Yet as wives and mothers, mill women enjoyed a certain respect and sense of security, and they had generally internalized the values that rationalized and exalted those roles for women. Besides, the alternatives available to them were generally unattractive.

Many women found genuine happiness in marriage and motherhood. Lucy Pace, the daughter of a North Carolina tenant farmer, went to work in a Durham cotton mill while she was a child and was still there when she married another mill worker about 1915. For a while she and her husband lived with his stepfather; they provided him meals, and he paid the rent. She continued to work intermittently. "When we needed a little more money, I'd go to work in the mill," she remembered. "My first child, Dorothy, was born in 1917, and of course I had to quit work and take care of her. . . . The younguns started coming and in no time we had five of them. . . . We loved children and we wish we could afford to have more. No Sir; I don't believe in stopping them. That's the Lord's business."

Mrs. Warren Edwards, whose husband was a carpenter at a mill in Wilmington in the years before World War I, was even more enthusiastic. "My old man and me had a grand life together," she said, looking back over their marriage. "I loved my home and was wild over my [five] babies. I was so crazy 'bout 'em that I could hardly wait fer 'em to be born. . . . It won't no trouble to care for 'em. No sir, mothers in them days didn't go galavanting off to the movies all the time, and here, there, and everywhere, twisting theirselves in crowds in the dime stores, brushing up against people, 'specially the men, and then go home tired and cross with everything to come their way, 'specially the poor little babies. That's why the world's so wicked this day and time, mothers won't stay home."

The validation such women derived from motherhood is evident.[12] "I think everybody in those days really thought that was the proper thing to do, is to raise a big family," Bessie Buchanan said. "You never heard tell of anybody ever taking anything to keep from getting pregnant." Mrs. M. A. Matheson, who was born in 1873 into a western North Carolina farm family, expressed similar views. "Birth control as they call it now, didn't bother people where we lived," said Mrs. Matheson, who was herself one of twelve

12. On the psychology of motherhood, see Shirley Ardener (ed.), *Perceiving Women* (London, 1975).

children. "Everybody had a big family. A baby was a blessing; the more babies there was, the more blessings there was." Harriet Echols, who was also born in western North Carolina, a generation after Mrs. Matheson, affirmed this sentiment. "A man's pride was in his family," she recalled. "He didn't think about what it was gonna cost to feed 'em, to clothe 'em, and give them a chance to go on their own in the world." It is interesting and perhaps significant that Mrs. Echols put the matter in man's rather than woman's perspective.[13]

Other women found childbirth unendurable and motherhood a burden. "Mother thought childbirth was about the worst thing a woman could go through," recalled Maxie Oakley, who moved with her family from a Virginia farm to a North Carolina hosiery mill in the early 1920s. Her mother's belief was no doubt one reason Mrs. Oakley herself never had any children. Mrs. J. C. Lawrence, whose father was a North Carolina tenant farmer, voiced economic concerns that many folk must have shared. "My parents were very poor," she said. "They had twelve children, ten of whom lived to be grown." Combining those circumstances, Mrs. Lawrence concluded that "large families are wicked. People oughtn't to have more children than they can educate and provide for."

That sentiment appeared only occasionally in the interviews. Some time after Nancy and William J. Owens, both children of North Carolina tenant farmers, married in 1907, William came to the conclusion, in his wife's words, that "the younguns was coming too fast and what with more mouths to feed and me not able to work half the time [because of pregnancies, childbirths, and child rearing] we'd soon find ourselves starving to death." Mrs. Owens believed this was why her husband began to drink heavily and talk of leaving her and his growing family; and she was understandably concerned when she "got big again." She recalled: "I would rather of done near 'bout anything than to had to tell him about it. . . . There was a old granny woman in our neighborhood—she's dead now—and she told me to drink cotton root tea. She swore that that would knock it up, and it did but I like to of died. William finally made me tell the truth and he cried and said that it was his sin instead of mine. William is funny like that. He didn't think it was wrong to cuss, drink, and work me to death, but he thought it was awful to git rid of a baby or to impose on a dumb animal."

Systematic studies of mill folk made subsequent to the New South era indicate that concern over an unwanted pregnancy was more widespread

13. "Harriet Echols," *Foxfire*, X (1976), 239.

than most of those interviewed suggested. In the 1940s, during her study of "Weaverton," one of the villages in York, South Carolina, Barbara Chartier learned that "women who find that they are pregnant often blame their husbands and openly express their dissatisfaction to other women at the mill." Chartier knew of at least one instance of abortion in the village and was convinced "that a large number of unwanted children" were born there.[14]

"WE HONORED OUR FATHERS AND MOTHERS."

Almost all mill folk welcomed babies. Whatever the problem presented by "another mouth to feed," they refused to take their worries out on the babies themselves. In the villages at York in the 1940s, John K. Morland found babies "accepted and loved with great affection, especially during infancy and early childhood," and his findings seem generally applicable to New South villages. At York, infants were constantly handled, caressed, and made the center of attention, and love for them was evident. One sign of the indulgence this affection produced was late weaning; a mother weaned her child nearer the age of two than one unless she became pregnant while nursing. In their study of 509 white infants born in a north Georgia county between March 1, 1916, and March 1, 1918, investigators for the Children's Bureau found that only 10 percent had been weaned by their first birthday and that more than half were still being breast-fed at eighteen months of age. In a low-country county in North Carolina, investigators from the same agency found that only 3 of 35 babies of white farm women were weaned before the age of twelve months, while 16 others were weaned between twelve and eighteen months, and the other 16 continued to be nursed after eighteen months. Of the pattern in a mountain county in North Carolina, the investigators said simply, "Weaning is commonly left to the inclination of the baby itself." Extended periods of breast-feeding impeded conception and thus functioned to space the children farther apart than would otherwise have been the case.[15]

14. Barbara Chartier, "Weaverton: A Study of Culture and Personality in a Southern Mill Town" (M.A. thesis, University of North Carolina, 1949), 69–70.

15. John K. Morland, *Millways of Kent* (Chapel Hill, 1958), 83–87; Department of Labor, *Maternity and Infant Care in a Mountain County in Georgia*, 28, and *Children in Selected Counties of North Carolina*, 38, 75. On the delay in conception caused by lactation, see Jeroen K. Van Ginneken, "Prolonged Breastfeeding as a Birth Spacing Method," *Studies in Family Planning*, V (1974), 201–206; and Alfredo Perez *et al.*, "First Ovulation After Childbirth: The Effect of Breast Feeding," *American Journal of Obstetrics and Gynecology*, CXIV (1972), 1041–47.

Before and after weaning, babies were indulged in what and when they ate. In two North Carolina counties in 1916, Children's Bureau investigators found commonplace "the custom of indulging children in the most undesirable habits of eating whenever and whatever they please." They wrote, "In many homes, the child is allowed to go to the 'safe' for leftovers whenever he can think of nothing else to do."[16]

There were still other customs in child rearing that caused investigators to cringe. In the north Georgia county just mentioned, they found many mothers giving their infants solid food at astonishingly early ages. "It would cry and I thought it was starved," said one mother "whose baby was fed pickled beans, eggs, meat, and other food from the table when he was 3 months of age." Another mother began giving her infant solid food at the same age because, she said, "it would watch me eat and it seemed like it wanted something, too." Investigators reported, "As early as the fifth month, there were more babies receiving mixed diet than receiving mother's milk exclusively." In the two North Carolina counties, the same pattern prevailed. "The average baby is given from an early age a taste of everything the mother eats," investigators wrote. "The mother's indulgence knows no bounds when it comes to feeding her baby."[17]

Even after weaning, this pattern of indulgence continued. John Morland observed children of three, four, and even five years of age using nursing bottles at York in the 1940s. "Apparently weaning is not a traumatic experience since it occurs when eating habits are well established," he concluded. This indulgent attitude applied as well to other areas of life. Toilet training was relaxed and unscheduled, and toddling children were given as much freedom as possible. Mill parents were too busy to worry over such things as dirtiness, and small children got along with a minimum of supervision. Discipline at this age was largely a matter of teasing and frightening with scare stories.[18]

Young children suffered more from neglect than from abuse. Their mothers sometimes returned to work within months, occasionally even weeks, of their children's birth, and infants and toddlers were not always properly attended. Babies were sometimes left in the custody of siblings who were too young to care for them, and adult babysitters sometimes committed gross neglect. Harry Hughey, for example, was an able-bodied but unem-

16. Department of Labor, *Children in Selected Counties of North Carolina*, 42.
17. Department of Labor, *Maternity and Infant Care in a Mountain County in Georgia*, 25, 30, and *Children in Selected Counties of North Carolina*, 75.
18. See Morland, *Millways of Kent*, 83–87; and Chartier, "Weaverton," 81–90.

ployed man whose wife left their two-year-old child in his custody while she worked in an Atlanta shirt factory. Hughey "went off and left the child alone and locked up in a room where it often spent the time in crying." His neighbors complained, and one day in 1905 police arrested him. Mrs. Joseph Carter's four children, all under six years of age, suffered a different kind of neglect when she became ill in the summer of 1903 and was unable to provide for them. Mrs. Carter worked in an Atlanta cotton mill, and her elderly, partially disabled, and apparently ne'er-do-well husband contributed almost nothing to the family's income. She made $3.50 a week when she worked, $1.20 of which was paid to the factory nursery to keep the children (5 cents a day per child). Not long after Mrs. Carter became ill, police were summoned to her home and found her and her "four children hungry with not a bite in the house."[19]

Child neglect was not always willful. Nora I. Oates, whose husband was "sick all the time," continued to work in a North Carolina mill "right on up to the night [her] baby boy was borned." She recalled, "I sat around home for about six weeks after the baby came, then left it with my mother and went back to work." Her mother, however, "was one of them old women that thought you ought to feed the babies. So she used to chew up food and feed that baby with it before he was six months old. . . . One day I come in to get my dinner (the baby was then about 18 months old) and Mama was chewing up collards and sweet potatoes and feeding the baby. He didn't live a week after she done it." This practice of chewing food for babies was sufficiently widespread for the North Carolina Board of Health to include it in a list of "don'ts" the board compiled in 1911 advising mothers on improper child-rearing practices.[20]

As children grew older, the indulgence diminished. By the age of five or six, they were introduced to the harsh but erratic discipline that characterized child rearing among plain folk, and they began as well to have chores and responsibilities of their own. At this age, their discipline was largely a matter of prohibited behavior rather than of positive example, enforced by "whoopings"; and that pattern continued into adolescence. Mary Gattis, who was born in 1909 in the village of Bynum, made a typical assessment in recalling her childhood. "We were brought up the hard way," she said. "We were disciplined. We knew to respect [that is, obey] our parents." Jessie Lee Carter recalled similarly: "We had to behave. We had to say 'yes, m'am,'

---

19. Atlanta *Constitution*, August 23, 1905, July 29, 1903.
20. North Carolina State Board of Health, *Health Bulletin*, XXIX (July, 1914), 62.

and 'no, m'am'; 'yes, sir' and 'no, sir.' Lord if we ever said 'what' to anybody, we would have got a whipping then. Everybody was raised that way then. . . . Lord, I never spoke back to my parents. . . . We knew to mind." Walter Vaughn, whose family lived near Conestee Mill in South Carolina and combined farm and mill work, had an equally disciplined childhood. "I had a daddy that made you walk the chalk line," recalled Vaughn, who was born in 1909. "You did what you were told. You talk back to him, you were tore all to pieces. And I appreciate it. He learnt me."

Discipline was enforced by corporal punishment. Younger children were slapped and spanked with the hand; older ones were beaten, sometimes brutally, with a switch, belt, or "strop." "They'd lay the hickory on me," was the way Alice P. Evitt summarized her parents' response to her misbehavior as a child. Emma Clark Williams, who grew up at Carrboro, was less laconic in her recollection. "My mother kept a switch about a yard long, two yards long, or something," Mrs. Williams recalled. "That was to intimidate us, I suppose, mostly, but I didn't get it many times, and none of us got it often. But, boy, it was there, and she'd speak once and that was fine." Jessie Lee Carter remembered "hundreds" of whippings when she was a child, all from her mother, mostly for "slipping off" to visit her grandmother. One can guess, however, that such frequent whippings were not severe. Perhaps Mrs. Carter's mother disciplined all the children in her family, or all the girls. That was frequently the case. In Dolly Hollar Moser's family, however, her father was the disciplinarian, and her mother was lenient.

A large part of discipline was work. "I was eleven in the family," recalled George W. Dyer, the son of a Virginia farmer. "We all had to work when we got big enough to work. We couldn't lay around and play off like something was wrong with us. [Father] made us work. That's the way people was brought up years ago." This was universally the case among mill folk, and the most successful aspect of child discipline. Folk who discussed their childhood often spoke of being punished for disobedience but never for refusing to work. Children learned at the outset that work was a part of life, and they worked without questioning the idea that they should do so. This suggests that the integration of small children into the family work force through the assignment of regular chores had positive effect. Those chores—for the very young, bringing in stove wood, weeding the garden or yard, drying dishes, sweeping floors, and for older children, milking the cow, washing dishes, fetching water, slopping the hogs—contributed to the child's sense of belonging, for he made meaningful contributions to family well-being. Chores also conditioned the child to go willingly to the field or into the mill at the proper time.

Because—or in spite—of work and discipline, mill children were generally obedient to and respectful of their parents. "I had a good mother and daddy, and they wasn't strict with us," Vinnie Partin recalled, apparently meaning that her parents rarely whipped their children. "They taught us right from wrong, and they always taught us that . . . a good name was better than anything in the world to have, and they always wanted us to live up to it. . . . They wasn't strict with us, but when we were told something, and we were told what time to be in, we were there, and there was no questions asked about it. . . . We honored our father and mother. And we respected them."

Evidence of the love these remarks imply is not abundant. "I had a mighty good mother," Flossie Moore Durham observed. "She was a good clean Christian woman. So was my father." Lessie Bowden Bland, whose mother died when Lessie was four, expressed her affection for her step-mother more explicitly. "We loved her like we did our mother almost," Mrs. Bland said. "She was so good to me." No doubt the chief indication of this love was the hard work mothers did for their children; but mothers expressed their love in many ways. "If she used to think we were hungry," Theotis Johnson Williamson recalled of her mother, "she would bring us something up there to the mill."

"HE WAS DISOBEDIENT, AND HAD FAULTS, I FEARED WOULD GROW TO BE CRIMES."

Despite the general equilibrium that prevailed, there were many problems between parents and children. Parents could be indulgent, ineffectual, and inconsistent, and even insensitive or brutal. Teenage children could be disobedient, willful, and sources of great sorrow to their parents. A woman identified only as Mrs. Thornton in the Federal Writers' Project interviews moved to Olympia mill village in 1907 at nineteen and was still there more than thirty years later. "I tried to raise my children right," she told an interviewer; but in spite of her every effort, she may have been an indulgent, ineffective parent. "I always kep' 'em in the yard; I never allowed them to say 'yes' an' 'no' to people, but I taught 'em to say 'yes, ma'am' an' 'no, ma'am.['] An' I wouldn't let 'em sass nobody nor quarrel with nobody nor fight among themselves. It's the way the parents raise 'em," Mrs. Thornton continued. "If you raise 'em right, you'll have good children. Yes ma'am, if you lay the pattern right in front of them, they'll carry the pattern on with 'em. But you got to start the saplin' right while it's young. Dont the Bible say, 'Spare the rod an' spoil the chile'? I taken my children to preachin' an' to Sunday School every Sunday."

Yet by her own account, Mrs. Thornton's efforts had failed, at least with her son who was still at home and working in the mill at the time of the interview. He was a chronic, heavy drinker and a great disappointment to his mother, who loved him and excused his drinking. "When they're little they're trampin' on your toes," she said of children with a certain resignation, "an' when they're big they're trampin' on your heart."

One problem of parents, especially mothers without husbands, was disobedient teenage sons. Information on their handling of these adolescents is scant but highly suggestive. So desperate did at least a few mothers—and fathers—become that they committed their sons to the state reformatory. Several of those parents in South Carolina wrote Governor Blease when they wanted their sons released. "I am writing you in regard to my boys—Hollis and Jerrell Jennings—which I sent to the Reformatory at Florence July 23, 1912," Eugenia Jennings of Pelzer wrote, apparently in late 1913. "They were Not sent there for any crime or offence[.] Mr Jennings thier Father died May 14, 1912. I was unable to controle them at that time and thought it best to send them for awhile." Now Mrs. Jennings was "satisfied" that her sons were "ready to come home." Inevitably, a part of her concern was economic. "My family consist of six children four too small to work," she wrote Blease. "I have too daughters at work in the mill and thier wages are not sufficient to support my family." Thus, her two sons' "help is badly needed in this home," and she asked that they be released.[21]

Similarly, Edna Cresswell, "a *poor* widow" who had "nothing but the wages of [her] children," of whom "only three can work one of them is not stout hardly work half time," asked Blease to arrange the release of her son John, whom she had sent to the reformatory more than a year earlier. "He was disobedient, and had faults, I feared would Grow to be Crimes," she explained. "So I sent him down there from Pelzer."[22]

Desperate mothers occasionally had adolescent sons arrested. Guyton Asher, "a youth who works in a cotton factory," was arrested by Atlanta police in 1905 at the behest of his "very poor" mother, who earned a

21. Mrs. Eugenia Jennings to Coleman L. Blease, n.d., in 1913 Spartanburg County folder, in Coleman L. Blease Papers, South Carolina State Archives.

22. Mrs. Edna Cresswell to Blease, date illegible, in 1914 Greenville County folder, Blease Papers.

"pittance" sewing. Young Asher's offense was "idling and loitering about the streets." After he spent a night in jail, his mother had him released. "I did not want to lock you up, but told the officer to get you and keep you for me," she told her son as he was freed. "You are not angry with mother for that, are you?" According to a reporter who witnessed this scene, "The boy was sullen and half pushed his mother away."[23]

Occasionally parents brutalized their children. In the summer of 1903, police in Atlanta arrested W. J. Holt for whipping his eighteen-year-old daughter Doretta "in a cruel manner, leaving marks on her body which were black and blue." The girl "worked in a factory twelve hours a day" to help support her family; and her father, a sixty-five-year-old Confederate veteran who worked only occasionally as a peddler, demanded absolute obedience from her and his other adult children. At his arraignment, Holt "drew a leather strap from his pocket, and said, with a great show of pride, that he had 'strapped' his girl because she wouldn't say 'Ma'am,' when answering her mother." Asked if he thought it right to whip a grown daughter, he said he "most certainly" did. "As long as any of my children stay under my roof and don't do to suit me, I'm going to whip them," he told the court. At that point, another of Holt's daughters, about thirty years old, spoke up. "Pa whips me," she said, "and I am older than my sister here. Pa ought to whip us, and I am glad he whips me when I don't do right." Still another daughter volunteered the information that Holt also whipped his married daughter. "I do it," Holt admitted, "because she is under my roof. The cause of all the trouble, Judge, is that my son-in-law gets mad when I whip his wife."[24]

Mothers could also be cruel. In the fall of 1906, Atlanta police arrested Jane Redd for brutally beating her fourteen-year-old daughter, Lena, who worked at Fulton Bag and Cotton Mills. At Mrs. Redd's trial, police exhibited "a leatherstrop full of small holes, with which the little girl had been beaten several times." Lena was sometimes whipped by her twenty-year-old ne'er-do-well brother with her mother's concurrence. Apparently, the beatings were prompted by Lena's desire "to go with other girls and visit Ponce de Leon," a nearby park, and by her brother's desire to have full control of her earnings. Neighbors, rather than Lena, reported this incident to police, and despite the brutality the trial revealed, the judge at Lena's request dismissed the charges against Mrs. Redd and refused to order Lena re-

23. Atlanta *Constitution*, April 17, 1905.
24. *Ibid.*, July 21, 1903.

moved from her custody. "I want to go home," Lena told the court after learning of a proposal to place her in a foster home. "I love my mamma."[25]

Not all brutalized children reacted in this way. In Atlanta in 1903, Corinne Earnest ran away from home and asked to be removed from her father's authority. "I am sixteen years old," she told a magistrate, "and ever since I was 8 I have toiled all day in the cotton mills. If I was late getting to work I was beat for it. Every cent I made my father took. I bore with it all until he married again, and now my stepmother makes life at home unbearable." The magistrate accepted her plea and placed her in a "home for the friendless."[26]

It is difficult to know how much stress to place on child abuse among plain folk, for it is difficult to draw a satisfactory line between acceptable punishment and abuse. The two incidents just described clearly involved abuse, but the disciplining and punishing of children vary so much among societies that the psychological consequences of punishment must vary as well. In some societies, shaming and other forms of nonphysical punishment function effectively to achieve desired behavior among children, and in such societies, corporal punishment is unnecessary and in varying degrees unacceptable. Among plain folk, shaming was widely used to discipline children, but so also was physical punishment. The impact of neither is assessable. Presumably, every society rationalizes certain forms of punishment, and misbehaving children expect those forms rather than others. Presumably also, this expectation eases somewhat the psychological consequences of receiving "acceptable" punishment. Yet plain folk and their children did not understand the consequences of the punishment they administered and received, and could not discuss them in the interviews.

The extensive modern literature on child abuse is, however, highly suggestive when read with plain folk in mind. According to that literature, child abuse tends to coexist with the kinds of family problems plain folk had—financial difficulty, unemployment, inadequate housing, broken families, alcoholism, and the like; and that tendency suggests that the punishment of children among plain folk was excessive and even abusive in large numbers of instances. More suggestive, however, is the association of child abuse with certain personality characteristics and authoritarian social attitudes that are themselves often, even generally, rooted in the mistreatment abusing parents themselves received as children. "Abusive parents are

25. *Ibid.*, September 20, 21, 1906.
26. *Ibid.*, August 19, 1903.

lonely people, yearning for love and understanding, yet plagued by a deep sense of inferiority and inability to have any confidence in being lovable or in finding real understanding and help," psychologist Brandt F. Steele wrote of abusive parents he had studied. "The deep conviction of helplessness and ineffectuality are frequently hidden beneath attitudes of righteous certainty about their ideas and actions and strong expressions of their right to run their own lives without interference." Such parents, Steele continued, "felt deeply crushed by disapproval" in their own childhood. "From their earliest years on, they felt the necessity to be alert and sensitive to parental needs, no matter how excessive, and to attempt to meet them. At the same time they felt their own desires, feelings, and thoughts were largely disregarded or belittled." This is a formula for frustration deeply felt. The abusing parents Steele studied "had rarely been able to disagree openly with their parents or rebel against them, and had developed the pattern of submitting to parental criticism and punishment without open complaint. Intense feelings of anger and resentment toward the parents were [therefore] common."[27] These patterns of feeling and behavior cannot be documented among plain folk, but much of what is known about the actions of plain folk in disciplining their children suggests the patterns were fairly common.

"I WAS FIFTEEN YEARS OLD BEFORE I EVER KNEWED WHAT A BABY CAME FROM."

Despite instances of parental abuse, most children grew up in an environment that encouraged some sense of social security. Chores and mill work lent purpose to their lives, and growing up near large numbers of relatives and other people of similar culture and circumstance contributed to feelings of identity and belonging. Most folk therefore remembered their childhood positively and described it in ways that stressed the security they felt.

Puberty and the emergence of sexual feelings mark a distinct evolution toward complexity. In and out of the villages, folk had difficulty with sexuality. In respectable circles, they never talked of it candidly, and theirs was a society of sexual repression. Inevitably, this atmosphere sustained ignorance and encouraged the association of sexuality with shame, immorality, and weakness. In concert with a double standard that permitted men but not women to indulge in irregular sex, this association resulted in a shadowy

---

27. Brandt F. Steele, "Parental Abuse of Infants and Small Children," in Anthony and Benedek (eds.), *Parenthood*, 454–56.

demimonde of "bad" women and prostitution that existed at the margins of village life.

Parents never talked to children about sex; indeed, the concept of sex education was alien to them. "Girls them days didn't talk and know things like they do now," Mrs. M. A. Matheson recalled of her youth in western North Carolina in the 1880s and 1890s. "I'd never asked my mammy anything about having babies like my daughter, who is eighteen, asks me; I guess she'd had a stroke. Things like that were spoken in whispers." Bessie Buchanan remarked in a similar vein: "I was fifteen years old before I ever knowed what a baby came from. People didn't tell children things like that. Now after a girl started menstruating, their mother would take them down and tell them these things. But until then you didn't hear things like that."

To some girls raised in this way, the onset of menses was frightening. Donna Redmond, who grew up in a mill village in Georgia where her mother worked, recalled just such an incident involving her grandmother: "Granny told me that when she started menstruating, it was in the middle of the winter and the snow was real deep. She was down at the stream getting water and it started and the blood was in the snow. She didn't tell T'aint Sally [who ran the orphan's home where she grew up] for about three months because she was scared to death. She thought she was going to die. She didn't know the first thing about it, didn't even know that animals did it. She thought T'aint Sally would think she'd done something bad or was dying."[28]

That reaction was no doubt rare. Surely girls learned of such things from older sisters or friends. Adolescent social life, however, revolved around sexual pursuits largely in the sense of seeking marriage partners. Unfortunately, village life was imperfectly suited to that effort. There were few social and recreational activities because plain folk were unfamiliar with activities organized for diversion alone and feared such activities might involve immorality or sin. "There wasn't anything to do," Jessie Lee Carter recalled of social activity at the village in Greenville where she grew up. "They didn't have places like they have now. You just stayed at home and you went to church." In response to a question about social life at Carrboro in the second decade of the twentieth century, Mrs. Bertram Andrews said: "Do nothing. Sit on the front porch and see people pass." Moral inhibitions were a part of the problem. "No mam! No cards, my mother would not have cards in the house," Alice Thrift Smith recalled vividly. "No, no dancing."

28. Quoted in Kathy Hahn, *Hillbilly Women* (New York, 1973), 113.

"WE'D GET OUT, TAKE WALKS, AND HAVE A LOT OF FUN."

There were, of course, some social activities. "That's all the recreation people had back in them days," Nannie Pharis recalled of village life in her youth. "Different neighbors would have dances at their homes. They'd invite their friends in." Flossie Moore Durham recalled going to dances in the country but not in the village where she lived. "I enjoyed it," she said. "And they weren't drinking or cutting up. No, they didn't do anything dirty at them dances, either." In the villages, youths "had music" at their socials "a lot of times on Saturday nights," Mrs. Durham also recollected. "And children would play together over there on the hill a lot of times, games at night, in the evening, things like that. Oh, they fared all right."

Others had positive memories, too. "I'd go to some of my friends' house, or they'd come to mine," Rose Bowden Humphreys remembered of social life after the day's work in the mill. "We'd get out, take walks, and have a lot of fun. Somebody'd have a party every once in a while. We had a good time." Annie Grady Emerick, who was "nearly grown-up" when she went to work in a mill in Athens, also had fond memories of her youth. "We had mighty good times then," she said. "Our riding was done in buggies and wagons, and we had our churches and church sociables. All Sunday schools had picnics every year and everybody went, old and young. . . . We had parties and candy pullings. I don't look now like I was ever able to do it, but I've danced all night many a time at those old square dances and not be tired even, then I'd work all the next day and think nothing of it."

Because social activity was limited, special events, sometimes involving the entire village, were milestones in village life. Scattered over the year were holiday celebrations, Sunday school picnics, "big dinners" at revival time, traveling shows, Saturday afternoon excursions, political rallies, picture shows, even funerals. Vinnie Partin remembered that at Roxboro, North Carolina, the mill gave each family a turkey every Thanksgiving and Christmas and presents to all the children at Christmas. Many mills followed this or a similar custom. Many observed a holiday one Saturday late in the spring or on the Fourth of July or Labor Day, and sponsored all-day outings for their operatives and families. Through the New South era, for example, mills in Columbus shut down for a holiday in the spring and again on Labor Day. On May 9, 1896, all major industries in that city, including the cotton mills, closed in observance "of the time honored custom of suspending on a Saturday in May that their operatives might take their families out and enjoy the invigorating country air, and partake of the festivities of the picnic." During that observance, "the largest crowds" ever flocked to nearby parks "and from early morning until late in the afternoon" enjoyed themselves. "Baskets of sumptuous dinners had been prepared," and interspersed through the feasting were baseball, sack racing, and other entertainments, including contests and prizes for the youngest infant, prettiest woman, and handsomest, ugliest, and oldest men.[29]

Labor Day festivities followed the same pattern. In 1898, for example, the major industries in Columbus again closed, and "the working people celebrated." There was boating and bathing for them that day, picnicking, baseball, and contests and prizes again for the most popular young lady, young man, and married woman as well. There was an ugly-man contest too, a footrace, a bottle-breaking contest, a watermelon-eating contest, and an address by Will W. Winn, state organizer for the textile union.[30] This annual event had begun in 1882.

At Monaghan Mills, the Fourth of July was a festive occasion. In 1914 plans for the celebration included dinner on the ground and a parade with floats, clowns, and marching groups from village fraternal organizations and their women's auxiliaries. Woodmen of the World, Red Men, Odd Fellows, Masons, Woodmen Circle, and Pocahontas had marching groups. There was also to be a baseball game between teams from Monaghan Mills and nearby Mills Mill, and another matching the "fats" and the "leans." After the games, there would be a fiddler's contest, though "no one who plays a violin by note will be allowed to compete," the sponsors announced. "It is only for those who play by ear."[31]

"I COULDN'T [LEAVE MY HUSBAND]. I HAD TWO LITTLE 'UNS AND ANOTHER COMIN', AND NOWHERE TO GO."

Beneath these special events ran the fundamental currents of social life. Folk society was man centered in appearance and ideal. A man was the head of his family and household, and due the respect that position suggested. Mill policy encouraged this ideal, which in most families had at least some substance behind it. Almost all those interviewed who commented on the subject remembered their fathers as dominant, often authoritarian figures. "In those days mothers didn't assert themselves," Maxie Oakley said with

29. Columbus *Enquirer-Sun*, May 10, 1896.
30. Columbus *Sunday Herald*, September 11, 1898.
31. Greenville *Daily News*, June 27, 1914.

her family in mind. "[My mother] went along with Daddy's decision." Even irresponsible fathers elicited obedience if not respect. "Pa didn't take a bit of responsibility for raising us," Eva Truelove, one of twelve children, said of her father, a North Carolina farmer. "He never tried to learn us a thing about right and wrong. . . . When he wanted us to do something he'd just say do it and give no reason, and when he didn't want us to do a thing he just said we'd damned better not unless we wanted the hell beat out of us."

Yet there were too many female-headed families, too many single adults who supported themselves, and too many ineffectual fathers and husbands for male dominance to prevail in all cases. Moreover, some fathers and husbands voluntarily shared their authority with mothers and wives. "Whatever my mother said went in our family but she was not bossy," Rosa Kanipe said. Her family moved from a farm to a mill in North Carolina while she was still a child. "Father respected her wishes just like us young-uns did."

As these disparate examples suggest, family relationships did not flow automatically from social roles. On the contrary, personality and social values did much to determine the dynamics within each family. The resulting variety was especially evident in the relationship between husbands and wives, which was inherently stressful. Poverty, children, in-laws, crowded housing, and numerous other things were potential or actual sources of strain. The anxieties and disappointments these things engendered could explode at any time in compulsive behavior, for many folk, especially men, had difficulty verbalizing and therefore rationalizing and controlling emotions. In time, concrete problems might appear—drinking, desertion, or other forms of irresponsibility. Even couples who avoided those problems had to weather repeated stresses.

Because the imperatives of men and women were different, the anxieties and frustrations of the sexes were dissimilar. And since the burdens of family living were unequally divided between them, husbands and wives often looked upon the most elemental aspects of family life—sex, having another child, child-rearing responsibilities, and the like—in different ways. The result was not merely disagreement but something like a war between the sexes—a war that manifested itself not just, or even chiefly, in obvious actions like desertion and violence but in the day-to-day struggles of couples trying to live together. Disagreement was a fundamental feature of village life, coexisting with love and respect as well as with the opposites of those feelings. It was difficult to live together in the villages. The only thing more difficult was to live apart.

One reason for this difficulty was the inequities of married life. The social and economic dependence of women on their husbands was greater than their husbands' on them. Men had more social freedom than women in the world of plain folk, and were much less defined by their marital and family status. Women bore a disproportionate share of the consequences of sex—pregnancy, childbearing, nurturing and rearing children. Neither their own nor their society's rationalization of motherhood completely compensated for these burdens. Marriage thus had far greater meaning for women than for men, as married women often warned their unmarried sisters. "Most of the women complain of the hard life which a married woman leads," Lois MacDonald wrote of women she interviewed in villages in the Carolinas in the 1920s, "and are full of advice to unmarried women to remain single. Their feelings have not been crystallized into principles, however."[32] By the latter remark, MacDonald meant that the feelings of the women about marriage were ambivalent. While their own experience had been problematic, the mill women still felt that marriage and motherhood were the proper roles for women and the only roles that promised fulfillment.

Plain folk seemed not to expect happiness as an absolute state, for their lives were too full of care and boundedness. That fact affected their attitudes toward each other in marriage. Since they were reticent about their emotions, however, the essential nature of the marriage relationship remains elusive. Even folk with agreeable relationships tended to understatement in discussing their marriages and spouses. "We are right foolish over each other," Fanny Bowers Maddrey said after more than twenty years of happy marriage to Herman Maddrey. "Not havin' no children of our own has made us real childish about each other and about stayin' apart at night. He don't even want to eat nobody else's cookin' but mine." Thomas Sizemore, who grew up on a South Carolina tenant farm before the turn of the century, spoke similarly of his wife of more than thirty-five years. "We have grown old together and I ain't never seed no woman yet I'd swap [Lily Bird] for," he said. "We've had good times and hard, she's always carried her share of the burdens and she does now, getting up early to give me a good breakfast."

Ella and Will Cheek, who began married life as tenant farmers and then moved to a mill, had an equally happy marriage. "Me and him's had a heap of hard times together, but then we've had a heap of quiet peace too," Mrs. Cheek said. "We've not had money to spend but we've enjoyed bein' with

32. Lois MacDonald, *Southern Mill Hills: A Study of Social and Economic Forces in Certain Textile Mill Villages* (New York, 1928), 77–78.

one another. He's never left me no time of a night and I've never left him but two or three nights when Pa was bad off four years ago." Mrs William J. Sadler, whose husband had been a molder, was equally satisfied with her marriage of more than four decades. "He was a good hearted man and worked hard all his life," she said of her husband. "We had our fusses and quarrels, just like I reckon all married folks do, but we lived together almost forty-two years without a thought of being separated or divorced."

These assessments convey more respect and adjustment than love and passion, though there is no reason to doubt these marriages were characterized by love. Still, no information is available on their sexual dimension, or even on what women, especially, regarded as sexually satisfactory in marriage. Did fear of pregnancy cause them often to resist, or try to resist, their husband's advances? If so, with what consequence? To what extent, also, was sexual activity influenced by the thought that women were, or were supposed to be, less enamored of sex than men and less demonstrative in sexual activity?

Obviously, many marriages were not happy, and sexual dissatisfaction was no doubt a contributing factor. Many women believed infidelity among men was common, and they might have been correct. "Eugene wa'n't no different from most men," Rachel Lester, a mill worker, said of her philandering husband of many years. "Taint many that don't have their women." Perhaps some women believed that because their husbands were poor sexual performers.

Some husbands were brutes, and their violent behavior might have been sexually related. Jennie Rowe, who grew up on a tenant farm in western North Carolina and moved with her family to a cotton mill, remembered that her father brutally beat her mother many times. "I come home from the cornfield to cook dinner one day," Mrs. Rowe recalled, "and there on the porch lay my Mammy. She was bleedin' at the mouth and bruises was all over her face. Big knots was swole up all over her head." She had been beaten with a bucket stave by her husband. As a result of such beatings, Mrs. Rowe's mother lived in dire fear. She "told us we better dassent not tell anything on Pap," Mrs. Rowe remembered.

Lonnie Williams, who was born in 1892 into a North Carolina tenant farmer's family, married a tenant farmer when she was seventeen. "I knowed he was a drunkard but he said he'd quit for me," she said. He did "quit for about two weeks" but then began drinking heavily. He "got drunk several times before I said much to him and he didn't offer to hit me," Mrs. Williams continued. "We'd been married four months and I found out that

I was going to have a baby. He didn't like younguns and he was mad about it so when he got drunk the first time after he knowed it he beat me. . . . I lost that one and like to of died, but he was so sorry that he done it I had to forgive him. . . . The next time he beat me I was six months gone. He knocked me down and stomped on my stomach. I lost that one, too, and never did git over it." After this beating she left her husband, and as soon as she had enough money, she got a divorce.

Lillian Holbrook's problem was not an abusive husband but a weak one. The two were working in a North Carolina mill when they married, and they were happy until they were laid off and their children began to arrive. Her husband began staying away from home and seeing a "bad woman." Mrs. Holbrook recalled, "A lots of the menfolks in the mill section went to her house at night, an' lots of 'em married men, too." She despaired. "I reckon most women would've give up and quit [that is, leave their husband], right there, when their husband done like that," she continued. "But I couldn't. I had two little 'uns and another comin', and nowhere to go without [my husband]. I just hung on and prayed that he'd see his wrong 'fore it was too late. It hurt an awful lot."

Other husbands abused their wives by overwork. "I fell in love with [Leonard] when I was sixteen, and I married him against my parents' better judgment just before I was seventeen," Bessie Warwick said of her marriage to a North Carolina tenant farmer in 1913. "He took me at once to the fifty acres he had rented for the year, and the second day after the wedding he put me in the cotton patch chopping cotton. I chopped ten hours that day. [Leonard] said I might as well git used to it, and he lay out in the shade and slept while I cooked in the hot kitchen." Mrs. Warwick continued: "He acted like he had intended to marry a machine to do his work and that he was very well satisfied with the results. He'd leave me at home to look after the tobacco barn and sucker tobacco while he went to town, and hardly ever he'd ask me to go."

Fannie Miles's husband was an irresponsible man who eventually deserted her and their children. Mrs. Miles had made the familiar trek from tenant farm to cotton mill with her family while she was still a child. At the turn of the century, when she was twenty, she married a fellow mill worker. Her husband "couldn't see an inch from his nose, and I told him he went backwards 'stead of forwards," Mrs. Miles recounted of their marriage. "He was a pretty good sort of a man, just thought he knowed it all. His worst habit was gambling. Sometimes he'd win a little and then he'd lose more than he'd won. When [one of her sons] was a baby, I decided I just couldn't keep draggin' the children around, so [my husband] got where he would go off without me. Sometimes he'd send money to help us along an' sometimes he wouldn't. Finally he quit coming home at all." She learned to live without him. "I worked, an' the children got big enough to work some," she recalled, and they managed.

"HELP ME FIND MY HUSBAND WHO LEFT ME AND MY POOR LITTLE CHILDREN."

Brutality may have been a bigger problem on the farm than in the village. Perhaps some women who brought their children to the villages were fleeing violent husbands. Perhaps also the proximity of neighbors in the villages served to protect women from violence. On the other hand, desertion seems to have been a larger problem in the villages than on the farms. Many of the deserted women in the villages, however, might have been forsaken on the farm or elsewhere before they went to the villages. In the census schedules of mill families, there are numbers of women listed as married and having children with no husband present, and some of them lived with their parents and had their parents' last name. Census takers were not always consistent in their listings, and the categories of unwed mothers, widows, and deserted women cannot be satisfactorily separated. There is therefore no way of calculating rates of desertion. John K. Morland knew of 22 deserted women in about 300 families in the mill villages of York in the 1940s and was certain there were others. That seems a rather high incidence. On the other hand, there were only 2 deserted wives and 1 unwed mother in 168 families at Saxon mill village in the 1920s, which seems a rather low rate.[33] Desertion was not, however, always a static state. Some women were left for a time and then their husbands returned, and others were sporadically deserted for varying periods. An unknown number remarried after a while without bothering to get divorced.

Desertion was especially difficult for women with small children. Ozella Barton of Greenville must have been reminded of that fact on Christmas Eve in 1913, for she chose that day to write Governor Blease "to help Me find My husband who left Me and My poor little children." She wrote: "Mr. Gov., he lef Me and 3 little children and the people of Greenville has gave us a living[.] I am not able to Work and My Mother is a Wido and Not able to

33. Morland, *Millways of Kent*, 66; Marjorie A. Potwin, *Cotton Mill People of the Piedmont: A Study in Social Change* (New York, 1927), 74.

keep us up. Just think if You have some little children that could Not have so Much as a orange and an appel [at Christmas] for them[.] I dont want to live with Mr Barton[.] But I Want you to advise Me and help me Make him support Me."[34]

The problems of deserted women were exacerbated by the difficulties of getting a divorce. South Carolina prohibited divorce absolutely, and in Georgia and North Carolina, divorce and legal separation were difficult, costly, and time consuming. Pearl Hinson, who worked at Judson Mill in Greenville, was fourteen in 1908 when she married a thirty-two-year-old man who already had a wife. "He stayed with me 2 months and left me," she wrote Governor Blease in 1914. "I have not Sean are herd from him in 6 six years[.] [T]here is a lot of peapol herc in Greenville that know he was married When he married me. When I married this man he made me beleave he was devorsed from his first wife." The truth was, "His first wife had given him a little truble beafore he went of[f] and he got a way and she was after him. . . . [H]is name was L. F. Hilton[.] [H]is ocapation was instruction hand and carpanters trade[.] I would like for you to give me some information a bout whether law of this state holds me under any oblagation to him if I was to marrie a gane are not[.] I sirtnlay feal free from him and do not bcaleave God holds me under eny oblagation."[35]

Addie Brown, who lived in the country outside Jefferson, wrote Blease asking "if thir is eny way that you can give Me afreedom from my husban[.] [H]e is gone and left me[.] [T]his is the third time that he has treated me that way," she explained. "He has mistreated me so Much untill I dont think that I can Be treated that way eney M[or]e[.] I have Bin Married 6 years[.] [H]e has lived with Me about 20 Months[.] I will Be so glad if you Can give me afreedom from him[.] I am ayoung girl and that the life that I havto live in this way is so Misible to me it seems like if I had afreedom or a dvorse from him I would feel better."[36]

Annie Williamson had more complicated problems, involving disappointed love, premarital pregnancy, a "shotgun" marriage, a runaway husband, and a father whose concern was not his daughter's happiness but social appearance and his own main chance. "I was deceved by A man who clamed to be a preacher," Mrs. Williamson wrote the governor. "We were to be married and he deceved me. [A]nd left home. [B]ut promos me when he got A place that he would take me. [B]ut when he got off from me, then he

34. Mrs. Ozella Barton to Blease, December 24, 1913, in Blease Papers.
35. Pearl Hinson to Blease, July 10, 1914, in Blease Papers.
36. Addie Brown to Blease, September 10, 1913, in Blease Papers.

fell in love with A nother girl who had some propity so they say, and I could not hear from him. So when my Father found out what he had don, he went to Wagner and had a Wornt taken out for him, for a Marge [marriage] Contract, and when they brought him to Wagner, Father toald him if he would marrie me and take me he would Stop it are if not that he would have to go to Jail and stand A trial." Mrs. Williamson continued: "So he agreed willingly to marrie[.] [W]ent on to Akain [Aiken] and bought is Linens his self and we were married Sept 27th 1913. [S]o he left me at his Brothers and went back to work. Promos me to get A place for me but did not. [S]o on Dec 24th 1913, he marries the other Girl and they go to Columbus Miss, and I am poore and had no money to bother them. [S]o now he had to come back, and got his Brother to get my Father to make me sign some Kind of A paper for $300.00 so he says he is not married to me." Mrs. Williamson wrote: "I had to sign the paper. Father sead if I would not sign them that I had to give my baby away and leave home, and go to work for my self. [S]o Lawer Starkey of Orangeburg, S.C. fixed some Kind of papers, and I sign them. [H]e sead that it would have to go through Coart in March and be sign by the Judge. Now, I want to Know if I will have to let him go on and live with the other girl[.] [T]hey are living A bout Six miles from me." She entreated: "Now Governor Please tell me Know what to do. [M]y Father has blamed me with it all, and treates me verry badly, and wont do any thing for me. [T]he girl that he married last knew that he was married to me but sead that she would leave with him. . . . Mr Starkey did not wread A word of the papers to me. I dont Know what I have sign. I Know that I only did it to keep my baby which is now three months old." Mrs. Williamson wrote this letter five months after her marriage.[37]

Emily Poteat's problems were less complicated, but they too stemmed from the dependence of women. "I am Very unhappy and I believe if you only will You can help me," she wrote Blease. "I will tell you My trouble[.] I married a Man 7 years ago last June and he left me 7 years ago last Sept[.] I do not Know Where he is or have not seen or heard from him since he left. . . . I have met a man that I truly love and he loves me but they Wont Give us lisence to Mary and you can give a Ida [idea] how unhappy We are[.] Mr Blease place your self in my place Married to a Man Who cares Nothing for me have a Mother and Child depending on me for living[.] I am not Very stout and I have no one in the World to turn to Care for me no Way[.] It

37. Annie Williamson to Blease, February 16, 1914, Blease Papers.

seems some time I can not bear it and live." Mrs. Poteat continued: "Mr Bleese you may know that I love him or I Would not ask you for help[.] I am bound hand and foot[.] I have no Money to go any Where to get devorce[.] [I]t takes What I make to live on and he is a poor Working Man Just like my self[.] [A]ll we have is our love for each other."[38]

Such incidents were apparently rather numerous. At least a few men took advantage of the ease with which mill folk could move from job to job and simply went from village to village and wife to wife as the notion struck them. In the early spring of 1912, for example, R. Luther Hawkins married Lizzie Tucker at Lindale, Georgia, the village of Massachusetts Mills. A few days later, Hawkins "departed for an unknown destination." Someone hired "private detectives" to track him down. Within weeks, the detectives found him in Greenville, where he had married again, this time to Georgia Ayers; and they found, too, that he had no fewer than six wives in Georgia, Alabama, and the Carolinas.[39]

If desertion was often an act of irresponsibility, it was also at times a pragmatic adaptation to the difficulties of divorce.[40] Divorce entailed hiring a lawyer and going through legal proceedings, which cost more money than plain folk could afford and confronted them with legal and bureaucratic mysteries they did not understand. Traditionalists, most folk knew little of the ways of the modern state, and few comprehended that marriage was a legal contract. No doubt many of them thought leaving marriage should be as easy as entering into it. What outsiders saw as casual disregard for the sanctity of marriage might therefore have been to mill folk a necessary and convenient act of well-being. "We kind of fell in love and decided we'd get married," Abel Starnes recalled of his marriage to a young widow with four children at a South Carolina mill village just after World War I. But after a while, Starnes and his wife "quarreled all the time. She didn't want me to have one word to say about managing the children," he said, "and she wasn't satisfied with the little bit of money I could get. Well, I stood it six years, and then I just left her. Didn't get no divorce. I didn't have no money to pay for one, so I didn't do nothing but walk off." Soon thereafter, he married again.

38. Emily Poteat to Blease, November 4, 1913, in Blease Papers.
39. Atlanta *Constitution*, June 12, 1914.
40. For a contemporary study, see Carroll D. Wright, *A Report on Marriage and Divorce in the United States, 1867–1886* (Washington, D.C., 1889).

"SHE RAND A WAY WITH A NOTHER MAN 2 YERS A GO AND I HAVE GOT 2
GIRLS THAT I NEAD A WIFE TO HELP TO RASE."

The war of the sexes took many forms. If men generally took advantage of
women, women sometimes took advantage of men. "I was force to Marry a
young lady by the name of Miss Kelley of Bennettsville who was Not a *lady*,"
J. D. Berry of Tatum wrote Governor Blease in 1914. "Soon after we were
married a child was born. She then went back to her father Chief Kelley of
Bennettsville. In a few months the child died. . . . Some time afterwards
she Married another Man in Some part of this State. . . . I do not believe
[her] child belonged to me. As other boy had been going with this Girl."
Berry did nothing about this situation, however, until he decided to remarry
and found himself unable legally to do so. "Please help Me that I can Marry
again in the near future," he pleaded with Blease. "I am . . . a poor clerk in
a General Mdse Store."[41]

J. A. Craig of Lancaster had a different problem. "I have Been Maried for
7 years," he told the governor, "and My wife left about 2 Years a go and went
to augusta G.A. and i have not saw her Since and have not heared from her in
a year and i Want you to tell me is thir no way to get free from her with out
goin to sum other state [where divorce is legal.]" S. P. Burkett of Pendleton
had also been deserted by his wife. "I have Maired the second time and She
Rand a Way With a Nother man 2 yers a go and i have got 2 girls that i nead a
Wife to help to Rase[.] Plese give me some ad vise[.] [I] dont Wants leve my
old home to go to a Devorsed State[.] . . . [I] can git as mind witness as you
Want to Prove her conduct[.] She is Bad[.] [H]er Madon name was Addie
Daves."[42]

This problem of deserted husbands was far less widespread than that of
deserted wives. Occasionally, men and women who were married, but not to
each other, deserted their families and ran away together. That is what
L. M. Poteet and Carrie Westmoreland, both operatives in Spartanburg, did
in 1907. They were later found living as husband and wife and working in
the mill at Alabama City, Alabama. "Poteet's wife was left in destitute
circumstances with four small children" as a result of her husband's desertion, "and Mrs. Westmoreland had left a husband and a six year old
daughter. Police arrested them for bigamy."[43]

41. J. D. Berry to Blease, November 30, 1914, in Blease Papers.
42. J. A. Craig to Blease, February 14, 1912, and S. P. Burkett to Blease, March 27, 1913, in
Blease Papers.
43. Atlanta *Constitution*, January 9, 1907.

Occasionally, such episodes took unexpected turns. In 1904 John R. Haynes was married and living in Anderson, South Carolina, when he fled to Gainesville, Georgia, leaving his wife behind. At Gainesville he married again, and after a while he and his new wife, the former Maud Owens, who was seventeen years old, moved to Atlanta, where Haynes went to work at Exposition Mills. One day, his first wife appeared there, and when he saw her, he "uttered an exclamation" and "lit out of the back door." This time he fled to Mobile, where authorities apprehended him and returned him to Atlanta to face charges of bigamy. At his trial Haynes said he had hired a lawyer to get a divorce from his first wife, but when he returned to the lawyer and asked if his divorce was final, the lawyer told him he would have to pay an additional twenty dollars to find out. Haynes refused to pay, he said, and assumed he was legally divorced. The judge ruled that Haynes's first wife was his legal spouse, which prevented her from testifying at his trial. Both wives, however, declared their loyalty to Haynes. "He is a nice man and a gentleman," his second wife told the court, "and I intend to stick to him to the last, and, if possible, to get him out of trouble. I love him." Afterwards, Haynes, who seems to have been a likable rogue, said "he was not sure whether he possessed hypnotic powers or not, 'but I have been told,' said he, 'that I was a very remarkable person, possessing a certain charm to which ladies are especially susceptible.'"

Perhaps Haynes was right. He was acquitted of bigamy in Georgia, but South Carolina authorities charged him with the same offense and asked for his extradition. At a hearing on the request, Haynes's wives appeared together and asked the governor of Georgia to deny it.[44]

This was not the only unexpected twist in the battle of the sexes. If many men beat their wives, some wives beat their husbands. In Columbus in 1906, for example, Minnie Bentley had her husband, C. W. Bentley, arrested on charges of beating her, claiming he had "struck her with his hand, slapping her in the face." Bentley, however, countercharged that his wife "was the aggressor, using harsh language toward him, striking him with her hand, kicking him on the shin, striking him with a home-made poker, and starting for the pistol, and that all he did was shove a copy of a newspaper in her face and tell her to stop it." The court believed Bentley, and the charges were dropped; but his wife filed suit for divorce and asked for alimony. Bentley was "a cotton mill employee," a reporter noted, "who out of a comparatively modest salary had saved enough money to buy a home."[45]

44. *Ibid.*, August 17, 18, 19, October 13, 1905.
45. *Ibid.*, April 15, 1906.

Also in Columbus, in 1904, another mill operative, H. E. Mendall, battled with his wife and came out the loser. One day the Mendalls were walking down the street when they "disagreed on some subject, and being [at] a rocky place of the street, they began to hurl missels [sic] at each other," several of which "took effect." Mendall, "getting the worst of the battle, pulled out an 8-inch knife and pursued his wife down the street, without, however, getting an opportunity to use it." Perhaps this episode was part of an ongoing battle. Not long before this fight occurred, Mendall, his wife, and his mother-in-law had each been fined five dollars for disorderly conduct. Mendall's defense on that occasion was that "his mother-in-law got after him with a piece of lightwood."[46]

D. A. Gosnell, who worked at Poe Mills, was equally ineffectual in dealing with his wife. In 1913 he was desperate enough to solicit Governor Blease's help "to see if I could get My child from My Wife or else her live With me. [H]er father and Mother persuaded her not to live with me any more," Gosnell wrote. "So I thought would write and see you about it. I have tried to get her to live with me every Way in the World and she Will Not. I offered to support her and the child too and she Wont come back With Me. [I]f I can get papers to get my child I wish you would notify me."[47]

"IT IS HARD . . . TO GET A HUSBAND TO DO WHAT THEY WANT."

These episodes illustrate what could happen, not what did happen, to the average woman. Taken together, however, the misfortunes of marriage were so prevalent that they must have had an impact on all women. Women who did not lose their husbands or find themselves married to irresponsible or otherwise disappointing spouses knew other women who had those problems. That knowledge plus the stresses in their own marriage and the generally dependent condition of females, must have fed the insecurities all women knew.

One can only speculate, however, as to the content of those insecurities for the average woman. As girls, females learned to be passive in their relationships with men. During courtship, a woman could say no to a man's advances, but after marriage she lost much even of that right. Perhaps the impressions sociologist Lee Rainwater and his colleagues drew from their

---

46. *Ibid.*, March 14, 1904.
47. D. A. Gosnell to Blease, April 26, 1913, in Blease Papers.

study of wives of blue-collar workers in the 1950s offer insight into what this type of relationship meant for women folk of an earlier generation. "The working class woman sees men as dominant and controlling," Rainwater and his associates wrote. "She is hopeful that her own husband will be benign toward her, but she counts it as a blessing rather than her natural right when he is. . . . She is inclined to see [men] as insensitive and inconsiderate, sometimes teasing, sometimes accusing, sometimes vulgar, and always potentially withholding of affection."

For such women, marriage was not hell but a state of insecurity. "It is hard, these women believe, to get a husband to do what they want or to change his ways," Rainwater and his colleagues continued. "Men go their own ways and as often as not the wife feels she has little influence. She seems unable to free herself altogether from the view that men are quite independent and can easily leave."[48]

The attitude of average men folk to their wives and marriages is even more a matter of speculation. Although the burdens of marriage and household were heavier for women than for men, men had other burdens that they often bore less well than women bore theirs and that therefore explain much of their social irresponsibility. It seems certain that men had more difficulty than women in the transition from farm to factory. Men in the New South were expected not only to provide for their families but to be independent, assertive, and if necessary aggressive in all social relationships. Yet the situation of men folk in the mills and often, too, their position within the family prevented them from fulfilling those expectations to their own satisfaction. For many, feelings of personal inadequacy compounded this problem. This combination of circumstances, as many studies have shown, is a formula for compulsive, aggressive behavior to compensate for inner frustrations. "As a protective device," sociologist Glen H. Elder has written, "social camouflage of inner dependencies may take the form of aggression and bravado." Another scholar has remarked, "The pose of tough rebellious independence, often assumed by the lower-class person, frequently conceals powerful dependency cravings."[49]

Such observations must be used warily by the historian, but the behavior

48. Lee Rainwater, Richard P. Coleman, and Gerald Handel, *Workingman's Wife: Her Personality, World and Life Style* (New York, 1959), 70–71.

49. Glen H. Elder, "Adolescent Socialization and Development," in Edgar F. Borgatta and William W. Lambert (eds.), *Handbook of Personality Theory and Research* (Chicago, 1968), 280; Walter B. Miller, "Lower Class Culture as a Generating Milieu of Gang Delinquency," *Journal of Social Issues*, XIV (1958), 13.

they describe is consistent with much of the social irresponsibility men displayed in the villages. For the vast majority of men, however—those who were not alcoholics, "mill daddies," wife beaters or deserters, and the like— this irresponsibility was a matter of degree only. The social inadequacies of mill villagers, like the social problems of their villages, were not unique. On the contrary, they existed among all peoples in all places. Only their specific combinations were distinctive. The villagers constituted functioning communities, not collections of social or psychological misfits.

"SO HARD IS THE FORTUNE OF ALL WOMANKIND!/THEY'RE ALWAYS CONTROLLED THEY'RE ALWAYS CONFINED."

The content of folk songs confirms the nature of relationships between men and women and the position of women in folk society. Many of the songs sung by folk across the New South, whether survivals from the Old World or products of the New, described just such incidents as those pictured above. That should not be surprising, for the culture of plain folk was conservative and traditional, and only partially overlapped that of southern society as a whole. And since that culture was predominantly oral, traditional folk songs were especially important expressions of its basic forms. "[Folk] music is a magical summing-up of the patterns of family, of love, of conflict, and of work which give a community its special feel and which shape the personalities of its members," folklorist Alan Lomax wrote some years ago. "Folk songs call the native back to his roots and prepare him emotionally to dance, worship, work, fight, or make love in ways normal to his place."[50]

It is not always possible to know who sang which songs, but the South was a single folk culture area, and Appalachia, where that culture was best preserved and where most of the songs mentioned herein were collected, was the home of large numbers of mill folk. And as Lomax has also observed of southern folk culture, "The lowland poor whites shared the song preferences of their mountaineer cousins."[51]

Taken together, the songs that deal with courting picture it as a veritable minefield of danger, deceit, and disappointment. "The Gosport Tragedy," for example, tells of the betrayal of a virgin by a ship's carpenter in a way mill girls would have readily understood. At first the young woman refuses

50. Alan Lomax, *The Folk Songs of North America* (New York, 1960), xv.
51. *Ibid.*, 153.

the carpenter's sexual advances because she knows most men are untrustworthy, and in a society of double standards, she knows, too, they lose respect for "easy" women. "Young men are fickle, I see very plain," she tells her suitor. "If a maiden is kind they soon her disdain." The carpenter continues his importuning, and she continues to resist. "The state of a virgin, sweet William I prize,/For marriage brings trouble and sorrow likewise," she says. "I'm afraid for to venture [that is, submit to his sexual advances] for fear/I will never wed with a ship carpenter." Eventually, however, she gives in to his entreaties and becomes pregnant, whereupon the young man takes her away and murders her.[52]

In the songs there is the presumption that happy, faithful love is rarely attained and, if attained, rarely endures. If one or the other partner is not untrue, parents, fate, or something else intervenes to bring disappointment and tragedy. Again and again in the songs, one lover tries to take advantage of the other, or one of the pair is in love and the other is not, or one is willing to sacrifice love and lover for wealth or fame. The songs are therefore replete with betrayals, partings, long separations, and broken hearts. Perhaps the attraction of the songs was not that they described reality but that they mirrored fear. Folk, apparently, were insecure in love.

These themes appear in various forms. Love is always portrayed as impermanent. "Oh, love is sweet and love is charming / And love is pleasant when it's new," run the lines of "Little Sparrow." But "love grows cold as love grows old, / And fades away like the mountain dew." The songs picture women in a variety of roles, almost all of them unattractive. Typically, women are victims—of brutal or deceitful lovers, of parents or husbands, sometimes of their own vanity or coldheartedness. The classic statement of woman's plight is the traditional, doleful ballad "The Waggoner's Lad."

> So hard is the fortune of all woman-kind!
> They're always controlled they're always confined,
> Controlled by their parents until they're made wives
> Then slaves for their husbands the rest of their lives.[53]

The songs also picture marriage as a battlefield, on which women are either the cause or the victims of hostility. "The Wife Wrapt in Wether's Skin" tells the story of a woman who would not perform her household duties and of her husband's success in reforming her. When her husband

---

52. Newman I. White (ed.), *The Frank C. Brown Collection of North Carolina Folklore* (7 vols.; Durham, 1952–64), II, 235–40, gives 5 versions of this song.
53. *Ibid.*, III, 291, 276.

comes "in from the plow" for his dinner, the uncaring woman tells him: "There's a piece of bread a-lying on the shelf. / If you want any more you can bake it yourself." With that remark, her husband gets "a hickory as long as [his] arm" and thrashes her to great effect. The next time he comes for his dinner, she "flew all around and spread the board / And 'Yes, my dear husband' was her every word. / And ever since then she has been a good wife."[54]

Among the difficulties of marriage appearing in the songs is that of the woman who wants to control her husband. "Devilish Mary" is a witch of a woman who wants that control. "She jumped and kicked and popped her heels," her husband says of her, "and swore she'd wear my britches." If the songs have any relation to reality, they reveal that men folk were especially concerned with that problem. "Wife, O wife, make no objection," a husband says in another song. "Wife, O Wife, I do declare / That the britches I will wear!" The theme of desertion also appears frequently. "Every night when I go home, / My wife I try to please her," a man sings in "Shady Grove." "The more I try the worse she gets, / Damned if I don't leave her."[55]

The other major theme of the marriage songs is that of women as victims of overwork or of uncaring or brutish husbands. For women, love inevitably degenerates into the responsibilities of housework and the disappointments or sufferings of marriage. "I Wish I Were Single Again" exists in many versions, in one of which a wife laments her marriage to a drunkard. "The drunkard, the drunkard is a man of his own," she cries, "always a-drinking and away from home." In another version, the singer focuses on the burdens of a loveless marriage. "Wash them and strip them and put them to bed," she sings of her children, "Before your husband curses them and wishes you were dead." In another verse of this song, the woman sings: "When I was single I eat biscuit and pie, / Now I am married it's cornbread or die."[56]

54. *Ibid.*, II, 185–87, 188.
55. Lomax, *The Folk Songs of North America*, 188–89; White (ed.), *The Frank C. Brown Collection of North Carolina Folklore*, II, 477–78; Lomax, *The Folk Songs of North America*, 235.
56. White (ed.), *Frank C. Brown Collection of North Carolina Folklore*, III, 55; Cecil J. Sharp, *English Folk Songs from the Southern Appalachians* (6 vols.; 1917; rpr. London, 1932), II, 33.

11
MORALITY

From the beginning of mill communities, mill owners imposed restrictions on the conduct of villagers. The restrictions reflected the moral and social conventions of Victorian society; and contemporaries, including mill folk, found them acceptable, even desirable, as social ideals. This was the day of Anthony Comstock, of societies for the suppression of vice and the rescue of "fallen" women, of the Mann Act, the Anti-Saloon League, and the first national efforts to control narcotics. Crusades against gambling, prizefighting, fortune-telling, cigarette smoking, snuff taking, and billiard playing had much the same nature as those better-known endeavors. These were vices of the poor, and removing them, reformers thought, would bring economic as well as moral and social improvement.

Efforts to regulate the conduct of mill villagers fitted readily into this pattern, though the villages had their own special circumstances. Mill owners could impose regulations and punish offenders without political or judicial interference; and the image of "poor whites" as naturally inclined to immorality and irresponsibility strengthened their resolve to do so. As congregations of "poor whites," mill villages were especially inviting targets for moral reform.

The owners' goal was villages in which social purity was attainable if not attained. The first step toward that goal was to exclude, or try to exclude, everyone and everything deemed undesirable—"loose" women and sexual immorality; liquor drinking and drinkers; gambling and gamblers; cardsharps, loan sharks, and fortune-tellers; labor "agitators," recruiting agents, and "floating" workers; "tainted" ideas, uncensored movies, and unapproved reading material; even traveling salesmen, itinerant preachers, and strolling entertainers. According to one report, officials at Pelzer Mills barred from their villages all lawyers, editors, actresses, and blacks.[1]

"THE HOUSES OF ILL FAME ARE FULL OF FACTORY GIRLS."

Sexual immorality was a special concern (*actress* was a popular euphemism for *prostitute*). Certain features of mill life heightened this concern, which had deep roots. In the traditional South, white women and girls worked, or were supposed to work, only at home or on the family farm. Many people, including many plain folk, believed the employment of women elsewhere, especially indoors under supervision by strange men, was morally compromising. Factory work for females was thus intrinsically suspect; and since most mill operatives were women or girls and all of them worked under male supervisors, cotton factories were especially problematic places. "The close and constant association with men and the natural influence of a man who is in authority over them," the *Southern Textile Bulletin* said of female mill workers in 1911, "has a tendency to cause the weak ones to err." A North Carolinian wrote in 1904, "A working woman at night, surrounded by men, is subject to temptations of all kinds, and some have fallen." A foundry worker added, carrying the idea to its conclusion, "The houses of ill fame are full of factory girls, and the Mayor's court of the men, and on election day the candidate that puts up the most money gets the vote of the whole mill."[2]

Reinforcing these impressions were certain facts of mill demography. Teenage girls and unmarried young women were overrepresented in mill work forces and thus in village populations. In addition, mill employment attracted families of deserted wives and of some unmarried mothers as well. To outsiders, these things had moral significance. According to a line of reasoning that harked back to Eve's tempting of Adam in the Garden of

1. *Manufacturers' Record*, May 7, 1903, p. 323.
2. *Southern Textile Bulletin*, October 5, 1911; North Carolina Bureau of Labor Statistics, *Annual Report, 1904*, 201, *Annual Report, 1891*, 282, hereinafter cited as NC *Labor Report* by year.

Eden, women were morally weak and potential sources of temptation and corruption unless restrained by the authority of virtuous male relatives. As one North Carolina mill owner said in 1891, "We prefer families with daughters presided over by a good father to promiscuous girls boarding."[3]

The first guarantee of village morality was excluding "bad" women. When Hambright Black asked Cleveland Cotton Mills for employment for his family in 1889, officials there received an anonymous letter concerning the Blacks. "I warn you of the Black family," the letter read. "They are bad stock. Moved to Henrietta Mills and had to move out the next day. His women are bad." H. F. Schenck was always on the lookout for laborers. Nevertheless, he sent the anonymous letter to Black. "If these things are so," he wrote in a covering note, "it would be useless for you to come here. I cannot afford to keep any bad women here."[4]

That was announced policy in all villages, apparently, but was not always the reality. For reasons that are unclear, "bad" women were not always banished, even from small rural villages. Henderson Fowler recorded instances of fornication and illegitimacy at Alamance, North Carolina, in the 1880s, for example, with no indication that the women involved either left the village voluntarily or were expelled. "Geo Wilson guilty of basterdy with Tish Isley," Fowler wrote on one occasion, "& left for parts unknown Monday night June the 5. 1882." Wilson's flight and Miss Isley's plight were elements of a pattern that occurred with some frequency, though in this instance the aftermath was happier than usual. "Geo Wilson come home the 8th of June 1882," Fowler noted in his diary, "& married to Tish Isley the second Sunday in June by Rev J L Buck." A few years later, Fowler recorded another incident. "Cath Isley's child borne May 14th 1887," he wrote laconically. "Said to be J G Sharps."[5]

What subsequently happened to Cath Isley's private life is unknown, but if she and her child remained in the village, their lives were likely marked to some degree by the stigma attached to unwed mothers and their children. The experience of Sim Parsons, whose mother worked in a tobacco-bag factory in Durham, North Carolina, was probably representative of the general pattern. "Sim did try to go to school once," his wife told an interviewer in the 1930s, "but the other boys shunned him and teased him 'cause

3. NC *Labor Report* (1891), 153.

4. H. F. Schenck to Hambright Black, July 19, 1889, in H. F. Schenck Papers, Manuscript Department, Duke University Library, Durham, North Carolina.

5. Henderson Monroe Fowler Diary and Account Books, Vol. IV, in Southern Historical Collection, Louis R. Wilson Library, University of North Carolina at Chapel Hill.

he had no father and Sim is very sensitive about that. I think sometimes that he would've gone to school enough to have learned to read and write if it hadn't a-been for that."

Shame, ostracism, flight, and expulsion made the problem of "bad" women easy for moralists to deal with. The much larger number of women living outside the authority of fathers, husbands, or other male relatives presented more complicated problems, which moralists never solved to their own satisfaction. These women—widows, single "girls," abandoned wives—might be morally suspect, but the mills could not operate without their or their families' labor. The congregation of these women in the mills and villages nevertheless contributed to popular prejudices against mill folk.

"Mill girls"—teenagers and young unmarried women—were most affected by these attitudes. "You know," recalled Sallie Jane Stephenson, who began work at Anderson Mills about 1899, "when I was young some folks thought all cotton mill girls was loose. A crowd of us could be standin' on the fair grounds or some place like that payin' no attention to any man, and some fellow might walk up and say, 'Would one of you girls like to go for a ride?' I've cussed out many a man for askin' me that question."

This image probably contributed to the difficulties mills had recruiting labor, especially in the early years, when most workers were girls or young women. Mill officials apparently recognized the problem, for many of them acted to avoid the appearance of immorality in their mills. When Atlanta Cotton Mill opened in 1879, its announced policy was to employ "nothing but gentlemen" as supervisors and to take care that female workers were protected from sexual risk. "The girls are treated with kindness and consideration, and are thoroughly protected from insult," a reporter wrote of the mill's policies. "No loafers are permitted in or about the mill, and no man is admitted except on a ticket issued by the president or superintendent, who of course would not issue one to a drunken or improper person. The girls are just as safe in the mill as they could be anywhere."[6]

Such policies seemed to have effect. At least there is no evidence of sexual misconduct in the workplace. "We have a good Christian superintendent in our mill," a Catawba County mill employee wrote the North Carolina labor commissioner in 1896. "He is a man who looks after the welfare of his employees and does not keep any but good moral families, and therefore we have no trouble to keep good help." Similarly, Holland Thompson found

6. Atlanta *Constitution*, November 20, 1879.

that "many managers" of North Carolina mills were "strict moralists of an old-fashioned type who hold themselves responsible for the conduct of their operatives and attempt to control it in some particulars. Only those families who are willing to observe the regulations are kept, and the village often takes on a somewhat austere tone."[7]

Despite this caution on the part of mill owners, reports of misconduct involving supervisors and female workers circulated widely. The activities they described, however, were adultery or fornication, not sexual exploitation of employees. In 1911, for example, an editorial in the *Southern Textile Bulletin* lamented "the immorality of some superintendents and overseers with the women in their employment." That was "a growing evil," the writer reported, for "an unusually large number of cases have come to light in the past few months." He noted, "Scarcely a week has passed recently, but that some competent superintendent has not suddenly left his position" because he "got into trouble with a woman."[8]

No doubt most of these incidents involved activities of consenting adults outside the workplace. The folk interviewed spoke often, if generally, of village immorality but said virtually nothing of immoral conduct in the workplace. Two exceptions were Dewey and Gladys McBride, who began working in North Carolina mills in 1915 and 1920, respectively. They remembered that during World War I, when wages rose substantially and mill work became more attractive, a "girl" could get and keep a mill job only if she agreed to "go out" with the boss who hired and supervised her.

That condition for employment was obviously exceptional, as were the scattered incidents of indecency in the mills. In 1903, a foreman at Fulton Bag and Cotton Mills was arrested for "circulating obscene notes among some of the young girls in the mills." The arrest, made on the complaint of a sixteen-year-old girl to her father, caused "a very decided sensation in the mill district." After the incident came to light, many workers "severely criticized" the foreman "for permitting such indecent literature to be handed around among a lot of girls and boys." But before the complaint was made, "a large number" of employees had known of the notes, and "a number of girls" had read them without apparent offense.[9]

More important than such random incidents is the striking absence of evidence of direct forms of sexual exploitation in the workplace—demands

7. NC *Labor Report* (1896), 71; Holland Thompson, *From the Cotton Field to the Cotton Mill: A Study of the Industrial Transition in North Carolina* (New York, 1906), 165.
8. *Southern Textile Bulletin*, October 5, 1911.
9. Atlanta *Constitution*, September 2, 1903.

for sexual favors as the price for getting or keeping a job, or for transferring into better-paying or otherwise more desirable work. The lack of evidence suggests strongly that such demands were not widespread, as may be inferred from the circumstances of village life. The villages were small communities in which "affairs" of any kind could not be long concealed, and any effort to extort sexual favors from employees would have been not only exposed but made the subject of sensational scandal. Moreover, incidents involving nonsexual mistreatment of female workers suggest that even the appearance of sexual exploitation would have provoked mob violence. The risks were therefore overwhelming, as supervisors surely knew. It was much safer to find a woman who bestowed her favors voluntarily, in which case exposure meant swift flight and loss of employment, but not, usually, bodily harm.

Supervisors and employees did socialize a lot in and out of the mills. Most overseers and second hands, the levels of supervisors of immediate concern to workers, were former operatives and from the same socioeconomic class as workers. Status differences between them and their employees were small. Several of those interviewed, Flossie Moore Durham, for example, married overseers under whom they worked at the time of their marriages; and others reported familiar social relationships with supervisors. Lelia Bramblett, who went to work at Princeton Mill in Athens, Georgia, in the late 1880s, had fond memories of one of her overseers half a century after she had worked for him. "The boss was my sweetheart," she recalled. "Me and his sister run together, and I went with him 'til he got married. The reason I didn't marry him was that I didn't want him. . . . He was a heap older'n me."

Although sexual exploitation was rare in the workplace, petty forms of what is today called sexist behavior, especially flirting and sexually suggestive chatter on the part of male workers as well as supervisors, was probably a staple in the lives of unmarried female workers. This was a society of male prerogative and double standards in which men had some leeway in approaching unmarried women and in which unmarried women were assumed to be eager for compliments as well as marriage, and thus tolerant of at least some suggestiveness on the part of potential suitors. Congregation in the mills of young people who knew one another well encouraged not just the romancing that led to so many marriages between mill workers—Marjorie A. Potwin reported in the 1920s that a hundred such marriages had occurred over the years at Saxon Mills—but more casual familiarities as well.[10] Yet evidence of these familiarities, unlike that of the marriages, is scanty.

"USUALLY GOOD ORDER AND BUT LITTLE DRINKING"

Contemporary assessments of village morality varied widely. A decade after he began ministering to mill congregations in 1914, the Reverend Benjamin H. Smith reported that gambling and prostitution were common in mill communities and that authorities there were indifferent to the presence of professional gamblers and "traveling expert" prostitutes. "These immoral women have others make dates for them at specified places near the mill village," Smith wrote of the prostitutes. "Often the hotel near the mill becomes a debauched place because of this traveling element," and "many of the young men are ruined for life by this pernicious vice."[11]

In the fall of 1900, the Augusta *Chronicle* published a series of articles on living conditions among mill folk in that city, the exposures of which were more convincing because the paper was never unfriendly to mill interests. Based largely on information provided by John Chipman, an Episcopal minister active in the mill district, the articles detailed the kinds of poverty and social disorganization that characterized urban mill slums. There were scores of men and women in the district, the reporter wrote, who had separated from legal spouses and "without even the semblance of divorce" married others. Many folk of both sexes had done this "several times," and some of them had "three or four living husbands and wives." The number of desertions, usually of wives by husbands, was also "enormous" and, according to Chipman, was the cause of much of the "destitution and distress" in the district. "The favorite time for desertion," Chipman told the reporter, "is when the wife is in her most serious trouble and about to become the mother of the second or third babe."[12]

Other assessments were more positive. Holland Thompson thought "sexual immorality [was] not common" in the villages he visited in North Carolina; and investigators for the 1907–1908 labor study believed "the moral standard [was] high," especially in "country" villages, because per-

10. Marjorie A. Potwin, *Cotton Mill People of the Piedmont: A Study in Social Change* (New York, 1927), 74.
11. Benjamin H. Smith, "The Social Significance of the Southern Cotton Mill Community" (M.A. thesis, Emory University, 1925), 23–24.
12. Augusta *Chronicle*, September 2, 9, 16, 1900.

sons and families of known or suspected immorality were expelled by mill owners or pressured into leaving by village opinion. There was "usually good order and but little drinking" in the villages, the investigators wrote, and seldom any "need for a civil officer to make an arrest." Villagers "as a body," therefore, were "sober and well behaved."[13]

Mill owners often made what appear to be exaggerated claims of moral purity in their villages, but such claims might have been valid for some communities. "We exercise a strict discipline over the morals of all in the mills or connected with them in any way," one North Carolina owner said at the turn of the century, "do not allow man or woman to remain in the service of the company unless they are virtuous, honest and of good character— hence we have no better people, morally, in our section than the mill people in our employ." Publicists often echoed these claims. "There are no police in the mill villages and the order is excellent," August Kohn wrote in his report on South Carolina mills in 1907. "Loose morals, unfaithfulness or indecent living are not tolerated," he observed, and "it is quite in order" for villagers to ask officials to expel individuals or families for unbecoming conduct. "Sometimes the operatives themselves take matters in hand" and "discipline" wayward villagers. Still, Kohn admitted, "drinking of liquor and the resulting festivities" were problems, as were wife desertion and illegitimacy.[14]

These disparate assessments mirrored the variety of conditions. Overall, the villages and mill districts had a full measure of the social problems then ascribed to immorality and human weakness and today associated with poverty and social disorganization. The villages probably had more than a proportionate share of some of those problems, especially ones related to drinking and wife desertion. Most of the problems did or could disrupt family income and thereby upset the precarious state of material and social well-being. That, indeed, was their real significance.

"WITHOUT SOME KIND OF STANDARD, PEOPLE'S LIVES DETERIORATED."

To understand moral and social conditions in the villages, it is necessary to understand folk thought concerning morality. That thought is one of the fundamentals of folk identity, concerning on one level matters of social

13. Thompson, *From the Cotton Field to the Cotton Mill*, 167; *Senate Documents*, 61st Cong., 2nd Sess., No. 645, Vol. 1, p. 589.

14. Raleigh *News and Observer*, December 9, 1900; August Kohn, *The Cotton Mills of South Carolina* (Charleston, 1907), 177.

status and differentiation, and on another, questions of right and wrong, sin and virtue, and, ultimately, the nature of human nature. In social morality, and in turn cultural fundamentals, mill folk were indistinguishable from other plain folk—indeed in many respects from all other southerners.

Plain folk were uncomfortable with ambiguities of any sort, and thought of people in terms of good and bad. "Good" people were neighborly, morally conventional if not necessarily religious, and "clever" (in an earlier English sense of friendly or personable) as opposed to "curious" (eccentric and unfriendly). They shunned the sins of common concern—drinking, dancing, making and selling liquor, swearing in public or in sexually mixed company, "frolicking" with "sorry" folk, violating sexual conventions. They also lived according to prescribed social roles. Men worked and supported their families as best they could, disciplined their children, and controlled but did not beat their wives. Women were dutiful wives and mothers and lived more exacting moral lives.

These patterns of conduct were measures of social status. In the larger southern society, status derived from wealth, family, occupation, income, education, or some combination thereof, but plain folk were too much alike in those things to use them as sources of status distinction among themselves. Status is a matter of differentiation, and what set plain folk apart from one another, sharply so in their own calculation, was personal conduct. "People in the village [judge each other] by their ethical standards," Sybil V. W. Hutton wrote of Victor mill village in the 1940s; and her observations might aptly be applied to villages in the New South. "Among some, a woman is judged by how well she gets along with her husband and how conscientious she is about training her children to be 'good,'" Hutton explained. "The husband is judged by his sobriety, the way he provides for his family, and his attitude toward his wife and family—such as faithfulness." Standards, in other words, were highly conventional. "It is probably safe to say that most of the people in the village disapprove of card playing (associating it with gambling), dancing, rough language, drunkenness, and 'wild parties,'" Hutton continued. "The way the people uphold their standards is by social ostracism—not associating and not allowing their children to associate with those whose standards are lower."[15]

These were ideals, not actualities; for many villagers complained of their neighbors' conduct. "I just couldn't live on the other side of the mill again,"

15. Sybil V. W. Hutton, "Social Participation of Married Women in a South Carolina Mill Village" (M.A. thesis, University of Kentucky, 1948), 18.

one woman told Hutton of a newer, less desirable section of the village. "The people over there, or most of them, are just ignorant. They drink and smoke, even the women do, and even wash clothes on Sunday. You wouldn't believe it, but they do. They curse, and just don't know how to get along with people." Another woman had similar complaints. "Some of the people are nice, but the others are terrible," she told Hutton of folk in the "bad" section of the village. "When we lived over there, the people in front of us were so filthy the painters refused to go in and paint their house. They drank and smoked, made music and danced on up into the morning. I almost had a nervous breakdown. The children had lice and all kinds of diseases and it nearly ran me crazy trying to keep my children at the back of our house away from those children."[16]

These comments are revealing, suggesting what were normative standards while also indicating that many villagers fell short of those standards. The space between the normative and the actual constituted a fault line in village life. That line might divide one section of a village from another, as was apparently the case at Victor Mills, but more often it divided people according to conduct—life-style, we would say today—and sometimes according to elements of their very being, as in the case of the families at Victor Mills who were "just ignorant." Because men and women often differed in important matters of social conduct, a given fault line, such as that between drinkers and nondrinkers, might divide women and men, even husbands and wives.

The villages, like other places then and now, had "moral majorities," folk who were uncomfortable with the individual freedom of other people in areas of personal conduct about which they were sensitive and insecure. These folk nurtured the tendencies toward authoritarianism and social repressiveness that grew from southern culture and fed on the insecurities of folk themselves. They wanted a wide range of social activity proscribed. Thus, when the North Carolina labor commissioner asked workers in his state what could be done to improve the condition of the working classes, mill folk offered a variety of suggestions for constricting social behavior. A Cumberland County mill worker, for example, thought the biggest need was night schools in the villages. These, he explained, would keep children "off of the streets where the larger boys and loafers congregate and use vulgarity as well as profanity. We cannot expect any better of the small boy

16. *Ibid.*, 48.

than to become dissipated," this man told the commissioner, "when he has nothing to do but stroll about the streets at night with loafers who have no respect for themselves or any one else."[17]

Others had similar suggestions. "The making and smoking of cigarettes should be prohibited," urged a Roberdel operative, who also thought "there ought to be a general law prohibiting all young people from being on the streets, in stores, or at public gathering places after night[fall]." Another mill worker wanted the legislature to enact "a law to stop livery stables from hiring out teams on Sunday for boys to sport with."[18]

Plain folk and other workers outside the mills shared these concerns. Many workers inside and outside the mills also answered the commissioner's query with proposals for repressive measures and blamed the working classes for many of their own problems. There were too many loafers, one man complained; there was too much drinking and wasting of time and money, others insisted. "I know nothing that would so much improve the working people just now as the removal of all whiskey and intoxicants from the land," a Caswell County farm tenant told the labor commissioner. "So far as the wage-earners are concerned," a Lenoir County wage earner wrote, "nothing but economy and temperance (that is, abstinence from strong drink) will ever do the majority of them any good."[19]

The repressiveness inherent in these views manifested itself in many ways, among which was the exaggerated concern of girls and young women with their moral reputations. In this repressed society of the double standard, being "talked about"—having a questionable reputation—was something every "nice girl" feared, all the more so because of the popular image of "mill girls" as morally suspect. "You didn't go out with people you didn't know," Alice P. Evitt recalled. "We didn't; we never was allowed to." And the restrictions were efficacious. "Wasn't very many back in them days talked about," Mrs. Evitt added, " 'cause they tried to do right. They's raised right."

Others recalled this concern. "If you wasn't in by nine o'clock you was disgraced," Nannie Pharis remembered of her courting days in a Virginia mill village. "If you wore a skirt above your ankles you was [also] disgraced." And "nice girls"—or their parents—insisted that suitors who called on them leave at a respectable hour. To allow a beau to stay later than

---

17. NC *Labor Report* (1896), 191.
18. *Ibid.* (1904), 203, and (1900), 153.
19. *Ibid.* (1887), 125, and (1906), 129.

9:00 or 9:30 P.M., even on Saturday nights, recalled James W. Pharis, who married Nannie in 1911, was "awful"—"just terrible" for the girl's reputation. In the villages, as this attitude suggests, everyone knew what everyone else was doing, and that fact worked to enforce social conventions.

This concern for reputation was one reason so many villagers approved the regulations imposed on them. Pauline Phillips Griffith, whose family moved to Judson Mill in 1915, was one such villager. "The mill people [that is, the owners] had a good standard that the people had to live by," Mrs. Griffith recalled. "There was no roughnecks allowed in the village. They were choice people. You didn't even have to lock your doors. . . . They just simply wouldn't have anybody that wasn't the best type of people. And it was a good thing. Because without some kind of standard, people's lives deteriorated. They're just not up to par, and it affects communities in the ways they don't want to be affected. We had lots to be thankful for in that."

Another manifestation of the tendency toward repressiveness was the willingness of plain folk to endorse coercion in matters of social conduct. "Parents who don't send their children to school should be dealt with as criminals," a mechanic told the North Carolina labor commissioner in 1901. Another worker thought the state should have a law "compelling ablebodied men to work for a living"; still another wanted the legislature to "compel [all] young men to learn some trade." A man from Burke County supported legislation "to compel the wage-earner to hold his job, or, in other words, comply with his contract." No worker, this man thought, should be able to quit his job without giving fifteen days' notice. A Kings Mountain man would require "wage-workers [to] show a certificate of good morals and not be in the habit of drinking" in order to get a job. Thus only those with "good morals" could find employment.[20]

Perhaps it was this urge to coerce that prompted so many folk to ask Governor Blease for jobs in law enforcement and to equate law enforcement with coercion in personal conduct. "I have drank lots of Whiskey," a Laurens County man wrote Blease, listing his qualifications for a job as "Whiskey Constable." He stated: "I think I can Make you a good Constable. . . . I Know all the ropes how to catch up with a man who handles the stuff[.] I Know lots of Dives such as Gambling Whiskey and other low down things are going on." Others made similar requests. "I would like for you to Give Me a Job catching Whiskie Men and Gamblers and other Meanness

20. *Ibid.* (1901), 278, 284, (1900), 144, and (1906), 124, 125.

done in the State," one wrote Blease. "I have suprted [you] in the last to races and I think You aught to give me the Job[.] . . . [I]f you give Me a Job Please Send Me a Badge and Oblige."[21]

Such sentiments could eventuate in vigilantism. Thus, in Chester County, South Carolina, in the winter of 1888, a band of twenty-five young men calling themselves Jay Hawk Regulators was "organized for the purpose of purifying morals and regulating conduct in and about the neighborhood" of the Fishing Creek factory. One object of their concern was Louis Batton, "a good looking young man" who some months earlier had come to the factory from Rockingham, North Carolina. Batton "appeared to be a young man of great piety, and manifested deep interest in Sunday school and church work." He also became "enamored with Miss Nancy Kee, a pretty girl at the factory," and in January, 1888, the two were married. Shortly thereafter, word came that Batton already had a wife and three children in Rockingham, whereupon the Jay Hawk Regulators "took the matter in hand." On the night of February 10, "They called Batton out of his house, marched him off to the woods, stripped him to the waist and bound him to a pine tree. Batton begged piteously for mercy, but his appeals were unheard by the regulators, who deliberately gave him fifty lashes over the bare back with a rawhide, almost every stroke of the lash drawing the blood and invoking piteous howls of pain from the victim." When the mob released him, Batton left "for parts unknown," his new wife "almost heartbroken."[22]

At the village of Massachusetts Mills, a similar incident occurred in 1905, involving George Fitzpatrick. Arrested on the charge of wife beating, Fitzpatrick was seized from the arresting officer, "taken into the woods and stripped," and "whipped almost to insensibility by a mob of masked men." Before the beating, he was "harrangued by an oratorical member of the mob upon the evils of wife beating and general cussedness." The day afterwards, "A huge placard was hung, by unknown hands just outside the big gate at the Lindale mills, where all the hands could see it when they came out from work for dinner, reciting the crime, and also stating that the treatment accorded Fitzpatrick would be handed out to all other such characters around Lindale." The placard, which stated that wife beating and rowdy

21. C. P. White to Coleman L. Blease, May 28, 1911, W. D. Gunter to Blease, October 29, 1913, in Coleman L. Blease Papers, South Carolina State Archives.
22. Atlanta *Constitution*, February 11, 1888.

drunkenness had to stop in Lindale, was signed by "Jim Beatem," who identified himself as "King of the Kuklux Clan."[23]

"IT TAKES A MISTAKE OR TWO TO LEARN PEOPLE THAT THE BEST THING TO DO IS TO DO RIGHT."

If their attitudes encouraged plain folk to categorize people as good or bad, experience forced them to add a third category, "weak"—referring to "good" people who succumbed to temptation or the frailties of human nature. "Weak" relatives, especially, made an impression on folk attitudes, sometimes turning condemnation into intolerance but often also arousing compassion. Husbands who drank too much, beat or deserted their wives, or made and sold liquor; daughters who bore illegitimate children or refused to live with improvident or abusive husbands; ne'er-do-well sons who failed to work steadily, became violent, or broke the law; children of either sex who ignored parental advice or married "sorry" mates; and friends and neighbors who did any of these things were in every extended family or neighborhood and so had to be tolerated.

As victims of compulsions or problems they could not control, "weak" people were frequently objects of sympathy and understanding. A personal experience with "weakness" could be especially humanizing. "I'm not going to pertend I didn't sin once," said Ann Page, speaking of her premarital pregnancy. Mrs. Page began working in a North Carolina mill in the 1870s while she was a child, and worked off and on in the mills for most of her life. Looking back in old age, however, she made her "sin," not her work, the pivot of her life. Her experience made her tolerant of human weakness and led her over the years to help a number of women in the same situation. "I've jest took in many a pore gal," she said, "whose feelin's got a leap ahead of 'em 'cause the boy lied 'bout his'n, then he'd git scared plum to death an' run away; then the gal's paw an' maw was too good to know anything 'bout pore human nature an' got madder an' madder till they run her away from their home an' I'd take her in an' take keer of her till she had her baby."

It was refreshingly liberating. "I wouldn't a-missed my experience," Mrs. Page said. "I believes in experience, an' I believes I'se a better Christian 'cause I knows I'se weak as anybody. But I'se a Baptist an' goes to church regular. But I never could've helped my pore gals like I did if I didn't

23. *Ibid.*, March 10, 1905.

know jest how it were. You know, it takes a mistake or two to learn people that the best thing to do is to do right."

"I learned my lesson," the largehearted woman continued, putting a positive gloss on the experience. "Spite of ever' thing, lovin' is the finest thing can happen to us. You gits up in the mornin' an' you don't know an' don't keer whether you had any breakfus' or no. You starts to work, an' when you gits outdoors the sun shines brighter an' the air smells sweeter. Then you gits on to the mill an' starts work, an' 'stead of the spindles crackin' and bangin' down they soun's different to you, an' seems to fair play a tune."

Such generosity of spirit is everywhere rare, including among the plain folk, though there is some evidence the folk were more tolerant of illegitimacy than other southerners. "Sexual immorality is discounted to a greater extent among mill villagers," Liston Pope wrote of mill villagers in Gastonia two decades after the New South era ended, "and illegitimate children are generally accepted without serious penalty."[24] Pope interpreted and condemned that attitude as evidence of moral laxness, but it might have indicated a tolerance of spirit not always apparent to outsiders.

Not all folk shared that tolerance. For every Ann Page there were probably several Ida Maynards. Mrs. Maynard was born about 1880 into the family of a small North Carolina farmer, and at fifteen she married Peter Maynard, a landless farmer who "worked out" a fifty-acre farm of his own. Mrs. Maynard was a "righteous" person by her own reckoning, though others would probably call her self-righteous. In an interview in the 1930s, she came across as a woman whose lifetime of repeated tragedies and disappointments had turned her into an embittered shrew. At sixteen her oldest daughter, Sarah, became pregnant, and Mrs. Maynard had none of the sympathy for her that humanized Mrs. Page. "I've wished many a time that God had took her when she was little," she said of her daughter more than a quarter century after the pregnancy. "I tried to make the best of it but the disgrace was almost more than I could bear. I hated Sarah and I hated Thomas [Sarah's illegitimate son] from the minute I found out that my daughter had fell so low." Indeed, Thomas was "the living proof of [Sarah's] sin," and though he was a grown man at the time of the interview, Mrs. Maynard still thought him "as hardheaded and stubborn as I expected him to be" before he was born. "I still hate him," she said.

This was not the extent of her tragedy and bitterness. Mrs. Maynard's

---

24. Liston Pope, *Millhands and Preachers: A Study of Gastonia* (New Haven, 1942), 66.

second son grew up to be "too lazy to move" and not "worth the salt that went into his bread." Moreover, his wife gave birth to a child four months after their marriage, and that, too, was unforgivable. "I hate her," Mrs. Maynard said of her daughter-in-law; "she had no business having a baby like that." Her third son, Bill, was at the time of the interview serving a second prison term for robbery and other crimes, compounding her embitterment. "I hope he'll stay in prison the rest of his life," Mrs. Maynard said. "I hate him too." Even her fourth (and youngest) son, who had died a few years previously in an accident, did not escape her bitterness. "He might of turned out like Bill," she said. "I'd rather he was dead." As for her youngest daughter, recently married at sixteen, Mrs. Maynard "believe[d] she would of turned out like Sarah did if she hadn't of married so young." Even her late husband, whom she professed to love, did not escape her hatefulness. "He died a member of the church," she said of him, "but I'm afraid he died in sin. He cussed me out just a few weeks before he died."

"PELZER S.C. IS NOTHING MORE OR LESS THAN AN OPEN BARROOM."

The contrasting examples of Ida Maynard and Ann Page illustrate not only the range of folk attitudes on a vital subject but the prevalence of "immoral" conduct as well. In spite of the efforts of officials and the stern values of most folk, the mill villages had significant social problems. The cause, or manifestation, of many of those problems was drinking, or drinking too much.

Mill owners prohibited the buying, selling, and consuming of alcohol wherever they could, but liquor was apparently available in or about all the villages and mill districts. In the vicinity of every village, it seems, were blind tigers and other places in varying degrees of nonconformity to the law where liquor, licit or illicit, was available in whatever form and amount one desired. The villages and their environs were not "open" places in the manner of Wild West towns in the old movies. Probably none of them was what the town of Fort Valley, Georgia, was alleged to be in 1889. There, according to a newspaper report, in spite of a countywide prohibition ordinance, "Anyone who has the money and will announce themselves in favor of the sale [that is, the purchase of whiskey], from fourteen years old up, can buy just as much as they desire." The report read, "The vile stuff is sold . . . in quantities and a man can find a drink of whiskey for sale much easier than he can find a pound of country butter."[25]

25. Atlanta *Constitution*, January 26, 1889.

The balance between several factors determined the situation in most villages—state and local laws regulating or prohibiting the selling and consumption of liquor, the diligence of law enforcement officials, and the hoary custom in the South of making, selling, and consuming untaxed bootleg whiskey. During the New South era, bootlegging confronted the spreading Prohibition movement. By the 1880s, Georgia and the Carolinas had local option laws permitting counties and towns to ban alcohol, and more and more communities took advantage of those laws. That development served the purpose of mill owners, who wanted to keep liquor from their villages and operatives. By the time Georgia and North Carolina enacted statewide prohibition laws in 1907 and 1908, respectively, more than three-quarters of the counties in those states were already dry, and liquor was increasingly difficult to get. A system of state dispensaries made the situation in South Carolina distinctive, but even there local option and illicit liquor presented the same combination of problems found elsewhere in the New South.

These developments compounded the difficulties of mill folk who wanted to drink. Prohibition laws reduced the availability of alcohol and closed the places where it could be openly and legally consumed. These laws certainly reduced the amount and frequency of drinking but had other consequences as well. They drove drinkers into furtive places where other forms of illegal activity might also flourish. One thing the laws did not do was to stop determined folk from getting a drink.

What were probably typical conditions in villages near towns and cities can be discerned from letters mill folk wrote Governor Blease. "I heard two men talking," Mrs. S. J. Vaughn wrote the governor from Sampson mill village at Greenville in 1914. "They said they could order as large amount of whisky as they wanted rite here in Greenville [illegible word] at the wholesale house & they had seen them sell it in the resterrants rite in the presents of 2 Police[.] I tell you the big men are deeling in the stuff all the time[.] [T]his place you call Greenville is perfectly rotten[.] [T]hey pay the Police a little hush money and all they can drink & that settles it[.] [T]hey have a powder in the drug store they can put in the lickor that Kills the sent."

The situation, Mrs. Vaughn suggested, was part of a larger problem. "We have not got any officers fit for a heathern town," she told the governor, and other mill villages, she felt, were no better. "Pelzer S.C. is nothing more or less than an open barroom," she wrote. "The officers there have got scared or careless I dont Know which[.] Police Cox's son cut up an old man all to pieces in his face & he Cox would not even arrest him[.] . . . [Y]ou send some trust worthy Detectives here that cant be bought over & you will see for your Self it is surprising." She continued: "I do not think if the rich Merchants are going to be aloud to Sell lickor & make a big profit to pile up dollars on top of dollars the poor man ought to have a little showing too not that I am in favor of the poison stuff but the poor man has as much right as the rich man or he ought to have."[26]

The letter is revealing. Pelzer was one of the model villages, ostensibly well policed, socially harmonious—and free of liquor. And even though Mrs. Vaughn was something of a snoop and misanthrope, other letters to Blease substantiate her allegations. "Here in West Pelzer is a Bad Plase to get Whiskey and also Cider," W. E. Summey had written Blease two years earlier, "and the cider that is being sold here in this Plase Makes father drunk every day in the Week. I seen the Police here this Week and told him the condinion. I am told that the Big Stores of town sends Whiskey out in dray Wagons and I am told that even the overseers in the Mill seels Whiskey and I have told Mr Cox the Police all a Bout it and he dont seem to care a dern who seels Whiskey and Who dont. [F]or Gods Sacke do something."[27]

These letters suggest not just official indifference to illegal activity but corruption as well. "I was living at Pelzer at the time they were 10 or 12 Boys an men Caught gambling," Hamp Fullbright wrote Blease, offering what might be evidence of official collusion, or at least indifference to an injustice. "I Wer Bording With the Poliece and they thout i were the Wane [one] that told one [on] them[.] [T]hay Wer mad and tried evry Way to get me en to sompthing." Fullbright even moved away from the village for a while, but at the time of a return visit, trouble developed. "A croud of these same felers Went and Swore i was ther and sold 1 quart Whisky," he wrote. "The Poliece sed he Wante me to come down the next morning and Wee Wood look into hit[.] [T]hey were just mad and did hit fer spite and through males [malice][.] [H]it Went one [on] and i got Mr Dagnell [a lawyer or official?][.] [H]e sed they cold not do eny thing With me[.] [O]f corse he Wer talking for his end of hit[.] [B]ut I wer not guilty and i dont think you Will punish Me for hit." Fullbright had, however, been convicted, which occasioned his plea to Blease. Since he could not pay his fine, he faced a term on the chain gang.[28]

Blease received other complaints about drinking and indifferent police. In the Spartanburg County file of the governor's papers, for example, there is a petition signed by 144 people from "Arkwright Mill Village and the lower end of South Church Street" asking him "to close three 'Near Beer

26. Mrs. S. J. Vaughn to Blease, January 5, 1914, in Blease Papers.
27. W. E. Summey to Blease, July 13, 1912, in Blease Papers.
28. Hamp Fullbright to Blease, March 21, 1911, in Blease Papers.

Houses' just outside of Spartanburg City limits on South Church Street car line, established here to evade the city laws, as there is no police protection here." About three-fifths of the petitioners were women, which seems significant in view of the fact that women folk engaged in so little activity of a political nature. The petition was on Arkwright Mills stationery and was forwarded to Blease by J. R. Dean, a mill official. "The drunkenness and rowdyism last Saturday night was the worst that I ever saw here," Dean wrote the governor, "and I have lived here for five years being secretary of mill."[29]

This petition, too, is revealing. Since it was on company stationery, it almost certainly originated with mill officials, probably Dean himself. (Mill secretaries were administrative assistants to chief executive officers.) It therefore shows that mill officials could not always control drinking and its consequences ("rowdyism") among their employees—could even at times be desperate enough to motivate mill folk to appeal to Blease, the political bête noire of mill owners. The petition also shows two of the common devices for sidestepping the prohibition ordinances: locating saloons "just outside" dry jurisdictions and just beyond mill villages, and establishing near-beer houses as fronts for the sale of prohibited substances (one could not become drunk on near beer). The petition suggests other things, too: that police officers were not always subservient to mill officials and might subvert their efforts to control drinking; that many mill folk wanted more, not less, police regulation in the villages and prohibition laws enforced; and that drinking and not drinking were bases of social contention in the villages.

These points bear further illustration. "I would like to call your attention to the facts that there is a Great Deal of Gambling going on here Just out side the City Limit," J. R. Gosnell, a "citisin" of Arkwright mill village wrote Blease in 1913. "It can be caught Most anytime on Saturday afternoon and Sunday Most all day Just in 200 to 300 yards of the vilage of Arkwright Mills[.] [T]his Matter has been reported both to Sheriff White and Rural Policeman Vernon Som 2 Months ago[.] [T]hey Promised to attend to it but up to Now if they have Ever Ben down here only the one time the day it Was Reported No one Knows Any thing about it[.] We have no Police Protection here at all Except Rural [policeman] and dont think he Ever come to see any thing about Same."[30]

Complaint followed complaint. "It be comes Some ones duty to inform

29. The petition is in the 1911 Spartanburg County folder in Blease Papers.
30. J. R. Gosnell to Blease, July 21, 1913, in Blease Papers.

you that there are as Much as three Concerns at Spartanburg [illegible word] that are Selling Whisky Beer Ect. for a livelyhood In open defiance of all Law," T. C. Nichols of Saxon Mills wrote Blease. "They are going to ruin all the boys of Saxon Mill Village if Not Stoped. It seems like the officers here cant do Nothing[.] If You Will Send a private Detective he can work [?] the thing in no time[.] Lots of familys are on Suffernce Whare the Men of them Spends all they Make [illegible word]. These concerns paying [charging?] $1.00 per pint for the low grade stuff."[31]

Occasionally, mill officials joined the complainants. "We are having no end of trouble at the mill on account of the selling of liquor to the operatives and drunkenness is prevalent," President B. E. Wilkins of Mary Louise Mills, also in Spartanburg County, wrote, asking the governor to appoint a magistrate for the locality to help correct the situation.[32]

"BOOTLEG WHISKEY WAS PLENTIFUL, AND I LIKED IT MIGHTY WELL."

Drinking, at least among men and grown boys, was perhaps more extensive than among workers in other occupations. Abel Starnes, who went to work in a mill in Columbia, South Carolina, during World War I, recalled what was apparently a representative situation. "I was only seventeen years old, and wild, too, I reckon," he said. "Them days, bootleg whiskey was plentiful, and I liked it mighty well." By his own admission, Starnes "wasted" all the money he had on illegal liquor.

So, too, did many other workers. Historian W. E. Woodward, who grew up in the 1880s at Graniteville, where the company prohibited liquor and drinking, remembered that operatives went to the "suburb" of Madison, half a mile away, to do their imbibing. There were three saloons in Madison, Woodward recalled, and liquor was plentiful and cheap. "Saturday was pay day," he wrote, "and the big drinking took place that night. For many a mill hand getting drunk on Saturday night was a regular custom. Around midnight the noisy topers could be heard coming home from Madison, screeching and singing, sometimes quarreling and fighting." For more discreet folk, the saloons had deliverymen who went about Graniteville "quietly taking orders and delivering the whisky." According to Woodward, "many women bought liquor in this manner."[33]

31. T. C. Nichols to Blease, August 23, 1911, in Blease Papers.
32. B. E. Wilkins to Blease, July 11, 1911, in Blease Papers.
33. W. E. Woodward, *The Way Our People Lived: An Intimate American History* (New York, 1944), 334.

In the mill district of nearby Augusta, Georgia, where drinking was legal, similar conditions existed. There were "8 or 10 bar-rooms" in that district at the turn of the century, all of them, or so the Reverend John Chipman thought, tempting mill folk into lives of "billiards," "lust," and "political debauchery." Yet Chipman's understanding of the appeal of barrooms could well have been learned by Prohibitionists and other moralists. "The bar-room is the poor man's club house, his parlor, his theatre, his music club," Chipman said, and despite its evil influence, mill folk went there because such a place "fill[ed] real needs" that they had no alternative ways of satisfying.[34]

Drinking itself was one of those needs. For many men (and some women, too) drinking was the one "vice" they permitted themselves—even their only indulgence in pleasurable public activity besides the use of tobacco or snuff. Plain folk did not much engage in organized recreation or socially diverting group activity, for they tended to view such things as juvenile or morally questionable. For many men, however, drinking was acceptable—and manly—especially if done with discretion and not to excess, despite the protests of nagging wives and censuring neighbors. Will Conner, a North Carolina sharecropper, pointedly expressed the views of such men in an interview in the 1930s. "I drink licker, if that's sinful," Conner said. "I don't what-you-might-say get drunk, but I'll tell anybody I take a drink when I please. It's the only pleasure I got, all I ever had. I never went to a movin' picture in my life. I never went to a fair but once or twice, never went to school none, never hunted nor fished, never went to Norfolk and Richmond like other folks, never done nothin' but hard work all my life." And, he added, "I love the taste o' licker."

This was probably the attitude of typical drinkers. They were not drunkards, and certainly not alcoholics, though they might sometimes drink to excess. They drank because it was pleasurable in multiple ways. Liquor was cheap, available, of known effect, and socially acceptable among other drinkers, and drinking could be done away from women, mill officials, and prying neighbors.

The problem was that many drinkers lacked the self-control that made these considerations socially valid. There seem to have been a few chronic alcoholics in most villages, many of them "mill daddies" of classic stereotype. Much more important as a source of social concern, however, were the large numbers of grown boys and young men who drank to excess

34. Augusta *Chronicle*, September 9, 1900.

whenever the occasion presented itself and who used drinking as a prelimi-
nary to and excuse for boisterous, sometimes riotous, and occasionally even
deadly activity that intruded upon other folk and caused a variety of social
difficulties. The story of Enoch Ball, who began working in a North Carolina mill at eleven early in the twentieth century, illustrates one of the
patterns. When he was eighteen, Ball left home and moved into a boardinghouse, and promptly "got to runnin' 'round with a hard drinkin' set of mill
boys" of the sort found in many villages. "I drank considerable those days,"
he recalled. "I could get whiskey at 14 different saloons. We boys used to
make the rounds of them all, drinkin' at each one. A lot of drunken factory
workers used to gather round the Southern depot with their guns. They'd
shoot at the feet of the people that would pass by, 'makin' them dance,' they
called it. . . . At night, drunken crowds used to go up town and tear down
awnin's, and do other devilment. Nobody was safe in those days, even in
jail. Great big fat women would get drunk on the town square."

Ball's story had a common ending. He soon experienced a religious conversion, saw the error of his ways, and gave up drinking. That was not
always the case, however. Spurred along by excessive drinking, youthful
escapades could end in violence and crime and the consequences thereof.
When Leo Chumley was orphaned as a youth, for example, he went to
Enoree, South Carolina, to work in a cotton mill, and took up with the kind
of boys with whom Enoch Ball had associated. "I was thrown in all kinds of
people and became careless whom I Kept company with," Chumley wrote
Governor Blease of his experience. "You know how boys are at Mills when
they have no parents." By his own account, young Chumley drifted from
rowdyism to crime, and his letter to Blease was a plea for parole from
the Spartanburg County chain gang where he was serving a two-year
sentence.[35]

"MY HUSBAND IS A MAN THAT TAKES TOO MUCH STRONG DRANK."

As Chumley's misfortune suggests, the significance of drinking among mill
folk stemmed from the social problems it created or signified. In conjunc-
tion with certain features of folk temperament—tendencies toward psychological frustration, social irresponsibility, and compulsive violence, for example—drinking could cause or occasion great tragedy. Accounts of violent

35. Leo Chumley to Blease, June 23, 1913, in Blease Papers.

incidents involving mill folk almost invariably note that one or more of the participants were drinking, often to the point of drunkenness and unknowing irresponsibility. One night in 1905, for example, Walton Gulley, who worked at Whittier Mills near Atlanta, and another youth were arrested and charged with assaulting Ida and Belle Collins, two teenage girls who worked at the same mill. Gulley and his companion denied the charge as well as suggestions that they were too drunk to remember the incident. "We were both drinking some," Gulley admitted after his arrest, "but we were not so drunk that we did not know what we were doing."[36] Whether this was truly their condition or not is unknown. Gulley and his companion were almost lynched for attempting to waylay two girls who not only resisted their clumsy advances but knew who they were and promptly identified them to authorities.

Equally instructive was an incident involving Joseph Meisheimer, a weaver who worked in mills in North Carolina and Virginia. One night in 1907 after he had been drinking, Meisheimer went late to supper at his boardinghouse in a Lynchburg, Virginia, mill village only to find that his landlady had "allowed another boarder to occupy his seat at the supper table." Thereupon, according to a newspaper account, "Words followed and Meisheimer drew his gun and began firing." He shot twice, one bullet killing his landlady and the other "probably fatally" wounding her mother.[37]

In another violent incident, two young men, Jim Culpepper and John Riley, were walking down the street in Columbus, Georgia, one night in 1904 when they encountered Jim Howard and two of his friends. For unknown reasons, Howard, who had been drinking, turned to Riley and said, "I don't like you anyhow, and am going to kill you." With that statement, "He drew a long dirk from his pocket" and "badly" cut both Riley and Culpepper. Culpepper ran to his home nearby and grabbed his shotgun, with Howard in pursuit. Thus armed, Culpepper turned and confronted Howard, who, with the dirk in his hand, continued his advance despite Culpepper's warnings to stop. When Howard reached point-blank range, Culpepper shot him "almost through and through with a big charge of large shot." Both Culpepper, twenty-two, and Howard, eighteen, were mill operatives.[38]

36. Atlanta *Constitution*, November 9, 1905.
37. *Ibid.*, June 30, 1907.
38. *Ibid.*, December 5, 1904.

Such incidents occurred with frequency, and much of their significance stemmed from the problems they created for women and children. "I'm in distress as to Blind tiger Wiskey My Husband is drinking," Mrs. Dahlia Thrower of Ridgeville wrote Governor Blease in 1913. "I know he is trying as hard as he Can to Stop [drinking] for I know he is a good true man to me." But illicit whiskey was everywhere, and her husband could not resist it. "I beg you for help to try and help us get rid of this nuisance," Mrs. Thrower, who had five children, pleaded, *"for it is ruining my home."*[39]

This was a widespread problem. "The Last Week of Aug all the Mill in Greenville Stope and My husband is a Man that takes too much Strong Drank," Rosa Adams of Greenville wrote Blease in 1914, "and when he is Under the influence of Drank he can Be Persaded to do anything." In such a state, her husband, Claud J. Adams, who worked at Poe Mills, had committed an act of "Larnsey," for which he had been sentenced to ten months on the chain gang, from which Mrs. Adams asked that he be paroled.[40]

The problem these women faced was that drinking and its consequences had deprived them of the earnings of their family breadwinner. Mrs. Adams and her children had "no one to look to for healp" while her husband did his time on the gang. Ten months, she pleaded with Blease, "is a long time for a Lone Woman to hafter Struggle Along With 2 children And No Money and home."

Some women suffered more than Mrs. Adams. Mary Abbott had been working in North Carolina mills for several years when she married John Abbott, also an operative, not long after the turn of the twentieth century. Sometime thereafter, John "took to drinkin' . . . and spendin' his money for whiskey," and Mrs. Abbott "had to keep the house goin' " by working in the mill to support herself and their three children. "After drink got a holt on him, [John] never was much good," Mrs. Abbott said, recalling her problems. "He got mean to me and the girls. I've took a lot from him." The Abbotts had fights in front of their children and neighbors; and Mrs. Abbott finally did something few mill women did lightly: she left her husband. "Twan't only whiskey done it [to John]," she recalled, "but dope too."

The battering of wives and children, which was also a problem among mill folk, was often associated with drinking. The case of W. D. Hoffman of Atlanta, the father of "a family of little girls," illustrates the frequent link between drinking and family violence. "He not only mistreats Mrs.

39. Mrs. Dahlia Thrower to Blease, June 11, 1913, in Blease Papers.
40. Rosa Adams to Blease, February 24, 1914, and Claud J. Adams to Blease, April 4, 1914, in Blease Papers.

Hoffman," read an account of Hoffman's trial for wife and child abuse, "but he makes the little girls work in the mills and takes the money to buy whiskey with. After he has gotten drunk on his children's hard-earned money, he goes home and whips out the whole establishment." Many such instances appear in the record. In 1905, officer James M. Gloer of Atlanta "arrested and prosecuted . . . nine fathers of minor children" for "not working and properly caring for their families, some of them drinking and even taking the money earned by the children and drinking it up."[41] In popular thought—and in police consciousness—this problem was especially prevalent among mill folk, and for that reason probably most of the nine cases involved mill workers.

Women had various ways of dealing with drunkard husbands, none altogether satisfactory. Some saw drinking as an issue pitting women against men, and wanted to eliminate it as a means of controlling men. Mrs. T. H. Dent of Lexington, South Carolina, seems to have had such a view. "I have ofton thought that if you new every thing a bout it you Would Stop it," Mrs. Dent wrote Governor Blease in 1911 concerning "the Whiskey Trafic" in her neighborhood. "I doo hope that you Will look a little deeper after the matter and stop it as I am a Wife an a Mother an I know that there is Whiskey Sold a round Lexington S C[.] I dont think it is rite fore the men of Lexington Co to Vote a dry ticket and then break theare own law that they have Made[.] I have known men and boys to go to lexington Sober and come back home drunk and that is why I know that they got the Whiskey there." Mrs. Dent continued: "I trust that you will stop it[.] [O]h yes I wont to ask you if it is lawful fore the merchants to Sell that So called cider as they are doing out heare[.] [I]t is beaing Sould and so is that Stuff they call ncare beare[.] I dont think they aught to Sell eney thing that Will make a man drunk."[42]

Other women, Luella Thomas of Atlanta, for example, had their husbands arrested for brutality and lack of support. "This man is my husband," Mrs. Thomas told the judge hearing the charges she brought against J. J. Thomas in 1904. "We have four little children, the eldest of whom is only 13 and the youngest 3 years of age. I have worked so hard to keep them up that my health is broken. The two eldest have had to go to work in the hosiery mill. This man who calls himself my husband has been away from home for four months. During that time he hasn't given me a cent of

41. Atlanta *Constitution*, September 19, 1901, January 1, 1906.
42. Mrs. T. H. Dent to Blease, April 18, 1911, in Blease Papers.

money. . . . I have to wash and milk cows for a living. I even have to wash for negroes sometimes and I milk eleven cows twice a day." For neglect of his family, Thomas, who "loafed about the streets day and night, drinking mean whiskey," was convicted of vagrancy and sentenced to the chain gang, which is what Mrs. Thomas asked of the court.[43]

Wilma Cline had a different reaction to her own drunkard husband. Born into a mill family at Gaffney, South Carolina, Wilma went to work in a mill about 1908 when she was nine years old. After she married, her husband began drinking, and she simply ran him off. "I don't care nothin' about married life," she later said of the experience. "No siree, no married life for me when a man is all the time a-suckin' a bottle instead o' bringing home something to eat. When that happens I'm ready to quit. Some women will hang onto them for years, talkin', coaxin', and beggin' them to quit [drinking]. I look at it this way: If they aim to do better they'll do it without somebody wearing themselves out tellin' 'em to. If I got to go out and make the livin' for the family I don't want some drunken man a-lyin' 'round to help spend it. That's what I told mine and he got out."

HE "JUST DRANK ON TILL HE DIED."

Why was drinking so much of a problem for so many mill folk? Alcohol was cheap, available, and familiar, and a quick way of drowning one's cares. In the world of plain folk, drinking, even to excess, was also a way of demonstrating manhood. It was a largely male activity, and morally forbidden, and as such a means of expressing one's contempt for the carpings of women and moralists. It was, similarly, a way of rebelling against employers, of flouting their regulations and asserting independence. Moreover, for people whose social codes were strict and repressive, drinking provided a way of excusing otherwise inexcusable behavior. In these senses, drinking and its consequences—carousing and various forms of unaccustomed assertiveness—were functional and largely harmless acts of release (unless the men involved spent too much of family income reaching their happy state).

Plain folk were not a permissive people. On the contrary, the use even of tobacco and snuff they regarded as a sign of weakness if not sin; and drinking alcohol in any amount, respectable folk believed, was sin for men and disgrace for women. Folk therefore never socialized the use of alcohol—that is, they never contained drinking within effective social conventions.

43. Atlanta *Constitution*, October 16, 1904.

Even moderate drinking had to be done furtively if the drinker wanted to remain respectable. This encouraged the feelings of guilt or shame that come from violating a social norm, and most drinkers probably regarded drinking as a sign of their own inadequacy as human beings. This in turn intensified the problems that caused them to drink in the first place.

Since drinking was perceived as a sin rather than a social problem, the community had no machinery (and indeed, no desire) for dealing with it unless one counts the exhortations heaped upon abusers and alcoholics to cease their sinful ways. This indeed was part of the larger significance of alcohol abuse—it revealed in stark form the inability of folk communities to cope with social problems except by condemning and shunning "sinners." Such mechanisms, if they had ever worked, were not effective in the modernizing world the folk encountered in the New South; and in this and related areas of social concern, the welfare programs of mill paternalists did more to reinforce old attitudes than to devise new ways of addressing a problem of growing significance.

Mill folk—drinkers and their women folk alike—bore the cost of this misfortune. In the villages, the limits of moralizing as a solution to social problems were dramatically revealed. It is therefore easy to admire the fortitude if not the wisdom of those folk who endured without condemnation the stupors of those they loved and knew not how to help. "He never give me no trouble about goin' off when he was drinkin', or gettin' put in jail," Addie Gaines said of her husband. "He always brought his liquor home and kept on a-drinkin' till he got where he couldn't make out to reach for the bottle any more, then he'd sleep it off." He "just drank on till he died."

12

HEALTH

The villages were ecological settings as well as places to live, and major influences on the physical quality of life. On the farm, plain folk were among the unhealthiest groups of people in the United States, and though the nature and incidence of their maladies changed as they moved to the mills, the state of their physical well-being was not dramatically altered. That state derived not from sharecropping or cotton milling but from elemental factors of environment and life-style. When the Cotton Kingdom was peopled with whites and blacks in the generation after 1810, a combination of ecological and cultural factors combined to create for about a century in the southeastern United States the most disease-ridden environment over so large an area and for so long a time in all American history. The diseases of Africa, Europe, and North America came together and flourished in the warm, wet climate of the South, and poor blacks and whites were the chief victims. Folk endured a host of contagious, parasitic, insect-borne, and filth-related diseases, most of them chronic rather than acute, that undermined their health, sapped their energy, and encouraged the lethargy, anemia, and sallow-skinned appearance of the "poor white" stereotype.[1]

1. For a modern overview, see "Parasitism in Southeastern United States: A Symposium," *Public Health Reports*, LXX (1955), 957–75. For an earlier discussion, see John M. Swan,

All of these diseases—malaria, hookworm, pellagra, tuberculosis, typhoid fever, and the like—depend for their existence and perpetuation on specific features of environment and life-style. Malaria, for example, requires warm weather, *Anopheles* mosquitoes, and numerous pools of stagnant water. This type of mosquito breeds only in stagnant water and has a flying range of about a mile. The spread of the disease requires a unique interaction between mosquitoes and people. The malaria parasite enters the human body only through the bite of an infected mosquito, which acquires the parasite only by biting an infected person. Once deposited in its human host, the parasite lives only a short time unless it reenters the digestive tract of an *Anopheles* mosquito; this continued transition from man to mosquito and back is necessary to perpetuate the disease.[2]

The situation is much the same with hookworm. The worms (*Uncinaria americana*) lodge in the human intestines, where the females lay thousands of eggs. The eggs cannot hatch in the human body, however, and are discharged in feces. In a favorable environment of warm, moist, sandy soil, the eggs hatch. The larvae feed on bacteria and evolve into tiny, threadlike worms that die unless they find their way back into a human host. This they accomplish by boring through pores or hair follicles in tender areas of bare feet, producing a tingling sensation plain folk called "ground itch" or "dew poison." Hookworm disease thus occurs only where soil and rainfall are ideal and people go barefooted in areas where they deposit their feces.[3]

Typhoid fever is the product of bacilli that multiply in the human body, are discharged in feces and urine, and die unless they reenter a human host by being swallowed. Outside the body, the bacilli thrive in contaminated water and milk supplies, and are carried from place to place by houseflies. The disease thus exists only where living conditions are grossly unsanitary.

"Tropical Diseases and Health in the United States," *Southern Medical Journal*, IV (1911), 497–507.

2. See James R. Young, "The South and Malaria, 1900–1930: Social and Economic Consequences" (M.A. thesis, University of North Carolina, 1969); and H. R. Carter, "The Malaria Problem of the South," *Public Health Reports*, XXXIV (1919), 1927–35. On malaria and *Anopheles* mosquitoes, see William R. Horsfall, *Mosquitoes: Their Bionics and Relation to Disease* (New York, 1972), 44–307; and American Association for the Advancement of Science (AAAS), *A Symposium on Human Malaria with Special Reference to North America and the Caribbean Region*, ed. Forest R. Moulton (Washington, D.C., 1941).

3. Greer Williams, *The Plague Killers* (New York, 1969), 41–47; Asa C. Chandler, *Hookworm Disease: Its Distribution, Biology, Epidemiology, Pathology, Diagnosis, Treatment and Control* (New York, 1929); George Dock and Charles C. Bass, *Hookworm Disease: Etiology, Pathology, Diagnosis, Prognosis, Prophylaxis, and Treatment* (St. Louis, 1910). On soil type and hookworm, see Donald L. Augustine, "Studies and Observations on Soil Infestation with Hookworm in Southern Alabama from October 1923 to September 1924," *American Journal of Hygiene*, VI (1926), supplement, 63–79.

Amoebic dysentery, after malaria "the most widespread of all the endemic tropical diseases" in the New South, is also a product of unsanitary living, as are tuberculosis, typhus fever, and roundworm. These and other environmentally related diseases peaked in the spring and summer months of the New South era, when conditions were ideal. The sickness rate in twenty-four mill villages in South Carolina in 1917 was thus twice as high in May and June as in November and December.[4]

Insects were a major problem. In 1912, for example, a team of medical researchers looking for the cause of pellagra investigated the insect population of Spartanburg County in the heart of the mill region. They found mosquitoes "to a greater or less[er] degree" everywhere, though the county was "almost entirely free from malaria." The housefly "was present everywhere and was usually extremely numerous," and stable flies were "exceedingly abundant and generally distributed." Cockroaches, rats, and mice were likewise ubiquitous, as were cats and dogs, "practically always heavily infested with their respective fleas." At the village of Inman Cotton Mills, "practically every house" had bedbugs, and "practically every child" was or had once been infested with head lice.[5]

The most common of the filth-carrying insects was the housefly, and mill villages, like farm sites, swarmed with them. The villages in Spartanburg County had "no regulations regarding the keeping of domestic animals, including hogs." Cows were "pastured indiscriminately about streets and village lots," where "their droppings [were] a source, sometimes a prolific one, of fly breeding," and hogs were "frequently confined to small yards or pens" that "too often, [were] unsanitary in the extreme and highly attractive to house and blow flies." In Rome, Georgia, another mill center, health investigators in 1916 counted a thousand open-surface privies and "several

4. L. L. Lumsden, "Causation and Prevention of Typhoid Fever," *Public Health Bulletin No. 51* (Washington, D. C., 1912), 5; W. W. Cort, "Recent Investigations of the Epidemiology of Human Ascariasis," *Journal of Parasitology*, XVII (1931), 121–44; Marian Pearsall, "Some Behavioral Factors in the Control of Tuberculosis in a Rural County," *American Review of Respiratory Diseases*, LXXXV (1962), 200–10; R. E. Dyer, "The Control of Typhus Fever," *American Journal of Tropical Medicine*, XXI (1941), 163–83; William H. Deaderick and Lloyd Thompson, *The Endemic Diseases of the Southern United States* (Philadelphia, 1916), 399; Dorothy Wiehl and Edgar Sydenstricker, "Disabling Sickness in Cotton Mill Communities of South Carolina in 1917," *Public Health Reports*, XXXIX (1924), 1419.

5. Allan H. Jennings and W. V. King, "An Intensive Study of Insects as a Possible Etiologic Factor in Pellagra," in J. F. Siler, P. E. Garrison, and W. J. MacNeal, *Pellagra: First Progress Report of the Thompson-McFadden Pellagra Commission* (New York, 1917), 287 and *passim*. In nearby Spartan Mills village, the situation was the same. See Siler, Garrison, and MacNeal, "Relation of Pellagra in Spartan Mills, S.C., and Adjacent District," in *Pellagra*, 170.

public livery stables and numerous private stables" from which "the re-moval of stable manure was infrequent" and at which flies bred prolifically.[6]

The health problems of plain folk thus multiplied in the New South, and the cause was often "progress" itself in assorted guises of economic develop-ment and technological innovation. Economic development brought new roads, railroads, and sawmills, new factories and company towns, new mines and lumber camps, lands cleared for farming or simply denuded of trees by loggers. This construction and clearing scarred the land and opened ditches and scrapes where stagnant water collected and malarious mosquitoes thrived. Railroads cut ditches along roadways to hold back weed and brush growth, contributing unwittingly to the same problem. They also transported mosquitoes and people between infected and unin-fected areas. New factories, construction camps, and other work sites were often in unhealthful places or places soon made so by unsanitary practices that encouraged typhoid, hookworm, and other diseases. New work sites invariably brought about the movement of people and thus the mingling of populations infected and uninfected with various diseases, and often the result was the outbreak of epidemics or expanded areas of endemic infection.

Mill villages, for example, might be major agents in the spread of malaria. When Henry R. Carter of the Public Health Service made a malaria survey of Roanoke Rapids, North Carolina, in 1913, he found the town and some of its cotton and paper mill villages so positioned in relation to nearby marshes and stagnating waterways as to ensure a high incidence of the disease. In the Patterson cotton mill village, for example, dwellings were located on two ridges divided by a sluggish waterway in which *Anopheles* mosquitoes bred prolifically, and malaria rates in the village were high. At nearby Rosemary Mills village, however, "the natural breeding places for the Anophelines [were] more distant," and "comparatively little malaria occurred." The mills themselves contributed to the problem. "In almost every part of every riverlet and pool" Carter examined, including several into which the mills emptied liquid wastes, he found *Anopheles* larvae in some stage of development.[7]

6. Jennings and King, "An Intensive Study of Insects as a Possible Etiologic Factor in Pellagra," 105–106; L. L. Lumsden, "Rural Sanitation: A Report on Special Studies Made in 15 Counties in 1914, 1915, and 1916," *Public Health Bulletin No. 94* (Washington, D.C., 1918), 232.
7. R. H. Von Ezdorf, "Demonstrations of Malaria Control," *Public Health Reports*, XXI (1916), 615*ff.*

The humid, lint-filled air in mills adversely affected health as well; breathing it caused assorted respiratory ailments. Those ailments required time to reach serious proportions, however, and linking them to mill work was more difficult than locating mosquito larvae in stagnant water. Health investigators therefore gave the ailments little attention in the New South era. As late as 1933, the Public Health Service stated unequivocally that concentrations of dust and lint in cotton mills were too low to affect the health of workers, and it was a long time thereafter before researchers pinpointed byssinosis, or brown lung as it is popularly known, as the product of breathing cotton lint.[8] In 1908, however, British researchers had documented symptoms of that disease and related them to breathing lint. Mill workers experienced those symptoms in the form of labored breathing and hacking coughs, especially if they worked regularly. One of the heretofore unnoticed effects of high rates of absenteeism and irregular work habits was their benign impact on the worker's respiratory system.

Mill employment also increased the risk of tuberculosis, as was soon documented. A study of mill workers in Fall River, Massachusetts, made in connection with the labor investigation in 1907 and 1908, found levels of that disease far higher than in the general population. In southern mills, the practice of "promiscuous expectoration" significantly increased the risk of contracting tuberculosis, and in one North Carolina village in 1915, an extreme example, the death rate from the disease was reportedly eight times the national average.[9]

FOLK SIMPLY "WORE THEIR CHILLS OUT."

The characteristic diseases of plain folk were malaria, hookworm, and pellagra. These are diseases of poor people (almost exclusively so in the case

8. "The Health of Workers in Dusty Trades," *Public Health Bulletin No. 208* (1933), 21–23; U.S. Department of Health, Education and Welfare, *Publication No. (NIOSH) 75–118, Occupational Exposure to Cotton Dust* (1974), 23, 27. For recent studies of the nature and incidence of byssinosis in textile plants, see Eugenia Zuskin and Arend Boukwys, "Byssinosis: Airway Responses in Textile Dust Exposure," *Journal of Occupational Medicine,* XVII (1975), 357–59; Zuskin and F. Volic, "Change in the Respiratory Response to Coarse Cotton Dust over a Ten-Year Period," *American Review of Respiratory Diseases,* CII (1975), 417–21; and F. F. Cinkotai, M. G. Lockwood, and R. Rylander, "Airborne Micro-Organisms and Prevalence of Byssinotic Symptoms in Cotton Mills," *American Industrial Hygiene Association Journal,* XXXVIII (1977), 554–59.

9. *Senate Documents,* 61st Cong., 2nd Sess., No. 645, Vol. 14, *Causes of Death Among Woman and Child Cotton Mill Operatives;* L. B. McBayer, "A Resumé of a Tuberculosis Survey of a Silk Mill Village in North Carolina," *American Review of Tuberculosis,* IV (1921), 920–25.

of hookworm and pellagra), and their common features gave a distinctive quality to the health problems of plain folk. All were chronic and debilitating rather than acute or generally fatal, and as such, they made their victims anemic, listless, and unable to work with vigor or efficiency.

Debilitating illness made many casual, undriven plain folk appear to be lazy, even stuporous. Certain features of the diseases exaggerated these unflattering effects. The most insidious and widespread of the diseases, malaria and hookworm, were also chiefly rural, often backwoods, ailments, whereas pellagra was a disease associated with the very poor. Poverty, filth, "backwardness," and lethargy might thus exist together with grossly unappealing effect.

"Malaria is responsible for more sickness among the white population of the south than any disease to which it is now subject," an observer wrote in 1903; and modern authorities have echoed that judgment. There is little reason to challenge the recent conclusion that during the New South era "malaria was unrivaled as the most prevalent disease." In his study of Roanoke Rapids in 1913, Henry R. Carter found an astonishing incidence of the disease. A physician there told Carter that 75 percent of the residents had had malaria in the summer of 1910, the first year the physician had lived in Roanoke Rapids; and the incidence was almost as great each of the next three summers. Carter contacted every person living in a 4-block area of the town and found that almost half of them (46.6 percent) had had chills and fever sometime between June 1 and October 15, 1913. During that period, an average of 50 people each day in this town of 4,100 saw a doctor concerning malaria, and about 200 were sick in bed with the disease from October 1 to October 5. Blood tests of 400 schoolchildren who had no visible signs of the disease showed that 1 in 7 was infected.[10]

Malaria results from parasites invading the bloodstream and destroying red blood cells. If the victim harbors enough parasites (has been bitten often enough by infected mosquitoes), he develops anemia and other problems, including an enlarged liver and spleen. The disease manifests itself in parox-

10. Glenn W. Herrick, "The Relation of Malaria to Agriculture and Other Industries of the South," *Popular Science Monthly*, LXII (1903), 523; Young, "The South and Malaria, 1900–1930," 1; W. S. Leathers, "The Importance of Malaria from a Public Health and Economic Standpoint," *Southern Medical Journal*, XI (1918), 542; John W. Trask, "Malaria," *Public Health Reports*, XXI (1916), 3445; Deaderick and Thompson, *The Endemic Diseases of the Southern United States*, 35; H. R. Carter, "Malaria in North Carolina," *Public Health Reports*, XXVIII (1918), 2743; R. H. Von Ezdorf, "Endemic Index of Malaria in the United States," *Public Health Reports*, XXXI (1916), 819; Von Ezdorf, "Demonstrations of Malaria Control," 614–31.

ysms of chills and fever that vary in length and intensity. The victim might collapse and be bedridden for a time, or suffer reduced energy but continue with daily routines. Repeated infection produces a tolerance, but the tolerance is purchased at a high cost in energy and well-being.

Since malaria was not usually a cause of death—the most common form in the South at this time was the mild strain known as vivax malaria—its significance in the social history of plain folk lies in the debility it produced. Each attack left accumulating aftereffects and reduced the body's capacity to withstand infections and other hazards. Chronic malaria reduced the ability of pregnant and lactating women to nourish their children and stunted the physical and intellectual growth of children, who suffered more from the disease than did adults. A malarious population was therefore likely to be "physically and educationally subnormal according to the degree of prevalence of the disease," and this effect was compounded in a population whose diet was not fully nutritious.[11]

The economic and social consequences of the disease were enormous. "During September, 1912," the treasurer of Roanoke Mills wrote Henry R. Carter after the latter's effort against malaria was completed, "we averaged 66 looms standing [that is, idle] per day for the want of weavers; during September, 1913, we averaged 25 looms standing per day for the want of weavers; during September, 1914, after the antimalarial work had been completed, we had no difficulty in running our looms, and during September, 1915, we have had the greatest abundance of help." Translated into productivity, that meant significant gains. "In September, 1913," the treasurer continued, "we worked 26 days and produced 238,046 pounds of cloth; during September, 1914, we worked 26 days and produced 301,151 pounds of cloth; during September, 1915, we worked 26 days and produced 316,804 pounds of cloth." The increase in two years was one-third. The mill thus reaped huge returns on the thousand dollars it invested in work against malaria; and its operatives benefited as well. Officials estimated that employee efficiency at the mill had been 40 to 60 percent in the malaria season before 1913, and was 90 to 95 percent after the disease was eliminated.[12]

Part of the tragedy in this story is that health professionals knew how to eliminate malaria. The disease had long been treated by quinine, but not

---

11. Trask, "Malaria," 3445, 3450. See also Herrick, "The Relation of Malaria to Agriculture," 521. On malaria and nutrition, see Macfarlane Burnet and David O. White, *Natural History of Infectious Diseases* (Cambridge, U.K., 1972), 235.

12. Von Ezdorf, "Demonstrations of Malaria Control," 623–24; H. R. Carter, "The Malaria Problem of the South," 1932.

until the second decade of the twentieth century was the world supply of that drug sufficient and the cost low enough for poor folk to get adequate supplies; and not until then did medical researchers understand the proper dosing.[13] Before that decade, many folk simply "wore their chills out," at great cost to their physical well-being. Also, quinine treated symptoms only; to eradicate malaria it was necessary to eliminate *Anopheles* mosquitoes by destroying their breeding places. Once understood and undertaken, that task was less daunting than might be imagined, in part because of the short flying range of the mosquitoes. In nearly one hundred communities across the South where control work was undertaken from 1910 to 1920, the incidence of malaria dropped 75 to 95 percent within a year. During the next generation, the disease virtually disappeared.[14]

"THERE WON'T NO HOCKY HOUSES IN OUR NEIGHBORHOOD NO PLACE."

The story of hookworm among plain folk is more dramatic, in part because publicists and others associated the disease with southern poverty and backwardness. Indeed, when Charles W. Stiles documented the widespread existence of the disease in the South in 1902, journalist Irving C. Norwood promptly labeled the tiny worm the "germ of laziness"; and others were soon using the disease to account for whatever they found lacking or undesirable in the South.[15]

Stiles, then with the Bureau of Animal Industry in the Department of Agriculture and later with the Hygenic Laboratory of the Public Health Service, accomplished his feat on a trip from Washington, D.C., to Ocala,

13. North Carolina Board of Health, *Sixteenth Biennial Report, 1915–16*, 53; Carter, "Malaria in North Carolina," 2742. On how quinine combats malaria, see Erwin E. Nelson, "Cinchona and Its Alkaloids in the Treatment of Malaria," in AAAS, *Symposium on Human Malaria*, 11. See also Charles C. Bass, "Studies on Malaria Control," *Southern Medical Journal*, XII (1919), 190–94; and Dale C. Smith, "Quinine and Fever: The Development of the Effective Dosage," *Journal of the History of Medicine and Allied Sciences*, XXXI (1976), 343–67.

14. A. W. Fuchs, "Economic Losses from Malaria," *Public Health Bulletin No. 125* (Washington, D.C., 1921), 137; "Transactions of the Fourth Annual Conference of Malaria Field Workers," *Public Health Bulletin No. 137* (Washington, D.C., 1923); Ernest C. Faust, "The Distribution of Malaria in North America, Mexico, Central America and the West Indies," in AAAS, *Symposium on Human Malaria*, 11.

15. On the origin of the expression "germ of laziness," see Charles W. Stiles, "Early History, in Part Esoteric, of the Hookworm (Uncinariasis) Campaign in Our Southern States," *Journal of Parasitology*, XXV (1939), 296. For a statement blaming the ills of the Solid South on hookworm, see William H. Skaggs, *The Southern Oligarchy* (New York, 1924), 214. For one that blames the section's "exuberant lawlessness" on hookworm, see Chandler, *Hookworm Disease: Its Distribution, Biology, Epidemiology*, 254.

Florida, in the fall of 1902. His subsequent work, "Report upon the Prevalence and Geographic Distribution of Hookworm Disease," is an important document in the history of plain folk in the New South. "There are about 60 white 'hands' on this farm," he wrote in Kershaw County, South Carolina, in a passage that typified his findings. "Going to a field I found 20 at work. These 20 persons, men, women, and children, corresponded in more or less detail to the description of the so-called dirt-eaters and resin-chewers. A physical examination showed also that they corresponded to cases of uncinariasis." Stiles wrote, "The owner of the plantation informed me that it would be a waste of my time to examine the remaining 40 'hands,' as they were in exactly the same condition as the 20 already examined." The common symptoms in all twenty workers were anemia and its sequelae, and in every case he examined microscopically, Stiles found "exceedingly heavy infections."[16]

Because of Stiles's extensive investigation, his conclusions were persuasive. "The disease," he wrote, "is primarily a 'poor man's' malady, and in frequency it far exceeds even the most extreme limit which theoretical deductions seemed to justify before commencing the field work." He continued, "Among the whites of the rural sand districts, uncinariasis is apparently the most common disease found." The pale skin, anemia, bloated stomach, diarrhea, and extreme lethargy so widespread among poor folk could now be understood, as could the "ground itch" produced by worms boring into the tender skin between the toes. That itch was "exceedingly common," Stiles found, occurring "at some period in the life of practically every person" in sandy rural districts. Subsequent investigation substantiated the findings of Stiles and other early researchers, and documented the existence of the disease in virtually every county in Georgia and the Carolinas.[17]

The physical effects of hookworm disease, like those of malaria, accumu-

16. Charles W. Stiles, "Report upon the Prevalence and Geographic Distribution of Hookworm Disease (Uncinariasis or Anchylostomiasis) in the United States," *Hygenic Laboratory Bulletin No. 10* (Washington, D.C., 1903), 36, 39–40. On Stiles's role in the campaign against hookworm disease, see John Ettling, *The Germ of Laziness: Rockefeller Philanthropy and Public Health in the New South* (Cambridge, Mass., 1981), 7–48; and James H. Cassedy, "The 'Germ of Laziness' in the South, 1900–1915: Charles Wardell Stiles and the Progressive Paradox," *Bulletin of the History of Medicine*, XLV (1971), 159–69.

17. Stiles, "Report upon the Prevalence and Geographic Distribution of Hookworm Disease," 36, 80, 63; Rockefeller Foundation, International Health Board, *Eleventh Annual Report (1924)* (Washington, D.C., 1925), 130. See also Rockefeller Sanitary Commission for the Eradication of Hookworm Disease, *Fifth Annual Report, 1914* (Washington, D.C., 1915), 13, 17.

late gradually. Attached to the intestines of their victims, the worms feed on blood, often changing places with one another, thereby producing minute hemorrhages and further depleting the blood supply. In direct proportion to the extent of infestation—the number of worms the victim harbors—the hemoglobin count is lowered and the number of red blood cells decreased, resulting in iron-deficiency anemia. The victim's system works to produce more blood, which generates a growing strain as the number of worms increases, but the lost iron can be replaced only through medication or diet. For people who eat poorly, the effects are thus compounded.

The physical consequences of hookworm disease are straightforward. Growing undernourishment produces a gradual sapping of vitality and a stunting of physical and mental growth. The victim becomes pale, anemic, sickly, passive, lacking in energy and alertness. His heartbeat accelerates as his system works to produce more blood, his skin turns sallow and dry, and he develops intestinal disorders and becomes increasingly susceptible to other diseases.[18] Heavy infestation (500 or more worms) was relatively unusual in the New South; light (less than 100 worms) or moderate cases were the rule. Large numbers of people seem to have had light infestation without ever knowing it, and after they became adults or began to wear shoes, the worms they harbored died within a few years.

Effects of the disease were especially harsh on women and children. Among women, infestation interfered with the normal flow of the menses and was particularly harmful during pregnancy, when it increased the possibility of miscarriage or stillbirth and made labor more difficult. It also interfered with lactation. Among children, who had by far the highest incidence of the disease because they walked barefooted more often than adults, heavy infestation was particularly harmful. The condition stunted growth and delayed the onset of puberty—children of ten or twelve might look no more than seven or eight. Children and youths often appeared so much younger than they were that reformers frequently overstated the extent of child labor in the mills by understating the age of children. Charles W. Stiles studied the case histories of thirty-three cotton mill youths who, in his judgment, looked three or more years younger than they actually were,

18. For recent summaries of the symptomology and pathology of the disease, see Marcel Roche and Miguel Layrisse, "The Nature and Causes of Hookworm Anemia," *American Journal of Tropical Medicine and Hygiene*, XV (1966), 1032–1100; and Harold W. Brown and Franklin A. Neva, *Basic Clinical Parasitology* (5th ed.; New York, 1983), 119–26. See also Robert W. Twyman, "The Clay Eaters: A New Look at an Old Southern Enigma," *Journal of Southern History*, XXXVII (1971), 439–48.

and accounted for their condition by "severe hookworm infection contracted before puberty." The degree of stunting, he thought, correlated with the intensity of infestation and the number of years since infestation began.[19]

A special problem for children and youths was the impact of the disease on mental development. Infestation interfered with alertness and concentration and thus with ability to learn and perform in school. "In severe cases the dullness of mind is one of the most outstanding clinical symptoms," one authority wrote. "Apathy, stupidity, and inability to concentrate are all present in marked degree, and . . . heavily infested [children], without treatment, are practically hopeless in school." In the second and third decades of the twentieth century, a number of studies affirmed this judgment, showing clearly that infestation and poor school performance were correlated. "The general rule is that the heavier the hookworm infestation, the lower the Intelligence Quotient," reported two authors, summarizing conclusions reached by a number of researchers.[20] What they meant by "Intelligence Quotient" was performance on standardized tests that measured school achievement.

Environmental and cultural factors compounded the effects of hookworm disease. Victims often lived in malarious or otherwise unhealthful areas, and ate inadequate or imbalanced diets. "If superimposed on faulty, or inadequate diet, hard labor and unhygenic surroundings," declared one authority, hookworm disease "must inevitably have a marked effect on [worker] efficiency."[21]

Charles W. Stiles carried this point further, for he was more concerned than most researchers with the social consequences of the disease. "It is exceedingly difficult to escape the conclusion that in uncinariasis, . . . we

19. Chandler, *Hookworm Disease: Its Distribution, Biology, Epidemiology*, 277*ff;* Charles W. Stiles, "The Influence of Hookworm Disease upon the Apparent Age of Children in the Cotton Mills," *Southern Medical Journal*, IV (1911), 325; W. G. Smillie and D. L. Augustine, "Hookworm Infestation: The Effect of Varying Intensities on the Physical Condition of School Children," *American Journal of Diseases of Children*, XXI (1926), 151–68.

20. Chandler, *Hookworm Disease: Its Distribution, Biology, Epidemiology*, 259; W. G. Smillie and Cassie R. Spencer, "Mental Retardation in School Children Infested with Hookworms," *Journal of Educational Psychology*, XVII (1926), 319. See also Edward K. Strong and Charles W. Stiles, *Effects of Hookworm Disease on the Mental and Physical Development of Children* (New York, 1916); and Charles A. Kofoid and John P. Tucker, "On the Relationship of Infection by Hookworm to the Incidence of Morbidity and Mortality in 22,842 Men of the United States Army at Camp Bowie, Texas, from October 1917, to April 1918," *American Journal of Hygiene*, I (1921), 112–16.

21. Chandler, *Hookworm Disease: Its Distribution, Biology, Epidemiology*, 281.

have a pathologic basis as one of the most important factors in the inferior mental, physical, and financial condition of the poorer classes of the white population of the rural sand and piney wood districts which I visited," he wrote in his 1902 report. "These people are suffering from a handicap in life which practically removes them from a fair chance in competition."[22]

The causes of hookworm disease—the lack of toilet facilities and the unsanitary disposition of human feces—were likewise cultural as well as environmental. In the five years of its existence, 1909 to 1914, the Rockefeller Sanitary Commission for the Eradication of Hookworm Disease surveyed 250,680 dwellings in 653 counties in 10 southern states and found that half (125,584) had no privies and almost all the others (113,682) had open-surface privies that offered no sanitary protection. Where there was no privy, people defecated wherever they found the degree of privacy they sought, and there as in open-surface privies, their feces were accessible to animals and chickens, which rooted and scratched about in them and ate from them, scattering hookworm ova, typhoid germs, or whatever else they contained. "Defecation occurs at almost any place within a radius of 50 meters from the house or hut," Stiles wrote of his observations of rural districts in the South Atlantic states, "and as a result the premises become heavily infested with the [hookworm] embryos."[23] Plain folk recalled this situation. "There won't no hocky houses in our neighborhood no place," remembered Sarah Strickland Faison of her childhood in rural North Carolina in the 1870s and 1880s. "Never seed one till I was a grown girl. The pure stuff was all 'round the place."

Because conditions were so bad on the farm, the move to mill villages, all of which had privies, even if unsanitary ones, significantly reduced exposure to hookworm disease. "I never seed a toilet in my life 'till we moved to Raleigh in '97," one sharecropper's son recalled. "Nor had I ever used one. I had heard of backhouses but had never seed one."[24]

In the mill villages, folk "soon abandon[ed] former habits of promiscuous defecation for the approved types of toilets provided for them," one researcher wrote after studying four mill villages in southern Georgia and Alabama. Consequently, "From the time the families move into the mill

22. Stiles, "Report upon the Prevalence and Geographic Distribution of Hookworm Disease," 97.
23. Rockefeller Sanitary Commission for the Eradication of Hookworm Disease, *Fifth Annual Report, 1914,* 13; Stiles, "Report upon the Prevalence and Geographic Distribution of Hookworm Disease," 35.
24. Quoted in W. T. Couch (ed.), *These Are Our Lives* (Chapel Hill, 1939), 99.

village practically no new infestation is acquired, and the hookworms previously acquired die in from three to five years." There was thus some correlation between the length of time folk had been in the mill village and the incidence of hookworm among them. "In general, the physical condition of the people improves with their residence in mill villages, due largely to the fact that the change from life on the farm to life in the mill village results in a very great improvement in sanitary conditions," Stiles wrote after a 6-month investigation that included visits to 116 cotton mills in Georgia, the Carolinas, Alabama, and Mississippi. The "cotton mill anemia" so widely ascribed to unhealthful conditions in the mills was, in Stiles's view, due to hookworms acquired before the workers went to the mills.[25]

One reason for the improvement in health was the development of a cheap, effective treatment and the encouragement of efforts against hookworm disease by mill officials.[26] The campaign against hookworm by the Rockefeller Sanitary Commission was the largest, most systematic public health effort in the New South era. Much more than the campaign against malaria, which was largely the work of public authorities, the effort to eradicate hookworm touched plain folk in highly personal ways. It not only required their cooperation in medical cures they found embarrassing and unpleasant but made many of them aware of health and their own unhealthful habits as they had never been before. The effort must also have helped folk see a connection between the way they lived and the way they felt, and caused at least some of them to believe they could influence their own well-being.

The success of the commission was often dramatic and deeply felt. In all except the most extreme cases, elimination of the worms caused immediate improvement in vitality and well-being and thus in energy, motivation, and outlook. The individual gained weight (and height, too, if a youth), and his complexion and general appearance improved, as did his alertness and school performance. His anemia disappeared, and with it the physiological problems it induced. His circulatory and respiratory systems worked bet-

25. Donald L. Augustine, "Hookworm Disease in Cotton Mill Villages of Alabama and Georgia: A Study of the Value of Sanitation in a Soil Province Heavily Infested with Hookworm," *American Journal of Industrial Hygiene*, VIII (1926), 382–91; Charles W. Stiles, *Hookworm Disease Among Cotton-Mill Operatives* (Washington, D.C., 1912), 9 and *passim*.

26. On the treatment, see Rockefeller Sanitary Commission for the Eradication of Hookworm Disease, *Second Annual Report, 1911* (Washington, D.C., 1912), 105; Stiles, "Report upon the Prevalence and Geographic Distribution of Hookworm Disease," 86–89; and Ettling, *The Germ of Laziness*, 166–67.

ter, as did his digestive system. Within a short time, he felt and acted like a different person.

The economic consequences of treatment could be equally impressive. In 1910 two researchers reported that a cotton mill manager, after reading in a newspaper that hookworm was the cause of laziness, had the sixty-two children in his mill examined for the disease. Fifty-six were infested, and after treatment all of them improved remarkably. Months later, the manager was still boasting of the results. "The time keeper had been absent nearly three months," he wrote, "and on his return he found that many of the children had changed so much he had to ask the names of some whom he had previously known well. The working capacity of the hands has been increased at least 25 percent," he estimated. The small expense of the treatment, he reported, was insignificant in light of the resulting benefits for the mill and its employees.[27]

"PELLAGRA MAKES THEM VERY CROSS AT TIMES AND EXCITABLE AND GIVES THEM FUNNY NOTIONS."

Pellagra is especially important to the social history of plain folk. It is a disease of dietary deficiency, and its incidence relates to economic conditions as well as to culturally based eating patterns. Its emergence in 1906 or 1907 as a major health problem was, however, the consequence of technological innovations in the milling of grain. Until the 1870s, the process of grain milling had remained unchanged for as long as anyone could remember. Farmers brought corn and wheat to local gristmillers who, at water-driven mills, transformed the grain into coarse, gray meal or flour by a simple process of crushing the grain between stones. Cornbread was generally made by adding water or buttermilk and salt to the meal, and biscuits or "flour bread" was made by mixing buttermilk or water and lard with the flour. In these forms, the bread contained all the nutritive elements of whole grain and had always been a basic source of nutrition for plain folk.

Each element of the milling system changed during the New South era with nutritionally devastating effects. New roller mills increased milling capacity, thereby lowering the cost of commercial meal and flour and gradually driving local millers out of business. Commercial millers were able to refine meal and flour much more highly than in the past by a process that

27. Dock and Bass, *Hookworm Disease: Etiology, Pathology, Diagnosis*, 124–25.

separated the germ and bran of the grain from the starchy endosperm and discarded the former while grinding the latter finely. (The milling of grits and rice was similarly affected.) The new products were attractive to housewives because they produced a whiter, fluffier bread and to merchants because they had a much longer shelf life. But the refining process robbed the meal and flour of most of their protein, fat, and vitamin content, including valuable trace elements. "In a few years," one authority wrote of the development, "the staple cereal food of millions of people changed from what was essentially a whole grain to a highly refined carbohydrate that carried little to facilitate its utilization." Among the essential elements removed from the bread were niacin and riboflavin, the loss of which significantly increased the risk of pellagra among people with the kind of imbalanced diets plain folk had.[28]

A change in the method of making bread compounded these effects. Housewives found that refined meal and flour produced lighter bread if they added baking soda as a leavening agent. At cooking temperatures, however, the soda produced a chemical action that destroyed even more of the remaining vitamin content. The use of buttermilk instead of water to mix the bread neutralized that action, but the poorest folk often had no cow and so made their bread with water.

The method of cooking beans and peas, other traditional sources of nutrients for plain folk, also changed at this time with deleterious results. During the New South era, plain folk found that baking soda caused beans and peas, especially the dried ones they ate through the winter, to cook much faster. Cooking time was a vital consideration for women who had to prepare meals as well as work in the fields or mills, but beans and peas thus cooked lost much of their food value—again, essential vitamins and trace minerals. In combination with the changes in bread, this development increased the danger of dietary-deficiency diseases.[29]

28. V. P. Sydenstricker, "The History of Pellagra, Its Recognition as a Disorder of Nutrition and Its Conquest," *American Journal of Clinical Nutrition*, VI (1958), 410. See also Carl Voeglin, M. X. Sullivan, and C. N. Myers, "Bread as Food: Changes in Its Vitamine Content and Nutritive Value with Reference to the Occurrence of Pellagra," *Public Health Reports*, XXXI (1916), 935–43; Worth Hale, "The Bleaching of Flour and the Effect of Nitrites on Certain Medicinal Substances," *Hygenic Laboratory Bulletin No. 68* (Washington, D.C., 1910), 5–39; and Casimir Funk, "Studies on Pellagra: The Influence of the Milling of Maize on the Chemical Composition and Nutritive Value of Meal," *Journal of Physiology*, XLVII (1913), 389–92. On niacin deficiency, see Edward B. Vedder, "Dietary Deficiency as the Etiological Factor in Pellagra," *Archives of Internal Medicine*, XVIII (1916), 138–42.

29. On the connection between diet and pellagra, see Elizabeth W. Etheridge, *The Butterfly Caste: A Social History of Pellagra in the South* (Westport, Conn., 1972), 65–69 and *passim;*

The diet of plain folk was imbalanced and marginally nutritious apart from these considerations. Its staples were meat (pork in any form), bread, syrup or molasses, and a few vegetables, especially corn, peas, beans, and potatoes, supplemented according to taste and season by a few other foods. The folk's diet was monotonous, but it varied enough from season to season to give a cyclical pattern to outbreaks of ailments related to dietary deficiency. The privations of winter might be followed in spring and summer by the appearance of skin sores or the initial stages of pellagra, which then disappeared as a result of improved diet.

The content of this diet was due to cultural choice as well as poverty. Like all other people, plain folk had become acculturated to the foods they ate, and they centered their diets on pork, bread, molasses, and a few vegetables because those were the foods they liked. A study of the eating habits of seventy-five white families in east Tennessee and north Georgia between 1901 and 1904 by researchers from the Department of Agriculture pointedly revealed that fact. The families dwelt in the country and in the towns, on the farm and off the farm; they included both poor and working-class people. There was enough difference in their circumstances and income to permit meaningful variation in their food consumption, yet investigators were struck by the remarkable sameness of the dietaries of all the families. Cornmeal, wheat flour, and fat, cured pork made up "about three quarters of the total diet," to which "a few other materials," mostly vegetables, were added "in varying proportions." What explained this sameness? "The occupation of the wage-earners apparently had little effect upon either the amount or the kind of food purchased," the investigators reported. "Nor do the families of farmers who cultivate their own land, including gardens, use as a rule a greater variety of vegetables than those who must pay cash for all their supplies." Moreover, there was "little connection between the size of [family] income and the amount spent for food." In many cases, "The families in the best financial condition spent very little for food, while those of very poor means often spent more than the average."

The controlling factor was taste. "Habit has much to do with the variety of food desired," the investigators concluded. "People accustomed for years or generations to eating only a few kinds of food, as are the families in these

Vedder, "Dietary Deficiency as the Etiological Factor in Pellagra," 137–72; and Joseph Goldberger, "The Relation of Diet to Pellagra," *Journal of the American Medical Association*, LXXVIII (1922), 1679–82. On the nutritional importance of enriching refined-grain products, see Russell M. Wilder, "Brief History of the Enrichment of Bread and Flour," *Journal of the American Medical Association*, CLXII (1956), 539–41.

studies, can relish a diet which would be irksome or even repellent to those accustomed to different ways of living. In several cases where the diet consisted of only three or four articles, the families were undoubtedly quite able to afford more variety had they craved it."[30]

The Tennessee families about whom these remarks were written would no doubt have agreed with F. B. Brewer, a North Carolina tenant farmer. "Good beans, corn bread, fat back, and cabbage," Brewer exclaimed, years after the above study was made, "there ain't no better farm food than that. Some folks eat so much of that fancy food that I don't see how they get along. I just have got to have something solid to work on."

These preferences continued in the mill villages. The 1907–1908 labor study included an in-depth investigation of eating patterns among twenty-one representative cotton mill families in Georgia and the Carolinas. "Corn bread, biscuit, pork, and coffee form a large part of the diet of all families," investigators reported after studying a week of family menus. The pork was largely salted and fat. Breakfast in these families was typically coffee, bread, syrup, and pork; dinner consisted largely of bread, pork, and one or more vegetables; and supper was usually leftovers from dinner.[31]

Cooking methods added to the nutritional deficiency of this diet. Meat was usually fried in lots of grease, and vegetables were always boiled, thoroughly, also in grease and often with pieces of fat pork. "When we used to cook vegetables," Lula Demry remembered of her childhood in South Carolina in the 1870s and 1880s, "we didn't think they was fit to eat unless the grease was laying on the top of them thick as that first joint of my finger." Vegetables were also not "fit to eat," folk thought, unless they were cooked almost to mush. The pot liquor containing much of the food value was usually thrown out, though it was especially favored by some folk and often eaten like soup with floating chunks of cornbread. Those who consumed it reaped a nutritional bonus.[32]

Pellagra, to which all of these things contributed, was a disease of families, or rather of households. Its significance was greatest in mill villages, mining camps, and poor agricultural districts, though its incidence was highest in insane asylums, orphanages, and almshouses, where it sometimes

30. U.S. Department of Agriculture, Office of Experiment Stations, *Bulletin 221: Dietary Studies in Rural Regions in Vermont, Tennessee and Georgia* (1909), 106, 107. This study was restricted to food consumed at regular meals.

31. Wood F. Worcester and Daisy W. Worcester, *Family Budgets of Typical Cotton-Mill Workers* (Washington, D.C., 1911), 23ff.

32. See Margaret L. Keller and A. X. Minot, " 'Pot Liquor': A Neglected Source of Vitamin C for the Feeding of Infants," *Southern Medical Journal*, XXXIV (1941), 163–64.

reached epidemic proportions. Because of the connection between diet and pellagra, logic suggests that the disease existed before H. F. Harris of Atlanta documented the first case in the South in 1902; and investigators subsequently developed evidence of its prior existence. Yet it became widespread only in 1906 and 1907, when physicians in several state hospitals and orphanages in Georgia, the Carolinas, and elsewhere in the section diagnosed numerous cases. Thereafter, documented cases grew rapidly, and estimates of the number of pellagrins in the South in 1915 ranged between 75,000 and 165,000.[33]

The disease was most concentrated in mill villages. In 1917, in 24 villages in South Carolina with a population of 22,653 people divided into 4,104 households, Joseph Goldberger and his associates diagnosed 1,146 cases of pellagra in 761 households, using relatively rigorous standards. This was a gross rate of 50.6 per 1,000 people and one or more cases in 18.5 percent of the households. The incidence, however, varied widely among the villages, from 19.6 to 100.8 per 1,000 people, and from 8.6 percent to 36.2 percent of the households.[34]

One problem in determining the incidence is that the definitive symptom of pellagra, a dermatitis characterized by marked eruption and bilateral symmetry, does not appear until weeks after the onset of the disease if it appears at all. Since most pellagrins in the mill villages experienced only the earliest stages of the disease and it disappeared after a short period of adequate diet, many cases must have gone undiagnosed. During their study of the South Carolina mill villages, Goldberger and his associates found that in average cases, "very definite clinical improvements may be observed after about 10 days or two weeks of appropriate diet." They also found many instances in which other symptoms of pellagra antedated the appearance of the skin eruption, and that "the great majority of all cases of the disease are quite mild," especially in children, "most of whom on casual examination present little or nothing more than the telltale eruption."[35]

Goldberger's studies were an effort to discover the cause of pellagra. The

33. On the history of pellagra in the South, see Etheridge, *The Butterfly Caste;* and Daphne A. Roe, *A Plague of Corn: A Social History of Pellagra* (Ithaca, 1973). On the early incidence of the disease, see Sydenstricker, "The History of Pellagra, Its Recognition as a Disorder of Nutrition and Its Conquest," 409; and Joseph F. Siler and Philip E. Garrison, "An Intensive Study of the Epidemiology of Pellagra: Report of Progress," *American Journal of Medical Sciences,* CXLVI (1913), 240.

34. Joseph Goldberger *et al.*, "A Study of Endemic Pellagra in Some Cotton Mill Villages of South Carolina," *Hygenic Laboratory Bulletin No. 153* (1929), 8–9.

35. *Ibid.*, 5–7, 10.

disease is a product of niacin (nicotinic acid) deficiency. A diet heavy in corn and corn products induces chemical actions in the body that increase the need for niacin even while blocking its endogenous production. Those chemical actions produce pellagra unless other foods supply the necessary amount of niacin. Lean meat, milk, eggs, fresh vegetables, and even coffee all contain niacin. It was the absence of such foods in proper balance from the diets of plain folk that placed them at risk.[36]

Goldberger provided the first demonstration of the connection between pellagra and the unbalanced diet of plain folk in 1915, when he fed a group of convicts who had never had the disease a diet of fat pork, cornbread, biscuits, rice, grits, gravy, sugar, cane syrup, sweet potatoes, and small amounts of turnips, cabbage, and collards. Within six months, six of the eleven convicts had contracted the disease.[37]

The symptomology of pellagra varies according to the stage of the disease. In the initial stages, which many mill folk experienced, the symptoms are general feelings of being unwell—listlessness, indigestion, diarrhea (or, sometimes, constipation). One might also experience a loss of appetite and weight, feelings of nervousness or irritability, headaches, pain in the neck or back, burning sensations at various places on the body, and dermatitis. Jessie Lee Carter, who lived most of her life in Brandon mill village in Greenville, developed a mild form of the disease after she married and moved to the country. "I had it six months," she told an interviewer years later. "Lord, you'd break out. You was scaley" on "[your] arms and hands and on [your] face. . . . It burned. It was scaley like a fish." In this form, the disease was more irritating than debilitating. "I wasn't sick with it," Mrs. Carter continued. "I never did go to bed with it. . . . I stayed up and done my housework and cooking and everything." She never knew the cause or

36. Knowledge and speculation about the disease before its dietary basis was known are summarized in *Southern Medical Journal*, V (March, 1912), which is devoted to pellagra. See also Edward J. Wood, *A Treatise on Pellagra* (New York, 1912). The medical nature of the disease is summarized briefly in nontechnical terms in Sydenstricker, "The History of Pellagra, Its Recognition as a Disorder of Nutrition and Its Conquest," 409–14. The food chemistry is summarized in Clara Mae Taylor and Orrea F. Pye, *Foundations of Nutrition* (6th ed.; New York, 1966), 270–80; and Kenneth F. and Virginia H. Kipple, "Black Tongue and Black Men: Pellagra and Slavery in the Antebellum South," *Journal of Southern History*, XLIII (1977), 410–28.

37. The basic study setting forth the relationship of diet to pellagra is Joseph Goldberger, G. A. Wheeler, and Edgar Sydenstricker, "A Study of the Relation of Diet to Pellagra Incidence in Seven Textile-Mill Communities of South Carolina," *Public Health Reports*, XXXV (1920), 648–713.

how she contracted the disease. "It came from overseas," her doctor told her.

Irritability was the characteristic that most impressed those who lived with pellagrins. "The reason I got started on diet was because my husband developed pellagra," Mrs. John S. Hale, who grew up in North Carolina at the turn of the century and married a lumber mill worker about 1911, recalled. "Of course I think he got the disease from what he ate [at work], and when he came home I would have the things he liked and I didn't know any better. Then I learned to give him leafy vegetables and keep him off starchy foods, and I expect he'd be dead or in the asylum if I hadn't. . . . Pellagra makes them very cross at times and excitable and gives them funny notions. That's all the difference in the world when he's fed right."

The victims of pellagra were disproportionately small children and women between twenty and fifty. In their investigations, Joseph Goldberger and his colleagues found the disease almost nonexistent among nursing infants but occurring with "great frequency" among children between two and fifteen years old. They found its occurrence "about twenty times" more frequent among women between twenty and fifty than among men between fifteen and forty. Among men in this age group, the disease was quite rare. Yet, strikingly, among elderly people, men had a higher incidence than women.[38]

This was not the extent of the variations. The incidence among married, widowed, and deserted women was more than four times higher than among single women; and among married women it was six times higher than among married men. Moreover, in cotton mill villages, where the most systematic studies were made, folk who did not work in the mills were about ten times more likely to have the disease than those who did.[39]

What explains these variations? Since pellagra is a disease of households, the simplest answer is the wide differences in eating patterns within the mill folk's households. Nursing babies avoided the disease because their diet of mother's milk was nutritionally adequate. But once the child was weaned, the nutritional value of his diet might drop notably, and thus pellagra

38. Goldberger *et al.*, "A Study of Endemic Pellagra in Some Cotton Mill Villages of South Carolina," 14–15.
39. *Ibid.*, 19; Joseph Goldberger, G. A. Wheeler, and Edgar Sydenstricker, "Pellagra Incidence in Relation to Sex, Age, Season, Occupation, and 'Disabling Sickness,' in Seven Cotton-Mill Villages of South Carolina During 1916," *Public Health Reports*, XXXV (1920), 1662. See also Katherine Dodd, "Pellagra in Childhood," in Seale Harris (ed.), *Clinical Pellagra* (St. Louis, 1941), 341–56.

appeared often in two- or three-year-olds. In families with inadequate food supplies, wage earners seem to have had first claim on the food available, and so mill workers avoided the disease while housewives and children too small to work did not.

When children went into the mills, pellagra rates among them dropped markedly as they became wage earners and ate more adequately. As those who did not earn wages, housewives simply sacrificed; and when men no longer worked because of advancing age and no longer had priority claim on the food supply, pellagra rates among them increased. Boarders and single adults also fit this pattern. As sources of income for the household, they, too, had a claim on the food supply.

Pellagra rates were thus tied to the family cycle in revealing ways. Over the life of mill families, there were marked fluctuations in income and in demands made on that income.[40] The fluctuations followed a pattern of alternating sufficiency and want that, given dietary preferences and norms, directly influenced the incidence of pellagra. When two young people married, both were likely to work in the mill until their first child was born. With two wage earners and no dependents, the family had an income that in relation to need was high, or at least sufficient for an adequate diet. But during her first pregnancy, the wife quit work in the mill, significantly reducing family income just as family size was increasing. As additional children were born, the demands of child rearing kept the wife at home and off the payroll (unless her mother, mother-in-law, or some other relative was available to keep the children), and during this period the family was especially vulnerable to pellagra. But as the children became old enough to work in the mills, the vulnerability diminished. Family income rose as children went to work, and continued to rise until the older children married and left home. At that time, the process reversed itself. Again, family income declined, but because the size of the family also declined and the income of experienced workers was higher than that of inexperienced ones, this decline was not as serious as the earlier one, at least not until the parents were alone and too old to work.

Instructive though they are, these patterns do not fully explain the sudden increase in pellagra about 1907. Because the diet of plain folk was only marginally adequate, it was vulnerable to fluctuations in economic conditions. Specifically, the incidence of pellagra in mill villages often correlated

40. Edgar Sydenstricker, Willford I. King, and Dorothy Wiehl, "The Income Cycle in the Life of the Wage Earner," *Public Health Reports*, XXXIX (1924), 2133–40.

with economic conditions within those communities. Thus, a few months after Saxon Mills shut down for a while in 1910, "There was a very considerable increase in the amount of pellagra among [its] operatives." At the nearby village of Newry, in contrast, where there was no shutdown and only one confirmed case of pellagra, the diet of the operatives was "undoubtedly distinctly above the average" diet of cotton mill workers.[41]

The increase in pellagra after 1906 and 1907 was also related to general economic conditions. One would expect that after refined meal and flour were in common use, an increase in pellagra would occur during the next downturn in the economy, and that is what happened. Following the panic of 1907, plain folk were caught in an economic squeeze. In that year cotton mill wages probably fell in real terms because of rising food prices, and they remained down for a few years. After 1907, then, mill workers were forced to spend a greater share of their income on food while also buying a larger quantity of cheap foods such as cereals and fat pork. "I was informed by several physicians who had been in practice many years in Spartanburg County," wrote a medical investigator in 1916, "that they were certain that as a general rule less fresh meat is eaten now than was the case ten years ago, this fact of course being due to the great increase in the cost of meat."[42]

"SOME NEW CASES [OF] TYPHOID ON THE HILL. SCARCE OF HELP."

Most sickness among mill folk involved lesser ailments than pellagra, hookworm, and malaria. Information on sickness patterns in individual villages over long periods of time seems to be lacking. However, surviving letterbooks make it possible to glimpse the situation at Cleveland Cotton Mills for a while in the early 1890s. "About the full force of hands was in the mill all week," Superintendent John F. Schenck wrote in the late fall of 1891, "while during almost every preceding week several were out and missed days and half days on account of sickness and other causes." The problem thus existed throughout the fall. In early December, "about 12 hands" at the larger of the company's mills were "out of the Spinning Room" with chicken pox, and a few days later, the mills were still "having a storm of

41. Vedder, "Dietary Deficiency as the Etiological Factor in Pellagra," 163, 161. Saxon Mills shut down about half the time between July and October, 1910.

42. *Ibid.*, 169. For information on this economic squeeze, see U.S. Commissioner of Labor, *Eighteenth Annual Report, 1903: Cost of Living and Retail Prices of Food* (2 vols., 1892); *Senate Documents*, 62nd Cong., 1st Sess., No. 22; and National Industrial Conference Board, *The Cost of Living Among Wage-Earners: Greenville, South Carolina, Pelzer, South Carolina, Charlotte, North Carolina. Special Report No. 8* (1920).

Grip & Chicken Pox—15 hands out of No 2 yesterday and today the same plus four mill hands who have gone to visit a Sister at Double Shoals who is said to be dieing of Pneumonia. Stopping part of Spinning room at No. 2."[43]

Illness might thus have a major bearing on productivity. "Production fell off considerably this week," the Schencks also reported in December. "No rope was made. Two spinning frames stopped half day Friday—and all day Sat. A good many changes had to be made in Mill, i.e., taking hands from their regular work and putting them on other work which was standing because of sickness of hands and the change in some instances was necessarily awkward to some of the hands."[44]

During the winter, the problem diminished. "Hands at No. 2 are in very fine health," H. F. Schenck reported in February, "so much so that [labor] expense rose above usual last week, because so many were in." The good health continued through the spring. "We have never before had such prompt attendance in the mill by the hands as we have had during the last several weeks," the superintendent reported in May, 1892. "We have had more help at times than we know how to keep busy, but we are reluctant to dismiss hands, especially at this season when sickness like last Summer's may return and cut down our help to our great disadvantage."[45]

The concern was a valid one, for that summer the village experienced an outbreak of typhoid fever. President H. F. Schenck bemoaned its effects on production. "We have been extremely short of hands," he reported in early July. "We have had out of the mill from 12 to 18 or 20 hands [in a work force of perhaps 115] every day on account of sickness in families." In addition, two village families had taken this occasion to move elsewhere.[46]

The problem continued for several weeks. On August 1, Schenck was still reporting "some new cases [of] Typhoid on the Hill," as a result of which the mill was "scarce of help." In addition to typhoid, the workers suffered from "summer trouble of bowels," which Schenck thought was brought on "by eating excess of vegetables &c." They also suffered from "rheumatism, general break-down from Exceedingly hot weather, and other causes," and some workers were "out because sickness in the family

43. John F. Schenck to J. E. Reynolds, November 28, 1891, H. F. Schenck to Reynolds, December 12, 1891, in H. F. Schenck Papers, Manuscript Department, Duke University Library, Durham, North Carolina.
44. "Report of Cleveland Cotton Mills," for week ending December 12, 1891, in Schenck Papers.
45. H. F. Schenck to Reynolds, February 2, 1892, "Report of Cleveland Cotton Mills," for week ending May 14, 1892, in Schenck Papers.
46. H. F. Schenck to Reynolds, July 5, 1892, in Schenck Papers.

demanded some help to wait on those who were helpless." The big problem that summer was typhoid, however. "I can find only one thing to attribute fever to at the mill," President Schenck wrote of that malady. "The cases nearly all originated in one house (4)—One in an adjoining house. The family brought a Milk cow and put her in a small stable on the back of their lot. Kept her there about 3 months and never took her out nor cleaned the stable. Milked her in the filthy stall and I think milk must have absorbed the germs. . . . They now stake her out and no new cases have occurred."[47]

As was usually the case, the illnesses eventually ran their course. "Yesterday is the first day in about 2 months when we have had a mill full of hands," Superintendent Schenck reported on August 3. "We have a few from No. 1 helping [in Mill No. 2] at present. But we will not need these after this week provided more at No. 2 do not get sick."[48]

"I HAVE FOUND A PREJUDICE IN FAVOR OF PROMISCUOUS DEFECATION."

Folk dealt with sickness, and with doctors and medical reformers, too, in ways determined by culture and tradition. In 1912, the North Carolina Board of Health took note of many people who "actively resisted" the advice of medical experts. "A favorite exercise for this is to question [the doctor's] diagnosis" and then go to "an irregular physician," or "kick doctor," who affirmed the patient's own notions and thus undermined the efforts of regular physicians.[49]

This behavior was one manifestation of the persistence of faith in folk medicine. The New South was a society in which folk medicine, popular medicine (patent folk medicine), and scientific medicine coexisted. It was also a society in which modern medicine was making rapid advances and gradually superseding traditional treatments. In such a society, few people subscribe exclusively to one system of medicine; instead, most people accept elements of all three systems, assigning credence to each as experience or inclination suggests. In a study of the relationship between folk and modern medicine in a similar society (that of northern India in the mid-twentieth century), anthropologist Harold A. Gould found the two forms coexisting and overlapping with little tension among people who partook of both. "Folk medical practices were being employed whenever the person's

47. H. F. Schenck to Reynolds, August 1, July 26, July 6, 1892, in Schenck Papers.
48. John F. Schenck to Reynolds, August 3, 1892, in Schenck Papers.
49. North Carolina Board of Health, *Fourteenth Biennial Report, 1911–1912*, 182–83.

complaint was classifiable as chronic nonincapacitating dysfunction," he reported, whereas scientific medicine was used to treat incapacitating diseases. The division was thoroughly pragmatic. Where traditional medicine was least effective, it gave way to modern practices, but it persisted for ailments that were diffuse and not altogether physical and for those for which scientific medicine had little to offer.[50]

This division is helpful in understanding the attitudes and practices of plain folk in the New South. Many of their ailments—anemia, chills, listlessness, indigestion, rheumatism, and the like were not incapacitating. And many of their incapacitating illnesses—consumption, pneumonia, the grippe, dysentery, typhoid, and the childhood diseases—were not readily curable by modern medicine. Folk attitudes toward health and medicine were thus functional even as advances in scientific medicine were rendering them less so. Folk medicine was decaying as its cultural underpinnings lost authority; and at the same time, food and drug researchers were exposing patent medicines as often valueless and sometimes harmful.

Yet folkways change slowly. Anthropologists have recognized two varieties of folk medicine that flourished in the New South. The first was nature based and stressed the curative powers of herbs, roots, and homemade potions; the second was derived from religion and the occult, and functioned through charms, spells, and ritualized behavior. Neither form was merely superstition, for superstition is simply a way of looking at things, and both forms contained much that was efficacious. Many herbs, roots, and homemade remedies do have curative qualities, and the faith many folk invested in magico-religious practices often produced satisfying results. This, indeed, is always the case where cultural practice endorses particular curing processes. As anthropologist Allan Young has observed, "People maintain their medical traditions because they affect undesirable biological states in expected ways, and because they are effective ways for dealing with disruptive events that cannot be allowed to persist."[51]

Both forms of folk medicine had long traditions. For plain folk in the piedmont and lowland areas of Georgia and the Carolinas, those traditions went back to Britain, but the long sojourn in America had adapted them to New World conditions. "Herbs and weeds of the field," said Harriet Echols,

50. Harold A. Gould, "The Implications of Technological Change for Folk and Scientific Medicine," *American Anthropologist*, LIX (1957), 507–16. On popular medicine, see Don Yoder, "Folk Medicine," in Richard M. Dorson (ed.), *Folklore and Folklife* (Chicago, 1972), 191–215.

51. Allan Young, "Some Implications of Medical Beliefs and Practices for Social Anthropology," *American Anthropologist*, LXXVIII (1976), 5; Yoder, "Folk Medicine," 191–215.

who was born in Murphy, North Carolina, in 1896 and moved to Tignall, Georgia, when she was five years old, "that's where our medicine came from." She recalled that her mother "would go to the woods and fields and gather the wild plants" and make her own medicines. Young Harriet, like so many of her generation, never learned the recipes and remedies, however, and many of the secrets were lost.[52]

But until they were no longer remembered, the recipes and remedies remained the staple of medical care for plain folk, for they were part of a belief system that held disease to be the result of natural imbalance, supernatural phenomena, or both. If the first, natural products could redress the problem. "In our old kitchen down on the farm, nailed to the wall was a medicine cabinet," Rosa Kanipe remembered of her childhood on a small North Carolina farm at the turn of the century. "In this cabinet was castor oil, salts, liniment, a bottle of good whiskey for snake bites, cough medicine made from cherry bark and whiskey and sugar, a tonic made from Sampson's snake root. Bitter tanay tea grown in the garden, boiled down with whiskey to preserve. The tanay was bitter as quinine. Ma gave me this for monthly periods."

The line separating nature-based and magico-religious healing was far from clear-cut, and was sometimes obscured altogether. The latter form of folk medicine had especially old roots, going back to medieval Europe, where assorted forms of magic had thrived, and running through Protestant Britain, where efforts to eradicate magical belief and practice had instead driven them underground.[53] This tradition expressed a world view based on the unity of all things while positing a dualism within that unity. The dualism was good and evil; the agents of each were, on the one hand, the Holy Trinity and healers, and on the other, the devil and his servitors, including all who could bewitch, "work roots," or otherwise invoke the forces of evil. In this tradition, disease was the product not of natural imbalances but of evil forces, and could be cured by counterforces invoked by spells, amulets, or ritualized behavior prescribed by someone with the power to command such things. "She cured a knot on the back of my neck once by puttin' three grains of corn in a handkerchief and rubbin' them on the knot and makin' me take 'em out and bury them in the ground," Homer L. Pike remembered of his great-grandmother in the early years of the twentieth century, before he and his sharecropping family moved to a cotton

52. "Harriet Echols," *Foxfire*, X (1976), 239.
53. See Keith Thomas, *Religion and the Decline of Magic* (New York, 1971); and Alan MacFarlane, *Witchcraft in Tudor and Stuart England* (New York, 1970).

mill. "She'd talk fire out of people, too, when they'd burn themselves. She'd take their hand or whatever part they burnt, and blow on it and whisper and mumble somethin' to herself and just talk it out."

In the medical beliefs of plain folk, magico-religious elements seem to have been stronger than those derived from nature-based healing. At the center was a conviction that illness, like other misfortune, was the work of God, usually as punishment for something, with the implication that individuals by themselves have little or no control over their physical well-being. One corollary to that idea was the belief that illness was inevitable, which led some parents knowingly to expose their children to a childhood disease to "get it over with." Another corollary was that modern medicine might be an intrusion into the work of God. "The Lord made us and He's going to take us away when he wants to," said Addie Norton, who even in 1975 did not "believe in" modern surgery. She stated, "You're never as strong after one part of your body's took away," because God "put in your body what he wants you to have. . . . I believe in keeping everything the Lord put in my body."[54]

It followed from such views that the world was a dangerous place and that people needed supernatural help in surviving. The source of help for most folk was God, and thus the widespread practice of praying for the sick and the belief even among the irreligious that prayer is or might be efficacious. For many people, the resulting attitude was one of fatalism, but for others the admonition that God helps those who help themselves was controlling; and the latter sought additional sources of help. "We have brought up with us various forms of superstition," the North Carolina Board of Health complained in 1916. "We don't like to sit down with thirteen at the table; we hang horseshoes over our doors; we carry buckeyes to keep off rheumatism and to cure piles; and we take the gallstone of the deer, moisten it, and stick it on the fresh bite of rabid animals to prevent hydrophobia."[55]

To folk, illness was something to be endured or exorcised, not approached scientifically. The ways of doctors and health officials were strange and thus threatening and, since they often did not work anyway, might be ignored or actively resisted. Doctors suggested cause-and-effect relationships that sometimes seemed bizarre or even ludicrous, and only when they produced dramatic results or accommodated their offerings to folk belief were they and their offerings accepted.

54. "Aunt Addie Norton," *Foxfire*, X (1976), 196–97.
55. North Carolina Board of Health, *Sixteenth Biennial Report, 1915–1916*, 55.

To medical reformers, folk were an endless source of despair—obstructionists or irresponsibles whose perversity and out-of-date customs stood in the way of medical reform and improved public health. In their every effort, whether to improve sanitation, to prevent the spread of disease, or to otherwise better the public's health, reformers ran into the folk; and in their exasperation, they, like other reformers, turned to coercion. The resistance they provoked is one measure of the vitality of folkways in the New South.

In one of their early efforts, the reformers tried to motivate folk to install and use sanitary privies. The effort was laudable, for the absence of sanitary privies, or any privies at all, and the consequent practice of "promiscuous defecation," were major health hazards. But the controlling fact was that plain folk had their own ways of "voiding their excreta," to use another of the reformers' euphemisms, and saw no need to change. Men and boys often refused to use privies even where they were available, though women and girls accepted outhouses as useful for the convenience and privacy they afforded. None of the folk were much concerned about whether their methods of elimination were sanitary, however, and all were alternately bemused and offended by the idea of indoor water closets.

Reformers thus faced a problem. Many folk had never used privies and refused to do so when they found the structures in the mill villages to which they moved. "Many families are not only unaccustomed to the privy, but many of them are opposed to it," Charles W. Stiles wrote in connection with his effort to have sanitary closets installed in the villages. "I have seen families which actually had to be 'house broken' to use of the privy. Such people will stool around and under their houses, or even on the privy floor, rather than use the privy properly; and not only have people themselves of this class told me that they disliked their use, but I have seen the effects of this dislike, and, further, mill managers have repeatedly told me of the difficulties with which they have had to contend in order to stop promiscuous defecation." Stiles continued: "I know at least one mill which starts in the families newly imported from the country in certain houses on the outskirts of the mill village, and does not move them into the better situated houses until after some time, a few months or a year or so, when the families have become less dirty in their habits." Stiles noted that "mill hands defecate on the floor or seat of newly installed [indoor] privies," the results of which he had "seen on several occasions."[56]

During World War I, military authorities encountered the same problem

56. Stiles, *Hookworm Disease Among Cotton-Mill Operatives*, 25, 33.

with troops from the rural South. The men "show an unusual amount of illiteracy, general ignorance and ignorance of personal hygiene," reported doctors at Camp Jackson, South Carolina, where those inducted were "mainly rural in origin" and largely from the Carolinas and Florida. "An illuminating example of the state of sophistication is the fact that classes [had to be] formed and instruction given in the use of water closets and toilet paper."[57]

Perhaps the strongest evidence that indoor privies were culturally taboo was the fact that their use caused emotional or physiological problems. "When a family followed the advice of the health authorities and installed toilets," Stiles found, "constipation very commonly resulted and people then reverted to 'dog sanitation' as compared with 'cat sanitation.' This resulted in the important observation that the seats on most toilets were too high."[58] The position of toilet seats might have been more important than one imagines. Warren Edwards, chief carpenter for a Wilmington, North Carolina, cotton mill village for several years before World War I, found building privies, in his wife's words, "the worstest work he ever done." The problem was making the height and size of the holes just right. " 'Taint no quick job cutting holes to fit folks," Edwards' wife continued. "The folks made a lot of fuss 'bout one hole being too small or too big fer little Buster or little Mary Jane. Holy mackerel, but my old man was driv almost crazy."

Because folk were indifferent or opposed to the installation of sanitary, indoor privies, Stiles, like other reformers, decided coercion was necessary. "Soil pollution should be made a 'crime,' and as such it should be punished by law," he wrote exasperatedly; and the Southern Medical Journal agreed. "It would seem justifiable that State legislation should be called in to pass laws demanding better privies," the journal editorialized after Stiles revealed the extent and cause of hookworm infection. "It is absolutely necessary that laws be passed and enforced, because of the ignorance of this class of tenant whites and the absolute indifference of the negro population throughout the South in all matters pertaining to public health."[59]

The idea of coercion became a routine part of the reformers' solutions to

57. Victor C. Vaughan and George T. Palmer, "Communicable Diseases in the National Guard and National Army of the United States During the Six Months from September 29, 1917, to March 29, 1918," *Journal of Laboratory and Clinical Medicine*, III (1918), 698.

58. Stiles, "Early History, in Part Esoteric, of the Hookworm (Uncinariasis) Campaign in Our Southern United States," 298.

59. Charles W. Stiles, "Some Underlying Causes of the Existence of Soil Pollution in Rural Districts," *Southern Medical Journal*, IV (February, 1911), 160; "The Hook Worm Disease in the South," *Southern Medical Journal*, II (1908), 1049–50.

health problems. "Put your hands on them with the law and make them do," a Charlotte, North Carolina, physician told his colleagues of folk whose unsanitary practices contributed to tuberculosis. "You talk about educating the laymen to do this," he continued; "it isn't worth a cent. Do something. Put your hands on them with the law and make them do; that is the way to teach the people to do things." The South's leading medical journal urged the same method in its fight against that "arch enemy, the house fly," "one of the most frequent, insidious and ever-present factors in the dissemination of [typhoid fever]." The *Southern Medical Journal* editorialized, "It is all well enough to advise persons to live in screened houses, but why not compel them to screen all earth closets and manure heaps and thus destroy the principal breeding places?"[60]

"I WON'T ALLOW MY CHILDREN TO BE VACCINATED ANYWHERE AS LONG AS I CAN HELP IT."

These ideas influenced another reform effort, the endeavor to make small-pox vaccinations and medical examinations of schoolchildren compulsory. The effort challenged deeply held values of plain folk and southern ideas concerning the proper role of government as well. By 1900 or 1915, vaccination was a safe, generally effective means of preventing the spread of many diseases, even if it did cause very sore arms; and a large majority of folk children had never had a medical examination.

Still, both aspects of the effort engendered intense opposition. The experience of North Carolina with compulsory vaccination was representative. In 1893 the state adopted a law permitting local jurisdictions to require smallpox vaccination, and as they began to do so, opposition appeared. In 1900 the state board of health took note of an "unreasonable prejudice" against vaccination among "many people chiefly of the more ignorant classes," and three years later the board was still complaining of the same thing. "Many refuse to submit to vaccination," the president of the board reported in 1903, "because of the serious [that is, sore] arms which have followed the practice, and that in turn seems to have been the result of very bad vaccination."[61] The opposition, however, was more deeply rooted than

60. North Carolina Board of Health, *Eleventh Biennial Report, 1905–1906*, 46; editorial, *Southern Medical Journal*, III (1910), 611.
61. North Carolina Board of Health, *Eighth Biennial Report, 1899–1900*, 160–61, and *Tenth Biennial Report, 1903–1904*, 18.

the president realized, for vaccination challenged folk beliefs that advocates of vaccination refused to accommodate.

Like other reformers, proponents of mandatory vaccinations selected cotton mill villagers as special objects of their concern. Perhaps they perceived the villagers as especially unhealthy or sensed that they were more resentful than other people of the vaccination campaign. Mill villages were sometimes virtually invaded by vaccinators supported by the force of law. "With two or three assistants Dr. Gibson invaded the mill districts and began calling for bared arms," read an item in the Atlanta *Constitution* from the cotton mill district of Macon in 1903. "With astonishing rapidity Dr. Gibson and those with him made many a sore upper portion of the arms which within a few days will call for a multiplicity of slings." Without offering detail, the item continued, "The opposition to vaccination was clearly shown, and the indications are that there may be many revolts against the work within a short time." Perhaps one such revolt had occurred four years earlier in Columbus, Georgia, another cotton mill center. The annual report of the Columbus police commissioner included this notation in the list of arrests made during 1899: for "refusing to be vaccinated, 43 cases."[62]

So strong was this fear of vaccination that one mill villager, Lola Campbell of Whitmire in Newberry County, wrote Governor Blease, asking his help. "Thay are trying to forse the people to Bee vacnated and I wish you would Please let me Know for I am not in a helthey condisun to Bee vacnated," she wrote. "Thay say thay are going to start next Week[.] Please let me Know at once where ti is Law or not[.] [T]hay say that the s[m]all Pocks is her[e] on the Place but I have Not Seen Eny thing But the chicken Pocks[.] [W]ill you pleas let me Know Where it is law or Not."[63]

This apprehension was widespread. One of the families Edgar R. Rankin interviewed in Gastonia in 1914 found vaccination so objectionable that it was leaving the mill after eighteen months and returning to the farm. "It is unhealthy in the mills," the mother of the family told Rankin, "and they try to vaccinate my children here. I won't allow my children to be vaccinated anywhere as long as I can help it." Similarly, Bessie Van Vorst found that twenty pupils withdrew from a mill village school in Griffin, Georgia, when vaccination there became mandatory.[64]

62. Atlanta *Constitution*, November 14, 1903; Columbus *Enquirer-Sun*, December 17, 1899.
63. Mrs. Lola Campbell to Coleman L. Blease, n.d., in 1914 Newberry County folder, in Coleman L. Blease Papers, South Carolina State Archives.
64. Edgar R. Rankin, "A Social Study of One Hundred Families at Cotton Mills in Gastonia North Carolina" (M.A. thesis, University of North Carolina, 1914), 20; Bessie Van Vorst, *The Cry of the Children: A Study of Child Labor* (New York, 1908), 134.

Perhaps the most instructive episode in the effort to impose medical examinations on schoolchildren occurred in South Carolina. There, in January, 1913, state legislators debated a bill requiring such examinations, but because of widespread opposition, they dropped the compulsory feature before passing the bill. Despite endorsements from the state's medical community and a variety of Progressive reformers, Governor Blease vetoed the measure, for which reformers then and historians since have condemned him. Yet to plain folk, his veto was an act of statesmanship. Whatever the merits of his action, Blease was more sensitive to the cultural values of plain folk than any other politician in the New South, and he used those values to justify his veto.

Blease wrote the legislature that the bill would take "from the parents of the child the right to attend to the physical condition of their own children." This Blease considered "a most outrageous intrusion" into family life, for it would permit "any physician to examine [a] child and expose its deformity or condition to the world." Such an act, he stated, was an invasion of privacy and a potential source of embarrassment or ridicule. "Do you not think that every man in this State is able to care and has love enough for his children to care for and protect them?" Blease asked the legislators. "Have all the people and all classes of the people become imbeciles and children that the Legislature at every turn must pass acts creating guardianships?" Blease hoped not. "People have a right to control their own children," he insisted. "Do you wish to . . . force every poor man to bow down to the whims of all the professions?"

Blease's remarks were an exemplary statement of the conflict between traditional folk and modernized professionals, and between "old-fashioned" ideas of propriety and morality and the demands of the modern state. "Do not say that every young girl in the State from 12 years old and up, without her consent, must be forced to be examined," Blease admonished, "and her physical condition certified by her physician to some school teacher, to be heralded around as public property."[65]

Whatever its degree of demagoguery, Blease's message touched values deeply held by plain folk. The folk did not understand and were therefore fearful of modern medicine and doctors, and as Blease sensed, they also resented intrusions into their lives, perhaps for the same reasons. They

65. L. Rosa H. Gantt, "Medical Inspection of Schools in South Carolina," *Southern Medical Journal*, VI (1913), 239–43. Blease's veto message is printed on 240–41. See also Jno. A. Ferrell, "The Need of Medical Inspection in Public Schools," *South Atlantic Quarterly*, XI (1912), 295–300; and David J. Hill, "First Measures Needed for Child Welfare upon the Part of Municipal and Educational Authorities in the South," *Southern Medical Journal*, II (1911), 99–104.

feared and resisted whatever they did not comprehend, in part because they feared exposure and humiliation. Blease's reference to the fear of ridicule was therefore especially relevant, for a profound sense of modesty, even shame, was one reason for the opposition to compulsory medical examination. Many folk simply refused to submit to a procedure they considered intimate to the point of embarrassment and positively indecent when performed by a stranger.

A recent study of the medical beliefs of a group of Appalachian women who migrated to Detroit illuminates this point. During the years of the Great Society, these women partook of little of the medical care available to them, even during and after pregnancy, unless they experienced serious complications. They even preferred to have their babies at home and went to the hospital for delivery only because their doctors refused to make house calls. "Most of them retain a basic distrust of physicians as well as a traditional modesty," Ellen J. Stekert wrote, explaining these findings. "Prenatal and postnatal examinations were regarded as humiliating" and were resisted because of "intense" modesty. In her study of the locality from which these women had come, Stekert found "that older women often changed clothes by simply putting on a dress over one already being worn" and that many women believed "it was unusual for persons to disrobe in front of others, even those of the same sex." Not surprisingly, then, "Most of the women expressed acute embarrassment about the pelvic examination. Several felt they had been physically hurt by it, and one woman commented that it 'somehow wasn't right,' having a strange man 'handle' and 'see' her just as if he were her husband." Where these women were raised, Stekert observed, "Prenatal counsel is given by a woman."[66] These kinds of attitudes and habits made Blease's veto message appealing to plain folk.

"MUCH DIPLOMACY IS REQUIRED IN DEALING WITH THEM."

Although most efforts in health reform won little support from plain folk, one endeavor did win their grudging endorsement. That was the campaign against hookworm of the Rockefeller Sanitary Commission, which eventually gained the cooperation of hundreds of thousands of folk despite the fact that it forced them to confront and accept some embarrassing and otherwise disagreeable things. The reason for the effort's success was sim-

66. Ellen J. Stekert, "Focus for Conflict: Southern Medical Beliefs in Detroit," in Americo Paredes and Ellen J. Stekert (eds.), *The Urban Experience and Folk Tradition* (Austin, 1971), 111.

ple: the people directing the campaign understood that what they were trying to do would be ignored or resisted unless plain folk did not find their methods threatening or patronizing.

All southerners resented outsiders coming in and telling them what they should and should not do, especially in sensitive matters of life-style. The Rockefeller commission's task was in the medium as well as in the message, and in accomplishing that task, its leaders borrowed eclectically from things plain folk knew and understood—the devices of religious revivalism, political rallies, traveling road shows, and all-day socials. The historian of the effort has compared it to a religious crusade, and the metaphor is apt. The campaign, John Ettling has written, incorporated "all the features of the old evangelical notion of sin" and "employed the methods of evangelical Christianity to wage war on hookworm disease."[67]

To avoid the image of outsiders, campaign leaders worked through local people of influence, asking them to endorse the effort, visit clinics and exhibitions, and otherwise show their support. The campaign entered cotton mill villages only when mill officials actively cooperated, and there as elsewhere, editors, teachers, preachers, and employers worked to assure the skeptical. Through exhibits and illustrated lectures, campaign workers described hookworm disease in language laymen could understand. Wherever people congregated—at school and church, in town on Saturday afternoon, at county fairs across the South—campaign workers appeared, frequently having arranged for entertainment and picnicking. At clinics and traveling dispensaries, individuals could look at hookworms through microscopes. They might also have their pictures taken, hear testimonials from those already freed of the parasites, and find themselves objects of public praise for their cooperation. "Those needing [hookworm] treatment most are generally poor, ignorant, and superstitious and much diplomacy is required in dealing with them," wrote a Mississippi doctor active in the campaign, "but when the confidence of one of this class is gained he generally becomes a powerful factor in his little circle in inducing others to be examined and treated."[68]

The effort was more difficult than this statement suggests, for the obstacles were great. "The announcement that hookworm is prevalent in the States was not taken seriously," one of the Rockefeller Sanitary Commission's early reports said. "Many people resented the suggestion of their

67. Ettling, *The Germ of Laziness*, 222–23.
68. Louis Kolheim, "Some Intestinal Parasites of North Mississippi," *Southern Medical Journal*, V (1912), 485.

386 PLAIN FOLK IN THE NEW SOUTH

being infected and refused to be examined and treated, even when they knew they were ill and when every indication pointed to hookworm disease." It was difficult to make people believe they were "wormy," for "they have taken their anemia, their lack of vitality, their feeling 'puny' and 'out of sorts,' as a matter of course." It was even more difficult to motivate them to bring in a specimen of their stool. In the mill villages, Stiles found it "frequently necessary to go to the house two to four times before the specimen could be obtained, as at the time there was widespread popular prejudice against or distrust of the examinations."[69]

Even after they learned they had hookworms, some folk refused the medication. "I have seen family after family where they tell me they have visited the clinics, had been told they had hookworm disease, had taken the medicine home, but were afraid to take it," Stiles also wrote. Many others who did take the medication refused to do what was necessary to prevent reinfection, and according to one estimate, "three out of every four children that we cured of this disease would have it again within a year after we cured them."[70]

Plain folk were intensely conservative in matters of social custom, and most had little of the ego strength or social experience that eases the kind of social reckoning the hookworm campaign demanded of them. Rejecting help was the easiest way of coping with a situation in which many of them felt insecure. It was a means of gaining self-assurance by asserting control of themselves and confounding those who aroused their anxieties with offers of help.

One mark of the commission's achievement was its successes in overcoming these obstacles. Another was the adoption of its techniques by other public health campaigns. A drive to improve sanitation and health in Greenville County in 1916, for example, included the sermon "The Gospel of Health," based on the text "Now that ye know and do not these things, ye have sinned against God and man." The campaign also included essay contests for schoolchildren, a "Sanitation Day" parade with floats depicting health themes, and an exhibit of sanitary privies at the county fair. Concluding the festivities was a drawing in which the prize was one of the privies on display.[71]

69. Rockefeller Sanitary Commission for the Eradication of Hookworm Disease, *First Annual Report, 1919* (Washington, D.C., 1920), 13; Stiles, *Hookworm Disease Among Cotton-Mill Operatives*, 13.

70. Stiles, quoted in Ettling, *The Germ of Laziness*, 165; Frederick Eberson, "Eradication of Hookworm Disease in Florida," *Journal of the Florida Medical Association*, LXVII (1980), 736.

71. Lumsden, "Rural Sanitation," 222.

PART IV

CULTURAL PERSISTENCE AND SOCIAL CHANGE

13

RELIGION

Plain folk were a religious people. "Sacred symbols function to synthesize a people's ethos," Clifford Geertz has written, "the tone, character, and quality of their life, its moral and esthetic style and mood—and their world-view—the picture they have of the way things in sheer actuality are, their most comprehensive ideas of order."[1]

Whether plain folk were "saved" or "lost," churched or unchurched, religion was the wellspring of their understanding of things, the taproot of their value system, their guide to right and wrong and to life itself. Yet the fundamental position of religion in their lives is more easily recognized than demonstrated, for plain folk were not given to systematic thought. They never spoke of first principles except in phrases they heard endlessly repeated by self-taught preachers whose purpose was to affirm their faith and warm their hearts. They never probed the logic, coherence, or implications of even basic beliefs, and never thought through their convictions from premise to conclusion. Instead, they "felt" and "believed in" things, which thereby made

1. Clifford Geertz, "Religion as a Culture System," in Michael Banton (ed.), *Anthropological Approaches to the Study of Religion* (New York, 1966), 3.

them true for the folk, and did not "feel" or "believe in" other things, which thereby made them false or irrelevant.

Folk accepted religion; they did not analyze, critique, or even much ponder it. In his study of a white farm community in southwest Tennessee in the 1930s, sociologist Frank D. Alexander encountered a phenomenon that pointedly illustrates this. "Will you make a statement of what religion means to you?" Alexander asked people in the community. They were taken back. The question had never occurred to them, and they had no ready, substantive answers to it. "A whole lot," some of them responded revealingly, "lots." Alexander saw their reaction as evidence of "the small degree" to which people in the community had rationalized their religion and of the "vague, generalized" nature of their belief.[2] He was no doubt correct. To most folk, and probably most other southerners too, religion was a given of life, not something to look into inquiringly.

Yet plain folk were not a pious, worshipful, or churchly people. Of all major socioeconomic groups in the New South, they were the least likely to join a church, attend worship services, pray as a family, or say grace at mealtime.[3] Probably more than half of the plain folk had little or nothing to do with organized religion. At the village of Aragon-Baldwin Mills in Whitmire, South Carolina, in 1926, for example, 45 percent of the male heads of families were not church members, and in a quarter of the families (23.2 percent) neither husband nor wife belonged to a church. In almost half the families (45 percent), neither spouse attended church regularly, and only a quarter of the mothers and a sixth of the fathers were regular churchgoers. "In a great many cases the thought of church never enters their minds," Alexander R. Batchelor, who collected these figures, wrote of village families. "In many homes the wife did not know whether her husband was a member of the church or not. 'She had never heard him say.'"[4]

These facts complicate the problem of generalizing about folk religion.

2. Frank D. Alexander, "Religion in a Rural Community of the South," *American Sociological Review*, VI (1941), 241–42.
3. Information on religious practices among plain folk is skimpy for the New South era, but it all points in the same direction. Eighty percent of tenant farm families in the Tennessee community studied by Frank D. Alexander in the 1930s never said grace at the table and 92 percent never prayed as a family. In these categories as in church attendance, their worship activity was significantly less than that of farm owners (*ibid.*, 244–45). For similar results in a survey of 855 farm families in 8 cotton-growing counties in Oklahoma in 1926, see Otis D. Duncan, "Relation of Tenure and Economic Status of Farmers to Church Membership," *Social Forces*, XI (1933), 541–47.
4. Alexander R. Batchelor, "A Textile Community" (M.A. thesis, University of South Carolina, 1926), 21–25.

So also does the widespread belief in signs and other forms of magic, superstition, and luck that was at least partly religious in nature and function. This belief appears in the interviews less than one might expect, but in quite conventional form.[5] Like the religious convictions to which it was culturally related, it helped folk understand fundamental things and thereby control or mediate events. "We allus planted corn on the first dark of the moon in March," Julie West, the wife of a North Carolina sharecropper recalled of her youth. "Crops planted on the bright of the moon grows spindling. The corn shoots up tall and goes all to leaves. The ears are stunted. Mustard planted on the bright of the moon goes all to stems. Plant it on the dark of the moon, and it grows low, and bushy, with plenty of leaves."

Such beliefs were universal, but they were not rivals and certainly not alternatives to religion. On the contrary, they complemented and supplemented it. To plant crops, kill hogs, or wean babies according to signs of the zodiac was no evidence of paganism or unbelief. Rather, for guidance in some activities, one prayed, followed the Bible, or talked with the preacher; for help with others, one read the signs and the almanac that explained them, took whatever steps were necessary to counteract ill omens, or sought out one of the old women who had mysterious powers to do certain things. "Planted my corne the Second day of May," Henderson Fowler recorded in his diary at Alamance Mills in 1887. "Little Moon down in the Virgin 5 dayes before the full Moon one fourth guano in the hill."[6]

Belief in signs was more widespread and socially significant than belief in ghosts and spirits. The latter survived more in the form of controllable fears than in the form of coherent social thought. "My parents believed in witches and ghosts," recalled Andrew King, who grew up on a North Carolina farm at the turn of the century. "I've knowed them to put pins around the bed, lay the broom in front of the door, and do other silly things. They also believed in brownies. I never believed in any of it but ghosts, and I didn't believe in them much until a ghost rode my back down Crabtree Hill

5. For representative collections and commentaries, see B. A. Botkin, *A Treasury of Southern Folklore: Stories, Ballads, Traditions and Folkways of the People of the South* (New York, 1949); Botkin (ed.), *Folk-Say: A Regional Miscellany* (Norman, 1930); Botkin, "Folk and Folklore," in W. T. Couch (ed.), *Culture in the South* (Chapel Hill, 1934), 570–97; Harry M. Hyatt, *Hoodoo Conjuration, Witchcraft, Rootwork: Beliefs Accepted by Many Negroes and White Persons These Being Orally Recorded Among Blacks and Whites* (4 vols; Cambridge, Md., 1971–74); Vance Randolph, *Ozark Superstitions* (New York, 1947).

6. Henderson Monroe Fowler Diary and Account Books, Vol. IV, in Southern Historical Collection, Louis R. Wilson Library, University of North Carolina at Chapel Hill.

once. I've seen two or three since then. They don't bother you except the first three nights when the moon is new. I stay in them nights."

Credulity of this sort was generally submerged, though extraordinary events brought it rapidly to the surface. In the summer of 1914, the village of Massachusetts Mills was "thrown into a fever of excitement" for two weeks by midnight appearances of an apparition "about the size and shape of a white calf or a large dog." After the Reverend J. E. Smith, pastor of the village Baptist church, confirmed the appearances, villagers organized "a volunteer posse, armed with shotguns, revolvers, and army guns" and for several nights searched for the "ghost." They found a large, white, deaf dog that had the habit of appearing fleetingly in the moonlight and scampering away whenever anyone approached.[7]

"I'M A GOD FEARING WOMAN, BUT I GOT TO HAVE MY SNUFF."

Plain folks were generally Baptists or Methodists.[8] Their religion revolved around a core of unambiguous beliefs that all their lives they heard repeated at church, camp meeting, and revival. Their God was the anthropomorphic being of the Old Testament. He interested himself in their individual lives, punishing their sins and rewarding their faith. His wrath had been mediated by the sacrifice of his son, Jesus Christ; and by accepting Christ and the salvation his sacrifice made possible, the individual would earn eternal bliss in heaven, "the good place." This was accomplished by professing one's faith, joining the church, and living according to required standards of moral conduct. Rejecting the offer of salvation, refusing to accept Christ as one's personal Savior and persisting in a "life of sin," doomed the unbeliever to eternal punishment in hell, "the bad place." These essentials of Christian theology came to folk through a long history, the milestones of which included the Calvinism that influenced English and Scottish Protestantism in the seventeenth century, the recurrent waves of revivalism set off by the Great Awakening, the Wesleyan Methodism that spread through the South during and after the revolutionary war era, and the leveling Arminianism preached in camp meetings and backwoods revivals throughout the nineteenth century.

7. Atlanta *Constitution,* July 10, 14, 17, 1914.
8. On these churches in the New South era, see Rufus B. Spain, *At Ease in Zion: Social History of the Southern Baptists, 1865–1900* (Nashville, 1967); Hunter D. Farish, *The Circuit Rider Dismounts: A Social History of Southern Methodism, 1865–1900* (Richmond, 1938); John Lee Eighmy, *Churches in Cultural Captivity: A History of the Social Attitudes of Southern Baptists* (Knoxville, 1972); H. Shelton Smith, *In His Image but . . . Racism in Southern Religion, 1780–1910* (Durham, 1972).

The resulting religion was democratic, hopeful, and affirming, as well as otherworldly, mysterious, and demanding in matters of personal conduct. Even the lowliest person, it taught, was precious in the eyes of the Lord and of Christ, too, whose atonement made salvation available to all. Everyone had freedom of choice in this most vital of all matters, and had, too, the prospect of God's help through prayer. These things the Bible set forth in inerrent terms believers must know and accept.

The Bible was also an inerrent guide to right and wrong, sinlessness and sin. These were not philosophical or sociological constructs but categories of moral absolutes largely concerned with individual conduct. Nowhere was the personal, concrete nature of folk religion more evident than in its understanding of sin. Murder and other gross crimes were of course sinful (unless committed in a social context that justified them, such as the preservation of white supremacy or of female virture). But plain folk were not concerned with gross crimes when they spoke of sin. Of far more importance were ordinary matters of personal conduct, especially those involving sex and abuse of "the temple of the body." These were crucial areas of behavior because human nature was weak and inclined to self-indulgence and because the Devil was everywhere, tempting, promising, seducing. Sex was the Devil's special lure, and any conduct associated with it, even suggestive of it, outside marriage was actually or potentially sinful. Adultery, fornication, and prostitution, like gross crimes, were obviously anathema. But other activities were problematic because the sin they involved seemed potential rather than actual and was therefore less apparent. They were the more to be avoided for that reason: they were lures the Devil used to trap the innocent. Dancing and partying, especially where there was drinking, were thus absolutely forbidden, as were the kinds of immodesty manifested in the new pastime of men and women swimming together in revealing bathing suits, and the sorts of unbecoming conduct that led to easy familiarity between men and women. Anything that abused the body—except perhaps overeating—was likewise sinful or at least morally questionable. Next to sexual incontinence, drinking was the worst of ordinary sins, so bad that any activity in places where it might be present—card playing, gambling, and billiard playing, for example—was also forbidden to decent people. Smoking, chewing tobacco, and dipping snuff were also abuses of the body, but they were so widespread that the degree of their actual sinfulness was a matter of debate. Breaking the Sabbath, using profanity, telling lies, gossiping, dishonoring one's parents, beating one's wife, and brutalizing one's children were also sins of special concern.

Joined to the belief that sin was the consequence of personal depravity or weakness, these attitudes turned religious energies inward, onto believers themselves, rather than outward toward social and economic problems. This discouraged conventional kinds of social activism, though it did focus attention on some real problems—drinking, wife beating, and child abuse, for example. By helping believers control their own conduct, these attitudes enabled them to use their religion efficaciously. This offered them the enlarged self-esteem that comes from living a "good" life, as well as the psychological securities of salvation.

Most folk did not live a "good" life, however. By their own reckoning, they were sinners to some degree. That is, after accepting a standard of conduct as ideal and righteous, folk failed to live according to that standard. They readily acknowledged that their violations of it were sins, which they regretted and apologized for. "I'm a God fearing woman," Mrs. Warren Edwards said, "but I got to have my snuff."

Evidence of this disparity between belief and practice is abundant. "I used to belong to the Baptist Church," Nancy Owen said, acknowledging a division in her life she regretted, "but I've always been used to cussing, drinking, and working on Sunday." Such dissonance fed the sense of guilt and inadequacy folk experienced, but the religious belief that created the dissonance offered a rationalization that rendered it tolerable. People were weak, the rationalization held, and the Devil was strong and constantly at work even among the saved. "Backsliding"—falling from salvation back into sin—was therefore frequent and understandable. "I quit snuff once for twelve year," a North Carolina mill worker said. "I never even wanted to dip while I was saved but when I backslid I took it up again." Why did she backslide? "Don't know," she answered. "Devil got in me, I reckon. Nothin' but the Devil made me take up snuff again. I know it's a sin because the Bible says 'Cleanse yourself from all filthy habits.' Dippin's sure a filthy habit."[9]

Another longtime mill worker had much the same experience. "I wish I could've holt on to my religion," Lil Pepper said of her own fall from good standing in a Holiness church, "but I 'lowed myself to get mad with two fool women in the mill—hypocrites was what they was—and I ain't been right with the Lord since. Tain't a good feelin' neither. If I was to die tonight I know I'd go as straight to hell as a bee martin to his hole. But you can't push the spirit, no sir, not to save your life you can't push the spirit."

This failure to live righteously was not the same as indifference to organized religion, which was also quite widespread. "We're Baptists but I

9. Unnamed person in FWP interviews, reel 3.

never paid much attention to religion," "Pa" Carnes, a North Carolinian, told an interviewer in the 1930s. "I don't understand much of the Bible when I read it, so I leave that to the women folks and the preachers." He also left to his wife teaching their children about religion. "Of course I've got no objection to religion," he said. "I really like a good sermon." These views and practices were commonplace, and might have been typical. They were those of folk who gave no evidence of unbelief and made no mockery of religion but who attended church only occasionally, perhaps at revivals or camp meetings, where opportunities to socialize and experience emotional release were especially great.

Many folk shared this respect for religion and indifference to churches. "It's been a good while since I thought of religion," Nancy Owens said. "I stopped going to church mostly way back when the younguns was little. You see I didn't have nothing to wear for me nor them. It was a good ways to go and William won't go with me nor keep the younguns for me to go. He never did care for churches nor religion and atter a while the hard life took everything outen me 'cept cussing, I reckon."

Plain folk, then, worshiped far less than is suggested by their reputation as zealous denizens of the Bible belt. For reasons of social insecurity and inexperience, most folk were not joiners or ready participants in organized activities. In the presence of other people, many of them were sensitive about their clothes and shoes, and felt, no doubt rightly, that better-off churchgoers looked down on them because of their appearance, speech, and social ways. Their frequent movement from place to place also affected their participation in churches, for those who moved every year or every two or three years spent much of their lives about strangers in strange places. This helps explain why so many folk belonged to churches in communities where they no longer lived. Many mill folk, for example, remained members of rural churches. Almost a quarter (23.2 percent) of the members John K. Morland counted in villages in York in the 1940s were in this category. Many rural folk also joined a church once, probably in the community they grew up in or thought of as home, and never changed their membership after they moved away.[10]

This pattern suggests that folk associated church membership with rootedness and that many of them thought of themselves as sojourners away from home. It suggests, too, that they expected to move again in the future.

10. John K. Morland, *Millways of Kent* (Chapel Hill, 1958), 108. Frank D. Alexander found that about a third of the husbands and wives in the tenant families (34 percent and 30 percent, respectively) were members of churches outside the community in Tennessee where they resided in the 1930s ("Religion in a Rural Community of the South," 245).

Whether it also related to the tendency among many folk to distinguish between religion and the people who professed it most prominently is an open question. That tendency, however, was pronounced. The folk view of what constituted a religious life was extraordinarily literal. To them, true Christians, especially those who put themselves forth as religious examples by assuming prominent roles in church, must live according to popular religious precepts literally interpreted. Of course no one could live that way, but many folk took the failure of church people to do so as proof of hypocrisy and reason not to associate with "that church crowd." What saved folk from hypocrisy in their own minds was that they never pretended to be anything but weak and human, and never set themselves up as examples for other people to follow.

"THE METHODIST PREACHER WOULD PREACH ONE SUNDAY AND THE BAPTIST THE NEXT."

These were major contours in the religious background of mill folk, and what the folk brought from that background to the mills largely determined the nature and content of village religion. Outside of work itself, religion was the first aspect of village life to be organized. At the outset, the larger villages had one or more church buildings and congregations, but in smaller communities, arrangements were initially makeshift. If there was a church nearby, villagers worshiped there for a time or invited the preacher to come to them under whatever arrangements they could make. Early in the life of every village, religious folk set about the task of organizing themselves into congregations and arranging for places of worship and preachers to serve their needs. For a number of reasons, mill owners were anxious to help them accomplish these goals. The villagers wanted churches of their own, and helping them get places of worship was a sure way of raising morale. Also, many owners were themselves professed Christians for whom establishing churches in their villages was a religious obligation. In addition, all owners, religious or otherwise, were certain that religious folk were better workers than those who were not. Religious belief, paternal instinct, and economic interest all encouraged the same course of action in mill owners' minds.

The owners' contributions to village religion were substantial.[11] Many

11. A survey by the South Carolina Manufacturers' Association in 1902 found that in the villages of 65 mills in South Carolina, there were 93 church buildings valued at $159,000. Of this value, the mills had contributed $82,595; and the mills contributed a total of $5,483 annually to operating costs of churches in their villages (*Manufacturers' Record*, January 30, 1902).

owners built and equipped churches from their own funds; others donated two, three, or more dollars for every dollar raised for that purpose by villagers. When the structures were completed, mill owners often deeded them and the land they stood on to the congregations. They also hired and paid preachers or, more often, paid a specified portion of the preacher's salary or made substantial annual contributions to churches in their villages. Some assisted in the purchase of Sunday school literature, new songbooks, or a church organ. Those who lived in or adjacent to their villages often attended church with their operatives, and many who did not encouraged mill officers and supervisors to attend. A few owners and officers taught Sunday school classes, and some of their wives and relatives also assisted in church work.

Details varied from village to village. Since most mills were small and operated with limited capital, building and supporting one or more churches represented a substantial expense. The first sanctuary in many villages was therefore a converted residence, but even after a proper edifice was built, it was likely to be used by Baptists and Methodists alike. At the village of Victor Mills, for example, where Methodists organized a congregation in 1898 and Baptists followed suit a year later, the two groups shared a church for several years. "We all went to the same church," an older resident remembered in the 1940s. "We had a union Sunday School and the Methodist preacher would preach one Sunday and the Baptist the next—until 1909 when the Baptists drew out and built a church on the other side of the street." Meanwhile, the mill built parsonages for the free use of each congregation.[12]

At Brandon village in Greenville the same sharing of facilities occurred. "They didn't have it separate," Jessie Lee Carter recalled of the situation there early in the twentieth century. "Like this Sunday our preacher would preach—the Baptist preacher—then next Sunday the Methodist preacher would preach. . . . Everybody went. The church was always full on Sunday."

At their village at Lawndale, the Schencks repeated this process. "We are nearly done [building] our little chapel," H. F. Schenck wrote his business partner in 1891, listing the furnishings he needed to complete the interior of the structure. "We want a small chapel organ for S School and worship. A Small 4 lamp Chandileer—a Bible and a couple of Suspension Lamps. These I propose to get by contribution." He then asked his partner for a

12. Sybil V. W. Hutton, "Social Participation of Married Women in a South Carolina Mill Village" (M.A. thesis, University of Kentucky, 1948), 14.

donation. A few years later, John F. Schenck described the chapel as "a good church—at which all denominations are allowed to hold services."[13]

This easy interdenominationalism was facilitated by the similarities of Methodism and Baptism and the absence of sectarian rivalries among mill folk. In performing baptisms, Methodists "sprinkled," as folk said, and Baptists "dunked." Methodists were also somewhat more organized as a denomination; Baptists were thoroughly congregational. But both churches were open to all save wanton sinners and were essentially the same in things that mattered to folk. "Don't make no difference what church you belong to though, jest so you lives right," remarked Sarah Strickland Faison, the daughter of a North Carolina farmer and a lifelong Baptist. "Doing what God tells us to do is what gits us to the good place, and that's 'xactly where I wants to go."

"Living right," rather than denominational loyalty, was what religion was about to Mrs. Faison and other folk in and out of the villages. "My people was mighty good," Mrs. Faison recalled of her parents, illustrating the way religious folk used religion to order their daily lives. "They wouldn't go to dances and parties where they drunk. They didn't care nothing 'bout shows, and I never been to half a dozen shows in my life. I think most dances and shows is the devil's work. Pappy wouldn't let his chillun go to dances and such, and my husband always preached against such things." This conduct was what the Bible stipulated, Mrs. Faison believed, and she, like Methodist and Baptist folk across the New South, used the Bible as an infallible guide to life. "I don't believe in keeping from having chillun," she also said. "It's God work and 'cording to what the Bible says we should let what happen happen. The Bible say multiply the earth. I can't read the Bible but I love it, and I gits people to read it to me. It's God's word, and I believe every word in it."

Most villages eventually developed a full array of church activities—Baptist and Methodist services with full- or part-time resident preachers, Sunday schools, and midweek prayer meetings. Easily the highlight of the year was the annual revival, held, as in the country, in late summer between "laying by" time and "cotton picking" time. Villages with two or more congregations enjoyed a season of revivals, during which saved and sinner alike sat spellbound before visiting evangelists exhorting them to "take up the cross" and return to the verities of old-time religion.

13. H. F. Schenck to J. E. Reynolds, December 16, 1891, statement by John F. Schenck, September, 1898, in H. F. Schenck Papers, Manuscript Department, Duke University Library, Durham, North Carolina.

The churches played important but not dominating roles in village life. Most folk joined one of them, a few married in them, and almost all passed through them on the way to the graveyard and eternity. But many things undermined the centrality they and their preachers tried to achieve. The presence of mill owners and officers eclipsed the preacher's significance, and schools, community houses, and other places provided social alternatives for the nonreligious. Larger villages commonly had one or more active fraternal organizations. At Lindale in 1904, for example, there were lodges of Masons, Knights of Pythias, Odd Fellows, and Red Men.[14] The nature and duration of mill work also encouraged mill folk to make Sunday a day of rest and diversion; and many folk simply had no interest in church.

Yet in many villages, the church was the only institution of significance outside the family and the mill, and the only source of group activity. Church, Sunday school, Bible school, choir practice, youth programs, socials, revivals, and even funerals constituted the core of social life for many villagers. Church sponsorship of picnics and other excursions removed the qualms many folk had about such activities and made participation not only acceptable but even commendable. At such events, young people did much of their courting, and adults found occasion for socializing and showing off new clothes and babies.

But churches and religion provided much more than social activities. They were important sources of solace and strength. "I look to put my trust in the Lord about what comes on us," said Mary Abbott, whose lifetime in the mills had been especially full of care. "There's nothin' anyways folks kin do about death a-comin'. I mind Ma sayin' she'd put her trust in the Lord when Pa was took and how it was her comfort. We're took away when He feels like it's best and I never let myself to worry over them younguns [her grandchildren] bein' took up to Heaven."

Religion was also a way of ordering and explaining things, and therefore a source of certainty in an uncertain world. "I believe good as I'm settin' here that the boll weevil is sent on folks because of the ways they do," Fanny Bowers Maddrey, wife of a North Carolina sharecropper and a onetime mill worker, said in the 1930s. "Instead of goin' to church, they pile in a car and go to the movin' pictures and bathin' pools. It's too fast a life nowadays. The Lord means to cut 'em down with the boll weevil or somethin'." Commenting on the hard times the mills experienced in the 1920s and 1930s, Joseph

14. *Manufacturers' Record*, October 13, 1904, p. 298.

A. Michaels said similarly, "I've always thought it was the Lord showing his disapproval of our evil ways."

Most folk accepted the ways of the world in which they grew up, and throughout their lives used those ways as moorings against which to measure social and moral change. Any significant departure from familiar norms they viewed as threatening and therefore objectionable. In this sense, most of them were backward looking in their social views, which explains why so many children thought of their parents as old-fashioned or "old timey," and why older folk generally thought the younger generation was becoming increasingly immoral. "Seems like too many people are going to the bad now," F. B. Brewer said in the 1930s after a lifetime of tenant farming. "I wouldn't be caught at one of these beaches or swimming holes that they keep open on Sunday, but I have heard talk of them that has been caught there. It ain't so good. When I was a boy they got along without so many amusements they think so necessary now. I guess the car is the cause of it all."

"THE VALUE OF RELIGION AS AN AID TO DISCIPLINE IS FULLY RECOGNIZED."

Was village religion an instrument of social control? Certainly the owners' support of churches and preachers was substantial and almost universal. Certainly, too, all owners believed religion made workers more conscientious, sober, stable, and reasonable to deal with; and they were surely correct in the belief. "The value of religion as an aid to discipline is fully recognized," Holland Thompson wrote of mill owners in a contemporary assessment; and he and subsequent scholars used that fact and the economic advantage it gave mill owners to interpret village religion as an endeavor by which self-serving, even cynical, owners manipulated helpless, ignorant folk into actively furthering their own victimization. "The clergymen of the denominations most active in mill villages naturally believe and preach doctrines which would be acceptable in the main to a capitalist employer," Harriet Herring wrote a generation after Thompson, "a gospel of work, of gratitude for present blessings, and of patience with economic and social maladjustment as temporal and outside the sphere of religious concern."[15]

Later scholars carried these views much farther. "The greatest contribu-

15. Holland Thompson, *From the Cotton Field to the Cotton Mill: A Study of the Industrial Transition in North Carolina* (New York, 1906), 176; Harriet L. Herring, *Welfare Work in Mill Villages: The Story of Extra-Mill Activities in North Carolina* (Chapel Hill, 1929), 99.

tion of the churches to the industrial revolution in the South undoubtedly lay in the labor discipline they provided through moral supervision of the workers," sociologist Liston Pope wrote in his major study *Millhands and Preachers*, focusing on Gaston County, North Carolina. "Methods used in helping to convert an atomistic assemblage of rural individualists into a disciplined labor force, amenable to a high degree of social control, consisted of the inculcation of personal virtues (stability, honesty, sobriety, industry)" and giving mill folk "an emotional escape from the difficulties of life in a mill village." Herbert J. Lahne was even more explicit. The village church, he wrote in 1944, was "little more than an adjunct to the employer—just one of the channels through which the employer has sought to make complete his hold on the workers." And, Lahne believed, the churches would never be anything else until they rid themselves of "the necessity of relying on the mill management for financial aid."[16]

Assessing these conspiratorial, starkly economic interpretations is another way of learning about the realities of village religion. There is a level on which the interpretations are true, but the level is abstract and the truth theoretical. That is the level at which all religions affirm the social order in which they function. Even religions committed to social change may at that level be said to be affirming in that they relieve grievances that might otherwise produce pressure for social change. Whatever their value, however, interpretations of social phenomena that are abstracted enough to be universally applicable have little room for context and do little to illuminate the particularities of individual cases. Yet for all its concern with regularities and patterns, history is a discipline of context, a study of the particular and the specific. From that perspective, the important issue is not whether village religion was otherworldly, escapist, or affirmative of the social and economic status quo. It is, instead, how and to what extent mill folk molded a religion of their own and how they used that religion to make their lives more meaningful and tolerable.

The indictment of village religion is weakened by testing it against the religion of rural folk. No one has made a systematic study of the religion of sharecroppers or claimed that religion was a major instrument in keeping them docile or subservient. The logic of social control, however, suggests that religion functioned in that way. The religion of mill folk and farm folk was the same. The two groups were culturally identical and received their

16. Liston Pope, *Millhands and Preachers: A Study of Gastonia* (New Haven, 1942), 29; Herbert J. Lahne, *The Cotton Mill Worker* (New York, 1944), 60.

religion from the same kinds of preachers in the same denominations. Yet rural churches were not underwritten by individual or even groups of land-lords for the benefit of croppers. Although there was no doubt some social and economic stratification among rural churches in the New South, segregation into congregations based on land tenure was not a primary fact. On the contrary, landlords and tenants attended the same churches if they attended at all, and tenants stayed away from churches at which they felt unwelcome or uncomfortable. This explains the low rates of religious participation among farm tenants.

There seems to have been no parallel effort among landlords to use religion as mill owners are said to have used it to discipline and control their employees. It might be argued that landlords were more sure of their economic and social position than mill owners and thus had no need for social manipulation. It might also be argued that mill work required more social discipline than sharecropping, or that the congregation of large numbers of folk in mill villages increased the threat of indiscipline to property owners. Still, it is difficult to see how a religion that kept sharecroppers "an atomistic assemblage of rural individualists," to use Liston Pope's words, could make those same folk "a disciplined labor force" in the mills.

There are other problems with interpretations of village religion as a vehicle of social control. Mill folk chose their own religious affiliations, and in choosing Baptism and Methodism they also chose the religious message they wanted to hear. The choice was exercised by the simple act of staying away from unappealing churches and preachers. It is therefore difficult to believe that mill preachers aimed their message at mill owners rather than mill folk, or preached as they did from cynical self-interest. A large minority of the preachers had been or still were mill workers, and part of their appeal was that they spoke the idiom of the folk and made folk comfortable at church. More important, they had been reared in the religion they preached, and had internalized its deepest precepts and values. They therefore preached what they believed in their heart of hearts, as they would have said, and not what they were paid to preach. Or rather, they were paid to preach what was in their heart.

It might be said in opposition to this point that mill owners hired only preachers with "correct" views. That statement is abstractly true but implies that there were preachers about with "wrong" views and that mill officials dispensed to their employees religious views they did not believe themselves. There is no evidence to support either implication. On the contrary, owners, preachers, and mill workers shared the same basic religious beliefs (though they did not express them the same way in worship services). In supporting village churches and preachers, mill owners had multiple motives, and the fact that their religious and economic interests coincided only affirmed their faith in the correctness of their religion. Theirs was a faith that honored economic enterprise, accumulation, and activities that encouraged those ends, but it honored social uplift and moral crusading, too, and to make one of these sets of values their entire concern is an act of fundamental distortion. Mill owners did not live for philanthropy alone, but neither did they live only for bread, and the truth about their motivations in supporting mill churches lies in the ways they joined those disparate concerns.

The conclusion that village religion was largely an exercise in social control thus rests on only part of the relevant information. It incorporates what mill owners said about the social functions of religion, assesses the economic interest in the owners' "investment" in religion, assumes that wherever an economic interest is involved it is automatically controlling, and reads otherworldly Christianity for its escapist content alone. Also relevant were what mill folk gained from the preaching they heard and how they applied religion besides in escapism, and even whether they heard the preaching at all. Recent studies of slave religion show that the ostensible message of a religion controlled by an economic elite and the uses social out-groups make of that message can be entirely separate.[17] Mill owners never fully succeeded in making mill folk into disciplined workers or model citizens. To the extent that they failed, village religion (among other things) was ineffective as an instrument of social control. Mill folk themselves decided the content of their religion, and only part of that content facilitated the goal of social control. What they wanted from religion was solace and strength to live their lives and the promise of salvation in heaven. They wanted preachers whom they respected and who respected them, who berated them for their sins and offered them hope of salvation in sermons afire with commitment and emotion. They wanted, too, an experience of fellowship and sense of belonging to something larger than themselves.

Folk did not understand religion to be an instrument of reform or revolution. Indeed, they were not interested in reform or revolution by religious or other means. Wages, hours, and working conditions were of this world, not

17. See, for example, Lawrence W. Levine, *Black Culture and Black Consciousness: Afro-American Folk Thought from Slavery to Freedom* (New York, 1976); Eugene D. Genovese, *Roll, Jordan, Roll: The World the Slaves Made* (New York, 1974); and Albert J. Raboteau, *Slave Religion: The "Invisible Institution" in the Antebellum South* (New York, 1978).

the next. Religion was a matter of hope, salvation, and right conduct. To critics with other values, this view is evidence of brainwashing—a model of how capitalist elites control lower classes through the hegemonic devices posited in the formulations of Antonio Gramsci.[18] Yet the folk's reading of Christianity was hardly distinctive. And in implementing that reading, mill folk did what Christian groups have always done. From the multiple offerings of a complex and immensely malleable religion, they picked things that were meaningful and functional to them and made those things into a set of beliefs and practices that served their needs as defined by the folk. In this sense, Liston Pope was correct in insisting that the village church was "a distinctive type of religious institution." Pope, however, saw this as a negative quality and blamed it on the fact that town people and mill folk in Gastonia were segregated into separate congregations.[19]

That segregation, an important aspect of village religion, is often misunderstood and overstated. Of the church members John K. Morland counted at York in the 1940s, a quarter (24.8 percent) were members of town churches, and some outsiders worshiped in village churches. At the same time, Sybil V. W. Hutton found half the members of the Baptist church and a tenth of the members of the Methodist church at Victor Mills in 1947 living outside the village.[20] Many of these outsiders were mill folk who lived near the village, but the larger point remains: the religious segregation of mill folk was far from absolute.

Yet mill folk did generally prefer to attend their own churches. They did this not to please mill owners and not because they had internalized the message of social control. Rather, like all distinctive social groups, whether black Americans, Orthodox Jews, Pennsylvania Amish, or upper-class Episcopalians, they wanted to worship their own God in their own way among their own kind of people. Mill churches are therefore best understood not as evidence of enforced isolation and social manipulation but as a reflection of the social stratification and ethnocultural separatism that characterize American Protestantism and keep it vital.[21]

18. See Frederick A. Bode, "Religion and Class Hegemony: A Populist Critique in North Carolina," *Journal of Southern History*, XXXVI (1971), 417–38.

19. Pope, *Millhands and Preachers*, 84.

20. Morland, *Millways of Kent*, 108; Hutton, "Social Participation of Married Women in a South Carolina Mill Village," 15.

21. See H. Richard Niebuhr, *The Social Sources of Denominationalism* (New York, 1929); H. J. Demerath, *Social Class in American Protestantism* (Chicago, 1965); Andrew M. Greeley, *The Denominational Society: A Sociological Approach to Religion in America* (Glenview, Ill., 1972).

That mill folk found in mill churches what they wanted was evident even to Liston Pope, who deplored the religious segregation their preferences produced. Mill folk "desire[d] churches of their own in which they could feel perfectly at ease," Pope wrote. That "was partly because of a desire for independence and self-respect" and partly because of a desire to participate in church activities and avoid the condescensions they encountered in town churches. Churches of their own had other attractions, too. Attending them was one of the ways mill folk achieved status and respectability among themselves; and church services at which they could be themselves provided a valuable emotional outlet for those whose lives were otherwise repressed. Above all, as Pope saw, "The worker . . . looks to his church to find transvaluation of life, which may take the form of reassurance or of escape, or both. By affirmation of values denied in the economic world, the church provides comfort and ultimate assurance." Because mill churches provided these benefits, they became, in Pope's words, "focal centers around which to integrate" village life.[22]

The cultural creativity folk religion involved was especially evident in worship services, for to mill folk the medium was as important as the message. According to Pope, services in village churches were "more intense in mood than those" among whites elsewhere. "Lack of social security is compensated for by fervor of congregational response, and the degree to which all worshippers participate in the service is much higher," he reported. "A larger number of persons, relatively, sing in the choir, serve as ushers, offer personal testimonies, shake hands with each other. Music is more concrete and more rhythmic; it conjures up pictures rather than describes attitudes or ideas, and it appeals to the hands and feet more than to the head. The entire service in mill churches has an enthusiasm lacking in the more restrained worship of the 'respectable people' uptown."[23]

Mill churches were equally distinct from town churches in their message. "Their religion is intimately related to the everyday struggles and vicissitudes of an insecure life," Pope wrote of the churches. This religion " 'work[ed]' and 'chang[ed] things' " and was more infused with "superstitions" than that of town churches. Mill folk, Pope thought, more often believed in signs and in direct punishment for sin than did whites in town. "A strong admixture of magic is often found in the popular religion of mill workers," he wrote. "They trust devoutly in the power of prayer to get

22. Pope, *Millhands and Preachers*, 72–73, 87–91.
23. *Ibid.*, 86.

results." And when prayers were unanswered, they blamed their own sin-fulness. They "show no interest in theological questions at all," Pope also reported; that statement is certainly false unless theology is defined as akin to systematic philosophy. As Pope noted, the religious beliefs of mill folk were sometimes inconsistent or contradictory when analyzed logically. To folk, however, religion was a thing of faith, not logic, and they would not have been surprised at the inability of a scholar like Pope to see the design in what they believed.[24]

"PREACHERS WHO 'SIDE WITH THE PEOPLE' . . . ARE REWARDED WITH AN INCREASING NUMBER OF ADHERENTS."

Late in the New South era, village religion underwent a major evolution, the nature of which reinforces the picture of mill churches as institutions of cultural creativity. That evolution, which grew from contemporary changes in American religion as a whole, was the emergence of Holiness and charis-matic sects and the relative decline of Baptism and Methodism. Mill owners generally did not approve of or support the new sects. Their emergence is therefore further evidence that owners did not control the content of folk religion and that village churches were imperfect instruments of social control.

Figures for Gaston County, which became a major textile center during the New South era, illustrate the trend. All village churches established there before 1901 were Baptist and Methodist except for one, which was Presbyterian. Between 1901 and 1920, however, ten of thirty new village churches belonged to the newer sects, and from 1921 to 1939, twenty-six of forty-four. In view of the general poverty of mill folk and the refusal of mill owners to "contribute to any significant extent to the salaries of preachers of the newer Holiness and Pentecostal sects," this was impressive growth indeed.[25]

The disdain of owners for the new sects was widespread. In her study of North Carolina villages in the 1920s, Harriet Herring found that the only churches mill owners objected to were Pentecostal or Holiness, especially the former, whose members they disparaged as "Holy Rollers." They "stay up half the night" worshiping, one mill manager told Herring of Pen-tecostals, "and go to sleep on the job the next day." Besides, he added, they were a poorer class of people the mills did not like to hire.[26]

24. *Ibid.*, 103.
25. *Ibid.*, 36–41.
26. Herring, *Welfare Work in Mill Villages*, 100.

Over the course of the New South era, the Baptist and Methodist denominations became increasingly middle class, and as they did so, their ministers became more educated and the emotionalism of their services diminished. The denominations thus began losing their appeal to the lowest economic classes. Many poor folk wanted emotional, participatory worship services conducted in the manner of old-time religion. Their need was for a religion of the heart, and only preachers whose educational and social levels were close to their own could deliver it in ways they found comprehensible and fulfilling.

At York in the 1940s, John K. Morland found specific evidence of social stratification in the churches. At "Crownwell," for example, the congregation of the Baptist church was notably more "respectable" and better dressed than those of the two Holiness churches. Among the members of the Baptist congregation were the "best" folk in the village and some of the mill foremen as well, none of whom belonged to Holiness congregations. Services at the Baptist church were relatively subdued, whereas those at the Holiness churches involved shouting and congregational participation.[27]

This transition of Baptism and Methodism explains the contemporary impression that mill churches were losing their appeal. "The testimony is universal that the churches are losing their hold upon the mill population," Holland Thompson wrote in 1906. At least part of the explanation for lower rates of attendance, Thompson thought, was that "workers are tired on Sunday, and the day is more and more devoted to rest and recreation." One may speculate, however, that the cause was that the churches were not offering what many folk wanted. Liston Pope thought Baptists and Methodists lost favor in the villages in direct proportion to the rising educational level of their ministers. Education, he explained, opened a gap between preachers and villagers, who found educated preachers uninspiring and generally condescending toward mill folk. "A mill church with a disappointed, condescending pastor is doomed to disintegration," Pope wrote. "In contrast, preachers who 'side with the people' and reveal genuine enthusiasm with their work are rewarded with an increasing number of adherents."[28]

The absence of educated preachers among the Holiness and charismatic sects was thus significant. "The newer sects in [Gaston] county are led by ministers almost wholly uneducated," Pope wrote of the 1930s. "Several of them find it necessary to have some more literate person read the Scriptures

27. Morland, *Millways of Kent*, 108.
28. Thompson, *From the Cotton Field to the Cotton Mill*, 178; Pope, *Millhands and Preachers*, 114.

in their services. Others did not go beyond the fourth or fifth grades," and "most of them are on sabbatical leave from jobs in cotton mills."[29]

A class division thus developed in village churches and in the villages themselves, perhaps growing in part from the evolution of cotton manufacturing. The division appeared late in the New South era and was clearer by the 1920s and 1930s. By then, many mills and villages were three or four generations old, and many workers and folk had become acculturated to village life. As wages and educational levels increased over the years, some folk were pulled toward the mainstream of southern life—a fact reflected in the changing nature of the Baptist and Methodist churches in which they worshiped. Other folk, perhaps newer to mill life and more vulnerable to the economic difficulties that plagued the industry between the two world wars, remained closer to their cultural roots, and for them old religious forms were still appealing. In 1910, a villager in Gastonia wrote a local newspaper denouncing the "tongue exhorting" and "holy dance" he witnessed at a church in his village. The exhorting he blamed on persons "claiming that they are possessed of gifts of the Holy Ghost." The dancing, he believed, was a product of "demonism."[30]

"I JUST GAVE MY WHOLE SELF AWAY TO THE LORD."

As a child, Brother Fisher, as he is called in his Federal Writers' Project interview, moved with his family from a farm in western North Carolina to a mill village in Gastonia in 1904 or 1905. Poor mountaineers, Fisher and his family experienced more than the usual cultural dislocation as a result of the move. "When we went to church up there [in the mountains] all we needed was a clean pair of overalls and that was good enough," Fisher recalled, "but we sorta felt out of place in a city church with everybody dressed up in store-bought clothes. That in itself was one reason we started goin' to a tent revival that the Church of God was holdin'. We felt more at home and wasn't ashamed of our clothes." But that was not the only attraction of the new church. "There seemed to be *more power* in their meetin's," explained Fisher, whose family had been Baptists. "Of course we had seen shoutin' before, but not the kind that they were doin' there."

This "power" was visited on Fisher, and at sixteen he was converted. "I never will forget the night I was saved," he recalled. "We'd been attendin'

29. Pope, *Millhands and Preachers*, 109.
30. *Ibid.*, 129.

the revival for several nights and had witnessed a number of souls saved. After about four nights I felt the pull of the altar. Well, I didn't go up right away. I never will forget when Mother came from her seat up near the front back to where I was sittin' with some of the neighbor boys, and I can hear her now sayin' as she looked at me with tears runnin' down her cheeks, 'Son, give your heart to the Lord, *now!'*

"I made a step toward the aisle," Fisher remembered, "and, with her arm around me, mother and son walked down the sawdust trail to lay my sins and burdens at the feet of Jesus.

"He was there that night as surely as there is a God," Fisher continued. "There on that crudely built altar I poured out my soul to Him. I had been under conviction for two or three nights, and my built-up emotions and feelin's came surgin' out as I sobbed and cried for the blood of Jesus and its cleansing power. It wasn't long before I felt that He was there, extendin' His holy hand and biddin' me to follow Him. Then I knew that the debt had been paid and my slate was as clean as snow." Fisher recalled: "Oh, my, was I happy! It's good to think of that hour even today, and to know that it was from that moment that life started all anew. Why, yes, to the person that doesn't have that feelin', all that sounds light and unimportant, but to me it's real—as real as a headache is to you—or a sorrow is to one who has lost a loved one. It's real!"

Folk acknowledged their conversion and their profession of faith by joining a church and being welcomed into its congregation. The resulting sense of fellowship and belonging, which came from membership in a body of like believers, was one of the chief sources of strength for churches and church members alike. "They treated me as a brother and made me appreciate the joys that were to be had in Christian fellowship," Fisher recalled of his entry into the Church of God. "Every night I attended the services, enjoyin' more and more the newfound life." Presently, he sought "sanctification"—"the second blessing" his church promised all believers who prayerfully sought it. When asked about it later, he answered: "I don't know how to tell, except that—well, I just gave my whole self away to the Lord and was submissive to His every impulse and let Him have His way. What I did I don't remember, but they say I was joyous in the spirit."

Saved and sanctified, Fisher continued to work in the mill, but after a while he felt the call to preach. He took a Bible course to learn more of the mysteries of his faith, and at its conclusion, still working in the mill, he set about organizing a Church of God congregation. That took him five years, and he succeeded not by winning converts from established churches but by proselyting among folk those churches did not reach. "Many of the fellow workers in the mill attended," Fisher said of his effort, "and some of our greatest victories for the Lord was with some of the hardened sinners of the mill who had never been church-goin' men because of their clothes, which might not be as good as other people's. . . . In fact, I think you'll find that to be the reason there is such a large number of sinners around the mill sections. They are self-conscious about their appearances and standin', when they are not on 'mill hill.'"

Like all churches in the new sects, Fisher's was successful because its teachings and the worship services were attractive to poor, uprooted folk. All the sects incorporated elements of the Holiness and charismatic (Pentecostal) movements.[31] The Holiness movement, which had a major impact on the Protestantism that flourished among poor folk in the New South, grew from Methodism in the last generation of the nineteenth century. It appealed to those who thought the Methodist church was becoming too secular, too much at ease with the world, and too little concerned with the deepest meaning of salvation. Its particular emphasis was on sanctification, an inner state of blessedness that carried the believer much farther toward perfect grace than did baptism and profession of faith alone. Baptism and profession of faith helped the believer overcome outward sins. Sanctification, however, was an inner matter, "an experience of grace accompanied by emotional exuberance which enabled the one so sanctified to forsake inward sins such as pride and covetousness and to renounce [the] unholy practices" those sins encouraged.[32]

The charismatic sects were those with greatest appeal to mill folk. Among those whose members included folk were the Assembly of God, the Church of God, and the Pentecostal Holiness Church. Charismatics developed the idea of sanctification more than the Holiness groups, the largest of which was the Church of the Nazarene. Subsequent to conversion, accord-

31. On these churches, see Robert M. Anderson, *Visions of the Disinherited: The Making of American Pentecostalism* (New York, 1970); Charles E. Jones, *Perfectionist Persuasion: The Holiness Movement and American Methodism, 1867–1936* (Netuchen, N.J., 1974); Arthur C. Piepkorn, *Evangelical, Fundamentalist, and Other Christian Bodies*, vol. IV of Piepkorn, *Profiles in Belief: The Religious Bodies of the United States and Canada* (San Francisco, 1979); Timothy P. Weber, *Living in the Shadow of the Second Coming: American Premillennialism, 1875–1925* (New York, 1979); George M. Marsden, *Fundamentalism and American Culture: The Shaping of Twentieth Century Evangelicalism, 1870–1925* (New York, 1980); Nils Bloch-Hoell, *The Pentecostal Movement: Its Origin, Development, and Distinctive Character* (New York, 1964); and William W. Wood, *Culture and Personality Aspects of the Pentecostal Holiness Religion* (The Hague, 1965).

32. Piepkorn, *Evangelical, Fundamentalist, and Other Christian Bodies*, 4.

ing to charismatics, the believer experienced a "baptism in the Holy Spirit," during which he was "filled with the Spirit" and received one or more of the spiritual gifts described in the New Testament, among them the ability to speak in unknown tongues, the power to perform divine healing, and the ability to prophesy. To charismatics, "tongue speaking" was especially significant, a sure sign of baptism in the Spirit and of "the Second Pentecost," and certain evidence of the imminent Second Coming of Christ. To them, "The ultimate religious experience [was] to possess or be possessed by divine power evidenced by extraordinary sensations and physical manifestations."[33]

The new sects were also millennialist, and as such believed the world was in the final corrupt days before Christ returned to establish his thousand-year kingdom on earth, at the end of which would come the final day of judgment. Because, according to their beliefs, the Second Coming was imminent and this world, its governments, and most of its people were corrupt, charismatics dissociated themselves from every secular activity possible and worked for their own salvation. Thus they and their churches avoided politics and social movements.

The theology of the sects was much like that of Protestant fundamentalism. Their members believed in the inerrancy of the Bible, the efficacy of prayer, the virgin birth, and the substitutionary atonement, physical resurrection, and literal second coming of Jesus Christ. They also practiced a pronounced puritanism in personal conduct, eschewing not only dancing, drinking, and smoking but everything they associated with the sin of pride, from jewelry, cosmetics, and brightly colored clothes to "bobbed" hair among women.

The sects stressed emotionalism and congregational participation as essential features of worship. Their services began with music that was much more rhythmic and fast paced than that of mainstream churches. The music borrowed the honky-tonk and hillbilly styles popular among plain folk, and the singing, handclapping and swaying movements that accompanied it encouraged worshipers to drop their reserve and become involved in the service. "Testifying," praying, and individual outbursts of ecstasy punctuated the "song service" and underscored the participatory nature of worship itself. The sermon was the central feature of every service, and by the time it began, the congregation was aroused, involved, expectant. The preacher's task was to carry his listeners to higher levels of participation and fulfill-

33. Anderson, *Visions of the Disinherited*, 27.

ment. In accomplishing this, his voice, demeanor, and style of delivery were important, because his message would not be new. On the contrary, regulars in the congregation would have heard it countless times, with variations only in illustrative details. Its purpose was to affirm their faith.

To hold the congregation's interest, the preacher had to impress its members with the earnestness of his conviction and the intensity of his presentation. The listeners were prepared to be impressed. A standard, highly effective technique was the use of rhythm, making the sermon an alternating mixture of booming crescendos, dramatic climaxes, and whispered downbeats delivered in the singsong style that set preaching apart from the other forms of public speaking. The members of the congregation fixed on the preacher's every word and move, and as he shouted his message, they responded in multiple forms of approval. The preacher and some in his audience might burst into the unintelligible ecstasies of unknown tongues or be seized by the jerking, shaking frenzies that gave the "Holy Rollers" their name. The sermon climaxed with a call for sinners and unbelievers to come forth and be saved, and at that time the emotional outpourings assumed a new purpose. The preacher pleaded, the congregation sang dolefully of the perils of hell or happily of the promises of heaven, and here and there a relative or friend might go sobbingly to a lost loved one and plead for him to "come to Christ." The preacher himself might approach a member of his congregation, especially if he knew that person was "under conviction"—had recently become aware of his sinfulness and was "wrestling with the Devil" over the state of his soul. If anyone came forth to be saved, there was another round of testifying and ecstatic rejoicing at the Lord's victory and the Devil's defeat. The service lasted three or four hours, and the believers left cleansed, strengthened, and exalted.[34]

The Church of God is "free from all man-made creeds and traditions," Brother Fisher said, explaining the attractions the church had for him. "Take the New Testament, or law of Christ, as your only rule of faith and practice; givin' each other equal rights and privileges to read and interpret for yourselves as your conscience may dictate. . . . Intellectuals and would-be high elements call us 'Holy Rollers' and 'fanatics.' . . . They put their worshippin' on a strict intellectual basis, void of all emotional elements, whereas we solicit and give way to the emotional blessin's of the spirit." He remarked, "They criticize our speakin' in unknown tongues."

34. On the meaning of such experience, see Andrew M. Greeley, *Ecstasy: A Way of Knowing* (Englewood Cliffs, N.J., 1974); William Sargant, *The Mind Possessed: A Physiology of Possession, Mysticism, and Faith Healing* (Philadelphia, 1974).

Like others of his faith, Fisher was especially offended by criticism of speaking in tongues, for to all charismatics the Bible was perfectly clear on the practice. "These signs shall follow them that believe. In my name shall they cast out devils; they shall speak with new tongues," St. Mark wrote. "They were all filled with the Holy Ghost, and began to speak with other tongues as the Spirit gave them utterance," the author of Acts of the Apostles also wrote. "And when this was noised abroad, the multitude came together, and were confounded, because that every man heard them speak in his own tongue."[35]

The Church of God also appealed to Fisher because it insisted that members set themselves apart from the corrupt world by maintaining proper standards of personal conduct. "In daily livin' our philosophy is one of restraint, while the trend of the modernist is that of givin' way to impulses," Fisher said. "None of our members are allowed to smoke or use tobacco in any form. We are definitely against the use of alcohol in any way. Our members are not permitted to attend picture shows or theaters or ball games or dances. Neither do we believe in showin' unnecessarily any parts of our bodies, such as appearin' on bathin' beaches. While attendin' our church you will notice that none of us every wear any ornaments or jewelry of any kind."

"WE TRIED NOT TO TAKE SIDES IN THE STRIKE, OUR WORK NOT BEIN' MILL WORK BUT THE SALVATION OF SOULS."

Emotional, otherworldly religion served mill folk in many positive ways, but it also helped bind them to a system that treated them inequitably. This was probably inevitable given their history, circumstance, and mind set, for no other religion appealed to them; and had they forsworn all religion, their socioeconomic condition would likely have remained the same. Yet Christianity does include the potential for social reform, as the more recent examples of Martin Luther King and his Southern Christian Leadership Conference suggest. That that potential went untapped in mill villages in the New South was due in part to the nature of village Christianity and of the men who preached it, and the inability or unwillingness of those men to turn their religion to social purposes.

In 1899 an unusual incident occurred at Fulton Bag and Cotton Mills that

35. Mark 16:17, and Acts 2:4, 6. See also 1 Cor. 14. On this phenomenon, see Felicitas D. Goodman, *Speaking in Tongues: A Cross-Cultural Study of Glossolalia* (Chicago, 1972).

was indicative of the failure of mill religion to address social issues. In the late spring, officials of this mill had the Reverend Charles D. Bacon, a "street preacher," arrested for going repeatedly into areas of the district owned by the mill and "making incendiary speeches." Specifically, Bacon "publicly denounc[ed] the mill owners as robbers and thieves" and "predicted bloodshed unless the company treated the employees with more humane consideration." This kind of talk, mill officials insisted, exposed the district to dangers of "disorder, if not riot." At his trial, Bacon's defense was that his words were true. "The people are deceived," he told the court. "The poor are oppressed, and the earth groans and mourns with their cries because they are oppressed. I have said and I repeat it here, that the cotton mills are a curse for they take the labor of even little children and offer them a crust of bread for compensation; they keep little children from getting an education; their employees live like paupers while the owners live in luxury. That's what I said and that's what caused my arrest. If I would obey men, I might live like a king, but I prefer to obey God and live a poor man."[36]

It is easier to question Bacon's tactics than his sincerity, and his example may be used to raise the issue of social activism and the failure (if that is the correct word) of mill preachers to turn their religion in that direction even during this era of Progressive reform. What could the preachers have done to help mill folk, and what were the most promising ways of doing it? Surely one form of help was providing people the kind of religion they wanted. In view of the realities of power and property in the villages, the confrontational approach of the Reverend Mr. Bacon was unpromising certainly in the short run and probably in the long run, too, as the experience of textile unions suggests. Bacon's effort benefited neither him nor mill folk. Bacon was denied even the martyrdom he sought when the judge dismissed the charges against him; and it was surely significant that Bacon was an Englishman who had been in the United States only a few months. Was there not some promising middle way, some alternative to preaching otherworldliness or advocating revolution, that might have led to social melioration?

Mill preachers cared deeply about their flocks. Their concern was what brought them into the ministry, and one can easily imagine the good a man like Brother Fisher accomplished in his lifetime. That good was spiritual rather than material, but Fisher would have therefore considered it more valuable.

Almost certainly, however, Fisher could not have been equally helpful in

36. Atlanta *Constitution*, June 1, 1899.

material things.[37] Mill preachers read the New Testament, not Karl Marx or even Walter Rauschenbusch or Jane Addams. Their flocks were poor, they themselves were uneducated and innocent of the ways of social activism, and they and their churches were dependent on the money and goodwill of mill owners. The preachers' ability to do good depended on their jobs as ministers, and to keep their jobs they had to please their flocks, who wanted emotional affirmation of their faith, and not displease mill owners, who wanted no "trouble." The preachers were buffeted by other conflicts, too. Perhaps some were aware of the Social Gospel movement then touching American Protestantism, and all of them must have been sensitive to poverty and the social problems it caused. They were also influenced by biblical teachings on the evils of wealth and the wealthy and the virtues of poverty and the poor, for these teachings were favorite themes of their sermons.

These conflicting claims of faith and circumstance, of God and Caesar, fueled insecurities that encouraged conformity and the avoidance of controversy. Mill preachers were thus men with a dilemma. They were dedicated servants of God who were not certain what their duties were outside of purely religious affairs. Were they, in worldly things, doing everything their religion and role as preachers demanded of them? That question must have occurred to all of them, and appreciating the uncertainties the question embodied and the corroding effects of those uncertainties on the will of earnest, caring, unsophisticated men is essential to understanding the social role of mill preachers.

That the preachers were troubled in this way is suggested by the example of the Reverend David Brown. Born just before the turn of the twentieth century on a poor North Carolina farm, Brown went to work as a sweeper in a cotton mill when he was fifteen. He thus knew poverty and the problems of plain folk. "I'd seen hard times on the pore little farm where my father was struggling along with us six children and him ownin' nothin' but one little plug of a mule and a homemade carryall," Brown later recalled of his childhood.[38] In the mill, however, he "learnt fast" and in a few years was a weaver and then an overseer. But he found mill work unsatisfying, and at

37. On the conservative nature of the religious views of poor people in North Carolina in the 1960s, see John R. Hofley, "Lower Class Religion: 'The Moral Basis of a Backward Society' " (Ph.D. dissertation, University of North Carolina, 1968). See also Benton Johnson, "Do Holiness Sects Socialize in Dominant Values?" *Social Forces*, XXXIX (1965), 309–16.

38. The interview with Brown is printed in Tom Terrill and Jerrold Hirsch (eds.), *Such As Us: Southern Voices of the Thirties* (Chapel Hill, 1978), 157–69.

thirty-two, he answered what he believed was a call to become a Baptist preacher. His church, in a village in Greensboro, had been largely built with mill funds, the owner putting up four dollars for every dollar raised by the congregation, and in 1939 at the time of his interview, it still received an annual subsidy of five hundred dollars from the mill.

Brown was conscious of the problems of serving two masters, just as he was aware that spiritual help was not the only aid mill folk needed. He felt deeply his inability to help folk materially. In 1933, about three years after he became a preacher and during the depths of the Great Depression, he preached a sermon that showed the genuineness of his social concern and the way that concern dissipated into otherworldliness. His text was from the fifth chapter of the book of James, which, in Brown's words, "sets down hard on the rich." James wrote: "Go now, ye rich man, weep and howl for your miseries that shall come upon you. Your riches are corrupted, and your garments are moth-eaten. . . . Behold, the hire of the laborers who have reaped from your fields, which is of you kept back by fraud, crieth; and the cries of them which have reaped are entered into the ears of the Lord."[39]

"After finishin' with that scripture," Brown recalled of his sermon, "I began to preach. I say, 'Do the multi-millionaires of our country have a hard time now? No,' I answered, 'they have their palaces, they have their servants, they can write a check for a million dollars. But the day will come, brothers and sisters, the day will come.'" Developing the moral of his sermon, Brown turned to the mill workers in his congregation. "You run their looms," he said to them, "you run their cards, you keep their yards, and you live on a little weekly wage." And with that remark, he told his interviewer, "I start to warmin' up, sister. Then I say, 'But what does the Holy Bible teach? Hellfire is waitin' to receive the rich man who gives no thought to his soul but spends his time fillin' his storehouses with earthly goods, and you, you, the faithful, are storin' up treasures in heaven where neither moth nor rust doth corrupt and thieves do not break through to steal.'"

Brown was still pleased with this sermon years later. He had told the truth as he saw it and expiated the sense of restraining dependence he felt toward the mill owner. "That's straight talkin', sister," he said of the sermon, "but I've never been called down for it yet."

Brown's personal dilemma came to a head the year before his interview, and he resolved it in the only way he could, with an ambiguity that fed his

39. James 5:1, 4.

sense of inadequacy for being unable to do more. Workers in his village had gone on strike after a round of wage cuts reduced their income to levels they thought unlivable. After two weeks, however, sheer want had driven them back to work at the reduced wage, and they had emerged from the strike poorer and more dependent on management than ever. "We tried not to take sides in the strike," Brown recalled, showing how poorly his religion and his position equipped him for social activism, "our work not bein' mill work but the salvation of souls. It was natural, though, us bein' the pastor, that many of the brethren would come to us and talk their troubles over with us. We give them what comfort we could.

"While the strike was goin' on we done a lot of thinkin'," Brown continued. "We decided the South ought to be organized, but how? There's always a Judas to sell his people out. He'll get into the union and find out its secrets. Then he'll go to the company man and whisper in his ear. 'They're organizin'. They're plannin' to strike when you cut again.' Why does he do it? I don't know and you don't know, but gifts can be give at other times than Christmas." Brown went on: "The people are cut, they walk out, sayin' among themselves, 'We can't live on no less. We won't let nobody go in that mill to work until we get our old wage back.' What happens? The mill owner with his foot on the head of the law asks for help to open up his mill to let his people work, or he asks for help to keep his mill closed if that be his will at that time. Whichever way his fancy goes, he gets the help. The law comes out and fortifies him against the people. Ah, sister, it's a hard thing to do to get ahead of a power like that."

The outcome of the strike still rankled Brown. "Among themselves they muttered, 'A half a loaf is better than no bread at all,'" he said of the strikers forced back to work. "So the company started their wheels again with the promise of a bean, a bean today, a bean tomorrow, but never two beans on the same day. Aye, sister, it's a proposition. Bondage, slavery, a bean. The multi-million-airy is hard to beat."

There must have been other preachers like Brown, giving what comfort they could in times of trouble. They forged no social revolution and rarely even criticized the mills; and historians have been unkind to them. But to see them as emotional fools or minions of the mill owners who caused many of their insecurities is unjust as well as incorrect. It is also to miss the ambiguity and drama that infused the story of religion in the mill villages of the New South.

14
EDUCATION

Except for the church, the school was the most common village institution. But just as religion was more important than churches, so education was more significant than schools and schooling, which had little impact on plain folk in or out of the villages. In the sense of the transmission of knowledge from older to younger generations, education was a basic aspect of folk experience. Folk attended school only briefly and discontinuously. Probably the average adult in 1915 had no more than ten or fifteen months of schooling and only the rudiments of literacy. Certainly schooling had practically no impact on ways of living and thinking among plain folk. They did not value schooling, for they did not associate "book learning" with the needs of life.

During the New South era, folk experienced a social transition that made that attitude, and the lack of schooling it entailed, increasingly constricting. Defining literacy as the ability to write, census takers found a quarter (26.3 percent) of all whites over ten years of age in Georgia and the Carolinas illiterate in 1880; and though no meaningful estimates are available, it is probable that most plain folk said to be literate were only marginally so. This condition changed significantly during the New South era, but in 1910 about 1 of every 10 whites in the 3 states was still illiterate, and most plain folk were what we today call functionally illiterate.[1] Among mill folk, illiteracy was more widespread. Of 4,010 mill workers counted in 7 counties in the 1880 manuscript census listings, 35 percent were illiterate, as were 23.8 percent of 10,854 workers in 5 localities in 1900.[2]

In modern, industrial societies, the ability to read, write, and figure, and do these things well, is far more important than in traditional, agricultural societies. In the world of plain folk, the written word (the legal contract) was superseding the spoken word (the personal understanding sealed by a handshake) as the basic instrument of human relationships. In all their dealings with outsiders—landlords, employers, and credit merchants, as well as bureaucrats, reformers, and other agents of change—folk ran increasingly into the mysteries of the printed word. Even the right to vote now hinged on the ability to read a secret ballot unless one wanted to expose his illiteracy to election officials. About 1900, illiteracy and a lack of schooling became handicaps, even vulnerabilities, of a new sort.

Besides bringing risks of exposure and humiliation, the increasing importance of literacy also affected the ability of folk to deal with outside forces impinging on their culture and ways of living. The folk faced powerful forces of social change, and if they wanted to resist or channel those forces— if they wanted to maintain their culture and life-style—they needed the kinds of resources only a proper schooling could provide. Change was inevitable; the question was whether folk would be able to influence it or be overwhelmed by it. Unfortunately, the education they found in the spreading system of public schools had in their view no appeal.

Folk first encountered the public school system in the decades around 1900, at a critical point in their own history and that of the school system as well. In Georgia and the Carolinas, professional educationists had appeared, and as their influence spread, the school system was modernized and transformed. Small community schools were consolidated into larger, graded institutions with standardized curricula taught by men and women

1. *Tenth Census, 1880: Population,* 920. In 1910 actual figures for illiteracy among whites ten years old and over was 7.8 percent in Ga., 10.3 percent in S.C., and 12.3 percent in N.C. See U.S. Bureau of Education, *Bulletin 1913 No. 20: Illiteracy in the United States and an Experiment for Its Elimination,* 17.

2. Actual figures for 1880 were 1,399 illiterates in 4,010 mill workers, or 34.9 percent (Manuscript Census, 1880, Schedule 1, Muscogee and Richmond counties, Ga., Russell County, Ala., Aiken and Spartanburg counties, S.C., Gaston and Alamance counties, N.C.). The figures for 1900 were 2,584 illiterates among 10,854 workers. See *ibid.,* Alamance County, N.C., Muscogee County, Ga. (sample of every third mill household), Spartanburg County, S.C. (sample of every third mill household), Richmond County, Ga., and Gregg Township, Aiken County, S.C.

who learned the new educational methods and theories at teacher institutes and normal schools. Educationists were especially concerned to remove the schools from community influence—"politics," they called it—and assert their own control. They were also intent on making attendance at their schools compulsory.

These circumstances posed problems for plain folk. Just as their need for schooling increased, folk found the schools falling into the hands of people who were unsympathetic to their needs and even contemptuous of their being.

"THEY DIDN'T BELIEVE IN EDUCATION."

Plain folk were indifferent to schooling not because they were depraved or ignorant but because they were traditionalists. Most expected to follow the economic and social footsteps of their parents, and to have their children do likewise, and for that purpose schooling beyond the level of basic literacy was largely unnecessary. "Papa was a tenant farmer and him nor Mammy neither one had any learning," recalled Mrs. Lonnie Williams, who grew up in North Carolina at the turn of the twentieth century. "All they'd ever knowed was hard work. They didn't believe in education and they was superstitious, but they were good neighbors and they never repeated bad tales on nobody."

"They didn't believe in education"—that was the essence of what folk thought of schooling. The attitude was entirely pragmatic. Schools did not teach children how to live or make a living; and after they learned to read and write or were big enough to work (at home or in the field or the mill), children were better off working. Perhaps folk discerned what modern scholars know, that literacy and the elementary levels of schooling that produce it are not by themselves avenues to economic and social mobility, especially among groups not oriented toward mobility. Class, ethnicity, and gender, rather than literacy, were the correlates of success and mobility in nineteenth-century America.[3] To outsiders, "poor whites" and "lintheads" with the rudiments of literacy were still "trash"; and the prejudices of outsiders aside, plain folk did not center their lives on mobility and achievement.

3. See Harvey J. Graff, *The Literacy Myth* (New York, 1979). On the evolution of the meaning of literacy, see Daniel Resnick and Lauren B. Resnick, "The Nature of Literacy: An Historical Explanation," *Harvard Educational Review*, XLVII (1977), 370–85.

In traditional cultures, education is the process by which youths learn whatever is necessary to live in the culture into which they are born. In modern societies, in contrast, education is more likely to be an effort to overcome one's past in order to take advantage of social and economic opportunity. Some years ago, Margaret Mead drew this distinction between "primitive" and modern education in ways that illuminate the attitudes of plain folk. Among "primitives," according to Mead, the child is taught what is fixed and traditional, and the educational system rests on the consensual need to perpetuate the old and proven. Its function is explicitly conservative. To modernists, however, education is nearly the opposite. Shaped by "the will to teach, convert, colonize, or assimilate" out-groups, it is a device for creating something new, and it functions to create social and cultural discontinuities.

The change from "primitive" to modern education thus involves a "shift from the need for an individual to learn something which everyone agrees he would wish to know, to the will of some individual to teach something which it is not agreed that anyone has any desire to know." Much of the impulse for modern educational reform thus comes from the desire of people who feel culturally or otherwise superior to coax or coerce people they consider culturally or otherwise inferior to adapt their "superior" ways. "As soon as there is any attitude that one set of cultural beliefs is definitely superior to another," Mead wrote, "the framework is present for active proselytizing." When that occurs, "Education becomes a concern of those who teach rather than of those who learn," and one committed to "the acceptance of discontinuity between parents and children. Primitive education [in contrast] was a process by which continuity was maintained by parent and children." Forcing traditional people into modern education can therefore be emotionally as well as culturally dislocating. "Changing people's habits, people's ideas, people's language, people's beliefs, people's emotional allegiances," Mead observed, "involves a sort of deliberate violence to other people's developed personalities."[4]

To plain folk in the New South, the purpose of schools in the transmission of necessary knowledge was teaching literacy. The rest of education, despite the rather abstract hope of parents that life would be better for their children, was learning to work and live as one's parents worked and lived. In accord with the differing economic and social roles of men and women, boys

4. Margaret Mead, "Our Educational Emphases in Primitive Perspective," *American Journal of Sociology*, XLVIII (1943), 633–36.

learned to farm and girls to keep house, and while they learned, they did whatever they could to help their families live. Childhood and adolescence thus revolved around an education that was learning by doing rather than by sitting in classrooms or by serving formal apprenticeships. This form of education involved much labor and resulted in a great deal of learning, for making a living and other aspects of life were difficult matters for plain folk in the New South. The learning was not of mechanical tasks alone—how to plow a furrow, birth a calf, cure a side of meat, or hill a pile of potatoes—but of the collective knowledge and wisdom that made their doing effective. Youths had to learn to read the signs, seasons, and weather, to know when to plow and plant and wean the baby, and when it was bad luck to do those things. They had to learn medical lore—how to prepare home remedies and how to determine the remedies for particular ailments. They also had to learn how to deal with those who could help or harm them—landlords, credit merchants, preachers, employers, revenuers, and the like. Above all, they had to learn to make do with the limited income and resources that bounded their lives.

Teaching and learning these things were not conscious matters of education, and none of them were taught in school. But children began learning as soon as they were old enough to begin. The process was intensely conservative. Children were never encouraged to experiment, to seek new or more efficient ways of doing things, or to question the necessity of doing what they were told to do. Nor were they encouraged to develop skills their parents did not possess or ever, consciously, to think in terms of the future or of a "career." They were instead expected to learn what their parents knew and then duplicate their parents' lives.

This method of learning discouraged the qualities we today associate with individualism and achievement. Ambition and initiative were valued only in that folk encouraged children to be "smart," that is, to work willingly and well at whatever task was at hand. Children learned not to look critically at their situation and try to overcome it but to regard their place in life as fixed and natural. Not progress and mobility, and certainly not protest, but accommodation and adaptation were what they learned.

For these purposes, book learning was ineffectual and even harmful if it had the effect of alienating the child from things that made accommodation, adaptation, and "making do" easy. This is why folk thought educated people impractical misfits. Too much education could unfit one for the life plain folk knew. For all their book learning, educated persons might be unable to bridle a mule, sharpen a plowpoint, or mix turpentine and tallow in correct proportions, and such disabilities made life impossible as plain folk knew it. This impression was reinforced by the virtual lack of contact folk had with educated people. Those they knew—the preacher, the school-teacher, the landlord, and the credit merchant—never dealt with them in ways that were formally intellectual. Folk never heard ideas discussed abstractly and critically. Nothing in their experience encouraged them to think critically.

OF "RECIPROCATED LOVE" AND "REFLECTED GLORY"

Child rearing, not schooling, was the molding influence on the generations. Unfortunately, not much is known about the positive elements of raising children in the decade after the child's sixth birthday. In Erik H. Erikson's stages of human development, these years are marked by the prominence of "industry vs. inferiority" and "identity vs. role confusion" issues, the particular dangers of which are developing a sense of personal inadequacy and failing to resolve issues of personal identity. To compensate for tendencies in these directions, the individual might resort to a "constriction of his horizons to include only his work," Erikson suggests. "If he accepts work as his only obligation, and 'what works' as his only criterion of worthwhileness, he may become the conformist and thoughtless slave of his technology and of those who are in a position to exploit it."[5]

Among plain folk, the punishment of school-age children and youths for misbehavior was stern, physical, and occasionally brutal, and also erratic. How parents visualized the functions of such punishment is suggested by their belief in the biblical adage that to spare the rod is to spoil the child. Much more obscure are the ways parents functioned as role models and influenced the personalities and basic values of children. Parents were inept at verbalizing personal emotions, including the love, hopes, and fears they had for their children. The result might have been a perceived lack of parental empathy on the part of children, which discouraged open expression and sharing of such feelings as love, sympathy, shame, guilt, and doubt.[6]

The modern literature on child rearing offers suggestive bases for surmising the impact of these patterns on the child's personality, temperament, and outlook. Scholars have found significant differences between child-

5. Erik H. Erikson, *Childhood and Society* (2nd ed., rev.; New York, 1963), 260–61.
6. See Norman L. Paul, "Parental Empathy," in E. James Anthony and Therese Benedek (eds.), *Parenthood: Its Psychology and Psychopathology* (Boston, 1970), 337–52.

424 PLAIN FOLK IN THE NEW SOUTH

rearing practices in middle- and lower-class families, and have correlated them with differences of personality and social outlook among children in those classes. Working-class (lower-class) parents rely primarily on physical punishment to discipline their children. Parents of the middle class, in contrast, "use more symbolic and manipulative techniques such as reasoning, isolation, and appeals to guilt." They are also "more acceptant and egalitarian" in child rearing, whereas the practice of working-class parents is "oriented toward maintaining order and obedience."[7]

These differences seem to grow from differing degrees of social and psychological security. Working-class parents feel less able to control forces that shape their lives, and consider "rules and authoritative guidance" necessary to prepare their children for a world of uncertainty and anxiety. Thus, "Working-class and lower-class parents want conformity to external proscriptions while middle class parents want their children to become self-directing." In punishing misbehavior, therefore, "Middle class mothers are more concerned with the child's intent; working class mothers are more concerned with the overt consequences of the child's act." Similarly, "Middle class mothers tend to feel a greater obligation to be supportive of their children, whereas working-class and lower-class mothers are more attentive to the parental obligation to impose constraints."[8]

These findings, which generally conform to what is known of child-rearing patterns among plain folk in the New South, have a number of important implications. "In sociological and psychological theories," Glen H. Elder has written, "moral development is viewed generally as a process of decreasing reliance on external constraints manifested by evidences of internalized standards." That development is healthiest in individuals who feel they have control of their lives and are not living in chance situations. Many aspects of child rearing in working-class families, however, among them "erratic discipline and inconsistent rules, greater reliance on physical than on verbal methods, and infrequent attempts by parents to explain rules and discipline," encourage feelings of uncertainty. These practices emphasize adjustment to external controls rather than development of internal values, and they evidence the degree to which working-class parents see "obedience as a highly desirable quality in children." Elder has observed, "Working class parents tend to prefer 'obedience' over 'independent self-control' as a desired quality in their children," and obedience thus learned

7. Gerald Handel, "Sociological Aspects of Parenthood," in Anthony and Benedek (eds.), *Parenthood,* 95–99.
8. *Ibid.,* 95–99.

correlates with a choice of jobs entailing "close supervision, low autonomy," and work with things. This obedience is also apparently related to the "fatalism, distrust, and apathy [that] appear to be particularly common in the lower classes."[9]

These tendencies were perhaps worsened for the many children who grew up without a father. Sons seem especially to suffer from that condition. Sex-role conflicts, feelings of inferiority and mistrust, low levels of independence and assertiveness, and lack of curiosity about one's environment—all conditions that encourage resignation and apathy—correlate with father absence.[10] They are also among the conditions that caused many of the folk's social problems.

These psychological speculations are supported by findings of sociologists on child rearing and on the adaptations of workers to work. Lee Rainwater and his associates, for example, found workingmen's wives in the 1940s little interested in developing in their children the kinds of achievement orientation middle-class parents value so highly. They "do not feel there is anything basically wrong or undesirable with a working class life for their children," Rainwater and his associates wrote of women they studied. They "raise their children to the life they themselves know and in ways that seem natural to them." Furthermore, success to them was more a matter of morality, religious conviction, and right conduct in their children than one of ambition, economic success, or social mobility. "They are a fine set of children," Enoch Ball, son of a North Carolina day laborer, said of his fourteen offspring in 1939. "I've never seen them take a drink of liquor— not even of beer. I've never caught 'em smoking seegars or cigarettes. I've never heard of them dancing. They don't go away from home much." As a reward for properly rearing their children, parents such as Ball hoped for "reciprocated love," in the striking phrase of Rainwater and his associates, in sharp contrast to middle-class parents, who sought "reflected glory" in their children's achievements.[11]

Plain folk and their children had aspirations middle-class people considered low. Such expectations are molded early in life. "Certain basic components of the work personality appear to be laid down in the early school

9. Glen H. Elder, "Adolescent Socialization and Development," in Edgar F. Borgatta and William W. Lambert (eds.), *Handbook of Personality Theory and Research* (Boston, 1968), 295–97.

10. See Henry B. Biller, *Parental Deprivation: Family, School, Sexuality, and Society* (Lexington, Mass., 1974).

11. Lee Rainwater, Richard P. Coleman, and Gerald Handel, *Workingman's Wife: Her Personality, World and Life Style* (New York, 1959), 92–102.

years," W. S. Neff has written, "the ability to concentrate on a task for an extended period of time, the development of emotional response-patterns to supervisory authority, the limits of cooperation and competition with peers, the meanings and values associated with work, the rewards and sanctions for achievement and non-achievement, the effects (both positive and negative) which become associated with being productive."[12]

At an early age, then, the children of plain folk internalized attitudes and self-concepts that influenced the course of their lives. "A number of studies have shown that adolescents are attracted to occupations which they see as similar to their self-image, or as requiring skills which they believe they possess," psychologist Michael Argyle has written. "Those high in achievement motivation choose high-status and risky occupations," whereas those less motivated choose safer, more familiar work. In both cases, however, "People choose occupations which they think require the qualities which they think they possess," and they convince themselves of the merit of the work they choose. "Job satisfaction is related to a belief that the work done is important and useful," Argyle has observed, and "workers will often provide moral justification for their work."[13]

TEACHERS CALLED THEIR PUPILS " 'FOOLS,' 'LIARS,' 'VAGABONDS,' 'ILL-BRED,' 'POOR WHITE TRASH.' "

During the second half of the New South era, the public schools and their agents began to intrude themselves into the lives of plain folk, and the resulting face-off was an instructive episode in the history of both sides. In the early years of the New South, public schools were invariably small, scantly financed, and of little consequence. An overwhelming number were one-room, one-teacher affairs, most of which operated only a few weeks a year. In 1899, for example, there were 5,045 white public schools in Georgia staffed by 5,866 teachers and enrolling 251,093 pupils, 151,341 of whom attended on an average day. This was an enrollment of approximately 50 pupils per school and 43 per teacher, though attendance averaged a more manageable 30 per school and 26 per teacher.[14]

The vast majority of schools in Georgia and the Carolinas met in small, rudely built structures that offered little comfort to students and teachers and even less teaching equipment. Students supplied textbooks and some

12. W. S. Neff, *Work and Human Behavior* (New York, 1968), 161.
13. Michael Argyle, *The Social Psychology of Work* (New York, 1972), 63, 68, 70, 98.
14. Georgia Department of Education, *Twenty-Eighth Annual Report, 1900*, cclxvi.

other items themselves. In North Carolina in 1902, the average schoolhouse for whites was valued at $231.43, less even than the annual earnings of many mill workers. In 484 white districts in the state, the school buildings were "rude log houses," and in 625 districts there were no schoolhouses, the schools meeting wherever possible. "In one county in the State twenty schools had to be closed last winter because the children could not be kept warm in the houses," the state school superintendent reported that year; and "in many of the rural districts the houses are still rude, deskless and comfortless." Less than 7 of every 10 white school-age children enrolled in school in 1902, and on an average day when schools were in session, only 4 of those 7 were present.[15]

Over the course of a year, teaching paid much less than full-time mill work, and for that and other reasons, the profession attracted transient, poorly prepared young women and men waiting for more respectable and remunerative employment. Monthly salaries in Georgia in 1899 averaged between $20.70 and $35.31 for white teachers, depending on their credentials, and this salary was paid only during the few months the schools were in session. Turnover was therefore high, the average teacher moving as often as the average mill hand and teaching only a few terms altogether.[16]

Methods of instruction were traditional ones of drill and recitation. The teacher assigned a student a section of a textbook, which the student pored over in class while other students were at the front of the classroom reciting to the teacher what they had learned from the textbook. They read or spelled aloud, or answered questions requiring memorized knowledge of the text. The process was mechanical, involving little explanation and understanding.[17] "We didn't do no homework," Alice P. Evitt recalled. "We just studied over our lesson and wrote that up in school. Had to get up in line and stand in line. One'd read, then 'nother one read, 'nother one read, and that's the only kind of work we done. They'd give out spelling. We'd write that down in the school and they'd take it up and see what you got on it."

Boredom and incomprehension were problems of all students. Folk children had additional difficulties. Most entered school with none of the conditioning that prepares children for learning, and their encounter with seem-

15. North Carolina Superintendent of Public Instruction, *Biennial Report, 1900–02,* xiv, xlvi.

16. Georgia Department of Education, *Twenty-Eighth Annual Report, 1900,* cclxxvii.

17. For examples, see U.S. Bureau of Education, *Bulletin 1919 No. 50: The Public School System of Memphis, Tennessee,* Pt. 3, pp. 16–21, and *Bulletin 1920 No. 27: Survey of the Schools of Brunswick and of Glynn County, Georgia.*

ingly incomprehensible information was complicated by various consequences of poverty, including social prejudice. Middle-class teachers and
better-off pupils looked down on the children of folk because of who they
were and the badges of their identity—poor dress, poor speech, poor scholarship. "Some people are so poor that it seems they cannot provide for their
children suitable clothing and books, even if they desire to do so," the North
Carolina superintendent of public instruction reported in 1890. "When the
children of such parents do find their way into the schools they do not find
among many other children such forbearance and sympathy as to make the
school a desirable place, and consequently school is no pleasant place for
them."[18]

So obvious was this problem that it often appeared in the debate over
compulsory education. "I am in favor of having different schools for them,"
a farm owner wrote the North Carolina labor commissioner about children
of "the poor laboring class" in 1900. "The poorer class don't send their
children [to school] with a better class, or well-do-do children; they feel
cramped. If they had good teachers and class them off they would do better
and feel better satisfied."[19]

The differences alluded to in these remarks were cultural as well as
economic and social. This man was in effect suggesting that in school, as in
church, poor folk would feel more comfortable with institutions of their
own. Only there, he meant, could they escape the stigmas of poverty and
cultural distinctiveness; and providing them with separate schools, he
thought, was the likeliest way of motivating them to go to school. Another
farm owner had a different solution to the problem. "White people who are
not able, and who have not the means to clothe their children for school," he
wrote the commissioner, "their children should be compelled to attend
school during the months of August, September, and October, and the
county furnish one suit of cotton clothes for them for the three months."[20]
Many children avoided school because of the prejudice they encountered
there, and parents acquiesced in their action because they had no desire to
subject their children to humiliation.

Many folk could not afford textbooks, slates, and other equipment without which learning was impossible. This was more common with farm folk
than with mill folk, because the cash income of the former was almost

18. North Carolina Superintendent of Public Instruction, *Biennial Report, 1889–91*, xxiv.
19. North Carolina Bureau of Labor Statistics, *Annual Report, 1900*, 257, hereinafter cited
as NC *Labor Report* by year.
20. *Ibid.*, 260.

nothing. In 1886, for example, the North Carolina board of education recommended that teachers use the Holmes series of readers, the first four of which cost fourteen, twenty-four, thirty-six, and forty-eight cents, respectively. It also recommended primary and intermediate arithmetics costing twenty and thirty-six cents, respectively, and Goodrich's *Child's History of the United States*, which cost forty cents.[21] Although these prices seem low, farm folk had difficulty paying them, for the income of agricultural laborers and sharecroppers was largely in kind rather than in cash, and a family might have three, four, or more children of school age. The expense was alleviated to some extent by buying a set of texts for the oldest child and letting younger ones use them in turn. A new teacher might teach from a different set of books, however, and it was not unusual for students at the same level in the same school to be studying different texts. To avoid the cost a change of textbooks entailed, a new teacher sometimes agreed as a condition of employment to teach from the texts used by the previous teacher.

The cost of textbooks, however, remained a problem for poor children, and the advent of graded schools made it worse. "In many sections of the city there are Russian Jews and factory children and others who are too poor to buy even one set of books, and more often six or eight [sets] in one family are needed," the Atlanta *Constitution* reported when school opened in 1901. "An average set of books costs about $3.50. They range from $2 in the first grade to about $8 or $10 in the higher classes."[22]

Poor children might also receive a disproportionate share of the harsh punishment teachers used to maintain order. "Many of our school children are subject to . . . slander, abuse, chastisement and personal shame," two opponents of child abuse wrote in 1885. Such punishments, they said, "are eminently calculated to cower [the children's] spirit, crush their pride of character, and in no little degree diminish and corrupt their moral sensibilities." Teachers, the two observed, called their pupils, " 'fools, 'liars,' 'vagabonds,' 'ill-bred,' 'poor white trash,' 'without raising,' and such like reproachful epithets; and children are chastised in a shameful manner for very trivial offenses." They were "walloped" with "whips and books over the face and head which in some instances causes their noses to bleed. They are slapped on a sore head, in the face, jerked and dragged around." They received this treatment, according to the writters, "for simply getting a

21. North Carolina Superintendent of Public Instruction, *Biennial Report, 1885–86*, Appendix 5.
22. Atlanta *Constitution*, September 7, 1901.

drink of water, misspelling a word, for speaking, and in some instances for changing position upon the seat when tired."[23]

Lack of promotion—normal progress through textbooks and later through grades—was another problem for poor children. This was partly caused by absence, disinterest, and poor performance, and it helped convince plain folk that schools were alien places. In one-room schools, each child began with a first reader and remained "in" it until he mastered its contents, and then went on to the second and subsequent readers at his own pace, having meanwhile begun the same process with spellers, arithmetic books, and other texts. His progress might be uneven in various books. Wherever he stopped one day, he began the next time he returned to school. Because terms were short, periods between them were long, and learning was superficial, students sometimes forgot what they learned, and had to learn it again.

Throughout the New South era, states provided localities money to operate schools for only a short time, about three or four months per year in the 1880s. The localities could tax themselves to extend the term one or two months, but since school taxes fell on property owners, that effort was not always popular. Many districts extended their school terms only for students who paid a special tuition charge. In these districts, poor children could attend only part of the term and, when they returned the following year, were behind students who attended the tuition term. Many children went to school for several terms but never progressed beyond the first reader because they forgot so much between sessions. Some children remembered how to read but forgot how to figure or spell, in which case they would be in, for example, the third reader and the first speller or arithmetic.

This problem was more pronounced in graded schools, where children who attended irregularly or performed poorly were denied promotion to the next grade. Their failure was more conspicuous than it had been in one-room schools, where everyone studied together regardless of age. Children of tenant farmers suffered more of this retardation than did those of farm owners, but it was a problem for all classes of children. At the end of the 1923–1924 school year in North Carolina, for example, more than half (51.5 percent) of all first graders were denied promotion.[24]

23. *Ibid.*, June 22, 1885.

24. Information on lack of promotion is impressionistic for the New South era. For significant differences in this area between children of farm owners and those of tenant farmers in North Carolina schools in the mid-1920s, see Roy W. Morrison, "Some Inequalities of Educational Opportunities in North Carolina Elementary Schools" (Ph.D. dissertation, University of North Carolina, 1928), 31 and *passim*.

Despite all its shortcomings, however, this traditional system of school-ing, which endured in many localities into the twentieth century, had attrac-tions for plain folk that the new system, which emerged after 1900, did not have. The old system was voluntary, thus honoring parental authority and the role of the family. Unless they needed the young ones at home or in the field, many parents let their children decide whether and how long to attend. School districts were always small and schools were nearby since everyone had to walk, and children thus attended school with people they knew. The districts were often so small that children had a choice of schools—and teachers. "School district lines are not very definite," investi-gators for the Bureau of Education found in Appalachia in 1915, "and a boy or girl who does not like one teacher may try another school. One boy told with glee of having been 'fired' from three schools in two weeks time."[25]

The old system was therefore informal and flexible, and responsive to complaint. An unpopular teacher could be boycotted or removed, and a popular one retained regardless of what outsiders thought. The community, not distant educationists, set conditions of teacher employment and decided all matters related to the school. Where there were no school buildings, the site of the school could be changed from year to year; and disgruntled parents might even form a school district of their own. The community could also dictate what its children were taught on disputed subjects. In 1921 John C. Campbell, who spent many years in the schools of Appalachia, said he personally knew two teachers there who had been fired for teaching that the earth was round.[26]

"THOSE WHO HAVE LEARNED TO READ AND WRITE GIVE US LESS TROUBLE THAN THOSE WHO ARE IGNORANT."

In the villages, most folk were satisfied to have familiar kinds of schools and schooling, but their congregation in compact communities set in motion a series of important changes in their relationship to schools. Mill owners saw schools as devices for keeping young children off village streets and for making them better workers as well, so they made sure that schools were available to their villagers. For many children, the move to the mill thus meant that school was accessible for longer terms and that the training was

---

25. U.S. Bureau of Education, *Bulletin 1915 No. 11: A Statistical Study of the Public Schools of the Appalachian Mountains*, 11.
26. John C. Campbell, *The Southern Highlander and His Homeland* (New York, 1921), 266.

probably of better quality. The improvement over schools available to farm families attracted some folk to the mills.

Mill owners supported schools for the same reason they supported churches. They had the Progressives' faith in education and were certain it would improve and help them discipline their workers. "As a manufacturer I believe in educating the labor; give them every facility for it," a mill president told the Industrial Commission in 1900. "I believe they make better operatives, make better citizens. It elevates and dignifies labor, and I should like to see anything that would add to the education of the masses." Because formal education involved no more than a few terms in a village school for children under twelve, it is difficult to see what this idea rested on, yet it was a basic element of paternalist thought. "We find that it is far easier to manage people who are educated, and that they make far better operatives than persons who are not educated," Francis Coggin, superintendent of Augusta Factory, told a congressional committee in 1883. "Those who are ignorant are inclined to be superstitious, and think you never treat them right, but the educated ones understand matters better and make much better operatives. . . . Those who have learned to read and write give us less trouble than those who are ignorant."[27]

Village schools varied greatly. At first, small villages duplicated the one-room schools familiar to country folk, but as the years passed, graded schools became the rule. By the end of the New South era, a large majority of mill children had free access to school through perhaps the sixth grade, and a few of the largest mills had schools extending higher than the ninth grade. Not all these schools were in the villages. Mill children in or adjacent to towns generally attended town schools, though schools in mill districts might enroll mill children only. Urban mills generally had no schools of their own and contributed to education only or largely through the taxes they paid. In 1901, for example, the mills in Augusta paid $8,167.97 into the Richmond County school fund, and children of their operatives attended four public schools, one of which met in a building donated by Augusta Factory.[28]

Mill schools were financed in various ways. Some mills constructed schools of their own, especially in the early years of the New South era, before public funds were available in meaningful amounts. More often, mill owners had their villages and surrounding areas constituted as public school

27. *House Documents*, 57th Cong., 1st Sess., No. 184, Vol. 7, p. 504; *Senate Documents*, 48th Cong., 1st Sess., No. 91, p. 729.
28. Augusta *Chronicle*, November 17, 1901.

districts, which permitted them to control the school board and receive whatever public funds were available for their school. They usually supplemented those funds in order to pay teachers more than minimum salaries and to operate the schools longer, often significantly longer, than minimum terms. The use of public funds opened the schools to all white children in the district and resulted in some integration with children unassociated with the mills, though most of the latter shunned mill schools. The mills' contribution to the school was significant.[29]

At Graniteville, the company built and operated a school long before the public school system was introduced, and in the 1870s and 1880s spent one thousand dollars a year on its operation. In 1883, the school's enrollment was 125, all mill children, and the two or three hundred dollars received from public funds were a small share of total costs. Originally, mill officials built the school to oversee children too young for mill work, and for that reason made attendance mandatory. Parents whose children did not attend had five cents deducted from their wages each day. According to Hamilton H. Hickman, who was president of the mill from shortly after the Civil War until the turn of the twentieth century, this practice "gave a good deal of dissatisfaction, and the school was not a success." When Hickman took over the mill, he revoked the rule and made attendance voluntary. "It is a remarkable fact," he said later of his action, "that from that time the school has been a success."[30]

In 1899 enrollment at the mill school was 262 and average daily attendance about 75 percent. The school by then was graded, employed four teachers as well as a principal, and offered work through the ninth grade. Four graduates of the class of 1899 received teaching certificates and found jobs in public schools, and two others won scholarships to Winthrop Institute in Rock Hill. Although attendance was not mandatory, the company "made very effort to induce the children to attend" by making the school "as attractive as possible."[31]

At Pelzer, a school also grew with the mills and the village, and was a centerpiece of the paternalism practiced there. Early in the twentieth cen-

29. In 1907 a survey of 65 mills in South Carolina found that the mills had spent $74,975 for school buildings and $11,189 for school equipment. All except one of the mill schools at the time of the survey provided free tuition for an average term of almost nine months, twice as long as that of other schools in the state (*Manufacturers' Record*, January 30, 1902, p. 192).

30. *Senate Documents*, 48th Cong., 1st Sess., No. 91, pp. 744–45.

31. Graves L. Knight to H. H. Hickman, April 18, 1899, April 19, 1900, in Graniteville Manufacturing Company Papers, University of South Carolina at Aiken Library; *Manufacturers' Record*, October 13, 1904, p. 300.

tury, this village had a kindergarten and night school as well as a mandatory day school that operated ten months a year and was tuition free. Indeed, as a condition of employment, each family head signed a statement pledging not only that all his children past their twelfth birthday would work in the mills if they were needed but also that all of his children "between the ages of 5 and 12 years, shall enter the school maintained by said company at Pelzer, and shall attend every school day during the school session, unless prevented by sickness or other unavoidable causes." The company gave each child ten cents for each month's perfect attendance and altogether spent about five thousand dollars a year on the school. Everything related to the school was carefully supervised. "Every teacher is chosen with special reference to his or her capacity for this distinctive work," a visitor wrote of the Pelzer school in 1901. "Last year about 800 pupils were enrolled, and the examination papers showed an excellent average of scholarship. . . . Some children . . . work in the mills at stated hours of the day, at the expiration of which time certain positions of the machinery are shut down, and the children, having earned from twenty-five to fifty cents apiece for their half-day's labor, hie away to school, where special provision is made for them."[32]

At Gastonia in 1914, where there were a number of small mills rather than a few large ones, each village had a graded school with at least three grades, and one, at Loray Mills, had seven grades. These schools were in the public school system, and mill children could attend the only high school in Gastonia if, like other children, they paid a tuition charge. The village schools were open eight months a year, whereas rural schools in the county operated only five months. Attendance was voluntary, despite a state law requiring all children between eight and twelve to be in school four months a year.[33] Few mill children progressed beyond the fourth or fifth grade. Indeed, in 1914, graded schools were still relatively new in Gastonia. They had been introduced in the villages in 1901, though for some time before, the mills had employed first-grade teachers at their own expense in order to separate first graders from other students.

Mill officials used various strategies to encourage children to attend school. Only a few required attendance, because they, like mill folk, found that practice unappealing. "The subject of education touches every phase

32. See U.S. Bureau of Labor, *Bulletin No. 54: Housing of the Working People by Employers* (1904), 1224–26; Leonora B. Eillis, "A Model Factory Town," *Forum*, XXXII (September, 1901), 60–65; and *Manufacturers' Record*, February 21, 1901, pp. 78–80.

33. Edgar R. Rankin, "A Social Study of One Hundred Families at Cotton Mills in Gastonia, North Carolina" (M.A. thesis, University of North Carolina, 1914), 22–24.

and fiber of life. It is indispensable and inseparable from success," the president of the mill in Jonesville, South Carolina, said early in the twentieth century. "Before school opened in September I posted notices in each mill that it would be expected that at least one child from each family would attend school, and have been compelled to stop several machines for lack of help caused by reason of their attending school." At Arcade Mills in Rock Hill, it was "the business of the heads of the departments in the mill to see that the children attend" school. At Anderson, South Carolina, the Townsend, Cox, and Brogan mills pooled their resources to build and finance a school, and undertook to see that the children used it. At the Townsend mill, "All the children under 13 years of age are urged to go to school, and when they don't go it is the duty of the teacher to hunt them up and see why they don't go, and the parents are seen and asked to make them attend school." This was the practice also at Olympia, Granby, Richland, and Capitol City mills in Columbia, South Carolina. "Teachers are required to visit the families living in the villages and to solicit the pupils," an official of Richland Mill reported in 1904. "At the same time our overseers are instructed not to take children that should go to school, as it is our endeavor to in a manner force every child to attend school during the session."[34]

"OH, NO. I'D RATHER WORK THAN GO TO SCHOOL."

In the New South, educational standards and expectations were low, which influenced attitudes toward the schools. In his annual report for 1885, the school superintendent of Augusta, Georgia, reported construction of an "excellent" new school for children at Sibley and King mills in the city. The building had four rooms and was already crowded "to its fullest capacity" of 250 students. The superintendent was proud of the building and the enrollment, for they represented significant improvement. Still, there were problems. Not only were mill children "somewhat unambitious of an education," the superintendent reported, but "their parents are poor, many of them, and need to place them at work early in life." Thus, "The primary grades are principally needed and the children are from six to ten years old almost exclusively who attend the factory schools. To give a good idea of reading, spelling, writing and simple arithmetic is the best that can be done, and many are growing up ignorant of even these." He continued: "The trouble here, as it is in some other places, is that the parents of children are

34. *Manufacturers' Record*, October 13, 1904, pp. 297–301.

content for them to grow up with as little education as they themselves had. I have often been astonished to find that some people look upon education as a mere pastime, to be gained in spare hours, or until the child is old enough to work."[35]

Folk, then, brought to the mills attitudes shaped on the farm and in the mountains. "It is in the attitude of parents and children toward education rather than in the condition of school systems that a chief cause of the illiteracy and ignorance of the textile operatives, North and South, is to be found," investigators for the 1907–1908 labor study reported. Indeed, most parents "are indifferent or hostile to the schools," though a minority "do all they can to have their children get all the school training available."[36]

That range of attitudes suggests that new views were beginning to appear even though old ones were still dominant. Mill parents themselves had virtually no education and their children could manage without it, they told the investigators. Children old enough to work should help support the family, they insisted, and the family could not afford the cost of schooling. Cultural values reinforced these practical concerns. "Parents allege that school regulations are curtailments of their personal liberties," investigators reported. "They regard such requirements as that children shall be vaccinated or come to school properly dressed and clean as enough to condemn the whole school system as undemocratic." They "claim that the schools are worthless and that the time of the children spent there is lost." Those whose children attended school outside the villages also "claim their children are looked down upon by other classes of children and discriminated against by the teachers." Of the latter claim, investigators said, "There is ample evidence that this is true."[37]

Adding complexity to this situation was the failure of schools and teachers to adapt themselves to the needs and concerns of mill folk. Indeed, the folk's indifference to schooling often turned into active distaste as a result of experience with schools. Among the factors that caused this dislike were, according to the labor investigators, "the unattractiveness of the school, the inefficient teaching, the lack of mechanical aids to instruction, the physical discomforts of the school, and the irksomeness of school work." Furthermore, they continued, "The child feels it is useless to go to school when he knows he will go into the mill anyway before he learns much. . . . The mill is attractive to the inexperienced child. Its unrestraint, its crowd spirit, the opportunity which it affords to the child to do things with his hands rather

35. Augusta *Chronicle*, January 17, 1886.
36. *Senate Documents*, 61st Cong., 2nd Sess., No. 645, Vol. 1, p. 581.
37. *Ibid.*, 581–82.

than with his head, and its regularly recurring pay day make the child and parent believe he is better off than in school."[38]

The schools functioned as adjuncts to the mills through the desire of mill folk and of mill owners. Mill-operated nursery schools and kindergartens freed mothers to work; night schools enabled children to work in the mills during the day; the encouragement and, sometimes, the requirement of attendance to keep children off the streets made the schools policing agencies for mill owners. Many officials subordinated the schools to the mills in more explicit ways. Some mills divided the day into halves, and sent some children to work in the morning and to school in the afternoon and reversed that schedule for other children. Others treated the schools as reservoirs of labor, taking workers from them when a full component of operatives failed to show up in the morning. Occasionally, schools closed for the day because so many children were pressed into mill work. Families themselves often took one of their children out of school to substitute for a sibling or parent absent from the mill.

These circumstances added to the unattractiveness of teaching in mill schools. Because of the general prejudice against mill folk, there was some stigma attached to teaching their schools, and this was one reason mills supplemented teachers' salaries. Teachers had to move into isolated villages, and for them the mills built special houses so they would not have to live with mill folk. Such teachers generally remained in the villages only during school terms, and the social distance between them and the children they taught might have been a factor in the ineffectiveness of their schools. Investigators for the labor study of 1907 and 1908 thought the quality of mill teaching was low and that circumstances in mill schools made effective teaching impossible. Among the problems were "indifference, absenteeism, insubordination, lack of equipment, [and] interference from the mill," investigators reported, "and about everything else that can defeat a teacher's efforts." The average teacher faced oversized lower grades and undersized upper grades, and had "little or no public sentiment back of her." Many of the youngest pupils "are sent to school at a very early age quite as much for the purpose of being cared for and so relieving other members of the family from the charge of them as with the hope of their learning anything." And many of the older pupils had already worked in the mill and thus were "harder to teach because duller of comprehension and less amenable to discipline."[39]

38. *Ibid.*, 578.
39. *Ibid.*, 579–80.

The schools could not hold their pupils. In 1902 only two-fifths of school-age children in mill villages in North Carolina were enrolled in school, and only a fourth were in daily attendance. Educationists deplored these facts, which had an apparent cause: mill children preferred work to school. "I have repeatedly asked children who have gone from the school into the mill whether they would rather remain in the school or be in the mill," James L. Orr told the Industrial Commission in 1900, "and I have never found one who said he would not rather work in the mill than go to school."[40]

Parents acquiesced in this preference. "We send around to all the families and insist on their sending the children to the school," an official of Henrietta Mills near Charlotte reported in 1900. "We have a good many people who tell us they have lived all their lives without education and they think their children could get along as well as anybody." This official continued: "A man will say that he does not think we ought to force him to do something he does not want to do, that he is his own man, and if he does not want to send his children to school he does not see why any other individual should force him to do it."[41]

Perhaps, however, most parents wanted their children to go to school more than children themselves were willing to go. Those interviewed remembered mill work as children positively, but they had no such memories of school. "Oh, no. I'd rather work than go to school," said Jessie Lee Carter, who began spinning at Brandon Mill when she was twelve years old. "I never did learn to read and write. But I loved to work. Yes, I did." Significantly, young Jessie had been enrolled in school when she first went to work, but though she was twelve years old, she could not read or write.

Curtis Enlow, who was born into a mill family in 1904 and grew up at Poe Mills, had what was probably a typical experience. "I was about thirteen years old, and I decided I would go to work," Enlow recalled. "Well, I went to work [between school terms] and my dad says if I quit when school started, he'd let me work. When school started, I didn't quit. I went back to school, but I wasn't learning nothing—I didn't think I was. So I went and told him, and he says, 'All right, you ain't learning nothing. Well, you can go back to the mill.'"

The range of memories was, however, diverse. "When I got twelve years old, I wanted to quit school," recalled Alice P. Evitt, who had already learned mill work by helping her older sister. "My daddy didn't want me to quit, and he said, 'Well, if you quit school, you've got to go to work.' So I

---

40. North Carolina Superintendent of Public Instruction, *Biennial Report, 1900–02*, I; *House Documents*, 57th Cong., 1st Sess., No. 184, Vol. 7, p. 484.
41. *House Documents*, 57th Cong., 1st Sess., No. 184, Vol. 7, p. 494.

just quit and went to work." What had school been like? "They'd whoop you then. They'd get hickories," Mrs. Evitt remembered. "I never did get a whoopin', but I see'd a lot of them get a whoopin'." Folk had no such memories of mill work.

"NO HUMAN-HEARTED MAN CAN LONGER TURN A DEAF EAR TO THE CRY OF THE FACTORY CHILDREN."

Mill children and their parents subverted the intentions of educationists, reformers, and even mill owners. Those groups, however, were unwilling to let folk have their way in something so fundamental as schooling their own children. They therefore joined the movement to make school attendance compulsory, for that, they concluded, was the only way to ensure that children entered schools and were under the influence of those who would help them. Folk resisted this effort as an intrusion into their lives, and their resistance was one reason compulsory schooling made so little progress in the New South.

There were practical obstacles to compulsory schooling that went far beyond the concerns of plain folk, however. Schools were throughout the region inadequate to accommodate the school-age population. At the beginning of the 1900–1901 school year, for example, the Atlanta school system turned away four hundred white pupils because there was no room for them. Two years later, the school superintendent of North Carolina noted that inadequate facilities were a major obstacle to compulsory schooling in his state. "If all the children of school age were suddenly forced into the schools by a compulsory attendance law," he wrote in 1902, "the school houses would probably be overrun, the teachers overwhelmed, the demand for new houses and additional teachers" too great to meet.[42]

Opposition to compulsory schooling was especially strong among plain folk. Middle-class parents sent their children to school in far greater proportions and for far longer times than folk parents sent theirs, and they had more faith in the efficacy of schooling since they were oriented toward mobility and achievement. The compulsory attendance movement was therefore in important respects a weapon middle-class reformers and other disparagers of "poor whites" hoped to use to eradicate the culture and lifestyle of plain folk. In 1902, when J. Y. Joyner, the North Carolina school superintendent, wrote down the reasons he thought so many children failed

42. Atlanta *Constitution*, September 15, 1900; North Carolina Superintendent of Public Instruction, *Biennial Report, 1900–02*, xlix.

to attend school, he obviously had plain folk in mind: "Ignorance of parents, often rendering them incapable of appreciating the value of education"; "carelessness, indifference, and incompetence of parents to control the child"; "laziness, thriftlessness or selfishness of parents that lays the burden of family support upon the shoulders of the little children"; "honest and unavoidable poverty of parents." In what seems almost a postscript, he added a final reason: "poor schools and teachers."[43]

Joyner's was the characteristic stance of advocates of forced schooling: the problem was plain folk and their benighted ways, not the schools and what they had to offer. The schools' failures were thus caused by people who stayed away from them. This attitude was shared by many middle-class people. "Parents seem to take no interest in the public schools," a North Carolina farm owner complained in 1905. "The boys rabbit-hunt during the school season and drink whiskey—that is a large part of them do. So what we need is a better school law, and have it enforced." Another farm owner wrote the same year: "The greatest need of the wage earner is to improve themselves mentally, morally and industrially, that they may learn to have more regard for their obligations and thereby be better enabled to fulfill their obligations to those who employ them and to provide for themselves. I think that compulsory education is one of the great necessities of our people." A third farm owner insisted, "The poorer class of white people are too careless about sending their children to school, and if we furnish the means for them to send, they ought to be forced to utilize it."[44]

Most mill officials also endorsed compulsory attendance laws, at least for children too young to work in the mills. "We have built good schoolhouses, etc.," one official told the North Carolina labor commissioner in 1907, "but the great trouble is that the poor whites neglect to send their children to school, when there is not the least excuse for them not attending. There are certain people who do not seem to care whether their children get an education or not, and we think the state should see to it that the children all receive at least a common school education. We believe the State should protect the children from the carelessness of such parents."[45]

Mill folk were special targets of these advocates of compulsion. As "poor whites," they attracted attention from all reformers, and their concentration in villages made them and their indifference to schooling especially visible. Also, compulsory schooling was the natural concomitant of the child-labor laws then being advocated, for no opponent of child labor wanted to turn

43. North Carolina Superintendent of Public Instruction, *Biennial Report, 1900–02*, xlvii.
44. NC *Labor Report* (1905), 24–25, 27, and (1901), 78.
45. *Ibid.* (1907), 245.

children out of the mills only to have them wander the streets of villages, where all kinds of temptations were thought to lurk. Finally, the opposition of mill folk to compulsory schooling was open and especially disconcerting to educationists.

Some reformers thus urged special treatment for mill folk. In 1902, for example, the school superintendent of North Carolina still refused to endorse a statewide compulsory attendance law. "I fear that a State compulsory attendance law might generate so much friction that the general course of education might be retarded rather than advanced," the superintendent wrote, acknowledging the widespread opposition to proposed legislation. However, he would ignore the opposition of one group of North Carolinians. Mill folk, but not other people, the superintendent told legislators, should be forced to send their children to school. "No human-hearted man can longer turn a deaf ear to the cry of the factory children," he wrote, piggybacking compulsory schooling on child-labor reform. "The strong arm of the law must intervene" to help them. The superintendent therefore "earnestly" recommended that legislators prohibit the labor of all children under twelve in mills and factories and all those under fourteen who could not read and write. Such restrictions were advisable, however, only if children forced out of the mills were forced into the schools. "To make fully effective such a law," he wrote, "some legislation looking to compelling these children to attend the school while in session ought to be enacted. To take the children out of the mills and turn them loose in the mill villages in idleness, without parental oversight, while the grown people are all at work, might prove a greater evil than light employment in the mills."

These coercions, the superintendent assured legislators, were unnecessary for farmers (even though the vast majority of child labor in the state was done on farms, and much of it was harder work than that done by children in the mills). "The difference between the conditions and surroundings of the mill villages and those of the rural agricultural districts makes manifest, without discussion, the stronger reasons and greater necessity for a compulsory attendance law in the former," the superintendent wrote.[46]

Legislators resisted the superintendent's suggestion, perhaps partly because they recognized that many white people, including some mill folk, could not afford to send their children to schools. A mill official, alarmed at proposals to compel mill children but not farm children to go to school, endorsed this view. "The poor class of people are not able to support their children while at school," he wrote. To pass a law aimed at factory children

46. North Carolina Superintendent of Public Instruction, *Biennial Report, 1900–02*, l–li.

alone would therefore cause the poorest mill families to return to the farms and their children "to work in the fields, which is really harder labor and less remunerative than the factory."[47]

These considerations did not delay passage of child-labor laws, at least not for so long. Child-labor laws would not apply to the middle classes or farmers but only to mill folk and a few other groups whose interests and wishes could be ignored. Compulsory education and its concomitants—consolidated schools controlled by professional educationists rather than local communities, higher taxes to support those schools, education of blacks, and other weighty considerations—were entirely different matters. Southerners disliked laws that coerced themselves, but not necessarily laws that coerced other people, especially if they disapproved of the group being coerced. Educationists recognized that fact and knew that compulsory education would remain unacceptable in Georgia and the Carolinas until they could convince the political majorities in those states that it was a practice responsible citizens should impose on the irresponsible for the latter's own good. Child-labor reformers had used similar methods to accomplish their goals.

"I am not sure that this would be a wise course to pursue," the North Carolina school superintendent had said in 1890 as the debate on compulsory schooling was getting under way in his state. To increase school enrollment, he recommended, instead of compulsion, a campaign to persuade people of the desirability of schooling. After a dozen years of persuasion, however, another superintendent gave up on that option. "It is a tragic truth," he wrote in 1902, "that there are some parents so blinded by ignorance to the value and importance of education, and others so lazy, thriftless or selfish that they cannot be reached by the power of attraction and persuasion, or the mild compulsion of public opinion." Still, because opposition to compulsion was so strong in North Carolina, the superintendent thought it "wisest to be content to progress along the same safe, conservative lines [of persuasion and voluntarism] a while longer." He noted, "A compulsory law . . . would be ineffective without truancy officers," and "such officers would probably be out of accord with the past traditions and the present temper of our people."[48]

Two years later, the superintendent, J. Y. Joyner, changed his mind. "Knowing the conservatism and the independence of our people and their natural resentment at the suggestion of compulsion in anything," he had

47. NC *Labor Report* (1902), 170.
48. North Carolina Superintendent of Public Instruction, *Biennial Report, 1889–90*, xxlv–xxxv, and *1900–02*, xlix–l.

always supported voluntary schooling, Joyner wrote. But in 1904 he concluded "that non-attendance, irregularity of attendance and the resulting illiteracy will never be overcome except by reasonable, conservative compulsory laws." The superintendent thus transformed the "conservative" course of the education effort from voluntarism to compulsion. Despite years of intense effort, he told state legislators, school leaders had made no headway against parents who refused to see the benefits of schooling. He assured the legislators, however, that the people to be coerced were only those who needed coercion for their own good. "The majority of these illiterate children are the children of illiterates and perhaps the descendants of generations of illiterates," Joyner wrote. And "the intervention of the strong arm of the law is . . . the only hope of saving [those children and] also the children of literate, and, sometimes intelligent, parents, from the carelessness, indifference, incompetence, laziness, thriftlessness, or selfishness of such parents." Casting his argument for compulsion in a more appealing, libertarian guise, Joyner continued: "Every child has a right to have the chance to develop the power to make the most possible of himself in spite of his environment. No man, not even a parent, has any right to deprive any child of this inalienable right."[49]

Eventually, legislators succumbed to such arguments in piecemeal fashion, enacting legislation so full of loopholes and so indifferently enforced that it was not until after World War II that the three states had fully implemented compulsory education. North Carolina acted first. In 1907 its legislature adopted a law permitting localities to compel children between eight and fourteen to attend school for sixteen weeks a year. South Carolina adopted a similar law in 1915, making the compulsion applicable to the entire school term. A year later, Georgia required four months of schooling each year for children between eight and fourteen except those who were disabled, impoverished, or too far away to walk to school.[50]

These laws were not effectively enforced until long after the second decade of the twentieth century. "The four months compulsory school law is a farce," a North Carolina school official remarked a few years after its passage. "It isn't enforced." Even where efforts were made to enforce it, parents and children sabotaged them. "As it is written," the official continued, "a child may remain in the first grade for several years. After

49. *Ibid.*, 1904–06, 28–29.
50. The laws are summarized in Elizabeth H. Davidson, *Child Labor Legislation in the Southern Textile States* (Chapel Hill, 1939), 275–77. In its first year, the South Carolina local-option law covered 21 of 167 mills in the state (South Carolina State Superintendent of Education, *Report, 1916*, 116).

attending school for four months he leaves, goes to work and returns the next year no further advanced in grade. This performance keeps up until he is of age to leave entirely. There is no incentive to study and no attempt to complete school."[51]

Because of other people's tolerance, folk were generally able to evade the compulsory attendance laws when they wanted to. Local officials and grand juries gave little attention to enforcing the laws. "It has been almost impossible to induce persons to serve as district or township attendance officers," the North Carolina school superintendent reported in 1918. "Few are willing to incur the displeasure of their neighbors by enforcing the law. . . . Consequently the law has been laxly enforced in many counties and districts and has failed to reach those who most need to be reached." [52]

Children could be forced to enroll in school, but they could not be forced to attend regularly or to learn while they were there. At a school that served children of three mill villages in Gaston County in 1923 and 1924, for example, the school year was 170 days. Only 29 percent of the 707 students who enrolled that term attended as many as 130 days, however, and 38.6 percent attended less than 50 days. According to Bertha C. Hipp, who compiled these figures and who talked with teachers and officials at the school, this absenteeism was due not only to the frequent movement of families but to the indifference of parents and children alike. "Individual pupils playing hooky and parents keeping children out irregularly without lawful excuses constitutes the chief difficulty," Hipp wrote.

Under such circumstances no school could succeed, and at the end of the school year, only 287 of the 707 students (40.7 percent) were promoted, compared with 60.6 percent of all white students in the state. Most students in the school were thus older than average for their grade. Indeed, the average age of fourth-graders in the school was 12.3 years compared with the standard age of 9.5 years. Only one in seven (13.9 percent) of the students in the school that year had passed their fourteenth birthday compared with one in three (32.7 percent) statewide. Mill children, these figures show, quit school and went to work as soon as the law allowed. Child-labor and compulsory attendance laws delayed their entry into the mills about two to four years, during which the children attended school sporadically.[53]

51. Quoted in Theresa Wolfson, "Child Labor," in W. H. Swift (ed.), *Child Labor in North Carolina* (Chapel Hill, 1920), 211.

52. North Carolina Superintendent of Public Instruction, *Biennial Report, 1916–18*, 23.

53. Bertha C. Hipp, "A Gaston County Cotton Mill and Its Community" (MA. thesis, University of North Carolina, 1930), 53–60.

Mill children learned little at school. They expected to be mill workers or wives of mill workers, and for those roles the schools taught them very little.[54] Their indifference to schooling was reflected in the studies educational psychologists began making in the 1920s measuring intelligence and achievement among children in mill schools. Invariably, the studies found mill children educationally retarded and, in the confident opinion of those who made the tests, subnormal in intelligence. In a representative study, John H. Cook, an educationist, and J. A. Highsmith, a psychologist, tested several hundred eleven-year-olds in seven mill schools in North Carolina in the mid-1920s and found 92.1 percent of them with intelligence quotients of less than 100. Indeed, almost a third of the students (30.5 percent) were "feebleminded," as psychologists then labeled children who scored below 70 on their scale; and twice that proportion (61.6 percent) of the students, who scored between 70 and 99, were of "borderline," "dull," or "below average" intelligence.[55] The results of Cook and Highsmith's tests are a fitting monument to the efforts of educationists to force folk into schooling that they did not want, that did not serve their needs as folk saw them, and that even tried to destroy their identity as folk.[56]

54. For accounts of "textile schools" that did in fact try to teach mill work, see U.S. Bureau of Education, *Bulletin 1913 No. 25: Industrial Education in Columbus, Ga.*, and *Bulletin 1916 No. 6: A Half-Time Mill School;* and Walter A. Dyer, "Training New Leaders for the Industrial South," *World's Work*, XXVIII (1914), 285–92.

55. John H. Cook, *A Study of the Mill Schools of North Carolina* (New York, 1925), 18, 1. For other studies, see Graham B. Dimmick, "A Comparative Study of the Growth in Mental and Physical Abilities of the Mill and Non-Mill Children of the West Durham North Side School over a Period of Six Months" (M.A. thesis, University of North Carolina, 1927); L. H. Jobe, "A Study of the Intelligence Levels of a Group of Cotton Mill Village School Children" (M.A. thesis, University of North Carolina, 1922); Ray Armstrong, "The Mental Growth of Children Whose Parents Are Cotton Mill Operatives Compared with the Mental Growth of Children Whose Parents Follow Other Occupations" (M.A. thesis, University of North Carolina, 1926); and L. A. Williams, "The Intellectual Status of Children in Cotton Mill Villages," *Social Forces*, IV (1925), 183–86.

56. Compulsory schooling, J. S. Hurt has written in a study of the impact of this phenomenon on poor people in England, was "far from . . . the gift of a beneficent state"; it was "an infliction that reduced living standards [and] disrupted the normal pattern of life" (*Elementary Schooling and the Working Classes, 1860–1918* [London, 1979], 211).

15

POVERTY AND PREJUDICE

In the estimation of outsiders, most plain folk were "poor whites," that is, "trash," "lintheads," "rednecks," "crackers," or some other category of "sorry" people. They were therefore objects of a pervasive prejudice that had psychological as well as social and economic effects. All folk encountered this prejudice in some form, understood its nature and manifestations, and spent much of their lives avoiding situations that provoked it. Many even remembered their first encounter with this prejudice, and all knew the sense of inadequacy that it evoked. Jim Jeffrey, a sharecropper all his life, was "a little shaver" in north Georgia at the turn of the century when "a rich man's son got mad at him and said, 'You ain't nothing but pore whites.'" Jim asked his grandmother what that remark meant, and when she told him, he "made up his mind right then and there to leave Oconee County the first chance he got." The incident left an emotional scar, and flight became for Jeffrey a perennial means of avoiding situations that reminded him of it. "Nobody ever called him 'pore white' any more," his wife said much later, but "Jim still believes that people are thinkin' it." And this, she thought, was why he drank so heavily and moved every time he had a dispute with a landlord. "The only time he forgets that he came from pore folks is when he gits drunk," his wife said. "Boy! He's rollin' in clover then."

Many folk first encountered prejudice when they moved from the country to the mill. "I've always been shamed I can't talk good like other folks," Jennie Rowe, a Newton, North Carolina, mill worker, said in the late 1930s. "Seems like I can't get words together right. Pap wouldn't let us go to school. Said learnin' made girls crooked and made boys wuthless." Still, Jennie had not been conscious of her speech and illiteracy until she and her family moved from the mountains to Lawndale Mills near Shelby while she was still a child. "In that town everybody had education and there we was—not a one of us could read nor write," she recalled. "I was so shamed. . . . The mill people laughed at us." In a prejudiced world, the disesteemed clung to even the smallest margin of status.

More prejudice was shown, however, by outsiders. When Sallie Jane Stephenson and her family moved to a mill in Anderson County, South Carolina, about 1890, they endured the disdain of relatives who remained on the farm; and when Sallie Jane went to school in town, she was mocked by her classmates. "Sallie Jane from factory hill," the children chanted, "yonder comes old Sallie Jane from factory hill." Infuriated and humiliated, she shouted back, "It's good honest work and folks'd have a hard time gettin' along without cotton mills." But by her own account, she hardly believed what she said. "I was a grown and mature woman before I ever got to where I could honestly feel like that in my heart," she said years later.

That feeling was widespread among mill folk. "They feel themselves a class apart and looked down upon by others, even of no great means," labor investigators said of Alabama mill workers in 1907 and 1908. "And this is true." The investigators found mill workers who were ashamed of having to work in the mills and who never told outsiders they did so, who refused to live in mill villages or mix socially with other mill folk, and who expressed contempt for mill people as a group.[1] "I don't blame [people] for looking down on some of them," J. H. Reynolds said of mill folk after more than forty years of mill work, "for they are so sorry."

"I WOULD ALL MOST AS SOON DIE AS TO HAVE MY CHILD BORNED HERE IN THIS PLACE."

Prejudice and discrimination were triggered by "stigma symbols" (the opposite of status symbols) that marked the appearance of plain folk. The most obvious were the red necks of dirt farmers, the sallow, lint-tinged appearance of mill workers, and the coarse, ill-fitting clothes of the very

1. *Senate Documents*, 61st Cong., 2nd Sess., No. 645, Vol. 1, pp. 585–86.

poor. The sharecropper's sunburned skin was not a mark of health or ruddy good looks by the standards of the day but a symbol of having to "work like a nigger." The ideal skin was milk white, and farm women tried to protect themselves with bonnets and sleeves, for appearance was important to them. Hookworm and other sources of anemia sallowed the complexion, malaria gave it a jaundiced color, and snuff and chewing tobacco discolored the teeth. All added to the problem of self-image.

Clothing did, too. Women especially were sensitive about the lack of presentable clothing and frequently avoided church, town, or other places where their dress made them self-conscious. Sometimes the problem was no clothing at all. Thus, Henry T. Bramblett, son of a disabled Confederate veteran, never forgot the winter he had to go without shoes on the north Georgia farm where he grew up. Because of their poverty, Bramblett and his family moved to a cotton mill in Athens about 1890 when Henry was "nigh fifteen years old." He recalled of the experience: "One winter before then I hadn't had no shoes to wear, so I never took no chances on not having shoes that first winter I worked. Soon as I was paid enough, I bought myself two pairs of shoes, one pair to wear everyday and the other pair was for Sunday. Them was mighty tight times then, but one thing shore I ain't never had to go barefooted from that day 'til this."

Illiteracy was another stigma symbol when folk mixed with outsiders, and thus an added source of anxiety. Disputing charges of credit merchants, for example, might expose one's inability to read or figure, or to do so with ease, and thus bare vulnerabilities at the heart of feelings of inadequacy. For this reason, many folk refused to protest charges they thought were incorrect. According to investigators for the 1907–1908 labor study, some mill workers "suspected that they were cheated at company stores by short weights, false entries, bills charged again after payment, and other methods"; and in some localities, there was "considerable dissatisfaction on this score." Yet the complainants kept no record of their accounts and were unable to challenge the merchants' figures.[2]

Dealings with lawyers, bureaucrats, and others whose expertise lay hidden in the printed word were equally problematical. Again and again, "reform" and "progress" exposed the inadequacies of illiterates in a transforming world. Literacy qualifications, registration forms, and secret ballots revealed the problems of uneducated voters. Even the advent of motion pictures (silent films, with printed subtitles) was a reminder of the limita-

2. *Ibid.*, 603.

tions of illiteracy. "I've seed two shows in my life and that was before they done any talkin'," Lil Pepper, a North Carolina cotton mill worker, said. "I couldn't do no readin' so I just had to set up there and watch folks jump from one horse to another and gallop off like tarnation after some man they wanted to kill. Looked like a bunch of fools to me."

The chief stigma symbol, and the source of all others, was poverty. Plain folk were poor people in a society that demeaned poverty, and the psychological consequences of how they adjusted to the limiting effects of poverty were a major factor in their history. Their poverty was relative as well as absolute, which governed their response to it among themselves. Within their own circle, being poor was one of the givens of life, not something to fret over. "We were always poor, but so was everyone else we knew," Brother Fisher recalled of his family before they moved to a mill in Gastonia early in the twentieth century, "so we didn't mind."

Mill folk generally judged their circumstance by that of other folk similarly situated, and unless they fell below the levels made tolerable by that standard, they did not preoccupy themselves with economic hardship. As Lessie Bowden Bland remembered of villagers at Carrboro in the second decade of the twentieth century, everyone "was on the level," that is, in the same economic condition, and that neutralized the feeling of being poor. "It wasn't too bad," Mrs. Bland recalled. "We had enough to eat, and we had a warm place to stay, a good bed to sleep in, and food. We were all right."

This attitude predominated. Complicating the adjustments it represented, however, was the fact that many folk fell below the economic levels of other folk around them. So many folk fell below those levels at some time in the course of their lives that the fear of destitution was one of the realities of folk life. Folk who did not eat sufficiently or have minimally adequate housing, medical care, or other necessities were most numerous in urban mill districts and remote farming areas. But most families may have experienced want at some time, and even if not, all folk knew someone who had been or was destitute.

Thus, for example, the winter of 1886 was extraordinarily severe in Augusta, and it followed months of shutdowns and short time in the mills. The consequent suffering was great, and townspeople organized a special relief effort. Charity workers found "great destitution" near Enterprise Mill, for example; and the Augusta *Chronicle* publicized the need for help. "The charitable people of Augusta will find full scope for the exercise of their generosity among the operatives of the Sibley mills," the *Chronicle* said in one report. "The cases of illness are frequent and distressing, and the want and destitution is widespread and pathetic. Whole families are stricken down with fever, and in many cases food and fire are strangers to the sufferers." The need, the paper reported, was for "help, attention, sympathy, clothing and food."[3]

Such calamities had lasting effects, for they reinforced gnawing fears of falling into destitution and dependence. Folk feared having to live on charity, losing their children to an orphans' home, going to a poorhouse in old age, facing death with no prospect of proper burial—any circumstance that would bare their vulnerabilities.[4] Such situations brought shame and loss of self-esteem. People should take care of themselves, folk believed, and failure to do so was evidence of personal or family inadequacy.

Among the destitute, despair could be overwhelming, and some of them wrote Governor Blease of their problems. "I just thought I would Write you and See if there was any thing that you Could Give me to Do to make a few Dollars Extra," L. A. Few of Mollohon Mill in Newberry wrote in 1914. Few and his wife lived alone. She was bedridden and helpless, and when he went to work, there was no one to attend to her. "My Wages Are not sufficient to make Expences Just at This Time," he told the governor. "My Wife Has been Down for 9 Weeks and has not Walked a step." She "has White sweling and Cant move her self in bed."[5]

The letter of L. H. McKissick of New Brookland showed just how difficult medical problems could be for the destitute. "I am suffering from kidney and bladder trouble, and am not able to work," McKissick wrote. "I am a poor man, I have got a wife and little babe to support and I am not able to work a bit[.] I have tried to work and hold out long enough to get the Money to have an operation performed but my last hopes have vanished as I am not able to do any thing. I have been suffering for years and nothing has done me any good. I am passing pure blood in my urine all the time and some times it is cloted. I am so weak I cant hardly walk. *I have got nobody to look to help me* . . . I thought you would help me."[6]

Women, too, wrote of misfortune and despair. Minnie Beacham's husband had been sentenced to the chain gang while she was pregnant, and with no relatives to which she could turn, she had to go to the poorhouse.

3. Augusta *Chronicle*, February 28, 1886.
4. For descriptions of some of the conditions poor folk feared, see Roy M. Brown, *Public Poor Relief in North Carolina* (Chapel Hill, 1928); and annual reports of the North Carolina State Board of Public Charities during the New South era.
5. L. A. Few to Coleman L. Blease, February 25, 1914, in Coleman L. Blease Papers, South Carolina State Archives.
6. L. H. McKissick to Blease, July 23, 1911, in Blease Papers. Italics added.

"He was my only dependance for a liveing," Mrs. Beacham wrote Blease of her husband. "And they taken him and lefe me on the mercys of charity to do the best I can. [T]hare was No way left for Me only to Come to the County home. [S]o I am here. [A]nd it Will Cost the County More to suport Me and pay My Doctor bill and buy My Medicine than My husband's labor will be worth to the city. [B]esides the trouble it has brought on Me in My Condition. I am in the last stage of Maternity. Will be confined in about three & a half weeks." Mrs. Beacham continued: *[A]nd I would all most as soon die as to have My Child borned here in this place.* I was put here and have to stay because I have no relatives to go to. [A]nd I have to risk the danger of ruining my child. I am with people that look allmost inhuman. [A]nd have all kinds of queer actions but I am compelled to see them some in spite of pending danger. I have wearyed and grieved untill I am half insane now and I believe I will have to go to an asylum before he serves his time out."[7]

Hattie Freeman of Greer was also desperate because of her husband's imprisonment. "I am weeak and Sick Werey about my Husbend to night," she wrote in the spring of 1914. "I and My baby is by hour Silf[.] Mr Gov please give My Husbend a payrole please. I sure do need my Husbend help at home to Keep I and the baby up. My Husbend ant got good mine[.] [H]e was all way that way[.] [H]e can be good deeal help to me and the baby. Mr Gov I am living ind a little house by My Self and I ant got nuthing fit to ware and ant got nuthing for me and the baby to eat." Mrs. Freeman pleaded: "Mr Gov I hope you will helpe me please. Mr Gov I dont get nothing only what my nabro gave me[.] I ant able to work. . . . *Mr Gov we are White peaple[.]* My Husbend name is Bly Freeman[.] We have ben marrie about eaght year and my Husbend never has ben ind truble be fore. Will Wats got him ind this truble. My Husbend is able hard heardn he cant heare good. . . . Gov I am a poor Women and help my Self[.] I would get better paper [to write this letter on] but I ant got no money to by good paper[.] I done the Best I could."[8]

Elderly folk, too, had fears of destitution. "I am an old Confederate, one armed and 71 years old," D. F. Tippett of Langley wrote. "I have been Working in the Mills here for 17 years. [B]ut the Mill has only been working half time since March. My poor old wife is now helpless & sick and has been so far the past three Years. I took my little Pension and paid up every dollar I owed in the world, but I am not able to keep up and Keep straight any longer

7. Minnie Beacham to Blease, February 1, 1914, in Blease Papers. Italics added.
8. Mrs. Hattie Freeman to Blease, March 24, 1914, in Blease Papers. Italics added.

without help." He continued: "*I am not a beggar* & any one here can tell you so but the thought came to me that having done my full duty & given my blood for my State paid all taxes and other dues, it was time Now in My old age & helplessness for it to do something [for me]. . . . If there is any way in which I can be helped I beg that it be done & done Quickly or it will be of no good."[9]

J. M. Bright, apparently a farmer, who lived near Greer, was even more desperate and ineffectual in his effort to help himself. "I hav bin a flicked five years an hav Spent all," he told the governor. "Hav no on[e] to work [and support me.] I am pentioner But Dont Get [but] 22 00 a year[.] [N]ow I ask a faver of you[.] Will you be kind a nough to [see] if I Cant Get a Little Rais[?] I Cant think [illegible word] my famley fur years in the prime of life and then *Go to the poor house to Die*[.]" Bright wrote: "[P]leas think [about] it[.] [I]f I Liv til august 15 I be 78[.] Dont think I hav not tride to Get a Rais[.] [T]he County Board Wont for nothing unless I Last A [illegible word][.] [P]leas Rite me and Let me no Whether ther is eney chance[.] I Can git Good Refernc[.] I am in Grade need helpless."[10]

The most desperate words in these letters, italicized in the quotes above, express the deepest fears of folk and the profoundest effects of poverty. The fears were not of destitution alone or coupled with helplessness. The ultimate fear was of shame and the sense of exposure that came from being completely vulnerable.

"THAY TREET US LIKE WE WAS DOGS."

For folk who were not destitute, social and economic discrimination was a more pressing problem than economic desperation. The letters to Governor Blease provide many examples of the form of discrimination folk encountered in dealing with the multiplying agencies of government.

The writers had had unsatisfactory encounters with government or one of its agencies. Often they did not understand what had happened to them, and always they felt themselves unfairly treated. In writing to Blease, they were doing what they had traditionally done in comparable situations— turn to a paternal figure and ask him for help. "I woush to inform you of the way our competroler genral treats [illegible word] the vetrances," D. B. McClellan of Spartanburg wrote in a typical letter. "He hasent cent us alld

9. D. F. Tippett to Blease, August 15, 1911, in Blease Papers. Italics added.
10. J. M. Bright to Blease, July 7, 1913, in Blease Papers. Italics added.

vettrant iney pencian pension [*sic*] this yar yar [*sic*.] . . . [Y]ou wold be So kind as to ordor [him] to cend us all thats due us to[o] ald feleras [who] Stanes a [stand in] needs of all we can havest got or have. . . . I . . . cant Wright good plese escquese."[11]

When the convicted killer of his son received a short sentence and immediately petitioned Blease for a pardon, W. A. Mooney of Greer feared Blease would grant it. "I Am a poor man working in the Cotton Mill," he wrote the governor, "and on April the 14th/1911 My boy was Killed by three Men And he wasent Eightteen years of age[.] Ambrose Scrugs taken it all on his Self[.] Solisator Otts Nolprossed two of them and Scrugs maid witness out of them for himself[.] Scrugs got a Sentence of only Five years from the two Corts[.] [H]e has only been on his Job [on the chain gaing (?)] two weeks and I have been Informed that they have got J. B. Buttler there atorney and they have Got his Petition in circulation[.] Please dont Consider thears untill you receive mine."[12]

The experience of W. R. Passmore of Batesburg illustrates other difficulties poor folk encountered in court. In a series of events he did not understand, Passmore had been arrested, convicted, and bound to labor to a man who paid his fine. An illiterate, he asked J. A. Parrish, apparently a neighbor, to write Blease of his plight. "I have bin arested and carried Before the Mayor of Batesburg and fined ten Dollars & $1.00 [court costs]," Passmore told the governor, "without eny one apearing against Me[.] [T]hey Never red eny charge at all. [T]he case they had against Me Was by Me being in a Emty house[.] I scared a Woman[.] I am a poor cotton mill hand and cant get Justice[.] Will you Pleas advise me What to Do[?] I am out on some sort of Bond. [T]hey claim a Man Put up the Money and I am Working for him[.]" Parrish appended a note to this letter. "This Man never harmed eny one," he told the governor, "and in My Opinion they tricked him because he Was Easy."[13]

So apparent was the discrimination poor folk encountered in the courts that their employers sometimes interceded with Blease on their behalf. "L. L. Langley, an old man, who hails from Newberry, is in our employ as Night Watchman, and he makes us the best one we have ever had," B. B. Bishop, secretary of Inman Cotton Mills near Spartanburg, wrote the governor in 1911. A warrant had been issued for Langley's arrest, charging him with disposing of mortgaged property. Langley, who in Bishop's estimation

11. D. B. McClellan to Blease, n.d., in 1911 Spartanburg County folder, in Blease Papers.
12. W. A. Mooney to Blease, May 6, 1913, in Blease Papers.
13. W. R. Passmore to Blease, May 6, 1914, in Blease Papers.

was "an ignorant man" (by which he probably meant illiterate), denied the charge, and Bishop believed him. The man who brought the charge also wanted Langley to pay him $1.90 in costs, and the magistrate who endorsed the warrant requested an additional twenty-five cents despite the fact that he was paid by salary rather than by fee. "The reason I write you," Bishop told Blease, "is: that I have seen so much of just such cases vs. ignorant mill people where so much injustice has been done."[14]

Unfair treatment in the courtroom was the least problem of those who were convicted and sentenced to a chain gang. Harry Coleman was on a chain gang when he wrote Blease two letters in 1914. In one of the letters, he told of wearing a Blease campaign button on the gang only to have to take it off when guards threatened to punish him. "I am told by the boyes here," he wrote in the other letter, "that these gards sometimes curses them for all sorts of vial names and even cast reflection on the convicts mother who are sometimes dead and in her grave[.] What do you think of this[,] how they are treated [?] [H]ow can you stand for this[?] . . . We are Worked here on not even enough of What We do get to eat[.] We only Get Corn bread and it cold[.] [C]orn bread homney for breakfast. [C]orn Bread pees or collards for diner. Corn Bread mollasses for supper." He continued: "Sunday we get Beef and rice cornbread. We get a bat [bait, that is, a large portion] of wheat bread twice a Week[.] [I]t lookes like it been rubbed in sut [that is, soot.] . . . I much had rather be ded than in this Place so I am going to ask you to let me out."[15]

Experiences with other agencies of government are less abundantly illustrated in the letters to Blease. "We are Willing to Pay Street tax But We Want it to Come Back to our Cotton Mill Hill to Buill up our Streets and Side Walks," a Laurens County mill worker wrote Blease in 1911. "The town dont fix up our Streets at all[.] We Wont you to point Some Cotton Mill Man to Colect 1.00 Per Head and Put it on our Streets[.] We dont Want it to go to town[.] Thay treet us like We Was dogs."[16]

"THE LAWD GIVES ME ALL I NEED; ALL I WANT MIGHT NOT BE GOOD FOR ME."

Repeated encounters with prejudice and discrimination necessitated behavioral strategies to avoid humiliation and a consequent sense of inadequacy.

14. B. B. Bishop to Blease, July 25, 1911, in Blease Papers.
15. Harry Coleman to Blease, March 14, 1914, in Blease Papers.
16. J. H. L. Huckaby to Blease, n.d., in 1911 Laurens County folder, in Blease Papers.

The employment of these strategies was a major concern among plain folk and does much to explain their avoidance of risk and unnecessary contact with outsiders, as well as the uncompetitiveness and low aspirations that characterized their lives and the attractions paternalism had for so many of them.

Fear of exposure and rejection helped discourage folk from seeking or even accepting outside help if they could avoid it. One of their principal fears was of having to beg from outsiders. So intense was this fear that even the destitute turned to charity only as a last, humiliating resort. John Belk was born in the mid-1890s and spent most of his life working in cotton mills in North Carolina. In 1930 his wife suffered severe complications from the birth of twin sons and was bedridden and helpless for a long time thereafter. Belk stopped work to care for her and put his twelve-year-old daughter to work in his stead in the mill. After several weeks, however, the family was destitute, for his daughter earned only a pittance. At that point, Belk decided he had no choice but to go to the charity office in Charlotte, where the family was living, and ask for assistance. But because he was able-bodied and his daughter was working, the charity worker denied his plea. "You nor nobody," he told an interviewer years later, "won't ever know how I felt about them people at that place when they told me I couldn't get anything to eat just because my little girl had been tryin' and was still tryin', to save me, her Dad, from havin' to go down there to beg. Right now, I hate 'em. I hate to set down here and talk about it. I start to gettin' mad and feelin' like I did that day."

Thus rejected, Belk, like most folk in such situations, turned to his employer, and thus to the paternalist system, for help. There, the response to his plea was more sympathetic. "If it hadn't been for the Super down at the mill I don't know what we'd done," he recalled. "He dug down in his pocket four weeks and sent us groceries. He was a fine man." He was also someone whose advances could be repaid, and for that reason his help, in Belk's reckoning, was not charity. The "Super" helped Belk in a time of need, and Belk would repay the favor when he returned to work. In this way folk rationalized their acceptance of credit at the company store or in the landlord's name at a credit merchant's. The credit was part of a mutually obligating relationship from which both parties benefited.

Belk had suffered a painful humiliation. He had gone begging and been turned down. No wonder the experience rankled. He had bared his dependency to outsiders, and after his rebuff, which he felt was undeserved, he had no way to relieve his frustration. It was to obscure such dependency that plain folk often refused the help of outsiders. In 1892, for example, a local politician made a speech in which he charged that mill workers in Spartanburg County were treated worse than convict laborers in Siberia. At least some of the workers found the charge insulting. Statements comparing them to convicts and describing their employment as "grinding human flesh into money" reflected "upon our character as parents and citizens" as well as workers, eighty of them complained in a published statement. "We . . . deny that we or our children are inhumanly treated by the managers of Spartan Mills, but on the contrary we desire to state that their treatment of us has been better than convicts, [and] our condition is better in every way than if we were employed on farms."[17]

Psychological adjustments to the stresses of poverty thus varied widely. Most folk simply accepted what they thought they could not change, in ways that were functionally positive. "When I look back, things then didn't seem so hard," Mrs. J. W. Sadler recalled of growing up in a poor family in Raleigh in the 1870s and 1880s. "We just did without what we didn't have, and made the best of things as they were." Such an attitude precluded familiar forms of status anxiety and was not fatalistic. As Julie West remarked, looking back over her life as the wife of a day laborer and sharecropper, "We have had bad times, but we have had good times too. I guess the Lawd gives me all I need; all I want might not be good for me."

Some folk, however, did succumb to the kind of unprotesting resignation, even fatalism, that can be read into these statements. The difficulties of generalizing their reactions are substantial, however, as the example of the family of J. R. Everett illustrates. Everett's father, who sharecropped in North Carolina at the turn of the century, was "very poor and entirely uneducated." He was also, his son recalled, "without ambition" and economically ineffectual. "He could and did work," the younger Everett said of his father, "but he was a poor manager and seemed not to care whether he made anything more than a bare living." Young Everett's mother, on the other hand, "was most industrious." She "had some ambition for herself and for her family," and Everett followed her example. Poverty and insecurity became for him incentives to hard work and to the self-discipline that encouraged education, accumulation, and achievement. "I cannot remember when I did not have an ambition to rise above my childhood environment and early station in life," Everett said some years after he

17. Quoted in Charles D. Delorme, "Development of the Textile Industry in Spartanburg from 1816 to 1900" (M.A. thesis, University of South Carolina, 1963), 82.

became a Baptist preacher. Yet none of his six siblings "had any ambition for an education, or desire to accomplish anything more than to make a bare living." Everett's struggle had been difficult. "I was denied opportunity to develop the social graces and amenities so necessary to a full and well-rounded career in my vocation," he said of his youth. "Therefore, either from nature or because of early environment and lack of opportunities, I developed an inferiority complex, and I have always been, and still am, rather timid. I have not had sufficient self-confidence. But I have had great determination, and would never give up or admit defeat."

Everett's siblings, whose attitudes reveal the disabling effects of poverty, were probably more representative than Everett himself. "I'd like for my children to have a chance," Merton Rhodes, a North Carolina sharecropper and father of ten, said in the 1930s. "I can't do nothing about it though." Rhodes's fatalism might have been caused by the Great Depression, but plain folk were inured to hard times. Lillian Holbrook's reflections on a difficult life were probably characteristic. Daughter of a small farmer in North Carolina, Lillian ran away from home while still a teenager. She found employment in a cotton mill at Winston and married a mill worker, who in later years worked at a variety of things, including sharecropping. Within a few years after her marriage, Mrs. Holbrook experienced a series of disasters that shattered the brief period of happiness that followed her wedding. One of her children died of measles; and her husband became unfaithful, failed to provide for their growing family, and was eventually killed in an automobile accident. "I reckon it's 'bout the same as any other poor folks," she said later of her life, "just hard luck on top o' hard luck. Seems like it's God's will somehow."

John Belk's fatalism was even more pervasive. Son of a North Carolina tenant farmer, Belk had moved with his family to a Charlotte cotton mill in the "hard times" of 1904. "I was eight years old. Old enough to see that things didn't get no better," Belk recalled of his life after the move. "Dad knowed he'd got in a bind. . . . Y'see, he was *caught*. When I got to be fifteen Dad died and I had to leave school in the sixth grade and start in too, to help keep us all goin'. That's when I got caught. I don't know nothing else now. Don't you see. There ain't anything else I *can* do [but work in the mill]."

This sense of fatalism governed the hopes and expectations many plain folk had for their lives. Such folk did not expect much from life, at least in a material sense, because experience discouraged expectation, and they wanted to avoid the disappointment of unrealized hope. Since folk defined progress and success in terms derived from their own experience, their definitions were modest. In 1900, for example, Joe Morgan, identified as a mechanic in Concord, North Carolina—probably a cotton mill employee— suggested that laboring people needed shorter hours and better wages. His specific suggestion, however, was more revealing than his remark that conditions needed improving. "We have young ladies in our town," he wrote the state labor commissioner, "who work twelve hours a day for fifty and sixty cents, when they ought to get seventy-five or eighty [cents] for ten hours work." T. P. Almond, a mill worker, also from Concord, was equally modest. "We work seventy hours a week here," he wrote, "and I think sixty-six is enough at the very most." Mill workers, he thought, "would do as much work and better work in ten hours or eleven hours than they do in twelve hours and twenty minutes."[18]

Pride was similarly limited. "I allus wanted to be somebody," Julie West said. "Even when I didn't have a dress on my back, I wanted to be somebody." "Being somebody" was not a matter of fame or wealth, for plain folk did not think in such terms. It was instead a matter of self-respect and respect from the community, and of minimum economic security. As a sharecropper's wife told Margaret J. Hagood in the 1930s, "Renters can hold their heads as high as anybody if they live right."[19]

This attitude was functionally positive. Not only did it make the situation of plain folk tolerable but it made improvement, even success, possible. With this perspective, folk could view a job in a cotton mill as evidence of economic opportunity, the chance for their children to attend a one-teacher school for a few terms as educational progress, or the freedom to move from one farm or mill to another as evidence of individual freedom. Expectations among plain folk in the New South were rising, but only within limits permitted by low horizons.

By defining success in limited, realizable terms, plain folk could see their lives as improving, even successful. "Yes'um I had a hard time, but I got a lots to be thankful for," Nancy Nolan said, looking back over her life. Just before the turn of the century, Mrs. Nolan's husband died, leaving her and their three small sons with no choice but to move to an Alabama cotton mill. They were still there forty years later. "All my sons are well and strong, married and happy," Mrs. Nolan said. "I am well, excusing a little rheu-

18. North Carolina Bureau of Labor Statistics, *Annual Report, 1900*, 105, 106.
19. Margaret J. Hagood, *Mothers of the South: Portraiture of the White Tenant Farm Women* (1939; rpr. Greenwood, 1969), 86.

matics now and then. My grandchildren is members of the Boy Scouts, the band and the [sic] goes to school and kindergarten. They's don't work in the mills like they's Pas and Mas did [when children]. Ain't hit grand?"

These words reflect no sense of demoralization or degradation. In keeping their hopes low and expectations realistic, plain folk helped perpetuate the system that exploited them. But of the options open to them, the perspective they chose was not the worst. "When I came from the farm, I had nothing," an employee of Pacolet Mills wrote his employer in 1894. "You could have carried my things on your back. Now I would not be ashamed for any man in the State to come to my house, or to sit down at my table."[20] It was a modest claim proudly made, and whether it masked the sense of insecurity that plagued so many folk is unknown. "He's forty-five year old now and he's not spent air hour of his life in jail," Lula Bennett of Anderson mill village in South Carolina said of her son in the 1930s. "But I know taint never too late to get in trouble."

OF SHAME AND GUILT

The ultimate concern of plain folk was their self-image, and the battering effects of prejudice and insecurity upon their self-perception were substantial. Self-image is a product of many things, however, and not all of them relate to economic circumstance and the sense of how one is perceived by outsiders. Self-image is also a matter of individual and group perception and expectation, of ego strength and weakness, of temperament, gender, age, and individual experience.

Most folk did not view themselves as debased or helpless. The collective image that emerges from the interviews is one of people who were friendly and unpretentious but inured by experience to conditions they could not change. Only a few of those interviewed displayed the self-pity, debasement, or inertia that suggest demoralization. Most spoke readily on everything they were asked about, so much so that outspokenness is one of the traits the interviews document. When they were apologetic, as they often were, they were concerned not about who or what they were but about things they thought offended middle-class interviewers—unkempt houses, an inability to speak standard English, or such personal lapses as snuff

20. Quoted in Allen H. Stokes, "John H. Montgomery: A Pioneer Southern Industrialist" (M.A. thesis, University of South Carolina, 1967), 127.

dipping or lack of attendance at church. They were not outraged or embittered at life, even when they felt victimized; on the contrary, they were grittily determined to manage as best they could.

Yet there were contradictions in their very being according to their perspective, and that was the source of psychological difficulty. Folk shared many values with the rest of southern society. Their status as "poor whites," however, prevented them from doing and being some of the things those values presupposed. They were "free, white, and twenty-one" in a society in which such people were supposed to be independent, unrestrained, and beholden to no one. They were also Christians—or pervasively influenced by Christianity—but by their own admission, they were unable to abide by the standards their religion imposed on them. These contradictions were formulas for guilt and shame, and those feelings were widespread among plain folk.

The abundance of such feelings is more easily deduced than illustrated. "Whereas guilt is generated whenever a boundary (set up by the superego) is touched or transgressed, shame occurs when a goal (presented by the ego ideal) is not being reached," psychoanalyst Gerhart Piers has written. "Guilt anxiety accompanies transgression; shame, failure." Guilt, that is, results from an action, a "sin" or violation of an internalized social norm, whereas shame is the consequence of a state of being—of poverty, illiteracy, or powerlessness where those things are disesteemed, of being a "linthead" or "trash" or a "mill daddy." Guilt-ridden people fear hatred or punishment; the shame-ridden fear contempt—being shunned, segregated, despised. Since guilt is a result of doing "evil" and shame of doing poorly, the former is more easily shed than the latter. Confession and reformation might readily neutralize guilt, but the feelings of inadequacy that accompany shame are more difficult to expiate.[21]

Plain folk did not conceptualize their problems in these terms, but they might have been conscious of what Irving Goffman has called "stigma," or "spoiled identity," and of the threats that condition poses to self-image. Goffman used those terms to describe individuals who are not, and understand they are not, accepted by other people as they would be if they did not possess specific, stigmatized characteristics. This condition generates a

21. Gerhart Piers and Milton B. Singer, *Shame and Guilt: A Psychoanalytic and a Cultural Study* (New York, 1971), 24, 29. Most authorities seem to have abandoned the old effort to label cultures as characterized by either guilt or shame in favor of the idea that both guilt and shame exist in all cultures. See *ibid.*, 99, and Helen M. Lynd, *On Shame and the Search for Identity* (New York, 1958).

problem, according to Goffman, wherever a stigmatized individual identifies himself as normal and yet views his stigma according to the values of society. "The standards he has incorporated from the wider society equip him to be intimately alive to what others see as his failing, inevitably causing him, if only for moments, to agree that he does indeed fall short of what he really ought to be," Goffman wrote of the stigmatized individual. In such a situation, "Shame becomes a central possibility, arising from the individual's perception of one of his own attributes as being a defiling thing to possess, and one he can readily see himself as not possessing."[22]

One does not have to believe that plain folk were overwhelmed with shame or guilt, or consumed with self-hate, to see the significance of those feelings in their lives. As whites, Christians, individualists, and in many cases males, they felt entitled to the respect and assertiveness that were supposed to accompany those characteristics in the New South. But as "trash," "rednecks," "crackers," sharecroppers, "lintheads," or social deviants of other sorts, they risked the kind of contempt ostensibly reserved for blacks and other stigmatized groups. The dissonance between those states was one of the heavier burdens of poverty.

22. Irving Goffman, *Stigma: Notes on the Management of Spoiled Identity* (Englewood Cliffs, N.J., 1963), 7.

16
RACE

Whites held virtually all production-line jobs in cotton mills in the New South, but racial factors were nevertheless extraordinarily important in the lives of mill folk. Those factors involved not merely obvious matters of segregation and racial feeling but subtle features of economics, class, and according to most students of the subject, social control as well. They were therefore unexpectedly complex. Mill folk, who insisted that blacks be excluded from their workplaces, and the blacks they excluded were not the only groups involved in this racial issue. Mill owners and officials were also involved, as was the larger white community of the South. The exclusion of blacks from mill work was not simply an exercise in racial prejudice by mill folk, nor was it primarily a weapon mill owners used to control their employees by threatening to replace them with blacks. It was instead a policy that grew from and expressed the racial imperatives of the white South, and given those imperatives, there was no possibility that the policy, once implemented, would be altered until racial attitudes changed.

As cotton mills spread across the South between 1880 and 1915, the section underwent unprecedented changes in racial policy and circumstance. Historians have studied those changes widely as well as insightfully.[1] During these years, white southerners dismantled the structures Reconstruction Radicals had erected to protect the civil and other rights of blacks, and replaced them with an elaborate system of white supremacy, the cornerstones of which were segregation and disfranchisement. The system incorporated rigid barriers of social separation between the races, and a spreading segmentation of labor markets that reserved more and more jobs exclusively for whites or blacks. The social and political aspects of this system were written into law in the quarter century after 1890. The economic dimensions, however, were never so rigidly defined, nor were they the subject of inclusive legislation; and there remained significant areas of interracial competition for the unskilled and semiskilled jobs plain folk could fill.

This system was rationalized in starkly racist ideas and feelings that crested in the decades before and after 1900; and it was sustained as necessary by intimidation, coercion, and violence. Inevitably, the rawest outbursts of trouble occurred where racial interactions were fluid and racial feeling was intensified by economic rivalry. Mill folk had competed with blacks on and off the farm, and were especially concerned that this competition not follow them into the mills. In pursuing this purpose, they found support in southern racial ideology, which dictated that white women and girls not be employed indoors with black men and boys. They were also abetted by the idea, already in place in 1880, that mill employment should be reserved for poor whites as a philanthropic and paternalistic endeavor.

Their purpose was thus sustained by the weight of history. Before the Civil War, southern mills had often employed black as well as white operatives, and the two had worked together with no apparent friction. The blacks were slaves, however, which precluded questions of social equality just as it muted concerns about economic competition. Furthermore, the work had been in small, individually owned, local enterprises rather than in modern factories, and matters of status were governed by tradition and personalism. "Previous to and during the war the employment of colored persons was quite common in a number of cotton mills then in operation in

1. See, for example, C. Vann Woodward, *The Strange Career of Jim Crow* (3rd ed.; New York, 1974); Joel Williamson, *The Crucible of Race: Black-White Relations in the American South Since Emancipation* (New York, 1984); John W. Cell, *The Highest Stage of White Supremacy: The Origins of Segregation in South Africa and the American South* (Cambridge, 1982); and George M. Fredrickson, *White Supremacy: A Comparative Study in American and South African History* (New York, 1981).

Georgia and South Carolina," Otis G. Lynch of Enterprise Mills recalled in 1893. "They were generally in small establishments operated by individuals who owned the mills as well as the operatives. These mills without exception were engaged in making coarse goods, the machinery being invariably poor and crude in its construction; [and] the output was not very creditable."[2]

When larger mills appeared in the South, such as the one William Gregg opened at Graniteville in 1848, publicists for the industry, including Gregg himself, promoted cotton manufacturing as an economic opening for the section's large population of impoverished whites. The idea caught on, and since slaves could be used more economically at other tasks, mill workers were largely whites by the time of the Civil War. Still, the old pattern did not disappear at once, for as late as 1880, a traveler visited a small factory at Saluda, South Carolina, and found twenty-five blacks among its one hundred operatives. "He had worked mixed operatives with great advantage," the visitor wrote, summarizing the experience of the mill's superintendent. "The negro was as capable of instruction in the business as the white male or female, and could afford to work much cheaper, as they lived so much cheaper. The negro labor he found was easily controlled."[3]

"WE HAVE COLORED HELPERS, SWEEPERS, SCRUBBERS, YARD HANDS AND FIREMEN."

The Saluda factory was a survival, not a portent. By the 1880s, the mills reserved essentially all production-line work for whites, restricting blacks to menial and sweated jobs in the mill and to positions outside the mill. Mill owners took pride in this fact and used it to enhance their standing as paternalists. "I think that the preference should be given to the white labor, as long as we can get it," James L. Orr told the Industrial Commission in 1900, "because they have had a hard time in the South for a long time in competition with negro labor, and this is the only sphere, as it was, set aside for their benefit. As long as I can use the white labor to any advantage I intend to do it."[4]

2. *Manufacturers' Record*, September 22, 1983, p. 134.
3. Quoted in Broadus Mitchell, *The Rise of Cotton Mills in the South* (Baltimore, 1922), 214. On blacks in the mills generally, see Allen H. Stokes, "Black and White Labor and the Development of the Southern Textile Industry, 1800–1920" (Ph.D. dissertation, University of South Carolina, 1977).
4. *House Documents*, 57th Cong., 1st Sess., No. 184, Vol. 7, p. 482.

Within the general pattern of employment, there was some variation. At Eagle and Phenix Mills in 1883, there were 1,829 "hands," all whites, inside the mills, and 54, all blacks, working outside. At Graniteville in 1900, blacks were employed as pickers, "roustabouts about the yards, etc," and "none [worked] in the mill proper except to carry water, wash floors, and that class of labor." Also in 1900, the 1,300 employees at Henrietta Mills were "all white[s] except the scrubers, cotton handlers, etc"; and the mill at McAdenville, North Carolina, employed no blacks. At the latter, in the president's words, there were "no colored men about the mill who are employed by the mill. There are some few women around there—washer-women—who do not live inside the corporation, and a few men who chop wood and work for the different families; but they have no employment in the mill. Even my teamster is a white man."[5]

As these examples suggest, blacks were only a small portion of the mill work force. Of 152 mills in 1907, for example, none employed black men indoors, and only a few employed them outdoors. However, 18 of the mills had black women and girls on their payrolls; and altogether blacks were 5.5 percent of the adult work force and 2.8 percent of the child-labor force in and about the 152 mills.[6]

These patterns conformed to New South racial theory. Outdoors, especially among men, segregation of workers was unnecessary and probably not even the general practice. Certainly whites and blacks often worked side by side there and frequently for the same wage with no thought of social equality or white "degradation." Indoors, however, whites and blacks might work together only after white concerns about social equality were accommodated in appearance if not always in fact. This was done through some understanding, tacit or explicit, that the blacks were present only in menial or service capacities and were thus subordinate to the whites.

The much more rigid segregation in cotton mills was therefore distinctive. Why did the policy of hiring only whites, which began when the cotton industry was small and the supply of white labor abundant, continue after the industry became large and the supply of labor inadequate or problematical? And why did mill owners not take advantage of the potentially large supply of cheap black labor? There were several ways of employing blacks that would not have required integration. Employers might have divided mill jobs along racial lines in the manner of positions in

5. *Senate Documents*, 48th Cong., 1st Sess., No. 91, p. 508; *House Documents*, 57th Cong., 1st Sess., No. 184, Vol. 7, pp. 487, 492, 504.
6. *Senate Documents*, 61st Cong., 2nd Sess., No. 645, Vol. 1, pp. 188–89.

tobacco factories, compartmentalized their mills into all-white and all-black workrooms, or, indeed, have operated separate mills employing all-white and all-black work forces.

Yet none of these options were pursued on a meaningful scale. Most explanations emphasize the racial prejudices of mill folk and the willingness of employers to indulge, and even cultivate, those prejudices to ensure that their threats to hire black workers at lower wages would be taken seriously. In this way, these explanations run, employers kept workers insecure and therefore docile. Mill folk allowed themselves to be manipulated by employers who massaged their egos with rhetoric about white supremacy and racial kinship while robbing them of independence and economic well-being. "White cotton-mill workers in the South deliberately sacrificed their own living standard to keep blacks out of the mills," one scholar has written, implying that if poor whites and blacks had joined together in class solidarity they would have achieved higher wages and greater control of the workplace. "Mill officials shamefully encouraged the mill hands' hatred of the Negro and manipulated that hatred to their own ends," another has said, intimating that had mill owners been less callous and powerful, the racism of mill workers would have been less controlling and less damaging to workers themselves. "They preferred . . . to cultivate the racial phobias of white operatives and to exploit their fears of competition from blacks," a third has concluded about mill officials and their purposes. "This policy yielded considerable benefits to the owners, including possibly lower labor costs. It advanced the idea of an Anglo-Saxon kinship between management and labor and also reminded the white workers that the kinship did not allow them to challenge the owners' authority."[7]

A variation of these views stresses the psychological advantages mill folk derived from racial prejudice and from keeping blacks out of the mills. "They have an inferiority complex," an eminent authority wrote of mill workers in the 1930s. "It is safe to say that the workers in every industry felt above cotton mill workers and coal miners," and "the only group left for these to feel superior to was the negro." Another scholar wrote some years later, "The mill worker, with nobody else to 'look down on,' regards himself as eminently superior to the Negro. The colored man represents his last

7. The quotes are, respectively, from Philip S. Foner, *Organized Labor and the Black Worker, 1619–1973* (New York, 1974), 86; Melton A. McLaurin, *Paternalism and Protest: Southern Cotton Mill Workers and Organized Labor, 1875–1905* (Westport, Conn. 1971), 65; Stokes, "Black and White Labor and the Development of the Southern Textile Industry, 1800–1920," 8.

outpost against social oblivion." These scholars suggested that this feeling of inferiority led mill folk into various forms of racial extremism, including exclusion of blacks from the mills.[8]

Evidence supports these interpretations, but they are incomplete and therefore distorting. All of the interpretations rest in some degree on the twin ideas that mill workers were victims of employers with almost unlimited powers in racial matters and that mill folk were the only ones who had racial "phobias" and ego problems.

"THE NEGRO WAS PUT TO WORK AT ONE OF THE KNITTING MACHINES IN THE MIDST OF THE WHITE MEN."

By virtually any standard, mill folk were racists. To a person, apparently, they believed blacks were racially inferior to whites, that public policy must guarantee white supremacy and public practice uphold it, that blacks must stay in their "place" and act deferentially toward whites, and that every action necessary to guarantee those ends, including violence, was tolerable. Folk practiced racial discrimination in their everyday lives without reflection, except in times of tension or crisis. Some folk engaged in acts of violence against blacks, and all of them routinely spoke their prejudices. In neither their behavior nor their racial beliefs, however, were they exceptional in the white South. The overt forms their racism took were somewhat distinctive because of their circumstance as poor folk and mill workers, but that kind of variation was true of all groups of whites in the section. The situation John K. Morland discovered among mill folk at York in the 1940s was probably also true of those in the New South. "No evidence was found," Morland wrote, "that there is considerable difference between the attitude of millhands and that of the town and country [that is, urban middle classes and rural, landowning whites] toward the Negro. In some ways [for example, the possibility of blacks being permitted to vote] town and country appear more determined [than mill folk] to keep the Negro in his place."[9] Those prejudices, then, were conventionally southern.

At worst, the prejudices of plain folk incorporated the pitiable sense of inferiority often attributed to them. Thus, Rastus Swanger, "a poor man" with no lawyer to plead his case, asked Governor Blease for a pardon on

8. Harriet L. Herring, "The Industrial Worker," in W. T. Couch (ed.), *Culture in the South* (Chapel Hill, 1934), 347, 349; Liston Pope, *Millhands and Preachers: A Study of Gastonia* (New Haven, 1942), 69.

9. John K. Morland, *Millways of Kent* (Chapel Hill, 1958), 187.

grounds that his racial integrity was demeaned by the treatment he received in prison. "This is an awful hard place for a white man to stay," Swanger wrote, "as I have to sleep, eat, and work with negroes which puts me on a level with them." For much the same reason, H. W. Woodward wanted release from a chain gang in Orangeburg County. "I Want to no," he asked Blease, "if it is law for the Maire [mayor] to put me one [on] the Street and put Shalter [shackle?] on an Woirk me with the nigers."[10]

Whether Woodward or Swanger ever worked in a cotton mill is unknown, but mill folk often reacted as these men did to blacks in the workplace. They generally had no objection to blacks in and about the mills as long as the blacks' jobs were menial, sweated, or outdoors, and their presence otherwise conformed to standard racial arrangements. Typically, there were no blacks inside the mills except women and girls working in janitorial or other menial work, though occasionally small boys worked as sweepers, water carriers, and the like. Exceptions to this rule seem always to have evoked protest. "In Card room department of this mill we have two negroes running draw frames with people in same room," a Hartsville operative complained to Governor Blease in 1914. "They were asked to be moved by two white men the overseer refusing to do so claiming they were more to the company than the white people & the two whites sent out of mill that day to rest. Your office would of been notified long ago but 9/10 of the people owe the company & can not move & are afraid to mention same on acct of losing their work."[11]

Such reticence was exceptional. "We had a Negro Lynching here on August the 11th of which the Cotton Mill boys taken an active part," several workers from Laurens wrote Blease in 1913, "& the day following one of the Negroes that work in the mill had some verry rough talk about the Poor unlearned Cotton Mill people & the result was that some of the help immediately had him put out of the mill. [J]ust after this for fear of further trouble about (18) eighteen of the weavers went to Mr. W. S. Montgomery & Mr. Jno. M. Moore Supt. & asked them to please take the negroes out of the mill & their answer was they would as soon as they could get white help to take their places." The workers continued: "Then the negroes seem to get scared & they went on their own accord. [T]his was on Wednesday[.] [O]n Saturday following Mr Montgomery had the help up & said that he wanted all the help to assist him in protecting these Negroes[,] that he would get white

10. Rastus Swanger to Coleman L. Blease, April 5, 1914, H. W. Woodward to Blease, May 11, 1914, in Coleman L. Blease Papers, South Carolina State Archives.
11. G. T. McDaniel to Blease, January 5, 1914, in Blease Papers.

help as soon as he could[,] but all that would not agree to protect these Negroes had better ask for their time & none did this." The workers wrote: "On the following Monday he had them up one at the time & asked them if they would protect these negroes & upon refusal of some of them promptly dismissed 2 weavers that they suspected of being leaders leaders [sic] & about 35 weavers walked out with them. [T]hese negroes laid up filling & cleaned looms & swept the floor[,] & the loom cleaners had to go in the weavers alleys & the Girls all objected & of cours you know we would not stand for that. [T]here is about 23 negroes working in the mill. White men has applied for these jobs most of them & all has been refused."[12]

The workplace could thus be the site of considerable racial tension, between workers and management as well as between whites and blacks. As these letters suggest, mill folk were concerned on such occasions about jobs as well as racial prerogative, and in their minds those two considerations could not be separated. The folk were therefore prepared to do whatever was necessary to keep blacks out of production-line work and to command from those in other jobs appropriately deferential behavior. For those reasons, racially motivated episodes might occur wherever blacks were employed.

Accounts of such episodes in the public press were often distorted in favor of white participants. One spring day in 1887, two teenage boys, Johnnie Ryols, white, and Willie Harris, black, were spinning tops during a work break at Bibb Manufacturing Company. This was a game mill boys often played, sometimes with feeling. The feeling stemmed from the practice of one boy "nulling" another boy's top—that is, spinning his own against the other's already spinning top in a way that knocked the latter out of its spin. According to press accounts, Harris, a sweeper in the mill, nulled Ryols' top despite Ryols' admonition. In the altercation that ensued, "Harris grabbed a brick in his left hand and held his unopened knife in the other," whereupon Ryols drew his own knife "and the quarrel grew hotter." Presently, "Harris called Ryols a 'g-d d-m son of b-h,' which so enraged Ryols that he struck at Harris, and the keen blade of the pocket knife struck him in the breast, and was quickly withdrawn, and the warm blood came spurting out." Harris collapsed and died while Ryols fled the scene, and the town as well. He evidently escaped prosecution.[13]

This incident might have been representative. Minor events could fan the

---

12. Albert E. Sloan et al. to Blease, August 21, 1913, in Blease Papers.
13. Atlanta Constitution, April 27, 1887.

flames of racial feeling. A fellow worker justified Ryols' action in racial terms, and his view was likely shared by others. In investigating the incident, a reporter "had a talk with another employe of the factory who remarked that Ryols was the first boy that had ever dared lift a hand to protect himself from insult by the overbearing negro boys employed there." This worker "did not consider that Ryols had done more than assert his manhood in resenting the abuse and threats of the boy Harris."[14] The mere presence of blacks, it seems, might cause racial feelings to stir.

A different, but perhaps also representative, racial incident occurred in 1906. Two white operatives, Lula Norris and Ola Thomas, assaulted Henrietta Riddle, "a stout, middle-aged negro woman," while she was scrubbing floors at Fulton Bag and Cotton Mills. The cause of the assault is unclear. The women gave conflicting stories, and the judge before whom the three were brought believed the black woman's claim that she was unjustly attacked because she refused to close a door. "I was down on mer knees scrubbin' de floor," is the way a reporter rendered the account of Henrietta Riddle, "dey cummed after me and dey beat me ober de head wid two big hickory sticks." Witnesses, apparently white operatives, corroborated this account. "I saw the old nigger woman down on her knees quietly scrubbing the floor and I saw Miss Norris and Mrs. Thomas approach her with two big hickory sticks," one told the judge. "Mrs. Thomas remarked, 'Let me swipe her one first.' When Mrs. Thomas swiped old Henrietta the first one[,] I heard the skull pop just like a Fourth of July firecracker. Then they both hit onto that old nigger woman. After a while the old nigger woman took one of the sticks away from the white women and struck Mrs. Thomas with it. It was a warm affair." The court found the white women guilty and fined them, which was perhaps some consolation to their victim, whose injury required six stitches to close.[15]

No doubt this incident had a background. Perhaps the black woman had a reputation for "uppityness," though that seems unlikely in view of the willingness of some whites to testify in her behalf, or perhaps she and her attackers had had difficulties before. Either circumstance would explain the white women's claim that the black woman "cursed them and threatened to whip them" and would explain as well the black woman's refusal to close the door. The incident suggests that the lot of black workers was not an easy

14. *Ibid.*
15. *Ibid.*, July 8, 1906.

one, which might be one reason few blacks worked in the mills. The jobs black mill workers could get were much more difficult or disagreeable than those of whites, and that fact alone might have been sufficient cause to avoid mill work. But racial humiliation was apparently always a threat to black workers. In addition, many mill officials might have refused to hire blacks even for menial work because their presence in the mills could occasion difficulties that not only interrupted work schedules but, if white workers became sufficiently aroused, also generated challenges to management's authority in the workplace and brought opprobrium on mill officials for failing to honor racial customs.

Such an incident occurred at Massachusetts Mills in the summer of 1896, when the superintendent hired a black maintenance man, claiming no white man was available for a job that had to be done at once. White operatives immediately objected to the presence of the man inside the mill, and a group of them protested to the superintendent that white women and children should not have to work indoors with a black man. The superintendent rejected the protest, discharged the instigators, and ordered them to vacate their company housing. That was a routine way of handling insubordinate employees; but routine measures were not always effective where racial feelings were involved. The protesters refused to leave their homes, and the wrath of other whites was aroused against the superintendent. The incident threatened to get out of control, and the company, which found itself accused of violating racial custom, had to rush an official from its Massachusetts headquarters to resolve the difficulty.

As soon as the official arrived, he removed the black man from inside the mill and let it be known that he and the company were "quite in sympathy . . . with the general southern feeling against the introduction of the negro with white labor indoors, particularly where women and children are employed." He used the occasion to assure his employees that his northern-owned company had not intended to violate southern mores. "There are certain tasks about a cotton mill," he noted, "which are delegated by general consent in a large majority of southern mills under southern managers to negroes. . . . These are, besides roustabout work and the like, the scrubbing of floors, oiling the shafting and transferring the material from place to place in the building. For all indoors work except the scrubbing, we have preferred white labor, but in the case of men to oil the shafting, we have not been able to get people to stay on the work." He continued: "In an emergency, therefore, we followed the common course and put two negroes at the work, one only as a temporary hand to care for a hot box. No white man was discharged or displaced by our action, and there was no motive except to keep the mill in operation."[16]

An incident illustrating the volatility of racial matters occurred at Barnesville, Georgia, in the fall of 1899, when white operatives at Oxford Knitting Mills were aroused "because of the placing of a negro man at work among the white employees." Like most such occurrences, this one had a history. "For about eight months three other negroes have been working at the mill," a reporter found, "but in departments shut out from view of the white men and women. One was employed as engineer [that is, fireman] and the other two in the fleecing room, where the work is said to be of a nature that a white man should not be required to do. At various times, however, without the knowledge of the mill owners, these negroes have sought to exercise an unwarranted authority over the whites, and in many ways to make it unpleasant for the young ladies employed at the mill." The reporter observed: "The white people, while dissatisfied with the existing condition, have borne it without complaint. The climax came, however, when the negro was put to work at one of the knitting machines in the midst of the white men."

This account seems unconvincingly one-sided in blaming the blacks for the difficulty, but it is entirely plausible as a statement of the white operatives' view of the situation. Certainly white workers regarded the black man's presence as an affront. At once, "The young ladies [in the mill] approached Mr. Howard [the superintendent] and told him they could not tolerate the placing of the negro in their midst, and would not continue their work unless the negro was removed. Mr. Howard's reply to them, they say, was: 'Well, if you can not work with negroes, you can take your hats and go home.'" All of them followed his suggestion, and the mill had to close down.

Again, a mill official had insisted on upholding his authority in the workplace only to find himself accused of violating racial custom and forcing white women to mingle with black men. That was an intolerable position in the New South, and it forced the president of the mill to intervene in a dispute that had theretofore involved only the superintendent and the striking "ladies." The president called the protesting women together "and after assuring them there was no intention to humiliate or degrade them, but from necessity, that the negro was put at work, and, after promising to have

16. *Ibid.*, July 17, 27, 1896.

him removed at the earliest possible moment, secured their consent to return to work." After standing idle for several days, the mill reopened.

The president backed up his assurances by dismissing all black employees from the mill, but his action failed to quiet the racial feelings the incident had aroused. Someone posted numerous notices throughout Barnesville "warning negroes not to return" to the mill, and "several depredations" were "perpetrated on innocent negroes." When a group of blacks assembled to discuss protective measures against this intimidation, disapproving whites threatened to riot, and the mayor felt it necessary to call out the local militia, the Barnesville Blues, to preserve the peace.[17]

The sometimes violent consequences of racial "mingling" in the mills were apparent in a sequence of events that occurred at Kincaid Manufacturing Company in Griffin, Georgia, in the spring of 1899. With no apparent warning, three black men, who had worked for some time at the company mill, were taken from their homes one night "by a mob of twenty-five or thirty people and severely flogged." The men had menial jobs—one, indeed, was a personal servant of the superintendent, and the other two worked outside the mill—and "so far as known there were no charges [of wrongdoing] against [them.]" Their "only offense seems to have been working at the mill," and the purpose of their flogging was simultaneously to coerce black employees into leaving all of the mills in Griffin and to convince mill officials (and other local employers) that it was unwise to hire blacks for jobs whites could fill.

The incident therefore did not end with the beatings. The next day all blacks who worked at the Kincaid mill were "warned to leave, and most of them walked out at once." The campaign of intimidation continued, however, and that night another black, "who [had] the respect of all law-abiding whites, was taken from his home and brutally beaten." The president of the manufacturing company, a Confederate veteran, was "highly indignant" over these developments and joined law enforcement officials in promising to do everything possible to end the reign of terror. The mobsters persisted, however, and "an anonymous communication was sent to the superintendent of the mills stating that the mob would whip him and his overseer [that] night." For good measure, the president himself received a missive stating, in his words, "how [the anonymous authors] desired the president to conduct the affairs of his mills." The source of these threats, according to newspaper accounts, was "a collection of laborers in the mills, known as the

17. The preceding account is in *ibid.*, October 14, 17, 18, 1899.

'Laborers' Union Band,' who object[ed] to negro labor in the mills." Nothing substantial is known of this organization, which disappeared from public notice after the incident ended. "It is said the band was about 500 members," a reporter wrote, and was "determined to have things to suit themselves."

Such a membership seems fancifully large, but there was for a time organized opposition to black employment in the mills and other workplaces in Griffin, and the mayor of the town took the threatening letters seriously enough to call out the militia to protect mill officials. After intimidating blacks in the cotton mills, "The band then turned its attention to [other] employers of negroes in Griffin and warned them to dispense with colored labor and secure white men in their place." To advertise the warning, notice was posted throughout the town "stating that after next Saturday night no negro will be allowed to ask for employment at certain manufactories, and in fact should not have any employment that comes in competition with white labor."[18]

"ALL WE WANT YOU TO DO IS TO TAKE OUT THE NIGGERS."

The most important and spectacular incident involving black mill workers was the strike that occurred in the late summer of 1897 at Fulton Bag and Cotton Mills.[19] The strike shut down the mill for several days, and local labor groups rushed to the strikers' assistance. Yet the episode is best seen as a racial, not a labor, incident. It was occasioned by a racial development, sustained by the strength of racial feeling among whites in and out of the mill, and carried to a successful conclusion by the strikers' determination to preserve racial segregation and the jobs of white workers. The incident thus epitomizes the racial dimensions of mill experience and sheds considerable light on how the race issue functioned in the workplace. It dramatizes the intensity with which mill folk opposed black employment, and shows quite clearly that mill officials had little or no room to maneuver in racial matters. It also suggests that instead of mill owners manipulating the racial prejudices of their employees, mill folk forced their views on any owner who was prepared to sacrifice racial custom for immediate profit. The race issue, in short, was one tool mill folk could and did use successfully against their employers.

18. The preceding account is taken from *ibid.*, May 24, 25, 27, 1899.
19. The following account is taken from Atlanta *Constitution*, August 5–10, 1897, and Atlanta *Journal*, August 4–10, 1897.

In the summer of 1897, President Jacob Elsas of the Fulton mill faced a perennial problem, a shortage of labor that caused delays in filling orders and no doubt reduced his profits as well. The shortage was greatest in the folding department of his bag factory, which employed about 200 women and girls. For several weeks Elsas advertised for workers to fill vacant positions but to little avail, and he decided to solve the problem by employing a complement of about 25 black women (accounts disagree as to the exact number) and put them to work as folders in a segregated compartment in the mill. He had always employed blacks and had about 50 in his work force of perhaps 1,500 before the trouble arose. All of the 50, however, were in jobs traditionally open to blacks, and their presence was tolerable to whites in the mill. Now Elsas proposed to hire blacks in production-line jobs theretofore reserved for whites.

That Elsas understood the significance of the change and was apprehensive about its consequences is evident in the precautions he took to mute its effect. He took care to preserve all the forms of segregation. He not only prepared a separate workplace for the black folders but located it on a floor where no whites worked. He installed "separate toilet rooms" for the blacks and made "separate arrangements" to supply them "with water and other necessaries during their working hours." Elsas was also careful not to introduce black men into indoor work, and on the day before the new folders were to begin, he formally notified the white folders that black women would begin work the next day in an area completely apart from their own. Finally, on the fateful day, he had the blacks arrive early enough to be inside the mill and at their workplace before any whites appeared.

The precautions did not work. When the white folders arrived at the mill in the morning and learned the blacks were already inside, they refused to enter. When Elsas appeared and asked why they were outside, one of them, identified only as Miss Brooks in press accounts, told him they were waiting "to see if [he was] going to put the negroes to work." Elsas, who wanted to treat the issue as one of management prerogative, not racial policy, asked, "Are you running this business?" Miss Brooks riposted, "We are running this part of it, and if you are going to employ the negroes we are not going to work." Elsas refused to discuss the matter and went inside the mill. The women went home.

All but three of the workers in the folding department joined the walkout. Word of their deed spread spread quickly through the mill, and during the morning, the other white women and girls in the mill decided to join the strikers by not returning to work after dinner. As soon as this decision was known, the men and boys decided to join as well, and except for the room in which the black women were working, the mill was effectively shut down at lunchtime. As they left the mills, the workers congregated outside, and members of the unorganized crowd voiced their resentment against Elsas and the presence of the black folders in the mill. Some of the teenage boys hurled stones at the mill, and their arrest almost provoked a riot; but the leaderless crowd had assembled spontaneously, and no one had devised a course of action. Police reinforcements had no difficulty averting violence.

The crowd's resentment was evident. Walking about the scene, a reporter encountered "many lowering looks and muttered curses among the strikers, who felt they were being wronged." One man said, "We'll fix them niggers when they come out at 7 o'clock." Another agreed, "They'll be some fun this evening. We don't propose to hurt anybody, but they will have to git up and git from here." Still another said: "I wish old man Elsas would come out and try to cross the street. He's the man who is responsible for the whole trouble. We'd teach him to respect our wives and daughters." Authorities took such talk seriously. When the black women left the mill that night and when they returned again the next morning, they had a police escort.

The strike involved dual concerns of race and economics, and the strikers made little effort to separate the two. Even so stark a statement as that of the man who thought it a shame and an outrage for "our wives to be forced to work along side nasty, black, stinkin' nigger wimmin" must be read as an economic as well as a racial remark. "When we heard that the negro women were to be employed we all resolved to leave," one of the striking women said of their action. "Some of the men said that it did not make any difference about the negro women because they would be on a different floor, but we think that it makes a good deal of difference because we are all there together and the negroes would be considered employed with us just as much as if they had been on the same floor." Although this, too, seems a purely racial remark, it has an economic dimension. This woman continued: "It is all piece work and so far as we were informed all would be paid the same price. There was no question of difference in wages in the case."

Mill folk assumed that the introduction of blacks into production-line work would rob them of jobs as well as racial respect, and would in the long run bring lower wages as well. In the racial and economic milieu of the New South, they were surely correct on all three points, as suggested by the situation at Fulton Bag and Cotton Mills. The Fulton mill had a history of labor shortages caused in part by overbearing management—it seems to have been one of the most disagreeable workplaces in the New South. In this case, the company had advertised for white folders for some time, but the reponse was inadequate, and some of the women who responded quit after a short time. Because of racial custom, the company could not fill the shortage of white workers by inserting individual blacks wherever they were needed. This was the reason Elsas decided to hire a contingent of blacks large enough to staff a separate workroom. But his decision meant a reduction in the number of places available for white folders, and as he assembled the black work force, he turned away some whites who applied for work because there were no places for them to fill. His employment of the blacks therefore directly displaced some whites. "We knew that several white women had applied to the management for work yesterday and had been turned away, while they employed twenty-five negro women instead," one of the strikers said. "We supposed that the reason the white women were turned off yesterday was that the company was afraid that enough white women could not be secured and the management knew that a few white women would refuse to work besides the negroes, so they decided to employ negroes."

The concern over jobs was thus as real as racial feelings were deep. According to the strikers, the Fulton factory had tried once before to put blacks in operatives' jobs, but white workers had resisted and the plan had been abandoned. "The Elsas people have been trying to stick in negroes for a long time," a reporter wrote, summarizing the views of strikers he interviewed. "Before yesterday there were nearly fifty negroes employed at different points of the building."

This combination of racial and economic concerns magnified fears and gave credence to rumors of worse things to come. "One of the bosses by the name of Ward gave the place of 'opener' in the cotton mill to a negro when there was a white man who asked for the job," a striker told a reporter. As soon as the strike began, word circulated that blacks were applying for jobs in the idle mill and that a black second hand (assistant overseer) was already at work. "We want that nigger boss to git out of there," one of the strikers said. "There's a nigger second boss down there and he orders us about just like he owned us." Another added: "That's right. We want all of them niggers out of there, and that's what we are going to have."

The strike immediately attracted the attention of the Textile Workers Protective Union and the Atlanta Federation of Trades, with which the union was affiliated. Since the strike was spontaneous and the strikers were unorganized, those two organizations coordinated strike activity and oversaw negotiations with management. The women who began the strike and whose determination helped ensure its success therefore had no leadership role in its conduct. None of the speakers at the strikers' rallies were women, and no women seem to have served on negotiating committees. This was not surprising, for unions in the New South honored traditions concerning gender as well as race. For the Atlanta textile union, those traditions meant not only that women had a subordinate position in all matters of labor organization and leadership but that blacks were excluded from union membership altogether. Indeed, the union sought to turn the strike to its advantage by exploiting the racial issue and posing as a defender of white womanhood.

Although its spokesmen claimed about two hundred members at Fulton Bag and Cotton Mills before the strike began, the union apparently had no influence, or even presence, inside the mill. But since race was the only issue on which strikes could be won in the New South, the union was understandably anxious to seize the opportunity presented by the situation at Elsas' mill. Union strategists sought to fuse the strikers' racism and concern for jobs with their own interests in the union. They apparently hoped to induce all white workers at the Fulton factory to join the union in return for help during the strike, and then to demand of Elsas that he hire only union members. Since blacks were ineligible for union membership, this practice would exclude them from the mill not as blacks but as scabs.

The union encouraged racial feeling as well as economic fear. In a statement issued under union auspices, the strikers not only condemned management for long hours, low pay, and disagreeable working conditions but complained they were "subjected to such indignities as would meet the condemnation of every loyal white citizen of Atlanta." The statement read, "The effort of the Fulton mill owners to force the white women and girls employed there to work with the negro women who were placed among them is a deliberate attempt to eliminate the white wages-slaves from this avocation, and substitute black wages-slaves because they will work cheaper, although the white wages-slaves do not live but simply exist." Thus "the real question at issue is one of wages and not of prejudice. The mill owners know that the white workers are organizing and becoming more intelligent," the strikers declared, "and they are making an effort to keep them in subjection by employing cheaper labor and forcing the white workers out of employment." The action of the white folders in refusing to work with blacks was not one "originating in racial prejudice"; it was instead "a strike against the introduction of cheaper labor."

To take that statement seriously is to remove some of the racist sting from the strikers' words and actions and to see their position in its full complexity. "All we want you to do is to take out the niggers from this place, all except the scrubbers and the firemen," J. R. Owens of the strikers' committee told President Elsas. It is easy, even proper, to condemn such a statement for its inherent offensiveness. But Owens' concern was "niggers" not just as black people but as competitors for jobs that the striking women vitally needed. The fact that alternatives to mill work were more limited for women than for men might help explain why mill women were evidently more opposed to black workers than mill men were. "The whites will not work with the negroes," a mill owner told the Industrial Commission in 1900, "especially the women folk."[20]

By the time Owens made his demand, on the second day of the strike, President Elsas apparently recognized his mistake in placing the black women in the mill. He was unbecomingly accommodating to a delegation representing the strikers, agreeing at once to remove the blacks and to sign a pledge to that effect. But when the delegation returned later in the day with the written agreement, Elsas found it more comprehensive than the terms he had agreed to. The strikers now demanded "that all negroes in any capacity whatever . . . except the janitor and scrub women, be removed [from the mill] at once, and that none but white persons be employed" except as "yard hands or firemen, who may not be employed directly in the mill." According to this agreement, Elsas would have to dismiss not only the black women whose presence had provoked the strike—whom he was eager to discharge without regard for their interests—but also a number of blacks who had worked at the mill before the strike began. Sensing perhaps that his promise to remove the offensive workers had relieved him of the odium his action in hiring them had generated, and wanting no doubt to reassert his authority over his work force, Elsas refused to sign the proposed agreement. He had no justification, he insisted, for firing employees whose service was satisfactory and whose presence had never before given offense.

Elsas' position was reasonable, and since both sides wanted a settlement, a new agreement was arranged through the efforts of Hoke Smith, an Atlantan who had just concluded a term in Grover Cleveland's cabinet. Elsas agreed to dismiss the black folders and "remove the colored man from the machinery repairing department, transferring him to another department where his presence would be less objectionable." He also agreed that

20. *House Documents*, 57th Cong., 1st Sess., No. 184, Vol. 7, p. 492.

"if any other work done by other colored men or colored women is of a character to be offensive to the white operatives in contiguous work the particular instance may be brought to [his] attention . . . and each case . . . [would be] acted upon separately." Finally, Elsas promised to take no action against the strikers. Five days after it began, the strike ended on terms overwhelmingly favorable to the strikers.

What caused so swift and complete a victory? No other strike of mill workers in the New South had such a successful outcome. On the contrary, in disputes involving far less substantive issues and challenges to management prerogatives, mill owners rigidly resisted workers' demands and used all the resources they could command to force their workers into complete capitulation. Elsas himself employed that strategy on more than one occasion, and even in the aftermath of this strike, he failed to honor his pledge to take no action against the strikers. Yet he gave in completely and at once in the matter of the black folders and apparently never again sought to hire blacks for production-line jobs.

The reason for this denouement seems obvious: hiring black women to fill jobs customarily held by whites violated racial taboo and rendered Elsas' position untenable in the ensuing dispute. The violation of racial convention also made the strikers' cause universally popular in the white South, which strikers in nonracial situations were never able to achieve, and this popularity brought the strikers support in influential circles. "The sympathy of the white people of the South goes out to the striking women and girls," the Columbus *Enquirer-Sun* editorialized during the strike, lecturing Elsas, who was not a native of the section, on southern racial practices. "In the South it is not the custom for the races to be placed together in the same mills," the editorialist wrote, and anyone who violated that custom, as Elsas had done, "deserves just what they have received." Perhaps, the editorial suggested, a boycott of the products of Elsas' mill was in order.[21]

The Atlanta Painters Union was even more critical of the hapless president. "The action of Jacob Elsas . . . in placing negro women to work with white women and girls [is] emphatically condemned . . . as one of the most dastardly and disreputable acts ever perpetrated on the white working women in the South," read a resolution adopted by the union and printed in the newspapers. Elsas should "be required to do himself what he has endeavored to force white women to do—make social equals of negro women."

21. Columbus *Enquirer-Sun*, August 7, 1897.

In face of such withering criticism, Elsas surrendered. "It was never my intention," he said lamely, "to establish anything like social equality among the people, nor did I intend for them to associate or be thrown with colored people in any capacity." He added: "I have no desire to oppress any of the people, nor am I forced to take the advice of the Painters' Union. . . . I do not mind having my dinner served by a colored cook, but I don't say that they should sit down to my table."

"IF THIS NEGRO LABOR PROVES THE SUCCESS THAT WE THINK, THE COTTON MANUFACTURING IN THE SOUTH WILL BE REVOLUTIONIZED."

The Fulton strike occurred as public discussion of the potential of blacks as mill workers was increasing. The reaction to Elsas' employment of black operatives and his quick capitulation in the face of the ensuing outcry suggest that mill owners had no leeway in introducing blacks into production-line jobs, at least in mills staffed by white operatives. Other mill owners were surely aware of the predicament Elsas had created for himself, for the strike at his mill received newspaper coverage across the South.

That awareness might explain why mill officials who breached racial custom backed down immediately when employees challenged their action. When a child-labor law went into effect in Alabama in the spring of 1903, Lanett Mills, across the river from West Point, Georgia, dismissed 125 under-age children and replaced them with "several negro women." The blacks were placed in a side building so that they would not come in contact with the white workers. According to reports, white workers, however, "thought that the change would interfere with their positions and salaries and decided to walk out on a strike." In a short time, the entire force of 1,500 men and women was out. The strikers marched in a body to the large square in front of the main office of the mill and told the superintendent "that unless all negroes were immediately and permanently withdrawn from the mills they would not return to their work." The superintendent promptly notified the mill president, who "at once left his private office for the scene of the strike, where he addressed the laborers, agreeing to grant their request. This being the only grievance and as it was promptly settled, the laborers agreed to resume their respective position[s] at the usual time [the next] morning."[22]

Surely, then, practically all mill owners knew the risks of violating racial

22. Atlanta *Constitution*, April 28, 1903.

custom. Threats to replace white workers with blacks, at least on a significant scale, were therefore empty, which is no doubt why virtually no attempts were ever made to implement them. It is difficult to see wherein Elsas' actions—or those of other mill owners in analogous situations—can be read as an effort to manipulate the prejudices of employees.

There was another way of employing blacks in mills that did not violate segregation or subject white women and girls to the "degradation" of working with blacks. That was to operate mills staffed entirely by blacks. This possibility was widely discussed at the turn of the century by mill owners as well as publicists for the cotton manufacturing industry, and a group of the former undertook a calculated experiment to test its feasibility. Yet in retrospect the idea seems fantastic. Its most serious proponent was apparently the *Manufacturers' Record,* an influential booster of cotton manufacturing and other forms of economic development, whose editors saw black labor as a weapon against the twin threats of unionism and labor shortage. Thus, in the aftermath of a trip through the South by an agent of the New England textile unions, the publication warned that "persistent labor agitators, carrying on their work in the South, will force mill owners to supplant white laborers by colored." Union activity among white operatives would "only result in turning the attention of Southern cotton manufacturers to the employment of colored labor."[23]

The shortage of white labor was a more valid reason for looking into the possibilities of black labor. But that motivation would have required treating the subject as a matter of economics rather than race, which in the New South was difficult indeed. "The truth is, white labor is becoming scarce," read a newspaper editorial commenting upon the announcement that a mill employing black labor only would be built at Bamberg, South Carolina. "White and colored laborers and tenants are employed on the same farms, but they cannot and will not work together in the same factories," the editorialist noted. Thus the only way to utilize black labor was in separate mills. "We suspect some of the mill-owners already look with longing eyes upon the supply of cheap, easily-managed labor the Southern negro seems to offer."[24]

The suspicion was valid. D. A. Tompkins, who was a mill official as well as a newspaper editor and a publicist for the cotton industry, was one who

23. *Manufacturers' Record,* December 11, 1896, p. 324.
24. Greenville *News,* reprinted in *Manufacturers' Record,* May 15, 1896, p. 262.

cast those longing eyes, but he was also a realist on racial matters. "If the colored man is ever much employed in Southern cotton mills," Tompkins wrote in 1896, "it will probably be in mills organized throughout with colored labor" and as a supplement to rather than displacement of white labor.[25]

Despite their apparent potential, all-black mills faced serious obstacles. They were a threat to white jobs, and in view of the kinds of incidents described above, prospective investors had to worry about their reception by white operatives and neighboring communities. "We have received several letters from operatives located in the Western part of North Carolina," a Charlotte textile publication announced in 1897, after it became known that an all-black mill was to be erected at nearby Concord, "all of which give us to understand that the cotton-mill operatives throughout that quarter have taken an oath to destroy the negro cotton mill if it is ever erected. The letters come to us without any signatures."[26]

The financial risk in black mills was also substantial. There was no pool of experienced black operatives, and investors would have to withstand initial losses while workers were trained in numbers necessary to neutralize such problems as absenteeism and turnover. Moreover, officials had scant experience in disciplining black workers and exacting labor from them in a cotton mill. It was much safer to invest in mills with white workers, whose high rates of return were already proven.

Despite these difficulties, several mills employing blacks alone were organized, and some operated for varying periods of time at the turn of the century. These mills were generally small, apparently underfinanced, often poorly managed, and largely unsuccessful. When a New York *Times* correspondent surveyed the subject in 1898, he found three such mills in operation and no others planned. Among the all-black enterprises that operated in the early years of the twentieth century were a knitting mill at Beaufort, South Carolina; a hosiery mill near Columbia; the Elmwood Manufacturing Company, a small yarn mill, also at Columbia; a hosiery mill at Durham, which operated profitably for a number of years; and a silk mill at Fayetteville, North Carolina. All of these were financed by the capital of white investors and employed white supervisors. There were also a few efforts by blacks to finance and operate mills of their own, among them the Afro-

25. *Manufacturers' Record*, May 1, 1896, p. 225.
26. *Textile Excelsior*, quoted in *Manufacturers' Record*, March 26, 1897, p. 152.

Alabama Cotton Mill near Anniston and the celebrated enterprise of W. C. Coleman at Concord, North Carolina, which was organized in 1897 and operated from 1901 until its bankruptcy in 1904.[27]

None of these mills had appreciable impact, though the failures among them probably reinforced the sentiment among white mill owners that mills could not be operated successfully with black workers. Yet a few men were interested in the idea of all-black mills, apparently because of its promise of cheaper labor, and a group of these men in Charleston decided to give the idea a thorough test. In 1897, they bought out the Charleston Cotton Mill, reorganized its management, installed new equipment, and undertook to train an all-black work force under the direction of whites. This was the most ambitious, calculated, and closely watched experiment of its kind in the New South, and its failure ended the possibility that meaningful numbers of all-black mills would appear in the section.

The situation in Charleston seemed ideal for the experiment. The area had a black population large enough, investors believed, to guarantee an adequate supply of black operatives. The location was away from upcountry mill districts where white workers were concentrated, which would, the investors hoped, neutralize their opposition. The mill was already built, which reduced the initial investment; and when a group led by John H. Montgomery of Spartanburg took over the experiment in 1899, it was guaranteed sufficient capital and competent management by men who earnestly wanted the venture to succeed.

The Charleston mill had had a checkered career. Built some years before the experiment began, it had never been successful, and its problems were popularly attributed to the shortage of white workers in a largely black area. It had closed down entirely more than once, and each closing occasioned talk of staffing it with black labor. "It is believed that colored operatives can be obtained who will work regularly, and be satisfied with the market rate of wages," a Charleston newspaper observed in the aftermath of a closedown in 1887. Nothing came of that observation, however. Three years later, when

27. Blacks also worked in mills within the penitentiary system of South Carolina and Alabama. On the mills with all-black labor forces, see Stokes, "Black and White Labor and the Development of the Southern Textile Industry, 1800–1920"; Mitchell, *The Rise of Cotton Mills in the South*, 195–221; William K. Boyd, *The Story of Durham: City of the New South* (Durham, 1925), 125–26; Jerome Dowd, "Colored Men as Cotton Manufacturers," *Gunton's Magazine*, XXIII (1902), 254–56; New York *Times*, September 5, 1898; *Manufacturers' Record*, October 13, 1893, p. 179, November 1, 1895, p. 209, December 27, 1895, p. 329, August 7, 1896, p. 24, July 16, 1897, p. 420, October 14, 1898, p. 197; and Atlanta *Constitution*, September 4, 1904, July 16, 1905, November 4, 1906.

the mill experienced another labor shortage, the owners tried to solve it by placing blacks in jobs traditionally held by whites. But after "the number of them employed [had] been gradually increased from time to time," white operatives rebelled, and the result was "a race war on a small scale." In many departments "the negroes were working and doing work that had always been done by white boys," a reporter wrote of the background to that incident. "The management was evidently endeavoring to get negro labor in the mills gradually. Two or three rows occurred during the week [of the trouble] and the war culminated in a grand battle, which was won by the whites, who had gradually ran off the negroes. Today the last negro employed in the mill was discharged."[28]

In 1897 the new owners of the reorganized mill announced plans to reopen it as an experiment with an all-black labor force. "If the experiment [had] succeeded here mills all over the South would be open to [blacks]," one of the investors said after the test ended. John H. Montgomery, one of the most successful mill owners in the New South, was even more explicit concerning the purpose and significance of the endeavor. "The experiment is attracting widespread attention over the cotton states," Montgomery said when he took over the enterprise and renamed it Vesta Mills. "While I would not attempt to put negro help in my two mills in the upcountry, I believe that mill people everywhere would try it. . . . If our schemes prove successful it will mean great things." He repeated later, "If this negro labor proves the success that we think, the cotton manufacturing in the South will be revolutionized within the next three years."[29]

With so much at stake, the experimenters went about their tasks carefully. To recruit workers, they contacted local black ministers and asked them to recommend only those who were reliable. As superintendent they engaged "a thorough mill man" whose support of the venture was enthusiastic. To train the work force, they hired a corps of experienced whites, and they apparently retained some white operatives in segregated workrooms until enough blacks had been trained to run the entire mill.

Despite the hopeful publicity these efforts generated, the experiment had difficulty from the beginning. "The plan worked badly at first," according to one account, "and there was more or less trouble" of an unspecified nature. In the spring of 1899, continuing difficulties led the original inves-

28. Charleston *News and Courier*, December 16, 1887; Atlanta *Constitution*, September 15, 1890.
29. Mitchell, *The Rise of Cotton Mills in the South*, 217n; Atlanta *Constitution*, March 19, September 27, 1899.

tors to transfer the mill and the experiment to Montgomery, who seems to have believed he could make the endeavor successful. "The labor is cheap," Montgomery said at the time, "much cheaper in fact than white help, and heretofore the only difficulty which stood in the way was the uncertainty of the negro labor."[30]

On that uncertainty, according to press reports, the experiment foundered. "The negro operators have been found willing, but unsteady, and in many instances unreliable, and they cannot be depended on to stick to the places," one account of their performance read. "The lack of constancy is the great fault found here with the colored operatives." After learning the work, "and after they had been working perhaps for weeks, the negroes would quietly walk away at night and not return for work in the morning. . . . The 'breaking-in' work was necessarily slow and tedious, and it was a bit discouraging to train a great number of operatives and then quietly have them depart without notice."[31]

The labor difficulty was never solved. In early 1901, less than two years after he took over the experiment, Montgomery pronounced it a failure, closed the mill, and shipped the machinery to a new factory he was erecting near Gainesville. "The operation of the mills with negro labor has proven unsatisfactory and unprofitable," he said of his action, "and it has been deemed wise to employ white labor altogether."[32]

"We had the best management and fine machinery, and all the money necessary," one of the investors told Broadus Mitchell a few years later. This investor claimed that the labor had caused the failure. On one occasion, the superintendent spoke of another problem the experimenters had had. "They have been denounced," he said, "for giving employment to negroes when white men and women would be glad of the jobs."[33]

"THE HUM OF THE MACHINERY PUTS THEM TO SLEEP."

The failure of Montgomery's experiment ended the possibility that all-black mills would ever gain a foothold in the New South. Mill folk and their racial concerns had not caused that failure; but ironically, in view of the attention historians have given the racism of the folk, the racial attitudes of mill

30. Atlanta *Constitution*, March 19, 1899.
31. *Ibid.*, August 18, 1900.
32. *Ibid.*, January 24, 1901.
33. Mitchell, *The Rise of Cotton Mills in the South*, 218; Atlanta *Constitution*, August 18, 1900.

owners might have played a part in the experiment's outcome. The deficiencies Montgomery and others ascribed to black workers were very like those they attributed to white operatives and had learned to tolerate and even neutralize. Moreover, mills with all-black work forces promised higher profits because blacks were paid significantly lower wages than whites. At W. C. Coleman's factory, for example, black spinners received five or six cents a side, whereas white spinners in the area were paid twice that amount. At a more successful hosiery mill in Durham, which began operating in 1904, wages paid black operatives were "from 20 to 40 per cent lower than for white knitting mill hands"; and though the productivity of the blacks was reportedly lower than that of whites, the difference was "not so great as the difference in wages."[34]

Mill officials recognized this potential advantage. Thomas H. Rennie, the superintendent at Graniteville, told the Industrial Commission in 1900 that since black operatives in the Charleston mill were receiving only "about two-thirds of the wages of the whites," the success of Montgomery's experiment would "most assuredly" bring down wages of white operatives in other mills. Yet Rennie resisted the suggestion that the mills pay blacks the white scale of wages in order to avoid the hardship lowered income would cause white workers. To equalize wages for whites and blacks, he said, "would create another inequality. The colored man does not expend for his living or for his family what the white man does," Rennie explained. "It costs the white laborer more to live. The result is that if the colored labor received the same wages as the white man, he would have the advantage of the white man, even in his living."[35]

That the economic potential in this view did not result in large numbers of all-black mills must be attributed to racial influences, not the least of which was the racial attitudes of mill owners. Like other white southerners, mill officials supported segregation and white supremacy and shared the common belief in black inferiority. Most doubted that blacks could be made into satisfactory mill workers and that all-black mills would ever be profitable. They also took seriously their reputation as paternalists, which rested in no small part on the alleged benevolence involved in reserving mill work for whites. Such views might have been overcome by economic interest, of course, but combined with other factors, the racial view of mill owners

34. Holland Thompson, *From the Cotton Field to the Cotton Mill: A Study of the Industrial Transition in North Carolina* (New York, 1906), 263; Mitchell, *The Rise of Cotton Mills in the South*, 214, 220.
35. *House Documents*, 57th Cong., 1st Sess., No. 184, Vol. 7, p. 488.

made it impossible for black labor to receive a fair test in the mills. Mill owners, like mill folk, had ideas and feelings that governed their actions in racial matters. In dealing with those matters, they did not manipulate the racial prejudices of their employees; rather, they acted out their own prejudices in their own ways and in circumstances that gave them little room for maneuver.

The racial ideas of mill owners were conventional, though not uniform. Attempting to encourage discussion of the subject, the *Manufacturers' Record* occasionally asked mill representatives for their views on the potential use of blacks in the mills. The editors of that publication obviously believed the potential was great, yet most of the mill officials whose views they published disagreed.[36] Otis G. Lynch, superintendent of Enterprise Mill, was one of the exceptions. Lynch acknowledged the difficulties of employing blacks and thought the supply of white labor adequate, but said he would "have no hesitation about trying to run a mill successfully in the South on plain or medium goods with colored labor." Similarly, G. W. Williams, president of Swift Manufacturing Company at Columbus, saw "no reason why colored labor would not fill each and every place about a cotton mill if so trained." Williams was certain, however, that "the two races would not work well together in the same mill."[37]

Others expressed standard views. William Entwistle employed blacks in the dyehouse and yard at the Pee Dee Manufacturing Company in Rockingham, North Carolina, where he was superintendent, but "under no circumstances would [he] employ them in any department where white girls [were] employed." In addition, he did "not think they [were] adapted to the close confinement or capable of conforming to the system and discipline incident to factory labor." J. F. Iler, superintendent of Piedmont Manufacturing Company in South Carolina, had supervised slaves in mills before the Civil War and did "not think that the colored help would make good operatives." He explained: "In the first place they are lacking in intelligence, and are very unreliable and have no pride. In the second place . . . they do not want to work more than just enough to get bread to eat, and that is about half time."

E. T. McKinney employed no blacks at the mill in Trion, Georgia, where

36. The following quotations, unless otherwise indicated, are from *Manufacturers' Record*, September 22, 1893, pp. 134–35, and May 22, 1896, p. 280.

37. Mill officials who testified before the Industrial Commission in 1900 stressed the unwillingness of their white employees to work with blacks (*House Documents*, 57th Cong., 1st Sess., No. 184, Vol. 7, pp. 482, 487, 492, and 521).

he was superintendent, and thought black labor "would be very unsatisfactory." He wrote: "For carding, spinning, weaving and finishing, I think they would prove a failure, and would certainly cause trouble between themselves and white labor in Southern mills. They are too unreliable for cotton mills." Therefore, McKinney himself "would not undertake to run a mill with the colored help with whom [he had] come in contact." Hamilton H. Hickman held similar views. He was certain that "the white labor [would] not work with the negro at the machine," and for that reason, "you cannot mix them in a cotton mill." He would "shrink from being the owner or president" of a mill that employed blacks only. The problem was not necessarily the ability of blacks to do the work. "If we concede the fact of [their] capability," Hickman wrote, "unreliability would be sufficient cause for not employing them. . . . They would close the mill to go on a picnic or go off on a railroad excursion and spend the last dime in their pockets, and very many of them, as soon as they get ten dollars ahead, will walk quietly off without notice." An official at Isactta Mills in Augusta expressed these ideas succinctly. "The only objection we have heard to colored help," he wrote, "is that the hum of machinery puts them to sleep."[38]

BLACKS WERE "AFRAID TO GO IN THE NEIGHBORHOOD OF THE MILLS AFTER DARK."

The racial dimension of the mill experience was not restricted to events inside the workplace. Mill folk lived in a society in which racial concerns were never entirely absent. Apparently nowhere in the New South did blacks live in mill villages proper, but some mills built housing for black employees apart from the white village, and there were blacks in the vicinity of virtually all mill communities. Indeed, in many villages there were black domestics, washerwomen, wood haulers, and the like, and it is probable that all mill folk knew familiarly and interacted regularly with at least a few blacks.

This interaction was generally peaceable and even pleasant on the surface. "Between the whites and the twenty negroes now working at the mill, with an almost equal number of colored women employed as cooks and nursemaids by the operatives," Marjorie A. Potwin wrote of Saxon Mills, "there are bonds of mutual affection." The same feelings existed in mill villages across the New South. As long as blacks were in menial roles and

38. *Manufacturers' Record*, October 6, 1893, p. 163.

appropriately deferential, personal relations between them and mill folk were conventionally southern—outwardly friendly and forbearing but restricted to situations involving no questions of social equality. Even in the workplace, this was probably the general rule. President Rufus B. Bullock of Atlanta Cotton Mill seemed to suggest amiable relations when he told the Industrial Commission in 1900 that whites and blacks in his mill never mixed their work "except when the white help goes out to get a can of snuff and colored sweepers run the loom."[39]

Despite this general equilibrium, racial incidents in and about cotton mill villages were numerous. The worst of them dramatized the extremes to which mill folk went in defending white supremacy. Thus in the fall of 1900 at a mill village in Rock Hill, "an inoffensive negro" was shot by "a drunken factory operative, supposed to be Sid Smith, who is rather notorious." The shooting, according to press reports, was "the result of feeling which [had] existed for several weeks between a certain class of factory operatives and the negroes." During those weeks, so much violence had occurred that blacks were "afraid to go in the neighborhood of the mills after dark." A reporter wrote of the situation, "Livery men say they cannot get a colored driver to go that way at all."[40]

Interracial violence involving mill folk occurred with some frequency. Will Fambro, a black driver for Spalding Cotton Mills in Griffin, Georgia, "grossly insulted a lady and child" in the mill village while intoxicated one day in 1903, for which he was arrested, tried, and fined. But when a nearby farmer paid Fambro's fine and put him to work to pay off the debt, "a mob of unknown white men" went to Fambro's house, "fired hundreds of shots from guns, pistols and Winchesters into the room occupied by the negro, his wife and three children," and killed him. Whether any members of this mob were mill workers is unknown. In racial matters, mill folk were white people, not "lintheads," and in the defense of white supremacy, lines of employment and questions of social status were no barriers to cooperation. Thus when fifteen-year-old Maude Tomblin, who worked at Bibb Mills in Columbus, Georgia, was reportedly assaulted by a black man in 1902, white men from in and out of the mill community rallied to the defense of her honor. "The alarm was given and bloodhounds were procured," read a press account of the response to her report, and "a crowd of nearly two

39. Marjorie A. Potwin, *Cotton Mill People of the Piedmont: A Study in Social Change* (New York, 1927), 59–60; *House Documents*, 57th Cong., 1st Sess., No. 184, Vol. 7, p. 482.

40. Atlanta *Constitution*, September 30, 1900.

hundred men is on the scene tonight armed with guns and pistols, looking for the negro."[41]

Mill folk also participated in lynchings. In 1906, for example, George Hall, a cotton mill operative, was convicted of conspiracy and sentenced to fifteen years in prison for his role in the lynching of three blacks at Salisbury, North Carolina. He was convicted on the testimony of a deputy sheriff who saw Hall leading a mob of about thirty men, which stormed the jail and seized the blacks, accused of killing a white family.[42]

Gruesome as such incidents are, they were not exceptional racial events in the New South. This was a time of racial extremism and pervasive racial consciousness among nearly all white southerners, and the defense of white supremacy was one public activity in which mill folk participated free of social stigma. Like other groups in the New South, folk learned racism and racial awareness at an early age and acted out their beliefs as circumstances dictated. Perhaps some of their children participated in what might have been a unique incident, even in the New South. This was the "mimic imitation riot" a group of boys staged near the woolen mills in Atlanta in the spring of 1907. This incident, which occurred a few months after the great Atlanta race riot of 1906, suggested the pervasiveness of racial awareness at the time. The boys involved "had read and heard much about race conflicts, and . . . they decided . . . a riot between whites and blacks would be something unique and exciting to the highest degree." Accordingly, "Half of the boys blacked up so as to appear as negroes," using for the purpose "a copious application of soot"; and the other half took the role of whites. The object of the division was to "play riot," as one of the participants said later; but the stones the two sides began throwing at each other damaged a nearby store, the owner of which grabbed one of the boys and held him until police arrived, while the others fled the scene.[43]

Mill folk also joined, in their own way, the political campaigns waged in defense of white supremacy. In 1900, for example, North Carolina whites campaigned to preserve white supremacy by supporting a proposed amendment to the state constitution requiring the ownership of property, literacy, and other qualifications for voting. The idea was to disfranchise blacks by imposing qualifications a large majority of them could not meet. But many mill folk could not meet the requirements either. Therefore, honestly en-

41. *Ibid.*, February 25, 1903, November 12, 1902.
42. *Ibid.*, August 7–11, 1906.
43. *Ibid.*, March 23, 1907.

forced, the amendment would clearly reduce the voting potential of propertyless and illiterate whites as well as blacks.[44]

Yet many mill folk enthusiastically joined the campaign to adopt the amendment.[45] Some must have been members of "the White Supremacy club" at Pilot Mills, which met regularly during the campaign and whose members were "charmed" one night by speeches of politicians supporting the amendment. Others were no doubt in the audience that heckled Republican opponents of the amendment when they spoke one day at Proximity Mill. In the middle of the campaign, "a good sized audience of mill people and farmers" at Worthville listened approvingly while Ben R. Lacy, the state labor commissioner, assured them that "the amendment will take the right to vote from no white man, but will only undo a wrong and disfranchise the negro." When Lacy spoke a few nights later at Newton, the Newton Cotton Mills suspended its night shift to allow workers to attend. "This being the only mill [in Newton] running at night at present," a newspaper reported, "all the mill operatives were out to hear him." At Pittsboro, mill folk showed their support for the amendment by joining a public parade. Its first float featured "a huge white swan, drawn by four white horses and filled with thirty young factory girls in pure white, with their white supremacy badges and banners."

44. J. Morgan Kousser, *The Shaping of Southern Politics: Suffrage Restriction and the Establishment of the One-Party South, 1880–1910* (New Haven, 1974), 183–95.
45. Quotations in the following account are from Raleigh *News and Observer*, July 21, 8, 14, 19, 17, 1900.

17
CHILD LABOR

As historian James A. Henretta has observed, "The point of departure for the study of any cultural group must be its own values and aspirations."[1] To see child labor as mill folk saw and experienced it is to perform something of an act of will, for the perspective of virtually all scholarship on the subject—and the view sustained by one's own inclinations as well—is that not of the folk but of their nemesis, the child-labor reformers.[2] The difference between the perspectives of the two groups was substantial, and thus child labor is one of the most misunderstood subjects in the history of the mill experience.

Whether defined as the labor of children under sixteen, fourteen, or twelve, child labor was a pervasive feature of mill work.[3] So important was it that its virtual elimination in the years around World War I is one of the watersheds in the history of mill folk. The clash between child labor reformers and mill

1. James A. Henretta, "The Study of Social Mobility: Ideological Assumptions and Conceptual Bias," *Labor History*, XVIII (1977), 177.
2. See, for example, Walter J. Trattner, *Crusade for the Children: History of the National Child Labor Committee and Child Labor Reform in America* (Chicago, 1970); and Elizabeth H. Davidson, *Child Labor Legislation in the Southern Textile States* (Chapel Hill, 1939).
3. For a convenient summary of data on the subject, see Census Bureau, *Bulletin 69: Child Labor in the United States* (1907), 42–65.

folk that preceded this development was a singularly instructive episode in the story of mill work. In opposing child-labor reform and reformers, mill folk engaged in one of their earliest encounters with the modern state, and the outcome was a portent of things to come. Here was a new kind of adversary, one folk poorly understood and were ill equipped to confront. The new adversaries were cultural, not economic aggressors, bent not on extorting the fruit of one's labor but on forcing one to live in unaccustomed ways according to someone else's standards.[4] To mill folk, restriction of child labor was not reform but an effort to deprive them of income and control of their own children, and was thus an unwanted imposition on their lives by arrogant outsiders who held them in contempt and meant to do them harm.

"WEAZENED PIGMIES" AND "GAUNT GOBLINS"

The reformers' indictment of child labor bore little resemblance to the actualities of work by children as mill folk knew it, and took no cognizance of the economic needs of mill parents. Those actualities and needs caused mill folk to view child labor as "an actual social condition," in the words of one of their employers. The unwillingness or inability to acknowledge that condition led reformers to see child labor only in the light of abstract "humanitarian theory."[5]

That theory was born of Progressive urges to do good and to remake the institutions of lower-class life to fit middle-class imperatives, and of the efforts of labor-union leaders to raise wages. It fed on a growing unease among middle-class reformers concerning social and economic change in the New South, and on the failure of labor leaders to appreciate the immediate needs of poor parents whose children were at work. The theory derived special sustenance from elitist disdain for "lintheads" and other "poor whites." These feelings and attitudes encouraged reformers and labor spokesmen to see child labor in cotton mills as an acute social problem that had to be eliminated at once, whatever the wishes or needs of mill folk. Child labor was not a problem to study evenhandedly but a disgrace to expose sensationally. Only in that way could the public be aroused against it

4. The best discussion of this aspect of the history of mill folk is in David L. Carlton, *Mill and Town in South Carolina, 1880–1920* (Baton Rouge, 1982), 171–214.
5. James L. Orr, president of Piedmont Mills, quoted in *South Carolina House Journal,* 1901, p. 181.

and against the people responsible for it, including those "trifling, ignorant or careless" parents who put their children to work in the mills.[6] The reformers' depiction of children in the mills was thus grotesquely over-drawn, and did much to sustain the popular image of mill folk as degraded, morally insensitive people.

Irene Ashby-Macfadyen was a representative source of the distortion. Under auspices of the American Federation of Labor (AFL), this veteran labor organizer visited a number of mills after the turn of the century, and the kind of lurid reports she made of mill children became staples in the reformers' accounts of child labor. "The physical, mental, and moral effect of these long hours of toil and confinement on the children is indescribably sad, " Ashby-Macfadyen wrote in the *American Federationist* in 1902. She claimed that the mill children she encountered were "so stunted" by their labors it was impossible to tell their ages. Invariably they looked younger, often much younger, than they actually were, because of the dwarfing effects of long hours of monotonous toil in unhealthful workplaces, she stated.[7]

The physical toll of mill work took sometimes astonishing form. "A horrible form of dropsy occurs among the children," Ashby-Madfadyen reported; and, a doctor told her, 10 percent of the children who began mill work before their twelfth birthday contracted "active consumption" within five years. "The lint forms in their lungs a perfect cultivating medium for tuberculosis," she explained, "while the change from the hot atmosphere of the mill to the chill night or morning air, often brings on pneumonia." Children who escaped these scourges faced other hazards. "In one mill city in the South a doctor told a friend that he had personally amputated more than a hundred babies' fingers mangled in the mill," Ashby-Macfadyen wrote. She had herself heard a cotton merchant in Atlanta say that "he had frequently seen mill children without fingers or thumb and sometimes without the whole hand." No wonder "no mill children look[ed] healthy." How could they, these "child slaves," these "babies working for five and six cents a day?" Their entire appearance was "characterized by extreme pallor and an aged, worn expression infinitely pitiful and incongruous" and accen-

6. The phrase is from Irene M. Ashby, "The Fight Against Child Labor in Alabama," *American Federationist*, VII (1901), 150. Ashby used the name Ashby-Macfadyen in later articles.

7. Irene Ashby-Macfadyen, "Child Life vs. Dividends," *American Federationist*, IX (1902), 217. Excerpts from this article appeared in *Labor Advocate* (Birmingham), August 30, 1902, and *Journal of Labor* (Atlanta), January 18, 1907.

tuated by the utter hopelessness of their situation. "I scarcely ever found a mill child," Ashby-Macfadyen added, "who could read or write."[8]

This deplorable exaggeration rested on elements of truth: health and safety conditions in the mills were substandard, and many mill children were illiterate or underschooled. What mill folk needed, however, was sympathy for their needs and attention to the concerns that led them to place their children in the mills. What they received from middle-class reformers was caricatured misrepresentation that reinforced social prejudices against them. And labor spokesmen had adopted an approach that, as mill folk saw it, put the cart before the horse. Labor opposition to child labor was part of a larger effort to raise wages for adult workers. But until such raises occurred, the effort to abolish child labor was, to mill folk, a campaign to reduce their income.

Reformers gave little thought to the views of mill folk. Instead, they took the picture Ashby-Macfadyen painted and exaggerated it further. In 1905, for example, Elbert Hubbard, the New York editor and publicist, published, also in the *American Federationist*, a sensational account of the "weazened pigmies" he had recently seen on a tour of mills in South Carolina. Mill work "reduce[d] nervous sensation in a few months to the minimum," Hubbard wrote of the child laborer, who became an "automaton." As such, "The child does not think; he ceases to suffer—[his] memory is as dead as hope." Presently, he "sinks into a stupor and dies." Hubbard had seen "dozens of just such children" in a mill he visited, and "a physician who was with [him] said that they would all be dead probably in two years, and their places filled with others—there were plenty more. Pneumonia carries off most of them." Indicating some uncertainty over the life expectancy of the child laborer, Hubbard wrote: "In many mills death sets the little prisoner free inside of four years. Beyond that he cannot hope to live."[9]

Such hyperbole was widely repeated. In 1914, in a notable instance, three prominent Progressives, Edwin Markham, Benjamin B. Lindsey, and George Creel, published a muckraking exposé of child labor that featured "a gaunt goblin army of children," all of them "slaves of the loom," their lives reduced to "the grim grind of existence." Quoting someone who had written in the Washington *Post*, Markham and his coauthors observed, "It would be less cruel for a state to have children painlessly put to death than it is to permit them to be ground to death in this awful process." Indeed, "the

8. Ashby-Macfadyen, "Child Life vs. Dividends," 217–18.
9. Elbert Hubbard, "Slaughter of the Innocents," *American Federationist*, XII (1905), 205–206.

new slavery of the mills [was] worse than the old slavery of the cotton fields. For the negro of the old days was well fed and sure of shelter; [and] he did [his] work under the open sky, singing as he toiled." Better rural bondage, it seems, than factory servitude, for in the mills "the slavery of the white women and children sucks life dry of all vigor and all joy."[10] Working in the mills might also subject them to unexpected forms of cruelty. "I've seen little children strapped up by the thumbs because of their inability to perform their daily tasks," H. P. Barnes of the Loom Fixers Union in Columbus told a convention of the Georgia Federation of Labor in 1899.[11]

Such views tell more about the people who voiced them than about the actualities of child labor. By what standard was mill work worse than ante-bellum slavery? Apparently by one that justified different treatment for whites and blacks, especially if the whites were women and children; and apparently also by one that drew heavily on agrarian mythology. Mill folk were too familiar with farming to romanticize it. A conscious desire to avoid the hardships of farm life was one reason they were in the mills. Moreover, child labor, as they well knew, was far more pervasive and strenuous in agriculture than in cotton manufacturing. Yet reformers generally found child labor on the farms good. "Children in the farm do child's work . . . under the eyes of their parents," Alexander J. McKelway, a North Carolinian who headed the National Child Labor Committee, wrote in 1906, "and such work has helped to develop a large majority of the men who have contributed to the greatness of our country in peace and in war. But to compare this kind of work, familiar to all Americans whose good fortune it has been to be born on a farm, with the twelve-hour day or the twelve-hour night of the cotton mills, and the employment of children from six to twelve years of age for those hours is absurd on its face."[12]

C. T. Ladson, an Atlanta attorney who campaigned for child-labor laws on behalf of the Georgia Federation of Labor, was even more enraptured of farm work for children. "Is it possible," Ladson asked, urging the Georgia legislature to prohibit child labor in the mills, "that the farm boy who plows for six or eight months in the year, and goes to school three to five months in the winter; who is out in the fresh air all day long; who sings as he plows,

10. Edwin Markham, Benjamin B. Lindsey, and George Creel, *Children in Bondage: A Complete and Careful Presentation of the Anxious Problem of Child Labor—Its Causes, Its Crimes, and Its Cure* (New York, 1914), 40–49. For another example of this literature, see Bessie Van Vorst, *The Cry of the Children: A Study of Child Labor* (New York, 1908).

11. Atlanta *Constitution*, April 28, 1899.

12. A. J. McKelway, "Welfare Work and Child Labor in Southern Cotton Mills," *Charities and the Commons*, XVII (1906), 272.

who goes fishing and hunting, and has all manner of vacations in his labor; who grows sturdy, whose blood becomes red with the labor of his own stout arms out in the fields, amid sunshine and birds, and flowers, [is] to be compared to" the pitiful children in the mills?[13]

It was not child labor in general, then, but child labor in cotton mills that upset reformers. Their attitude was based on the harmful physical effects they ascribed to mill work, as well as the hurtful moral atmosphere many of them found in the mills. There "boys and girls are pushed into the company of coarse men who are big with oaths and reeking jests," Edwin Markham and his coauthors wrote in 1914, and the result was moral degeneration. "Torrents of foul profanity from angry overseers wash over the souls of the children, till they too grow hardened in crusts of coarseness. Piled on all these are the fearful risks that the young girls run from the attentions of men 'higher up,' especially if the girls happen to be cursed with a little beauty." Charles L. Coon, secretary of the North Carolina Child Labor Committee, agreed. "Child labor breeds immorality," Coon insisted, citing as proof the testimony of a schoolman who deplored the demoralizing effects of mill work on school-age children. "In the factories they are associated with older children," the schoolman had told Coon. "That gives them a desire to adopt certain vices which are always bad; but at that time of life are absolutely ruinous." Soon, the moral sense of young workers "seems badly wrong. They have but little regard even for the decent relations of the sexes, and only slight ability to see the point in many a question of right and wrong."[14]

The immoralities of work were compounded by those of mill life itself. Nowhere was the reformers' special combination of arrogance and ignorance more apparent than in their suggestions that the congregation of large numbers of plain folk in mill villages was itself a source of immorality. "Is it not likely," John C. Campbell asked in the *Child Labor Bulletin*, "that active immorality will become more active, and an unmoral state pass into an immoral one more readily where many people of the same social grade are closely grouped together?" Markham and his coauthors were alarmed over the "moral degeneration" they traced to "white loafers" attracted to mill communities by the prospect of living in idleness on the earnings of their wives and children. C. T. Ladson of the Georgia Federation of Labor, on the other hand, said the problem was not that the mills attracted "loafers" but that they created temptations that turned workingmen into idlers. Testify-

13. Atlanta *Constitution*, December 3, 1899.
14. Markham, Lindsey, and Creel, *Children in Bondage*, 50–51; Charles L. Coon, "The Dinner Toter," *Annals*, XXXVIII (July, 1911), supplement, 89.

ing before the Georgia legislature, Ladson told the story of three industrious farmers who moved their families to Dalton and "put all their children in the mill, big and little, old and young." Suddenly able to live without working, the three men rapidly degenerated into loafers, Ladson said, and not one of them had "struck a lick of work" since moving to the mill.[15]

Perhaps such stories should be attributed to the demands of advocacy, which are not always served by the ambiguities of truth. They had a larger significance, however, for the campaign against child labor caught mill folk in a crossfire between southern elites. Mill owners and their apologists and publicists, who opposed child-labor legislation for economic and other reasons, found appeals to sectional and racial prejudices useful in their effort to discredit the reform movement. The reformers, whose views on sectional and racial matters were no different from those of their critics, responded in kind, and suddenly an issue that mattered to mill folk was an object of controversy between competing elites, each bent on purposes of its own. To ward off charges that child-labor reform was a scheme of northern capitalists or New England textile unionists to undermine the South's advantages in cotton manufacturing, reformers not only stressed their southern origins—the National Child Labor Committee and its efforts in the southern states were directed by southerners—but couched many of their arguments against child labor in exaggeratedly sectional terms. Overemphasizing the extent of northern investment in southern mills, a speaker expressed those arguments succinctly at a Labor Day celebration in Columbus, Georgia, in 1903. In recently voting down a child-labor bill, the speaker said, the Georgia legislature had shown itself "willing to swap Georgia babies for yankee dollars."[16]

Such discourse was unedifying but a part of the indictment of child labor. Like almost everyone who mentioned the subject, child-labor reformers frequently pointed out that mill folk were native Americans of "pure" Anglo-Saxon or other desirable racial stock, and thus the exploitation of mill children (and women) was doubly deplorable. Despite this respect for their racial ancestry, however, mill folk were not consulted about child labor.

There were other, more important racial arguments against child labor. Irene Ashby-Macfadyen for example, pointed out that mill work deprived

15. John C. Campbell, "From Mountain Cabin to Cotton Mill," *Child Labor Bulletin*, II (1913–14), 80; Markham, Lindsey, and Creel, *Children in Bondage*, 51; Atlanta *Constitution*, December 3, 1899.

16. Atlanta *Constitution*, September 8, 1903.

white children of schooling while black children, who were excluded from the mills by racial policy, were being educated. "There will be a generation of illiterate whites surrounded by educated negroes," she warned. Yet "the only possible way to secure the absolutely essential leadership of the black by the white race, is to guarantee the education of the whites." A Georgia legislator, Madison Bell of Atlanta, repeated this warning. "While the little white children of Georgia are going to the cotton factories six days out of the seven in the week," Bell said, urging his fellow legislators to pass a child-labor bill, "the little negro children are trooping to school, and are being educated out of the school fund paid in by the white taxpayers of Georgia."[17]

"MANY PARENTS ARE NEITHER SENSIBLE NOR CHRISTIAN."

The opposition of mill folk to child-labor reform presented problems for reformers. Sighs by the latter that mill folk did not know their own interest dramatized the cultural chasm—and differing economic circumstances—between the folk and their would-be uplifters. "Not much will be done till these people do for themselves and quit having it all done for them," W. H. Swift of the North Carolina Child Labor Committee said in 1914. Swift meant not that mill folk should have a say in child labor or other concerns but that they should cease relying on the paternalism of mill owners and turn instead to the enlightenment of men like himself. "There is just one more job awaiting somebody—that of shaking up the mill operatives," Swift continued. "The sooner these people are made to realize that all is not well with them, the better."[18] Few reformers had the patience necessary to accomplish, or even undertake, the educational task to which Swift's statement seemed to point. Most reformers began with the premise that parents who permitted their children to work in the mills were heartless loafers or moral monsters and in either guise were unfit to be consulted on an issue so pressing as child-labor reform.

This unflattering portrait was a staple of reform literature. In 1902 the *Labor Advocate*, official voice of organized labor in Birmingham, ran an article denouncing "crackers" who "invert the moral order of things by calling upon their progeny to support them in lieu of supporting their

17. Ashby, "The Fight Against Child Labor in Alabama," 154; Atlanta *Constitution*, August 3, 1905.
18. W. H. Swift, "The Campaign in North Carolina," *Child Labor Bulletin*, II (1913–14), 100–101.

offspring." Such parents had to be prevented from exploiting their children. "One preacher has said it might be left to sensible Christian parents and mill managers," Swift remarked in 1914, "but all of us know that many parents are neither sensible nor Christian."[19]

The social bias behind such statements prevented reformers from appreciating the views of mill folk on child labor—indeed, from knowing they had views worth appreciating. Not even obvious economic considerations moved reformers. "I know of no employment in the South for girls under 14 that pays so well as work in the cotton mills," Alexander J. McKelway wrote in 1913, "and only one employment for boys, the demoralizing messenger service." McKelway added, "[Mill] wages are comparatively high, considering the ages of the children."[20]

Such remarks might have produced some sympathy for parents who put their children in the mills, especially in specific instances in which the income of poor families included meaningful contributions from child laborers. The investigative reports of reformers are replete with such examples. In one of his exposés, McKelway described the case of Sam Bowles, an eleven-year-old employee he found in 1913 at White City Manufacturing Company in Georgia. Sam, who earned 40¢ a day, and a thirteen-year-old sibling who made 75¢ a day, worked under a special permit granted their mother as a widow. At work in the same mill were another of Sam's siblings, who was fifteen years old, and the children's mother, a weaver. Together, the four earned $3.15 a day, a not inconsiderable wage, 37 percent of which was contributed by the two underage children. Such a family might have impressed McKelway with its industry and determination to "make do," as folk would say, in difficult circumstances. But what chiefly impressed him was his discovery that Sam's mother had remarried and that the employment of her two youngest children was therefore illegal.[21]

It seems not to have occurred to McKelway that Sam and his mother had legitimate interests in the situation he described, or that Sam's employment might have been justifiable. Others shared McKelway's narrow perspective. "It is perfectly useless to say that the operatives don't want it," a reformer said of the abolition of child labor. "There are only two classes of operatives that would oppose it—those who want to work their little children, and

19. *Labor Advocate* (Birmingham), August 30, 1902; W. H. Swift, "The Last Stand of the One Business Which Opposes Child Labor Legislation in the South," *Child Labor Bulletin*, III (1914), 87–88.

20. A. J. McKelway, "Child Wages in the Cotton Mills: Our Modern Feudalism," *National Child Labor Committee Pamphlet No. 199* (n.p., 1913), 3–4.

21. A. J. McKelway, "Child Labor in Georgia," *Child Labor Bulletin*, II (1913), 64–65.

those who are under the influence of higher authorities [that is, mill owners] who may be opposed to it, and are overpersuaded by them." Neither group, in this view, could be trusted to act in the best interest of their children.[22]

Nor could working children be trusted to know what was best for themselves. Children viewed mill work in ways reformers found incomprehensible. Most children found mill work preferable to the other options available to them—school, housework, or farm work—and viewed their circumstance as far from intolerable. Historian Holland Thompson seems to have captured the essence of their attitude. "Many hate the work," Thompson wrote of mill children in 1906, "but the general attitude of the children is not one of rebellion. On the farms the children worked, and they accept their occupation as a matter of course. They take pride in being wage earners and treasure a word of approval from an overseer or superintendent. Their ambition is to be transferred to the looms, where they make larger wages. Many prefer the mill to the school, and will attend [school] only under compulsion."[23]

Reformers had difficulty accepting the positive aspects of this view; and in trying to discredit these aspects, they turned even the pride mill folk took in their work against them. "One of the saddest cases was that of little Savannah, a frail eleven-year-old," a child-labor investigator wrote of a girl he found in the mill in 1912. Among the "sad" characteristics of the child was the enthusiasm she and her father displayed in her work. "The boss says she's a crackerjack at spinnin'," her "gaunt father" had proudly told the investigator. "She ain't satisfied unless she's in the mill."[24]

That attitude shocked reformers. "Almost incredible as it may seem," Edwin Markham and his coauthors acknowledged, "nine out of ten child workers prefer their toil to school attendance." Such a preference, which these authors found among child laborers in all types of work, revealed as much about schools, no doubt, as about workplaces. It also documented the cultural differences between reformers and the folk they wanted to reform. What prompted the disbelief of Markham and his associates was a survey of 500 child laborers in Chicago, 412 of whom said they preferred work to school. Among the reasons for their preference were many that southern mill children would have agreed with: "because you get paid for what you

22. Quoted in Elizabeth H. Davidson, "The Child-Labor Problem in North Carolina, 1883–1903," *North Carolina Historical Review*, XIII (1936), 114.
23. Holland Thompson, *From the Cotton Field to the Cotton Mill: A Study of the Industrial Transition in North Carolina* (New York, 1906), 323–33.
24. *Journal of Labor* (Atlanta), February 23, 1912.

do in a factory"; "because it's easier to work in a factory than 'tis to learn in school"; "you never understand what they tells you in school, and you can learn right off to do things in a factory"; "they ain't always pickin' on you because you don't know things in a factory"; and "the boss he never hits you, er slaps yer face, er pulls yer ears." According to reformers, children with such values had to be made over. "No child," wrote Markham, Lindsey, and Creel, "should be permitted to practice sabotage upon his own life."[25]

Child labor, folk believed, was economically necessary and therefore simply a fact of life. The practice was also customary and thus culturally and socially sanctioned, and involved a decision parents should make for their own children. "The attitude of parents toward laws restricting the employment of children illustrates clearly the fact that earnings of the child are considered indisputably the parents rightful due," investigators for the 1907–1908 labor study found. "The fathers and mothers vehemently declare that the State has no right to interfere, if they wish to 'put their own children to work,' and that it is only fair for the child to 'begin to pay back for his keep.' "[26] To mill folk, then, child labor was not a social policy to be debated but an integral part of life. Everyone was supposed to work, and at whatever job one's circumstance permitted or dictated. Wives and mothers should work at home, men outside the home at men's occupations, and children, at their parents' behest, at whatever was available for them.

Reformers rejected such complacencies. "The State has a distinct duty when it comes to the protecting of her children," W. H. Swift wrote. "The child is the ward of the State and the State must protect the ward in its human as well as its property rights. . . . The rights of the community and of the State, and rights of the child . . . rise paramount to any right which any parent may claim to have."[27]

"WE BESEECH YOU TO LET US ALONE."

This clash of cultural values lay behind the campaign for child-labor legislation and the opposition of mill folk to it. The campaign began slowly. As early as the 1880s, occasional reformers and mill critics began sporadic efforts to urge legislatures to prohibit the labor of children, usually below

25. Markham, Lindsey, and Creel, *Children in Bondage*, 372–73.
26. *Senate Documents*, 61st Cong., 2nd Sess., No. 645, Vol. 1, p. 353.
27. Swift, "The Last Stand of the One Business Which Opposes Child Labor Legislation in the South," 87–88.

twelve years of age. Legislators were indifferent or opposed to such legislation, however, and nothing came of the efforts until after the turn of the
century. Then, between 1903 and 1906, the legislatures of Georgia and the
Carolinas adopted limited, ineffective laws proscribing the employment in
mills of most children under twelve; and over the next decade, they
strengthened those laws and raised the age of children excluded from employment to fourteen and then sixteen years of age. By the end of World War
I, these laws were being systematically enforced, and the labor of children
under sixteen in cotton mills had been largely eliminated.[28]

In prohibiting employment of children, the early laws granted exemptions to orphans dependent on their own earnings, children of widows or
disabled men, and children who could read and write or had attended
school for a term during the previous year. Even when the laws were
enforced and obeyed, these exemptions permitted large numbers of small
children to work because so many mill families were headed by women or
disabled men. The laws were not honestly enforced or obeyed, however, for
some years, because mill parents and owners alike disapproved of them and
wanted to keep underage children at work. In addition, the early laws had
no enforcement machinery—no factory inspectors and administrative bureaucracy with a stake in seeing the laws properly applied—and the exemptions became gaping loopholes through which children continued to work.
"I am confident that not over ten per cent of the mills observe [the child
labor law]," a mill official from Hickory wrote the North Carolina labor
commissioner in 1907. "I know this to be the case because so many
[families] come to me seeking employment and stating that they have children under twelve at work in other mills. I now have a family with four girls
nearly grown, all number-one hands, and they are going to another mill
because I will not employ a ten-year-old boy."[29]

The responses of mill folk to child-labor laws revealed not only general
opposition to the reform but a wide range of opinion within that opposition.

28. Davidson, *Child Labor Legislation in the Southern Textile States*, 275–77, lists by year of
passage all laws on the subject in the three states. For texts of the early laws, see U.S.
Commissioner of Labor, *Twenty-Second Annual Report, 1907*, 297–98, 962–63, and 1233–35.
By 1919 all children under fourteen were excluded from the mills, and only about 1 in 20 mill
workers in the 3 states was under sixteen. See George E. Newby, "The Cotton Manufacturing
Industry: New England and the South" (M.A. thesis, University of North Carolina, 1925),
117.

29. North Carolina Bureau of Labor Statistics, *Annual Report, 1907*, 245, hereinafter cited
as NC *Labor Report* by year.

Mill folk did not favor child labor but thought it a necessity and an option parents had the right to choose for their children. Within these parameters, however, mill folk could be highly critical of specific instances of child labor, especially those in which they thought children were compelled to go to work too young or in which mill owners required parents to send their children to work when the parents wanted them to stay home or go to school. In neither of those situations was the objection to child labor itself. It was, instead, to the abuse of small children on the one hand and interference with parental authority on the other. "There is one evil existing among our manufacturers," a Forsyth County carder told the North Carolina labor commissioner in 1890, "and that is the working of small children at about ten or twelve years of age twelve to fourteen hours per day." Others agreed. "Children are put to work entirely too young in some cases," an overseer wrote. "I have charge of a room in a factory. Most of the help in the room are children, and I think from my observation as to the effects on them, they are put to work too soon."[30]

Mill folk sometimes debated the precise age at which children were old enough to work. This was pointedly illustrated in a letter Mrs. S. J. Vaughn of Sampson mill village wrote Governor Blease in 1914. Mrs. Vaughn had recently sought employment for her thirteen-year-old daughter under the law, then in effect, permitting employment of children of that age whose mothers were widows. By 1914, however, South Carolina had several factory inspectors and an administrative bureaucracy committed to the exclusion of underage children from the mills. In pursuing that goal, the inspectors had successfully prosecuted a few mill owners and managers and many parents, and mill officials had become wary of employing children of questionable age. The mills sometimes refused to employ undersized children even after their parents secured the necessary permits. Mrs. Vaughn's daughter had been denied employment for that reason, though other underage children were, according to Mrs. Vaughn, permitted to work. "There are children workin in all the Mills that are not a bit over 9 years old," she wrote the governor, "& as I told you I am a widow & my little girl is 13 years old & they will not let her work at all[.] [S]he has a permit too but they say she is too Small[.] [I]t is awful to go in the mills & see the little tots in there & awful to hear the Parents tell a lie about their ages." She continued: "The way to get them [is] to go back & count up their age yourself[.] I have no way

30. *Ibid.* (1890), 83, 82.

to make a living only by keeping howse for people & I have to take her around with me[.] I thought she could work in the mill while I kept howse & we could make a good living."[31]

Clearly Mrs. Vaughn thought nine-year-olds too young for mill work and had no objection to the state excluding them from the mills. Yet she wanted her own thirteen-year-old daughter to work despite her small size and young appearance. Like many other parents, Mrs. Vaughn felt child labor reform dealt unfairly with her, and she clearly resented what she considered an injustice.

Not all parents wanted their children to work, however, and for them the problem was not reformers but mill owners in need of workers. "They just keep at a person until they have to let them work whether they want to or not," a woman told investigators in 1907 of the owner who had recently harassed her into sending her ten-year-old son into the mill. "I don't want them to know I've got another gal [age nine]," she said. "They'd have her right in that mill, and I want her to help me [at home]." Another woman told the same investigators that she had recently had to take her sons, ages eleven and fourteen, out of school and send them to the mills for fear her husband would otherwise lose his job.[32]

Such instances were probably numerous. It was the custom in all mill communities for children to go into the mills as soon as they were old and large enough to work, usually about the age of twelve. This custom was no doubt honored in the breach at times, but agreeing to it was often a condition of mill employment. Since parents wanted and expected their children to go to work in due course, owners who insisted that young children do so despite parental objection probably acted because they were short of labor. But rules on the matter were not always rigid or rigidly enforced, and families had at least some control over when their children went to work. Some of them alternated their school-age children between mill and school, sending one to school while another worked and reversing the arrangement during the next school term, or sending a schoolchild to the mill temporarily whenever the mill was short of help. Since school terms were measured in weeks rather than months through much of the New South era, many children worked as well as attended school over the course of a year.

There might have been other dimensions to the complaints of mothers forced to send their children to the mills. Since the custom was for children

31. Mrs. S. J. Vaughn to Coleman L. Blease, January 5, 1914, in Coleman L. Blease Papers, South Carolina State Archives.
32. *Senate Documents*, 61st Cong., 2nd Sess., No. 645, Vol. 1, p. 209.

to go into the mills about the age of twelve, officials inquiring about individual children might have been, in their own minds at least, simply reminding parents of that custom. The line between suggestion and threat could have been a fine one, and one owners and parents perceived differently. In addition, it was clearly false economy for an owner short of workers to dismiss an entire family over the employment of a ten- or twelve-year-old child, and mill folk no doubt understood that fact. Thus the complaint that owners "just keep at a person" indicates that parents did resist the owners' importunings at least for a time.

The claim that many mill folk opposed child-labor legislation and the exclusion of children from the mills is supported by the petitions thousands of them signed opposing such legislation in the early twentieth century and by their widespread violation of the laws once the legislatures acted.[33] Mill workers were not simply victims. One may apply to them the conventional rule of historical study which holds that what groups of people say and do over periods of time can be taken as evidence of what they believe and desire. Historians have never before taken at face value the fact that thousands of mill workers signed petitions opposing child-labor legislation. The apparent reason for their attitude is the surmise that such petitions were so self-evidently contrary to the interest of the signers that they must have been products of coercion. That is, mill owners, who also opposed the legislation, must have used their power to force employees into signing petitions the signers misunderstood or were helpless to resist. The opportunity for coercion was, of course, present, and perhaps some mill folk signed the petitions from fear of actual or perceived reprisals. Those who originated the petitions, which came from mill districts across South Carolina, are unknown, though it is likely that they began with management (just as another, much smaller set of petitions supporting child-labor laws probably began with union or would-be union groups). Certainly the cooperation or acquiescence of management is implied by the large number of petitions submitted over the years to legislators.

The potential for coercion in the petition campaign seems less important than the fact that petitions against child-labor legislation expressed the views of most mill folk on the subject. That those views coincided with the interests of mill owners should not obscure the reality that the signers agreed with what their signatures (or marks) endorsed. The signing was a

33. According to one count, 4,864 operatives signed petitions to the South Carolina legislature in 1901 protesting child-labor legislation, and 1,230 signed petitions favoring such legislation (*ibid.*, Vol. 6, p. 153).

deliberate choice just as refusing to sign these statements and signing petitions supporting the legislation were deliberate choices of other folk. The
number of signers was too small to signify the use of systematic intimidation. Surely if the coercive power of mill owners was as great as critics of the
petitions said, more workers would have been obliged to sign.

The petitions incorporated the objections mill folk had to child-labor
laws.[34] In South Carolina, where the petition campaign was most extensive
and successful, a group of Glendale operatives asked legislators in 1901
"that no law be passed interfering with" cotton manufacturing and that the
petitioners as mill workers "be permitted, as others are, to make our own
contracts, control our own families, and pursue our chosen calling as we
consider best for our interest." Another group, from McColl, had other
reasons for opposing legislation. "To pass a law prohibiting the Mills of this
State to employ children under twelve years of age would be a great hardship to us," they petitioned. "The work engaged in by children [in the mills]
is of a character that they can easily do, and it aids a number of widows and
crippled parents to make an honest living."[35]

The point that child labor was essential to the livelihood of many families
was especially appealing to legislators. Reformers dismissed it as a rationalization of the selfish interests of parents and owners alike, but the
composition of mill families gave it considerable validity. It is appropriate to
take the petition of forty-one widows from Pelzer Mills at face value. "We
found we could not make a living on the farm," the widows told legislators,
"and of necessity came to the mill, where we are contented and our children
have many benefits that they did not have on the farm. Our lot in life is hard
enough as it is and we beseech you to let us alone."[36]

These petitions were made before South Carolina lawmakers had passed
any legislation on child labor, and the petitions might have had some influence in delaying legislation for several years and in shaping the substance of
early laws. New South legislators generally opposed "paternal" legislation,
as they called laws that intruded the state into the lives of white citizens.
This was one reason southern reformers had difficulty getting their proposals enacted. But reformers were resourceful, determined people, and
legislators gradually succumbed to the pressures they generated. The early
child-labor laws, however, were written in ways that enabled mill folk (and

34. For examples of the petitions, see *South Carolina House Journal, 1901*, 127–57, 184–
201, 231–35, 276, 347, 387, 418, 437.
35. *Ibid.*, 129, 231.
36. *Ibid.*, 233.

their employers, too) to sidestep them. No doubt mill owners were largely responsible for the ineffective laws, but the coincidence of views among owners and operatives must have made watered-down, unenforceable legislation attractive to legislators buffeted by conflicting pressures.

Reformers, however, were not placated by such legislation, and year after year they returned to the legislatures, pressing relentlessly for stringent laws. Mill folk continued to oppose their efforts. "We believe our children will be better off in the mill than loafing the streets and at present the schools have not room for more," a group of Inman Cotton Mills operatives petitioned in 1913 while the South Carolina legislature debated proposals to raise the legal age of mill employment from twelve to fourteen. "To further extend the age limit now will force many of us to go back to the farms where we do not live as well as we do here." Another group, from Piedmont, told legislators the same year, "We do not think that we should be forced to keep our children out of the mills until fourteen years old when other citizens are permitted to work their children on farms at any age."[37]

Such ideas seemed axiomatic to mill folk. "We have children working in cotton mills, do not regard the work as at all detrimental to them, and think, as parents who are alone responsible for their well being, that we have a right to a say-so in the matter," a group of workers at Lancaster Cotton Mill declared. "We do not regard it as any greater hardship on our children to work in factories than on farms or at other employment. We regard employment as a benefit both to the children and the family. . . . We do not want to be over-legislated. . . . No doubt agitators have the welfare of humanity at heart, but in our opinion are over-zealous. We, at least, claim the right to a say-so in the matter as to how our children shall be occupied, as their support, control and advancement does not rest on the State of South Carolina, but on us as parents."[38]

"THE HANDS THEMSELVES, NOT THE MILLS ARE CHIEFLY RESPONSIBLE."

Mill parents violated child-labor laws whenever and however they could. Their violations were abetted by management, which engaged in open and widespread collusion with them to continue employing underage children. Thus, labor investigators in 1907 and 1908 reported that recently enacted laws were "openly and freely violated in every State" and in most of the

37. *South Carolina House Journal*, 1913, 236, 387.
38. *Ibid.*, 387.

mills they visited in the South. In 97 of 126 mills in Georgia and the Carolinas, for example, they found "clear and indisputable proof of violations" and counted 673 children illegally employed. Other sources confirm this picture. Charles W. Stiles estimated in 1911 that 2 to 5 percent of the employees in the mills he visited were less than twelve years old. Child-labor reformers were reliable authorities on this point. They regularly visited mills across the South and not only found underage children at work almost everywhere but dramatized that fact by including in their exposés large numbers of compelling photographs of such children.[39]

Mill folk circumvented the law in many ways. The most important circumvention grew from a traditional feature of mill employment, the helper system, by which small children were introduced to mill work. "In a number of cases I have found children 4 or 5 years old playing on the spinning room or spool room floor," Stiles wrote in 1911. "The children's mothers were at work, and they brought their children with them for the simple reason that they saw no other place open to them." President Orr of Piedmont Mills said similarly in 1901: "Work in our mills is largely by families and not individuals. [Some] parents take their children in the mill to have them under their eyes, others to keep them off the streets and the chances of bad company, others from dire necessity to secure their share of the family living." Still other small children came to the mills on their own because they found the mills fascinating places and wanted to learn the work or help out a parent or older sibling.[40]

These small children rarely appeared on the payrolls, and neither their parents nor the mills considered them employees. They were "helpers"—a category that seemed an ideal device for evading the new laws against child labor. Children would remain in the mills; but as helpers rather than employees, their status might be legally obscured.

This system rationalized most of the employment of underage children after child-labor laws were enacted. The "so-called helpers ordinarily are in fact regular employees," labor investigators in 1907 and 1908 reported; and there is little reason to doubt the correctness of their report. Nor is there reason to doubt that mill folk had a large hand in perpetuating the system. Stiles was probably correct when he wrote in 1911 that the helper system

39. *Senate Documents*, 61st Cong., 2nd Sess., No. 645, Vol. 1, p. 171; Charles W. Stiles, "The Influence of Hookworm Disease upon the Apparent Age of Children in the Cotton Mills," *Southern Medical Journal*, IV (1911), 326; McKelway, "Child Labor in Georgia," 53–97.
40. Stiles, "The Influence of Hookworm Disease upon the Apparent Age of Children," 327.

was not only "an invasion [evasion] of the law" but one "for which the hands themselves, [and] not the mills were chiefly responsible."[41]

This situation existed because parents desired or needed the earnings of their children or, for some other reason, wanted their children in the mills. And to the degree those preferences are legitimate, removing the children from the mills, as the new laws required, was debatable social policy. "For the mills to prohibit [working] mothers from bringing [their] young children into the mills," Stiles wrote on one aspect of the issue, "would mean increasing a widow's difficulty in her efforts for self-support. . . . Is it charity to forbid her from taking her child to the mill? Or is it greater charity on the part of the mill to permit her to bring her child with her?" The circumstances that prompted these questions were real. "It is a pity for children of tender years to be compelled to do physical labor of any kind," James L. Orr remarked on other aspects of that reality, "but they must be fed and clothed, and if their parents are unable to provide for them they must work, and there is no employment where a child, from ten to twelve, can make as much for their labor as in a cotton mill."[42]

Orr could have helped matters in his own mills by paying his workers more and thus removing the chief cause of the condition he deplored. But to suggest a pay increase as a solution to the problem of mill folk is to deal in fantasy, not social analysis. When the helper system came under the pressure of mounting criticism, parents turned to other strategies to evade the law and keep their children at work. Chief among these was the extensive use of the exemption provisions of the child-labor laws. Because of the distinctive composition of mill families, the exemptions permitted large numbers of underage children to continue working, and that fact provided a cover for parents of children who were not exempted or whose standing under the law was uncertain. The latter category included children whose age was unrecorded and unknown, and those who because of disease or debility looked so much younger than they actually were that their right to work was questionable.

Both of these groups were large. None of the three states required birth registration, and probably most mill families had no record of the births of their children, not even entries in a family Bible, which was the most common way of recording vital events. Birth dates were thus forgotten or

41. *Senate Documents*, 61st Cong., 2nd Sess., No. 645, Vol. 1, p. 189; Stiles, "The Influence of Hookworm Disease upon the Apparent Age of Children," 327.
42. Stiles, "The Influence of Hookworm Disease upon the Apparent Age of Children," 327; *South Carolina House Journal, 1901*, 179–81.

remembered imprecisely by illiterate folk. "One of the noticeable results of illiteracy was the inability of some mothers to give their exact age," investigators from the Children's Bureau of the Department of Labor found in a study of maternity and infant care in a north Georgia county in 1918. " 'In our family we never had our ages put down,' stated one mother who did not know how old she was. Another who hesitated in giving the dates of birth and death of her baby said: 'I can't read to keep up with the days on the calendar.' "[43] Under the early child-labor laws, children of uncertain age and those entitled to exemption could work if their parents or guardians signed affidavits attesting to their age or to circumstances that made their employment legal. This procedure placed most of the responsibility for violating the law on parents or guardians who swore falsely rather than on mill owners who employed underage children. The affidavits, which were kept on file in the mills, provided legal protection for owners who went to the trouble of gathering them.[44]

Many parents did swear falsely, and many children (and employers) supported or acquiesced in the perjury. "The average child in a cotton mill family seems anxious for the time to come when he can go with the older children to the mill," noted Stiles. And to do so, "Many of them will practice deception in regard to their ages." Stiles thought it "sometimes amusing to see what a large number of children are *just above the legal age* for mill work."[45]

The amusement was justified. "Doubtless parents frequently deceive mill officials concerning the age of their children," labor investigators concluded, though "the attitude of . . . mill officials was often such as to encourage misrepresentation." This suggests an ironic effect of child-labor legislation. The mutual effort to sidestep the law joined mill folk and their employers in still another alliance—a conspiracy to violate the law and keep children at work. Evidence that the conspiracy was pervasive is extensive and convincing. In 1907 in a single South Carolina mill, for example, investigators found 60 children with work permits on file in the mill office attesting that their fathers were "totally disabled," but the fathers of 22 of the children were at work in the same mill. Altogether, in the 1,567 families these investigators studied in detail, a quarter (24.6 percent) of the children

43. U.S. Department of Labor, Children's Bureau, *Publication No. 120: Maternity and Infant Care in a Mountain County in Georgia* (1923), 24.
44. For copies of such affidavits, see File 601, Graniteville Manufacturing Company Papers, University of South Carolina at Aiken Library.
45. Stiles, "The Influence of Hookworm Disease upon the Apparent Age of Children," 327.

under twelve were at work either as payroll employees or as unlisted full- or part-time helpers, including 1 in every 12 (8.2 percent) of those between six and nine years of age.[46]

When the states finally appointed mill inspectors and undertook to enforce the laws, large numbers of children were forced to quit work. In 1909, for example, the first year of systematic enforcement in South Carolina, inspectors found 231 underage children at work and ordered them dismissed, even though managers and parents tried to keep such children away from work when "it was known that the mill would be inspected." Two years later, when the legislature placed an absolute ban on employment of children under twelve, another 410 children were ordered dismissed. The ban provoked another effort to evade the law. Parents inundated the state labor commissioner with "an avalanche of applications" for reinstatement of the dismissed children on grounds they had previously misreported their ages. "Many parents discovered that they had made 'mistakes' " in earlier statements of their children's ages, the commissioner reported. But in an instructive encounter with the growing enforcement machinery, the parents learned that their previous statements were still on file in the commissioner's office, and their requests were summarily denied.[47]

As this incident suggests, mill parents were no match for an aggressive, resourceful bureaucracy, especially one unhampered by legal niceties or even ordinary decencies. "I found a child, Velma Holt, working in that mill under sworn statement of age, showing her to be about twelve years of age," a South Carolina inspector wrote from one of the Pacolet mills in 1914. "Upon questioning both child and mother [no doubt without informing them of the purpose of the questioning] they both admitted that the child was under twelve years of age. After the noon hour I went to the child's house to see the family Bible record, which I found they had. Upon looking at this record I found that there had been an attempt to change the date of the child's birth. The mother then claimed the child to be over twelve years of age." The inspector continued: "Upon looking at this record through a magnifying glass it was seen by the old writing that the child was under twelve years of age. A warrant was sworn out for the parent, who pleaded guilty, and [she] was fined ten dollars."[48]

46. *Senate Documents*, 61st Cong., 2nd Sess., No. 645, Vol. 1, pp. 208, 213, 237.

47. South Carolina Commissioner of Agriculture, Commerce and Industries, Labor Division, *First Annual Report, 1909*, 15–16, and *Fifth Annual Report, 1913*, 47.

48. South Carolina Commissioner of Agriculture, Commerce and Industries, Labor Division, *Sixth Annual Report*, 1914, 40.

Similarly, Marshall and Lila Raley were working at Lancaster Cotton Mill "under sworn statements of age, showing that both were over twelve years of age." Believing the statements to be false, the investigator looked into the family situation of the children and found the parents were separated. Since the mother had sworn that the children were twelve, the investigator "secured affidavit from the father that these children were below twelve years of age." He believed the father rather than the mother despite the obvious potential for malice in the estranged man's statement and, with affidavit in hand, "swore out warrants against the mother who had put [the] children to work and she was convicted of violation of child labor laws, and fined ten dollars."[49]

OF BUREAUCRACIES, REFORMERS, AND THE MODERN STATE

Incidents of this type show what happened to mill folk as they began to encounter the modern state. Except for the "law"—the sheriff or constable and perhaps a revenue agent—mill folk had never had much dealing with government and its representatives. Before the first decade of the twentieth century, what governments did was of little concern to them, for it benefited them not at all, and they had no experience with political organization or policy formulation and administration. Their method for coping with difficulties was to attach themselves to paternalist landowners or employers or to flee from unpleasant situations by moving from farm to farm or mill to mill. Such devices worked in that they afforded a sense of security or relieved an immediate source of irritation. But against the new adversaries—bureaucracies, reformers, and other representatives of the modern state—such devices were ineffectual.

Whatever one thinks of the merits of the changes these adversaries sought, all of them represented cultural assault to mill folk. Folk saw reformers in a way reformers never saw themselves—as arrogant agents of oppressive elites, a bevy of outsiders as contemptuous of mill folk as their nostrums were threatening or harmful. "It may be that the factory is a better place than the home," Chancellor James H. Kirkland of Vanderbilt University said of the impact of child labor on children whose family life he disapproved of, "but it is never better than the school; and it is just where parental obligation has failed, just where the home has disappeared from

49. *Ibid.*, 41. For other examples of such cases see *ibid.*, 39–43, *Eighth Annual Report, 1916,* 52–53.

the life of the child, that the school must step in as another home and the teacher must take the place of the parent who has deserted his charge." Such parents could not be trusted to bring up their children properly, and could not therefore be permitted to decide when or if their children should quit school and go to work. Permission to work must not be granted "on the unsupported affidavits of parents, who may be unscrupulous in their desire to gain from the child's labor," Kirkland continued, "but the responsibility should be placed in the hands of men and women who are interested in the child and its education."[50]

Mill folk were no match for Chancellor Kirkland and his kind. The reformers had too many advantages, too much familiarity with the workings of modern institutions, too much access to levers of power, influence, and organized self-righteousness, too great facility in arousing public prejudices against mill folk and their ways. In resisting the reformers, mill folk had no choice but to turn once more to their employers, who in their own fight against child-labor legislation showed far more respect for the cultural forms and social conventions—and wishes—of mill folk than did reformers. Given the limited choice between what their employers and the reformers offered concerning child labor, mill folk chose the former.

One easy way to understand why they did so is to consider the case of eleven-year-old Wade Hayes and his mother and their encounter with Charles L. Coon, who was superintendent of schools in Wilson, North Carolina, as well as secretary of the North Carolina Child Labor Committee. In the 1910–1911 school year, Wade dropped out of Coon's school and went to work in a nearby cotton mill. Coon found out and had the child dismissed from his job, for North Carolina law prohibited mill employment for all children under twelve. The Hayes family then moved to Goldsboro, where Wade again went to work, but soon thereafter, for unknown reasons, returned to the Wilson mill, where Coon again had Wade dismissed from his job.

Just why young Hayes quit school and went to work is unclear. Perhaps he disliked school or felt it a waste of his time, for at eleven he was still in the first grade. More likely, his family needed his earnings. About a year earlier, Wade's father had died and his two oldest brothers had married and moved on their own, leaving his widowed mother with six children still at home. The three oldest of those children worked in the mill, and their earnings

50. James H. Kirkland, "The School as a Force Arrayed Against Child Labor," *Annals*, XXV (May 1905), 145, 147.

were probably the family's entire income, for Mrs. Hayes, with three children under twelve years of age, was not employed outside the home. Because of the recent loss of the earnings of the father and the two oldest sons, the family income had no doubt dropped significantly, which might explain why Mrs. Hayes put Wade, the oldest child not yet at work, in the mill. Given her family circumstance, she probably thought Wade's employment was a necessary, sensible way of dealing with an immediate problem.[51]

The experience of Wade and his mother was instructive. Whether Coon's relentless effort to remove Wade from the mill and place him in the classroom was simply a schoolman's effort to use child-labor reform to enlarge his own constituency is unknown. But his pursuit of the boy illustrates how child-labor reform could become a weapon in the hands of a zealous reformer and why mill folk often saw themselves as victims of that weapon.

51. The story is taken from Charles Piehl, "White Society in the Black Belt, 1870–1920" (Ph.D. dissertation, Washington University, 1979), 108–10.

PART V

CLASS THEMES

18
RESISTANCE

The folk brought no sense of group identity to the mills, and conditions there discouraged development of class consciousness and labor organization. Economic dependence and the disorienting effects of social change increased the attractions of paternalism and traditional ways, and undermined the efforts of those who would organize workers into cadres of self-conscious proletarians. To most folk, union organizers, like reformers and educationists, were threatening and alienating, for the things they advocated risked one's job. If unionization was to be successful, these attitudes would have to be changed. Mill folk would have to forsake traditional ways for those of modern economic men.

For cultural reasons deeply implanted, most folk found the prospect of surrendering traditional ways unattractive or impossible, and that was one reason union organizers had limited success among them. What unions represented and tried to accomplish in the lives of mill folk is poorly understood. The assumptions that inform most accounts of the encounter between unions and mill folk do not conform to what labor organizations actually were in the New South. Moreover, those accounts approach unions, strikes, and related subjects from the perspectives of labor activists and therefore perceive incorrectly the imperatives—and role—of mill folk in the matters of labor activism.

Implicitly or explicitly, there runs through much of the literature on unions and mill folk an interpretation of human behavior that is alien to what mill folk were and wanted. According to that interpretation, people are largely defined by the work they do, and in their work, they are chiefly concerned with bettering their economic condition. Because betterment depends on higher wages and other economic improvements, the relationship between employees and employers is inherently adversarial. When it is also exploitive, as was the relationship between mill workers and mill owners, workers view their situation rationally and act accordingly. That is, they develop a sense of grievance and class consciousness, organize themselves, and challenge their employers for higher wages, shorter hours, and greater control of the workplace.

Moreover, the interpretation continues, their effort will be effective unless employers and other agents of power (the law, the courts, the police, political and economic elites) combine to crush them. Since unions and strikes among mill folk in the New South invariably failed (except when racial issues were involved), the cause of the failure must be found in the owners' ruthless use of their power. The result of that use was the victimization of mill folk. "Management's economic, political, and social power simply overwhelmed the organized operatives and cowed those who sympathized with them," one scholar was written. "Shackled by ignorance, poverty, and racial prejudice and faced with laissez-faire dogma as rigid as any slave code, the operatives were no match for the aristocracy of the New South."[1]

"I HAVE NEVER BEEN INSIDE A COTTON MILL."

Labor activism is part of the larger subject of resistance, which encompasses the continuum of widely varying activities through which mill folk protested and resisted things that bothered them. The range of these activities was much broader than strikes and other forms of labor militance. Indeed, militant endeavors were to mill folk what conspiracies and uprisings had been to slaves in the Old South—exceptional, even extreme, acts in which relatively few people engaged.

The literature on slave resistance is helpful in understanding this point. "To equate resistance with violence," anthropologist Sidney W. Mintz has

---

1. Melton A. McLaurin, *Paternalism and Protest: Southern Cotton Mill Workers and Organized Labor, 1875–1905* (Westport, Conn., 1971), xvii, xviii.

written of slaves in the New World, "is to impose on slave consciousness a rigidity and unresourcefulness that misrepresents both the nature of the institution of slavery and the capacities of the slaves themselves." Much more important then violence, Mintz suggests, were the multiple ways slaves resisted the daily impositions of slavery and withstood its emasculating pressures. Thus defined, slave resistance ranged from "immediate, open and unplanned violence by newly-arrived Africans to the myriad techniques of covert resistance, some employed by individuals and others by organized groups." Historians of resistance, Mintz insists, should not limit themselves to acts of violence and confrontation. They should instead "ask of the historical record how the slaves resisted" their condition, and they "should be neither surprised nor disappointed in the discovery that considerable resistance involved as its precondition some process of cultural change, of adaptation on the part of the slaves themselves." They must also remember "that the slaves, like all human beings everywhere, were beset by all of the ordinary demands of living—to sleep, to love, to eat, to understand and to explain, [and] to survive."[2]

Despite the vast differences between the circumstances of mill folk and those of slaves, Mintz's remarks illuminate the matter of resistance among the folk. They suggest that resistance, an important facet of mill experience, centered in unspectacular matters of day-to-day resentment and protest rather than in dramatic episodes of labor militance. Among the components of this protest were the behavior and attitudes mill folk used to maintain traditional ways and resist efforts to make them disciplined workers and citizens. They included frequent absence from work and movement from mill to mill, the bothersomeness and indiscipline of which mill officials complained, and the determined refusal to honor the values of the work ethic. Resistance, in other words, was rooted in traditional rather than modern ways.

For years, historians and social scientists have been studying the impact on workers of the transition from traditional to modern society and from preindustrial to industrial work. Their studies not only document the controlling role of culture in that transition but offer insight into the processes by which traditional ways have changed and persisted in the new environment.[3] Two historians, Alan Dawley and Paul Faler, have developed an

2. Sidney W. Mintz, "Toward an Afro-American History," *Journal of World History*, XIII (1971), 321–22.

3. See, for example, Herbert G. Gutman, *Work, Culture, and Society in Industrializing America: Essays in Working Class and Social History* (New York, 1976); Daniel Walkowitz,

explanatory model that is especially helpful in understanding those processes among mill folk in the New South. The Industrial Revolution, Dawley and Faler wrote, "gave birth to a new person among the laboring classes of Europe and America, one who put his/her own needs ahead of the demands of kin and community, who acknowledged no master but the self, and who located the virtues of self-control, self-denial, and self-improvement at the center of the moral universe." This "new person" abandoned tradition in favor of modern ways—ways that encouraged material and other kinds of success in industrial, capitalist society.

The transition this evolving perspective demanded of workers was difficult. "This new individualism fomented a fundamental challenge to customary ways of living," wrote Dawley and Faler. "It divided people along cultural lines between the traditionally minded, who clung to old values and beliefs, and the modern minded, who adopted the new personality." Success in the new order "demanded industry (labor aimed at self-improvement), frugality (economic self-sacrifice) and temperance (sensual self-denial)." Many workers, however, "clung to preindustrial values," refusing "to give up their casual attitudes toward work, their pursuit of happiness in gaming and drinking," and their attachment to other things that impeded economic success. They "still deferred to the silk vest"—honored paternalistic values—and to modern-minded people, they appeared hopelessly backward.[4]

This "cleavage within the working class" manifested itself in the labor history of mill folk. Most folk remained traditionalists. Some, however, became "modernists" or made varying degrees of movement toward modernism. To the latter, unions and labor activism were appealing. The efforts of organizers, themselves "modernists," to spread unionism among mill folk are therefore best understood as attempts to transform traditional folk into a modern, self-conscious working class.

A cultural chasm separated most folk from union activists. Unions were organizations to join, and their leaders were outsiders who had little understanding of mill folk and their ways. Moreover, the effectiveness of unions depended on paying dues for abstract or threatening purposes. It also

---

Worker City, Company Town: Iron and Cotton Worker Protest in Troy and Cohoes, New York, 1855–1884 (Urbana, 1978); Alan Dawley, *Class and Community: The Industrial Revolution in Lynn* (Cambridge, Mass., 1976); and Tamara Hareven and Randolph Langenbach, *Amoskeag: Life and Work in an American Factory-City* (New York, 1978).

4. Alan Dawley and Paul Faler, "Working-Class Culture and Politics in the Industrial Revolution: Sources of Loyalism and Rebellion," *Journal of Social History*, IX (1976), 466–68.

required individuals to subordinate themselves and their right to work to a group and its collective interest, at great risk and with no assurance of success.

Leaders of organized labor compounded these drawbacks by following their own interests rather than those of mill folk. That is, labor leaders in Georgia and the Carolinas supported many policies that mill folk opposed and would have been harmed by, at least in the short run, and many other practices that promised folk little or no advantage. This was not sinister, or even surprising. Unions in the New South were largely organizations of skilled workers—railway engineers, printers, machinists, and the like—and they served the interests of those who dominated them. The Knights of Labor, which appeared briefly in the 1880s, gave more attention to the situation of mill operatives than most unions, but its practice of enrolling workers of all occupations in integrated locals had the effect of subordinating mill workers to others with more experience in labor organization.

Near the turn of the twentieth century, union groups in Georgia and the Carolinas federated themselves into state and local organizations, which constituted the core of the labor movement in these states. In North Carolina, these federations and their leaders "tended to be extremely conservative," in the words of one historian, and had "relatively little interest in questions of social policy." For years, their chief concerns were child-labor laws (which most mill folk opposed) and state examinations for entry into skilled crafts (which would have made it more difficult for unskilled workers to move into those crafts). In Georgia, leaders of the labor movement "appear to have been of very conservative temperament," another scholar concluded. In politics they were regular Democrats and on racial matters "ku klux klannish." With these views, labor leaders "maintained economic and social respectability."[5]

The organizations were products of their time and place and of the men who controlled them. They were thus southern in their interest and outlook, and class-conscious only in the sense that skilled craftsmen sought to use unions to guard their interests. Not surprisingly, many of their activities were detrimental to working-class solidarity. The unions tried to enforce conventional morality among their members, for example; tried to use apprenticeship programs to protect the places and prerogatives of their members against other workers; used white supremacy and segregation

5. Harry M. Douty, "The North Carolina Industrial Worker, 1880–1930" (Ph.D. dissertation, University of North Carolina, 1936), 287; Mercer G. Evans, "The History of the Organized Labor Movement in Georgia" (Ph.D. dissertation, University of Chicago, 1929), 215.

laws against black workers; and were nativist on matters concerning immigration and immigrant workers and chauvinist during such events as the Spanish-American War.

The unions were poorly equipped to look sensitively upon the concerns and wishes of mill folk. Their organizational structure, by craft rather than industry, was ill suited to unify mill workers. When the National Union of Textile Workers sent organizers into the South in the 1890s, for example, they set about organizing mill workers along job lines. Thus at Augusta at the turn of the century there were at least seven separate unions among mill workers. There was a union of men weavers, another of women weavers, and still another of weavers and helpers, as well as one of carders, spinners, and spoolers, one of carders and spinners, and one of loom fixers, too, all of them affiliates of the Augusta Central Federation of Textile Workers and, in turn, of the Augusta Federation of Trades.

This structure was more limiting than might appear. One of the problems of labor activists was their inability to motivate workers in individual mills to unite and remain united for common purposes. Almost invariably, workers divided during strikes or other activity, some walking off the job, for example, while others remained at work. This undermined the efforts of activists, which were usually abortive. One reason for the failure of activists' efforts was that mill workers did not think in collective terms or recognize a common interest with other workers. Mill owners used this tendency to advantage. They often made wage adjustments in piecemeal fashion—for example, lowering or raising piece rates for weavers or carders on one occasion, and doing likewise for loom fixers or spinners on another. Reducing wages in this way had the advantage for owners of discouraging protest throughout the mill. Spinners, for example, were unlikely to resist a reduction in pay for loom fixers, in part because their own pay was unaffected and in part, too, because loom fixers made much more money than spinners. If the loom fixers acted collectively to protest a pay cut and enough walked out to shut down the mill, spinners, who would lose their wages from the shutdown, might look unfavorably on the loom fixers' action. If the strike were long, their disfavor might turn to resentment, because even if the strike was eventually successful only loom fixers would benefit. The organization of workers by job categories rather than by factories might have facilitated this divisiveness.

The gulf between organized labor and mill folk was also evident in platforms adopted by labor groups in the three states. Delegates to the organizing convention of the Georgia Federation of Labor in 1899, for example, adopted resolutions endorsing child-labor laws and compulsory education, both of which mill folk opposed. The delegates also endorsed the eight-hour day, which if made mandatory would have caused substantial pay cuts for mill workers, most of whom were paid by the piece. The delegates wanted, too, a state labor bureau and factory inspector, whose duties would include the enforcement of laws mill folk found intrusive and objectionable. Other resolutions adopted at the convention would, if made law, positively affect skilled workers, but not mill folk, among them the branding of products made by convict labor, requiring the state government to contract for printing with union printers only, and compelling streetcar companies to place vestibules on their cars. The delegates also wanted employers to "pay the same wages to women doing the same work as men"—an ideal more nearly realized in cotton mills than in any other area of employment.[6]

This was hardly a platform mill folk would rally around. Nor was the one adopted the following year. In 1900 the convention of the Georgia Federation of Labor endorsed a mixture of Progressive, socialist, and other reform measures, among them initiative and referendum, and public ownership of banks and utilities. It also endorsed the eight-hour day, weekly wage payments, equal pay for women, prohibition of child labor under sixteen, compulsory education, and "payment of wages in lawful money and abolition of truck pay."[7]

As these platforms suggest, labor leaders had little understanding of labor issues that mattered to mill folk. When the Industrial Commission held hearings in Atlanta in the spring of 1900, the men who testified on behalf of labor were leaders or affiliates of the Georgia Federation of Labor. They spoke often of mill workers, but only as victims of callous employers. "I have never been inside a cotton mill in Atlanta," H. F. Garrett, a machinist employed by the Western and Atlantic Railroad and president of the Georgia labor organization, told the commission. Yet by his own testimony, Garrett knew more about mill conditions in Atlanta than about those anywhere else. Those conditions, he said, were "bad; awfully bad," both in the workplace and in the housing workers were forced to rent from the mills. Garrett was especially concerned that workers were "discharged immediately" for joining a union and that so many young children worked in the mills. But in numerous instances, he said, idle, whiskey-drinking fathers were more responsible for child labor than were the mills. "They go down

6. Atlanta *Constitution*, April 29, 1899.
7. *Ibid.*, April 21, 1900.

when the children get paid and get the money," Garrett told the commissioners, "and buy the children something and the balance goes for whisky."[8]

C. C. Houston, editor of the *Journal of Labor*, the organ of the Georgia Federation of Labor, was concerned about the housing of mill workers in Atlanta and Augusta. In Atlanta, he said, Fulton Bag and Cotton Mills charged "exorbitant rent and [took] it out of the wages." The mill company also advanced travel expenses for workers to move to Atlanta and deducted those costs from their wages, and workers often received little or no pay on payday. Houston was also upset that there were so many children in the mills and with the general condition of mill workers. "I have never found any that were satisfied with their lot," he said of the workers.[9]

Such views help explain why union organizers had difficulty reaching mill workers. "I have been working hard to get a Textile Workers union here for the last three months," J. C. Hudson, an AFL organizer reported from Rock Hill in 1901, "but it is rather slow, because it takes a good deal of time to get the Southern working people interested and impress upon them the necessity of organizing and keeping up the union in good shape."[10]

The problem, a labor newspaper said of mill workers in Alabama in 1902, was that workers fresh from the farm were backward and were easy prey to unscrupulous employers. "It has been charged, and rightfully," a writer in the *Labor Advocate* reported, "that the employes were ignorant and unskilled. A majority were recruited from the cotton fields by tempting promises . . . and the glamor of community life, and a lack of knowledge as to their fate" after they arrived at the mills. "They are first robbed of all independence, planted in company houses, often fed from company stores and worked at the company's will. The result is that the spirit of organization has hard ground to work over." Not even "Mother" Mary Jones had been able to reach them. A few years previously, the fabled Mrs. Jones had gone to Avondale Mills in Birmingham and worked as a weaver "trying to lay ground plans for an organization." She had failed, however, and given up the effort. "The time was not ripe," the *Labor Advocate*'s writer said ruefully.[11]

8. *House Documents*, 57th Cong., 1st Sess., No. 184, Vol. 7, pp. 542–49.
9. *Ibid.*, 549–55.
10. *American Federationist*, VIII (1901), 377.
11. *Labor Advocate* (Birmingham), February 22, 1903. For a more recent instance of the failure of union spokesmen to understand and appreciate the culture and values of mill folk, see Solomon Barkin, "The Personality Profile of Southern Textile Workers," *Labor Law Journal*, XI (1960), 457–72.

"I DONT APPRECIATE NO MAN . . . CALLING ME 'SCABS' AND ESPECIALLY A
'SON OF A BITCH,' BECAUSE I CONSIDER MY MOTHER DECENT."

The difficulty unionists had with mill folk was part of a larger problem. Most, perhaps even a large majority, of the workers in the New South were indifferent or opposed to unions. Union spokesmen accounted for these attitudes by the oppressiveness of employers who tried to keep organizers away from their workers, and by the fear workers had of losing their jobs if they joined a union. In the case of mill workers, these were factors of importance. "We are in Trouble here," T. S. Bowers, who was head of a Knights of Labor assembly at Pelzer, wrote Terence V. Powderly, national leader of the organization, in 1886. "We have organized a assembly of Knights of labor[.] [T]he Mill Managers is doing every thing in their power to Suppress it [.] [T]hey are discharging every one as fast as they can get his name[.] I cant See how they get our names but they do doit[.] [T]hey discharged one the Second day I was elected Master Workman of this assembly and they have found out my name Some how and have discharged me[.] I dont know what to do but to confer with you."[12]

Mill owners, then, were prepared to use their power. All of them—there is no known exception—adamantly opposed organization among their workers. "Nothing but the most determined and firm stand taken and maintained by the Mill owners in that immediate locality will prevent ruin and disaster to us all," Henry P. Hammett, president of Piedmont and Camperdown mills in South Carolina, wrote an Augusta mill owner shortly after a Knights of Labor assembly appeared in that city. "Such a stand by the Mill owners there, firmly held, would crush the Knights beyond resurrection in two or three weeks. Any wavering will encourage them to other and larger demands, which if yielded to, will result in disaster and ruin to all the Mill interests in the Southern States and the depreciation of the value of their stock as an investment."

Hammett then advised the Augusta mills on how to crush the local branch of the organization. "All that is necessary is, that when a demonstration is made in one of the Mills," he wrote in a preview of the strike and lockout then impending there, "to suddenly and finally shut down and close them all, until the Knights starve out and beg to return to work upon any terms." When that occurred, the workers would "get tired of and lose

12. T. S. Bowers to Terence V. Powderly, October 16, 1886, in Terence V. Powderly Papers, microfilm edition, Georgia State University Library.

confidence in outside influences and be willing to return upon such terms as the Mill owners dictate." Hammett's concern went far beyond economic self-interest, though that was important to him. "If the mills cant manage their own business, in their own way," he wrote, "and according to the dictates of their best judgment without being dictated to by their help, the sooner they shut down permanently the better—for everyone who has their money invested in the property."[13]

These sentiments were virtually universal among mill owners in the South. In other places where employers were also powerful and determined, however—in midwestern coalfields and New England textile centers, for example—unions were much more successful than they were among mill folk in the New South. The opposition of employers was therefore only one of the reasons for the failure of textile unions there.

Also contributing to their failure was the unwillingness or inability of unions to respond understandingly to the concerns and values of the workers. The task of organizers was not just to offer union membership to mill workers but also to foster conditions that would make that membership attractive and efficacious. Unionists had little awareness of what that task entailed. Reading labor newspapers from the New South era, one is repeatedly reminded that unions were always fighting "apathy" among workers, which they blamed on the workers rather than on themselves. "There are women employed, who do not care to identify themselves with a labor union," the *Journal of Labor* complained in 1904; "it would bring them in too close contact with their real position in life. They are deluding themselves with the idea that labor of today with them is only temporary but as time creeps on, the falsity of their position is apparent."[14] Although that statement contains truth, there was more to the refusal of working-class women to join unions than its author allowed. For cultural and social reasons, such women deferred to men on many issues, and a lot of the women deliberately avoided so "public" an act as joining a union. Unionists who wanted to organize mill women were insensitive to their reasons for resisting organization.

This problem, in multiple variations, recurred repeatedly. Andrew Mulcay, an AFL organizer in Augusta and one of the leaders of the mill strike there in 1898 and 1899, told the Industrial Commission in 1900 that the home was the "common and natural place" for married women. "Where

13. Henry P. Hammett to N. E. McCoy, June 19, 1886, in Henry P. Hammett Papers, South Caroliniana Library.
14. *Journal of Labor* (Atlanta), November 25, 1904.

the woman is the mother of a family, and she goes into the factory," Mulcay said, "she lives an unnatural life."[15] Surely such views affected Mulcay's dealings with the large numbers of married women, widowed mothers, and female heads of households who worked in the mills of Augusta. Was his union an "unnatural" place for those women?

This failure of vision was most evident in the attitudes of union spokesmen toward workers who rejected unions, sided with employers in labor disputes, or worked as strikebreakers. If unions were to succeed in the New South, they would have to sway these workers. Yet unionists dealt with them chiefly by calling them "scabs," the ultimate epithet in their view, and otherwise denouncing them as lackeys of management and traitors to their class. Employing this strategy was the greatest weakness and biggest error of unionists in the New South, for the people unionists described as scabs were a majority of working folk in the New South. *Webster's New Collegiate Dictionary* defines *scab* variously as "one who refuses to join a labor union," a "union member who refuses to strike or returns to work before a strike has ended," a "worker who accepts employment or replaces a union worker during a strike," and "one who works for less than union wages or on non-union terms." In the broadest of these meanings, most workers in the New South were scabs.

The history of working people in that region cannot be written without treating scabs at length and with understanding. They and not unionists will be the focus of any definitive history of working people there—provided, that is, that the history of working people (as distinct from that of organized labor) should focus on what workers actually did and thought and felt.

Who were these scabs? "The non-unionist, or scab workman," the *Journal of Labor* editorialized in 1906, "has no elevating principle; no love for his fellowman; no helping hand to extend to an unfortunate and needy brother. He has no desire to see his fellowman prosper and better his condition in life; he is concerned about himself only; he is not his brother's keeper, and he cares not whether the lot of his fellowman is poverty or plenty, misery or happiness." Referring to workers who returned to work at a South Carolina mill in 1902 while others remained on strike, another labor newspaper commented: "God pity the poor devils at Vaucluse. They used to be rated as union people, but 'scabbed' at the very first opportunity. Evidently they were not made of the right kind of stuff. They were not brave enough to

15. *House Documents*, 57th Cong., 1st Sess., No. 184, Vol. 7, p. 568.

stand and fight." Rather, "Trembling in every limb, they renounced the union principles, and, getting down on their knees to their masters, they licked their hands, like puppies, and begged for work at any price." In so doing, they "sold themselves into slavery" and showed themselves "possessed of a superfluity of jackassibility." The newspaper told the strikebreakers, "Get off your knees, stop holding your hat in your hand, take your eyes from your master's feet."[16] Such criticism was hardly calculated to make the workers look kindly upon unions.

This was, of course, a difficult, vital matter for unions as well as for mill folk. Unions regularly lost strikes, including the one at Vaucluse, because workers refused to join strikers, returned to work while other strikers were still out, or came in from outside the mill's work force and took the jobs of strikers. Occasionally these acts followed a long work stoppage that spread deprivation, and starved workers had little choice but to return to work. More often, as at Eagle and Phenix Mills in July, 1900, and at Erwin Mills a month later, strikers received so little support from fellow workers that the mills remained open and their strikes collapsed.[17]

It is impossible to know the motives of individual strikebreakers—those, for example, who braved the imprecations and threats of massed strikers when the mills reopened during the strikes at Augusta in 1886 and 1898. Apparently no one interviewed the strikebreakers or wrote down their concerns. Perhaps they were desperate for work. Perhaps they had had unfortunate experiences with unions or believed workers were better off without organization. Or perhaps the meaning of their action for striking workers was unclear to them. But perhaps of foremost significance is the admonition of Sidney W. Mintz that the first concern of slaves was survival. So it was with mill folk; and individually and collectively, they were surely entitled to make their own judgment about activities they linked to so vital a concern.

In all the studies of strikes in the New South, strikebreakers as individual human beings have received little attention and less understanding. The scattered instances in which they have spoken for themselves suggest that in their own minds they had honorable, compelling motives. Those instances also suggest that the strikebreakers' actions were consonant with cultural

16. *Journal of Labor* (Atlanta), July 6, 1906; *Voice of Labor* (Augusta), quoted in *Labor Advocate* (Birmingham), May 31, 1902.

17. On the Eagle and Phenix strike, see Atlanta *Constitution*, July 10–12, 1900, and Columbus *Enquirer-Sun*, July 10–12, 1900. On Erwin Mills's strike, see Raleigh *News and Observer*, August 18–26, 1900.

values deeply planted. Except for those whose concern was sheer want, strikebreakers seem to have acted chiefly on the principle of what today is called the right to work. They refused to surrender their freedom of choice on this vital matter to someone they might not know for purposes they might not understand or support. For such people, labor solidarity was less important than other values, obligations, or imperatives.

What is known of strikebreakers who were not mill folk sheds light on this subject. Arthur D. Price returned to work in the midst of a strike against Jay Gould's southwestern railway system in 1886. "I said when I married my wife I had taken an obligation to keep my wife," Price told a meeting of strikers who demanded an explanation for his action, "and I thought that obligation was superior to any obligation I had ever taken, and I was going back to work and earn sufficient to support my wife and family; and I could not make a living by tramping." The strikers were unsatisfied with this explanation. When they undertook to throw Price out a window, he "tried to shoot some of them" but was arrested for carrying a pistol.[18]

F. Ludolph, foreman of a cleaning crew, also returned to work during the southwestern strike. His superior had told him that he would lose his job if he did not return to work. Because of that threat, Ludolph felt he had had no choice in the matter, and his consequent expulsion from the Knights of Labor, he thought, was unfair. "I have just bought me a little home and gave notes on said home to be paid in monthly installments to support my wife and three children," Ludolph wrote Powderly, protesting his dismissal. "A man is forced to work to support his family. If this strike was a just one I would suffer death rather than give up—but I know it is not just—as I know the whole beginning—and done my best to prevent [it]."[19]

Price and Ludolph do not fit the image of cringing bootlicks unionists tried to attach to strikebreakers. Their motive in returning to work was explicitly traditional—fulfilling their obligations to their families—and therefore honorable. They were not traitors to their class, for they had no class. As E. P. Thompson insisted some years ago, class is not an objective condition but something that "happens" when people develop a consciousness of common interests as against the interests of other people.[20] Mill folk would have understood that formulation. Strikebreakers and antiunionists were workers who clung to traditional values; and when labor activity forced them to choose between those and modern (union) values,

18. *House Reports*, 49th Cong., 2nd Sess, No. 4174, Pt. 3, p. 294.
19. F. Ludolph to Terence V. Powderly, April 13, 1886, in Powderly Papers.
20. E. P. Thompson, *The Making of the English Working Class* (New York, 1966), 9–10.

they opted for the former. They were, in the formulation of Alan Dawley and Paul Faler, workers who had not made the transition to modern ways.

This was strikingly revealed in the testimony of two men, Elzie Teal and his son Durward B. Teal, concerning their anti-union activity during a strike at the American Thread Company's plant in Tallapoosa, Georgia, in the late 1940s. The Teals's situation was much like that of mill folk in the New South. Both men and their wives were operatives in the thread mill, and both had farmed before going to the mill. The elder Teal still lived in the country and commuted to his job in town. He had belonged to the Brotherhood of Railway Trainmen in the late 1920s, perhaps being forced to join as a condition of employment, and the experience had hardened his antipathy to unions. "The only thing I got out of it—the only thing I done was to pay out money," he recalled years later, the memory still fresh in his mind.[21]

In the strike at their plant, the Teals actively opposed the union and its organizers, and were accused of roughing up union sympathizers, kidnapping a union organizer, and otherwise acting as company goons. The Teals's explanation of their activity shows the cultural roots of anti-union sentiment among mill folk. "I don't think so," the elder Teal answered when asked if he thought there should be labor organizations of any sort. "I think a man ought to be free—a free country. . . . If they don't like the job, they can quit; that is the way I figure. I figure I can quit my job. I farmed before it."

That statement was a striking embodiment of folk attitudes toward organizations demanding that folk subordinate themselves to a group and do things that were unfamiliar and perceived as unnecessary or undesirable. Just as they resisted the "help" of child-labor reformers and educationists, so many folk consciously declined that of union organizers. They did not want to be "helped." They wanted to do as they had always done; and to do so, they had to be left alone. Obviously Teal—and most other folk—knew as little of the purposes of unions as union spokesmen knew of the ways of folk, and the failure of communication was therefore mutual. Did Teal have "a fixed feeling" concerning unions? "If they come around interfering [with me], I have," he said. "So long as they don't interfere, I don't care what they do. . . . I like to be left alone at home and on the job and on the streets and different places." Unions did not permit that. "They come around the sidewalks, sticking papers at you, pushing you, call you scabs and different

21. The following account is taken from U.S. Senate, 81st Cong., 2nd Sess., *Hearings: Labor-Management Relations in the Southern Textile Manufacturing Industry,* August 21–24, 1950, pp. 75–134.

stuff." They also brought "strikes and fights and killings," and where they appeared, "you . . . have to come out on strikes."

Teal's position was rooted in social and cultural experience, not intellectual inquiry. "I tried to keep it off my mind all I can," he responded when asked if he had thought about unions. "I have forefathers raised without it. They got by. I figured I could get by. . . . I do not think it is necessary for labor to go ahead and work out money and give it over to [union officials] to drink and have big times on, spend and spring around on."

Because these values were deeply embedded, they passed on to Durward Teal, who at twenty-nine was the father of four children and a doffer at the thread mill, earning $1.05 a hour. "I don't appreciate no man or woman or anybody else bumping me around and calling me 'scabs' and especially a 'son of a bitch,' because I consider my mother decent," the younger Teal said, discussing his encounters with union activists outside the mill gates. "They were there, lined up on the sidewalk, pushing people, not only me but other people, I would say a good many of them pushed around, women as well, rubbing papers [that is, leaflets] in your face, calling you scabs and other vile names because you didn't join the union, and said if we didn't join it peaceably we would be forced to join it, that they would picket the fence and see that we did join it."

Union activists had challenged the Teals in ways that roused their concerns of manhood and self-respect. The "backwoods individualism" of folk, to use the phrase of one scholar, dictated that no man should have to do against his will the bidding of another. That outlook meshed nicely with the purposes of mill owners. But in following their own imperatives and rejecting unions, folk like the Teals did not embrace their employers. "I don't bother with their part of it," Elzie Teal said when asked if he sided with management in the labor dispute. What he did bother with was his own "part of it."

"I HAVE STRUGGLED LONG, HARD AND DESPERATELY AGAINST THE COCA AND BROMEDIA."

A major problem of textile unions in the New South was the dearth of responsible, experienced leaders. Many of the men who found themselves in key positions at crucial times and places in the struggle with management had little understanding of how effectively to channel the dissatisfactions of the workers they organized or of how to avoid those devastating, demoralizing defeats unions suffered in confrontations with management. Far too often for the long-range success of the union movement, organizers went into mill villages and districts, made unrealistic promises about the fruits of organization, and led workers into confrontations they had no prospect of winning. When a particular confrontation was over, the organizers departed, the union died, workers suffered, and mill folk became more disillusioned with and fearful of unions. This failure was due in part to unrealistic assessments by leaders or would-be leaders of the mill workers' situation and their ability to challenge mill owners.

Faulty assessment was one of the problems at Augusta during the prolonged strike and lockout in 1886, which is arguably the most important incident in the history of labor activism among mill folk in the New South era. Workers were led into the debacle by J. S. Meynardie, master workman of Knights of Labor Assembly 5030. Meynardie was not a mill worker but a Baptist preacher, and apparently had no experience in organized labor until he joined the Knights of Labor assembly in Augusta and, early in 1886, was elected its leader. A young, enthusiastic man untested in crisis leadership, Meynardie was apparently inspired by union theory rather than by Christian ideals. He voiced no religious sentiments in either his public or private statements during the strike. According to those statements, he earnestly believed that mill workers in Augusta could, if organized, force management to raise wages, improve working conditions, and concede some of its control over the workplace. Organization meant strength—how much strength depended on the number of workers who joined the union and the willingness of leaders to use the workers' commitment for constructive purposes.

Meynardie was prepared to do just that. "Augusta, is *so ripe* for organization, and will rot, unless organized very soon," he wrote Powderly soon after becoming head of the Augusta Knights of Labor. "I have worked hard & earnestly to awaken the people to a sense of duty; and I am happy to say, my most sanguine expectations have be[en] realized." His work had been done "quietly, peacefully, most discretely and secretely [sic]"; and he unmodestly (and no doubt wrongly) credited his work for a recent wage increase in some of the mills. "It was done by earnest & most respectful solicitation of the employes to employer," he said of the pay raise. "It was, to all appearance, granted in as good spirits as the request was made." Meynardie should have worried that the Knights of Labor had kept their existence secret and that his own identity as leader of the assembly had not yet been publicly announced. "Please do not mention my name as yet to the public," he cautioned Powderly in late February, 1886.[22]

Meynardie was not oblivious of the problems he and his organization faced. "The 'Bosses' are exceedingly tyrannical in many instances," he reported in April, after the union's existence was publicized. "Many of our members are victimized, and they can not obtain work in the city & some have already had to leave; and others about to leave. If one dare leave the mills without a pass he or she will not get work here [at any mill in Augusta] until they go back to work out two weeks notice." And even then workers might not be given a pass. The Knights of Labor, Meynardie thought, could end the pass system "by stopping the mills," but that, he told Powderly with evident seriousness, he did "not wish to do."[23]

As that comment suggests, Meynardie had little understanding of the realities of labor-management relations or of the nature and role of economic power. And he did not understand that the very victimization he complained of undermined the ability of mill workers to challenge management. "There are hard and robust men here, who work for 60 cents per day," he wrote. "Ladies some of them are working for 44 & 5 cts per day. And the least flaw found in their cloth they are made to pay for it. The people here are very poor & work hard from 6, a m. to 6,30 P.M. If one gets sick he must be supported by charity." Meynardie thought these conditions could be sources of strength for the Knights of Labor, for he, like other unionists, was certain that exploitation pulled workers toward unions, and the greater the exploitation the more avid would be their commitment to the union cause. "The mill men are under the impression that we are weak. [O]n account of our conservative course," he told Powderly. "But they are mistaken & badly too. I have labored night & day to organize this city. And my most sanguine expectations have been realized. Many visiting brethren complement us upon our government. Our members are well up on the labor questions of the day. I deliver a lecture twice a week. We are very well drilled."[24]

Events preceding the strike are not altogether clear. Perhaps his confidence encouraged Meynardie to press for confrontation despite the lack of strike funds and the policy of the national Knights of Labor organization to give no assistance to local assemblies until six months after their affiliation

22. J. S. Meynardie to Powderly, February 25, 1886, in Powderly Papers.
23. Meynardie to Powderly, April 13, 1886, in Powderly Papers.
24. *Ibid.*

was effective. "I know that we are never going to gain a single inch not an iota with out a step down and out for a while," he told Powderly on April 13. "The mill men are fully organized and have been for sometime; and they are unrelenting as can be. They say the mill hands cannot stay out any length of time as they are too poor. And they argue we can get no assistance until the expiration of six months. I know if we are to depend on our resources we can never do anything here. If we are not assisted[,] then we are not benefited by the K of L."[25]

By the time Meynardie wrote this letter, his assembly had petitioned the mills for a wage increase and changes in work rules, including abolition of the pass system, to take effect May 1. Clearly he feared the petition would be denied, with the result that the local Knights of Labor would have to strike or have their organization exposed as ineffectual, in which case it would surely disintegrate. Yet at this late date he evidently had no plan of action. "Please advise me what to do, when to do, and how to do it," he pleaded with Powderly. "I want to take no step, that I cannot maintain. I want to carry every thing judiciously, expediently & legally. If we fail to carry our point we are done. . . . Should I make a misstep and loose [sic] the battle or lose the aim of purpose involved in our petition, then we are a ruined people."[26]

Meynardie, then, did anticipate the problems that occurred. "I cannot sleep at night on account of the present situation & the one now pending," he wrote Powderly in the same letter. Yet whether he pressed for confrontation or waited on events, his organization and the mills were on a collision course. The mill owners denied the petition and refused even to meet with representatives of the Knights of Labor. Several minor disturbances in May and June reflected the growing tensions. The Knights of Labor, meanwhile, developed a strategy that, in view of their weakness and determination to press the issues of their petition, was as good a one as they could have devised.

In early July, fourteen pickers in Augusta Mill walked off the job when management refused their request for a wage increase. Their action forced the superintendent to close the mill because he could not find replacements, no doubt because of organizing work by the Knights of Labor. With one mill shut, the union was prepared to wait on management. The mill would remain closed until management recognized and negotiated with the labor

25. *Ibid.*
26. *Ibid.*

organization, and granted the pay increases and other changes it wanted. When that was accomplished at Augusta Factory, the process would be applied in turn to each of the other factories; and the success of the Knights of Labor in Augusta would carry the union triumphantly across the South. By striking one factory at a time, the union hoped to avoid the deprivations a long strike would create. Dues and contributions from members working in other mills would sustain those on strike at Augusta Factory.

The plan was theoretically sound, even brilliant. Its success, however, depended on the cooperation of the presidents of the Augusta mills and was thus doomed to failure. The presidents had an organization of their own and resources that dwarfed those of the local Knights of Labor, and they were determined not to let themselves be defeated one at a time. They soon announced that unless the pickers returned to work at Augusta Factory all other mills in the district would close until they did return. The resulting shutdown commenced in early August and lasted into November, by which time deprivation and the coming of winter forced workers to give up their struggle and go back to work. They had suffered greatly and lost completely. When the confrontation was over, their employers were stronger than ever, their union had disintegrated, and Meynardie had disappeared from the historical record.[27]

Meynardie's disappearance was not due entirely to the defeat of the Knights of Labor. There is an additional facet of his story that is relevant to the subject of union leadership and its role in the failure of textile unionism in the New South. In early October, as the strike began to disintegrate, Meynardie went to Richmond, Virginia, to attend a Knights of Labor convention. Unexpectedly, on October 12, he returned to Augusta "completely prostrated from mental exhaustion," in the words of his physician, Dr. O. B. Sally, "from overtaxing his brain." Those who saw Meynardie when he arrived at the Augusta train station thought he had the look "of a man who was under the influence of liquor, though [a reporter noted] he was not for he detests it." Dr. Sally, according to press reports, "shaved the patient's head and applied poultices and blisters" to treat him for fever. The physician also took care to let no one see Meynardie "because he gets excited and almost crazy whenever he speaks concerning the mills."[28]

This secrecy fueled rumors. One man who saw the local labor leader at this time told a reporter that Meynardie was "almost a raving maniac,"

27. For Meynardie's description of the deprivation, see Meynardie to Powderly, August 30, 1886, in Powderly Papers.
28. Augusta *Chronicle*, October 13, 1886.

"perfectly sane" one moment and "raving mad" the next, his nourishment consisting largely of "milk punches." In the wake of this report, someone, probably Dr. Sally, issued a statement to the newspapers. Meynardie had been "in a state of intense activity" for six months, the report read, and the result was "a prostration that temporarily overshadowed his brain, and he was without consciousness of his acts until after his return to Augusta." Because of his condition, "Stimulants were necessary to revive him, but after a temporary prescription, he was able to dispense with them entirely." Since his breakdown, Meynardie "has been excessively weak; walks very slowly and with much effort, but is careful and exact in his use of words, and utterly free from anything like wandering of the mind." He had in one or two instances manifested "the usual aberrations that accompany fever," and "during one of these states of hallucinations produced by high fever he was seen by the witness whose account of his condition gave rise to the report that his mind was gone."[29]

If the author of this report was Dr. Sally, he was covering up his own role in Meynardie's breakdown. Sally was not only the personal physician of Meynardie but also a close friend and a member of the executive committee of the Knights of Labor assembly. The assembly paid him one hundred dollars a month to provide health care to its members. For these personal reasons, and because of the damage it would do the organization's cause while the strike was still on, Sally would have wanted to conceal the truth about his patient. So, too, did his patient. When Meynardie appeared in public for the first time after the incident, nine days after his sudden return to Augusta, it was to accept his removal as master workman. He did so with no explanation and no investigation despite rumors of charges against him, including allegations of gross irregularities in the management of the strikers' relief fund.[30]

The truth, apparently, was never exposed. Under the pressures of his role in the strike, Meynardie had become addicted to narcotics—a "dope fiend," mill folk would have said. Somehow, Powderly learned of the addiction and, while Meynardie was in Richmond, confronted him with it, ordered him dismissed from the Knights of Labor, and forced his sudden return to Augusta. Humiliation and drugs were thus the causes of Meynardie's breakdown.

This explanation is documented in a long letter Meynardie wrote

29. *Ibid.*, October 21, 22, 26, 1886.
30. *Ibid.*, October 30, November 18, 1886.

Powderly on the day he left Richmond. "Having lost so much sleep & the taxation upon my mental forces was so exceedingly great," he said of the origin of his addiction, "Dr. O. B. Salley prescribed 'Fluid Extract Coca' for me. This not being strong enough, I bought & mixed with it 'Bromedia.' The two combined has about dethroned reason, & have about recked my life. I have striven with main and might to put my foot upon it: but to no purpose." The distraught Meynardie told Powderly, "Your accusations *doubtless are true*. . . . The torture torment I had suffered since, being face to face with you, is more than those of blood can tell. . . . Whatever accusations are brought against me, I cannot deny. My life has been & empty dream for several days; and my God, in this lucid moment, I cry in the anguish of my heart—what have I done?"

Desperate, Meynardie pleaded that his misfortune be covered up. "I have a wife—for God sake save her. Oh dont say one word that would reach her at home." He also asked Powderly's help in explaining his sudden return to Augusta. "Will you not say it was most expedient for me to be in Augusta in the present crisis[?] . . . Do for God sake, be careful how you instruct the party you send to Augusta [to handle the Knights' assembly and Meynardie's removal], hundreds yearn & long for my *down fall*. They have striven hard to bring me to naught. Do for pity sake, dont lend any material for my injury."

Clearly fearing what Powderly might do, Meynardie repeated his plea. "If you only knew my mental & nervous affliction inside[?], I inherited from my father, I know you would deal gently and charitably with me," he entreated. "Do let the past be buried in the past. . . . I have struggled long, hard and desperately against the Coca & Bromedia, but it has bound me but God being my helper I will break loose from it. The Drs put me on it. They must help me off of it."[31]

The plight of the unfortunate Meynardie was not the essential feature of the Augusta strike and lockout of 1886, but it was symptomatic of the problem of union leadership. W. H. Mullen, who was sent by Powderly to control the damage caused by Meynardie's affliction and loss of the Augusta strike, offered what seems a reasonable assessment. "Mr. Meynardie was never the proper man to lead those people," Mullen wrote Powderly, "for he done everything he could and held out every inducement to them to stop work. I saw this when I was in Augusta the first time [before the strike occurred], and told him that he should not encourage the people to stop

31. Meynardie to Powderly, n.d. (probably October 11 or 12, 1886), in Powderly Papers.

work but should rather encourage them to continue work. He lead the people to believe that they could get a million dollars [in strike assistance] if necessary." Mullen continued: "He told me in glowing terms how much money and provisions he could raise in Augusta if all the mill hands went out, and I told him that he would find if the crisis came that the promises would be all he could get from the people of Augusta."[32]

The strike and lockout had been a debacle, and if mill folk in Augusta suffered immediate consequences, others across the South were affected by the affair's long-range impact on the union movement. "If the affairs of the Order had been settled in Augusta as they should and could have been, it would have been the means of spreading the Order over the entire South," Mullen also wrote Powderly, perhaps too hopefully. "As it is the Order has been almost shattered in Augusta and unless something is done to save it it will be a total wreck."[33]

"I BELIEVE IN FREEDOM TO DO WHAT YOU WANT TO DO."

The appearance of unions inevitably brought confrontation with management, and since the unions were unable to protect their members in the resulting struggle, those workers faced real difficulties. That circumstance reinforced the cultural values that encouraged folk to disapprove of unions. Martin Lowe, who began work at Poe Mills in 1912, remembered that some of his fellow workers once decided to go on strike. "They came through, and I was running a section in the card room at that time," Lowe recalled. "A fellow come along through and knocked my motors off. I just went right behind and started them back up again. He said, 'Well, we're on strike.' 'Well,' I said, 'go ahead and strike, but don't touch one of my motors again.' I said, 'I look to my job for a living. Get off of my job.' And he went too. If he hadn't, I'd have let him have it with my hammer."

Bessie Buchanan, who worked in mills in North Carolina in the early twentieth century, was similarly caustic in her reminiscences. "I never have joined a union, and I don't believe in it. I can't go for it, because wherever there's a strike there's always damage. I just can't go for that. I believe in freedom to do what you want to do. If you want to work, work; and if you don't want to work, quit. And that's the way I am." Mrs. Buchanan was expressing the same right-to-work sentiment that led Elzie Teal into anti-

32. W. H. Mullen to Powderly, February 18, 1887, in Powderly Papers.
33. Mullen to Powderly, January 27, 1887, in Powderly Papers.

union activism in the 1940s. "Not a bit in this world," Mrs. Buchanan answered when asked in union activity had helped mill workers. "It's made it harder and harder, to my opinion. Now they've helped in bringing the wages up a lot, but it's killing to people. So what have they gained by it?" These remarks reveal another way in which unions and mill folk saw things differently. The unions wanted higher wages and shorter hours, and beginning in the 1920s and 1930s management began to concede those things, partly to undermine the unions' appeal. But officials also speeded up the machines and increased the number each worker tended, and as a result, according to Mrs. Buchanan, work was more harassing and demanding than it had been in the slower, longer days of the past.

Everette Burchell was born into a mill family in Virginia in 1902 and worked in mills there and in North Carolina most of his life. He, too, never joined a union, but his attitudes toward labor organization were more complex than those of Elsie Teal and Mrs. Buchanan. "I just never did care anything about it. I was getting along all right," he said. "But if anybody wants to organize, that's their business." That was the other side of the right-to-work view voiced by Mrs. Buchanan, Elzie Teal, and others. This approach did not always lead to unionism, however. "I don't like that union business," Stella Foust Carden, another longtime mill worker, said. "If it was carried out right, maybe it'd be all right, but you look at what kind of shape other things get into before you think about striking. Well, now, he goes on strike for a few cents more, and it drags on and on; and how long does it take them when they go back to work to make up all that time they've lost? I just don't think it's right."

This belief in individual choice was the shoal on which the union idea foundered. Sallie Smith Johnson, who began working as a spinner in 1904 in North Carolina when she was ten years old and continued in the mills for fifty-five years, never joined a union, though her husband did. "If anybody wants to work I think they ought to be allowed to work," Mrs. Johnson said, voicing a principle mill folk accepted. "All the companies I've ever worked for, you didn't have to belong to something like that to be treated right." Lessie Bowden Bland, who moved with her family from a farm to Carrboro when she was a teenager, had much the same opinion. "Well, I don't know, she answered when asked why she never joined a union. "I just felt that as long as we had work, we should be satisfied with it, and not, you know, push it." Alice Thrift Smith, who began mill work as a child in 1911 and continued through much of her life, affirmed this view. "Some unions are all right, I reckon," she said. "But I figure it was this way: I went there and I knew what they would pay me when I taken the job and I didn't feel like it would be right for me to strike for higher wages when I knew what I would get when I first went to work there. . . . I feel like if you ask for a job, and they pay you what they'll pay you and give you a job, I feel that it wouldn't be right to strike for higher wages when you was making a right good living."

These views were so deeply entrenched as to be moral in nature. Occasionally, the workers interviewed gave them a religious cast. Ralph B. Simmons, born into the family of a North Carolina farmer in 1894, left the farm for work not in the cotton mills but in lumber mills and furniture factories. In the latter, he eventually became an overseer. "I never had no interest in it," he said when asked about union activity. "I always tried to be satisfied, and I didn't pay no attention to what anyone else said. If they said anything to me I considered it all the way though, what that would be or what we had at the present time. And I don't believe in force. If you read your Bible, you'll see in there that you're supposed to be satisfied with your wages. It don't say how much or how little." Therefore, Simmons continued, "I don't believe in the union. I don't believe that anyone can show me between the leaves of the Bible where it gives you a right to force anyone to pay you more money. . . . I believe in doing what's right. It don't make any difference what might happen to you here; it's what happens to you beyond the shore."

Simmons had still other objections to labor organization. "I don't believe in a union on this ground," he remarked. "They probably help some people, and some they don't. Whenever they go on these strikes, there may be some people that are not able to survive it, and they suffer from it." Unions also tried to force job classifications on management and to restrict workers to tasks specific to their classification. "That's not right," Simmons insisted, exhibiting again the influence of moral values on his thinking. "If I go down to Southern Furniture in the morning, why, I am supposed to use my time for the best of their advantage, regardless of how they treat me or anything, what they pay me, how much or how little." Employees, in other words, should do whatever employers asked of them. "You're supposed to keep on the go," Simmons said, "and make a day and make an honest day."

"WE ARE HAVING TWO BIG FIGHTS AT THE MILLS HERE ONE IS FOR BLEASE AND THE OTHER IS FOR THE I.W.W. LABOR UNION."

These views, which equated unions with "trouble," intrusiveness, and even immorality, were obviously a problem for unions. Organizers and other spokesmen sought to change these perceptions, and in doing so they might have created false impressions among folk as to what unions were and what the consequences of unionization would be. That possibility raises basic questions. What did unions represent to mill folk? How would they have defined the term *union?* Historians' discussions of unions have assumed that mill folk's concept of the organizations was the same as that of organizers and historians. That was not necessarily the case, however. The conservative, "southern" nature of unions in the New South contrasts sharply with the progressive image they have in history books, as does their subservience to the interests of skilled workers at the expense of the unskilled.

Mill folk had a pervasive sense of grievance about their lot in life, but only where that generalized feeling became focused on a specific issue did it cause workers to find concerted action attractive. That focusing was often accomplished by union organizers. "We the undersigned would earnestly beg of you to instruct us how to organize a Lodge of the K of L," W. H. Carden and four other workers at Graniteville wrote Powderly in the spring of 1886. "We have no Lodge here and we badly need one[.] [T]here is three Cotton factories within a radius of five miles viz the Graniteville Mf. Co, Vau Cluse, and Langly all large mills working eight or nine hundred hands[.] [A]nd of all the down trodden hands we are the worst off. [I]n fact the wages are so low that we can hardly procure the most Common necessaries of life[.] [A] mere pittience is all we can get[.] [A]t the same time the factories are selling all the goods they make with orders ahead[.] Consequently thay could pay us a fair price for our work if they would."

The grievance of Carden and his fellow workers was sharply focused, clearly rationalized, and the source of concrete resentment. Yet as their letter also indicates, they knew nothing of unions or how to organize them. Nor did they understand the nature of the struggle against management that successful unionization entailed. "We hear that there is a great many Knights in augusta," Carden and his coworkers continued. "It is only twelve miles from this place[.] Could you not get the Head man in augusta to come out and help us[?] [W]e cannot write more at this time[.] If you can help us to start in the right way you will confer lasting obligations in a down trodden people[.] We do not wish any trouble or hard feelings with our superiors[.] [A]ll we want is a fair compensation for our Labor and Skills."[34]

The potential for organizing such workers as Carden and his cosigners is apparent. How did organizers present unions to such folk and convince

34. W. H. Carden *et al.* to Powderly, April 13, 1886, in Powderly Papers.

them that the labor organizations were likely means of solving their problems? Did they urge folk to ponder the risks and difficulties of union
membership, or did they exaggerate the promises of easy gains from unionization? Did they explain to folk such as Carden that successful unionization was impossible without "trouble or hard feelings" with management?
Did organizers, in other words, so tailor their appeals to mill folk that folk
joined unions without knowing just what was involved? Mill folk knew their
own minds, of course, but they knew of unions only what organizers and
experience told them; and many who joined unions must have done so
because organizers promised to redress their grievances, not bring them
"trouble." If that was the case, many of those who joined unions did so
without preparation for the struggle their action made inevitable.

In appealing to mill folk, did organizers for the Knights of Labor stress
the fraternal, reformist nature of that organization and Powderly's warning
that strikes were the "most disastrous of all methods of obtaining a redress
of grievance?" Did Master Workman Meynardie say in public what he was
then saying in private as he worked to organize workers in Augusta? "I am
absolutely an[d] irreconcilably opposed to *strikes*, lockouts, violence or acts
baring [*sic*] any semblance to violence," Meynardie wrote the conservative
Powderly in February, 1886. "I constantly warn all members to let a high
moral principle, actuate them in every step taken; and let only kindness &
forbearance characterize their every action; a point thus gained will be a
good and lasting one." If Meynardie stressed that approach, what did mill
folk think they were joining when they joined his union? "We find some
very much opposed to our organization," Meynardie wrote. Was his ostensibly cautious stance designed to disarm that opposition; or was he concerned
to entice wary mill folk into his union without their appreciation of the
risks?[35]

Although there is enough evidence to raise such speculations, there is not
enough to resolve them. "The purpose of the American Federation of
Trades [that is, the AFL] is not to cause strikes, but to prevent them," E. L.
Cranfill, an AFL organizer and one of the leaders of the Augusta strike of
1898 and 1899, said late in the course of that strike. "The great objects of
trade unions are to raise wages, shorten hours and improve conditions, not
by antagonizing capital, but by co-operating with it. By organization we
establish fraternity and discourage selfishness and by so doing cheer the
homes and firesides of workers and make the world better."[36]

35. Melton A. McLaurin, *The Knights of Labor in the South* (Westport, Conn., 1978), 53;
Meynardie to Powderly, February 25, 1886, in Powderly Papers.
36. Augusta *Chronicle*, January 7, 1899.

That statement was abstractly true but was taken by mill folk as they took everything else—quite literally. The picture Cranfill presented of the aftermath of unionization was not one of suffering, protracted struggle, and probable defeat, but one of the happiness and harmony mill folk earnestly desired. If organizers on other occasions did warn mill folk of the changes successful unions would necessitate, the message was not effective. "Many textile workers rushed into the union under the spur of specific grievances," one scholar has written of the surge of union activity in North Carolina at the turn of the twentieth century. And "when these were adjusted, their interests lagged."[37]

Unions sometimes represented, even to enthusiastic members, things quite different from those they represent to historians today. A key to the appeal of labor organizers among mill folk was that folk heard what organizers said, filtered the message through their own culture and experience, and gave it their own meaning. "We are having two Big fights at the Mills here," S. M. Miller of Sampson Mill wrote Governor Blease in 1914. "One is for Blease and the other is for the I.W.W. Labor Union and if it is Not asking too Much I Wish you Would Recommend a Man to Suport for Governor and Give your opinion of the I.W.W."[38]

It is difficult to imagine a better illustration of the problem of what unions meant to mill workers than this man's joint enthusiasms for Blease and the Industrial Workers of the World (IWW). "We have hear and Some rummer [rumor] that i think is false," another mill worker who joined the IWW in Greenville wrote the governor. "There is Some who dose Not Like our union because we are working people and has said that you would not indorse Labor union[.] Would it be so you could i think it would Make our membership of Near 3000 Cotton Mill People of Greenville S.C. get more enthused with our Honorable Cole Blease Campagn."[39]

These examples should not be dismissed as aberrations. As mill workers adapted the IWW to their understanding of things, some, not surprisingly, found in that ostensibly radical organization commonalities with what they admired in tradition-directed Bleaseism. Both the governor and the IWW were iconoclasts, both agitated mill officials, and both told mill workers certain things they wanted to hear. It was not class-conscious, anticapitalist ideology that attracted some of Blease's supporters to the IWW. It was

37. Douty, "The North Carolina Industrial Worker, 1880–1930," 283.
38. S. M. Miller to Coleman L. Blease, April 26, 1914, in Coleman L. Blease Papers, South Carolina State Archives.
39. B. E. Brookshire to Blease, n.d., in 1914 Greenville County folder, in Blease Papers. Brookshire worked at Duncan Mills.

instead the very presence of the organization, the outrage it aroused against employers, and the us-against-them feeling that outrage generated. "The mill people in Greenville are the worst stirred up I have ever seen," two IWW members wrote Blease from the town early in 1914. "We have a Union Organized here now with something over two Thousand members[.] [A]ll the hard fight we have had with Lewis W. Parker an others who have fought our Union from the begining we have organized in spite of all there efforts to check us[.] [B]oth [news]paper are dead against us but we intend to carry this *thru*."[40] Joining the IWW could thus be entirely compatible with support for Blease, for joining meant not a mature decision to enter the class struggle but what the joiners thought it meant.

40. Deed Cobb and R. F. Langford to Blease, February 4, 1914, in Blease Papers. Cobb worked at Duncan Mills and Langford at Judson Mills.

19
MILITANCE

During peak periods of labor activity, sizable minorities of mill folk joined unions, and others looked with some degree of favor on union activity. A few joined actively in long strikes, and many more were locked out or otherwise idled by strikes of fellow workers.

There were two major periods of union activity, one from 1884 to 1887 involving the Knights of Labor, and another from about 1898 to 1902, when the National Union of Textile Workers (NUTW) made a much larger and more sustained effort to organize mill workers. Together, these periods encompassed most of the strike and union activity of mill folk in the New South, and the pattern of separated waves is explained by the defeat and virtual elimination of unions in each of the two periods. After the defeat of the Knights of Labor in Augusta in 1886, unions disappeared as meaningful forces in mill communities for a dozen years. Even in Augusta, the most prominent center of union activity in the New South, a concerted effort by AFL and NUTW organizers in 1898 failed completely until mill officials announced a large pay cut that workers considered unnecessary and unfairly allocated. The resulting confrontation was part of a larger unionizing campaign prompted chiefly by the desire of New England textile workers and their unions to neutralize the effects on themselves of low wages and long hours in southern mills. Before it ended, the campaign attracted several thousand workers into unions and occasioned prolonged strikes in Augusta in 1898 and 1899, and again in 1902, in Alamance County, North Carolina, in the fall of 1900, and in Columbia, South Carolina, the following summer, as well as a major strike in Danville, Virginia, and a number of briefer, less significant episodes in mills across Georgia and the Carolinas.

The results of these strikes were the same—workers lost, and their unions disappeared or became ineffectual. As Melton A. McLaurin, the most important historian of mill unionism in the New South, has concluded, "All attempts to organize Southern mill hands prior to 1905 eventually failed."[1] So complete was the failure that McLaurin ended his study with the year 1905. There were, however, a few labor incidents after that date and a few strikes, too, without union organization. In 1914 a prolonged strike occurred at Fulton Bag and Cotton Mills and a brief one at Monaghan Mills, for example; and without benefit of a union, weavers at Eagle and Phenix Mills staged a strike in the spring of 1896 that prompted a shutdown of several weeks.

There were about ten major strikes in Georgia and the Carolinas in the New South era—three in Augusta (in 1886, 1898 and 1899, and 1902), three involving Fulton Bag and Cotton Mills in Atlanta (two in 1897 and one in 1914), one at Eagle and Phenix Mills in Columbus in 1896, one in Alamance County in 1900, one in Columbia in 1901, and one at Monaghan Mills in 1914. There were, in addition, perhaps three or four dozen less significant incidents involving strikes, lockouts, shutdowns, or other disturbances of brief duration and local impact.[2]

1. Melton A. McLaurin, *Paternalism and Protest: Southern Cotton Mill Workers and Organized Labor, 1875–1905* (Westport, Conn., 1971), xvii.
2. There is no satisfactory study of any of these strikes. They are best followed in the running accounts in local and metropolitan newspapers. On strikes and union activity generally, McLaurin, *Paternalism and Protest* and *The Knights of Labor in the South* (Westport, Conn., 1978) are the most informative works. There is also useful information in Mercer G. Evans, "The History of the Organized Labor Movement in Georgia" (Ph.D. dissertation, University of Chicago, 1929); George S. Mitchell, *Textile Unionism and the South* (Chapel Hill, 1931); U.S. Commissioner of Labor, *Third Annual Report, 1887, Tenth Annual Report, 1894, Sixteenth Annual Report, 1901,* and *Twenty-first Annual Report, 1906;* Harry M. Douty, "The North Carolina Industrial Worker, 1888–1930" (Ph.D. dissertation, University of North Carolina, 1936); Andrew W. Pierpont, "Development of the Textile Industry in Alamance County, North Carolina" (Ph.D. dissertation, University of North Carolina, 1953); Richard H. L. German, "The Queen City of the Savannah: Augusta, Georgia, During the Urban Progressive Era, 1890–1917" (Ph.D. dissertation, University of Florida, 1971); Gustavus G. Williamson, "Cotton Manufacturing in South Carolina, 1865–1892" (Ph.D. dissertation, Johns Hopkins

What is the historian to make of this record? Was the total of strikes impressively large, given the weak, dependent condition of workers, or was it surprisingly small, given the degree of their exploitation? When considered in combination with other forms of resistance and the determination of mill owners to crush it, the record of labor activism leaves no doubt that mill workers were frequently aggrieved and tried to improve their situation. The strikes they staged had a significance beyond their numbers and outcome, for even the devastating defeats at Augusta and elsewhere may have had some positive results. Prolonged strikes invariably forced mill owners to take extreme measures—locking out nonstriking workers, for example, or forcibly evicting strikers from their homes—which compromised their stance as large-hearted paternalists. Press coverage of extended strikes regularly included interviews with strikers, whose accounts of conditions effectively countered those of mill owners. The largest single cause of strikes was dissatisfaction with pay—more specifically, pay cuts—and press coverage exposed the low wages mill officials paid their employees and sometimes also the suffering and deprivation among the poorest mill folk. Moreover, the realities of protest in one place might have made the threat of militance more effective in other places, and might have encouraged mill officials to forgo exploitive acts they would otherwise have authorized. Perhaps the willingness of workers to endure the hardships and defeat of prolonged strikes impressed their employers in ways that benefited the workers. Such an impression might explain why mill owners in Augusta, for example, gave their workers a 10 percent pay raise on January 1, 1900, thereby restoring most of the pay cut that had pushed the workers into the bitter strike and lockout of 1898 and 1899.[3]

The difficulty of evaluating the level of strike activity is paralleled by that of assessing the level of union membership. Melton A. McLaurin, the most thorough historian of the subject, has estimated that two or three thousand southern mill workers joined the Knights of Labor in the 1880s, mostly in 1886, and that more than five thousand joined unions during the flurry of activism about 1900.[4]

Those levels seem dwarfed by the total number of mill workers in the

University, 1954); and Denis R. Noland and Donald E. Jones, "Textile Unionism in the Piedmont, 1901–1932," In Gary M. Fink and Merl E. Reed (eds.), *Essays in Southern Labor History: Selected Papers, Southern Labor Conference, 1976* (Westport, Conn., 1977), 48–79.

3. The pay raise is noted in *House Documents*, 57th Cong., 1st Sess., No. 184, Vol. 7, p. 566.

4. McLaurin, *Paternalism and Protest*, 210.

New South, which rose from 16,741 in 1880 to 97,559 in 1900 (and from 11,491 to 78,757 in the three states), but the ratio of union members to the total work force was hardly a meaningful figure.[5] Child laborers did not join unions, which commonly restricted membership to workers past their sixteenth birthday. And women did not join unions at the same rates as men. The meaning of female membership in unions is uncertain. None of the women in the union that assisted strikers at Fulton Bag and Cotton Mills in 1897 took leadership roles, even though the strike was precipitated by women. In Augusta at the time of the strikes of 1898–1899 and 1902, there was a separate union with the name "Lady Weavers," an adaptation that might have been made to overcome the hesitancy of women to participate in public activity with men. There was, however, no separate union for female operatives in other jobs, and the adaptation might have been related to the apparent concentration of unionism among weavers, loom fixers, and other skilled mill employees.

During the New South era, women played an increasing role in public life, which was reflected in their greater visibility in textile unions. In 1899, for example, several women represented the Augusta Lady Weavers at the organizing convention of the Georgia Federation of Labor, and a year later, several women attended the federation's convention as delegates from other Augusta unions as well. In 1900, Sadie Middleton of Augusta was elected one of nine vice-presidents of the federation. By the end of the New South era, women were playing an even larger public role. In 1914, for example, Samuel Gompers appointed Mrs. E. B. Smith of Atlanta, who apparently was not a mill operative, "to take local charge" of AFL activity in the strike then underway at Fulton Bag and Cotton Mills.[6]

Despite the prominent positions of some women in labor organizations, mill women generally deferred to their husbands, and it is likely that in most "union families" only husbands and fathers actually joined the union regardless of the number and sentiment of workers who made up the rest of the family. To the extent that this was the case, the significance of figures on union membership is enlarged. It is further enlarged by clear indications that union members were, disproportionately, adult males employed in skilled positions. When investigators for the 1907–1908 labor study asked 793 women mill workers about unions, they found the women had little knowledge of and even less interest in the subject. No less than 592 (75

5. C. Vann Woodward, *Origins of the New South* (Baton Rouge, 1951), 132.
6. Atlanta *Constitution*, April 15, 1900, June 20, 1914; Augusta *Chronicle*, April 25, 1899.

percent) had no opinion because they knew nothing about unions, and 126 of the others (16 percent) were indifferent or unfavorable to them.[7] This survey was made a few years after the wave of union and strike activity that occurred between 1898 and 1902. Was it possible that most mill folk were unaware of the great strikes at Augusta and elsewhere?

"DEPRIVATION SHOULD DEPRESS THE PROPENSITY OF WORKERS TO STRIKE."

Why did some mill workers join unions, go on strike, or otherwise become labor activists whereas most did not? And why, in view of the workers' exploitation, was there not more militance? To restate the questions in broader terms, what is it that causes militance at certain times and places, and quiescence, even peace, at others? Historians and social scientists have given these questions systematic attention in recent years, and their findings shed considerable light on what happened among mill workers in the New South. Traditionally, most explanations of strikes and other forms of labor militance focused on one of three causes. Some scholars stressed social breakdown and discontinuity—specifically, the dislocating effects of industrialization and of the move from preindustrial to industrial employment. Others pointed to accumulating miseries and deprivations among workers, and still others emphasized the emergence of class consciousness.

In recent years, the debate over these explanations has been superseded by the formulations Edward Shorter and Charles Tilly developed in their study of strikes in France in the nineteenth and twentieth centuries. According to Shorter and Tilly, social breakdown and economic deprivation reduce rather than increase the ability of workers to take collective action. "Long deprivation should depress the propensity of workers to strike," they have observed; "*a fortiori*, long-run immiseration of workers should be antithetical to strike activity." Furthermore, "To the extent that a given reorganization of production actually dissolves social bonds and controls personally affecting workers," there should be "a decline in strikes because of the increasing cost of collective action among those workers."

The incidence of labor militance was thus linked to many influences on mill folk in the New South. One of these influences was urbanization—not simply the degree of urbanization but the length of time workers had lived in cities. "Organization in large, dense places is easier than in small, diffuse, homogeneous places," Shorter and Tilly wrote. "The ties which bind and

7. *Senate Documents*, 61st Cong., 2nd Sess., No. 645, Vol. 1, p. 611.

criss-cross urban society hold its members more firmly in association than do the ties in other kinds of places." Stated another way, "The motors of militancy are set in motion not by the marginal, the unintegrated and the recently arrived [workers], but by the workers who belong to firmly established networks of long standing at the core of urban industrial society."

Other influences on militance and quiescence are the workers' degree of experience with unions and the strength and effectiveness of the unions that appear among them. "The scale and intensity of strike activity in a setting depend closely on the prior organization of workers in the setting," Shorter and Tilly remarked, "on the availability of a structure which identifies, accumulates and communicates grievances on the one hand and facilitates collective action on the other." Because all of these factors are involved, the incidence of strikes and other forms of militance is no guide to the degree of dislocation, deprivation, or exploitation of workers. On the contrary, "Dislocation and deprivation fix the attention of workers on survival from day to day, leaving them little disposed to risky collective action."[8]

These influences plus the strength of management, the attitude of government, and the general level of economic conditions, which Shorter and Tilly also emphasized, largely explain the dearth of strikes and other forms of labor militance among mill workers in the New South. Mill folk were deprived and economically insecure, dislocated by the move from the farm, unhabituated to urban ways, without experience in collective action. The unions that appeared among them were poor, ineffectively led, and unable to articulate or spark a clear sense of group consciousness. In addition, they faced a strong, well-organized management and a government hostile to their purposes.

The unions faced other problems, too. The mill labor force included too many women and children to be organized along conventional union lines, and unions offered no attractive alternatives to the paternalist tradition. Nor did the unions attempt to counter the folk alternative to labor militance— moving from one mill to another. The unions regularly encouraged striking workers to move elsewhere rather than stay and fight on or go back to work

8. Edward Shorter and Charles Tilly, *Strikes in France, 1830–1968* (New York, 1974), 8–9, 283, 272, 284–85. See also Neil J. Smelser, *Social Change in the Industrial Revolution: An Application of Theory to the British Cotton Industry* (London, 1959); Clark Kerr and A. J. Siegel, "The Interindustry Propensity to Strike—An International Comparison," in Kerr (ed.), *Labor and Management in Industrial Society* (Garden City, N.Y. 1964), 105–47; Craig Calhoun, *The Question of Class Struggle: Social Foundations of Popular Radicalism during the Industrial Revolution* (Chicago, 1982); and Sari Bennett and Carville Earle, "The Geography of Strikes in the United States, 1881–1894," *Journal of Interdisciplinary History*, XIII (1982), 63–84.

on management's terms. This alternative reduced the cost of relief among strikers and was one way of registering dissatisfaction, but it probably helped undermine the unions' larger purpose. "Movement through space, movement into and out of communities," historian Stephan Thernstrom has written of his studies of spatial mobility among American workers, "may retard the development of class consciousness in a manner somewhat analogous to movement into a higher social structure."[9]

The findings of Shorter and Tilly and other historians suggest not only why there were so few strikes among mill folk in the New South but why those few occurred where they did. The likeliest places of militance were cities, especially those in which mills were sufficiently concentrated to produce the critical mass of workers necessary to encourage organization and group consciousness, and cities, too, where mills had existed for the two or three generations necessary to give workers an urban experience and outlook. Augusta was the largest textile center in the New South, and its oldest mills predated the Civil War. So, too, did those of Columbus, another large textile center. Atlanta was the largest city in the New South, and Fulton Bag and Cotton Mills was located nearly at its center. In contrast to mills in these places, the new, decentralized town and rural mills scattered across the Piedmont experienced little or no significant labor disturbance. The exceptions were mills in Alamance County, where a prolonged, "unexpected" strike occurred in 1900. The county had been an antebellum textile center and had more than a score of mills at the turn of the century, but it included no sizable city, and its mills were relatively small even by New South standards.

"WE WANT TO WORK THROUGH THE MANAGEMENT OF THE MILL AND THE OFFICERS, AND BETTER OUR CONDITION."

These formulations require concrete illustration. The effort to establish a Knights of Labor assembly at Mississippi Mills at Wesson, Mississippi, in 1886; the effort by a group of anti-union beamers at Sibley Mill to raise their wages in 1905; and the effort of IWW members at Monaghan Mills to negotiate an overtime dispute with management in 1914 illuminate the nature and ineffectuality of the unions and unionism that sprang up among mill workers in the New South. The incidents also show something of how

9. Stephan Thernstrom, "Working Class Social Mobility in Industrial America," in Melvin Richter (ed.), *Essays in Theory and History: An Approach to the Social Sciences* (Cambridge, Mass., 1970), 224.

union and nonunion workers dealt with management, and of how mill workers molded unions in their own image, thus compromising the purposes of their militance.

In the spring of 1886, some of the men employed at Mississippi Mills formed an assembly of the Knights of Labor. Their number was apparently small compared to that of the total mill work force, though according to Recording Secretary R. M. Sasser, the growth of the "order" was "marvelous." The appearance of the organization alarmed the mill's manager, and his consequent moves to eradicate it dramatized the inability of workers to form effective unions. "Capt. Wm. Oliver, manager of Miss. Mills has ever been verry much predudiced [*sic*] against the order of the K. of L.," Sasser wrote Powderly in August, about three months after the assembly was organized. Oliver's reaction was grossly disproportionate to any threat the Knights of Labor posed to his power and prerogative, but it was typical of mill officials across the New South. "None of the brothers have ever allowed the order or their membership to interfere with their duties as laborers in the Miss. Mills," Sasser reported, "nor has Capt. Oliver ever been asked to make the time required for a days work shorter.[.] Nor has be been asked to make any concessions at all."

This caution might have been tactical, but the tone of Sasser's letter indicates that the Wesson Knights of Labor were conservative men who sought to avoid rather than provoke confrontation. Despite this, as Sasser wrote, "On the [word missing] day of June/86[,] mecha[n]ics who were Ks of L wer discharged. Oliver said on account of Scarcity of work. The real cause of their discharge they were Ks of L. Capt Oliver had said that he would work every K. of L. out of the mills."

In the face of this intimidation, the assembly continued to grow, according to Sasser, and Oliver became more determined to destroy it. On August 7, several weeks after dismissing the mechanics, Oliver told the head of the assembly, Master Workman W. J. Benning, who after fourteen years in the mill was a second hand, "that he could not work for the Mills & be a K. of L. that he would have to give up one or the other." Benning responded "that the K. of L. were an honorable society that they had asked for nothing at [Oliver's] hands; that they would much rather build the Miss. Mills up than do any thing against their interests." Oliver was insistent, however. "You cant work for the Miss Mills and be a K. of L," he said to Benning, telling the assistant overseer that unless he resigned from the Knights of Labor he could consider himself discharged.

Thus challenged, the assembly called a meeting "& appointed a committee of 5 to meet Capt O. & confer with him & see if the matter could not be adjusted." But like mill officials throughout the South, Oliver refused to meet the committee. At that point, the Knights of Labor were stymied by lack of resources, organizational strength, and experienced leadership. None of them knew what to do. "We can do nothing more & refer the matter to you," Sasser wrote Powderly despairingly. "Will further say that we would dislike to see a strike here not on account of the Ks. of L. so much as the poor women and children. The[y] would be bound to suffer. Capt. O. said to some Ks. of L. yesterday that he would break up the order in Wesson if he had to discharge every K of L in the Mills & if it was necessary he would close the Mills for 12 months. We expect others to be discharged at any time."

The discharges came the following day. "Since writing the above," Sasser added in his letter, "Capt. Oliver has gone through the Mills & told all the Ks. of L. that he would give them till Saturday night Inst to draw out of the Assembly & if they did not they would be discharged on Monday morning. He says he is determined to break up the Assembly. He has induced or Bull Dozed some till they have withdrawn. We want to hold a meeting Sat. night. Please advise us what to do."[10]

Sasser's letter is revealing. His union was apparently composed exclusively of men. He refers to its members as "brothers" and at one point counterposes the Knights to the women and children in the mill. Yet the work force at the mill, nearly a thousand people, was, in Sasser's words, "composed largely of widow women young girls and small children who have no other way of making a living except working in this factory." Moreover, the only Knights identified in Sasser's letter were mechanics (skilled machinists), rather than operatives proper, and the head of the assembly was an assistant overseer. Although there were certainly adult male operatives in the assembly, the union was in no sense representative of the work force. The organization was also small enough for Sasser to distinguish between its members and the work force generally, and small enough, too, for the manager to threaten to dismiss the entire membership and for Sasser and those "Bull Dozed" former members to take the threat seriously.

The weakness of the union was thus starkly revealed. Months after its organization, the assembly had made no demands, or even requests, of

10. R. M. Sasser to Terence V. Powderly, August 12, 1886, in Terence V. Powderly Papers, microfilm edition, Georgia State University Library.

management, its entire energies being consumed in remaining alive. Yet women and children earned no more than twenty-five to seventy-five cents a day, according to Sasser, for a workday of eleven hours and fifteen minutes. The Knights of Labor no doubt knew any demand or request they made would be denied, in which case they would have to back down or call a strike. But a strike, according to Sasser, was out of the question because it would hurt the women and children, whose livelihood depended on their work. A strike might also have been out of the question for other reasons. The union members were a small portion of the work force, and other workers were unlikely to join them in striking. In addition, the Knights of Labor themselves might have suffered from internal dissension and even betrayal. "They are talking of giving us all the Bounce Because we are K of L," Sasser wrote Powderly three weeks earlier than the letter just quoted. "How are we to act in consequence they Do. [A]nd we expell a member of Talking to mutch that is Said he was Going to Sell us out our names[.] [N]ow he Said he is going to give a Way all the Secret words he Noes[.] What Shal we Do?"[11]

This situation might have been typical wherever unions appeared, especially outside urban centers. If so, it seems appropriate to ask whether unions and the model of labor-management relations they provided were promising means for resolving the problems of mill workers. Was not Sasser's union so poorly equipped to help mill workers that workers (and labor activists who wanted to help them) should have sought other devices? A realization of the union's limitations might explain why so few workers joined the organization. If a union cannot strike, cannot negotiate with or even win recognition from management, cannot reach the vast majority of workers, and cannot protect its members from arbitrary dismissal merely for joining the union, is such an organization useful? Is it a union at all?[12]

Was there a more promising way of helping workers whose sense of grievance the unions tapped but could not assuage? Theoretically, the unions might have adapted themselves to mill conditions in advantageous ways. They might have renounced confrontation and strikes as counterproductive in view of their ineffectiveness and of the workers' depen-

11. Sasser to Powderly, July 23, 1886, in Powderly Papers.
12. Noting the frequency with which organizations of workers appeared, occasioned a strike, and disappeared when the strike was lost, anthropologist Anthony F. C. Wallace called such organizations "ad hoc strikers' groups" rather than unions (*Rockdale: The Growth of an American Village in the Early Industrial Revolution* [New York, 1979], 367).

dence, and worked for meliorative change within the framework of paternalism. Labor-management relations, in the final analysis, were matters of
power, which mill owners had and workers lacked. The appearance of
unions in mill communities did not redress that imbalance. Rather, it encouraged mill owners to exercise their power ruthlessly. Mill owners reacted
unsparingly because they felt threatened by unions and had the power to
respond in that way. Could the threat mill officials perceived from worker
organization have been neutralized?

Worker organizations that were not threatening to management—that
modeled themselves along fraternal lines, were organized perhaps like
church congregations on a family basis, and were dedicated explicitly to
cooperation rather than confrontation—might have accomplished more
than the unions. They might, for example, have tapped the humanitarian
component of paternalism to the workers' advantage. The often substantial
expenditures paternalists made for social, educational, and religious purposes suggest that many owners who could not be challenged might have
responded to other types of appeals. "I believe I could make a satisfactory
arrangement which would meet your views," Lewis W. Parker of Monaghan
Mills told a committee of workers during strike negotiations in 1914, "if you
would come to me without an arbitrary statement of what you require."
Parker, in other words, would concede nothing to workers demanding
changes from him, but he would allow himself to be appealed to in other
ways. To settle the 1914 strike, Parker relentlessly pursued a seemingly
trivial goal—to force striking workers to make up thirty-five minutes of lost
time by working overtime. Of importance to Parker was the fact that the
strikers had defied the order to work overtime. If they would go back to
work and obey the order, he told the strikers, then he would consider their
objections to making up lost time. Parker, who was a noted mill paternalist
and relentless enemy of unionism, was a man to whom mill workers could
appeal, but only if they came to him as supplicants. Not long before this
strike, he had granted a pay raise to petitioning loom fixers. He granted the
raise, he said, because that had been the "right" thing to do, and he promised to do the "right" thing in responding to future petitions and grievances. But he would concede nothing to workers who made demands of
him.[13]

The futility of union efforts at places like Mississippi Mills left workers

13. Greenville *News*, July 17, 18, 1914.

with two alternatives. They could forgo unions altogether and approach management as Parker suggested, through traditional avenues of paternalism, or they could work toward even more militant forms of unionism.

In the summer of 1905, a group of beamers at Sibley Mill tried the first of those options, sending the superintendent "a petition asking a small increase in wadges." The beamers were aggrieved because recent changes in their work, occasioned by new manufacturing processes and the pay adjustments such processes always brought, had resulted in longer hours and less pay, extending their workday about forty-five minutes and reducing their earnings from parity with those of loom fixers to below those of weavers. "In all places where this kind of work is run," their petition read, "beamers make as much as loom fixers or more, and [Sibley Mill] is the only place we know of where weavers make more than the beamers." The petitioners thus built their appeal on the ground that the recent adjustment had had inequitable results. "We refer to what the beamers made before this C. O. commenced to run the Sulpher Blue," they told the superintendent. "Compare our pay then and now and compare the weavers pay then and now to see if our pay has not been cut. While we were working by the piece we were allowed to [go] out at six o'clock, and now it is from 645 am to 645 pm Every day."

Obviously attuned to the psychology of paternalism, the petitioners were careful to present their plea in conservative, unthreatening terms. "We were holding off [with our complaint,]" they said, "thinking the work would get better so that we could go back on piece work, but there are no prospects whatever of that now. We only ask for a fifteen cent raise on the day." One reason for such caution was that two years earlier, union activity had caused a brief strike and lockout at the mill, memories of which were no doubt still fresh. "We are no members of the union nor no sympathisers," the petitioners assured the superintendent, "and we want this petition kept secret from any of the help in other parts of the Mill. We hope this will be given a due consideration[.] We pray the above will be given due consideration. Please notify us through our overseer as soon as possible. We remain your humble servants."[14]

Whether the petition was granted is unknown. Managers were probably more sympathetic to petitions in this form than to public, union-backed demands. At least they might receive and consider such petitions. The price

14. The petition is in File 656, Graniteville Manufacturing Company Papers, University of South Carolina at Aiken Library.

for that consideration was high, however. Requests had to be modest and obsequiously made, even by workers who felt themselves victimized by injustice. If the requests were accepted, the workers were bound further in the web of paternal dependence. If the requests were denied, the petitioners, like the Knights of Labor at Mississippi Mills, were at a dead end. They could accept management's decision and remain at work, or they could accept it and look elsewhere for work.

Workers who found these alternatives unacceptable could theoretically work for more radical organization than that offered by the Knights of Labor in the 1880s or the NUTW about 1900. The reputation of the IWW might have been part of its appeal when that "revolutionary" group sent organizers among mill workers in Greenville in 1914. The Greenville effort occurred not long after the IWW's involvement in the dramatic mill strikes at Lawrence, Massachusetts, in 1912 and Paterson, New Jersey, a year later, when the organization's reputation for radicalism was still at its height. How organizers presented the IWW to mill folk is unknown, but if their purpose was to spread radical, anticapitalist activism, they failed signally. Something like the reverse occurred. The organizers were so "successful" in Greenville that the union they created was no different from other textile unions in the New South. It was folk influenced, hesitant to challenge management, and ineffectual.

The nature of the local organization was pointedly illustrated in the only strike for which IWW members were responsible, at Monaghan Mills in the summer of 1914. The difficulty began on July 8, when the mill lost an hour and ten minutes in a power outage. In line with standing policy, mill supervisors announced shortly before the 6:00 P.M. closing time that employees would have to make up half the lost time by working that evening until 6:35. This policy was the source of longstanding grievance, and on that day most of the weavers refused to work overtime and instead walked out of the mill. The next morning, they congregated outside the mill and demanded as the condition of entering that the policy requiring the make-up of lost time be abandoned. The superintendent refused the demand, and since the mill could not operate without the weavers, he ordered it closed. After a week, the mill reopened with a reduced work force. Four days later, the strikers agreed to return to work, make up the lost time, and then petition management to change the objectionable policy.

This incident occurred after IWW organizers had been in Greenville several months, and apparently all the strikers were IWW members (their negotiating committees consisted exclusively of members). One would therefore expect the strike to have been conducted with the same determination that characterized the efforts at Lawrence and Paterson. But the strike was not even called by the union, though its presence no doubt emboldened the weavers.[15] Rather, like most work stoppages in the New South, this one began on the spur of the moment and thus without preparation. Joseph J. Ettor, a national official of the IWW, went to Greenville during the strike and addressed meetings of the workers, but mill officials refused to meet with anyone claiming to represent the IWW. As a result, neither Ettor nor A. F. Hunnicutt, who was head of the Greenville local and an operative in another mill, had any part in negotiations with management. Moreover, when Lewis W. Parker, who did the negotiating for the mill, said he would not meet with the strikers' committee if it claimed to represent the IWW, the head of the committee, whose name was Merritt, stated categorically that the group represented Monaghan workers and not the IWW.

The conservative conduct of the strike was evident. Among those who addressed the first meeting of the strikers were the sheriffs of Greenville and Anderson counties, who, like other speakers, urged caution and responsibility. On the second day of the strike, union leaders implored "the members to be peaceful and gentlemanly and to resort to nothing but parliamentary tactics" during the strike. The assembled strikers who heard this advice responded by electing a committee "to patrol the mill village and protect the mill property from any who might for one cause or another attempt to do damage." Strike leaders also urged that the sale of liquor be discontinued during the strike.

The negotiating committee, elected by the strikers, was equally conservative in its meetings with management. Its members made no threats or demands, or even any rhetorical outbursts. They sought instead to avoid confrontation and to play down their differences with management. Indeed, they were less insistent on the strikers' demands than were the strikers themselves. The negotiators, all of them loom fixers or weavers, stated repeatedly that the walkout had been precipitous and ill advised, and that the strikers should have remained on the job, made up the lost time as ordered, and then brought their grievance to management. Moreover, when Parker suggested that a speech by himself at one of the strikers' meetings might encourage the strikers to accept his proposition that they return to work and then come to him with their grievance, the head of the negotiating

15. The strike is covered in the Greenville *News*, July 11–18, 1914. A verbatim transcript of all negotiations between the strikers and Lewis W. Parker, chief executive officer of the mill, is printed *ibid.*, July 17, 18, 1914.

committee demurred. "I don't believe it would do any special good," he told Parker. "When you get a crowd of young people together, they will not consider things as we will and I just don't believe you could get anything from that crowd."

The committee members were always deferential and respectful in addressing Parker. "I don't think there is a man at Monaghan who would damage you," one of them told Parker. "We want to work through the management of the mill and the officers, and better our condition. . . . It is the interest of our people and the people of the State and our race to try to up-build any community in which we live." Such views were those of mill folk, not class revolutionaries. In stating the strikers' request for assurances that none of them would be dismissed or otherwise punished if they returned to work, the committee agreed that Parker should not have to make an absolute commitment. That might obligate him, they conceded, to retain lax or immoral workers. "We could not expect you to take men who will want to do as they please. In a short time, that would run us all out of business," the chief negotiator told Parker of lax workers. Also, "We had rather some people without good morals would be dismissed than for them to be allowed to work on. We do not stand by a man who does not stand for good morals, or ask you to work a man under those conditions."

The strikers made no extreme demands. All they asked was that the mill drop the policy that required them to make up lost time by working overtime. They even offered to let Parker "dock" their pay proportionately to the time they lost, so that if they were kept in the workplace during a stoppage, as often happened, they would not be paid for some of the time they were in the mill.

In the negotiations, Parker conducted himself masterfully. Head of perhaps the largest textile chain in the New South, he controlled sixteen mills at the time of the negotiations and was perhaps a man of overawing reputation to the employees with whom he "negotiated." Flanked in the sessions by the mill president and superintendent, he used the devices of paternalism with great effect. His refusal to deal with anyone except his own employees excluded outsiders who might have met him on a more equal footing. Recognizing his advantage he treated the negotiators paternalistically. He kept them on the defensive, alternately chiding and shaming them while proclaiming his willingness to forgive and forget if the miscreants returned to work, agreed to follow the rules (specifically, to make up the thirty-five minutes of lost time), and then came to him with their complaints. He also read to them with telling effect from IWW publications and bylaws. He chided them for joining an organization that said amorality and even sabotage were acceptable weapons in the struggle against employers, and one that admitted blacks to membership on equal footing with whites. The committee, whose chairman was a Sunday school teacher as well as a loom fixer, was clearly embarrassed by Parker's reading. Clearly, also, IWW representatives in Greenville had not dwelt on these aspects of the organization.

Parker surely had the measure of the committee members. He also understood his advantage over the strikers. Only a minority of the work force had refused to make up the lost time, and the weavers' strike had thrown out of work many operatives who thought work was more important than challenging management. Thus, on July 16, a week after the shutdown and while he was still negotiating with the committee, Parker reopened the mill with a reduced work force. The strikers made no attempt to prevent workers from entering the mill, and Parker's action brought the strike to a rapid end. On July 20, the strikers themselves returned to work, having accepted Parker's assurance that if they did so and made up the lost time, he would look into the disputed policy.

The Monaghan strikers had been smothered by paternalism, just as those in the three strikes at Augusta were whipped into capitulation by vengeful mill presidents. In all cases the workers lost, but the loss at Monaghan Mills entailed the least suffering. That outcome was due in part to Parker's reputation as a fair-minded paternalist, which none of the mill presidents in Augusta ever had.

"AT TIMES DOZENS OF EXCITED MEN AND WOMEN [WERE] TALKING AT THE SAME TIME."

If dealing with management was intrinsically difficult because of the imbalance of power, the difficulty was compounded by the way mill folk conducted their strikes. Their approach best illustrates the way in which their culture limited their ability to cope effectively in the modern world. How did mill folk decide to strike, set matters of policy once a strike was under way, select strike leaders, negotiate with management, sustain their commitment, accept defeat? Answers to these questions complete the cycle of evidence that strikes and unions were not effective weapons in the workers' struggle with management.

On March 27, 1896, officials at Eagle and Phenix Mills announced a reduction of about 10 percent in the rates of pay for weavers working on certain kinds of goods.[16] The reduction applied only to weavers in the company's largest mill, the same cut having already been made in another of its smaller mills. The cut in the smaller mill had prompted a dozen weavers to quit in protest, but several of them had returned the next day, and work had not been disrupted. Such actions regularly accompanied announcements of pay reductions, and officials were surprised when a more serious reaction followed notice of the cut in the larger mill. The weavers were incensed because they thought the reductions unnecessary and unfair, and some of them called an indignation meeting to be held that night at a hall in the mill district.

At the meeting, "The crowd was considerably wrought up and many loud denunciations of the proposed reduction, and some of the officers of the company, were heard." The protesting workers voted to assemble in front of the superintendent's office at dinnertime the next day; and they named a committee to present their objections to the superintendent at that time. At the resulting demonstration, the superintendent emerged from his office, but the committee's ineffectuality in making its complaint demonstrated the protesters' lack of experienced leadership. "Of the several men who appeared in the front rank there was not one who felt the right of spokesmanship," according to a reporter who witnessed the scene. After a short time, "one young fellow found his tongue" and began presenting the weavers' case. The superintendent interrupted him to say that the cut had been forced on the mill by economic necessity— "the decline in the prices of the goods"—and was therefore final. At that point, the whistle ending the dinner break sounded, and the superintendent refused to continue the discussion. This further incensed the protesting weavers, and 270 to 300 of them refused to return to work.

This sequence of events was typical of the onset of mill strikes in the New South, and it shows the disadvantages with which workers began their contests with management. The strike was unplanned and therefore unprepared for. The strikers had no strategy, no resources for sustaining themselves, no organization or experienced leaders. Nor did they have the support of most workers in the mill. What they did have was a deeply felt grievance and the frustration that came from the inability to have it heard. The strikers also had the support of most weavers in the largest of the Eagle and Phenix mills, and if their ranks held firm, the mill would be unable to

16. This account is based on Columbus *Enquirer-Sun*, March 28 to May 17, 1896, and Atlanta *Constitution*, March 29 to May 24, 1896.

operate efficiently without them. "We have fully made up our minds," some of the strikers told a reporter as they left the mills, "and will not work for the Eagle and Phenix Company if the present wages are reduced."

The walkout occurred on Saturday, and mill officials announced that unless the weavers returned on Monday, all the company's mills would close. This warning, or second thoughts about staying off the job, weakened the resolve of some of the weavers, and to prevent them from returning to work, "bands of men posted themselves in the bridge [across the Chattahoochee River from Phenix City, where many of the weavers lived] and at the entrance of the mill yard." As a result, "Many operatives were turned back at the bridge, while the rest found impenetrable barriers in the bands at the mill gates." The effort was successful. Two-thirds of the looms in the giant mill were idled, though the number of other workers who joined the striking weavers or were prevented from going to work is unclear.

Mill officials were as good as their word. They closed all the Eagle and Phenix mills, including the knitting mill in Girard, Alabama, when it ran out of thread a few days later, idling altogether about two thousand workers, including the strikers. The officials insisted the shutdown would not hurt the mills, for, they said, the mills had recently run without profit and only to prevent hardship among the operatives. The mills' conduct during the strike and shutdown indicates there was probably some truth in that claim.

This response was typical of mills facing walkouts that meaningfully affected production. Partial operation was not economic, for with so large a number of looms idled the product of the company's spinning mills could not be processed. For mills in this situation, a shutdown might even be desirable if cotton prices were high, "conditions of trade" were bad, or the mill had a surplus of manufactured goods. Even if these conditions were absent, a mill could cushion the effects of even a long shutdown by contracting its orders to other mills or selling some of its cotton supplies. In short, the financial condition of most mills was quite strong, enabling them to withstand even extended strikes.

The workers had no such advantages. Shutting down an entire complex of mills when only part of the work force was on strike robbed the mill community of all of its income and prevented nonstrikers, who had nothing to gain from the protest, from helping strikers remain off the job. The policy also encouraged nonstrikers to pressure strikers to return to work. This pressure was not immediately effective, for the practice of holding back the wages of one pay period provided workers with at least one payday after a strike or lockout began. But it soon had accumulating effects.

The Eagle and Phenix weavers conducted their strike much like other striking mill workers across the New South. They held mass meetings at which they organized themselves, elected leaders, discussed their problems, and listened to advice from invited speakers. The daily meetings were generally restricted to strikers, and one of their primary functions was to sustain morale. Attendance was voluntary, and presumably those strikers who were most enthusiastic or concerned about the strike were most likely to attend. Not surprisingly, strike enthusiasts dominated the meetings, which might have had the effect of silencing voices of moderation or dissent. If so, decisions made at the meetings might have been more uncompromising than sentiment among rank-and-file strikers. The fact that strikers could officially end their strikes only by majority vote in a public meeting might have one reason many strikes dragged on long after they had been lost.

Decisions in the meetings were by majority vote, and every striker present could vote. This, too, worked to the advantage of the resolute. Workers not on strike but out of work because of the shutdown had no voice in the deliberations. They held no mass meetings and developed no organization, but waited instead on strikers and management to resolve differences. Among strikers, however, the conduct of business was astonishingly democratic. Leaders, those on negotiating committees, and others in responsible positions were elected at mass meetings and subject to replacement at any subsequent meeting; and all negotiating positions, offers to management, and proposals from management had to be approved in the same manner. No leader or negotiating committee was ever free to commit strikers to any position.

This pattern prevailed even where unions existed, and it had significant consequences for union organization and leadership. This manner of conducting union business, including strikes, prevented union leaders from entrenching themselves in their positions. Leaders retained their offices only as long as members approved their leadership. This was one reason strong leaders never emerged from mill unions and strikes. Workers decided everything individually. No one could bind anyone else to anything, and no one would follow any leader where he did not wish to be led, even in the middle of a strike.

This pattern made negotiations with management difficult. Negotiating committees were messenger groups that communicated strikers' proposals to management and management's response to the strikers. They were almost never authorized to modify the strikers' position or to approve or disapprove offers from management. Exceptions were made when outsiders from national unions came in to acknowledge the workers' capitulation after extended strikes. That happened in each of the strikes at Augusta.

The strikers' meetings embodied the atomistic individualism of mill folk and the equality they exercised among themselves. A reporter at the first meeting of Eagle and Phenix strikers in 1896 witnessed "at times dozens of excited men and women talking at the same time." Even after they settled down, the strikers took their own counsel. They regularly invited outsiders to advise them and then rejected the advice they received. The Eagle and Phenix strikers, for example, listened to the mayor of Columbus, E. H. Baker, who "counseled prudence and warned [them] . . . against the misfortunes that must necessarily result from a strike." However, "all" of the assembled workers "seemed to feel the weight of oppression and to have a strong conception of some grievance," and they voted unanimously to continue their walkout.

Despite this resolve, the strikers were never able to dispel the fog of injured innocence, moral superiority, and economic certitude in which Eagle and Phenix mill officials enveloped their actions and explanations of the pay cut. The mills invariably responded to strikers' complaints with talk of the necessity and equitableness of the reduction, of the strikers' rashness in following the advice of "outside agitators," and of the justness of company policies in dealing with employees. "We have never been harsh with the people," John S. Bigby, president of the mill, insisted during the strike. "They know it and when it became necessary for us to make the reduction, it was but right that they should yield to the occasion." Instead, "A few who listened to what Eugene V. Debs [of the American Socialist Party] had to say" on a recent trip to Columbus incited the weavers, and the result was the strike. "It was the insidious work of that man which is the prime cause of all this trouble," Bigby insisted.

When it became evident that the strikers would not return to work, mill officials waited for the shutdown to work its hardships. As they waited, the strikers met regularly and made confident assessments of their situation for reporters, who in turn wrote stories of the hopelessness of the strikers' position. Meanwhile, the shut-out workers despaired, and many moved elsewhere as the shutdown continued from late March into April and then into May. Strikers and management had no channels of contact, and each guarded its own deliberations. As a result, rumors abounded. The workers were hopeful or despairing according to the latest unverified reports—of the company losing large contracts because of the stoppage, of strikers leaving the city for jobs elsewhere, of strikebreakers coming in by the carloads, of the ebb and flow of the strikers' resolve.

On April 3, a week after the shutdown began, the strikers sent a delegation to talk to company officials. The delegates could only talk, not negotiate, however, and the meeting accomplished nothing. On April 9, another delegation brought a proposal that the old wages be restored and no employee be punished for joining the strike. Company officials rejected the proposal, but they did announce that the mills would resume operations when enough employees were willing to work. The resumption could not begin for ten days or two weeks, however, and then only in the woolen department. The other areas of the mills would not reopen until after May 1, which was three weeks away. The delay might have been due to the unwillingness of many weavers to return to work. When limited operations did finally resume in Mill No. 1 on May 11, "many more than the requisite number of operatives were on hand."

The strike collapsed. On May 13, the strikers agreed to return to work at the reduced wages, and the company pledged to restore the reduction when business permitted. All the mills were in operation by May 18, but they achieved full capacity only near the end of the month, probably because so many workers had left the city during the shutdown.

On May 17, Eugene V. Debs was again in Columbus, and in a public address spoke the meaning of this and most other strikes of mill workers in the New South. "I am opposed to strikes," Debs said. "It is the height of folly for laborers under almost any conceivable circumstance to strike now. . . . The odds against [the worker] are too great, and what he loses while idle is never replaced by an advance even if the strike succeed. . . . [Employers] can afford to close down and live on their capital while the striker exhausts his savings and either gives in or starves."[17] Debs's statement is a fitting reminder of the inability of mill workers in the New South to confront management through the devices of unions and strikes. It is also a measure of the extent to which they needed other devices for dealing with management from their position of weakness.

17. Columbus *Enquirer-Sun*, May 18, 1896.

POSTSCRIPT

The second decade of the twentieth century produced no sharp departure in the lives of mill folk. However, a series of overlapping transitions during and after World War I produced a significant evolution in the circumstances of mill life. By 1915 most mill villages were well-established communities, and most mill workers had spent at least a decade in the mills. The interchange between farm and mill thus became a less central feature of folk life. In addition, the marked rise in wages during the war brought to the mills people who had previously shunned mill employment, and as they remained when the war was over, the social composition of the work force was altered.

The accumulating effects of Progressive reform further altered the substance of mill life. The elimination of child labor radically changed the composition of the work force and much of the activity in the workplace as well. Educational and literacy levels increased; physical well-being improved (except that respiratory diseases continued to plague folk); welfare work and the kinds of social activity that it encouraged became more significant parts of village life. "Backwoods individualism" eroded.

More important, the paternal nexus of work and other aspects of mill life began to undergo a series of major transformations. Management became more "modern" and professionalized, and more concerned with efficiency, productivity, and cost accounting. The personalism that mediated mill life in the New South era diminished. The accumulating years of industrial employment modified important elements of folk culture, and more and more mill folk began to take on the trappings of industrial proletarians conscious of their grievances against employers, whom they increasingly perceived as having antithetical interests. Class consciousness became a more meaningful aspect of life.

Conditions in the cotton manufacturing industry in the years between the world wars accelerated these tendencies. Productive overcapacity, fluctuating markets, increasing competition from overseas and from new synthetic fibers, and the uncertain profit margins those conditions implied prompted management to introduce speedups, stretch-outs, and more discipline in the workplace, all of which helped transform the pace and nature of work. This transformation further undermined the appeal of paternalism; and union activity and the grievances that spawned it became more important features of mill life. In the 1930s, the Great Depression devastated the textile industry, and the lives of mill folk commenced another major evolution.

These were tendencies rather than sudden or absolute changes. Together, they set the interwar years apart from the New South era in the history of mill folk. The effect of these developments was such that folk who remembered the earlier time looked back upon it nostalgically. Seeing and appreciating life in that simpler age as mill folk saw and remembered it dispels the fog of prejudice and ignorance that has heretofore obscured and distorted the story of one of the most fascinating groups in American history.

APPENDIX

TABLE I
Employment of Plain Folk, 1890
(Georgia and the Carolinas)

		MALES	FEMALES
Number of gainfully employed whites (10 years old and older)		660,226	111,047
Percentage of gainfully employed whites (10 years old and older)		74.9	12.2

	NUMBER	% OF MALE WORK FORCE	NUMBER	% OF FEMALE WORK FORCE
Tenant farmers (including sharecroppers)	109,933	16.6	5,588	5.0
Agricultural laborers	152,875	23.1	31,588	28.4
Mill and factory operatives[a]	16,787	2.5	13,683	12.3
Nonagricultural laborers[b]	21,455	3.2	31,730	28.6
Totals	301,050	45.4	82,589	74.3

SOURCES: *Eleventh Census, 1890: Population,* xxxv–xxxviii, cxiv, 548–49, 592–93, 606–607; *Eleventh Census, 1890: Report of Farm and Home Ownership,* 566–70.

[a]This category includes workers in cotton, woolen, and other textile factories, sawmills and planing mills, and tobacco and cigar factories.

[b]For males, this category includes wood choppers, miners, lumbermen and raftsmen, common laborers, servants, draymen and teamsters, messengers, packers and porters. For females, it includes housekeepers, stewardesses, common laborers, laundresses, nurses and midwives, servants, dressmakers, and seamstresses. The category excludes all skilled and semiskilled craftsmen and workers not listed as laborers. It significantly understates the number of unskilled and untrained workers, especially among males.

TABLE II
Employment of Plain Folk, 1910
(Georgia and the Carolinas)

		MALES	FEMALES
Number of gainfully employed whites (10 years old and older)[a]		1,113,575	300,550
Percentage of gainfully employed whites (10 years old and older)		83.4	23.1

	NUMBER	% OF MALE WORK FORCE	NUMBER	% OF FEMALE WORK FORCE
Tenant farmers (including sharecroppers)	173,565	15.6	8,751[b]	2.9
Agricultural laborers				
Working off home farm	74,960		18,398	
Working on home farm	206,336		134,292	
Working on turpentine farms	1,240		11	
Total agricultural laborers	282,536	25.4	152,701	50.8
Mill and factory operatives[c]	53,930	4.8	43,571	14.5
Nonagricultural laborers[d]	54,014	4.9	33,784	11.2
Totals	564,045	50.7	238,807	79.4

SOURCES: *Thirteenth Census, 1910: Population*, I, 370, 392, 399, IV, 449–51, 499–501, 516–17; *Thirteenth Census, 1910: Agriculture*, 172.

[a]This category includes whites in nine basic occupational categories: agriculture, forestry, and animal husbandry; extraction of minerals; manufacturing and mechanical industries; transportation; trade; public service; professional service; domestic and personal service; and clerical occupations.

[b]Farmers were not classified by gender before 1920. In that year, women were 4.5 percent of all white tenant farmers in Georgia and North Carolina and 6.0 percent in South Carolina. In 1890 women were 4.8 percent of all farmers listed as operating rented farms in the three states. I have therefore estimated that 4.8 percent of all tenant farmers in 1910 were women.

[c]This category includes workers in cotton, knitting, and other textile mills, tobacco and cigar factories, furniture factories, and sawmills and planing mills.

[d]For males, this category includes garden laborers; draymen, teamsters, and expressmen; lumbermen, raftsmen, and wood choppers; laborers, porters, and helpers in stores; persons in domestic and personal service; laborers and helpers in brick, tile, and terra cotta factories, in sawmills and cotton and planing mills, in fertilizer factories and turpentine distilleries, in cigar, tobacco, and furniture factories, in paper and pulp mills, in tanneries, and in the buildling and hand trades; and all other workers listed as laborers. For females, this category includes dressmakers and seamstresses, common laborers, persons in domestic and personal service, and garden laborers.

TABLE III
Growth of White Farm Tenancy, 1890–1920
(Georgia and the Carolinas)

	ALL TENANTS		SHARECROPPERS ONLY	
	NUMBER	% OF ALL WHITE FARMERS	NUMBER	% OF ALL WHITE FARMERS
1890	115,530	37.4		
1900	147,735	38.7	99,516	26.1
1910	182,316	41.8	121,353	27.8
1920	194,721	42.6	146,276	32.0

SOURCES: *Eleventh Census, 1890: Report of Farm and Home Ownership*, 566–70; *Twelfth Census, 1900: Agriculture*, Pt. 1, pp. 69, 109, 119; *Thirteenth Census, 1910: Agriculture*, 172; *Fourteenth Census, 1920: Agriculture*, Pt. 2, pp. 226, 268, 292. Tenancy data in 1880 were not broken down by race. Separate data for sharecropping were not collected until 1900.

TABLE IV
Estimated Wealth Per Capita
(For Total Population)

	1890		1900		1904		1912	
	TOTAL ($)	% OF U.S. AVERAGE	TOTAL ($)	% OF U.S. AVERAGE	TOTAL ($)	% OF U.S. AVERAGE	TOTAL ($)	% OF U.S. AVERAGE
Georgia	464	44.8	422	36.2	493	37.4	802	41.1
North Carolina	361	34.8	360	30.9	420	31.9	740	37.9
South Carolina	348	33.6	362	31.1	414	31.4	811	41.6
United States	1,036		1,165		1,318		1,950	

SOURCE: *Statistical Abstract of the United States, 1923*, 738. Note that the absolute dollar gap widened considerably between the three states and the national average.

TABLE V

Estimated Personal Income Per Capita
(For Total Population)

	1880		1900		1920	
	TOTAL ($)	% OF U.S. AVERAGE	TOTAL ($)	% OF U.S. AVERAGE	TOTAL ($)	% OF U.S. AVERAGE
Georgia	86	49.1	86	42.3	348	52.9
North Carolina	64	36.6	72	35.5	354	53.8
South Carolina	72	41.1	74	36.5	336	51.1
United States	175		203		658	

SOURCE: Richard A. Easterlin, "State Income Estimates," in Simon Kuznets and Dorothy S. Thomas (eds.), *Population Estimates and Economic Growth: United States, 1870–1950* (Philadelphia, 1957), I, 753. For other estimates and information on this subject, see Easterlin, "Regional Income Trends, 1840–1950," in Seymour E. Harris (ed.), *American Economic History* (New York, 1961), 525–47; Easterlin, "Interregional Differences in Per Capita Income, Population, and Total Income, 1840–1950," in Conference on Research in Income and Wealth, *Studies in Income and Wealth* (Princeton, 1960), 73–140, vol. XXIV of *Trends in the American Economy in the Nineteenth Century*.

TABLE VI

Home Ownership, 1910
(White Population Only)

	TOTAL HOMES	NUMBER OWNED[a]	NUMBER RENTED	NUMBER WITH OWNERSHIP UNKNOWN	% RENTED[b]
North Carolina					
Number of homes	298,956	162,637	131,272	5,047	44.7
Farm homes only	179,446	119,276	59,906	264	33.4
Georgia					
Number of homes	289,920	125,380	158,275	6,265	55.8
Farm homes only	155,881	79,144	76,447	290	49.1
South Carolina					
Number of homes	135,608	60,574	71,588	3,446	54.2
Farm homes only	72,663	41,106	31,366	191	43.3
Total in the three states					
Number of homes	724,484	348,591	361,135	14,758	50.9
Farm homes only	407,990	239,526	167,719	745	41.2

SOURCE: *Thirteenth Census, 1910: Population*, 1308–1309.

[a]This category includes homes with mortgages.
[b]This category excludes homes with unknown ownership.

TABLE VII
Distribution of White Farmers by Age and Tenure,
1910
(Georgia and the Carolinas)

AGE	NUMBER OF WHITE FARMERS	% OWNERS	% TENANTS	% MANAGERS
Under 25	29,938	28.7	70.3	0.9
25–34	108,879	42.7	56.4	0.8
35–44	101,986	59.2	39.8	0.9
45–54	89,498	69.6	29.7	0.6
55–64	63,954	74.1	25.4	0.4
65 and over	31,087	80.6	18.9	0.4

SOURCE: *Fourteenth Census, 1920: Agriculture*, 367.

TABLE VIII
Average Value of Farmland and Farm Buildings
per Acre

	1880	1890	1900	1910
Georgia	$4.30	$6.03	$6.95	$17.78
North Carolina	6.07	8.12	8.56	20.35
South Carolina	5.10	7.52	9.06	24.64

SOURCE: *Thirteenth Census, 1910: Agriculture*, VI, 317, VII, 221, 495.

TABLE IX
Length of Residence at Current Farm
(White Farmers, Georgia and the Carolinas)

	ALL OWNERS		ALL TENANTS		SHARE AND SHARE-CASH TENANTS		CASH AND UNSPECIFIED TENANTS	
	1920	1910	1920	1910	1920	1910	1920	1910
Number reporting years at current farm	252,300	209,998	177,079	172,341	132,454	114,963	44,625	57,378
Less than 1 year at current farm	4.80%[a]	5.79%	24.05%	38.74%	26.07%	42.26%	18.05%	31.68%
1-2 years at current farm	8.28%	5.63%	27.67%	17.39%	29.34%	17.44%	22.71%	17.29%

2-5 years at current farm	15.54%	19.39%	28.20%	28.34%	27.30%	26.81%	30.86%	31.40%
5-10 years at current farm	17.06%	19.03%	11.71%	9.77%	10.35%	8.63%	15.72%	12.07%
10 or more years at current farm	54.30%	50.14%	8.35%	5.73%	6.90%	4.84%	12.64%	7.53%
Number not reporting years at current farm	7,845	40,787	17,642	9,975	13,822	6,390	3,820	3,585

SOURCE: *Fourteenth Census, 1920: Agriculture*, 418.

a All percentages are of the number reporting years at current farm.

INDEX